ROTHMANS RUGBY LEAGUE YEARBOOK 1991-92

Raymond Fletcher and David Howes

ROTHMANS

Queen Anne Press

A QUEEN ANNE PRESS BOOK

© **Rothmans Publications Ltd**

First published in Great Britain in 1991 by
Queen Anne Press, a division of
Macdonald & Co (Publishers) Ltd
165 Great Dover Street
London SE1 4YA

A member of Maxwell Macmillan Publishing Corporation

COVER PHOTOGRAPHS
Front Cover: Great Britain winger Martin Offiah in action for Widnes in the 1990 Greenalls Lancashire Cup final against Salford.
Back Cover: Great Britain and Wigan prop Andy Platt on Test duty against France at Perpignan in January 1991.

ACKNOWLEDGEMENTS
The compilers would like to acknowledge the assistance of the Rugby League Record Keepers' Club, club secretaries and individuals in providing material as a further source of reference for accuracy.

PHOTOGRAPHS
Modern day domestic photographs in this *Rothmans Rugby League Yearbook* are from the files of the *Rugby Leaguer.* The compilers acknowledge the co-operation of Chief Photographer Gerald Webster and his staff.
The colour photographs on the front and back covers, plus a number of black-and-white contributions — in particular from the 1990 Great Britain tour — are by freelance photographer Andrew Varley.

All rights reserved. No part of this publication may be reproduced, stored in a retrieval system, or transmitted, in any form or by any means, without the prior permission in writing of the publisher, nor be otherwise circulated in any form of binding or cover other than that in which it is published and without a similar condition including this condition being imposed on the subsequent purchaser.

British Library Cataloguing in Publication Data
Rothmans Rugby League Yearbook — 1991-92
    1. Rugby football — Great Britain —
    Periodicals
    796.33.3.0941 GV945.9.G7

ISBN 0 356 17852 8

Photoset by New Rush Filmsetters, London

Reproduced, printed and bound in Great Britain by
BPCC Hazell Books, Aylesbury and Paulton

Rothmans Rugby League Yearbook 1991-92

CONTENTS

EDITORIAL PREFACE

Rugby League performed on a world stage during the full 12 months of the 1990-91 campaign, Great Britain meeting all four international rivals in the Test arena. Even Russia got in on the act, a first-ever national line-up entertaining a combined Fulham and Ryedale-York side in the famous Dinamo Stadium in Moscow to round off a memorable year on the international scene.

We take pride and pleasure in reflecting the higher profile and increased awareness of world Rugby League, particularly the heroics of the British Lions tour to Papua New Guinea and New Zealand and of the Australians' visit to these shores. The Wembley Test deserved a chapter on its own!

In the constant search for new material we have chronicled for the first time the leading scorers for Great Britain and previewed the rebirth of the Welsh national side. Elsewhere, the desire for the highest degree of accuracy has once more been pursued and we again thank club officials, RLHQ staff, the RL Record Keepers Club and a few individuals for their assistance.

For the 11th season, sincere thanks go to our wives for unwavering support and understanding. Two new names also receive our grateful recognition, house editor Ian Marshall for an impressive debut campaign and young Ben Howes for his time-saving assistance in helping to compile the 1990-91 match analyses sub-section.

● Facts and figures in this *Rothmans Rugby League Yearbook* as at 1 June 1991.

RAYMOND FLETCHER, of the *Yorkshire Post*

DAVID HOWES, Rugby League Public Affairs Executive

COACHES SELECT XIII

For the third time, the coaches of the 14 clubs in the Stones Bitter Championship were invited to select their form team of the season as an exclusive feature of the 1991-92 *Rothmans Rugby League Yearbook*.

The coaches were asked not to include members of their own club sides and to base their choice on opposition performances during the 1990-91 campaign, while taking general form into account. It is based on individual form and does not necessarily represent their best team.

A total of only 45 players were nominated by the 13 coaches taking part, Peter Fox of Featherstone Rovers again declining the invitation. It compared with 69 put forward at the end of the season 1989-90 and 54 in 1988-89.

Eleven players were named from Wigan and nine from Widnes. Seven players were nominated in more than one position, Widnes utility back Jonathan Davies being named at full back, centre and stand off in his five votes. St. Helens packman George Mann received a creditable six nominations but failed to make the Select XIII as they were split between prop and second row.

Nine overseas imports were voted for, compared with previous totals of 15 and 16. There was also a tighter spread of candidates, with only two loose forwards, three scrum halves and four hookers being proposed. The largest number of nominations was 10 second row men.

In the Coaches Select XIII, only four players have achieved a 100 per cent appearance record over the three years of voting ... Martin Offiah, Andy Gregory, Phil McKenzie and Ellery Hanley.

The only tie in the voting was for the second centre spot, between Wigan's Dean Bell and Sheffield Eagles' skipper Daryl Powell.

Overseas representation increased to five from the three of the previous two seasons with the inclusion of New Zealanders Frano Botica, Kevin Iro, Bell and Emosi Koloto, plus ever-present Australian McKenzie.

Of the 14 Select players, nine had represented Great Britain during the season. Seven of them were debutants in the Select XIII ... Steve Hampson, Botica, Bell, Powell, 1991 Stones Bitter Man of Steel Garry Schofield, Karl Harrison and Koloto. Eight of the side were from League-Cup double winners, Wigan.

Great Britain and Wigan skipper Ellery Hanley received a 100 per cent poll from the 12 coaches eligible to vote for him, a repeat of 1988-89. Team-mate Andy Platt also earned all 12 votes, 11 for prop and one for second row. Scrum half Gregory tallied 11 nominations and Offiah 10.

Wigan and Great Britain full back Steve Hampson.

COACHES SELECT XIII

1. **Steve Hampson** (Wigan)
2. **Frano Botica** (Wigan)
3. **Kevin Iro** (Wigan)
4. **Dean Bell** (Wigan)
   Daryl Powell (Sheffield Eagles)
5. **Martin Offiah** (Widnes)
6. **Garry Schofield** (Leeds)
7. **Andy Gregory** (Wigan)

8. **Karl Harrison** (Hull)
9. **Phil McKenzie** (Widnes)
10. **Andy Platt** (Wigan)
11. **Denis Betts** (Wigan)
12. **Emosi Koloto** (Widnes)
13. **Ellery Hanley** (Wigan)

Wigan's New Zealand All Black RU import Frano Botica.

Wigan and New Zealand centre Kevin Iro.

NOEL CLEAL, Hull

1. Tait (Widnes)
2. Botica (Wigan)
3. Powell (Sheffield E.)
4. Davies (Widnes)
5. Offiah (Widnes)
6. Myler (Widnes)
7. Gregory (Wigan)
8. Sorensen (Widnes)
9. Cook (Sheffield E.)
10. Platt (Wigan)
11. Mann (St. Helens)
12. Koloto (Widnes)
13. Hanley (Wigan)

JOHN FIELDHOUSE, Oldham

1. Lyon (Warrington)
2. Hunte (St. Helens)
3. Loughlin (St. Helens)
4. Bell (Wigan)
5. Offiah (Widnes)
6. Myler (Widnes)
7. Gregory (Wigan)
8. Ward (St. Helens)
9. McKenzie (Widnes)
10. Platt (Wigan)
11. Betts (Wigan)
12. Mercer (Warrington)
13. Hanley (Wigan)

GARY HETHERINGTON, Sheffield E.

1. Hampson (Wigan)
2. Eastwood (Hull)
3. Iro (Wigan)
4. Watson (Hull K.R.)
5. Offiah (Widnes)
6. Schofield (Leeds)
7. Gregory (Wigan)
8. Ward (St. Helens)
9. Jackson (Hull)
10. Platt (Wigan)
11. Betts (Wigan)
12. Mann (St. Helens)
13. Hanley (Wigan)

Wigan and New Zealand centre Dean Bell.

Sheffield Eagles and Great Britain centre Daryl Powell.

DAVID HOBBS, Bradford N.

1. Hampson (Wigan)
2. Botica (Wigan)
3. Powell (Sheffield E.)
4. Bateman (Warrington)
5. Offiah (Widnes)
6. Davies (Widnes)
7. Gregory (Wigan)
8. Glancy (Wakefield T.)
9. Jackson (Hull)
10. Platt (Wigan)
11. Mann (St. Helens)
12. Koloto (Widnes)
13. Hanley (Wigan)

NEIL HOLDING, Rochdale H.

1. Lyon (Warrington)
2. Botica (Wigan)
3. Iro (Wigan)
4. Bell (Wigan)
5. Sullivan (Hull K.R.)
6. Watson (Hull K.R.)
7. Gregory (Wigan)
8. Ward (St. Helens)
9. McKenzie (Widnes)
10. Platt (Wigan)
11. Mann (St. Helens)
12. Koloto (Widnes)
13. Hanley (Wigan)

BRIAN JOHNSON, Warrington

1. Gay (Hull)
2. Sullivan (Hull K.R.)
3. Iro (Wigan)
4. Loughlin (St. Helens)
5. Offiah (Widnes)
6. Schofield (Leeds)
7. Gregory (Wigan)
8. Harrison (Hull)
9. Jackson (Hull)
10. Platt (Wigan)
11. Betts (Wigan)
12. Koloto (Widnes)
13. Hanley (Wigan)

DOUG LAUGHTON, Widnes

1. Hampson (Wigan)
2. Botica (Wigan)
3. Bell (Wigan)
4. Schofield (Leeds)
5. Quirk (St. Helens)
6. Edwards (Wigan)
7. Gregory (Wigan)
8. Mann (St. Helens)
9. Dermott (Wigan)
10. Platt (Wigan)
11. Betts (Wigan)
12. Dixon (Leeds)
13. Hanley (Wigan)

Widnes and Great Britain winger Martin Offiah.

11

Leeds and Great Britain stand off Garry Schofield.

Wigan and Great Britain scrum half Andy Gregory.

MIKE McCLENNAN, St. Helens

1. Hampson (Wigan)
2. Devereux (Widnes)
3. Iro (Wigan)
4. Bell (Wigan)
5. Sullivan (Hull K.R.)
6. Schofield (Leeds)
7. Gregory (Wigan)
8. Harrison (Hull)
9. McKenzie (Widnes)
10. Platt (Wigan)
11. Eyres (Widnes)
12. Nickle (Sheffield E.)
13. Hanley (Wigan)

ROGER MILLWARD, Hull K.R.

1. Hampson (Wigan)
2. Botica (Wigan)
3. Iro (Wigan)
4. Schofield (Leeds)
5. Offiah (Widnes)
6. Edwards (Wigan)
7. Gregory (Wigan)
8. Sorensen (Widnes)
9. McKenzie (Widnes)
10. Platt (Wigan)
11. Betts (Wigan)
12. Koloto (Widnes)
13. Hanley (Wigan)

JOHN MONIE, Wigan

1. Lyon (Warrington)
2. Devereux (Widnes)
3. Powell (Sheffield E.)
4. Davies (Widnes)
5. Offiah (Widnes)
6. Schofield (Leeds)
7. Ellis (Warrington)
8. Harrison (Hull)
9. McKenzie (Widnes)
10. Mann (St. Helens)
11. Mercer (Warrington)
12. Fairbank (Bradford N.)
13. Eyres (Widnes)

Hull and Great Britain prop Karl Harrison.

Widnes's Australian-born hooker Phil McKenzie.

Wigan and Great Britain prop forward Andy Platt.

Wigan and Great Britain second row man Denis Betts.

13

Widnes's Tongan second row man Emosi Koloto.

Wigan and Great Britain skipper Ellery Hanley.

DAVID TOPLISS, Wakefield T.

1. Davies (Widnes)
2. Hunte (St. Helens)
3. Powell (Sheffield E.)
4. Bell (Wigan)
5. Offiah (Widnes)
6. Schofield (Leeds)
7. Gregory (Wigan)
8. Crooks (Castleford)
9. McKenzie (Widnes)
10. Platt (Wigan)
11. Betts (Wigan)
12. Fairbank (Bradford N.)
13. Hanley (Wigan)

DARRYL VAN DE VELDE, Castleford

1. Tait (Widnes)
2. Nelson (Sheffield E.)
3. Powell (Sheffield E.)
4. Schofield (Leeds)
5. Offiah (Widnes)
6. Myler (Widnes)
7. Gregory (Wigan)
8. Harrison (Hull)
9. Jackson (Hull)
10. Platt (Wigan)
11. Medley (Bradford N.)
12. Fairbank (Bradford N.)
13. Hanley (Wigan)

DAVID WARD, Leeds

1. Tait (Widnes)
2. Sullivan (Hull K.R.)
3. Iro (Wigan)
4. Loughlin (St. Helens)
5. Offiah (Widnes)
6. Davies (Widnes)
7. Edwards (Wigan)
8. Lucas (Wigan)
9. McKenzie (Widnes)
10. Crooks (Castleford)
11. Betts (Wigan)
12. Platt (Wigan)
13. Hanley (Wigan)

Lions halt Roo giants

Record £2m deal for Championship

Three-division plan just wins the vote

Schofield honoured

Scarborough given rugby go-ahead

Hanley's shock gridiron move

MEMORIES

1990-91 HEADLINES
Behind the scoring feats and records of the 1990-91 season were a number of stories which made the headlines:

BISHOP IN DOUBLE DISPUTE
David Bishop was never out of the headlines during a remarkable week in October which began with an incident that resulted in calls for the former Welsh RU international to be banned for life and finished with him quitting Hull Kingston Rovers after a row with coach Roger Millward.

Playing full back, Bishop was sent off by referee Colin Morris for a tackle which fractured Charlie McAlister's cheekbone in the 35th minute of a Stones Bitter Championship match at Oldham on 7 October. Twelve-man Rovers went on to win 28-25 after trailing 16-10 at half-time.

Oldham director Jim Knox said the club would be demanding a life ban on Bishop if he were found guilty of an illegal high tackle. This outburst resulted in banner headlines and the Rugby League immediately imposed a ban on further comments about the incident.

A few days later the RL Disciplinary Committee found Bishop not guilty of any offence after studying a video and hearing his claims that McAlister's injury was caused by an accidental clash of heads.

The following evening Bishop was involved in an unrelated row with club coach Millward, who had dropped him to substitute for the weekend's match against Widnes and accused the player of a poor attitude during training. Bishop, who was not happy at losing his regular scrum half spot, then quit Rovers saying he would not play for them again while Millward was in charge. Rovers supported Millward by listing Bishop at £120,000.

Two days later Millward announced he would not be seeking a new contract at the end of the season, thus ending a 25-year stay at Rovers including 14 as coach. Rovers said

his decision was unconnected with the Bishop incident as he had indicated his plans much earlier.

Bishop did not play again during the season but was welcomed back by new coach George Fairbairn in May.

DONOHUE *SINE DIE* BAN
Leigh scrum half Jason Donohue was suspended *sine die* for a foul in a reserve team match, but had the sentence changed to a 12-match ban on appeal.

The 18-year-old received the original ban from the RL Disciplinary Commitee on 19 October after the case had been forwarded to them by the RL Board of Directors following a 'trial by video'.

Donohue had not been sent off by referee Alan Hunter, but was cited by Wigan for the high tackle in a Slalom Lager Alliance match on 6 September which left 17-year-old Mike Neal with a depressed cheekbone.

Donohue had already served a two-match ban after being sent off earlier in the season. The *sine die* suspension was changed to 12 matches on 2 November and by the end of the season Donohue had gained a regular place in Leigh's first team.

● Gary Charlton's *sine die* ban was lifted from 1 December, 1990, having been suspended since 10 December, 1989 following the Whitehaven forward's cheekbone-shattering tackle on Castleford's Graham Steadman.

SCARBOROUGH PIRATES WELCOMED
Scarborough were admitted to the Rugby Football League on 9 January by the narrowest possible margin — the exact two-thirds majority necessary.

Only 30 clubs were represented at the RL Council meeting at Headingley, Leeds, and they voted 20-9 in favour with one abstention. But Whitehaven, Workington Town and Carlisle said they would have backed Scarborough's entry had they not been held back by adverse weather. No reason was given for the absence of Bradford Northern and Keighley.

The application was made by Scarborough Football Club who would rent their McCain Stadium to the new club. Soccer chairman Geoffrey Richmond would have an identical role with the rugby club, which would be a separate company.

Former Test forward Len Casey was later appointed coach and they took the name of Scarborough Pirates after dropping Vikings which was already attached to a local RU club. Scarborough's entry brought the total of senior clubs to the century's record of 36, which was achieved briefly in the 1980s.

TUFFS WINS DRUGS APPEAL

Simon Tuffs of Bradford Northern was the centre of British Rugby League's first major drugs story, of which he was eventually cleared. It began after he failed a random drug test following the Stones Bitter Championship match at Leeds on 26 December when the forward went on as a 31st minute substitute.

The League did not name Tuffs in a statement issued on 22 January but confirmed that a drug test on a player had proved positive, showing traces of the stimulant amphetamine. It was the first time a positive drug test had been made public since random testing was introduced four years earlier. There had been a few positive tests for which a satisfactory explanation had been given, usually relating to medical purposes.

An inquiry into the case on 24 January was postponed when Tuffs claimed the positive test was the result of his drink being 'spiked' at a Christmas party. On 26 February Tuffs was found guilty and banned for two years.

But he appealed and on 16 April was cleared and the ban lifted after Tuffs produced the person who admitted spiking his drink.

● Brendon Tuuta of Featherstone Rovers received a severe reprimand on 24 January for failing to have a drugs test after being selected at random following the game against Wakefield Trinity on 30 December. The League accepted there had been some confusion when Tuuta was called to provide a sample.

MONARCHS LURE HANLEY

Ellery Hanley provided new American football club London Monarchs with an invaluable publicity coup when the Wigan and Great Britain captain announced he would sign for them.

The story broke on 5 March with headlines about the '10 million dollar man' but it proved to be little more than a superb publicity stunt. Hanley did train with the Wembley-based gridiron team but never played for them.

Earlier alarm that Rugby League could be losing its greatest player changed to indignation as Hanley boosted American football with interviews while continuing his refusal to speak to the Rugby League media.

THREE DIVISIONS ARRIVE

Three Divisions finally got the go-ahead — but only just — as clubs voted by the narrowest of margins for the 'Hetherington Plan' to be introduced for 1991-92.

The special general meeting at Leeds at Rugby League Headquarters on 17 April resulted in the exact minimum of 21 votes from 35 clubs needed to get the scheme passed.

Just six weeks earlier the same plan had failed to get the go-ahead after only a 19-15 vote in favour.

The three divisions plan had been instigated by Gary Hetherington, the Sheffield Eagles chairman and coach. It was for a First and Third Division of 14 clubs each and a Second Division of eight clubs playing each other four times.

A move for three divisions of 12, introduced by Castleford, was defeated after 25 clubs opposed it, while Whitehaven's moves for a 14-11-11 structure gained little support.

The Second Division Premiership was replaced by a Divisional Premiership. The top eight in the Third Division would play-off to provide four teams, to face the top four in the Second Division.

RUSSIA INVADED

Fulham and Ryedale-York made history in May by becoming the first teams to make a brief tour of the Soviet Union little more than a year after Rugby League had been introduced to the country.

The two teams drew 20-20 at Alma-Ata in Kazakhstan, Fulham winning 18-12 in Leningrad. The crowds were about 7,000 and 1,000 respectively.

The two Second Division clubs then combined to face the first-ever Soviet Union national side at the Dinamo Stadium, Moscow, on the evening of 23 May. A disappointing crowd of 3,200 saw the British XIII, captained by Ryedale-York's Stuart Horton, record at 42-10 victory, having held a 24-4 half-time lead.

Soviet Union 10 Bailive; Pisconove (1t), Dyatlove, Nichiave (1t), Olar; Parshow (1g), Kartzov; Zarnba, Ossachie, Strach, Lysove, Senin, Sókoluv. Subs: Sycophsky, Sharcoff, Tarran, Gloticov (all played), Rychcove (did not play).

British XIII 42 Sullivan★ (1t, 3g); Kettlestring★ (1t), Taylor†, Pitt†, Smith★; Browning†, Dobson★ (1t); Hayes★, Horton★ (1t), Rotheram†, Lee†, G. Price★, Pearce† (1t, 4g). Subs: Pinkney★ (1t), Maxwell★, Dwyer† (1t), Workman†, Render★ (all played).

★Ryedale-York. †Fulham.
Referee: Fred Lindop (England).

JUNE

Great Britain beat Papua New Guinea 40-8 in Port Moresby to collect two World Cup points .... Shaun Edwards signs a new one-year contract with Wigan .... Great Britain open the New Zealand leg of the tour with a 23-22 success over a President's XIII at Napier .... A Canterbury Select XIII beat Great Britain 18-10 at Christchurch .... Boost for Great Britain as Widnes winger Martin Offiah flies out to join the tour party .... Auckland defeat Great Britain 24-13 .... Arbitration ruling forces the League to accept that players from EEC countries do not count on the British quota system .... Widnes full back Alan Tait forced to return home from the Lions tour through injury .... Wakefield Trinity chase Sydney Premiership duo Paul Langmack and Michael Hagan .... Great Britain call up Warrington full back David Lyon into the tour party .... Hull K.R. list John Lydiat, Richard Pratt, David Laws, Malcolm Beall and Gary Sims at a total asking price of £90,000 .... Great Britain defeat Kiwi Colts 22-10 at Huntly .... Oldham offer loose forward John Cogger at £150,000 and prop Leo Casey at £160,000 .... Cash crisis club Halifax put in the hands of accountants Price Waterhouse .... Workington Town appoint Leeds scrum half Ray Ashton as player-coach .... Wakefield Trinity list centre Phil Eden at £75,000 .... Great Britain win the first Test against New Zealand at Palmerston North by 11-10 .... Leeds capture Bradford Northern scrum half Paul Harkin .... Trafford Borough demand £10,000 for Norman Turley, appointed player-coach at Whitehaven .... Widnes prop forward Joe Grima turns down a £50,000 move to Hull K.R. .... Oldham lose interest in Bramley winger Peter Lewis but sell prop Neil Clawson to the Villagers .... Great Britain suffer first-ever defeat by Wellington, 30-22 .... Bradford Northern sign RU centre Darrall Shelford from New Zealand .... Hull's Australian import Steve Folkes forced to retire with a hamstring injury .... Warrington list hooker Mark Roskell at £45,000 .... Great Britain winger David Plange put on the list at £85,000 .... Widnes agree terms with New Zealand prop Esene Faimalo .... Harry Jepson elected as President of the League .... Great Britain scrum half Bobby Goulding accused of assault in a bar in New Zealand.

JULY

Great Britain defeat New Zealand Maoris 20-12 at Rotorua .... Tribunal values Paul Harkin's move from Bradford Northern to Leeds at £65,000 .... Keighley appoint Tony Fisher as coach .... Hooker Andy Ruane priced at £35,000 by Oldham .... Great Britain beat Taranaki Invitation XIII 24-0 at New Plymouth .... Oldham sign Warrington utility player Ronnie Duane .... Great Britain scrum half Bobby Goulding ordered to pay £500 into a New Zealand court, £175 each going to the assaulted men and the remainder to charity .... St. Helens hand over £80,000 for Castleford's Test prop Kevin Ward .... RU scrum half Brett Iti signs for Bradford Northern from New Zealand .... Great Britain clinch the Test series with a 16-14 victory over New Zealand in Auckland .... International Board decide to reinstate Great Britain's traditional four-year tour cycle Down Under from 1992 onwards .... The Board also agrees to introduce four playing substitutes in Test football .... Former New Zealand RU All Black, London-born John Gallagher, given the Board's option to play for New Zealand or Great Britain .... South Sydney centre Brad Webb joins Hull .... Wigan sign Bradford Northern's Test prop Kelvin Skerrett .... Bramley recruit New Zealand duo Paul Nahu and Justin Wallace .... Great Britain round off their 15-match tour with a 21-18 defeat by New Zealand in the World Cup-rated third Test .... Hull sign French Test scrum half Patrick Entat .... Featherstone Rovers pay out a club record

£100,000 for Oldham prop Leo Casey .... French Test second row man Daniel Divet pulls out of move to Hull K.R. .... St. Helens sign New Zealand tour centre Tea Ropati .... Leeds utility back Ikram Butt joins Featherstone Rovers .... Hull's Kiwi winger Dane O'Hara moves to Doncaster for £8,000 .... Hull K.R. snubbed by Scottish RU back Scott Hastings.

AUGUST

Salford appoint prop forward Steve O'Neill as Alliance player-coach .... Wakefield Trinity sign Penrith captain Chris Mortimer .... Robin Whitfield appointed to take charge of the New Zealand Test encounter with Australia at Wellington .... Oldham take hooker Andy Ruane off the transfer list .... Warrington recruit stand off Chris O'Sullivan from Sydney Premiership winners Canberra Raiders .... £150,000-rated Australian loose forward John Cogger pledges to return to Oldham .... Halifax, £760,000 in debt, face creditors .... Sheffield Eagles sign Hull utility man Tim Wilby for around £6,000 .... Halifax takeover talks suspended because of a handful of players refusing to accept reduced terms .... The League sign a £1.5m three-year deal with British Aerospace to launch a satellite television service for pubs and clubs only, with the screening of 90 matches a season, one third of them live at 1pm on Sundays .... Gold Coast half back Bob Grogan signs for Rochdale Hornets .... Bradford Northern list Roger Simpson at £180,000 after failing to agree new contract terms .... Halifax sack Australian coach John Dorahy .... Leigh sign John Woods for a farewell season and take on New Zealand Test prop Peter Brown for a second spell .... Bramley list 10 players for failing to attend training, headed by Andy Gascoigne at £15,000 .... Leigh and Ryedale-York selected to take part in a three-match exhibition series of matches in the Soviet Union in the autumn .... Rochdale Hornets sign £95,000-rated Ian

Gormley from Salford, the fee to be decided by Tribunal .... Leeds capture Kenyan winger Eddie Rombo .... Canterbury prop forward Peter Tunks joins Salford .... Leigh offer Brian Dunn at £35,000 .... Halifax interview St. Helens scrum half Neil Holding for the player-coach role .... Hunslet sign Sheffield Eagles winger Steve Lidbury .... League back Australian counterparts' clampdown on drug-taking by refusing to allow clubs to sign banned players .... Whitehaven sign New Zealander Shane Horo .... Warrington skipper Mike Gregory ruled out for the early part of the season with a double-pinned finger suffered on the summer tour Down Under .... Ayr RU winger Phil Manning joins Carlisle .... Persistent groin injury forces Hull K.R. Test winger David Laws to retire .... Hull K.R. sign Blackheath RU winger Bob Sodje .... St. Helens forward Paul Forber advised to quit because of neck trouble .... Widnes record a hat-trick of Charity Shield wins by beating Wigan 24-8 in the CIS Insurance encounter at Swansea, watched by a crowd of over 11,000 .... Halifax back in business with a new board of directors and a new coach, 34-year-old Peter Roe who had just taken Dudley Hill to the BARLA National League title .... Leeds winger Norman Francis moves to Oldham .... The Soviet trip for Leigh and Ryedale-York postponed until May .... Leigh's £60,000-rated Alan Platt joins Halifax .... Doncaster sign Australian Ian French and New Zealander Tairie Tagaloa .... Kiwi Test prop Adrian Shelford joins Wakefield Trinity .... Former New Zealand Test scrum half Clayton Friend signs for Carlisle for a second time .... Castleford scrum half Roy Southernwood moves to Halifax .... Ex-Widnes and Barrow Tongan forward Bob Tuavao signs for Salford .... Great Britain tourist Terry Flanagan forced to quit Swinton because of neck trouble .... Sheffield Eagles recruit New Zealand Test back Sam Panapa for a second spell .... Kiwi tourist Brendon

Tuuta joins Featherstone Rovers .... Ten per cent increase in prize-money provides a record £44,000 for the 1990-91 Stones Bitter Champions .... Wigan installed by Corals as 5-4 favourites for the Stones Bitter Championship title, ahead of Widnes at 11-4 and 3-1 shots Leeds .... Leigh quoted as 5-4-on favourites for the Second Division title .... League announce that a recommendation for all-seater stadia would not apply to Rugby League clubs.

SEPTEMBER
Hull coach Brian Smith announces his departure to Sydney St. George club in January .... Hull immediately appoint fellow Australian Noel Cleal as his successor .... Hull K.R. sign Newcastle Knights' Kiwi Test prop forward James Goulding but delay a decision as to which of their quota of three overseas players to release .... Wigan coach John Monie extends his contract to 1991-92 .... Salford ask £60,000 for long-serving David Major .... Former Australian Test star Wayne Pearce turns down St. Helens offer .... Rugby League Council approves Runcorn Highfield's application to move to St. Helens Town FC ground .... Wigan sell utility back John Gilfillan to Salford for £20,000 .... Gary Atkins moves from Ryedale-York to Castleford for £15,000 .... Doncaster recruit Bramley full back Wayne Race in exchange for Ian Fletcher, Keith Jones and £10,000 .... Halifax ask £45,000 for Richard Milner .... Leigh sign Manly utility man Tony Iro on a short-term contract .... Halifax sign Leeds back Warren Wilson for £20,000 .... Kiwi tourist Tea Ropati proves his fitness and joins St. Helens for a second time .... Fulham make a bold move to line up Australian Test skipper Wally Lewis .... Hull K.R. release free-scoring Australian centre Greg Austin to make room for new signing James Goulding .... St. Helens receive £50,000 from Rochdale Hornets for scrum half Neil Holding ....

Warrington sign 10-cap Wales RU forward Rowland Phillips .... Triple blow for Australian tour selectors as Wally Lewis, Michael O'Connor and Bradley Clyde all ruled out by injury .... Halifax sign Hull K.R. centre Greg Austin and New Zealand Test threequarter Mark Elia .... Great Britain scrum half Bobby Goulding found guilty of bringing the game into disrepute on the summer tour Down Under and warned as to his future conduct .... Hull K.R. list centre Mike Fletcher at £80,000 and packman Colin Armstrong at £45,000 .... Leeds pay Wigan £60,000 for Great Britain prop forward Shaun Wane .... St. Helens forward Paul Forber advised to quit on medical advice with a neck injury .... Castleford beat neighbours Wakefield Trinity 11-8 to lift the John Smiths Yorkshire Cup .... Warrington's Under-21 prop forward Steve Molloy joins Leeds in £110,000 deal .... Neath centre Allan Bateman signs for Warrington on £100,000 contract .... Sheffield Eagles celebrate their first fixture at the Don Valley Stadium with a 34-6 victory over Wakefield Trinity .... Wigan utility back Ged Byrne moves to Wakefield Trinity for around £60,000 .... Widnes beat Second Division Salford 24-18 in the Greenalls Lancashire Cup final at Wigan.

OCTOBER

Australia arrive at Manchester Airport to herald a seven-week, 13-match British Coal tour of Britain .... Castleford sign Hull full back Paul Fletcher .... Leigh recruit ex-Fulham hooker Russell Bridge from Wigan .... Ex-Great Britain centre David Stephenson listed at £15,000 by Leigh .... Australia open the tour with an eight-try 34-4 hammering of St. Helens, celebrating 100 years at Knowsley Road .... Oldham demand a life ban for Hull K.R.'s David Bishop, sent off after Charlie McAlister suffers a broken cheekbone .... Four sent off and three sin binned as Australia beat Wakefield Trinity 36-18 .... Welsh RU international forward Mark Jones, of Neath, joins Hull .... Warrington offer Great Britain Under-21 stand off Rocky Turner for £120,000 .... Hull K.R. utility man David Bishop found not guilty of a high tackle at Oldham .... Leigh take hooker Mick Dean off the list .... Australia dispose of Wigan 34-6 .... Hull K.R. list David Bishop at £120,000 after a dispute with coach Roger Millward .... Featherstone Rovers sign RU forward Clarry Iti from New Zealand .... Great Britain call up Hull winger Paul Eastwood to replace injured Joe Lydon in training squad .... Australia beat Cumbria 42-10 under Workington Town's new floodlights .... Coach Roger Millward announces his end-of-season resignation at Hull K.R. after 25 years' playing and coaching .... Dave Chisnall quits as coach of Runcorn Highfield after losing all 38 matches in a 16-month reign .... Leigh's 18-year-old scrum half Jason Donohue given *sine die* ban after A-team dismissal for a high tackle .... Australia stave off determined Leeds challenge to win 22-10 .... Jonathan Davies left out of Great Britain's 19-man Wembley squad, Hull prop forward Karl Harrison being the only debutant .... Australian stand off Laurie Daley ruled out of the first British Coal Test with a broken hand sustained at Leeds .... Castleford capture England RU Under-21 winger Jon Wray .... British Test record 54,569 witness Great Britain's 19-12 victory over Australia at Wembley .... Hull's Welsh utility man Gary Pearce joins Sheffield Eagles on a month's loan .... Australia beat Warrington 26-6 .... All 29,000 seats for second British Coal Test at Old Trafford, Manchester, sold out within 72 hours of the Wembley spectacular.

NOVEMBER

Half back Paul Bishop given a free transfer after asking Warrington for a move .... *Sine die* ban of Jason Donohue reduced to 12

February . . . Kiwi forward George Mann wins his battle with the New Zealand Rugby League for permission to sign a three-year contract with St. Helens.

January . . . Regal Trophy final action with Bradford Northern second row man Paul Medley outstripping Warrington's Kevin Ellis.

May . . . Joyous Hull celebrate Stones Bitter Premiership success at Old Trafford.

matches on appeal .... Castleford fined £500 and ordered to pay £2,000 compensation after turning up 50 minutes late for a televised league match at Widnes .... Police make third British Coal Test at Elland Road, Leeds, all-ticket .... Centre Mark McGaw ruled out of the rest of the tour with torn knee ligaments as Australia beat Castleford 28-8 .... Great Britain recall Paul Loughlin and Andy Platt for the second Test .... St. Helens recruit Paul Bishop .... Grade two referee Stuart Cummings steps up from the crowd to take charge of the Wigan-Oldham league fixture after communications mix-up leads to lack of a replacement for referee Ray Tennant .... Second Division Halifax go down 36-18 to Australia .... Australia give Test debut to stand off Cliff Lyons as four players dropped from the defeated Wembley line-up .... Featherstone Rovers sign Keighley winger Owen Simpson .... Board of Directors announce lifting of Gary Charlton's *sine die* ban from 1 December .... Trafford Borough list eight players headed by half back Steve Griffiths at £10,000 .... Workington Town sign New Zealander Paddy Tuimavave .... British Lion and Llanelli winger Ieuan Evans rejects £150,000 offer from Featherstone Rovers .... Mal Meninga's last-second try seals 14-10 second Test victory for Australia over Great Britain at Old Trafford .... Hull open their new Threepenny Stand as Australia record 34-4 success .... Featherstone Rovers list Andy Fisher at £40,000, Alan Dakin and Paul Hughes at £20,000 each .... St. Helens put £30,000 price-tag on Cumbrian prop forward Jonathan Neil .... Dewsbury sign Bob Marsden from Rochdale Hornets .... New Zealand scrum half Stu Galbraith has his Trafford Borough contract taken over by Rochdale Hornets .... St. Helens offer winger Brimah Kebbie at £40,000 .... Leigh ask £60,000 for Kiwi Test prop Peter Brown .... Oldham list Des Foy at £100,000, Keith Newton at £50,000 and Andy Ruane at £20,000 .... Australia extend their unbeaten club record to three successive tours by defeating Widnes 15-8 .... Centre Steve McGowan priced at £125,000 by Bradford Northern .... Proposed David Bishop move from Hull K.R. shelved by Bradford Northern .... Second Division clubs stage a crisis meeting to discuss the contract system .... Leeds put eight players on the list at a total of £170,000 including, Rob Ackerman, Gary Lord, Gary Spencer, Chris Vasey and Neil James .... Great Britain recall Jonathan Davies for the third British Coal Test .... St. Helens discipline coach Mike McClennan and stand off Tommy Frodsham after a benefit dinner fracas .... Australia retain the Ashes with a 14-0 victory at Elland Road .... Trafford Borough list prop Steve Herbert at £9,000.

DECEMBER

Warrington sign Barrow prop forward Gary Tees for £30,000 .... Wakefield Trinity offer full back Kevin Harcombe for £45,000 .... Widnes protest at being televised by the BBC in successive Regal Trophy ties and earn 100 per cent increase in fee .... Andy Gregory retires from Test football .... Scarborough FC announce their intention to apply for membership of the Rugby League .... The 100th and final Rugby League Roadshow is staged, the grand total of more than £162,000 being raised for players' benefits .... Dewsbury sack coach Maurice Bamford, assistant Jack Addy taking over .... Cash crisis club Leigh list want-away David Ruane at £90,000, David Topping £80,000 and Andy Collier £70,000 .... League decide that Silk Cut Challenge Cup finals will kick off half an hour earlier at 2.30pm to maximise television coverage .... Oldham's John Cogger sent off in Regal Trophy tie at Batley for inciting the crowd and subsequently banned for two matches .... Bramley coach Barry Johnson resigns due to business transfer to the North East .... Fastest-ever sell out for the

Wembley Challenge Cup final with record £1.5m receipts .... Bradford Northern's veteran full back Keith Mumby joins Sheffield Eagles .... Board of Directors declare Scarborough's application as 'worthy of consideration' .... Australian referee Greg McCallum appointed for the forthcoming Anglo-French Tests, his third trip to Europe .... Wakefield Trinity list centre Phil Eden at £55,000 .... Cumbrian full back David Lightfoot offered at £40,000 after missing Christmas training.

JANUARY

Former All Black RU full back John Gallagher pledges his allegiance to Great Britain for future Test selection .... Sydney club Eastern Suburbs offer short term contract to Martin Offiah, but at a lower value than being asked .... Sheffield Eagles sign New Zealander Desmond Maea to replace the returning Australian Ian Russell on their quota .... Leigh bid to sell Hilton Park to raise money to clear debts and build a new ground .... Hull coach Noel Cleal retires as a player and replaces himself on the quota with Balmain centre Damien McGarry .... Hull bid farewell to Australian coach Brian Smith with a 34-14 defeat of Leeds at the Boulevard .... Former Kangaroo coach Frank Stanton flies in from Sydney for week-long talks with Hull K.R. regarding a 1991-92 appointment as coach .... Leigh list Mick Round at £65,000 while hooker Mick Dean threatens legal action for the club's non-fulfilment of his contract .... Scarborough accepted as Rugby League's eighth new club in 10 years .... Rugby League Council recommend the introduction of three divisions based on the 'Hetherington Plan' of 14 clubs in the First Division, eight in the second and 14 in the third .... Widnes cut the asking price on scrum half Andy Eyres from £40,000 to £25,000 .... Maurice Bamford joins Bramley as commercial manager .... Barrow exchange centre Mark Beckwith for Whitehaven prop Steve Maguire .... Ex-Kiwi Test back James Leuluai given a free transfer by Ryedale-York .... Warrington lift the Regal Trophy with a 12-2 defeat of Bradford Northern .... Uncapped St. John Ellis, Les Holliday and Anthony Sullivan named in 19-man Great Britain squad to face France in Perpignan .... Oldham sack coach Tony Barrow .... Wakefield Trinity re-sign full back Gary Spencer .... John Fieldhouse appointed caretaker player-coach at Oldham and asks Maurice Bamford for advice .... Jeannette Smith named as Great Britain Under-21 physiotherapist, Rugby League's first-ever female international appointment .... Doncaster sign James Leuluai .... Allan Agar quits as coach of Rochdale Hornets .... Don Gregoire joins Nottingham City from Dewsbury .... Halifax recruit Kiwi Test prop forward Peter Brown from Leigh .... Hull prop forward Karl Harrison receives four-match ban and fails in subsequent appeal, ruling him out of the Great Britain side to meet France, Ian Lucas of Wigan being called in for his Test debut .... Roy Dickinson appointed player-coach of Bramley .... Former Welsh international Brian Juliff named as caretaker coach of Rochdale Hornets .... Bradford Northern prop forward Simon Tuffs faces League drug inquiry and claims that amphetamine was in his blood because a drink was spiked, the case being adjourned .... Featherstone Rovers Kiwi import Brendon Tutta given severe warning after failing to take a post-match drug test, claiming confusion over the testing procedure .... Scarborough line up Hull K.R. director Len Casey, former coach of Hull and Wakefield Trinity, as first-ever supremo .... Record away scores as Great Britain beat France 45-10 in Perpignan and the Under-21s record a 48-2 success in Limoux .... Wales set for re-formation to meet Papua New Guinea at Swansea in October .... Castleford chase French Test centre David Fraisse .... Widnes swoop for New Zealand winger Ben Lia .... Great Britain Under-21s visit Lilleshall for a fitness-testing programme .... Hull K.R. offer coaching role to Australian Frank Stanton.

FEBRUARY

Castleford offer second row man Martin Ketteridge at £55,000 .... Full back Paul Topping asks to come off the list at Leigh .... Widnes block Rochdale Hornets' move to approach Kurt Sorensen to be player-coach .... Huddersfield list centre Stuart Cocker at £65,000 .... Rochdale Hornets fail in bid to re-sign John Woods from Leigh .... Scrum half Dean Marwood makes his peace at Barrow .... RL Council recommends three division set-up be introduced in 1991-92 season .... Swinton sign Trafford Borough prop forward Steve Herbert and take Tommy Frodsham on loan from St. Helens .... Keighley hand over £7,000 fee for Bradford Northern scrum half Heath Godfrey .... Newcomers Scarborough appoint Hull K.R. director Len Casey as coach .... Ex-Welsh RU scrum half Kevin Ellis, of Warrington, called up for his Great Britain Test debut after fewer than 20 first team games .... Whitehaven sign New Zealander Mike Toomata from Runcorn Highfield .... Snow forces the switch of the British Coal Under-21 international from Huddersfield to centrally-heated Wigan .... Barrow sack Steve Norton as coach after 11 months in charge .... Leigh offer John Woods at £30,000 and veteran Tony Cottrell at £10,000 .... Kiwi Test packman George Mann wins appeal to the New Zealand League and signs three-year contract with St. Helens .... Hull prop forward Andy Dannatt recalled by Great Britain after six-year absence .... Great Britain Under-21s crash 16-6 to the French at Wigan .... Leeds transfer list winger Vince Fawcett at £125,000 .... Barrow appoint Paul Kavanagh as coach .... Great Britain rewrite the record books with a 60-4 hammering of the French at Leeds .... Hull K.R. deal with former Australian Test coach Frank Stanton falls through .... The League announce the formation of an eight-club championship in Russia, to be launched in May .... Southern amateur club Hemel Hempstead apply to join the Slalom Lager Alliance .... Barry Seabourne quits as coach of Huddersfield .... The 1991 CIS Insurance Charity Shield to be staged at Gateshead International Stadium in August as catalyst of North East development programme .... Whitehaven and Huddersfield propose a three division set-up of 14-11-11 to commence in 1992-93 .... Bradford Northern prop forward Simon Tuffs banned for two years after drug test reveals amphetamine usage.

MARCH

Swinton offer full back Chris Johnson at £15,000 .... Featherstone Rovers ask £60,000 for loose forward Andy Fisher and £16,000 for prop John Bastian .... Newcomers Scarborough adopt the name Pirates .... Plans formulated to launch professional Rugby League in Stoke .... Ellery Hanley agrees to join new American football club London Monarchs .... Wigan insists that Hanley's first commitment stays with Rugby League .... Halifax sign Pontypool RU full back Matthew Silva .... Meeting of clubs fails by two votes to provide the required majority for a 14-8-14 three division system for 1991-92 season .... Talks break down for the £150,000 transfer of Wigan scrum half Bobby Goulding to Leeds .... League add cannabis to the list of banned drugs .... Fulham chosen to join Ryedale-York on three-match pioneer visit to Soviet Union in May .... Leeds packman Paul Dixon signs a summer contract with Winfield Cup side Gold Coast .... Wigan reject Manly move for Denis Betts, Ellery Hanley and Joe Lydon on close season contracts .... Halifax utility player

Simon Longstaff moves to Oldham .... Kippax referee John Holdsworth appointed for the Australia Test series with New Zealand .... Featherstone Rovers veteran forward Peter Smith is first recruit by Scarborough Pirates and appointed captain .... Canterbury-Bankstown agree terms with Widnes utility back Jonathan Davies for a summer contract .... Board of Directors give blessing to southern amateurs Hemel Hempstead joining the Slalom Lager Alliance .... Stoke bid to join the League thwarted by the Board of Directors because of financial circumstances .... Bradford Northern list reserve hooker Glenn Barraclough at £70,000 .... Warrington make an offer to Irish RU winger Simon Geoghegan .... Leeds duo Rob Ackerman and Neil James join Ryedale-York .... Leeds skipper Garry Schofield opts to have a summer lay-off and decides not to join Australian club Gold Coast .... Roger Millward bows out after 25 years at Hull K.R. with a 62-16 defeat at Sheffield.

APRIL

Sydney Premiership side Gold Coast sign Sheffield Eagles skipper Daryl Powell on a summer contract .... Wellington invite Salford coach Kevin Tamati to take the reins if admitted to the Sydney Premiership in 1993 .... Consortium offers £200,000 to take over financial crisis club Leigh .... Scarborough Pirates sign Hull K.R. winger Steve Hadi .... Wigan coach John Monie calls for four substitutes in British club matches .... Wigan beat Widnes 26-6 to become favourites to lift the Stones Bitter Championship title .... Wigan centre Kevin Iro signs for Australian club Manly .... Bradford Northern draw 18-18 at Wigan to leave the title still undecided .... Dewsbury play their last match at Crown Flatt after 115 years of rugby use .... Oldham appoint Australian Peter Tunks as coach .... Wigan beat Leeds at Headingley in the last match of the campaign

to earn a record £44,000 Stones Bitter title prize .... Rochdale Hornets, Oldham and Sheffield Eagles relegated, with Salford, Halifax and Swinton promoted .... Coach Norman Turley leaves Whitehaven by mutual consent .... St. Helens centre Paul Loughlin turns down a £20,000-plus summer contract with Australian club Gold Coast .... Bradford Northern prop Simon Tuffs is cleared of drug charges on appeal after producing the person who spiked his drink .... Clubs vote to introduce three divisions in season 1991-92 .... Rugby League Council working party recommends a limit of £60,000 per season on First Division clubs for the importing of overseas players .... Leigh club put in the hands of an administrator in a bid to find new owners .... Batley part company with player-coach Keith Rayne .... Wigan lift the Silk Cut Challenge Cup for a record fourth successive year, beating St. Helens 13-8 .... St. Helens sign Hull K.R. winger Anthony Sullivan for around £100,000 .... Huddersfield cut the asking price for centre Ian Thomas from £80,000 to £40,000 and stand off Stuart Cocker from £65,000 to £35,000.

MAY

Castleford list Test winger David Plange at £70,000 .... Halifax sign winger Henry Sharp from Bradford amateur side Dudley Hill after scoring six tries in eight trial games .... Sheffield Eagles follower John Lack chosen as 1991 Traveleads Top Fan, Rugby League's official Supporter of the Year .... The International Board, meeting in Cannes, introduce the 'blood bin', approve a new international seven-a-side tournament in Sydney and ban heading of the ball .... Brewers Matthew Brown announce a new £50,000 three-year sponsorship of reserve grade football, with a new title of the Younger's Alliance .... Oldham offer skipper Mike Ford for £150,000 .... Halifax sign Hull K.R.'s Kiwi Test back

Dave Watson .... Widnes packman Kurt Sorensen turns down a summer contract with Sydney club Cronulla .... St. Helens renew interest in Australian RU skipper Michael Lynagh .... Wales side to be re-formed after seven years to meet Papua New Guinea in Swansea as part of their five-match autumn tour .... French Test scrum half Patrick Entat decides not to return to Hull after breakdown of contract talks .... Wigan forward Gerard Stazicker seeks a move because of lack of first-team opportunities .... Great Britain and Leeds star Garry Schofield named as 1991 Stones Bitter Man of Steel .... Runcorn Highfield seek League approval for change of name to Highfield RLFC .... Hull K.R. decide not to renew contracts of overseas imports Bryan Niebling and James Goulding as part of cost-cutting exercise .... Hull become the first Yorkshire side to lift a major cup for four years by defeating favourites Widnes 14-4 in the Stones Bitter Premiership final .... Salford lift a Second Division Championship-Premiership double by beating Halifax 27-20 in the Old Trafford final .... Widnes turn down a transfer request from Test winger Martin Offiah .... Widnes coach Doug Laughton accepts team manager role at Leeds, coach David Ward quitting the Headingley club when asked to be number two .... Wigan named as Stones Bitter Team of the Year for fourth time in five years .... Long-serving full back George Fairbairn appointed coach of Hull K.R. .... Dewsbury pay £45,000 for Leeds duo, scrum half Paul Delaney and forward Paul Worthy .... Leeds angry at claim by England RU skipper Will Carling of a £1m offer to turn professional .... Sheffield Eagles sign first local recruit, 17-year-old Jason Davidson .... Oldham list five players after contract talks, Des Foy and Paul Lord at £25,000 each, John Henderson and Keith Newton at £20,000 each and Andy Ruane at £10,000 .... Coach Noel Cleal agrees a new one-year contract at Hull .... Swinton persuade coach Jim Crellin to continue for further two seasons .... Bass Brewers announce a new four-year £1.8m contract from 1992-96 .... Welsh RU centre Scott Gibbs rejects a contract from Wigan .... Peter Roe parts company with Halifax after being asked to re-apply for his coaching job .... Oldham offer former Test forward John Fieldhouse at £50,000 .... Featherstone Rovers release veteran prop forward Jeff Grayshon .... Huddersfield referee Colin Morris appointed for the Papua New Guinea Test with France .... Leigh forward Tony Cottrell puts in a bid for the crisis club .... Great Britain's 1992 tour itinerary to be the shortest ever with 17 matches, featuring a record five fixtures against Winfield Cup sides and first-ever staging of Friday night Tests in Australia .. Batley sign Sheffield Eagles prop Neil Kellett .... Great Britain Test man David Bishop returns to Hull K.R. after departure of coach Roger Millward with whom he had been in dispute .... Combined Ryedale-York and Fulham side beat Russian XIII 42-10 in challenge match in Dinamo Stadium, Moscow .... Wigan winger David Myers joins Sydney club Manly on a summer contract .... Ryedale-York line up two Soviet 20-year-olds, centre Alexandre Dyatlove and loose forward Peter Sokoluv .... Featherstone Rovers reduce the asking price for Mark Knapper from £40,000 to £10,000 .... Kiwi James Leuluai leaves Britain to coach Wellington side Petone .... St. Helens cut transfer fees on Andy Bateman to £40,000, Brimah Kebbie to £30,000 and Roy Haggerty to £19,000 .... Widnes offer player-coach role to Wigan scrum half Andy Gregory .... Widnes insistence on a fee for Kurt Sorensen cools Halifax interest in player-coach approach .... Hull talk to Manly scrum half Des Hasler .... Scarborough sign Mark Knapper from Featherstone Rovers and Malcolm Beall from Hull K.R.

A tough baptism for former All Black John Gallagher.

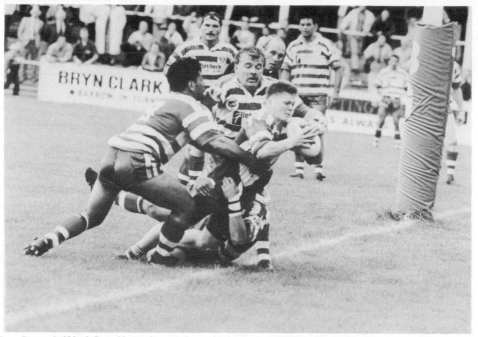

Barrow half back Dean Marwood crosses for one of six tries in a 1990-91 tally of 162 points for the Shipbuilders.

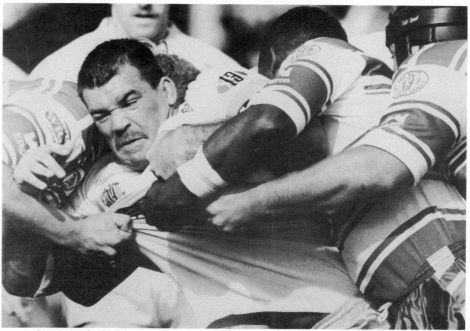

Crunch time for Castleford's Test prop Keith England, scorer of two tries in 31 appearances in 1990-91.

CLUBS

The following is a focus on the 36 professional Rugby League clubs, the section providing each club with a profile and an analysis of their 1990-91 campaign on a match by match basis with a summary for each first team player.

KEY
In the individual club profiles the following headings are featured:
First season refers to when the club gained senior league status. In some instances clubs have disbanded and re-formed, sometimes under different titles. For record purposes these changes are ignored except where there has been a break of more than one full season.
Honours. Until they were scrapped in 1970, the Yorkshire and Lancashire Leagues were among the honours in the professional game. Before 1903 they operated under the title of the Yorkshire and Lancashire Senior Competitions. Winners of these senior competitions are listed under Yorkshire and Lancashire League Champions. The pre-1903 Yorkshire Senior Competition should not be confused with the league operating for A-teams in Yorkshire which had the same title.
Regal Trophy is the new title for the John Player/Player's No. 6 Trophy competition.
Coaches. Changes in the appointment of a club's coach since 1 June 1990 are shown in brackets.
Attendances. Crowds in brackets are at neutral venue.
Appearances. Players' totals are based on official teamsheets submitted to the League after each first team match. + indicates playing substitute appearance.

In the match by match review for each club the following abbreviations are used:

YC	—	Yorkshire Cup	A	—	Away
LC	—	Lancashire Cup	W	—	Won
SBC	—	Stones Bitter Championship	L	—	Lost
SD	—	Second Division	D	—	Drawn
RT	—	Regal Trophy	dg	—	Drop goal
CC	—	Challenge Cup	Fr	—	France
PT	—	Premiership Trophy	Aus	—	Australia
SDP	—	Second Division Premiership	NZ	—	New Zealand
P	—	Preliminary Round	PNG	—	Papua New Guinea
H	—	Home	Pr	—	Probationer

BARROW

Ground:	Craven Park (0229-820273)
Colours:	Royal blue
First Season:	1900-01
Nickname:	Shipbuilders
Chairman:	John Gilbert
Secretary:	Susan Gaskell
Coach:	Steve Norton (May 1990-Feb 1991)
	Paul Kavanagh (Feb 1991-)
Honours:	**Challenge Cup** Winners, 1954-55
	Beaten finalists, 1937-38, 1950-51,
	1956-57, 1966-67
	Regal Trophy Beaten finalists
	1980-81
	Lancashire Cup Winners, 1954-55,
	1983-84
	Beaten finalists, 1937-38
	Division Two Champions, 1975-76,
	1983-84
Records:	Attendance: 21,651 v. Salford
	(League) 15 Apr, 1938
	Season
	Goals: 135 by J. Ball, 1956-57
	Tries: 50 by J. Lewthwaite, 1956-57
	Points: 305 by I. Ball, 1979-80
	Match
	Goals: 12 by F. French v.
	Maryport, 19 Feb, 1938; W. Horne
	v. Cardiff, 8 Sep, 1951; S. Tickle v.
	Kent Invicta, 8 Apr, 1984

Tries: 6 by V. Cumberbatch v. Batley, 21 Nov, 1936; J. Thornburrow v. Maryport, 19 Feb, 1938; F. Castle v. York, 29 Sep, 1951
Points: 28 by K. Jarrett v. Doncaster, 25 Aug, 1970; S. Tickle v. Kent Invicta, 8 Apr, 1984; D. Marwood at Runcorn H., 16 Apr, 1989
Highest score: 83-3 v. Maryport, 1937-38
Highest against: 90-0 v. Leeds, 1989-90

1990-91 PLAYERS' SUMMARY

	App	Tries	Goals	Dr	Pts
Archer, Darren	8	2	—	—	8
Beckwith, Mark	3 + 1	1	—	—	4
Blackwood, Mark	5 + 4	2	—	—	8
Burns, Paul	30	12	—	—	48
Cairns, David	18 + 2	3	—	—	12
Cartmel, Ian	19 + 7	1	—	—	4
Clayton, Stephen	15 + 1	—	—	—	—
Crarey, Paul	25	—	—	—	—
Dale, Graham	2	1	—	—	4
Dunn, Reg	23	2	2	—	12
Fletcher, Andrew	4	—	—	—	—
Hadley, Derek	3 + 4	1	—	—	4
Howse, Stephen	5 + 5	2	—	—	8
Jackson, Stephen	5 + 2	—	—	—	—
Jackson, Wayne	0 + 2	—	—	—	—
James, Mick	9	1	—	—	4
Kay, Tony	4	2	—	—	8
Kendall, Gary	26	5	—	—	20
Keresoma, Moses	16 + 2	1	—	—	4
Lupton, Graham	1	—	—	—	—
Maguire, Stephen	8 + 4	1	2	—	8
Marwood, Dean	26	6	67	4	162
Morrison, Steve	1	—	—	—	—
Moses, Alan	3	—	—	—	—
Mossop, Stephen	12 + 1	—	—	—	—
O'Neill, Ian	0 + 2	—	—	—	—
Pemberton, Keith	6 + 6	—	—	—	—
Rhodes, Stewart	11 + 4	1	—	—	4
Riley, Stephen	0 + 1	—	—	—	—
Roper, Kevin	9 + 2	—	—	—	—
Rowan, Stephen	7 + 5	—	—	—	—
Shaw, Neil	25 + 2	4	8	1	33
Simpson, Nigel	23	7	—	—	28
Spears, Kevin	1	—	—	—	—
Stott, Phil	3	—	—	—	—
Tees, Gary	2	—	—	—	—
Thompson, Philip	4	—	—	—	—
Townsend, David	17 + 1	10	—	1	41
Trainor, Pat	31	8	—	—	32
Westwood, Gary	1	—	—	—	—
Wild, John	5 + 1	—	—	—	—
TOTALS:					
41 players		73	79	6	456

Neil Shaw, scorer of 33 points for Barrow.

1990-91 MATCH ANALYSIS

Date	Competition	H/A	Opponent	Rlt	Score	Tries	Goals	Attendance	Referee
26.8.90	LC(1)	A	Wigan	L	8-70	Simpson	Marwood (2)	—	—
9.9.90	SD	H	Salford	L	0-31	—	—	1368	Carter
16.9.90	SD	A	Fulham	L	8-22	Burns	Marwood (2)	—	—
23.9.90	SD	H	Leigh	L	16-32	Dunn, Marwood	Marwood (4)	1206	Tidball
30.9.90	SD	A	Whitehaven	L	15-22	Townsend, Maguire	Marwood (3, 1dg)	—	—
7.10.90	SD	H	Dewsbury	W	12-11	Burns, Marwood	Marwood (2)	1313	Kendrew
14.10.90	SD	A	Salford	L	10-76	Townsend (2)	Marwood	—	—
21.10.90	SD	H	Bramley	W	26-7	Townsend (3), Simpson	Marwood (3), Maguire (2)	1100	J. Connolly
4.11.90	SD	A	Carlisle	L	26-44	Burns (2), Simpson, Kendall, Townsend	Marwood (3)	—	—
11.11.90	SD	H	Huddersfield	L	12-26	Rhodes, Burns	Marwood (2)	1030	K. Morris
18.11.90	SD	H	Trafford B.	W	10-6	Simpson (2)	Marwood	620	Cross
25.11.90	SD	H	Halifax	L	18-46	Marwood (2), Beckwith	Marwood (3)	1142	Asquith
2.12.90	RT(1)	H	Featherstone R.	L	16-54	Simpson, Dunn, James	Marwood (2)	1200	Campbell
9.12.90	SD	H	Ryedale-York	L	8-31	Trainor	Dunn (2)	621	Kendrew
23.12.90	SD	A	Leigh	L	4-40	Keresoma	—	—	—
26.12.90	SD	H	Carlisle	W	34-4	Townsend (2), Kendall, Archer, Trainor, Burns	Shaw (4, 1dg), Townsend (dg)	900	Burke
30.12.90	SD	A	Ryedale-York	L	0-34	—	—	—	—
6.1.91	SD	H	Keighley	L	10-14	Trainor, Shaw	Shaw	602	J. Connolly
27.1.91	SD	A	Bramley	L	14-16	Trainor, Kendall	Shaw (3)	—	—
10.2.91	SD	A	Hunslet	L	4-56	Kendall	—	—	—
17.2.91	CC(1)	H	Hunslet	W	13-8	Hadley, Townsend	Marwood (2, 1dg)	910	Crashley
24.2.91	CC(2)	A	Widnes	L	4-28	—	Marwood (2)	4643	Ollerton
27.2.91	SD	H	Hunslet	D	4-4	—	Marwood (2)	900	R. Connolly
3.3.91	SD	A	Huddersfield	L	10-18	Simpson	Marwood (3)	—	—
10.3.91	SD	A	Trafford B.	W	27-20	Blackwood (2), Burns, Shaw	Marwood (5, 1dg)	—	—
13.3.91	SD	A	Halifax	L	10-48	Cairns	Marwood (3)	—	—
17.3.91	SD	H	Fulham	L	8-20	Cairns	Marwood (2)	750	K. Morris
24.3.91	SD	A	Keighley	L	20-24	Trainor (2), Shaw, Marwood	Marwood (2)	—	—
29.3.91	SD	H	Nottingham C.	W	34-6	Burns (3), Howse, Dale, Trainor, Kendall	Marwood (3)	880	Tidball
1.4.91	SD	A	Nottingham C.	W	30-12	Shaw, Marwood, Howse, Burns	Marwood (7)	—	—
7.4.91	SD	H	Whitehaven	W	26-16	Trainor, Burns, Cairns, Kay	Marwood (5)	1040	Carter
14.4.91	SD	A	Dewsbury	D	19-19	Archer, Cartmel, Kay	Marwood (3, 1dg)	—	—

BATLEY

Ground:	Mount Pleasant (0924-472208)
Colours:	Cerise and fawn
First Season:	1895-96
Nickname:	Gallant Youths
Chairman:	Stephen Ball
Secretary:	Richard Illingworth
Coach:	Keith Rayne (May 1990-Apr 1991)
Honours:	**Championship** Winners, 1923-24
	Challenge Cup Winners, 1896-97, 1897-98, 1900-01
	Yorkshire League Winners, 1898-99, 1923-24
	Yorkshire Cup Winners, 1912-13 Beaten finalists, 1909-10, 1922-23, 1924-25, 1952-53
Records:	Attendance: 23,989 v. Leeds (RL Cup) 14 Mar, 1925
	Season
	Goals: 120 by S. Thompson, 1958-59
	Tries: 29 by J. Tindall, 1912-13
	Points: 281 by J. Perry, 1950-51
	Match
	Goals: 9 by W. Davies v. Widnes, 27 Mar, 1909; S. Thompson v. Keighley, 20 Sep, 1958
	Tries: 5 by J. Oakland v. Bramley, 19 Dec, 1908; T. Brannan v. Swinton, 17 Jan, 1920; J. Wale v. Bramley, 4 Dec, 1926 and v. Cottingham, 12 Feb, 1927
	Points: 26 by J. Perry v. Liverpool C., 16 Sep, 1951
	Highest score: 52-8 v. Widnes, 1908-09
	Highest against: 78-9 v. Wakefield T., 1967-68

1990-91 PLAYERS' SUMMARY

	App	Tries	Goals	Dr	Pts
Bailey, Howard	20 + 3	6	3	—	30
Bargate, Lee	3	—	—	—	—
Booth, Michael	31	6	—	—	24
Bownass, Mark	2 + 1	1	—	—	4
Child, Darren	6 + 6	1	—	—	4
Craven, Nigel	1	—	—	—	—
Crossley, John	4 + 2	—	—	—	—
Fortis, Mark	25 + 2	5	—	—	20
Gearey, Paul	7 + 3	—	—	—	—
Hamill, James	18	—	—	—	—
Hartley, Neil	16 + 7	2	—	—	8
Kay, Paul	15	1	—	—	4
McGrath, Damien	1 + 1	1	1	—	6
McLeary, Jack	5 + 3	—	—	—	—
Marshall, Paul	27	6	—	—	24
Parkinson, Andy	1 + 1	—	—	—	—
Parrish, Steve	14 + 4	7	15	1	59
Pratt, Richard	2	—	—	—	—
Rayne, Keith	22 + 2	5	—	—	20
Redick, Paul	19	3	—	—	12
Rees, Paul	4 + 6	1	—	—	4
Scott, Mark	14 + 1	5	—	—	20
Speight, Darren	4	—	—	—	—
Speight, Mark	33 + 1	1	—	—	4
Spendler, Mark	4 + 5	—	—	—	—
Stainburn, John	20 + 4	1	7	3	21
Storey, Paul	9 + 6	2	—	—	8
Thornton, Gary	31	5	—	—	20
Whakarau, Sonny	24 + 1	1	—	—	4
Williams, Andy	31 + 1	12	—	—	48
Wilson, Simon	29	3	38	5	93
Wragg, Nicky	0 + 2	—	—	—	—
TOTALS:					
32 players		75	64	9	437

Veteran Jeff Grayshon, a Batley recruit for 1991-92.

1990-91 MATCH ANALYSIS

Date	Competition	H/A	Opponent	Rlt	Score	Tries	Goals	Attendance	Referee
26.8.90	YC(1)	H	Huddersfield	W	17-10	Fortis, Marshall, Kay	Wilson (2, 1dg)	1734	Galtress
2.9.90	YC(2)	A	Dewsbury	L	8-18	Fortis	Wilson (2)	—	—
9.9.90	SD	H	Leigh	L	6-22	Fortis	Wilson	1735	K. Morris
16.9.90	SD	A	Keighley	L	14-21	Marshall, Speight	Wilson (3)	—	—
23.9.90	SD	H	Salford	L	10-21	Scott, Booth	Wilson	1375	Holgate
7.10.90	SD	H	Nottingham C.	W	17-0	Williams (2), Booth	Wilson (2), Stainburn (dg)	844	Steele
21.10.90	SD	H	Trafford B.	W	10-2	Scott	Wilson (2, 1dg), Parrish (dg)	761	Tidball
28.10.90	SD	A	Fulham	L	7-14	Williams	Wilson, Stainburn (dg)	—	—
4.11.90	SD	A	Halifax	L	3-28	—	Wilson (1, 1dg)	—	—
11.11.90	SD	H	Whitehaven	W	26-16	Parrish (2), Rayne, Marshall, Booth	Parrish (2), Wilson	702	Asquith
25.11.90	SD	H	Ryedale-York	L	14-26	Booth, Williams	Parrish (3)	1102	Holgate
2.12.90	RT(1)	A	Nottingham C.	W	35-6	Hartley, Storey, Marshall, Bailey, Williams	Parrish (6), Stainburn (1, 1dg)	—	—
9.12.90	RT(2)	H	Oldham	W	20-16	Rayne (3), Child	Stainburn (2)	2054	C. Morris
16.12.90	RT(3)	A	Widnes	L	6-56	Whakarau	Parrish	—	—
20.12.90	SD	A	Trafford B.	L	8-20	Parrish	Parrish (2)	—	—
23.12.90	SD	H	Carlisle	L	9-38	Fortis, Stainburn	Wilson (dg)	729	Cross
26.12.90	SD	A	Dewsbury	L	4-6	Hartley	—	—	—
1.1.91	SD	H	Dewsbury	W	12-6	Thornton, Booth	Parrish, Stainburn	2019	Smith
6.1.91	SD	A	Nottingham C.	W	16-15	Parrish (2), Redick, Williams	—	—	—
13.1.91	SD	A	Bramley	W	28-12	Thornton (2), Wilson, Marshall, Redick	Wilson (4)	—	—
20.1.91	SD	H	Halifax	L	0-12	—	—	3417	Crashley
27.1.91	SD	A	Hunslet	L	0-6	—	—	—	—
3.2.91	SD	H	Bramley	W	40-16	Wilson (2), Bailey (2), Rayne, Parrish, Williams	Wilson (6)	702	K. Morris
15.2.91	CC(1)	A	Salford	L	14-36	Redick, Parrish, Marshall	Wilson	—	—
24.2.91	SD	A	Carlisle	W	19-13	Bailey (2), Williams, Scott	Wilson (1, 1dg)	—	—
27.2.91	SD	A	Whitehaven	W	18-2	Williams (2), Booth	Wilson (3)	—	—
3.3.91	SD	H	Fulham	L	4-20	Rees	—	758	Tennant
10.3.91	SD	A	Ryedale-York	L	12-24	Scott, Bailey	Bailey (2)	—	—
17.3.91	SD	H	Keighley	W	22-12	Thornton, Storey, Williams, Fortis	Wilson (2), Bailey	629	Tidball
21.3.91	SD	A	Salford	L	14-32	Scott, McGrath	Stainburn (3)	—	—
24.3.91	SD	A	Leigh	L	6-28	Williams	McGrath	—	—
29.3.91	SD	A	Huddersfield	L	0-22	—	—	—	—
1.4.91	SD	H	Huddersfield	L	8-18	Bownass	Wilson (2)	1005	K. Morris
7.4.91	SD	H	Hunslet	L	10-14	Thornton	Wilson (3)	859	Whitelam

BRADFORD NORTHERN

Ground: Odsal Stadium (0274-733899)
Colours: White, red, amber and black
First Season: 1895-96 as "Bradford". Disbanded and became Bradford Northern in 1907-08. Disbanded during 1963-64 and re-formed for start of 1964-65
Nickname: Northern
Chairman: Chris Caisley
Coach: David Hobbs (Mar 1990-)
Honours: **Challenge Cup** Winners, 1905-06, 1943-44, 1946-47, 1948-49
Beaten finalists, 1897-98, 1944-45, 1947-48, 1972-73
Championship Beaten finalists, 1947-48, 1951-52
Division One Champions, 1903-04, 1979-80, 1980-81
Division Two Champions, 1973-74
War-time Emergency League Championship winners, 1939-40, 1940-41, 1944-45
Beaten finalists, 1941-42
Yorkshire League Winners, 1899-1900, 1900-01, 1939-40, 1940-41, 1947-48
Yorkshire Cup Winners, 1906-07, 1940-41, 1941-42, 1943-44, 1945-46, 1948-49, 1949-50, 1953-54, 1965-66, 1978-79, 1987-88, 1989-90
Beaten finalists, 1913-14, 1981-82, 1982-83
Premiership Winners, 1977-78
Beaten finalists, 1978-79, 1979-80, 1989-90
Regal Trophy Winners, 1974-75, 1979-80
Beaten finalists, 1990-91
Records: Attendance: 102,569 Warrington v. Halifax (RL Cup Final replay) 5 May, 1954
Home: 69,429 v. Huddersfield (RL Cup) 14 March, 1953

Season
Goals: 173 by E. Tees, 1971-72
Tries: 63 by J. McLean, 1951-52
Points: 364 by E. Tees, 1971-72
Match
Goals: 14 by J. Phillips v. Batley, 6 Sep, 1952
Tries: 7 by J. Dechan v. Bramley, 13 Oct, 1906
Points: 36 by J. Woods v. Swinton, 13 Oct, 1985
Highest score: 72-9 v. Doncaster, 1973-74; 72-12 v. Hunslet, 1984-85
Highest against: 75-18 v. Leeds, 1931-32

1990-91 PLAYERS' SUMMARY

	App	Tries	Goals	Dr	Pts
Barnett, Steve	2	—	—	—	—
Barraclough, Glenn	3	—	—	—	—
Cooper, David	6 + 2	1	9	—	22
Cordle, Gerald	39	14	—	—	56
Croft, David	3 + 6	1	—	—	4
Fairbank, Karl	35	7	—	—	28
Gill, Henderson	4 + 2	—	—	—	—
Green, Alex	0 + 1	—	—	—	—
Grogan, Bob	6	—	—	—	—
Gumbs, Hugh	13	3	15	—	42
Hamer, Jon	33 + 3	4	—	—	16
Hellewell, Phil	9 + 4	2	17	—	42
Hiley, Greg	0 + 1	—	—	—	—
Hobbs, David	35 + 3	5	49	6	124
Iti, Brett	29 + 2	13	—	—	52
McGowan, Steve	20	5	1	—	22
Marchant, Tony	23 + 4	6	—	—	24
Medley, Paul	35 + 2	17	—	—	68
Moxon, Darren	8 + 1	—	—	—	—
Mumby, Keith	2	—	—	—	—
Noble, Brian	37	—	—	—	—
Pendlebury, John	36 + 1	2	2	4	16
Richards, Craig	21 + 17	3	—	—	12
Rhodes, Paul	1 + 1	1	—	—	4
Shelford, Darrall	37 + 3	13	—	—	52
Simpson, Roger	34 + 2	9	—	—	36
Summers, Neil	21 + 6	6	—	—	24
Tuffs, Simon	3 + 4	—	—	—	—
Wilkinson, Ian	20	3	—	—	12
Wilson, Mark	5 + 8	1	—	—	4

TOTALS:
| 30 players | | 116 | 93 | 10 | 660 |

1990-91 MATCH ANALYSIS

Date	Com-petition	H/A	Opponent	Rlt	Score	Tries	Goals	Atten-dance	Referee
19.8.90	YC(P)	H	Sheffield E.	W	20-12	Cordle, Wilkinson, Cooper	Cooper (4)	3477	Whitelam
26.8.90	YC(1)	A	Leeds	W	24-16	Medley (2), Cordle, Wilson	Cooper (2), Hobbs (2)	—	—
2.9.90	YC(2)	H[1]	Castleford	L	12-42	Simpson, Cordle	McGowan, Cooper	7974	C. Morris
9.9.90	SBC	H	Widnes	L	10-14	Fairbank	Cooper (2), Hobbs (dg), Pendlebury (dg)	6203	Tennant
16.9.90	SBC	A	St. Helens	L	20-24	Iti (2), Marchant, Richards	Hobbs (2)	—	—
23.9.90	SBC	A	Featherstone R.	W	26-24	Wilkinson, Iti, Marchant, Fairbank	Hobbs (5)	—	—
30.9.90	SBC	H	Wigan	W	31-30	Cordle, Shelford, Simpson, Iti, Croft	Hobbs (5, 1dg)	8715	Whitfield
7.10.90	SBC	H	Leeds	L	12-21	Shelford, Pendlebury	Hobbs (2)	10,858	Smith
14.10.90	SBC	A	Rochdale H.	L	12-19	Medley, Summers	Hobbs (2)	—	—
21.10.90	SBC	H	Hull K.R.	W	26-10	Shelford (3), Cordle (2), Summers	Hobbs	4811	Kendrew
30.10.90	SBC	A	Sheffield E.	W	36-16	McGowan (2), Fairbank, Marchant, Medley, Iti, Cordle	Hobbs (4)	—	—
4.11.90	SBC	H	Warrington	W	25-16	Cordle, Marchant, Summers, Medley	Hobbs (4, 1dg)	4649	Ollerton
11.11.90	SBC	A	Oldham	W	18-16	Richards, Cordle, Medley	Hobbs (3)	—	—
18.11.90	RT(P)	A	Sheffield E.	W	12-8	Cordle, Hamer	Hobbs (2)	—	—
21.11.90	SBC	H	St. Helens	W	18-16	Shelford (2), McGowan	Hobbs (2, 1dg), Pendlebury (dg)	4151	Holdsworth
25.11.90	SBC	A	Hull K.R.	L	4-12	Summers	—	—	—
2.12.90	RT(1)	H	Workington T.	W	12-11	Marchant, Simpson	Pendlebury (2)	2850	R. Connolly
11.12.90	RT(2)	H	Bramley	W	28-0	Cordle (2), Simpson (2), Fairbank, Marchant	Hobbs (2)	1815	Whitelam
15.12.90	RT(3)	A	Wigan	W	12-6	Pendlebury, Medley	Hobbs (2)	—	—
22.12.90	RT(SF)	Leeds	Rochdale H	W	13-2	Fairbank, Shelford	Hobbs (2, 1dg)	(3788)	Smith
26.12.90	SBC	A	Leeds	L	8-26	Hamer, Medley	—	—	—
1.1.91	SBC	A	Castleford	L	0-9	—	—	—	—
6.1.91	SBC	H	Rochdale H.	W	23-16	Simpson (2), Hobbs (2)	Hellewell (3), Pendlebury (dg)	3251	Asquith
12.1.91	RT(F)	Leeds	Warrington	L	2-12	—	Hobbs	(11,154)	Smith
20.1.91	SBC	A	Hull	L	6-34	Hamer	Hellewell	—	—
27.1.91	CC(P)	A[2]	Leigh East	W	24-12	Shelford, Rhodes, Medley, Summers	Hellewell (4)	—	—
3.2.91	SBC	A	Warrington	W	13-12	Hellewell, Medley	Hellewell, Hobbs (1, 1dg)	—	—
17.2.91	CC(1)	H[1]	Leigh	W	50-4	Wilkinson, Cordle, Shelford, Hellewell, Gumbs, Simpson, Hobbs, Hamer, Richards	Hellewell (7)	3349	Gilmour
24.2.91	CC(2)	H	Leeds	W	5-0	Shelford	Pendlebury (dg)	9076	Whitfield
27.2.91	SBC	H	Sheffield E.	L	6-10	Iti	Hobbs	2444	Holdsworth
3.3.91	SBC	H	Oldham	L	10-37	Medley (2)	Hellewell	4272	Kershaw
10.3.91	CC(3)	A	Wigan	L	2-32	—	Hobbs	—	—
13.3.91	SBC	H	Wakefield T.	W	12-10	Gumbs, Iti	Gumbs (2)	3936	Asquith
17.3.91	SBC	A	Widnes	L	14-32	Cordle, Iti	Gumbs (3)	—	—
24.3.91	SBC	A	Wakefield T.	W	16-6	Medley, Iti, McGowan	Gumbs (2)	—	—
29.3.91	SBC	H	Castleford	W	24-14	Medley (3), McGowan, Gumbs	Gumbs, Hobbs	5653	Burke
7.4.91	SBC	H	Hull	W	28-16	Iti (2), Fairbank (2), Medley	Gumbs (4)	4949	Tennant
11.4.91	SBC	A	Wigan	D	18-18	Hobbs, Iti, Shelford	Gumbs (2), Hobbs	—	—
14.4.91	SBC	H	Featherstone R.	L	18-34	Shelford, Iti, Hobbs	Hobbs (3)	4667	J. Connolly
21.4.91	PT(1)	A	Widnes	L	10-46	Simpson, Summers	Gumbs	—	—

[1] at Bradford C. FC [2] at Leigh

BRAMLEY

Ground:	McLaren Field (0532-564842)
Colours:	Amber and black
First Season:	1896-97
Nickname:	Villagers
Chairman:	Jeff Wine
General Manager:	Maurice Bamford
Coach:	Barry Johnson (Mar 1989-Dec 1990)
	John Kear (Dec 1990-Jan 1991)
	Roy Dickinson (Jan 1991-)
Honours:	**BBC2 Floodlit Trophy** Winners, 1973-74
Records:	Attendance: 12,600 v. Leeds (League) 7 May, 1947
	Season
	Goals: 130 by J. Wilson, 1961-62
	Tries: 34 by P. Lister, 1985-86
	Points: 276 by G. Langfield, 1956-57

Roy Dickinson, appointed coach of Bramley in January 1991.

Match

Goals: 11 by B. Ward v. Doncaster, 1 Sep, 1974
Tries: 7 by J. Sedgewick v. Normanton, 16 Apr, 1906
Points: 28 by B. Ward v. Doncaster, 1 Sep, 1974
Highest score: 62-14 v. Dewsbury, 1988-89
Highest against: 92-7 v. Australia, 1921-22

1990-91 PLAYERS' SUMMARY

	App	Tries	Goals	Dr	Pts
Barnett, Gary	21 + 3	3	—	—	12
Bettney, Nev	8	1	—	—	4
Blankley, Dean	21 + 1	3	—	—	12
Brentley, Gary	15 + 2	4	—	—	16
Burdon, Nick	0 + 1	—	—	—	—
Burnell, Steve	0 + 1	—	—	—	—
Carroll, Steve	28	3	66	5	149
Charles, Marquis	12	8	—	—	32
Clawson, Neil	10	—	—	—	—
Connell, Phil	6 + 3	—	—	—	—
Devine, Paul	5 + 1	—	—	—	—
Dickinson, Roy	11	3	—	—	12
Durham, Steve	15 + 1	3	—	—	12
Edmondson, Steve	11	—	—	—	—
Ellis, Andy	3	—	—	—	—
Evans, Dave	14 + 1	5	—	—	20
Fletcher, Ian	2 + 1	—	—	—	—
Fletcher, Paul	0 + 1	—	—	—	—
Fraser, Paul	2	1	—	—	4
Gill, Henderson	6	—	—	—	—
Green, Karl	1 + 2	—	—	—	—
Haigh, Colin	2	—	—	—	—
Hall, Gary	16 + 4	1	—	—	4
Harker, Keith	11	2	—	—	8
Harwood, Dean	9 + 5	2	—	—	8
Hemingway, Neil	0 + 1	—	—	—	—
Hopkins, Calvin	4 + 6	—	—	—	—
Hunter, Damian	13 + 2	1	—	1	5
Jones, Keith	30 + 1	2	11	—	30
Kemp, Martin	0 + 5	—	—	—	—
Korn, Steve	3 + 1	—	—	—	—
Langley, Paul	3 + 2	—	—	—	—
Lewis, Peter	6	1	—	—	4
Lister, Peter	11 + 3	1	—	2	6
McCone, Steve	0 + 1	—	—	—	—
Nahu, Paul	9	4	—	—	16
Olpherts, Eric	4	—	—	—	—
Pitts, David	1 + 1	—	—	—	—
Race, Wayne	1	—	—	—	—
Raynor, Gary	2	—	—	—	—
Robinson, Simon	6 + 1	1	—	—	4
Sharp, Ronnie	18 + 1	3	—	—	12
Smith, Neil	9	1	—	—	4
Spedding, Paul	10 + 3	—	—	—	—
Timson, Andy	14	—	—	1	1
Vincent, Andy	20	4	—	—	16
Wallace, Justin	11	4	—	—	16
Walsh, Chris	1	1	—	—	4
Welbourne, Stewart	11 + 1	2	—	—	8

TOTALS:
49 players		64	77	9	419

1990-91 MATCH ANALYSIS

Date	Competition	H/A	Opponent	Rlt	Score	Tries	Goals	Attendance	Referee
26.8.90	YC(1)	A	Featherstone R.	L	4-36	—	Carroll (2)	—	—
16.9.90	SD	A	Swinton	L	19-34	Brentley, Sharp	Carroll (5), Lister (dg)	—	—
23.9.90	SD	H	Halifax	L	8-56	Evans	Carroll (2)	3596	Asquith
30.9.90	SD	A	Carlisle	L	15-44	Evans (2), Durham	Carroll (1, 1dg)	—	—
7.10.90	SD	A	Fulham	L	6-20	Wallace	Carroll	—	—
14.10.90	SD	H	Chorley	W	27-18	Hunter, Evans, Brentley	Carroll (7), Lister (dg)	452	K. Morris
21.10.90	SD	A	Barrow	L	7-26	Wallace	Carroll (1, 1dg)	—	—
4.11.90	SD	A	Salford	L	0-40	—	—	—	—
11.11.90	SD	H	Runcorn H.	W	44-6	Nahu (2), Wallace, Blankley, Durham, Brentley, Jones	Carroll (8)	385	Burke
21.11.90	SD	A	Halifax	L	12-42	Wallace, Nahu	Carroll (2)	—	—
25.11.90	SD	A	Nottingham C.	L	21-24	Durham, Carroll	Carroll (6, 1dg)	—	—
2.12.90	RT(1)	H	Dewsbury	W	30-16	Evans, Nahu, Blankley (2), Sharp	Carroll (5)	680	Cross
11.12.90	RT(2)	A	Bradford N.	L	0-28	—	—	—	—
16.12.90	SD	A	Runcorn H.	W	13-12	Lewis, Vincent	Carroll (2, 1dg)	—	—
23.12.90	SD	H	Doncaster	L	12-14	Barnett, Carroll	Carroll (2)	671	Holgate
30.12.90	SD	H	Hunslet	L	14-26	Bettney, Barnett, Robinson	Carroll	789	Crashley
1.1.91	SD	A	Hunslet	L	18-30	Lister, Vincent, Fraser	Jones (3)	—	—
6.1.91	SD	A	Doncaster	L	2-58	—	Jones	—	—
13.1.91	SD	H	Batley	L	12-28	Barnett, Vincent	Jones (2)	688	Whitelam
20.1.91	SD	A	Workington T.	L	9-52	Dickinson	Jones (2), Timson (dg)	—	—
27.1.91	SD	H	Barrow	W	16-14	Charles (2), Walsh, Harker	—	430	Asquith
3.2.91	SD	A	Batley	L	16-40	Charles (2), Harker	Carroll (2)	—	—
17.2.91	CC(1)	H	Oldham	L	6-38	Charles	Carroll	1257	Campbell
24.2.91	SD	H	Nottingham C.	W	29-6	Charles, Vincent, Dickinson, Jones, Carroll	Carroll (4), Hunter (dg)	349	Tennant
3.3.91	SD	A	Chorley	L	6-22	Welbourne	Carroll	—	—
10.3.91	SD	H	Huddersfield	W	14-12	Charles (2)	Carroll (3)	693	J. Connolly
17.3.91	SD	H	Swinton	L	10-17	Harwood	Carroll (3)	808	C. Morris
24.3.91	SD	H	Salford	L	18-27	Harwood, Dickinson, Brentley	Jones (3)	928	Cross
1.4.91	SD	H	Fulham	D	8-8	Smith	Carroll (2)	425	Allatt
4.4.91	SD	H	Workington T.	L	6-18	Welbourne	Carroll	436	Cross
7.4.91	SD	H	Carlisle	W	17-12	Sharp, Hall	Carroll (4, 1dg)	568	Tidball
10.4.91	SD	A	Huddersfield	L	0-20	—	—	—	—

CARLISLE

Ground:	Gillford Park (0228-401212)
Colours:	Blue, red and white
First Season:	1981-82. A Carlisle City team entered the League in 1928-29 but withdrew after 10 matches, winning one
Chairman:	Alan Tucker
Secretary:	Elsie Martlew
Coach:	Cameron Bell (Feb 1990-)
Records:	Attendance: 5,903 v. Workington T. (Div. 2) 6 Sep, 1981

Season

Goals: 113 by S. Ferres, 1981-82
Tries: 25 by M. Morgan, 1981-82; G. Peacham, 1984-85
Points: 242 by S. Ferres, 1981-82

Match

Goals: 10 by B. Vickers at Nottingham C., 11 Mar, 1990
Tries: 4 by G. Peacham v. Workington T., 25 Jan, 1987 and K. Pape v. Rochdale H., 11 Feb, 1987
Points: 24 by B. Vickers at Nottingham C., 11 Mar, 1990
Highest score: 60-0 v. Nottingham C., 1989-90
Highest against: 112-0 v. St. Helens, 1986-87

1990-91 PLAYERS' SUMMARY

	App	Tries	Goals	Dr	Pts
Armstrong, Ian	3	—	—	—	—
Brierley, Steve	33	2	—	—	8
Catton, Tony	1 + 1	—	—	—	—
Charlton, Gary	18 + 1	3	—	—	12
Coles, Colin	15 + 3	10	—	—	40
Cowgill, Dave	0 + 1	1	—	—	4
Davies, Lee	0 + 2	—	—	—	—
Denton, Kevin	15 + 1	3	—	—	12
Dorreen, Mike	5	2	—	—	8
Doyle, Mark	15 + 3	7	2	—	32
Friend, Clayton	31	5	—	3	23
Hepi, Brad	23	10	—	—	40
Hewer, Gary	0 + 1	—	—	—	—
Kavanagh, Mike	11 + 2	3	—	—	12
Kendall, Dave	7	—	—	—	—
Little, Alan	6 + 3	1	—	—	4
Lunt, Peter	0 + 1	—	—	—	—
McIntosh, Ken	1	—	—	—	—
Maclagan, Alan	2 + 6	—	—	—	—
McNicol, Tony	1 + 2	—	—	—	—
Manning, Phil	10 + 2	1	—	—	4
Murdock, Gary	1 + 5	—	—	—	—
Okesene, Hitro	18 + 1	10	—	—	40
Pape, Kevin	31	19	—	—	76
Perry, Mark	0 + 1	—	—	—	—
Pollard, Damian	3	1	—	—	4
Robinson, Paul	5 + 5	—	—	—	—
Rowe, Greig	17	8	—	1	33
Schubert, Gary	32	3	—	—	12
Scott, Tony	24 + 6	1	—	—	4
Seagar, Stuart	0 + 1	—	—	—	—
Southwell, Eddie	12 + 1	3	—	—	12
Thomason, Malcolm	30	8	—	—	32
Timoko, Nahu	8	2	—	—	8
Vickers, Barry	27 + 2	1	87	0	178
White, Nigel	3	1	—	—	4
Williams, Barry	21 + 7	7	27	4	86
TOTALS: 37 players		112	116	8	688

Kiwi Test half back Clayton Friend, five tries in 31 games.

1990-91 MATCH ANALYSIS

Date	Competition	H/A	Opponent	Rlt	Score	Tries	Goals	Attendance	Referee
26.8.90	LC(1)	H	Workington T.	W	38-18	Pape (2), Kavanagh, Denton, Doyle, Rowe	Williams (5), Doyle (2)	1104	Steele
2.9.90	LC(2)	H	Warrington	L	7-28	—	Williams (2), Vickers, Rowe (dg)	1596	Campbell
9.9.90	SD	H	Chorley	W	50-16	Pape (2), Coles (2), Okesene (2), Denton, Schubert, Pollard	Vickers (6), Williams	785	Campbell
16.9.90	SD	A	Dewsbury	W	24-13	Okesene (2), Coles, Southwell, Pape	Williams (2)	—	—
23.9.90	SD	H	Runcorn H.	W	44-13	Pape (2), Okesene (2), Rowe (2), Friend, Scott	Vickers (6)	839	Galtress
30.9.90	SD	H	Bramley	W	44-15	Coles (2), Williams, Thomason, Hepi, Friend, Doyle, Rowe	Vickers (4), Williams (2)	847	Carter
5.10.90	SD	A	Workington T.	W	13-8	Hepi	Vickers (4), Friend (dg)	—	—
14.10.90	SD	H	Ryedale-York	D	17-17	Hepi, Dorreen, Coles	Vickers (2), Williams (dg)	1150	R. Connolly
21.10.90	SD	A	Swinton	L	10-22	Pape, Cowgill	Vickers	—	—
4.11.90	SD	H	Barrow	W	44-26	Friend (2), Coles, Pape, Schubert, Kavanagh, Okesene	Vickers (8)	906	Gilmour
11.11.90	SD	A	Leigh	L	16-24	Coles, Hepi	Vickers (4)	—	—
18.11.90	RT(P)	H	Wakefield T.	L	10-28	Hepi, Doyle	Williams	1479	Galtress
25.11.90	SD	A	Chorley	W	12-8	Pape, Timoko	Vickers (2)	—	—
9.12.90	SD	H	Dewsbury	W	12-10	Williams, Kavanagh	Vickers (2)	573	R. Connolly
16.12.90	SD	H	Leigh	W	19-16	Thomason, Pape	Vickers (5), Friend (dg)	963	Tidball
23.12.90	SD	A	Batley	W	38-9	Okesene (2), Pape, Williams, Timoko, Coles, Brierley	Vickers (5)	—	—
26.12.90	SD	A	Barrow	L	4-34	Thomason	—	—	—
30.12.90	SD	H	Whitehaven	L	10-14	Pape, Dorreen	Williams	1004	Holgate
20.1.91	SD	A	Keighley	W	30-4	Brierley, Pape, Williams, Little, Denton	Williams (5)	—	—
27.1.91	CC(P)	H	Workington T.	L	8-9	Williams	Williams, Vickers	1911	Steele
3.2.91	SD	A	Runcorn H.	D	12-12	Coles, Pape	Vickers (2)	—	—
17.2.91	SD	H	Swinton	L	11-32	White, Pape	Williams (1, 1dg)	673	Tennant
24.2.91	SD	H	Batley	L	13-19	Thomason, Rowe	Vickers (2), Williams (dg)	480	Cross
3.3.91	SD	A	Ryedale-York	L	12-18	Pape, Thomason	Vickers (2)	—	—
10.3.91	SD	H	Keighley	W	32-18	Hepi, Rowe, Okesene, Thomason	Vickers (8)	495	Crashley
17.3.91	SD	A	Doncaster	L	7-14	Manning	Williams, Friend (dg)	—	—
24.3.91	SD	A	Trafford B.	W	52-14	Doyle (3), Hepi (2), Rowe, Pape, Williams, Friend	Vickers (8)	—	—
1.4.91	SD	H	Workington T.	L	5-12	—	Vickers (2), Williams (dg)	1210	J. Connolly
4.4.91	SD	H	Trafford B.	W	28-0	Vickers, Southwell, Doyle, Charlton, Schubert	Williams (4)	415	K. Morris
7.4.91	SD	A	Bramley	L	12-17	Hepi, Charlton	Williams, Vickers	—	—
10.4.91	SD	H	Doncaster	W	24-8	Charlton, Hepi, Rowe	Vickers (6)	590	J. Connolly
14.4.91	SD	A	Whitehaven	W	18-12	Pape, Thomason, Southwell	Vickers (3)	—	—
21.4.91	SDP(1)	A	Salford	L	12-26	Williams, Thomason	Vickers (2)	—	—

CASTLEFORD

Ground: Wheldon Road (0977-552674)
Colours: Yellow and black
First Season: 1926-27. There was also a
Castleford team from 1896-97 to
1905-06, inclusive
Nickname: Cougars
Chairman: David Poulter
Secretary: Denise Cackett
Coach: Darryl Van de Velde (July 1988-)
Honours: **Championship** Beaten finalists,
1938-39, 1968-69
Challenge Cup Winners, 1934-35,
1968-69, 1969-70, 1985-86
Yorkshire League Winners,
1932-33, 1938-39, 1964-65
Yorkshire Cup Winners, 1977-78,
1981-82, 1986-87, 1990-91
Beaten finalists, 1948-49, 1950-51,
1968-69, 1971-72, 1983-84,
1985-86, 1987-88, 1988-89
Eastern Division Championship
Beaten finalists, 1963-64
BBC2 Floodlit Trophy Winners,
1965-66, 1966-67, 1967-68, 1976-77
Regal Trophy Winners, 1976-77
Premiership Beaten finalists,
1983-84
Charity Shield Beaten finalists
1986-87

Records: Attendance: 25,449 v. Hunslet
(RL Cup) 3 Mar, 1935
Season
Goals: 158 by S. Lloyd, 1976-77
Tries: 36 by K. Howe, 1963-64
Points: 334 by R. Beardmore,
1983-84
Match
Goals: 17 by S. Lloyd v. Millom,
16 Sep, 1973
Tries: 5 by D. Foster v. Hunslet,
10 Nov, 1972; J. Joyner v. Millom,
16 Sep, 1973; S. Fenton v.
Dewsbury, 27 Jan, 1978; I. French
v. Hunslet, 9 Feb, 1986; S. Ellis at
Whitehaven, 10 Dec, 1989
Points: 43 by S. Lloyd v. Millom,
16 Sep, 1973
Highest score: 94-12 v.
Huddersfield, 1988-89
Highest against: 62-12 v. St.
Helens, 1985-86

1990-91 PLAYERS' SUMMARY

	App	Tries	Goals	Dr	Pts
Anderson, Grant	36	12	—	—	48
Atkins, Gary	3 + 2	1	—	—	4
Battye, Neil	7 + 7	3	—	—	12
Beardmore, Kevin	17	2	—	—	8
Boothroyd, Giles	5	1	—	—	4
Bragger, Ian	10 + 3	1	—	—	4
Clarke, Andy	3 + 7	—	—	—	—
Crooks, Lee	31 + 1	4	61	—	138
Ellis, St. John	31 + 1	8	—	—	32
England, Keith	30 + 1	2	—	—	8
Fletcher, Paul	8 + 2	2	—	—	8
French, Gary	24 + 2	6	—	—	24
Hardy, Jeff	36	6	—	—	24
Hay, Andy	0 + 1	—	—	—	—
Irwin, Shaun	28 + 2	10	—	—	40
Joyner, John	19 + 6	3	—	—	12
Ketteridge, Martin	6 + 11	1	—	—	4
Larder, Steve	20 + 4	10	—	1	41
McAllister, Terry	1 + 3	—	—	—	—
Plange, David	29	16	—	—	64
Roebuck, Neil	17 + 7	5	—	2	22
Sampson, Dean	34 + 1	2	—	—	8
Smith, Tony	8 + 2	4	—	—	16
Southernwood, Graham	18	3	—	—	12
Steadman, Graham	32 + 1	23	52	1	197
Wray, Jon	15	5	—	—	20
TOTALS:					
26 players		130	113	4	750

Shaun Irwin, 10 tries in 30 appearances.

1990-91 MATCH ANALYSIS

Date	Competition	H/A	Opponent	Rlt	Score	Tries	Goals	Attendance	Referee
26.8.90	YC(1)	A	Hull	W	10-6	Boothroyd, Ellis	Crooks	—	—
2.9.90	YC(2)	A¹	Bradford N.	W	42-12	Ellis (2), Larder, Steadman, Southernwood, Roebuck	Crooks (9)	—	—
9.9.90	SBC	A	Warrington	L	12-30	Irwin, Battye	Crooks (2)	—	—
12.9.90	YC(SF)	H	Hull K.R.	W	29-6	Ellis, Southernwood, Anderson, Larder, Steadman	Crooks (4), Larder (dg)	7940	Crashley
16.9.90	SBC	H	Wigan	L	18-38	Crooks, Steadman, Battye	Crooks (?), Steadman	9285	Kershaw
23.9.90	YC(F)	Leeds	Wakefield T.	W	11-8	Plange, Atkins	Crooks, Roebuck (dg)	(12,420)	Smith
26.9.90	SBC	A	Oldham	L	22-28	Plange (2), Irwin, Larder	Crooks (3)	—	—
30.9.90	SBC	H	Featherstone R.	W	24-19	Anderson (2), Roebuck, Plange, Larder	Crooks (2)	7293	Whitelam
6.10.90	SBC	A	Widnes	L	4-46	Larder	—	—	—
14.10.90	SBC	H	Wakefield T.	W	42-12	French (2), Plange (2), Larder, Hardy, Irwin, Steadman	Crooks (5)	7149	Whitfield
21.10.90	SBC	A	St. Helens	W	29-16	Steadman (3), Plange	Steadman (5, 1dg), Crooks (1)	—	—
4.11.90	Tour	H	Australia	L	8-28	Plange	Crooks, Steadman	9033	Kershaw
11.11.90	SBC	A	Featherstone R.	W	22-6	Steadman, Plange, Anderson	Crooks (5)	—	—
18.11.90	SBC	H	Oldham	W	28-10	Plange (3), Steadman, Anderson	Crooks (4)	5995	Smith
27.11.90	SBC	A	Leeds	L	16-41	Steadman, Plange	Steadman (4)	—	—
2.12.90	RT(1)	A	Fulham	W	14-8	Steadman, Larder	Steadman (3)	—	—
9.12.90	RT(2)	A	Wakefield T.	W	20-4	Steadman, Anderson, Joyner, Hardy	Crooks (2)	—	—
16.12.90	RT(3)	H	Rochdale H.	L	14-19	Larder, Joyner, Ketteridge	Crooks	4017	Gilmour
19.12.90	SBC	H	Warrington	W	22-18	Fletcher, Crooks, Roebuck, England	Crooks (3)	3594	Galtress
26.12.90	SBC	A	Hull	L	6-22	Steadman	Steadman	—	—
1.1.91	SBC	H	Bradford N.	W	9-0	Steadman	Steadman, Crooks, Roebuck (dg)	6190	Gilmour
6.1.91	SBC	H	Widnes	W	20-10	Sampson, Anderson, Plange	Steadman (4)	6259	Burke
20.1.91	SBC	H	Hull K.R.	W	30-2	Steadman, Wray, Bragger, Hardy, Anderson, Irwin	Steadman (3)	5575	Asquith
23.1.91	SBC	H	Rochdale H.	W	42-0	Steadman (3), Smith (2), Irwin, Crooks, Anderson	Steadman (4), Crooks	3842	C. Morris
27.1.91	SBC	A	Wakefield T.	W	12-8	Anderson, Crooks	Crooks (2)	—	—
3.2.91	SBC	H	Leeds	W	16-14	Irwin, Ellis	Steadman (4)	7814	J. Connolly
12.2.91	CC(1)	H	Wigan	L	4-28	Irwin	—	6749	Smith
24.2.91	SBC	A	Hull K.R.	W	16-12	French, Battye, Smith	Steadman (2)	—	—
3.3.91	SBC	A	Rochdale H.	W	76-12	Steadman (3), French (2), Ellis (2), Larder (2), Anderson, Beardmore, Sampson, Plange, Hardy	Steadman (10)	—	—
10.3.91	SBC	A	Sheffield E.	W	24-20	Irwin, Anderson, French, Roebuck	Steadman (4)	—	—
24.3.91	SBC	H	St. Helens	W	28-4	Steadman (2), Roebuck, Plange, Wray	Steadman (3), Crooks	6410	Asquith
29.3.91	SBC	A	Bradford N.	L	14-24	Irwin, Southernwood	Steadman (2), Crooks	—	—
1.4.91	SBC	H	Hull	L	14-16	Irwin, Smith, Wray	Crooks	6527	Galtress
7.4.91	SBC	A	Wigan	L	4-24	—	Crooks (2)	—	—
14.4.91	SBC	H	Sheffield E.	W	28-10	Wray (2), Hardy (2), Fletcher	Crooks (4)	4422	Whitfield
21.4.91	PT(1)	H	Leeds	L	20-24	Ellis, Joyner, England, Beardmore	Crooks (2)	6918	Smith

¹ at Bradford C. FC

CHORLEY

Ground: Victory Park (02572-41350)
Colours: Black and white
First Season: 1989-90
Chairman: Mike Livesey
Secretary: Brian Green
Coach: Bob Eccles (May 1990-)
Records: Attendance: 2,851 v. Oldham (League) 21 Jan, 1990. There was a crowd of 5,026 for a 'home' Lancashire Cup-tie against Wigan played at Leigh on 15 Sep, 1989

Season
Goals: 73 by M. Smith, 1989-90
Tries: 10 by D. Bacon, 1989-90
Points: 142 by M. Smith, 1989-90

Match
Goals: 6 by M. Smith v. Runcorn H., 1 Jan, 1990 and v. Nottingham C., 8 Apr, 1990
Tries: No player has scored more than 3
Points: No player has scored more than 12
Highest score: 46-12 v. Runcorn H., 1989-90
Highest against: 66-16 v. Oldham, 1989-90

1990-91 PLAYERS' SUMMARY

	App	Tries	Goals	Dr	Pts
Bacon, David	16 + 6	3	—	—	12
Bimson, Geoffrey	21 + 1	3	—	—	12
Bolton, Wayne	0 + 3	—	—	—	—
Briscoe, Carl	26 + 1	5	—	—	20
Duffy, John	12 + 4	1	—	—	4
Du Toit, Nick	1	1	—	—	4
Eccles, Bob	25	7	—	4	32
Edwards, Mark	29 + 1	2	—	—	8
Ellis, Jeffrey	2 + 1	—	—	—	—
Hankey, Steve	21 + 9	4	—	—	16
Hodson, Tony	26 + 1	2	—	—	8
Knight, Mark	22 + 4	7	—	—	28
Kolhase, Darren	1	—	—	—	—
Little, Peter	4 + 3	—	—	—	—
Marshall, Ken	1 + 1	—	—	—	—
Matautia, Vila	1	1	—	—	4
Mayo, John	15 + 2	—	—	—	—
Meadows, Kevin	27 + 1	6	—	—	24
Meyrick, Martin	1	—	—	—	—
Price, Billy	22 + 4	2	4	3	19
Ramsdale, Dennis	1 + 3	—	—	—	—
Roberts, Paul	16 + 6	5	—	—	20
Sedgwick, Peter	2	—	—	—	—
Sharkey, Tim	1	—	—	—	—
Shaw, Mark	2 + 1	1	—	—	4
Smith, Joe	3 + 1	—	—	—	—
Smith, Mike	27 + 2	—	56	3	115
Wakefield, Stuart	1	—	—	—	—
Whittaker, Aaron	24	6	—	1	25
Wilson, Walter	22	6	—	—	24
Wood, David	31	5	6	—	32
TOTALS:					
31 players		67	66	11	411

David Wood dives over for one of his five tries for Chorley.

1990-91 MATCH ANALYSIS

Date	Competition	H/A	Opponent	Rlt	Score	Tries	Goals	Attendance	Referee
26.8.90	LC(1)	A	Warrington	L	8-36	Eccles	Smith (2)	—	—
9.9.90	SD	A	Carlisle	L	16-50	Knight, Eccles, Roberts	Smith (2)	—	—
16.9.90	SD	H	Hunslet	W	27-23	Hodson, Bacon, Du Toit, Wood	Smith (5), Eccles (dg)	525	Tidball
23.9.90	SD	A	Ryedale-York	L	8-42	Bacon, Bimson	—	—	—
30.9.90	SD	A	Leigh	L	4-50	Whittaker	—	—	—
7.10.90	SD	H	Whitehaven	L	4-19	Eccles	—	514	Galtress
14.10.90	SD	A	Bramley	L	18-27	Hodson, Eccles, Price	Smith (3)	—	—
21.10.90	SD	H	Salford	L	2-50	—	Price	1609	Holgate
4.11.90	SD	A	Keighley	L	18-32	Wilson, Price, Hankey	Price (3)	—	—
11.11.90	SD	H	Nottingham C.	W	38-19	Whittaker (2), Meadows (2), Briscoe, Matautia, Wilson	Smith (5)	397	Steele
25.11.90	SD	H	Carlisle	L	8-12	Briscoe	Smith (2)	495	Tidball
2.12.90	RT(1)	A	Leigh	L	5-66	Meadows	Price (dg)	—	—
16.12.90	SD	A	Halifax	L	10-38	Shaw, Briscoe	Smith	—	—
23.12.90	SD	H	Keighley	L	10-14	Bimson	Smith (2, 2dg)	559	C. Morris
26.12.90	SD	A	Huddersfield	L	6-20	Eccles	Smith	—	—
1.1.91	SD	H	Trafford B.	W	9-8	Wilson	Smith (2), Eccles (dg)	391	Campbell
6.1.91	SD	H	Huddersfield	W	19-6	Knight (2), Roberts	Smith (2,1dg), Eccles (dg), Whittaker (dg)	625	Whitelam
20.1.91	SD	A	Hunslet	D	14-14	Wood, Whittaker	Smith (3)	—	—
3.2.91	SD	H	Leigh	L	12-30	Wilson (2)	Smith (2)	856	Holdsworth
19.2.91	CC(1)	A	Rochdale H.	L	10-14	Wilson, Hankey	Smith	—	—
24.2.91	SD	H	Fulham	L	2-36	—	Smith	502	Holgate
3.3.91	SD	H	Bramley	W	22-6	Briscoe (2), Wood, Whittaker	Smith (3)	376	Steele
10.3.91	SD	A	Whitehaven	L	16-21	Bacon, Hankey	Smith (4)	—	—
13.3.91	SD	A	Salford	L	2-46	—	Smith	—	—
17.3.91	SD	H	Halifax	L	13-22	Bimson, Edwards	Smith (2), Eccles (dg)	1717	Holgate
24.3.91	SD	H	Ryedale-York	L	20-24	Wood, Meadows, Whittaker	Wood (4)	605	Tennant
29.3.91	SD	A	Fulham	L	9-28	Roberts	Wood (2), Price (dg)	—	—
1.4.91	SD	A	Trafford B.	L	19-21	Knight (2), Roberts	Smith (3), Price (dg)	—	—
7.4.91	SD	H	Dewsbury	L	6-26	Edwards	Smith	483	Crashley
10.4.91	SD	A	Dewsbury	W	24-20	Eccles (2), Duffy, Hankey	Smith (4)	—	—
14.4.91	SD	A	Nottingham C.	W	32-17	Meadows (2), Knight (2), Roberts, Wood	Smith (4)	—	—

CLUBS

DEWSBURY

Ground:	Moved to Mount Pleasant, Batley (0924-472208) for 1991-92 season from Crown Flatt
Colours:	Red, amber and black
First Season:	1901-02
Chairman:	Rodney Hardcastle
Secretary:	Geoff Parrish
Coach:	Maurice Bamford (Dec 1988-Dec 1990) Jack Addy (Dec 1990-)
Honours:	**Championship** Winners, 1972-73 Beaten finalists, 1946-47 **Division Two** Champions, 1904-05 **Challenge Cup** Winners, 1911-12, 1942-43 Beaten finalists, 1928-29 **Yorkshire League** Winners, 1946-47 **Yorkshire Cup** Winners, 1925-26, 1927-28, 1942-43 Beaten finalists, 1918-19, 1921-22, 1940-41, 1972-73 **BBC2 Floodlit Trophy** Beaten finalists, 1975-76 **War League Championship** Winners, 1941-42. (1942-43 won final but championship declared null and void because Dewsbury played an ineligible player.) Beaten finalists, 1943-44
Records:	Attendance: 26,584 v. Halifax (Yorkshire Cup) 30 Oct, 1920 **Season** Goals: 145 by N. Stephenson, 1972-73

Tries: 40 by D. Thomas, 1906-07
Points: 368 by N. Stephenson, 1972-73
Match
Goals: 10 by J. Ledgard v. Yorkshire Amateurs, 13 Sep, 1947; N. Stephenson v. Blackpool B, 28 Aug, 1972; C. Wilkinson v. Huddersfield, 27 Mar, 1989
Tries: 8 by D. Thomas v. Liverpool C, 13 Apr, 1907
Points: 29 by J. Lyman v. Hull, 22 Apr, 1919
Highest score: 72-0 v. Doncaster, 1984-85
Highest against: 82-0 v. Widnes, 1986-87

1990-91 PLAYERS' SUMMARY

	App	Tries	Goals	Dr	Pts
Bailey, Dennis	33	14	—	—	56
Butler, Tim	11 + 1	1	—	—	4
Chapman, Mark	2	—	—	—	—
Cocks, Gary	12 + 3	2	—	—	8
Coen, Darren	21	—	—	—	—
Cooper, Andrew	1	—	—	—	—
Coughlan, Glen	28 + 2	7	—	—	28
Dickinson, Andy	23 + 10	7	—	—	28
Drummond, Barry	13	5	—	—	20
Durnin, Paul	11	3	—	—	12
Garforth, David	0 + 2	—	—	—	—
Garnett, Paul	9 + 2	1	—	—	4
Graham, Nathan	34	10	41	—	122
Haigh, Chris	3 + 1	—	—	—	—
Haigh, Mark	1	—	—	—	—
Hall, Dean	25 + 3	8	—	—	32
Howley, Pat	3 + 3	—	—	—	—
Hughes, Lee	14 + 2	2	—	—	8
Hughes, Paul	11 + 1	2	—	—	8
Jennings, Paul	4 + 1	1	—	—	4
Johnson, Willie	18	1	—	5	9
Jones, Kevin	8 + 2	6	—	1	25
Kelly, Neil	25 + 4	1	—	1	5
McCabe, Martin	10	2	—	—	8
Marsden, Robert	3	—	—	—	—
Mitchell, Tony	1	1	—	—	4
Moore, John	11 + 1	4	—	—	16
Shuttleworth, Greg	0 + 1	—	—	—	—
Shuttleworth, Paul	13 + 1	2	—	4	12
Spooner, Chris	0 + 1	—	—	—	—
Squires, Chris	13	5	—	—	20
Toole, Tim	8 + 1	—	—	1	1
Van Bellen, Gary	9 + 6	—	—	—	—
Vasey, Chris	9 + 1	2	5	—	18
Vincent, Andy	4 + 2	1	—	3	7
Watkinson, David	24 + 2	—	—	—	—
Whitehead, Craig	24 + 2	3	—	—	12
Wilkinson, Chris	16 + 1	1	30	5	69
Trialist	0 + 1	—	—	—	—
TOTALS:					
39 players		92	76	20	540

Winger Dennis Bailey, top tryscorer for Dewsbury.

1990-91 MATCH ANALYSIS

Date	Com-petition	H/A	Opponent	Rlt	Score	Tries	Goals	Atten-dance	Referee
26.8.90	YC (1)	H	Keighley	W	26-14	Hall, Johnson, Whitehead, Durnin, Dickinson	Graham (3)	1056	Kendrew
2.9.90	YC(2)	H	Batley	W	18-8	Shuttleworth, Dickinson, Squires	Graham (2), Shuttleworth (2dg)	2924	Tennant
9.9.90	SD	A	Halifax	L	6-38	Squires	Wilkinson	—	—
12.9.90	YC(SF)	A	Wakefield T.	L	2-25	—	Graham	—	—
16.9.90	SD	H	Carlisle	L	13-24	Vincent, Jennings	Graham, Vincent (2dg), Johnson (dg)	697	R. Connolly
23.9.90	SD	A	Workington T.	L	9-15	Bailey	Graham (2), Vincent (dg)	—	—
30.9.90	SD	H	Fulham	W	16-6	Graham, Bailey	Wilkinson (4)	605	Asquith
7.10.90	SD	A	Barrow	L	11-12	Dickinson, Coughlan	Wilkinson, Johnson (dg)	—	—
14.10.90	SD	H	Swinton	L	4-18	—	Wilkinson, Johnson (2dg)	935	Tidball
21.10.90	SD	A	Hunslet	L	10-19	Coughlan (2)	Wilkinson	—	—
4.11.90	SD	H	Doncaster	W	28-2	Mitchell, Graham, Dickinson, Durnin	Wilkinson (5, 2dg)	951	Steele
11.11.90	SD	A	Swinton	A	6-13	Wilkinson	Wilkinson	—	—
17.11.90	RT(P)	A	Dudley Hill	W	24-18	Bailey (2), Graham, Durnin, Kelly	Wilkinson (2)	—	—
25.11.90	SD	A	Fulham	L	10-14	Bailey	Wilkinson (3)	—	—
2.12.90	RT(1)	A	Bramley	L	16-30	Dickinson, Bailey, Butler	Wilkinson (1, 1dg), Shuttleworth (dg)	—	—
9.12.90	SD	A	Carlisle	L	10-12	Coughlan, Graham	Wilkinson	—	—
16.12.90	SD	H	Workington T.	W	7-6	Bailey	Wilkinson, Johnson (dg)	587	J. Connolly
23.12.90	SD	A	Nottingham C.	W	38-6	Graham (2), Moore (2), Bailey (2), Dickinson	Wilkinson (4, 2dg)	—	—
26.12.90	SD	H	Batley	W	6-4	L. Hughes	Wilkinson	1378	K. Morris
1.1.91	SD	A	Batley	L	6-12	Hall	Wilkinson	—	—
6.1.91	SD	H	Salford	L	2-50	—	Wilkinson	1053	Kendrew
20.1.91	SD	A	Doncaster	L	14-32	Coughlan, Bailey, Hall	Wilkinson	—	—
27.1.91	CC(P)	A[1]	Hensingham	W	24-7	Drummond (2), McCabe, Whitehead	Vasey (3), Toole (dg), Kelly (dg)	—	—
10.2.91	CC(1)	A	Leeds	L	20-40	Squires (2), Graham	Graham (2), Vasey (2)	—	—
17.2.91	SD	A	Huddersfield	W	28-16	Bailey (2), Coughlan, Moore, Squires	Graham (4)	—	—
27.2.91	SD	A	Salford	L	6-32	Bailey	Graham	—	—
3.3.91	SD	A	Runcorn H.	L	2-9	—	Graham	—	—
10.3.91	SD	H	Hunslet	W	15-12	Graham, Hall	Graham (3), Shuttleworth (dg)	800	Tidball
17.3.91	SD	H	Huddersfield	L	16-18	Hall (2), Graham	Graham (2)	804	Burke
24.3.91	SD	H	Runcorn H.	W	18-10	Garnett, Whitehead, Shuttleworth	Graham (3)	595	Gilmour
1.4.91	SD	H	Halifax	L	0-26	—	—	2640	Cross
4.4.91	SD	H	Nottingham C.	W	64-0	Jones (3), Cocks (2), Graham, P. Hughes, L. Hughes, Drummond, Vasey, McCabe, Coughlan	Graham (8)	465	Steele
7.4.91	SD	A	Chorley	W	26-6	Jones (2), Drummond, Bailey, Dickinson	Graham (3)	—	—
10.4.91	SD	H	Chorley	L	20-24	Moore, Hall, Vasey, Drummond	Graham (2)	539	Volante
14.4.91	SD	H	Barrow	D	19-19	Jones, Hall, P. Hughes	Graham (3), Jones (dg)	1321	Gilmour

[1] at Workington

DONCASTER

Ground:	Tattersfield (0302-390150)
Colours:	Blue and yellow
First Season:	1951-52
Nickname:	Dons
Chairman:	John Desmond
Secretary:	Granville Bowen
Coach:	Dave Sampson (May 1989-)
Records:	Attendance: 5,274 v. Wigan (RL Cup) 29 Jan, 1989. There was an attendance of 10,000 for a Challenge Cup tie against Bradford N. at York Road Stadium on 16 Feb, 1952

Season
Goals: 118 by D. Noble, 1985-86
Tries: 21 by M. Roache, 1989-90
Points: 250 by D. Noble, 1986-87

Match
Goals: 9 by D. Towle v. York, 9 Sep, 1967; D. Carroll v. Bramley, 6 Jan, 1991
Tries: 4 by V. Grace v. Rochdale H., 4 Oct, 1952; B. Tasker v. Leeds, 26 Oct, 1963; J. Buckton v. Rochdale H., 30 Aug, 1981; T. Kemp v. Carlisle, 23 Nov, 1986; N. Turner v. Keighley, 22 Nov, 1989
Points: 20 by K. Jones v. Whitehaven, 13 Mar, 1988; D. Noble v. Dewsbury, 2 Oct, 1988
Highest score: 58-2 v. Bramley, 1990-91
Highest against: 75-3 v. Leigh, 1975-76

Former Kiwi Test winger Dane O'Hara, struck by injury on his debut for Doncaster.

1990-91 PLAYERS' SUMMARY

	App	Tries	Goals	Dr	Pts
Abrahams, Steve	3 + 3	—	—	—	—
Armstrong, Mick	0 + 3	—	—	—	—
Barrett, Dale	0 + 2	—	—	—	—
Bowes, Tony	6 + 5	1	—	—	4
Carr, Alan	5 + 2	1	—	—	4
Carroll, Dean	30 + 1	4	61	13	151
Chappell, Simon	1	—	—	—	—
Close, David	7	1	—	—	4
Ellis, Mark	10 + 8	2	—	—	8
Evans, John	29	5	—	—	20
Firth, Steve	0 + 3	—	—	—	—
French, Ian	26	6	—	—	24
Hall, Carl	27	9	1	—	38
Heptinstall, Jason	0 + 3	1	—	—	4
Holmes, David	9	—	—	—	—
Holmes, Gary	3 + 3	—	—	—	—
Idle, Graham	25 + 2	1	—	—	4
Jasiewicz, Dick	25 + 2	10	—	—	40
Jones, Keith	0 + 1	—	—	—	—
Kass, Mark	0 + 1	—	—	—	—
Leuluai, James	12 + 1	1	—	—	4
Matautia, Vila	20 + 1	9	—	—	36
Miller, Tony	2 + 4	—	—	—	—
O'Hara, Dane	1	—	—	—	—
Patrick Shaun	4	—	—	—	—
Pell, Richard	7 + 1	—	1	—	2
Pennant, Audley	30	1	—	—	4
Price, Darren	18 + 2	12	—	—	48
Proctor, Wayne	20 + 8	3	—	—	12
Puckering, Neil	1	—	—	—	—
Race, Wayne	13	2	—	—	8
Ramsey, Neville	1	1	—	—	4
Rayne, Kevin	30	5	—	—	20
Roache, Mark	32 + 1	15	—	—	60
Sampson, Lee	2	—	—	—	—
Sheldon, Ian	23 + 6	2	—	—	8
Simms, Mark	1	—	—	—	—
Tomlinson, Paul	4	—	—	—	—
Zelei, Tony	16	4	22	1	61
Trialist	1	—	—	—	—
TOTALS:					
40 players		96	85	14	568

1990-91 MATCH ANALYSIS

Date	Com-petition	H/A	Opponent	Rlt	Score	Tries	Goals	Atten-dance	Referee
26.8.90	YC(1)	H	Halifax	L	4-40	Ellis	—	2989	Cross
9.9.90	SD	H	Hunslet	W	11-8	Roache	Zelei (3), Carroll (dg)	1890	Asquith
12.9.90	SD	A	Huddersfield	L	24-26	Roache (2), Sheldon, Hall	Zelei (4)	—	—
23.9.90	SD	H	Nottingham C.	W	38-14	Carroll (2), Zelei, Jasiewicz, Hall, Rayne	Zelie (7)	1404	Ollerton
3.10.90	SD	A	Salford	L	4-21	Price	—	—	—
7.10.90	SD	H	Keighley	W	14-11	Carroll, Evans, Price	Carroll (2dg)	1526	Carter
14.10.90	SD	A	Whitehaven	W	10-6	Zelie, Roache	Carroll (2dg)	—	—
21.10.90	SD	H	Huddersfield	W	29-20	Jasiewicz (2), Zelei, Proctor, Price	Zelie (4), Carroll (dg)	1059	Whitelam
4.11.90	SD	A	Dewsbury	L	2-28	—	Carroll	—	—
11.11.90	SD	H	Trafford B.	W	19-14	Price (2), Ramsey	Carroll (3, 1dg)	1330	Whitfield
14.11.90	RT(P)	H	Ryedale-York	W	14-12	French, Price	Carroll (2, 2dg)	1165	Whitfield
18.11.90	SD	A	Keighley	L	10-18	Proctor, Matautia	Carroll	—	—
25.11.90	SD	A	Hunslet	L	10-22	Matautia	Carroll (3)	—	—
2.12.90	RT(1)	A	Trafford B.	D	10-10	Raice, Roache	Zelie	—	—
5.12.90	RT(1) Replay	H	Trafford B.	W	19-7	Hall, Jasiewicz, Rayne	Zelie (3, 1dg)	1195	Crashley
12.12.90	RT(2)	H	Rochdale H.	L	10-14	Matautia	Carroll (3)	1341	Cross
16.12.90	SD	H	Fulham	L	0-4	—	—	1003	Allatt
23.12.90	SD	A	Bramley	W	14-12	Ellis, French, Bowes	Carroll	—	—
26.12.90	SD	H	Ryedale-York	L	4-11	Roache	—	1252	C. Morris
30.12.90	SD	A	Halifax	L	16-40	Carroll, French, Matautia	Carroll (2)	—	—
6.1.91	SD	H	Bramley	W	58-2	Matautia (2), Price (2), Hall (2), Rayne, Roache, Jasiewicz, Heptinstall	Carroll (9)	903	Allatt
20.1.91	SD	H	Dewsbury	W	32-14	Matautia (2), Race, French, Pennant	Carroll (6)	1746	Campbell
30.1.91	SD	H	Salford	L	12-14	French, Jasiewicz	Carroll, Pell	1602	Crashley
3.2.91	SD	A	Trafford B.	W	29-25	Jasiewicz (2), Hall, Roache, Price	Carroll (4, 1dg)	—	—
10.2.91	CC(1)	H	Widnes	L	4-30	Roache	—	3566	Cross
3.3.91	SD	H	Whitehaven	W	36-0	Price (2), Idle, Roache, French, Hall	Carroll (6)	1074	R. Connolly
10.3.91	SD	A	Leigh	W	20-16	Price, Leuluai, Roache	Carroll (2, 2dg), Hall	—	—
17.3.91	SD	H	Carlisle	W	14-7	Hall, Jasiewicz	Carroll (3)	1308	Whitelam
20.3.91	SD	H	Halifax	W	12-6	Roache, Evans	Carroll (2)	2332	Kershaw
24.3.91	SD	A	Nottingham C.	W	52-8	Roache (2), Evans (2), Sheldon, Jasiewicz, Rayne, Hall, Matautia	Carroll (8)	—	—
29.3.91	SD	A	Ryedale-York	L	7-15	Rayne	Carroll (1, 1dg)	—	—
7.4.91	SD	A	Fulham	W	12-6	Zelei, Proctor	Carroll (2)	—	—
10.4.91	SD	A	Carlisle	L	8-24	Carr, Roache	—	—	—
14.4.91	SD	H	Leigh	L	10-42	Close, Evans	Carroll	1557	Cummings (Pr)

FEATHERSTONE ROVERS

Ground: Post Office Road (0977-702386)
Colours: Blue and white
First Season: 1921-22
Nickname: Colliers
Chairman: Eric Gardner
Secretary: Terry Jones
Coach: Peter Fox (May 1987-)
Honours: **Challenge Cup** Winners, 1966-67, 1972-73, 1982-83
Beaten finalists, 1951-52, 1973-74
Championship Beaten finalists, 1927-28
Division One Champions, 1976-77
Division Two Champions, 1979-80
Second Division Premiership Beaten finalists, 1987-88
Yorkshire Cup Winners, 1939-40, 1959-60
Beaten finalists, 1928-29, 1963-64, 1966-67, 1969-70, 1970-71, 1976-77, 1977-78, 1989-90
Captain Morgan Trophy Beaten finalists, 1973-74
Records: Attendance: 17,531 v. St. Helens (RL Cup) 21 Mar, 1959
Season
Goals: 163 by S. Quinn, 1979-80
Tries: 31 by C. Woolford, 1958-59
Points: 375 by S. Quinn, 1979-80
Match
Goals: 13 by M. Knapper v. Keighley, 17 Sep, 1989
Tries: 6 by M. Smith v. Doncaster, 13 Apr, 1968; C. Bibb v. Keighley, 17 Sep, 1989
Points: 30 by M. Knapper v. Keighley, 17 Sep, 1989
Highest score: 86-18 v. Keighley, 1989-90
Highest against: 70-2 v. Halifax, 1940-41

1990-91 PLAYERS' SUMMARY

	App	Tries	Goals	Dr	Pts
Banks, Alan	7 + 1	5	—	—	20
Bastian, John	4	—	—	—	—
Bibb, Chris	27	5	3	—	26
Booth, Glen	0 + 1	—	—	—	—
Bugg, David	0 + 1	—	—	—	—
Burton, Chris	23 + 4	1	—	—	4
Butt, Ikram	32	10	—	—	40
Casey, Leo	24 + 1	4	—	—	16
Clark, Trevor	31 + 1	8	—	—	32
Fisher, Andy	4 + 18	4	—	—	16
Fox, Deryck	33	12	56	2	162
Gibbon, Mark	3 + 1	—	—	—	—
Grayshon, Jeff	28 + 2	1	—	—	4
Hughes, Paul	3	—	—	—	—
Iti, Clarry	15 + 6	4	—	—	16
Manning, Terry	33	12	—	—	48
Newlove, Paul	23	13	—	—	52
Newlove, Shaun	2	1	—	—	4
Pearson, Martin	15 + 6	10	47	—	134
Price, Gary	5 + 4	—	—	—	—
Rose, Gary	24 + 3	1	—	—	4
Sharp, Tim	10 + 11	3	—	1	13
Simpson, Owen	23	12	—	—	48
Smales, Ian	32	19	—	—	76
Tuuta, Brendon	28 + 1	4	—	1	17

TOTALS:
25 players		129	106	4	732

Great Britain centre Paul Newlove, 13 tries in 23 games.

1990-91 MATCH ANALYSIS

Date	Competition	H/A	Opponent	Rlt	Score	Tries	Goals	Attendance	Referee
26.8.90	YC(1)	H	Bramley	W	36-4	Bibb (2), P. Newlove (2), Fox, Sharp, Butt	Bibb (3), Fox	2445	Asquith
2.9.90	YC(2)	H	Hull K.R.	L	22-31	Manning (2), Banks, Casey, P. Newlove	Fox	4357	Kershaw
9.9.90	SBC	H	Hull K.R.	D	14-14	Bibb, Tuuta	Fox (3)	4275	Smith
16.9.90	SBC	A	Widnes	L	14-41	Smales, Banks	Fox (3)	—	—
23.9.90	SBC	H	Bradford N.	L	24-26	Manning, Fox, Clark, Casey	Fox (2), Pearson (2)	4898	Burke
30.9.90	SBC	A	Castleford	L	19-24	Pearson, Smales, Fox	Pearson (3), Fox (dg)	—	—
7.10.90	SBC	H	Sheffield E.	W	25-22	P. Newlove (2)	Pearson (8), Sharp (dg)	3963	Whitfield
14.10.90	SBC	A	Leeds	W	18-16	Fox, Tuuta, Banks	Pearson (3)	—	—
21.10.90	SBC	H	Rochdale H.	W	38-8	Smales (3), Clark, Fisher, Tuuta	Pearson (4), Fox (3)	3983	Ollerton
4.11.90	SBC	A	Hull K.R.	L	14-24	Smales, Rose, Grayshon	Pearson	—	—
11.11.90	SBC	H	Castleford	L	6-22	Simpson	Pearson	5760	Carter
17.11.90	SBC	A	Wigan	L	4-24	Smales	—	—	—
25.11.90	SBC	H	Hull	W	14-6	Pearson, Butt	Pearson (3)	4877	Ollerton
2.12.90	RT(1)	A	Barrow	W	54-16	Iti (2), Butt (2), Banks (2), Pearson, Manning, Sharp, Fox	Pearson (7)	—	—
11.12.90	RT(2)	H	St. Helens	L	16-33	Smales, Bibb, Pearson	Pearson (2)	3343	Asquith
26.12.90	SBC	H	Wakefield T.	W	14-8	P. Newlove, Butt, Simpson	Fox	5530	Holdsworth
30.12.90	SBC	A	Wakefield T.	W	16-8	Butt (2), Smales	Fox (2)	—	—
6.1.91	SBC	A	Oldham	W	20-18	P. Newlove (2), Simpson (2)	Fox (2)	—	—
9.1.91	SBC	A	Rochdale H.	W	26-12	Manning, P. Newlove, Simpson, Clark, Iti	Fox (3)	—	—
13.1.91	SBC	H	St. Helens	L	28-36	Clark (2), Simpson, Smales, Manning	Fox (4)	4879	Whitfield
20.1.91	SBC	A	Warrington	L	10-16	Simpson	Fox (3)	—	—
27.1.91	SBC	H	Oldham	W	28-20	Manning (2), Pearson, Fox, Simpson	Pearson (4)	4286	Smith
3.2.91	SBC	A	Sheffield E.	W	27-24	P. Newlove, Simpson, Fox, Clark, Smales	Pearson (3), Tuuta (dg)	—	—
17.2.91	CC(1)	A	Sheffield E.	L	12-19	Sharp, Pearson	Pearson, Fox	—	—
3.3.91	SBC	A	Hull	L	22-40	Fox (2), S. Newlove, Smales	Fox (3)	—	—
14.3.91	SBC	H	Warrington	H	22-8	Pearson, Casey, Manning, Fisher	Fox (2), Pearson	3113	Burke
17.3.91	SBC	A	St. Helens	L	38-54	Pearson (2), Fisher, Fox, Manning, Butt	Fox (6), Pearson	—	—
24.3.91	SBC	H	Widnes	L	22-27	Simpson, Fox, Butt, Casey	Pearson (3)	5247	Burke
29.3.91	SBC	H	Wigan	L	16-24	Smales, Tuuta, Iti	Fox (2)	5320	Asquith
7.4.91	SBC	H	Leeds	L	20-52	Fox, Smales, Pearson	Fox (4)	5261	Whitfield
14.4.91	SBC	A	Bradford N.	W	34-18	Smales (3), Simpson (2), P. Newlove (2)	Fox (3)	—	—
21.4.91	PT(1)	A	Wigan	W	31-26	Clark (2), Bibb, Manning, Smales, Burton	Fox (3, 1dg)	—	—
5.5.91	PT(SF)	A	Widnes	L	28-42	Butt, P. Newlove, Manning, Fisher, Smales	Fox (4)	—	—

FULHAM

Ground:	Crystal Palace National Sports Centre (081-659-4241)
Colours:	Black, red and white
First Season:	1980-81
Chairman:	Ray Stoner
General Manager:	Ross Strudwick
Coach:	Ross Strudwick (June 1989-)
Honours:	**Division Two** Champions, 1982-83
Records:	Attendance: 15,013 v. Wakefield T. (RL Cup) 15 Feb, 1981 at Fulham FC

Season

Goals: 136 by S. Diamond, 1982-83

Tries: 27 by J. Crossley, 1982-83

Points: 308 by S. Diamond, 1982-83

Match

Goals: 11 by S. Guyett v. Huddersfield, 23 Oct, 1988; G. Pearce v. Runcorn H., 26 Aug, 1990

Tries: No player has scored more than 3

Points: 22 by A. Platt, v. Mansfield M., 10 May, 1986; G. Pearce v. Runcorn H., 26 Aug, 1990

Highest score: 61-22 v. Huddersfield, 1988-89

Highest against: 72-6 v. Whitehaven, 1986-87

1990-91 PLAYERS' SUMMARY

	App	Tries	Goals	Dr	Pts
Abdurahman, Dazi	4 + 2	1	—	—	4
Browning, Russell	23 + 1	4	—	—	16
Callow, Steve	4 + 2	—	—	—	—
Churchill, Lachlan	4 + 3	1	—	—	4
Corcoran, Colin	8 + 2	—	—	—	—
Cruickshank, David	12 + 2	3	—	—	12
Dwyer, Tim	20	3	27	—	66
Grauf, Craig	29	7	—	2	30
Holderness, Kevin	0 + 1	—	—	—	—
Johansson, Lawrence	3 + 3	—	—	—	—
Keating, Noel	21 + 3	—	—	—	—
Lee, Mark	22	7	—	—	28
Leslie, Roy	19 + 1	4	—	—	16
Look, Tim	15 + 1	3	—	—	12
M'Barki, Hussein	20 + 1	7	—	—	28
Manthey, Greg	6	2	—	—	8
Mellors, Ian	20 + 9	3	—	—	12
Mohr, Shaun	0 + 2	—	—	—	—
Murphy, Kiernon	8 + 5	3	—	—	12
Noble, Mick	7 + 2	2	—	—	8
Pearce, Greg	23 + 1	5	74	—	168
Peart, Barry	1	—	—	—	—
Pitt, Darryl	14 + 2	10	—	—	40
Reinsfeld, Peter	11 + 1	1	—	—	—
Roberts, Steve	4 + 3	—	—	—	—
Rotheram, Dave	31 + 1	2	—	—	8
Sada, Adam	3	1	—	—	4
Scarlett, Richard	5 + 2	1	—	—	4
Scott, Conrad	4 + 3	—	—	—	—
Stevens, Andy	12 + 3	4	1	—	18
Taylor, Mick	29	5	—	—	20
Wilkins, Brent	15 + 2	1	—	—	4
Wilkinson, Bernie	1	1	—	—	4
Winborn, Doug	11 + 1	1	—	—	4
Winstanley, Chris	12 + 3	—	—	—	—
Wright, Bob	3 + 2	—	—	—	—
Trialist	5	4	—	—	16

TOTALS:

	App	Tries	Goals	Dr	Pts
37 players		85	102	2	546

1990-91 MATCH ANALYSIS

Date	Com-petition	H/A	Opponent	Rlt	Score	Tries	Goals	Atten-dance	Referee
26.8.90	LC(1)	H	Runcorn H.	W	50-0	Cruickshank (2), Murphy (2), M'Barki, Pitt, Rotheram	Pearce (11)	623	Ollerton
2.9.90	LC(2)	A	Leigh	L	8-40	Murphy	Pearce (2)	—	—
9.9.90	SD	A	Workington T.	L	4-9	—	Pearce (2)	—	—
16.9.90	SD	H	Barrow	W	22-8	M'Barki (2), Leslie, Browning	Pearce (3)	602	Ollerton
23.9.90	SD	H	Whitehaven	L	8-30	Pearce, Cruickshank	—	642	R. Connolly
30.9.90	SD	A	Dewsbury	L	6-16	Noble	Stevens	—	—
7.10.90	SD	H	Bramley	W	20-6	Mellors, Grauf	Dwyer (6)	557	Tidball
14.10.90	SD	A	Keighley	W	29-22	Grauf, Lee, Trialist, Rotheram	Dwyer (4), Grauf (dg)	—	—
21.10.90	SD	A	Runcorn H.	W	22-12	Trialist (3), Dwyer, Leslie	Dwyer	—	—
28.10.90	SD	H	Batley	W	14-7	Grauf, Pitt	Dwyer (3)	844	C. Morris
4.11.90	SD	A	Trafford B.	W	28-27	Pitt, Mellors, Lee, M'Barki	Dwyer (6)	—	—
11.11.90	SD	H	Ryedale-York	L	4-9	—	Dwyer (2)	586	Crashley
18.11.90	SD	A	Swinton	L	4-13	Stevens	—	—	—
25.11.90	SD	H	Dewsbury	W	14-10	Grauf (2)	Dwyer (3)	504	Whitelam
2.12.90	RT(1)	H	Castleford	L	8-14	M'Barki	Dwyer (2)	831	J. Connolly
16.12.90	SD	A	Doncaster	W	4-0	Leslie	—	—	—
6.1.91	SD	H	Trafford B.	W	13-6	Manthey (2), Sada	Grauf (dg)	504	K. Morris
20.1.91	SD	H	Leigh	L	20-23	Browning (2), M'Barki	Pearce (4)	720	Tennant
27.1.91	SD	A	Ryedale-York	L	4-22	—	Pearce (2)	—	—
3.2.91	SD	H	Swinton	W	26-10	Taylor (2), Pearce, Noble	Pearce (5)	820	Steele
17.2.91	CC(1)	A	Halifax	L	6-46	Wilkinson	Pearce	—	—
24.2.91	SD	A	Chorley	W	36-2	Lee (2), Stevens, Pitt, Grauf, Pearce	Pearce (6)	—	—
27.2.91	SD	A	Leigh	D	12-12	Pearce, Winborn	Pearce (2)	—	—
3.3.91	SD	A	Batley	W	20-4	Lee (2), Pitt (2)	Pearce (2)	—	—
10.3.91	SD	H	Workington T.	L	6-7	Browning	Pearce	467	Tennant
17.3.91	SD	A	Barrow	W	20-8	Taylor, Stevens, Churchill	Pearce (4)	—	—
24.3.91	SD	A	Whitehaven	W	20-16	Pitt, Stevens	Pearce (6)	—	—
29.3.91	SD	H	Chorley	W	28-9	Pitt, Taylor, Leslie, Abdurahman	Pearce (6)	524	Ollerton
1.4.91	SD	A	Bramley	D	8-8	Dwyer	Pearce (2)	—	—
7.4.91	SD	H	Doncaster	L	6-12	Mellors	Pearce	427	Galtress
10.4.91	SD	H	Keighley	W	28-16	Look (2), Pearce, Taylor	Pearce (6)	252	Asquith
14.4.91	SD	H	Runcorn H.	W	24-14	Scarlet, M'Barki, Wilkins, Dwyer	Pearce (4)	354	K. Morris
21.4.91	SDP(1)	A	Halifax	L	24-42	Pitt (2), Lee, Look	Pearce (4)	—	—

HALIFAX

Ground: Thrum Hall (0422-361026)
Colours: Blue and white
First Season: 1895-96
Nickname: Thrum Hallers
Chairman: Peter Marsland
Secretary: David Fleming
Coach: John Dorahy (June 1989-Aug 1990)
Peter Roe (Aug 1990-May 1991)
Roger Millward (May 1991-)
Honours: **Championship** Winners, 1906-07,
1964-65
Beaten finalists, 1952-53, 1953-54,
1955-56, 1965-66
Division One Champions, 1902-03,
1985-86
War League Beaten finalists,
1942-43, 1944-45
Challenge Cup Winners, 1902-03,
1903-04, 1930-31, 1938-39, 1986-87
Beaten finalists, 1920-21, 1940-41,
1941-42, 1948-49, 1953-54,
1955-56, 1987-88
Yorkshire League Winners,
1908-09, 1920-21, 1952-53,
1953-54, 1955-56, 1957-58
Eastern Division Championship
Winners, 1963-64
Yorkshire Cup Winners, 1908-09,
1944-45, 1954-55, 1955-56, 1963-64
Beaten finalists, 1905-06, 1907-08,
1941-42, 1979-80
Regal Trophy Winners, 1971-72
Beaten finalists, 1989-90
Premiership Trophy Beaten
finalists, 1985-86
Second Division Premiership
Beaten finalists, 1990-91
Charity Shield Winners, 1986-87
Beaten finalists, 1987-88
Records: Attendance: 29,153 v. Wigan
(RL Cup) 21 Mar, 1959
Season
Goals: 147 by T. Griffiths, 1955-56
Tries: 48 by J. Freeman, 1956-57
Points: 298 by C. Whitfield,
1986-87

Match
Goals: 14 by B. Burton v. Hunslet,
27 Aug, 1972
Tries: 8 by K. Williams v.
Dewsbury, 9 Nov, 1957
Points: 31 by B. Burton v. Hunslet,
27 Aug, 1972
Highest score: 82-8 v. Runcorn H.,
1990-91
Highest against: 64-0 v. Wigan,
1922-23

1990-91 PLAYERS' SUMMARY

	App	Tries	Goals	Dr	Pts
Atkinson, Colin	2	3	—	—	12
Austin, Greg	29 + 1	40	1	—	162
Barker, Andy	1	—	—	—	—
Beevers, Graham	1 + 4	—	—	—	—
Bell, Peter	24 + 4	4	—	—	16
Brown, Peter	15 + 2	7	14	—	56
Elia, Mark	16	14	—	—	56
Fairbank, Dick	16 + 2	3	—	—	12
Francis, Norman	2	—	—	—	—
George, Wilf	21 + 1	15	—	—	60
Grimoldby, Nick	1	—	—	—	—
Heslop, Simon	2	—	—	—	—
Hill, Brendan	30 + 2	11	—	—	44
Hutchinson, Rob	25 + 6	12	—	—	48
Irvine, Jimmy	19 + 1	9	—	—	36
Keebles, Mick	32 + 3	8	—	—	32
Lyons, John	12 + 4	1	1	1	7
McCallion, Seamus	9	2	—	—	8
Milner, Richard	13 + 4	3	—	—	12
Mitchell, Tony	3 + 2	1	—	—	4
Needham, David	2 + 4	—	—	—	—
Platt, Alan	23 + 7	5	91	—	202
Ramsey, Neville	0 + 1	—	—	—	—
Ramshaw, Jason	26 + 4	15	—	1	61
Richardson, Gary	6 + 1	1	—	—	4
Riddlesden, Eddie	10	6	—	—	24
Roberts, Lee	0 + 1	—	—	—	—
Robinson, Chris	2 + 1	2	—	—	8
Scott, Mick	20 + 12	2	—	—	8
Sharp, Henry	9	6	—	—	24
Silva, Matthew	4	1	13	—	30
Smith, Steve	32	6	20	—	64
Southernwood, Roy	34 + 1	9	—	—	36
Wilson, Warren	24	13	10	—	72
Wood, Martin	29 + 9	31	1	—	126
TOTALS:					
35 players		230	151	2	1,224

1990-91 MATCH ANALYSIS

Date	Com-petition	H/A	Opponent	Rlt	Score	Tries	Goals	Atten-dance	Referee
26.8.90	YC(1)	A	Doncaster	W	40-4	Atkinson (3), Wood, Keebles, Ramshaw, Southernwood	Platt (5), Smith	—	—
2.9.90	YC(2)	A	Wakefield T.	L	17-26	George (2), Wood	Platt (2), Lyons (dg)	—	—
9.9.90	SD	H	Dewsbury	W	38-6	Smith (2), Wood, Keebles, Ramshaw, Scott, George	Platt (5)	4993	Galtress
12.9.90	SD	A	Whitehaven	L	8-16	Wood	Platt (2)	—	—
16.9.90	SD	A	Leigh	W	16-6	Hill, Wood, Wilson	Platt (2)	—	—
23.9.90	SD	A	Bramley	W	56-8	Milner (2), Wood (2), Hill, Ramshaw, George, Austin, Fairbank, Wilson	Platt (6), Smith (2)	—	—
30.9.90	SD	H	Ryedale-York	W	26-18	Ramshaw (2), George, Wilson	Platt (5)	6888	Tidball
7.10.90	SD	A	Swinton	W	20-13	Elia, Hill, Austin	Smith (3), Platt	—	—
14.10.90	SD	H	Runcorn H.	W	82-8	Austin (4), Elia (2), Wood (2), Fairbank, Richardson, Platt, Ramshaw, Smith, George	Platt (13)	5283	Steele
21.10.90	SD	A	Ryedale-York	L	16-18	Elia, George, Southernwood	Platt (2)	—	—
4.11.90	SD	H	Batley	W	28-3	Platt, Hutchinson, Keebles, Elia, Fairbank, Austin	Platt (2)	4676	R. Connolly
6.11.90	Tour	H	Australia	L	18-36	Hutchinson (2), Austin, George	Smith	8730	Galtress
11.11.90	SD	A	Workington T.	L	16-24	Austin, McCallion, Keebles	Platt (2)	—	—
18.11.90	RT(P)	A	Leeds	L	6-58	Mitchell	Platt	—	—
21.11.90	SD	H	Bramley	W	42-12	Elia (2), Keebles, Southernwood, Riddlesden, Bell, Austin, Wood	Platt (5)	3035	Whitelam
25.11.90	SD	A	Barrow	W	46-18	Elia (3), Austin (2), Irvine, Hutchinson, Southernwood	Wilson (7)	—	—
16.12.90	SD	H	Chorley	W	38-10	Austin (2), Wood (2), George, Riddlesden, Hill, Irvine, Elia	Wilson	3645	Cross
26.12.90	SD	A	Keighley	W	12-6	Austin, Riddlesden	Wilson (2)	—	—
1.1.91	SD	H	Doncaster	W	40-16	Austin (2), Hutchinson, Wilson, Southernwood, Riddlesden, Irvine, Robinson	Platt (4)	4884	Whitfield
6.1.91	SD	A	Runcorn H.	W	62-0	Wood (3), Hill (2), Hutchinson (2), Wilson, George, Robinson, Riddlesden, Ramshaw	Platt (7)	—	—
20.1.91	SD	A	Batley	W	12-0	Riddlesden, Southernwood, Austin	—	—	—
17.2.91	CC(1)	H	Fulham	W	46-6	Austin (3), Southernwood, Elia, Brown, Platt, Wood	Platt (7)	4632	Carter
24.2.91	CC(2)	H	Whitehaven	W	46-12	Wilson (2), Hill, Austin, Wood, Elia, Platt, Southernwood, Irvine	Platt (5)	5549	J. Connolly
27.2.91	SD	H	Keighley	W	32-8	Wilson (2), Wood, Hutchinson, Ramshaw, Austin	Brown (2), Platt, Smith	3921	Burke
3.3.91	SD	A	Trafford B.	W	39-8	George (2), Elia, Hutchinson, Bell, Hill, Wood, Keebles	Platt (2), Smith, Ramshaw (dg)	—	—
6.3.91	SD	H	Whitehaven	W	56-6	Irvine (3), George (2), Austin (2), Sharp, Wood, Brown, Keebles	Brown (3), Smith, Austin, Lyons	2692	K. Morris

(continued on page 103)

CLUBS

HUDDERSFIELD

Ground: Fartown (0484-530710)
Colours: Claret and gold
First Season: 1895-96; added Barracudas to title from 1984-85 to 1987-88 inclusive
Nickname: Fartowners
Chairman: Jim Collins
Secretary: David Parker
Coach: Barry Seabourne (Mar 1990-Feb 1991)
Mick Blacker and Francis Jarvis (Feb 1991-)
Honours: **Championship** Winners, 1911-12, 1912-13, 1914-15, 1928-29, 1929-30, 1948-49, 1961-62
Beaten finalists, 1913-14, 1919-20, 1922-23, 1931-32, 1945-46, 1949-50
Division Two Champions, 1974-75
Challenge Cup Winners, 1912-13, 1914-15, 1919-20, 1932-33, 1944-45, 1952-53
Beaten finalists, 1934-35, 1961-62
Yorkshire League Winners, 1911-12, 1912-13, 1913-14, 1914-15, 1919-20, 1921-22, 1928-29, 1929-30, 1948-49, 1949-50, 1951-52
Eastern Division Beaten finalists, 1962-63
Yorkshire Cup Winners, 1909-10, 1911-12, 1913-14, 1914-15, 1918-19, 1919-20, 1926-27, 1931-32, 1938-39, 1950-51, 1952-53, 1957-58
Beaten finalists, 1910-11, 1923-24, 1925-26, 1930-31, 1937-38, 1942-43, 1949-50, 1960-61
Records: Attendance: 35,136 Leeds v. Wakefield T. (RL Cup SF) 19 April 1947. Home: 32,912 v. Wigan (League) 4 Mar, 1950
Season
Goals: 147 by B. Gronow, 1919-20
Tries: 80 by A. Rosenfeld, 1913-14
Points: 330 by B. Gronow, 1919-20

Match
Goals: 18 by M. Holland v. Swinton Park, 28 Feb, 1914
Tries: 10 by L. Cooper v. Keighley, 17 Nov, 1951
Points: 39 by M. Holland v. Swinton Park, 28 Feb, 1914
Highest score: 119-2 v. Swinton Park, 1913-14
Highest against: 94-12 v. Castleford, 1988-89

1990-91 PLAYERS' SUMMARY

	App	Tries	Goals	Dr	Pts
Boothroyd, Alan	25	—	—	—	—
Chapman, Chris	17 + 2	8	—	—	32
Chapman, Tony	6	—	3	—	6
Cocker, Stuart	24	15	2	—	64
Cook, Billy	3 + 1	—	—	—	—
Dick, Kevin	15 + 4	1	39	2	84
Edwards, Anthony	11	4	—	—	16
Gibson, Wally	27 + 1	12	1	2	52
Gregg, Carl	4 + 1	1	—	2	6
Hawkyard, Colin	1	—	—	—	—
Huck, Phil	28 + 1	1	—	—	4
Jowett, Bob	24	2	—	—	8
Mackintosh, Andy	2	1	—	—	4
McTigue, Mick	28	4	—	—	16
Mallinder, Paul	1 + 1	—	—	—	—
Maskery, Mark	9 + 8	2	23	—	54
Meillam, Paul	3	1	—	—	4
Mountain, Dean	5 + 3	—	—	—	—
Naidole, Joe	11 + 2	2	—	—	8
Parr, Chris	18 + 5	1	—	—	4
Riddlesden, Eddie	3	—	—	—	—
Royston, Paul	0 + 1	—	—	—	—
St. Hilaire, Lee	22 + 1	5	—	—	20
Sawyer, Aaron	3	—	—	—	—
Scholes, Damon	7 + 2	2	—	—	8
Seabourne, Peter	4	—	15	—	30
Senior, Gary	18	3	—	—	12
Sewell, Andrew	2 + 3	—	—	—	—
Shuttleworth, Greg	2	—	—	—	—
Siddall, Gary	24 + 3	1	—	—	4
Simpson, Andy	8 + 2	4	—	—	16
Stewart, Russell	23	—	—	—	—
Thomas, Ian	20 + 2	16	—	—	64
Ventola, Roy	1	1	—	—	4
Walker, Stuart	2 + 5	—	—	—	—
Wilson, Mick	2 + 2	—	—	—	—
TOTALS: 36 players		87	83	6	520

1990-91 MATCH ANALYSIS

Date	Competition	H/A	Opponent	Rlt	Score	Tries	Goals	Attendance	Referee
26.8.90	YC(1)	A	Batley	L	10-17	Cocker, Ventola	Dick	—	—
9.9.90	SD	A	Keighley	W	30-26	Gibson, Mackintosh, C. Chapman, McTigue, Senior	Dick (5)	—	—
12.9.90	SD	H	Doncaster	W	26-24	Cocker (4)	Dick (5)	1325	Tidball
16.9.90	SD	A	Whitehaven	L	8-11	C. Chapman	Dick (2)	—	—
30.9.90	SD	A	Runcorn H.	W	19-6	C. Chapman (2), Thomas	Dick (3, 1dg)	—	—
7.10.90	SD	H	Trafford B.	L	12-28	Parr	Dick (4)	1795	K. Morris
14.10.90	SD	H	Leigh	L	10-22	Gibson	A. Chapman (3)	2127	Ollerton
21.10.90	SD	A	Doncaster	L	20-29	Thomas (2), St. Hilaire (2)	Dick (2)	—	—
4.11.90	SD	H	Workington T.	D	16-16	Cocker (2), Jowett	Maskery (2)	1249	Crashley
11.11.90	SD	A	Barrow	W	26-12	St. Hilaire, Gregg, Senior, Cocker	Maskery (5)	—	—
25.11.90	SD	H	Runcorn	W	17-14	Cocker (3), Gibson	Gregg (dg)	1134	Cross
2.12.90	RT(1)	H	Keighley	L	13-15	Gibson, Huck	Cocker (2), Gregg (dg)	1256	Whitfield
16.12.90	SD	A	Ryedale-York	W	7-6	Thomas	Dick, Gibson (dg)	—	—
23.12.90	SD	H	Whitehaven	W	52-18	Thomas (4), Gibson (3), Cocker, McTigue	Dick (7), Gibson	1021	R. Connolly
26.12.90	SD	H	Chorley	W	20-6	Thomas (2), Dick, McTigue	Dick (2)	1187	Steele
1.1.91	SD	H	Keighley	L	8-10	Thomas	Dick (2)	1564	Tidball
6.1.91	SD	A	Chorley	L	6-19	Thomas	Dick	—	—
20.1.91	SD	H	Swinton	L	12-21	Thomas (2), St. Hilaire	—	1307	Cross
27.1.91	CC(P)	A	Warrington	L	4-22	—	Dick (2)	—	—
3.2.91	SD	A	Workington T.	L	17-28	Thomas, Jowett, C. Chapman	Dick (2, 1dg)	—	—
17.2.91	SD	H	Dewsbury	L	16-28	Edwards, Nadiole, Meillam, Gibson	—	1293	Cross
20.2.91	SD	H	Ryedale-York	L	10-14	Simpson	Seabourne (3)	873	K. Morris
24.2.91	SD	A	Trafford B.	L	22-23	Cocker, Edwards, Sidall	Seabourne (5)	—	—
3.3.91	SD	H	Barrow	W	18-10	Edwards, Cocker	Seabourne (5)	914	Allatt
10.3.91	SD	A	Bramley	L	12-14	Senior, Gibson	Seabourne (2)	—	—
17.3.91	SD	A	Dewsbury	W	18-16	Simpson, Edwards, C. Chapman	Maskery (3)	—	—
29.3.91	SD	H	Batley	W	22-0	Maskery, C. Chapman, Thomas, Gibson	Maskery (3)	1479	Steele
1.4.91	SD	A	Batley	W	18-8	Scholes, C. Chapman, Gibson	Maskery (3)	—	—
7.4.91	SD	A	Leigh	L	13-26	Gibson, Simpson	Maskery (2), Gibson (dg)	—	—
10.4.91	SD	H	Bramley	W	20-0	Nadiole, Simpson, Cocker	Maskery (4)	1022	Burke
14.4.91	SD	A	Swinton	L	18-42	Maskery, Scholes, St. Hilaire, McTigue	Maskery	—	—

HULL

Ground: The Boulevard (0482-29040)
Colours: Black and white
First Season: 1895-96
Nickname: Airlie Birds
Chairman: David Kirkwood
Secretary: Mike Stanley
Coach: Brian Smith (July 1988-Jan 1991)
Noel Cleal (Sep 1990-)
Honours: **Championship** Winners, 1919-20, 1920-21, 1935-36, 1955-56, 1957-58
Beaten finalists, 1956-57
Division One Champions, 1982-83
Division Two Champions, 1976-77, 1978-79
Challenge Cup Winners, 1913-14, 1981-82
Beaten finalists, 1907-08, 1908-09, 1909-10, 1921-22, 1922-23, 1958-59, 1959-60, 1979-80, 1982-83, 1984-85
Yorkshire League Winners, 1918-19, 1922-23, 1926-27, 1935-36
Yorkshire Cup Winners, 1923-24, 1969-70, 1982-83, 1983-84, 1984-85
Beaten finalists, 1912-13, 1914-15, 1920-21, 1927-28, 1938-39, 1946-47, 1953-54, 1954-55, 1955-56, 1959-60, 1967-68, 1986-87

Regal Trophy Winners, 1981-82
Beaten finalists, 1975-76, 1984-85
BBC2 Floodlit Trophy Winners, 1979-80
Premiership Winners, 1990-91
Beaten finalists, 1980-81, 1981-82, 1982-83, 1988-89
Records: Attendance: 28,798 v. Leeds (RL Cup) 7 Mar, 1936
Season
Goals: 170 by S. Lloyd, 1978-79
Tries: 52 by J. Harrison, 1914-15
Points: 369 by S. Lloyd, 1978-79
Match
Goals: 14 by J. Kennedy v. Rochdale H., 7 Apr, 1921; S. Lloyd v. Oldham, 10 Sep, 1978
Tries: 7 by C. Sullivan v. Doncaster, 15 Apr, 1968
Points: 36 by J. Kennedy v. Keighley, 29 Jan, 1921
Highest score: 86-0 v. Elland, 1898-99
Highest against: 64-2 v. St. Helens, 1987-88

Andy Dannatt, four tries in 25 appearances.

1990-91 PLAYERS' SUMMARY

	App	Tries	Goals	Dr	Pts
Blacker, Brian	5 + 8	—	—	—	—
Busby, Dean	2 + 9	2	—	—	8
Charles, Marquis	2	—	—	—	—
Cleal, Noel	0 + 8	3	—	—	12
Dannatt, Andy	25	4	—	—	16
Dixon, Michael	4 + 14	—	—	—	—
Durham, Steve	6 + 1	1	—	—	4
Eastwood, Paul	33	11	101	—	246
Entat, Patrick	29	4	—	—	16
Feather, Steve	1	—	—	—	—
Gay, Richard	31	7	—	—	28
Hanlan, Lee	2	1	—	—	4
Harrison, Karl	28	4	—	—	16
Jackson, Anthony	0 + 1	—	—	—	—
Jackson, Lee	31 + 1	5	—	—	20
McGarry, Damien	16	8	—	—	32
Mackey, Greg	33	6	—	3	27
McNamara, Steve	11 + 8	4	—	—	16
Marlow, Ian	28 + 3	1	—	—	4
Nolan, Gary	1 + 3	3	—	—	12
Nolan, Robert	25 + 2	10	—	—	40
Price, Richard	4 + 2	1	—	—	4
Sharp, Jon	31	4	—	—	16
Turner, Neil	17 + 2	7	—	—	28
Walker, Russell	29 + 4	4	—	—	16
Webb, Brad	32 + 1	8	—	—	32
Welham, Paul	1	—	—	—	—
Windley, Phil	2 + 1	—	—	—	—
TOTALS: 28 players		98	101	3	597

1990-91 MATCH ANALYSIS

Date	Competition	H/A	Opponent	Rlt	Score	Tries	Goals	Attendance	Referee
26.8.90	YC(1)	H	Castleford	L	6-10	Webb	Eastwood	6591	Smith
9.9.90	SBC	H	St. Helens	W	20-14	Mackey, Cleal, R. Nolan	Eastwood (4)	6026	Burke
16.9.90	SBC	A	Leeds	W	24-22	Cleal (2), Turner, Mackey	Eastwood (4)	—	—
23.9.90	SBC	H	Widnes	W	32-6	McNamara (2), Eastwood, Mackey, R. Nolan	Eastwood (6)	7769	Holdsworth
30.9.90	SBC	A	Rochdale H.	W	30-18	R. Nolan (2), Turner, Sharp, Webb	Eastwood (5)	—	—
7.10.90	SBC	H	Wigan	W	24-4	Marlow, Eastwood, Turner	Eastwood (6)	10,926	Allatt
13.10.90	SBC	A	Warrington	W	3-2	—	Eastwood, Mackey (dg)	—	—
21.10.90	SBC	H	Sheffield E.	W	34-6	Eastwood (2), Gay, Walker, Webb, Turner	Eastwood (5)	6997	Carter
3.11.90	SBC	A	Wakefield T.	L	6-22	Webb	Eastwood	—	—
14.11.90	Tour	H	Australia	L	4-34	Turner	—	13,081	Campbell
18.11.90	SBC	H	Warrington	W	17-8	Eastwood, Dannatt	Eastwood (4), Mackey (dg)	5566	J. Connolly
25.11.90	SBC	A	Featherstone R.	L	6-14	Gay	Eastwood	—	—
1.12.90	RT(1)	A	Widnes	L	16-24	Dannatt, R. Nolan, Mackey	Eastwood (2)	—	—
16.12.90	SBC	H	Oldham	W	31-4	Harrison, R. Nolan, Gay, Jackson, Mackey	Eastwood (5), Mackey (dg)	5189	Whitfield
26.12.90	SBC	H	Castleford	W	22-6	Entat, Eastwood, Price	Eastwood (5)	5207	Ollerton
1.1.91	SBC	A	Hull K.R.	L	8-20	Eastwood, Turner	—	—	—
6.1.91	SBC	H	Leeds	W	34-14	R. Nolan (2), McGarry, Webb, Walker, Sharp	Eastwood (5)	7591	Carter
20.1.91	SBC	H	Bradford N.	W	34-6	Dannatt (2), McGarry, Walker, Gay, Eastwood	Eastwood (5)	6443	Burke
30.1.91	SC(P)	A	Sheffield E.	L	6-19	—	Eastwood (3)	—	—
3.2.91	SBC	H	Rochdale H.	W	28-8	Jackson (2), Durham, R. Nolan, Eastwood	Eastwood (4)	4697	Gilmour
18.2.91	SBC	A	St. Helens	L	10-12	R. Nolan, Webb	Eastwood	—	—
27.2.91	SBC	A	Widnes	L	2-28	—	Eastwood	—	—
3.3.91	SBC	H	Featherstone R.	W	40-22	Entat (2), McGarry, Busby, Webb, Gay, McNamara, Harrison	Eastwood (4)	5441	Whitfield
13.3.91	SBC	A	Wigan	L	12-34	Jackson (2)	Eastwood (2)	—	—
17.3.91	SBC	H	Wakefield T.	L	6-14	Harrison	Eastwood	5621	Smith
24.3.91	SBC	A	Sheffield E.	W	16-6	McGarry, Hanlan	Eastwood (4)	—	—
29.3.91	SBC	H	Hull K.R.	W	28-16	Sharp (2), McGarry (2), Eastwood	Eastwood (4)	9618	Whitfield
1.4.91	SBC	A	Castleford	W	16-14	McGarry, Mackey, Webb	Eastwood (2)	—	—
7.4.91	SBC	A	Bradford N.	L	16-28	McGarry, McNamara	Eastwood (4)	—	—
14.4.91	SBC	A	Oldham	L	14-19	Harrison, Eastwood, G. Nolan	Eastwood	—	—
21.4.91	PT(1)	H	St. Helens	W	28-12	Entat, Gay, Busby, Turner	Eastwood (6)	5630	Tennant
5.5.91	PT(SF)	H	Leeds	W	10-7	G. Nolan	Eastwood (3)	9964	Whitfield
12.5.91	PT(F)	Man U. FC	Widnes	W	14-4	Gay, Walker, G. Nolan	Eastwood	(42,043)	Holdsworth

HULL KINGSTON ROVERS

Ground: Craven Park (0482-74648)
Colours: Red, blue and white
First Season: 1899-1900
Nickname: Robins
Chairman: Max Gold
Secretary: Ron Turner
Coach: Roger Millward (Mar 1977-May 1991)
             George Fairbairn (May 1991-)
Honours: **Championship** Winners, 1922-23,
             1924-25
             Beaten finalists, 1920-21, 1967-68
             First Division Champions,
             1978-79, 1983-84, 1984-85
             Second Division Champions,
             1989-90
             Challenge Cup Winners, 1979-80
             Beaten finalists, 1904-05, 1924-25,
             1963-64, 1980-81, 1985-86
             Regal Trophy Winners, 1984-85,
             Beaten finalists, 1981-82, 1985-86
             Premiership Winners, 1980-81,
             1983-84, Beaten finalists, 1984-85
             Second Division Premiership
             Beaten finalists, 1989-90
             Yorkshire League Winners,
             1924-25, 1925-26
             Yorkshire Cup Winners, 1920-21,
             1929-30, 1966-67, 1967-68,
             1971-72, 1974-75, 1985-86
             Beaten finalists, 1906-07, 1911-12,
             1933-34, 1962-63, 1975-76,
             1980-81, 1984-85
             BBC2 Floodlit Trophy Winners,
             1977-78
             Beaten finalists, 1979-80
             Eastern Division Championship
             Winners, 1962-63
             Charity Shield Beaten finalists,
             1985-86
Records: Attendance: 22,282 v. Hull,
             7 Oct, 1922. There was a crowd of
             27,670 for a League match v. Hull
             at Hull City FC's Boothferry Park
             on 3 Apr, 1953

Season
Goals: 199 by M. Fletcher, 1989-90
Tries: 45 by G. Prohm, 1984-85
Points: 450 by M. Fletcher, 1989-90
Match
Goals: 14 by A. Carmichael v.
Merthyr Tydfil, 8 Oct, 1910; M.
Fletcher v. Whitehaven, 18 Mar,
1990; C. Armstrong v. Nottingham
C., 19 Aug, 1990
Tries: 11 by G. West v. Brookland
R., 4 Mar, 1905
Points: 53 by G. West v. Brookland
R., 4 Mar, 1905
Highest score: 100-6 v. Nottingham
C., 1990-91
Highest against: 68-0 v. Halifax,
1955-56

1990-91 PLAYERS' SUMMARY

	App	Tries	Goals	Dr	Pts
Armstrong, Colin	1 + 4	—	14	—	28
Austin, Greg	4	7	—	—	28
Bishop, David	5	—	—	—	—
Chatfield, Gary	8 + 1	—	—	—	—
Clark, Garry	10	3	—	—	12
Cook, Graham	3	—	—	—	—
Ema, Asuquo	24 + 2	4	—	—	16
Fletcher, Mike	23 + 5	3	59	—	130
Fletcher, Paul	12 + 4	5	—	—	20
Goulding, James	18 + 4	3	—	—	12
Hadi, Steve	15	3	—	—	12
Hallas, Graeme	20 + 3	6	32	3	91
Harrison, Des	22 + 3	4	—	—	16
Hoe, Sean	14 + 2	2	—	—	8
Irvine, Jimmy	5 + 5	3	—	—	12
Jackson, Wayne	0 + 4	—	—	—	—
Lightfoot, David	7 + 1	1	—	—	4
Lydiat, John	8 + 2	4	—	—	16
Lyman, Paul	23 + 2	11	—	—	44
Niebling, Bryan	23 + 1	2	—	—	8
O'Brien, Craig	1	—	—	—	—
Parker, Wayne	18	1	—	—	4
Robinson, Steve	6	2	—	—	8
Rudd, Chris	19	1	—	—	4
Schultz, Stuart	1	—	—	—	—
Smith, Mike	12 + 2	1	—	—	4
Sodje, Bright	9	1	—	—	4
Speckman, Paul	8 + 9	1	—	—	4
Sullivan, Anthony	29	22	—	—	88
Thompson, Andy	27	—	—	—	—
Vannet, Paul	11 + 4	2	—	—	8
Watson, Dave	29	13	—	—	52
Wildbridge, Mark	1	—	—	—	—

TOTALS:
33 players		105	105	3	633

1990-91 MATCH ANALYSIS

Date	Competition	H/A	Opponent	Rlt	Score	Tries	Goals	Attendance	Referee
19.8.90	YC(P)	A[1]	Nottingham C.	W	100-6	Austin (6), Sullivan (5), Ema (2), Lightfoot, Harrison, Clark, Hoe, Irving	Armstong (14)	—	—
26.8.90	YC(1)	A	Ryedale-York	W	10-0	Hallas, Sullivan	Hallas	—	—
2.9.90	YC(2)	A	Featherstone R.	W	31-22	Sullivan (2), Austin, Speckman, Irvine	Hallas (5, 1dg)	—	—
9.9.90	SBC	A	Featherstone R.	D	14-14	Hoe	Hallas (5)	—	—
12.9.90	YC(SF)	A	Castleford	L	6-29	Irvine	Hallas	—	—
16.9.90	SBC	H	Warrington	W	20-14	Sullivan (2), Goulding, Watson	Hallas (2)	4895	Whitfield
23.9.90	SBC	A	St. Helens	L	10-42	Clark, Sullivan	Hallas	—	—
30.9.90	SBC	H	Wakefield T.	L	12-18	Hallas, Lyman	M. Fletcher (2)	5203	Allatt
7.10.90	SBC	A	Oldham	W	28-25	Lyman, Sullivan, Vannet, Parker	Hallas (6)	—	—
14.10.90	SBC	H	Widnes	W	22-20	Sullivan, Watson, Goulding	Hallas (4, 2dg)	5583	Crashley
21.10.90	SBC	A	Bradford N.	L	10-26	Watson	Hallas (3)	—	—
4.11.90	SBC	H	Featherstone R.	W	24-14	Hallas, Sullivan, Watson, Lyman	Hallas (3), M. Fletcher	4977	Galtress
13.11.90	SBC	H	Wigan	L	6-36	Watson	Hallas	5642	Smith
18.11.90	SBC	A	Rochdale H.	W	32-18	Watson (2), Lyman, Sullivan, Sodje	M. Fletcher (6)	—	—
25.11.90	SBC	H	Bradford N.	W	12-4	Niebling, Lyman	M. Fletcher (2)	4882	Carter
2.12.90	RT(1)	A	Leeds	L	22-26	Watson (2), Lydiat, Sullivan	M. Fletcher (3)	—	—
19.12.90	SBC	A	Widnes	L	8-28	Sullivan	M. Fletcher (2)	—	—
29.12.90	SBC	H	Sheffield E.	D	16-16	Lydiat, Watson	M. Fletcher (4)	3255	Asquith
1.1.91	SBC	H	Hull	W	20-8	M. Fletcher, Lyman, P. Fletcher	M. Fletcher (4)	8557	Holdsworth
6.1.91	SBC	A	Warrington	L	12-30	Goulding, Lyman	M. Fletcher (2)	—	—
13.1.91	SBC	H	Oldham	W	42-14	Lydiat (2), Hadi, P. Fletcher, Sullivan, Ema, Lyman	M. Fletcher (7)	4499	Carter
20.1.91	SBC	A	Castleford	L	2-30	—	M. Fletcher	—	—
27.1.91	SBC	H	St. Helens	D	26-26	Watson, Ema, Robinson	M. Fletcher (7)	4335	C. Morris
2.2.91	SBC	A	Wigan	L	4-34	Lyman	—	—	—
17.2.91	CC(1)	A	Workington T.	L	12-18	Sullivan (2), Clark	—	—	—
24.2.91	SBC	H	Castleford	L	12-16	Smith, Harrison	M. Fletcher (2)	4210	C. Morris
3.3.91	SBC	A	Leeds	L	18-24	M. Fletcher, Robinson, Sullivan	M. Fletcher (3)	—	—
10.3.91	SBC	A	Wakefield T.	L	6-26	P. Fletcher	M. Fletcher	—	—
17.3.91	SBC	H	Leeds	L	16-28	M. Fletcher, Hallas, Lyman	M. Fletcher (2)	4926	J. Connolly
24.3.91	SBC	H	Rochdale H.	W	48-14	Watson (2), Hadi, P. Fletcher, Sullivan, Rudd, Harrison, Lyman, Vannet	M. Fletcher (6)	4010	Galtress
29.3.91	SBC	A	Hull	L	16-28	Harrison, Hallas, P. Fletcher	M. Fletcher (2)	—	—
31.3.91	SBC	A	Sheffield E.	L	16-62	Hallas, Niebling, Hadi	M. Fletcher (2)	—	—

[1] at Doncaster

HUNSLET

Ground: Elland Road (0532-711675)
Colours: Myrtle, flame and white
First Season: 1895-96. Disbanded at end of
1972-73. Re-formed as New
Hunslet in 1973-74. Retitled
Hunslet from start of 1979-80
Chairman: Graham Lisle
Secretary: Mabel Grainger
Coach: Paul Daley (May 1990-)
Honours: **Challenge Cup** Winners, 1907-08,
1933-34
Beaten finalists, 1898-99, 1964-65
Championship Winners, 1907-08,
1937-38
Beaten finalists, 1958-59
Division Two Champions, 1962-63,
1986-87
Second Division Premiership
Beaten finalists, 1986-87
Yorkshire Cup Winners, 1905-06,
1907-08, 1962-63
Beaten finalists, 1908-09, 1929-30,
1931-32, 1944-45, 1956-57, 1965-66
Yorkshire League Winners,
1897-98, 1907-08, 1931-32
Records: Attendance: 54,112 v. Leeds
(Championship final) 30 Apr, 1938

Veteran forward Keith Bell, 19 appearances in his debut season for Hunslet.

Season
Goals: 181 by W. Langton, 1958-59
Tries: 34 by A. Snowden, 1956-57
Points: 380 by W. Langton,
1958-59
Match
Goals: 12 by W. Langton v.
Keighley, 18 Aug, 1959
Tries: 7 by G. Dennis v. Bradford
N., 20 Jan, 1934
Points: 28 by T. Lumb v. Runcorn
H., 7 Oct, 1990
Highest score: 75-5 v. Broughton
Rec., 1896-97
Highest against: 76-8 v. Halifax,
1972-73

1990-91 PLAYERS' SUMMARY

	App	Tries	Goals	Dr	Pts
Bell, Keith	19	1	—	3	7
Bettney, Neville	3	—	—	—	—
Bowden, Chris	15 + 4	3	—	—	12
Brook, David	1 + 2	—	—	—	—
Brook, Richard	1	—	—	—	—
Burrow, Paul	25	12	—	—	48
Carlyle, Brendan	5 + 1	1	—	—	4
Cartwright, Phil	3	—	—	—	—
Clifford, John	2	1	—	—	4
Coates, Jed	8 + 2	2	—	—	8
Coyle, Mick	8 + 3	1	—	—	4
Daniels, Alan	2	—	—	—	—
Halafihi, Nick	8 + 1	2	—	—	8
Jackson, Michael	27	5	—	—	20
Jones, David	1	—	—	—	—
Kay, Andy	1	—	—	—	—
King, Graham	8 + 5	4	—	—	16
Langton, Steve	18	5	—	4	24
Lidbury, Steve	1	—	—	—	—
Liles, Richard	0 + 1	—	—	—	—
Lowes, James	26 + 1	3	—	—	12
Lumb, Tim	28	9	84	1	205
Lyons, Paddy	5 + 5	1	3	1	11
Marson, Andrew	7 + 6	1	—	—	4
Mason, Keith	2	—	—	—	—
Mitchell, Keith	19 + 3	3	—	—	12
Moore, Herbie	13	4	—	—	16
Morgan, Paul	3 + 8	—	1	—	2
Newman, Dave	11	3	—	—	12
Oldroyd, Tommy	0 + 1	—	—	—	—
Penola, Colin	5	—	—	—	—
Petch, Andy	11 + 1	2	—	—	8
Precious, Andrew	0 + 2	—	—	—	—
Raw, Andy	4 + 1	—	—	—	—
Sampson, Roy	30	6	—	—	24
Waites, Brian	16	6	—	—	24
Warrener, Stan	9	1	—	—	4
White, Paul (Australian)	20	13	—	—	52
White, Paul (ex-Ryedale)	2	—	—	—	—
Wilkinson, Shaun	7 + 3	1	—	—	4
Wood, Mark	28 + 2	2	—	—	8
Wright, Jason	1	—	—	—	—
TOTALS:					
42 players		92	88	9	553

1990-91 MATCH ANALYSIS

Date	Com-petition	H/A	Opponent	Rlt	Score	Tries	Goals	Atten-dance	Referee
26.8.90	YC(1)	A	Wakefield T.	L	18-28	Wilkinson, Jackson, Lumb	Lumb (3)	—	—
9.9.90	SD	A	Doncaster	L	8-11	Newman	Lumb (2)	—	—
16.9.90	SD	A	Chorley	L	23-27	Langton, Mitchell, Sampson, Newman	Lumb (3), Langton (dg)	—	—
26.9.90	SD	H	Trafford B.	W	17-10	Warrener, Burrow, Sampson	Lumb (2), Langton (dg)	596	C. Morris
30.9.90	SD	A	Keighley	W	44-14	Burrow (3), White, Petch, King, Langton	Lumb (8)	—	—
7.10.90	SD	H	Runcorn H.	W	52-12	Lumb (3), Mitchell, Wood, Petch, Langton, Burrow, Lyons	Lumb (8)	707	J. Connolly
14.10.90	SD	A	Trafford B.	L	26-48	Sampson, White, Mitchell, Newman, Langton	Lumb (3)	—	—
21.10.90	SD	H	Dewsbury	W	19-10	White, Clifford, Burrow	Lumb (3), Langton (dg)	976	Gilmour
30.10.90	SD	H	Leigh	L	16-24	Lumb, Sampson, Lowes	Lumb (2)	850	Galtress
4.11.90	SD	A	Runcorn H.	W	11-10	Burrow, White	Lumb, Langton (dg)	—	—
11.11.90	SD	H	Keighley	L	6-14	—	Lumb (3)	785	Cross
18.11.90	SD	A	Whitehaven	L	7-12	Lumb	Lumb (1, 1 dg)	—	—
25.11.90	SD	H	Doncaster	W	22-10	Jackson, Bell, Moore	Lumb (5)	904	K. Morris
2.12.90	RT(1)	A	Wakefield T.	L	8-40	Marson	Lumb (2)	—	—
16.12.90	SD	A	Swinton	L	10-22	Moore, Burrow	Lumb	—	—
23.12.90	SD	A	Workington T.	L	12-22	White, Langton	Lumb (2)	—	—
30.12.90	SD	A	Bramley	W	26-14	White (2), Sampson, Lumb	Lumb (5)	—	—
1.1.91	SD	H	Bramley	W	30-18	Lumb (2), Burrow (2), White	Lumb (5)	721	R. Connolly
6.1.91	SD	H	Whitehaven	W	17-8	Bowden, Waites, White	Lumb (2), Bell (dg)	585	Campbell
20.1.91	SD	H	Chorley	D	14-14	Waites (2), Jackson	Lumb	644	R. Connolly
27.1.91	SD	H	Batley	W	6-0	Coates	Bell (2 dg)	936	Cross
10.2.91	SD	H	Barrow	W	56-4	White (4), Lowes (2), Burrow, Moore, Sampson, Bowden, Jackson	Lumb (6)	421	McCallum (Aus)
17.2.91	CC(1)	A	Barrow	L	8-13	—	Lumb (4)	—	—
24.2.91	SD	A	Leigh	L	24-31	Waites (2), Moore, Coyle	Lumb (4)	—	—
27.2.91	SD	A	Barrow	D	4-4	—	Lumb (2)	—	—
10.3.91	SD	A	Dewsbury	L	12-15	Carlyle, Bowden	Lumb (2)	—	—
15.3.91	SD	A	Ryedale-York	L	10-24	King (2)	Morgan	—	—
24.3.91	SD	H	Swinton	L	12-16	Halafihi (2)	Lumb (2)	812	Campbell
1.4.91	SD	H	Ryedale-York	L	6-20	Burrow	Lumb	931	Carter
7.4.91	SD	A	Batley	W	14-10	Coates, Waites	Lyons (2), Lumb	—	—
14.4.91	SD	H	Workington T.	W	15-14	Wood, Jackson, King	Lyons (1, 1dg)	875	Allatt

KEIGHLEY COUGARS

Ground: Lawkholme Lane (0535-602602)
Colours: Green, scarlet and white
First Season: 1901-02. Added Cougars to title at start of 1991-92.
Nickname: Lawkholmers
Chairman: Colin Farrar
Secretary: Betty Spencer
Coach: Tony Fisher (June 1990-)
Honours: **Division Two** Champions, 1902-03
Challenge Cup Beaten finalists, 1936-37
Yorkshire Cup Beaten finalists, 1943-44, 1951-52
Records: Attendance: 14,500 v. Halifax (RL Cup) 3 Mar, 1951
Season
Goals: 155 by B. Jefferson, 1973-74
Tries: 30 by J. Sherburn, 1934-35
Points: 331 by B. Jefferson, 1973-74

Six tries in 31 games for Keighley skipper Andy Gascoigne.

Match
Goals: 11 by R. Walker v. Castleford, 13 Jan, 1906; H. Cook v. Hull K.R., 31 Oct, 1953
Tries: 5 by I. Jagger v. Castleford, 13 Jan, 1906; S. Stacey v. Liverpool C., 9 Mar, 1907
Points: 24 by J. Phillips v. Halifax, 5 Oct, 1957
Highest score: 67-0 v. Castleford, 1905-06
Highest against: 92-2 v. Leigh, 1985-86

1990-91 PLAYERS' SUMMARY

	App	Tries	Goals	Dr	Pts
Bardgett, Paul	4 + 3	1	—	—	4
Burks, Jake	1	—	—	—	—
Burke, Mick	7	2	1	—	10
Butterfield, Jeff	20 + 1	4	—	—	16
Chick, Stuart	2	—	—	—	—
Collis, John	5	—	—	—	—
Coulter, Gary	15 + 3	—	—	—	—
Cox, Dave	9 + 4	—	—	—	—
Cummins, Shane	1	—	—	—	—
Dixon, Keith	30	6	71	3	169
Dixon, Paul	0 + 1	—	—	—	—
Donnelly, Jason	24	6	—	—	24
Fairbank, Andy	2 + 4	1	—	—	4
Fairbank, Mark	24	8	—	—	32
Farrell, Carlton	29	7	—	—	28
Fiechter, Murray	3	1	—	—	4
Gascoigne, Andy	30 + 1	6	—	—	24
Godfrey, Heath	10	2	—	—	8
Hiley, Greg	23	3	—	—	12
James, Tony	14 + 1	9	—	—	36
Johnson, David	0 + 2	—	—	—	—
Kelly, Haydn	21 + 1	3	—	—	12
Lee, Jason	0 + 1	—	—	—	—
McLean, Brian	2	—	—	—	—
Malcolm, Trevor	2	—	—	—	—
Mirfin, Phil	3 + 1	1	3	—	10
Mitchell, Pat	24 + 2	7	—	—	28
Moses, Paul	18 + 4	1	1	2	8
Needham, Dave	0 + 1	—	—	—	—
Nelson, Dave	1	—	—	—	—
Palelei, Aaron	17 + 1	8	—	—	32
Plath, Andre	3	—	—	—	—
Priestley, Ray	8 + 8	1	—	—	4
Proctor, Rob	2	—	—	—	—
Race, Wayne	7	—	—	—	—
Ragan, Mark	2 + 1	—	—	—	—
Rose, Kevin	26 + 4	2	—	—	8
Simpson, Owen	7	8	—	—	32
Stephenson, Andy	5	2	—	—	8
Stephenson, Phil	2 + 3	—	—	—	—
Thompson, Julian	13 + 2	8	—	—	32
Tyrers, Andy	6 + 3	—	—	—	—
Walsh, Tim	3 + 2	—	—	—	—
Wasyliw, John	2	—	1	—	2
Winterbottom, Ricky	2 + 2	—	—	—	—
TOTALS:					
45 players		97	77	4	547

1990-91 MATCH ANALYSIS

Date	Competition	H/A	Opponent	Rlt	Score	Tries	Goals	Attendance	Referee
26.8.90	YC(1)	A	Dewsbury	L	14-26	Simpson (2), Kelly	Dixon	—	—
9.9.90	SD	H	Huddersfield	L	26-30	A. Fairbank, M. Fairbank, Donnelly, Simpson	Dixon (5)	1110	Holgate
16.9.90	SD	H	Batley	W	21-14	Simpson (2), Burke (2)	Dixon (2), Moses (dg)	986	J. Connolly
23.9.90	SD	A	Swinton	L	16-22	Mitchell (2), Moses	Dixon (2)	—	—
30.9.90	SD	H	Hunslet	L	14-44	Farrell (2), Mitchell	Dixon	882	Steele
7.10.90	SD	A	Doncaster	L	11-14	Gascoigne, Rose	Burke, Dixon (dg)	—	—
14.10.90	SD	H	Fulham	L	22-29	Simpson (3), Dixon	Dixon (3)	696	Galtress
21.10.90	SD	A	Workington T.	L	0-42	—	—	—	—
4.11.90	SD	H	Chorley	W	32-18	Butterfield, Gascoigne, James, Farrell, Mitchell	Dixon (6)	616	Asquith
11.11.90	SD	A	Hunslet	W	14-6	Fiechter	Dixon (5)	—	—
18.11.90	SD	H	Doncaster	W	18-10	Hiley, James, Bargett	Dixon (3)	1012	Gilmour
2.12.90	RT(1)	A	Huddersfield	W	15-13	Donnelly, Palelei	Moses, Dixon (dg)	—	—
9.12.90	RT(2)	A	Wigan	L	16-36	James, Palelei, M. Fairbank	Dixon (2)	—	—
16.12.90	SD	H	Nottingham C.	W	38-6	James, Kelly, Donnelly, Palelei, Farrell, Rose, Dixon	Dixon (5)	700	Crashley
23.12.90	SD	A	Chorley	W	14-10	James	Dixon (5)	—	—
26.12.90	SD	H	Halifax	L	6-12	Butterfield	Dixon	2519	J. Connolly
1.1.91	SD	A	Huddersfield	W	10-8	Palelei, Thompson	Dixon	—	—
6.1.91	SD	A	Barrow	W	14-10	M. Fairbank, Thompson	Dixon (3)	—	—
20.1.91	SD	H	Carlisle	L	4-30	Donnelly	—	901	Kershaw
3.2.91	SD	A	Nottingham C.	W	24-2	Farrell, Palelei, Gascoigne, James	Dixon (4)	—	—
14.2.91	CC(1)	H	Runcorn H.	W	36-4	Butterfield (2), M. Fairbank (2), Thompson, Palelei, Farrell	Dixon (4)	574	Whitelam
17.2.91	SD	H	Runcorn H.	W	33-16	James (2), Dixon (2), Thompson (2), Donnelly	Dixon (2), Moses (dg)	668	J. Connolly
24.2.91	CC(2)	H	Warrington	L	10-42	Dixon, Farrell	Dixon	2472	Gilmour
27.2.91	SD	A	Halifax	L	8-32	Thompson (2)	—	—	—
3.3.91	SD	H	Salford	L	21-22	Kelly, Dixon, James	Dixon (4, 1dg)	1020	Burke
7.3.91	SD	H	Workington T.	L	10-15	Priestley	Dixon (3)	714	K. Morris
10.3.91	SD	A	Carlisle	L	18-32	Gascoigne, Palelei, Mitchell	Dixon (2), Wasyliw	—	—
17.3.91	SD	A	Batley	L	12-22	M. Fairbank, Palelei	Dixon (2)	—	—
24.3.91	SD	H	Barrow	W	24-20	Mitchell (2), M. Fairbank, Godfrey, Gascoigne	Dixon (2)	782	Kershaw
31.3.91	SD	A	Runcorn H.	L	16-54	Hiley, Gascoigne	Dixon (4)	—	—
7.4.91	SD	H	Swinton	W	14-10	Mirfin, Thompson, Stephenson	Mirfin	1179	Gilmour
10.4.91	SD	A	Fulham	L	16-28	Stephenson, M. Fairbank, Godfrey	Mirfin (2)	—	—
14.4.91	SD	A	Salford	L	0-30	—	—	—	—

CLUBS

LEEDS

Ground:	Headingley (0532-786181)
Colours:	Blue and amber
First Season:	1895-96
Nickname:	Loiners
Chairman:	Dennis Greenwood
Chief Exec:	Alf Davies
Coach:	David Ward (Sep 1989-May 1991)
	Doug Laughton (May 1991-)
Honours:	**Championship** Winners, 1960-61, 1968-69, 1971-72
	Beaten finalists, 1914-15, 1928-29, 1929-30, 1930-31, 1937-38, 1969-70, 1972-73
	League Leaders Trophy Winners, 1966-67, 1967-68, 1968-69, 1969-70, 1971-72
	Challenge Cup Winners, 1909-10, 1922-23, 1931-32, 1935-36, 1940-41, 1941-42, 1956-57, 1967-68, 1976-77, 1977-78
	Beaten finalists, 1942-43, 1946-47, 1970-71, 1971-72
	Yorkshire League Winners, 1901-02, 1927-28, 1930-31, 1933-34, 1934-35, 1936-37, 1937-38, 1950-51, 1954-55, 1956-57, 1960-61, 1966-67, 1967-68, 1968-69, 1969-70
	Yorkshire Cup Winners, 1921-22, 1928-29, 1930-31, 1932-33, 1934-35, 1935-36, 1937-38, 1958-59, 1968-69, 1970-71, 1972-73, 1973-74, 1975-76, 1976-77, 1979-80, 1980-81, 1988-89
	Beaten finalists, 1919-20, 1947-48, 1961-62, 1964-65
	BBC2 Floodlit Trophy Winners, 1970-71
	Regal Trophy Winners, 1972-73, 1983-84
	Beaten finalists, 1982-83, 1987-88
	Premiership Winners, 1974-75, 1978-79

Records: Attendance: 40,175 v. Bradford N. (League) 21 May, 1947
Season
Goals: 166 by B.L. Jones, 1956-57
Tries: 63 by E. Harris, 1935-36
Points: 431 by B.L. Jones, 1956-57
Match
Goals: 13 by B.L. Jones v. Blackpool B., 19 Aug, 1957
Tries: 8 by F. Webster v. Coventry, 12 Apr, 1913; E. Harris v. Bradford N., 14 Sep, 1931
Points: 31 by B.L. Jones v. Bradford N., 22 Aug, 1956
Highest score: 102-0 v. Coventry, 1912-13
Highest against: 71-0 v. Wakefield T., 1945-46

1990-91 PLAYERS' SUMMARY

	App	Tries	Goals	Dr	Pts
Ackerman, Rob	2	—	—	—	—
Anderson, Paul	1	—	—	—	—
Bentley, John	21 + 3	9	—	—	36
Butt, Tony	1	—	—	—	—
Creasser, David	10 + 5	3	—	—	12
Delaney, Paul	3 + 6	1	—	—	4
Divorty, Gary	10 + 15	4	—	1	17
Dixon, Paul	25 + 2	10	—	—	40
Fawcett, Vince	10	1	—	—	4
Ford, Phil	29 + 1	17	—	—	68
Gallagher, John	30	13	—	—	52
Gibson, Carl	33	10	—	—	40
Gunn, Richard	13 + 5	1	—	—	4
Harkin, Paul	31	1	—	2	6
Heron, David	8 + 7	1	—	—	4
Heugh, Cavill	25	9	—	—	36
Irving, Simon	26	11	99	—	242
James, Neil	2	—	—	—	—
Kuiti, Mike	25 + 4	11	—	—	44
Lord, Gary	8 + 11	—	—	—	—
Maloney, Francis	0 + 2	—	1	—	2
Maskill, Colin	24	6	3	—	30
Molloy, Steve	25 + 1	1	—	—	4
Powell, Roy	28 + 3	—	—	—	—
Rombo, Eddie	9	4	—	—	16
Schofield, Garry	30	20	22	4	128
Spencer, Gary	1	—	—	—	—
Wane, Shaun	21	—	—	—	—
Young, David	4 + 1	—	—	—	—
TOTALS:					
29 players		133	125	7	789

1990-91 MATCH ANALYSIS

Date	Competition	H/A	Opponent	Rlt	Score	Tries	Goals	Attendance	Referee
26.8.90	YC(1)	H	Bradford N.	L	16-24	Ford (2), Schofield	Irving, Maskill	13,968	Crashley
9.9.90	SBC	A	Oldham	L	22-32	Heugh, Gibson, Bentley	Irving (5)	—	—
16.9.90	SBC	H	Hull	L	22-24	Irving (2), Gibson, Dixon	Irving (3)	11,408	Allatt
23.9.90	SBC	A	Warrington	W	22-10	Dixon, Gibson, Gallagher	Irving (5)	—	—
30.9.90	SBC	H	St. Helens	W	23-4	Schofield, Irving, Gallagher, Ford	Irving (2), Schofield, Harkin (dg)	12,760	C. Morris
7.10.90	SBC	A	Bradford N.	W	21-12	Dixon (2), Irving	Irving (4), Schofield (dg)	—	—
14.10.90	SBC	H	Featherstone R.	L	16-18	Heugh, Ford	Irving (4)	11,937	Holdsworth
21.10.90	Tour	H	Australia	L	10-22	Gallagher, Dixon	Irving	16,087	Tennant
3.11.90	SBC	A	Widnes	L	8-26	Ford, Irving	—	—	—
11.11.90	SBC	H	Rochdale H.	W	64-4	Dixon (3), Schofield (2), Creasser (2), Irving, Gallagher, Ford, Divorty	Irving (10)	8038	Kendrew
18.11.90	RT(P)	H	Halifax	W	58-6	Schofield (2), Kuiti (2), Irving, Ford, Creasser, Maskill, Dixon, Delaney	Irving (9)	9761	Burke
27.11.90	SBC	H	Castleford	W	41-16	Kuiti (2), Molloy, Schofield, Irving, Gallagher	Irving (5), Schofield, Harkin (dg)	11,221	Campbell
2.12.90	RT(1)	H	Hull K.R.	W	26-22	Schofield (2), Gallagher, Heugh	Irving (5)	9753	Kendrew
8.12.90	RT(2)	A	Widnes	L	6-22	Ford	Irving	—	—
16.12.90	SBC	A	Sheffield E.	W	24-6	Ford, Schofield, Heugh, Gibson	Irving (2), Schofield (2)	—	—
23.12.90	SBC	A	Wigan	L	16-22	Gallagher (2), Bentley	Schofield (2)	—	—
26.12.90	SBC	H	Bradford N.	W	26-8	Heugh (2), Harkin, Bentley	Schofield (5)	13,962	Kershaw
1.1.91	SBC	H	Oldham	W	28-12	Ford, Bentley, Gallagher, Divorty	Irving (6)	11,587	Ollerton
6.1.91	SBC	A	Hull	L	14-34	Irving, Ford	Irving (3)	—	—
13.1.91	SBC	H	Sheffield E.	W	38-16	Gibson (2), Maskill (2), Kuiti, Bentley	Irving (7)	9146	Gilmour
20.1.91	SBC	A	St. Helens	L	16-22	Ford, Divorty	Irving (4)	—	—
30.1.91	SBC	H	Warrington	D	20-20	Kuiti, Divorty, Irving	Irving (4)	8505	C. Morris
3.2.91	SBC	A	Castleford	L	14-16	Schofield, Kuiti, Rombo	Irving	—	—
10.2.91	CC(1)	H	Dewsbury	W	40-20	Bentley (2), Rombo (2), Schofield (2), Kuiti, Gibson	Schofield (4)	4239	Asquith
17.2.91	SBC	H	Widnes	L	0-38	—	—	12,313	Asquith
24.2.91	CC(2)	A	Bradford N.	L	0-5	—	—	—	—
3.3.91	SBC	H	Hull K.R.	W	24-18	Schofield (2), Ford (2), Gibson	Schofield (2)	8041	Asquith
10.3.91	SBC	A	Rochdale H.	W	34-20	Maskill (2), Kuiti (2), Gibson, Heron, Rombo	Maskill (2), Maloney	—	—
17.3.91	SBC	A	Hull K.R.	W	28-16	Gallagher (2), Schofield, Heugh, Gibson	Schofield (4)	—	—
29.3.91	SBC	H	Wakefield T.	W	7-0	Schofield	Schofield, Divorty (dg)	10,139	Galtress
1.4.91	SBC	A	Wakefield T.	D	14-14	Schofield (2)	Irving (3)	—	—
7.4.91	SBC	A	Featherstone R.	W	52-20	Ford (3), Gallagher (2), Irving, Maskill, Heugh, Bentley	Irving (8)	—	—
13.4.91	SBC	H	Wigan	L	8-20	Bentley	Irving (2)	15,313	Holdsworth
21.4.91	PT(1)	A	Castleford	W	24-20	Heugh, Fawcett, Dixon, Schofield	Irving (3), Schofield (dg)	—	—
5.5.91	PT(SF)	A	Hull	L	7-10	Gunn	Schofield (1, 1dg)	—	—

LEIGH

Ground: Hilton Park (0942-674437)
Colours: Red and white
First Season: 1895-96
Coach: Alex Murphy (Mar 1990-)
Honours: **Championship** Winners, 1905-06
Division One Champions, 1981-82
Division Two Champions, 1977-78, 1985-86, 1988-89
Challenge Cup Winners, 1920-21, 1970-71
Lancashire Cup Winners, 1952-53, 1955-56, 1970-71, 1981-82
Beaten finalists, 1905-06, 1909-10, 1920-21, 1922-23, 1949-50, 1951-52, 1963-64, 1969-70
BBC2 Floodlit Trophy Winners, 1969-70, 1972-73
Beaten finalists, 1967-68, 1976-77

Records: Attendance: 31,324 v. St. Helens (RL Cup) 14 Mar, 1953
Season
Goals: 173 by C. Johnson, 1985-86
Tries: 49 by S. Halliwell, 1985-86
Points: 400 by C. Johnson, 1985-86
Match
Goals: 15 by M. Stacey v. Doncaster, 28 Mar, 1976
Tries: 6 by J. Wood v. York, 4 Oct, 1947
Points: 38 by J. Woods v. Blackpool B., 11 Sep, 1977
Highest score: 92-2 v. Keighley, 1985-86
Highest against: 60-8 v. Salford, 1940

John Woods, who amassed a Leigh club record of 2,272 points before retiring during the 1990-91 season.

1990-91 PLAYERS' SUMMARY

	App	Tries	Goals	Dr	Pts
Beardmore, Bob	13 + 4	4	20	—	56
Blakely, Michael	1	—	—	—	—
Booth, Simon	6 + 2	4	—	—	16
Bridge, Russ	10	1	—	—	4
Brown, Peter	13	1	—	—	4
Burrill, Craig	3	4	—	—	16
Case, Brian	29	1	—	—	4
Collier, Andy	29 + 1	6	—	—	24
Cottrell, Tony	1 + 13	2	—	—	8
Cruickshank, David	11	2	—	—	8
Dean, Mick	9	—	—	—	—
Donohue, Jason	11 + 2	5	1	—	22
Earner, Adrian	3 + 1	—	—	—	—
Entwhistle, Paul	2	—	—	—	—
Evans, Andy	6 + 2	—	—	—	—
Evans, Stuart	0 + 1	—	—	—	—
Gamble, Paul	1	—	—	—	—
Hill, David	17 + 4	7	—	—	28
Iro, Tony	10 + 4	4	—	—	16
Jeffrey, Ian	34 + 1	17	—	—	68
Johnson, Kevin	1	—	—	—	—
Johnson, Phil	2 + 2	—	—	—	—
Lang, Shaun	3	1	—	—	4
Ledger, Barry	22	10	—	—	40
Mellor, Terry	2 + 3	—	—	—	—
Myler, John	5 + 1	1	7	—	18
O'Toole, David	2 + 6	—	—	—	—
Potter, Ian	23 + 9	—	—	—	—
Ropati, Peter	36	8	—	—	32
Round, Mike	19	13	—	—	52
Ruane, David	30 + 1	18	—	—	72
Sawyer, Aaron	7 + 3	—	—	—	—
Sheals, Mark	28 + 2	7	—	—	28
Standish, Wayne	8	4	—	—	16
Stephenson, David	1 + 2	—	—	—	—
Sullivan, Andy	17 + 1	3	—	—	12
Topping, Paul	34	18	67	8	214
Valentine, Peter	0 + 1	—	—	—	—
Waterworth, Keith	0 + 2	—	—	—	—
Westhead, John	5	1	—	—	4
Woods, John	14	8	34	—	100
TOTALS: 41 players		150	129	8	866

1990-91 MATCH ANALYSIS

Date	Competition	H/A	Opponent	Rlt	Score	Tries	Goals	Attendance	Referee
26.8.90	LC(1)	H	Swinton	W	26-6	Jeffrey (2), Beardmore, Case, Ledger	Woods (2), Topping	3137	K. Morris
2.9.90	LC(2)	H	Fulham	W	40-8	Jeffrey (3), Woods (2), Westhead, Round, Topping	Topping (4)	2909	Burke
9.9.90	SD	A	Batley	W	22-6	Woods, Jeffrey, Cottrell, Ledger	Woods (3)	—	—
12.9.90	LC(SF)	A	Salford	L	7-16	Round	Topping (1, 1dg)	—	—
16.9.90	SD	H	Halifax	L	6-16	—	Woods (3)	3475	Burke
23.9.90	SD	A	Barrow	W	32-16	Lang, Standish, Iro, Ropati, Hill	Woods (6)	—	—
30.9.90	SD	H	Chorley	W	50-4	Round (4), Topping (2), Jeffrey, Sheals, Ledger	Woods (7)	1812	J. Connolly
14.10.90	SD	A	Huddersfield	W	22-10	Bridge, Ruane, Ledger	Woods (5)	—	—
21.10.90	SD	H	Nottingham C.	W	56-6	Ropati (3), Topping (2), Collier, Ruane, Woods, Ledger, Jeffrey	Woods (8)	1853	Burke
30.10.90	SD	A	Hunslet	W	24-16	Topping, Standish, Booth, Ledger, Ruane	Topping (2)	—	—
11.11.90	SD	H	Carlisle	W	24-16	Ruane (2), Woods, Round, Ledger	Topping (2)	1882	R. Connolly
18.11.90	SD	A	Nottingham C.	W	52-14	Jeffrey (2), Woods (2), Iro (2), Ledger (2), Ruane, Topping	Topping (6)	—	—
25.11.90	SD	H	Swinton	L	12-20	Topping, Beardmore	Topping (2)	2617	Whitfield
2.12.90	RT(1)	H	Chorley	W	66-5	Round (3), Jeffrey (3), Ruane (2), Cottrell, Standish, Iro, Brown	Beardmore (9)	1313	K. Morris
9.12.90	RT(2)	A	Warrington	L	6-11	—	Beardmore (3)	—	—
16.12.90	SD	A	Carlisle	L	16-19	Woods, Beardmore	Beardmore (4)	—	—
23.12.90	SD	H	Barrow	W	40-4	Sheals (3), Round (2), Booth (2), Ruane	Beardmore (4)	1403	Allatt
1.1.91	SD	A	Runcorn H.	W	32-11	Ruane (4), Topping, Sullivan	Topping (4)	—	—
6.1.91	SD	A	Workington T.	L	3-10	—	Topping (1, 1dg)	—	—
9.1.91	SD	H	Salford	L	4-20	Sheals	—	2218	Carter
20.1.91	SD	A	Fulham	W	23-20	Jeffrey, Collier, Standish	Topping (5, 1dg)	—	—
30.1.91	SD	H	Workington T.	W	18-12	Collier (2), Hill	Topping (2, 2dg)	1083	Kershaw
3.2.91	SD	A	Chorley	W	30-12	Ruane (2), Burrill (2), Hill, Jeffrey	Topping (3)	—	—
17.2.91	CC(1)	A[1]	Bradford N.	L	4-50	Burrill	—	—	—
24.2.91	SD	H	Hunslet	W	31-24	Topping, Burrill, Ropati, Jeffrey, Hill	Topping (5, 1dg)	1691	Whitelam
27.2.91	SD	H	Fulham	D	12-12	Hill, Round	Topping (2)	1122	Campbell
3.3.91	SD	A	Swinton	L	6-7	Topping	Topping	—	—
10.3.91	SD	H	Doncaster	L	16-20	Jeffrey, Collier, Ropati	Topping, Myler	1480	Gilmour
24.3.91	SD	H	Batley	W	28-6	Ruane (2), Donohue, Hill, Topping	Topping (4)	1520	Crashley
29.3.91	SD	A	Salford	L	11-18	Topping	Topping (3, 1dg)	—	—
1.4.91	SD	H	Runcorn H.	W	42-6	Topping (4), Cruickshank, Hill, Ledger, Sullivan	Topping (5)	1085	Holgate
7.4.91	SD	H	Huddersfield	W	26-13	Booth, Beardmore, Ruane, Collier	Topping (5)	1832	Asquith
10.4.91	SD	A	Halifax	L	18-24	Donohue, Sullivan, Sheals	Topping (3)	—	—
14.4.91	SD	A	Doncaster	W	42-10	Donohue (3), Ropati (2), Myler, Cruickshank	Myler (6), Donohue	—	—
21.4.91	SDP(1)	A[2]	Ryedale-York	W	11-6	Sheals	Topping (3, 1dg)	—	—
5.5.91	SDP(SF)	A	Halifax	L	8-32	Topping	Topping (2)	—	—

[1] at Bradford C. FC [2] at Scarborough FC

NOTTINGHAM CITY

Ground: Harvey Hadden Stadium
(0602-691666)
Colours: Green and yellow
First Season: 1984-85 as Mansfield Marksman.
Moved and became Nottingham
City at start of 1989-90.
Chairman: Paul Tomlinson
Secretary: Joan Tomlinson
Coach: Mel Wibberley (Mar 1990-Feb 1991)
Arnold Hema (Feb 1991-June 1991)
Mark Burgess (June 1991-)
Records: Attendance: 2,545 v. Halifax
(Div. 2) 1 Oct, 1989
Season
Goals: 63 by C. Sanderson, 1984-85
Tries: 13 by S. Nicholson,
K. Whiteman, 1984-85
Points: 136 by C. Sanderson,
1984-85
Match
Goals: 7 by B. Holden v. Keighley,
10 Mar, 1985; by W. Sanchez v.
Hunslet, 2 Oct, 1988
Tries: 4 by K. Whiteman v.
Doncaster, 4 Nov, 1984
Points: 18 by B. Holden v.
Keighley, 10 Mar, 1985;
M. Howarth v. Dewsbury, 17 Jan,
1988
Highest score: 54-10 v. Doncaster,
1984-85
Highest against: 100-6 v. Hull
K.R., 1990-91

1990-91 PLAYERS' SUMMARY

	App	Tries	Goals	Dr	Pts
Andrews, Brent	9 + 1	—	—	—	—
Bennett, Paul	8	—	—	—	—
Bennett, Phil	8	—	2	—	8
Blackman, Richard	2 + 1	2	—	—	8
Bowie, Iain	19 + 2	4	2	—	20
Burgess, Mark	10	—	—	—	—
Busby, David	8 + 1	1	—	2	6
Butler, Lee	5	1	—	—	4
Chappell, Tony	29 + 1	5	—	1	21
Clever, John	1	—	—	—	—
Cooper, Colin	1	—	—	—	—
Cooper, Paul	4	—	—	—	—
Coup, Chris	2 + 1	—	—	—	—
Crellin, Martin	9	1	—	—	4
Cummins, Shane	1	—	—	—	—
Edridge, Lee	2 + 5	—	—	—	—
Fraser, Mark	1	—	—	—	—
Gillespie, Mike	3 + 3	—	—	—	—
Gregoire, Don	17 + 1	3	—	—	12
Hare, Tyrone	0 + 1	1	—	—	4
Hema, Arnold	23 + 1	3	3	—	18
Holland, Mike	4 + 1	—	1	—	2
Hutchinson, Lee	3	1	—	—	4
Jackson, Darryl	19 + 8	2	—	—	8
Jackson, Dean	5 + 2	—	—	—	—
Keresoma, Moses	2	1	—	—	4
Kite, Kerry	9	—	—	—	—
McGrath, Barry	0 + 1	—	—	—	—
Machee, Loi	11 + 2	4	—	—	16
Meehan, Gary	1	—	—	—	—
Mitchell, Tony	2	—	—	—	—
Moore, John	4 + 1	—	—	—	—
Moulden, Darren	14 + 1	—	—	—	—
Oates, David	26 + 1	6	48	1	121
Portz, Karl	12 + 1	1	—	—	4
Powell, Paul	5	—	—	—	—
Quinn, John	13 + 2	2	—	—	8
Rex, Ian	2	1	—	—	4
Riley, Malcolm	7 + 5	—	—	—	—
Roberts, Howard	7 + 1	1	—	—	4
Robson, Duncan	2 + 1	—	—	—	—
Rudd, Neil	11 + 2	1	—	—	4
Sanderson, Mark	1 + 1	—	—	—	—
Schumkell, Glen	2	—	—	—	—
Simpson, Andy	1	—	—	—	—
Smith, Andy	7 + 2	—	—	—	—
Stones, Chris	1 + 1	—	—	—	—
Sutton, Tommy	16	2	—	1	9
Swift, Tony	1	—	—	—	—
Taylor, Adrian	5 + 1	—	—	—	—
Toder, Jai	11 + 2	—	—	—	—
Townsend, Jeff	3 + 1	—	1	—	—
Welsh, Gavin	2	—	1	—	2
Willis, Chris	13 + 1	1	1	1	7
Wilson, Sean	18	1	—	—	4
Wood, Richard	1 + 3	—	—	—	—
TOTALS: 56 players		47	56	6	306

*Tony Chappell, five tries and a drop goal in 30 games for
Nottingham City.*

1990-91 MATCH ANALYSIS

Date	Com-petition	H/A	Opponent	Rlt	Score	Tries	Goals	Atten-dance	Referee
19.8.90	YC(P)	H[1]	Hull K.R.	L	6-100	Jackson	Willis	1010	Tidball
9.9.90	SD	A	Ryedale-York	L	8-36	Rex	Oates (2)	—	—
16.9.90	SD	A	Trafford B.	L	4-42	Keresoma	—	—	—
23.9.90	SD	A	Doncaster	L	14-38	Machee, Bowie	Oates (3)	—	—
30.9.90	SD	H	Swinton	L	27-35	Bowie (2), Wilson, Chappell	Oates (5), Busby (dg)	301	K. Morris
7.10.90	SD	A	Batley	L	0-17	—	—	—	—
14.10.90	SD	H	Workington T.	L	12-23	Portz	Oates (4)	203	Kershaw
21.10.90	SD	A	Leigh	L	6-56	Hema	Welsh	—	—
4.11.90	SD	H	Ryedale-York	L	14-24	Gregoire (?)	Hema (2), Willis (dg), Sutton (dg)	330	Whitfield
11.11.90	SD	A	Chorley	L	19-38	Oates, Willis, Chappell	Oates (2, 1dg), Hema	—	—
18.11.90	SD	H	Leigh	L	14-52	Sutton, Oates	Oates (3)	327	Crashley
25.11.90	SD	H	Bramley	W	24-21	Sutton, Busby, Blackman, Machee	Oates (4)	162	R. Connolly
2.12.90	RT(1)	H	Batley	L	6-35	Blackman	Oates	367	Gilmour
16.12.90	SD	A	Keighley	L	6-38	Oates	Oates	—	—
23.12.90	SD	H	Dewsbury	L	6-38	Machee	Oates	305	Tidball
6.1.91	SD	H	Batley	L	15-16	Machee, Hema	Oates (2), Holland, Busby (dg)	239	Steele
20.1.91	SD	H	Whitehaven	L	14-28	Chappell, Hutchinson	Oates (3)	193	Whitelam
23.1.91	SD	A	Whitehaven	L	10-20	Bennett, Quinn	Oates	—	—
27.1.91	SD	A	Swinton	L	4-16	Quinn	—	—	—
3.2.91	SD	H	Keighley	L	2-24	—	Oates	227	Holgate
17.2.91	CC(1)	H	Whitehaven	L	10-26	Oates	Oates (3)	141	Tidball
24.2.91	SD	A	Bramley	L	6-29	Bennett	Oates	—	—
3.3.91	SD	A	Workington T.	L	4-38	Butler	—	—	—
10.3.91	SD	H	Runcorn H.	W	20-14	Oates (2), Roberts, Bowie	Oates (2)	150	Cross
17.3.91	SD	H	Trafford B.	L	12-48	Crellin, Gregoire	Oates (2)	178	Ollerton
24.3.91	SD	H	Doncaster	L	8-52	Rudd	Oates (2)	606	Whitelam
29.3.91	SD	A	Barrow	L	6-34	Chappell	Oates	—	—
1.4.91	SD	H	Barrow	L	12-30	Hema	Oates (4)	195	Tidball
4.4.91	SD	A	Dewsbury	L	0-64	—	—	—	—
7.4.91	SD	A	Runcorn H.	L	0-42	—	—	—	—
14.4.91	SD	H	Chorley	L	17-32	Chappell, Hare, Jackson	Bowie (2), Chappell (dg)	153	Smith

[1] at Doncaster

OLDHAM

Ground: Watersheddings (061-624-4865)
Colours: Red and white
First Season: 1895-96
Nickname: Roughyeds
Chairman: John Chadwick
Chief Exec: Ian Carr
Coach: Tony Barrow (Nov 1988-Jan 1991)
John Fieldhouse (Jan 1991-Apr 1991)
Peter Tunks (Apr 1991-)
Honours: **Championship** Winners, 1909-10, 1910-11,1956-57
Beaten finalists, 1906-07, 1907-08, 1908-09, 1921-22, 1954-55
Division One Champions, 1904-05
Division Two Champions, 1963-64, 1981-82, 1987-88
Second Division Premiership Winners, 1987-88, 1989-90
Challenge Cup Winners, 1898-99, 1924-25, 1926-27
Beaten finalists, 1906-07, 1911-12, 1923-24, 1925-26
Lancashire League Winners, 1897-98, 1900-01, 1907-08, 1909-10, 1921-22, 1956-57, 1957-58
Lancashire Cup Winners, 1907-08, 1910-11, 1913-14, 1919-20, 1924-25, 1933-34, 1956-57, 1957-58, 1958-59
Beaten finalists, 1908-09, 1911-12, 1918-19, 1921-22, 1954-55, 1966-67, 1968-69, 1986-87, 1989-90
Records: Attendance: 28,000 v. Huddersfield (League) 24 Feb, 1912
Season
Goals: 200 by B. Ganley, 1957-58
Tries: 49 by R. Farrar, 1921-22
Points: 412 by B. Ganley, 1957-58
Match
Goals: 14 by B. Ganley v. Liverpool C., 4 Apr, 1959
Tries: 7 by Miller v. Barry, 31 Oct, 1908
Points: 30 by A. Johnson v. Widnes, 9 Apr, 1928
Highest score: 67-6 v. Liverpool C., 1958-59
Highest against: 67-11 v. Hull K.R., 1978-79

1990-91 PLAYERS' SUMMARY

	App	Tries	Goals	Dr	Pts
Allen, Shaun	0 + 6	—	—	—	—
Anderson, Tony	17	2	—	—	8
Atkinson, Keith	12 + 7	3	13	—	38
Barrow, Tony	3 + 1	—	—	—	—
Blackman, Richard	1	—	—	—	—
Clark, Brett	32	11	—	—	44
Cogger, John	12 + 9	1	—	—	4
Donegan, Austin	16 + 5	3	—	—	12
Duane, Ronnie	18 + 4	1	—	—	4
Fairbank, John	9 + 5	1	—	—	4
Fieldhouse, John	22 + 1	2	—	—	8
Ford, Mike	33	10	1	3	45
Foy, Des	10 + 2	4	—	—	16
Francis, Norman	16	4	—	—	16
Henderson, John	15	3	—	—	12
Hyde, Gary	2 + 2	1	1	—	6
Irving, Richard	21 + 4	6	—	—	24
Joynt, Chris	1	—	—	—	—
Longstaff, Simon	1 + 1	—	—	—	—
Lord, Paul	21 + 1	8	—	—	32
McAlister, Charlie	25 + 4	7	2	—	32
Martyn, Tommy	17 + 3	8	9	3	53
Newton, Keith	6 + 4	1	—	—	4
Platt, Duncan	29	5	84	—	188
Pyke, Derek	5	—	—	—	—
Robinson, Steve	6	1	—	—	4
Round, Paul	32	19	—	—	76
Ruane, Andy	18	2	—	3	11
Russell, Richard	29 + 3	5	—	—	20
Warburton, Steve	0 + 1	—	—	—	—
TOTALS:					
30 players		108	110	9	661

John Fieldhouse, player-coach of Oldham for a four-month stint at the start of 1991.

1990-91 MATCH ANALYSIS

Date	Com-petition	H/A	Opponent	Rlt	Score	Tries	Goals	Atten-dance	Referee
26.8.90	LC(1)	A	Salford	L	24-27	McAlister, Round, Martyn	Platt (5), Ford	—	—
9.9.90	SBC	H	Leeds	W	32-22	Clark, McAlister, Martyn, Round, Newton	Platt (4), Martyn (1, 1dg), Ford (dg)	6388	Holdsworth
16.9.90	SBC	A	Wakefield T.	L	12-17	Platt, Irving	Platt (2)	—	—
26.9.90	SBC	H	Castleford	W	28-22	Round (2), Clark, Martyn, Francis	Platt (4)	5101	Whitfield
2.10.90	SBC	A	Widnes	L	16-24	Ford, Lord, Donegan	Platt (2)	—	—
7.10.90	SBC	H	Hull K.R.	L	25-28	Round (2), Lord, Ford	Platt (2), Martyn (2, 1dg)	4710	Tennant
14.10.90	SBC	A	Sheffield E.	W	24-14	Martyn, Francis, Fairbank, Clark	Martyn (4)	—	—
20.10.90	SBC	H	Warrington	W	4-2	—	Platt (2)	4099	Holdsworth
4.11.90	SBC	A	Wigan	L	15-38	Round, Anderson	Platt (2), Martyn (1, 1dg)	—	—
11.11.90	SBC	H	Bradford N.	L	16-18	Martyn (2), Round	Martyn, Hyde	5874	J. Connolly
18.11.90	SBC	A	Castleford	L	10-28	Hyde, Lord	McAlister	—	—
25.11.90	SBC	H	Widnes	L	18-24	Platt, Clark	Platt (5)	5541	Galtress
2.12.90	RT(1)	H	Salford	W	26-6	Russell, Donegan, Francis, Irving	Platt (5)	4932	Carter
9.12.90	RT(2)	A	Batley	L	16-20	Russell, Round, Lord	Platt (2)	—	—
16.12.90	SBC	A	Hull	L	4-31	Lord	—	—	—
26.12.90	SBC	H	Rochdale H.	W	18-13	Donegan, Francis, Russell	Platt (3)	4818	Gilmour
1.1.91	SBC	A	Leeds	L	12-28	McAlister, Clark	Platt (2)	—	—
6.1.91	SBC	H	Featherstone R.	L	18-20	Clark, Lord, Round	Platt (2), Atkinson	4753	Galtress
13.1.91	SBC	A	Hull K.R.	L	14-42	Martyn (2)	Platt (3)	—	—
20.1.91	SBC	H	Wakefield T.	W	26-22	Round, Henderson, Clark, Atkinson, Couger	Platt (3)	4754	Whitefield
27.1.91	SBC	A	Featherstone R.	L	20-28	Platt, Atkinson, Russell	Platt (4)	—	—
3.2.91	SBC	H	St. Helens	L	16-20	Russell, Anderson, Clark	Platt (3)	5189	Asquith
17.2.91	CC(1)	A	Bramley	W	38-6	Ruane (2), Foy, McAlister, Round, Irving, Ford		—	—
24.2.91	CC(2)	A	Workington T.	W	20-15	Platt, Round, Duane	Platt (4)	—	—
3.3.91	SBC	A	Bradford N.	W	37-10	Ford (2), Foy, Clark, Fieldhouse, Round	Platt (6), Ford (dg)	—	—
10.3.91	CC(3)	H	Salford	W	40-3	Irving (2), Ford, McAlister, Round, Henderson, Clark	Platt (3), Atkinson (3)	6503	Galtress
13.3.91	SBC	A	St. Helens	L	22-33	Round (2), Foy	Atkinson (4), McAlister	—	—
17.3.91	SBC	H	Sheffield E.	W	27-20	Platt, McAlister, Ford, Round	Platt (5), Ruane (dg)	4206	Carter
23.3.91	CC(SF)	Bolton	Wigan	L	16-30	Henderson, McAlister, Ford	Atkinson (2)	(19,057)	Smith
29.3.91	SBC	A	Rochdale H.	W	30-12	Lord (2), Fieldhouse, Ford, Atkinson	Atkinson (3), Platt (2)	—	—
1.4.91	SBC	H	Wigan	L	4-10	Irving	—	7399	Tennant
7.4.91	SBC	A	Warrington	L	14-22	Round, Foy	Platt (2), Ford (dg), Ruane (dg)	—	—
14.4.91	SBC	H	Hull	W	19-14	Ford, Clark, Robinson	Platt (3), Ruane (dg)	3397	Galtress

73

ROCHDALE HORNETS

Ground: Spotland (0706-48004)
Colours: White, blue and red
First Season: 1895-96
Nickname: Hornets
Chairman: Dick Bonser
Secretary: Paul Reynolds
Coach: Allan Agar (July 1989-Jan 1991)
        Neil Holding (Jan 1991-Apr 1991)
        Stan Gittins (Apr 1991-)
Honours: **Challenge Cup** Winners, 1921-22
        Lancashire League Winners, 1918-19
        Lancashire Cup Winners, 1911-12, 1914-15, 1918-19
        Beaten finalists, 1912-13, 1919-20, 1965-66
        Regal Trophy Beaten finalists 1973-74
        BBC2 Floodlit Trophy Beaten finalists 1971-72
Records: Attendance: 41,831 Wigan v. Oldham (RL Cup Final) 12 Apr, 1924
        Home: 26,664 v. Oldham (RL Cup) 25 Mar, 1922
        Season
        Goals: 115 by K. Harcombe, 1985-86
        Tries: 30 by J. Williams, 1934-35
        Points: 243 by S. Turner, 1988-89

Match
Goals: 14 by S. Turner v. Runcorn H., 5 Nov, 1989
Tries: 5 by J. Corsi v. Barrow, 31 Dec, 1921 and v. Broughton Moor, 25 Feb, 1922; J. Williams v. St. Helens, 4 Apr, 1933; N. Brelsford v. Whitehaven, 3 Sep, 1972
Points: 32 by S. Turner v. Runcorn H., 5 Nov, 1989
Highest score: 92-0 v. Runcorn H., 1989-90
Highest against: 79-2 v. Hull, 1920-21

1990-91 PLAYERS' SUMMARY

	App	Tries	Goals	Dr	Pts
Abram, Darren	24	12	—	—	48
Bamber, Simon	1	—	—	—	—
Belle, Adrian	7	2	—	—	8
Blackburn, John	16	—	—	—	—
Calland, Matt	0 + 3	—	—	—	—
Cheval, Robert	3 + 2	3	1	—	14
Cowie, Neil	26 + 1	5	—	—	20
Dean, Mick	2	—	—	—	—
Fox, Phil	15	1	—	—	4
Galbraith, Stuart	11 + 3	3	—	—	12
Gallagher, David	5	1	—	—	4
Garrity, Brian	14	2	—	—	8
Gartland, Steve	6	2	—	—	8
Gormley, Ian	19 + 5	2	—	—	8
Grogan, Bob	18 + 2	2	—	—	8
Hall, Martin	30	6	—	—	24
Hall, Robert	11 + 6	—	—	—	—
Halsall, Ian	1	—	—	—	—
Higgins, John	12	2	—	—	8
Holding, Neil	22 + 4	3	1	4	18
Hulme, Mike	0 + 1	—	—	—	—
Humphries, Tony	26 + 2	3	—	—	12
Kay, Martin	1 + 1	—	—	—	—
Lever, David	0 + 2	—	—	—	—
Lord, Mark	25	10	—	—	40
McDermott, Paul	6 + 3	1	—	—	4
Malloy, Dale	1 + 1	—	—	—	—
Marriott, Karl	9 + 5	1	—	—	4
Marsden, Bob	4 + 3	—	—	—	—
Myler, Chris	5 + 1	—	—	—	—
Myler, John	2 + 1	—	—	2	2
Nixon, Mark	22	4	—	—	16
O'Neill, Mike	25	3	—	—	12
Pitt, Darren	5 + 5	—	—	—	—
Sullivan, Andy	3	—	—	—	—
Turner, Steve	12 + 7	1	21	—	46
Viller, Mark	7 + 6	1	—	—	4
Viller, Paul	4	—	—	—	—
Whitfield, Colin	29	4	32	—	80
Williams, Mike	0 + 2	—	—	—	—
TOTALS: 40 players		74	55	6	412

Neil Holding, player-coach of Rochdale Hornets for the last four months of the 1990-91 campaign.

1990-91 MATCH ANALYSIS

Date	Com- petition	H/A	Opponent	Rlt	Score	Tries	Goals	Atten- dance	Referee
19.8.90	LC(P)	H	Salford	L	12-41	Whitfield	Whitfield (4)	2049	R. Connolly
9.9.90	SBC	A	Wakefield T.	L	6-42	Viller	Myler (2dg)	—	—
16.9.90	SBC	H	Sheffield E.	L	20-24	McDermott, Grogan, Gallagher	Whitfield (4)	2048	Holdsworth
23.9.90	SBC	A	Wigan	L	2-24	—	Holding	—	—
30.9.90	SBC	H	Hull	L	18-30	Turner, Gormley	Turner (5)	3402	Crashley
7.10.90	SBC	A	Warrington	L	9-26	Nixon	Turner (2), Holding (dg)	—	—
14.10.90	SBC	H	Bradford N.	W	19-12	Hall, Higgins, Cowie, Lord	Turner, Holding (dg)	3626	Burke
21.10.90	SBC	A	Featherstone R	L	8-38	Humphries	Turner, Whitfield	—	—
4.11.90	SBC	H	St. Helens	L	18-30	Whitfield, Fox, Hall, Lord	Whitfield	3652	J. Connolly
11.11.90	SBC	A	Leeds	L	4-64	Abram	—	—	—
18.11.90	SBC	H	Hull K.R.	L	18-32	O'Neill, Abram, Cowie, Grogan	Whitfield	1729	Ollerton
25.11.90	SBC	A	St. Helens	L	14-44	Abram, Humphries	Whitfield (3)	—	—
30.11.90	RT(1)	H	Saddleworth R.	W	30-10	Cowie (2), Humphries, O'Neill, Marriott, Galbraith	Whitfield (3)	2434	Tidball
12.12.90	RT(2)	A	Doncaster	W	14-10	Hall (2), Lord	Whitfield	—	—
16.12.90	RT(3)	A	Castleford	W	19-14	Whitfield, Galbraith, Lord	Whitfield (3), Holding (dg)	—	—
22.12.90	RT(SF)	Leeds	Bradford N.	L	2-13	—	Whitfield	(3788)	Smith
26.12.90	SBC	A	Oldham	L	13-18	Abram, Nixon	Whitfield (2), Holding (dg)	—	—
6.1.91	SBC	A	Bradford N.	L	16-23	Abram, Lord, Nixon	Whitfield (2)	—	—
9.1.91	SBC	H	Featherstone R.	L	12-26	Lord, Holding, Gormley	—	1862	Smith
20.1.91	SBC	A	Sheffield E.	L	16-30	Whitfield, Lord, Abram	Whitfield (2)	—	—
23.1.91	SBC	A	Castleford	L	0-42	—	—	—	—
30.1.91	SBC	H	Widnes	L	6-60	Abram	Whitfield	2571	Ollerton
3.2.91	SBC	A	Hull	L	8-28	Garrity, Lord	—	—	—
19.2.91	CC(1)	H	Chorley	W	14-10	Galbraith, Nixon, Garrity	Whitfield	952	R. Connolly
24.2.91	CC(2)	H	Wigan	L	4-72	Hall	—	6492	Galtress
27.2.91	SBC	H	Warrington	L	10-18	Abram (2)	Whitfield	1480	Carter
3.3.91	SBC	H	Castleford	L	12-76	Lloyd (2), Abram	—	1741	J. Connolly
10.3.91	SBC	H	Leeds	L	20-34	Gartland, Belle, Cheval	Turner (4)	2072	Carter
17.3.91	SBC	H	Wigan	L	16-44	Belle, O'Neill, Cheval	Turner (2)	3751	Asquith
24.3.91	SBC	A	Hull K.R.	L	14-48	Abram, Holding, Higgins	Turner	—	—
29.3.91	SBC	H	Oldham	L	12-30	Cheval, Holding	Cheval, Turner	3355	J. Connolly
10.4.91	SBC	H	Wakefield T.	L	6-25	Abram	Whitfield	2443	Smith
14.4.91	SBC	A	Widnes	L	20-44	Gartland, Cowie, Hall	Turner (4)	—	—

CLUBS

RUNCORN HIGHFIELD

Ground: Hoghton Road (0744-812817)
Colours: Yellow, red, green and black
First Season: 1922-23 as Wigan Highfield. Became London Highfield in 1933-34. Became Liverpool Stanley in 1934-35 and changed to Liverpool City in 1951-52. Became Huyton in 1968-69 and changed to Runcorn Highfield in 1984-85. Became Highfield in 1991-92.
Chairman: Terry Hughes
Secretary: Ian Swann
Coach: Dave Chisnall (June 1989-Oct 1990) Alan Bishop (Oct 1990-Apr 1991) Chris Arkwright (Apr 1991-)
Honours: **Lancashire League** Winners, 1935-36
Records: Attendance: 14,000 v. Widnes (Championship semi-final) 2 May, 1936 at Prescott Road
Season
Goals: 126 by P. Wood, 1984-85
Tries: 28 by J. Maloney, 1930-31
Points: 240 by P. Wood, 1984-85

Match
Goals: 11 by P. Wood v. Batley, 21 Oct, 1984
Tries: 5 by J. Maloney v. Bramley, 25 Apr, 1931
Points: 30 by N. Barrow v. Keighley, 31 Mar, 1991
Highest score: 59-11 v. Bramley, 1933-34
Highest against: 92-2 v. Wigan, 1988-89; 92-0 v. Rochdale H., 1989-90

1990-91 PLAYERS' SUMMARY

	App	Tries	Goals	Dr	Pts
Arkwright, Chris	15	1	—	—	4
Ashcroft, Keith	2 + 1	—	—	—	—
Ashcroft, Simon	26 + 1	6	—	—	24
Ball, Jimmy	2 + 2	—	—	—	—
Barrow, Norman	13 + 1	8	27	2	88
Barrow, Sean	28	4	—	—	16
Beckett, Peter	1 + 3	—	—	—	—
Bradshaw, Phil	2 + 1	—	—	—	—
Brown, Andy	6 + 1	2	—	—	8
Burrows, Alan	4	3	—	—	12
Chappell, Simon	10 + 1	1	—	—	4
Clayton, Richard	1	—	—	—	—
Cooney, Paul	11 + 1	1	1	—	6
Dean, Geoff	25	—	—	—	—
Dolan, Sean	26 + 1	3	—	—	12
Dooley, Jimmy	2 + 4	—	—	—	—
Fenney, Paul	3 + 1	—	—	—	—
Fenney, Steve	1	—	—	—	—
Forber, Gary	11	1	—	—	4
Goodier, Frank	25 + 3	—	—	—	—
Goulding, Dean	12 + 3	—	1	—	2
Grady, Mike	5	1	—	—	4
Hibberd, Craig	1	—	—	—	—
Higgs, Bradley	4	2	—	—	8
Hine, David	15 + 5	5	—	—	20
Hitano, Bradley	0 + 1	—	—	—	—
Hoey, Robert	4 + 1	1	—	—	4
Honey, Chris	1	—	—	—	—
Hunt, David	1	—	—	—	—
Johnson, Willie	11	1	—	1	5
Jones, Charlie	1	—	—	—	—
Langley, Tony	0 + 1	—	—	—	—
Littler, Paul	8 + 3	1	—	—	4
Lowrie, Jason	1	—	—	—	—
Martin, Floyd	4 + 1	—	—	—	—
O'Gara, Kevin	4 + 3	—	3	—	6
Platt, Billy	17	3	22	3	59
Platt, Brian	13 + 4	3	2	—	16
Price, Phil	5	—	—	—	—
Rawlinson, Tommy	25 + 1	4	—	—	16
Rose, Terry	15 + 3	—	—	—	—
Southward, Phil	14 + 8	2	—	—	8
Tinsley, Eddie	5 + 2	1	—	—	4
Toomata, Mike	4	1	—	—	4
Tuavo, Armand	1	—	—	—	—
Turner, Stuart	8	3	—	—	12
Wakefield, Stuart	7	—	6	—	12
Wilton, Rob	3	—	—	—	—
TOTALS:					
48 players		58	62	6	362

Frank Goodier, 28 appearances for Runcorn Highfield.

1990-91 MATCH ANALYSIS

Date	Competition	H/A	Opponent	Rlt	Score	Tries	Goals	Attendance	Referee
26.8.90	LC(1)	A	Fulham	L	0-50	—		—	—
9.9.90	SD	A	Trafford B.	L	12-20	Dolan	W. Platt (4)	—	—
16.9.90	SD	H	Ryedale-York	L	10-22	S. Barrow	W. Platt (3)	420	Holgate
23.9.90	SD	A	Carlisle	L	13-44	S. Barrow, Hoey	W. Platt (2, 1dg)	—	—
30.9.90	SD	H	Huddersfield	L	6-19	Southward	W. Platt	815	Holdsworth
7.10.90	SD	A	Hunslet	L	12-52	W. Platt, B. Platt	W. Platt, O'Gara	—	—
14.10.90	SD	A	Halifax	L	8-82	Hine	O'Gara (2)	—	—
21.10.90	SD	H	Fulham	L	12-22	Ashcroft, Toomata	N. Barrow (2)	400	R. Connolly
4.11.90	SD	H	Hunslet	L	10-11	Higgs	N. Barrow (3)	500	Allatt
11.11.90	SD	A	Bramley	L	6-44	Rawlinson	W. Platt	—	—
18.11.90	SD	H	Salford	L	6-26	W. Platt	W. Platt	1540	Steele
25.11.90	SD	A	Huddersfield	L	14-17	Higgs, Tinsley	W. Platt (3)	—	—
2.12.90	RT(1)	A	Warrington	L	7-33	Hine	W. Platt (1, 1dg)	—	—
16.12.90	SD	H	Bramley	L	12-13	W. Platt, Arkwright	W. Platt (2)	300	K. Morris
23.12.90	SD	A	Ryedale-York	L	0-34	—	—	—	—
1.1.91	SD	H	Leigh	L	11-32	B. Platt	W. Platt (3, 1dg)	1000	Cross
6.1.91	SD	H	Halifax	L	0-62	—	—	1600	Crashley
20.1.91	SD	H	Trafford B.	L	6-10	Forber	N. Barrow	500	Tidball
22.1.91	SD	A	Salford	L	6-50	Southward	N. Barrow	—	—
27.1.91	SD	A	Whitehaven	L	14-22	Dolan, N. Barrow	N. Barrow (2, 2dg)	—	—
3.2.91	SD	H	Carlisle	D	12-12	Ashcroft	N. Barrow (3), Cooney	300	Tennant
14.2.91	CC(1)	A	Keighley	L	4-36	S. Barrow	—	—	—
17.2.91	SD	A	Keighley	L	16-33	B. Platt, S. Barrow, Grady	W. Platt (2)	—	—
3.3.91	SD	H	Dewsbury	W	9-2	Littler, Johnson	Johnson (dg)	330	Crashley
10.3.91	SD	A	Nottingham C.	L	14-20	N. Barrow, Turner	Wakefield (3)	—	—
17.3.91	SD	H	Whitehaven	L	16-30	N. Barrow, Rawlinson, Ashcroft	Wakefield (2)	200	Allatt
24.3.91	SD	A	Dewsbury	L	10-18	Brown, Hine	Goulding	—	—
31.3.91	SD	H	Keighley	W	54-16	N. Barrow (3), Turner (2), Chappell, Dolan, Rawlinson, Burrows	N. Barrow (9)	350	Asquith
1.4.91	SD	A	Leigh	L	6-42	Burrows	N. Barrow	—	—
7.4.91	SD	H	Nottingham C.	W	42-0	Ashcroft (2), N. Barrow (2), Cooney, Rawlinson, Hine, Burrows	N. Barrow (5)	600	R. Connolly
14.4.91	SD	A	Fulham	L	14-24	Ashcroft, Hine, Brown	Wakefield	—	—

RYEDALE-YORK

Ground:	Monks Cross Stadium (0904-634636)
Colours:	Amber and black
First Season:	1901-02 as York. Moved and became Ryedale-York at start of 1989-90
Nickname:	Wasps
Chairman:	John Stabler
Secretary:	Ian Clough
Coach:	Gary Stephens (Apr 1988-June 1991)
Honours:	**Division Two** Champions, 1980-81 **Challenge Cup** Beaten finalists, 1930-31 **Yorkshire Cup** Winners, 1922-23, 1933-34, 1936-37 Beaten finalists, 1935-36, 1957-58, 1978-79
Records:	Attendance: 14,689 v. Swinton (RL Cup) 10 Feb, 1934 **Season** Goals: 146 by V. Yorke, 1957-58 Tries: 35 by J. Crossley, 1980-81 Points: 318 by G. Steadman, 1984-85

Match

Goals: 11 by V. Yorke v. Whitehaven, 6 Sep, 1958; C. Gibson v. Dewsbury, 28 Sep, 1980
Tries: 6 by R. Hardgrave v. Bramley, 5 Jan, 1935; D. Kettlestring at Keighley, 11 Mar, 1990
Points: 26 by G. Steadman v. Batley, 25 Nov, 1984; G. Sullivan at Keighley, 11 Mar, 1990
Highest score: 70-8 v. Keighley, 1989-90
Highest against: 75-3 v. Warrington 1950-51

1990-91 PLAYERS' SUMMARY

	App	Tries	Goals	Dr	Pts
Ackerman, Rob	4	1	—	—	4
Ake, Basil	23	9	—	—	36
Barrett, Anthony	1	—	—	—	—
Carlyle, Brendan	1 + 1	1	—	—	4
Craven, Stephen	5 + 1	1	—	—	4
Dickinson, Rob	0 + 1	—	—	—	—
Dobson, Steve	21 + 1	6	—	3	27
Faumuina, Mark	12	2	—	—	8
Fellows, Darren	2	—	—	—	—
Fowler, Ricky	7	1	—	—	4
Hayes, Richard	16 + 4	1	—	—	4
Horton, Stewart	31	4	—	1	17
Hutchinson, Paul	19 + 1	2	—	—	8
James, Neil	2 + 3	—	—	—	—
Kettlestring, David	23	5	3	—	26
Laws, Mark	5 + 2	—	—	—	—
Leuluai, James	7	2	—	—	8
Lidbury, Steve	5	2	—	—	8
Maxwell, Paul	21 + 1	2	—	—	8
Miles, Paul	3 + 4	—	—	—	—
Morris, Stuart	3	1	—	—	4
Nikau, Tawera	25	3	—	—	12
Patterson, Michael	2	—	—	—	—
Paver, Ian	22 + 2	1	—	—	4
Pinkney, Nick	31	14	—	—	56
Pryce, Geoff	19 + 4	7	—	—	28
Pryce, Steve	2 + 5	—	—	—	—
Render, Nick	7 + 7	2	—	—	8
Shaw, Matthew	3 + 6	—	—	—	—
Smith, Adrian	20 + 3	5	—	—	20
Stephens, Gary	9	—	—	—	—
Sullivan, Graham	31	13	90	4	236
Timson, Andy	2	—	—	—	—
Vasey, Chris	5 + 1	1	—	—	4
Vines, Simon	2	1	—	—	4
Warters, Mick	0 + 1	—	—	—	—
Warrener, Stan	1	—	—	—	—
Wheatley, Steve	1 + 1	—	—	—	—
Wilkinson, Shaun	3	—	—	—	—
Williams, Dean	20 + 5	9	—	—	36
TOTALS:					
40 players		96	93	8	578

Kiwi James Leuluai, scorer of two tries in seven appearances for Ryedale-York before moving to Doncaster.

1990-91 MATCH ANALYSIS

Date	Competition	H/A	Opponent	Rlt	Score	Tries	Goals	Attendance	Referee
26.8.90	YC(1)	H	Hull K.R.	L	0-10	—	—	2264	Holdsworth
9.9.90	SD	H	Nottingham C.	W	36-8	Kettlestring (2), Ake (2), Carlyle, Sullivan	Sullivan (6)	1391	R. Connolly
16.9.90	SD	A	Runcorn H.	W	22-10	Morris, Pryce, Ake, Pinkney	Kettlestring (3)	—	—
23.9.90	SD	H	Chorley	W	42-8	Maxwell, Leuluai, Ake, Pinkney, Williams, Pryce, Horton	Sullivan (7)	626	R. Connolly
30.9.90	SD	A	Halifax	L	18-26	Kettlestring, Leuluai	Sullivan (5)	—	—
7.10.90	SD	H	Salford	L	12-19	Pryce	Sullivan (4)	2444	Ollerton
14.10.90	SD	A	Carlisle	D	17-17	Ake, Sullivan	Sullivan (4, 1dg)	—	—
21.10.90	SD	H	Halifax	W	18-16	Smith (2), Paver	Sullivan (3)	4947	Crashley
4.11.90	SD	A	Nottingham C.	W	24-14	Sullivan (3), Kettlestring, Vasey	Sullivan (2)	—	—
11.11.90	SD	A	Fulham	W	9-4	Pryce	Sullivan (2), Dobson (dg)	—	—
14.11.90	RT(P)	A	Doncaster	L	12-14	Dobson, Sullivan	Sullivan (2)	—	—
18.11.90	SD	H	Workington T.	W	22-0	Pinkney, Williams, Faumuina	Sullivan (5)	1509	R. Connolly
25.11.90	SD	A	Batley	W	26-14	Faumuina, Kettlestring, Williams, Sullivan	Sullivan (5)	—	—
9.12.90	SD	A	Barrow	W	31-8	Ake (3), Pinkney, Pryce, Hayes	Sullivan (3)	—	—
16.12.90	SD	H	Huddersfield	L	6-7	Williams	Sullivan	1746	Steele
23.12.90	SD	H	Runcorn H.	W	34-0	Williams (2), Sullivan (2), Dobson, Trialist	Sullivan (5)	1523	Whitelam
26.12.90	SD	A	Doncaster	W	11-4	Horton, Nikau	Sullivan (1, 1dg)	—	—
30.12.90	SD	H	Barrow	W	34-0	Sullivan (2), Hutchinson, Dobson, Horton, Nikau	Sullivan (5)	1599	Galtress
6.1.91	SD	A	Swinton	L	6-12	—	Sullivan (3)	—	—
20.1.91	SD	A	Salford	L	12-22	Smith, Render	Sullivan (2)	—	—
27.1.91	SD	H	Fulham	W	22-4	Pryce, Render, Pinkney, Lidbury	Sullivan (3)	1351	Gilmour
17.2.91	CC(1)	H	Warrington	L	1-8	—	Sullivan (dg)	2825	Whitfield
20.2.91	SD	A	Huddersfield	W	14-10	Craven, Smith, Trialist	Sullivan	—	—
24.2.91	SD	H	Swinton	D	12-12	Pinkney, Nikau	Sullivan (2)	1984	Allatt
3.3.91	SD	H	Carlisle	W	18-12	Pinkney (2), Williams	Sullivan (3)	1397	Ollerton
10.3.91	SD	H	Batley	W	24-12	Hutchinson, Pinkney, Dobson, Horton, Sullivan	Sullivan (2)	1474	Allatt
15.3.91	SD	H	Hunslet	W	24-10	Williams, Pinkney, Lidbury, Pryce	Sullivan (4)	1469	Steele
24.3.91	SD	A	Chorley	W	24-20	Pinkney (2), Dobson, Williams	Sullivan (4)	—	—
29.3.91	SD	H	Doncaster	W	15-7	Sullivan, Smith, Ackerman	Sullivan, Dobson (dg)	2540	Allatt
1.4.91	SD	A	Hunslet	W	20-6	Pinkney (2), Maxwell	Sullivan (3, 1dg) Horton (dg)	—	—
7.4.91	SD	A	Workington T.	L	6-12	Dobson	Sullivan	—	—
21.4.91	SDP(1)	H[1]	Leigh	L	6-11	Ake	Sullivan	956	J. Connolly

[1] at Scarborough FC

ST. HELENS

Ground: Knowsley Road (0744-23697)
Colours: Red and white
First Season: 1895-96
Nickname: Saints
Chairman: Eric Latham
Secretary: Geoff Sutcliffe
Coach: Mike McClennan (Feb 1990-)
Honours: **Championship** Winners, 1931-32,
1952-53, 1958-59, 1965-66, 1969-70,
1970-71
Beaten finalists, 1964-65, 1966-67,
1971-72
Division One Champions, 1974-75
League Leaders Trophy Winners,
1964-65, 1965-66
Club Championship (Merit Table)
Beaten finalists, 1973-74
Challenge Cup Winners, 1955-56,
1960-61, 1965-66, 1971-72, 1975-76
Beaten finalists, 1896-97, 1914-15,
1929-30, 1952-53, 1977-78, 1986-87,
1988-89, 1990-91
Lancashire Cup Winners, 1926-27,
1953-54, 1960-61, 1961-62, 1962-63,
1963-64, 1964-65, 1967-68, 1968-69,
1984-85
Beaten finalists, 1932-33, 1952-53,
1956-57, 1958-59, 1959-60, 1970-71,
1982-83
Lancashire League Winners,
1929-30, 1931-32, 1952-53, 1959-60,
1964-65, 1965-66, 1966-67, 1968-69
Regal Trophy Winners, 1987-88
Premiership Winners, 1975-76,
1976-77, 1984-85
Beaten finalists, 1974-75, 1987-88
Western Division Championship
Winners, 1963-64
BBC2 Floodlit Trophy Winners,
1971-72, 1975-76
Beaten finalists, 1965-66, 1968-69,
1970-71, 1977-78, 1978-79
Records: Attendance: 35,695 v. Wigan
(League) 26 Dec, 1949
Season
Goals: 214 by K. Coslett, 1971-72
Tries: 62 by T. Van Vollenhoven,
1958-59
Points: 452 by K. Coslett, 1971-72

Match
Goals: 16 by P. Loughlin v.
Carlisle, 14 Sep, 1986
Tries: 6 by A. Ellaby v. Barrow,
5 Mar, 1932; S. Llewellyn v.
Castleford, 3 Mar, 1956 and v.
Liverpool C., 20 Aug, 1956;
T. Vollenhoven v. Wakefield T.,
21 Dec, 1957 and v. Blackpool B.,
23 Apr, 1962; F. Myler v.
Maryport, 1 Sep, 1969; S. Cooper
v. Hull, 17 Feb, 1988
Points: 40 by P. Loughlin v.
Carlisle, 14 Sep, 1986
Highest score: 112-0 v. Carlisle,
1986-87
Highest against: 78-3 v.
Warrington, 1908-09

1990-91 PLAYERS' SUMMARY

	App	Tries	Goals	Dr	Pts
Bailey, Mark	20 + 12	11	—	—	44
Bateman, Andy	1 + 4	1	—	—	4
Bishop, Paul	15 + 2	5	13	4	50
Connolly, Gary	22 + 2	4	—	—	16
Connor, Ian	2 + 2	—	—	—	—
Cooper, Shane	37	10	—	1	41
Cosgrove, David	1 + 3	1	—	—	4
Devine, Sean	15 + 2	6	22	—	68
Dwyer, Bernard	27 + 1	—	—	—	—
Evans, Stuart	17	2	—	—	8
Fairclough, Andy	4	1	—	—	4
Forber, Paul	8 + 4	3	—	—	12
Frodsham, Tommy	0 + 2	—	—	—	—
Griffiths, Jonathan	28 + 3	8	—	—	32
Groves, Paul	25 + 5	2	—	1	9
Haggerty, Roy	8 + 1	1	—	2	6
Harrison, John	27 + 1	5	—	—	20
Hunte, Allan	32	26	—	—	104
Jones, Paul	5 + 10	—	—	—	—
Kay, Tony	1	—	—	—	—
Kebbie, Brimah	3 + 1	2	—	—	8
Large, David	2 + 1	—	—	—	—
Loughlin, Paul	27	8	94	—	220
McCormack, Kevin	1	—	—	—	—
Mann, George	26 + 3	7	—	—	28
Neill, Jonathan	13 + 4	1	—	—	4
O'Brien, Darren	1 + 1	—	—	—	—
Quirk, Les	32	26	—	—	104
Ropati, Tea	29 + 2	12	—	—	48
Tanner, Dave	3 + 3	2	3	—	14
Veivers, Phil	32 + 1	3	—	—	12
Ward, Kevin	30	2	—	—	8
TOTALS: 32 players		149	132	8	868

1990-91 MATCH ANALYSIS

Date	Competition	H/A	Opponent	Rlt	Score	Tries	Goals	Attendance	Referee
26.8.90	LC(1)	H	Trafford B.	W	56-24	Bailey (2), Quirk, Evans, Groves, Ward, Haggerty, Cooper, Griffiths, Bateman	Loughlin (8)	4827	Holgate
2.9.90	LC(2)	A	Salford	L	7-21	Quirk	Loughlin, Haggerty (dg)	—	—
9.9.90	SBC	A	Hull	L	14-20	Veivers, Loughlin	Loughlin (3)	—	—
16.9.90	SBC	H	Bradford N.	W	24-20	Hunte (2), Fairclough	Loughlin (6)	6932	Whitelam
23.9.90	SBC	H	Hull K.R.	W	42-10	Quirk (3), Hunte (2), Loughlin, Griffiths, Cooper, Harrison	Loughlin (3)	6558	Kershaw
30.9.90	SBC	A	Leeds	L	4-23	—	Loughlin (2)	—	—
7.10.90	Tour	H	Australia	L	4-34	Quirk	—	15,219	Holdsworth
21.10.90	SBC	H	Castleford	L	16-29	Mann, Kebbie, Cooper	Devine (2)	6977	Galtress
4.11.90	SBC	A	Rochdale H.	W	30-18	Ropati, Mann, Quirk, Devine, Cooper	Loughlin (5)	—	—
11.11.90	SBC	H	Sheffield E.	W	34-17	Bailey (2), Loughlin, Cooper, Mann, Forber	Loughlin (5)	6155	Kershaw
21.11.90	SBC	A	Bradford N.	L	16-18	Devine, Mann, Cooper	Devine (2)	—	—
25.11.90	SBC	H	Rochdale H.	W	44-14	Devine, Mann, Cooper, Forber, Cosgrove, Bailey, Ropati, Hunte	Devine (6)	5482	Kershaw
2.12.90	RT(1)	A	Swinton	W	31-7	Connolly (2), Cooper, Hunte, Bailey	Bishop (5, 1dg)	—	—
11.12.90	RT(2)	A	Featherstone R.	W	33-16	Ropati, Hunte, Evans, Mann, Forber, Devine, Bailey	Loughlin (7), Bishop (dg)	—	—
16.12.90	RT(3)	A	Warrington	L	12-18	Hunte, Bailey	Loughlin (2)	—	—
23.12.90	SBC	A	Sheffield E.	L	8-18	Devine, Quirk	—	—	—
26.12.90	SBC	H	Wigan	L	15-28	Loughlin, Veivers	Loughlin (3), Cooper (dg)	13,226	Whitfield
1.1.91	SBC	A	Widnes	L	8-14	Cooper, Ropati	—	—	—
6.1.91	3DC	H	Wakefield T.	W	36-14	Quirk (3), Veivers, Harrison, Ropati	Devine (6)	5950	Ollerton
13.1.91	SBC	A	Featherstone R.	W	36-28	Hunte (2), Connolly, Kebbie, Mann, Ropati	Devine (6)	—	—
20.1.91	SBC	H	Leeds	W	22-16	Quirk, Devine, Ropati	Loughlin (5)	8188	Holdsworth
27.1.91	SBC	A	Hull K.R.	D	26-26	Quirk (2), Griffiths (2)	Loughlin (5)	—	—
3.2.91	SBC	A	Oldham	W	20-16	Hunte (2), Ropati	Loughlin (4)	—	—
10.2.91	CC(1)	A[1]	Swinton	W	18-8	Harrison, Ropati, Bailey	Loughlin (3)	—	—
18.2.91	SBC	H	Hull	W	12-10	Ropati, Quirk	Loughlin (2)	6893	Galtress
23.2.91	CC(2)	H	Wakefield T.	W	16-2	Hunte, Harrison	Loughlin (4)	4586	Burke
3.3.91	SBC	A	Warrington	L	20-34	Quirk (2), Tanner, Hunte	Bishop (2)	—	—
10.3.91	CC(3)	A	Halifax	W	24-16	Hunte (2), Bishop, Quirk	Loughlin (4)	—	—
13.3.91	SBC	H	Oldham	W	33-22	Quirk (2), Bailey, Tanner	Loughlin (8), Bishop (dg)	6772	J. Connolly
17.3.91	SBC	H	Featherstone R.	W	54-38	Bishop (2), Hunte (2), Loughlin, Groves, Bailey, Griffiths, Harrison, Quirk	Loughlin (7)	7173	Galtress
24.3.91	SBC	A	Castleford	L	4-28	Loughlin	—	—	—
30.3.91	CC(SF)	Wigan	Widnes	W	19-2	Griffiths (2), Hunte	Loughlin (3), Groves (dg)	(16,109)	Holdsworth
1.4.91	SBC	H	Widnes	L	12-20	Bishop, Cooper	Bishop (2)	7289	Asquith
4.4.91	SBC	A	Wigan	L	14-28	Ropati, Quirk	Tanner (3)	—	—
7.4.91	SBC	A	Wakefield T.	W	22-8	Ropati, Connolly, Quirk, Hunte	Bishop (2, 1dg), Haggerty (dg)	—	—
14.4.91	SBC	H	Warrington	W	62-16	Hunte (4), Quirk (3), Loughlin (2), Griffiths, Neill, Bishop	Loughlin (7)	8490	Carter
21.4.91	PT(1)	A	Hull	L	12-28	Ward, Hunte	Loughlin (2)	—	—
27.4.91	CC(F)	Wembley	Wigan	L	8-13	Hunte	Bishop (2)	(75,532)	Smith

[1] at Man City FC

SALFORD

Ground: The Willows (061-737-6363)
Colours: Red and white
First Season: 1896-97
Nickname: Red Devils
Chairman: John Wilkinson
Secretary: Graham McCarty
Coach: Kevin Tamati (Oct 1989-)
Honours: **Championship** Winners, 1913-14, 1932-33, 1936-37, 1938-39
Beaten finalists, 1933-34
Division One Champions, 1973-74, 1975-76
Division Two Champions, 1990-91
Challenge Cup Winners, 1937-38
Beaten finalists, 1899-1900, 1901-02, 1902-03, 1905-06, 1938-39, 1968-69
Lancashire League Winners, 1932-33, 1933-34, 1934-35, 1936-37, 1938-39
Lancashire Cup Winners, 1931-32, 1934-35, 1935-36, 1936-37, 1972-73
Beaten finalists, 1929-30, 1938-39, 1973-74, 1974-75, 1975-76, 1988-89, 1990-91
Premiership Beaten finalists, 1975-76
Second Division Premiership Winners, 1990-91
Regal Trophy Beaten finalists, 1972-73
BBC2 Floodlit Trophy Winners, 1974-75
Records: Attendance: 26,470 v. Warrington (RL Cup) 13 Feb, 1937
Season
Goals: 221 by D. Watkins, 1972-73
Tries: 46 by K. Fielding, 1973-74
Points: 493 by D. Watkins, 1972-73

Match
Goals: 13 by A. Risman v. Bramley, 5 Apr, 1933 and v. Broughton R., 18 May, 1940; D. Watkins v. Keighley, 7 Jan, 1972; S. Rule v. Doncaster, 4 Sep, 1981
Tries: 6 by F. Miles v. Lees, 5 Mar, 1898; E. Bone v. Goole, 29 Mar, 1902; J. Hilton v. Leigh, 7 Oct, 1939
Points: 39 by J. Lomas v. Liverpool C., 2 Feb, 1907
Highest score: 78-0 v. Liverpool C., 1906-07
Highest against: 65-0 v. Castleford, 1989-90

1990-91 PLAYERS' SUMMARY

	App	Tries	Goals	Dr	Pts
Bantley, Keith	2 + 2	1	—	—	4
Betts, Darren	0 + 1	—	—	—	—
Birkett, Martin	30 + 6	14	4	—	64
Blease, Ian	31	13	—	—	52
Bradshaw, Arthur	23 + 5	8	—	—	32
Brown, Shaun	3 + 3	—	—	1	1
Burgess, Andy	34 + 2	9	—	—	36
Cassidy, Frank	27 + 7	6	—	5	29
Clare, Jeff	1 + 2	1	—	—	4
Conroy, Tony	5 + 5	—	—	—	—
Dean, Mick	9 + 3	1	—	—	4
Evans, Tex	26 + 2	15	—	—	60
Fell, David	33 + 5	21	—	—	84
Gelling, Bryan	1	1	—	—	4
Gibson, Steve	30 + 1	17	—	—	68
Gilfillan, John	30 + 2	13	—	—	52
Hadley, Adrian	38	31	—	—	124
Hansen, Shane	21 + 9	2	—	—	8
Howard, Tony	3	1	—	—	4
Kerry, Steve	41 + 1	20	170	7	427
Lee, Mark	30 + 2	2	—	10	18
Leota, Francis	10	—	—	—	—
Mercer, Andy	1	—	—	—	—
Moran, Mark	1	—	—	—	—
O'Loughlin, Jason	5 + 1	3	—	—	12
O'Neill, Paul	6 + 4	8	—	—	32
Quigley, Jonathan	1	—	—	—	—
Shaw, David	5 + 2	—	—	—	—
Sherratt, Ian	27 + 3	2	—	—	8
Stephenson, David	0 + 1	1	—	—	4
Tamati, Kevin	5 + 2	—	—	—	—
Tunks, Peter	6 + 2	1	—	—	4
Walsh, Joe	4 + 3	—	—	—	—
Whiteley, Chris	11	—	—	—	—
Williams, Peter	26 + 5	5	—	—	20
Worrall, Mick	20 + 1	5	—	—	20

TOTALS:
36 players		201	174	23	1,175

1990-91 MATCH ANALYSIS

Date	Com-petition	H/A	Opponent	Rlt	Score	Tries	Goals	Atten-dance	Referee
19.8.90	LC(P)	A	Rochdale H.	W	41-12	Hadley (2), Fell, Williams, Evans, Lee, Gibson	Kerry (6), Lee (dg)	—	—
26.8.90	LC(1)	H	Oldham	W	27-24	Burgess (2), Hadley, Gibson, Birkett	Kerry (3), Brown (dg)	4236	Carter
2.9.90	LC(2)	H	St. Helens	W	21-7	Evans, Birkett, Gibson, Hadley	Kerry (2), Lee (dg)	5574	Whitfield
9.9.90	SD	A	Barrow	W	31-0	Blease (2), Birkett, Bradshaw, Gibson, Evans	Kerry (3), Lee (dg)	—	—
12.9.90	LC(SF)	H	Leigh	W	16-7	Fell (2)	Kerry (4)	6939	Allatt
16.9.90	SD	H	Workington T.	W	30-8	Evans (2), Kerry, Hadley, Fell, Bradshaw	Kerry (3)	2011	Kendrew
23.9.90	SD	A	Batley	W	21-10	Bradshaw, Cassidy, Evans, Gilfillan	Kerry (2, 1dg)	—	—
29.9.90	LC(F)	Wigan	Widnes	L	18-24	Williams, Blease, Fell	Kerry (3)	(7485)	Burke
3.10.90	SD	H	Doncaster	W	21-4	Gilfillan, Clare, Hadley	Kerry (4, 1dg)	2237	J. Connolly
7.10.90	SD	A	Ryedale-York	W	19-12	Gilfillan, Sherratt	Birkett (4), Kerry (dg), Cassidy (dg), Lee (dg)	—	—
14.10.90	SD	H	Barrow	W	76-10	Gilfillan (3), Gibson (2), O'Neill (2), Fell (2), Evans, Blease, Bradshaw, Burgess, Hadley	Kerry (10)	2360	Asquith
21.10.90	SD	A	Chorley	W	50-2	Burgess (3), Hadley (2), Bradshaw (2) Gibson	Kerry (9)	—	—
30.10.90	SD	H	Trafford B.	W	38-12	Kerry (2), Cassidy, Burgess, Blease	Kerry (8, 1dg), Lee (dg)	2376	R. Connolly
4.11.90	SD	H	Bramley	W	40-0	Hadley (2), Gilfillan, Birkett, Fell, Tunks, Evans, Gibson	Kerry (4)	2158	Campbell
18.11.90	SD	A	Runcorn H.	W	26-6	Hadley, Gilfillan, Evans, Fell, Gibson	Kerry (3)	—	—
25.11.90	SD	H	Whitehaven	W	40-6	Fell (3), Gilfillan, Sherratt, Gibson, Kerry	Kerry (6)	2042	C. Morris
2.12.90	RT(1)	A	Oldham	L	6-26	Gibson	Kerry	—	—
16.12.90	SD	A	Whitehaven	W	38-12	Blease, Worrall, Cassidy, Gibson, Kerry, Evans	Kerry (7)	—	—
1.1.91	SD	H	Swinton	W	13-0	Cassidy, Hadley	Kerry (2), Cassidy (dg)	4647	Asquith
6.1.91	SD	A	Dewsbury	W	50-2	Kerry, Burgess, Williams, Hadley, Birkett, Gilfillan, Evans, Gibson, Bradshaw	Kerry (7)	—	—
9.1.91	SD	A	Leigh	W	20-4	Williams, Blease, Fell	Kerry (4)	—	—
20.1.91	SD	H	Ryedale-York	W	22-12	Kerry, Hadley, Blease	Kerry (5)	2521	Ollerton
22.1.91	SD	H	Runcorn H.	W	50-6	Blease (3), Kerry (2), Lee, Evans, Hansen, Hadley, Gilfillan	Kerry (5)	1702	Steele
27.1.91	CC(P)	H	Cutsyke	W	44-4	Birkett (2), Fell (2), Evans, Kerry, Hadley, Worrall, Bradshaw	Kerry (4)	1788	Campbell
30.1.91	SD	A	Doncaster	W	14-12	Gelling, Kerry	Kerry (2), Cassidy (dg), Lee (dg)	—	—
15.2.91	CC(1)	H	Batley	W	36-14	Fell (2), O'Neill, Worrall, Blease, Hadley	Kerry (6)	2050	Kershaw
24.2.91	CC(2)	A	Sheffield E.	W	19-16	Kerry, Hansen, Fell, Burgess	Kerry, Lee (dg)	—	—
27.2.91	SD	H	Dewsbury	W	32-6	O'Neill (3), Kerry (2)	Kerry (6)	1837	Allatt
3.3.91	SD	A	Keighley	W	22-21	Hadley (3), Birkett	Kerry (3)	—	—
10.3.91	CC(3)	A	Oldham	L	3-40	—	Kerry (1, 1dg)	—	—
13.3.91	SD	H	Chorley	W	46-2	Kerry (2), Gilfillan, Howard, Birkett, Cassidy, O'Loughlin, Stephenson	Kerry (7)	1472	K. Morris

(continued on page 103)

SHEFFIELD EAGLES

Ground: Don Valley Stadium (0742-610326)
Colours: Red, white, gold and black
First Season: 1984-85
Nickname: Eagles
Chairman: Gary Hetherington
Secretary: Julie Bush
Coach: Gary Hetherington (July 1986-)
Honours: **Second Division Premiership**
Winners, 1988-89
Records: Attendance: 8,636 v. Widnes
(League) at Sheffield U. FC, 8 Oct, 1989
Season
Goals: 148 by M. Aston, 1988-89
Tries: 28 by D. Powell, 1988-89
Points: 307 by M. Aston, 1988-89
Match
Goals: 12 by R. Rafferty at Fulham, 21 Sep, 1986
Tries: 5 by D. Powell at Mansfield M., 2 Jan, 1989
Points: 32 by R. Rafferty at Fulham, 21 Sep, 1986
Highest score: 80-8 v. Wigan St. Patricks, 1988-89
Highest against: 62-11 v. Warrington, 1985-86

1990-91 PLAYERS' SUMMARY

	App	Tries	Goals	Dr	Pts
Aston, Mark	22	6	58	2	142
Bateman, Andy	3 + 2	2	—	—	8
Broadbent, Paul	26 + 1	3	—	—	12
Close, David	3	—	9	—	18
Cook, Mick	29	3	—	—	12
Dickinson, Andy	6 + 3	1	—	—	4
Farrell, Anthony	18 + 5	2	—	—	8
Gamson, Mark	22 + 1	3	—	—	12
Grimoldby, Nick	11 + 1	1	—	—	4
Halafihi, Nick	3	—	—	—	—
Johnson, Dean	0 + 2	—	—	—	—
Kellett, Neil	0 + 8	2	—	—	8
Leota, Francis	6	—	—	—	—
Lewis, Peter	4	2	—	—	8
Maea, Des	5 + 6	6	—	—	24
Moore, Thomas	0 + 1	—	—	—	—
Mumby, Keith	14 + 1	—	—	—	—
Mycoe, David	29 + 1	2	16	—	40
Nelson, David	31	8	—	—	32
Nickle, Sonny	21	9	—	—	36
Panapa, Sam	24	14	—	—	56
Pearce, Gary	4	—	11	3	25
Picksley, Richard	7	1	—	—	4
Powell, Daryl	29 + 1	7	—	4	32
Price, Richard	6	—	—	—	—
Rhoades, Simon	0 + 1	—	—	—	—
Russell, Ian	16 + 1	3	—	—	12
Tunks, Peter	13 + 2	1	—	—	4
Waddell, Hugh	24 + 7	2	—	—	8
Wilby, Tim	11 + 8	—	—	—	—
Young, Andy	16 + 6	6	—	—	24
TOTALS:					
31 players		84	94	9	533

SCARBOROUGH PIRATES

Ground: McCain Stadium (0723-375094)
Colours: Royal, purple and gold
First Season: 1991-92
Chairman: Geoffrey Richmond
Secretary: Roy Morton
Coach: Len Casey (Feb 1991-)

Anthony Farrell, two tries in 23 appearances for Sheffield Eagles.

1990-91 MATCH ANALYSIS

Date	Competition	H/A	Opponent	Rlt	Score	Tries	Goals	Attendance	Referee
19.8.90	YC(P)	A	Bradford N.	L	12-20	Aston, Powell	Aston (2)	—	—
9.9.90	SBC	A	Wigan	D	18-18	Gamson, Dickinson, Powell	Aston (3)	—	—
16.9.90	SBC	A	Rochdale H.	W	24-20	Aston (2), Russell, Nelson	Aston (3), Mycoe	—	—
26.9.90	SBC	H	Wakefield T.	W	34-6	Nickle, Panapa, Gamson, Young, Powell	Close (7)	7984	Tennant
30.9.90	SBC	H	Warrington	L	18-20	Nickle (2), Broadbent	Close (2), Mycoe	4920	Smith
7.10.90	SBC	A	Featherstone R.	L	22-25	Nelson, Nickle, Kellett	Mycoe (5)	—	—
14.10.90	SBC	H	Oldham	L	14-24	Panapa, Gamson	Mycoe (3)	5189	Whitelam
21.10.90	SBC	A	Hull	L	6-34	Panapa	Mycoe	—	—
30.10.90	SBC	H	Bradford N.	L	16-36	Kellett, Powell	Pearce (4)	4119	Kendrew
11.11.90	SBC	A	St. Helens	L	17-34	Waddell, Nickle	Pearce (3, 3dg)	—	—
18.11.90	RT(P)	H	Bradford N.	L	8-12	Panapa	Pearce (2)	2788	Campbell
25.11.90	SBC	A	Warrington	L	8-30	Nelson	Pearce (2)	—	—
16.12.90	SBC	H	Leeds	L	6-24	Cook	Mycoe	4714	Asquith
23.12.90	SBC	H	St. Helens	W	18-8	Mycoe, Panapa	Mycoe (4), Aston (2dg)	3111	Carter
29.12.90	SBC	A	Hull K. R.	D	16-16	Nelson (2), Powell	Aston (2)	—	—
6.1.91	SBC	H	Wigan	L	4-46	Young	—	4814	Kershaw
13.1.91	SBC	A	Leeds	L	16-38	Lewis, Cook, Russell	Aston (2)	—	—
20.1.91	SBC	H	Rochdale H.	W	30-16	Panapa (2), Broadbent, Russell	Aston (7)	2160	Galtress
30.1.91	CC(P)	H	Hull	W	19-6	Lewis, Maea	Aston (5), Powell (dg)	2847	J. Connolly
3.2.91	SBC	H	Featherstone R.	L	24-27	Panapa, Nickle, Powell, Tunks	Aston (4)	3206	Whitfield
17.2.91	CC(1)	H	Featherstone R.	W	19-12	Nelson, Farrell, Panapa	Aston (3), Powell (dg)	2910	Holdsworth
24.2.91	CC(2)	H	Salford	L	16-19	Aston, Farrell	Aston (4)	1990	Smith
27.2.91	SBC	A	Bradford N.	L	10-6	Aston, Panapa	Aston	—	—
3.3.91	SBC	A	Widnes	W	23-14	Waddell, Bateman, Maea, Nelson	Aston (3), Powell (dg)	—	—
6.3.91	SBC	A	Wakefield T.	L	4-12	Bateman	—	—	—
10.3.91	SBC	H	Castleford	L	20-24	Young (2), Mycoe, Aston	Aston (2)	3840	Asquith
17.3.91	SBC	A	Oldham	L	20-27	Maea (2), Panapa	Aston (4)	—	—
24.3.91	SBC	H	Hull	L	6-16	Maea	Aston	3104	J. Connolly
31.3.91	SBC	H	Hull K.R.	W	62-16	Panapa (3), Nickle (2), Nelson, Powell, Young, Broadbent, Maea, Grimoldby, Cook	Aston (7)	2684	Kershaw
6.4.91	SBC	H	Widnes	L	13-18	Picksley, Nickle	Aston (2), Powell (dg)	2578	C. Morris
14.4.91	SBC	A	Castleford	L	10-28	Young	Aston (3)	—	—

SWINTON

Ground: Station Road (061-794-1719)
Colours: Blue and white
First Season: 1896-97
Nickname: Lions
Chairman: John Way
Secretary: Wayne Dore
Coach: Jim Crellin (July 1989-July 1991)
Honours: **Championship** Winners, 1926-27, 1927-28, 1930-31, 1934-35
Beaten finalists, 1924-25, 1932-33
War League Beaten finalists, 1939-40
Division One Champions, 1962-63, 1963-64
Division Two Champions, 1984-85
Second Division Premiership Winners, 1986-87
Beaten finalists, 1988-89
Challenge Cup Winners, 1899-1900, 1925-26, 1927-28
Beaten finalists, 1926-27, 1931-32
Lancashire League Winners, 1924-25, 1927-28, 1928-29, 1930-31, 1960-61
Lancashire War League Winners, 1939-40
Lancashire Cup Winners, 1925-26, 1927-28, 1939-40, 1969-70
Beaten finalists, 1910-11, 1923-24, 1931-32, 1960-61, 1961-62, 1962-63, 1964-65, 1972-73
BBC2 Floodlit Trophy Beaten finalists, 1966-67
Western Division Championship Beaten finalists, 1963-64
Records: Attendance: 44,621 Wigan v. Warrington (RL Cup SF) 7 Apr, 1951
Season
Goals: 128 by A. Blan, 1960-61
Tries: 42 by J. Stopford, 1963-64
Points: 283 by A. Blan, 1960-61
Match
Goals: 12 by K. Gowers v. Liverpool C., 3 Oct, 1959
Tries: 5 by T. Bevan v. Morecambe, 10 Sep, 1898; W.

Wallwork v. Widnes, 15 Dec, 1900; J. Evans v. Bradford N., 30 Sep, 1922; H. Halsall v. St. Helens, 24 Jan, 1925; R. Cracknell v. Whitehaven Rec., 11 Feb, 1928; R. Lewis v. Keighley, 12 Jan, 1946; J. Stopford v. Bramley, 22 Dec, 1962; A. Buckley v. Salford, 8 Apr, 1964; J. Ropati v. Nottingham C., 21 Jan, 1990
Points: 29 by B. McMahon v. Dewsbury, 15 Aug, 1959
Highest score: 76-4 v. Pontefract, 1906-07
Highest against: 76-3 v. Huddersfield, 1945-46; 76-16 v. Castleford, 1987-88

1990-91 PLAYERS' SUMMARY

	App	Tries	Goals	Dr	Pts
Allen, John	22 + 2	1	—	—	4
Ashall, Barry	22 + 1	3	9	8	38
Best, Brian	1	—	—	—	—
Boucher, Phil	1	1	—	—	4
Clark, Jason	1	—	—	—	—
Daintith, Ian	4 + 1	—	1	—	2
Edwards, Logan	20 + 5	11	—	—	44
Frodsham, Tommy	5	4	—	—	16
Graziano, Joe	1	—	—	—	—
Griffiths, Danny	11 + 2	2	—	—	8
Hancock, Mike	3 + 3	1	—	—	4
Herbert, Steve	4 + 3	—	—	—	—
Hudson, Julian	1	—	—	—	—
Jackson, Steve	3	—	—	—	—
Johnson, Chris	15	2	45	1	99
Kennett, Paul	0 + 1	—	—	—	—
Kerr, John	4 + 1	2	—	—	8
Leyland, Martin	1	1	—	—	4
McNichol, Tony	4	1	—	—	4
Melling, Alex	24 + 2	1	—	—	4
Mellor, Paul	7 + 1	—	1	—	2
Morrison, Tony	30	3	—	—	12
Murdock, Gary	3	—	—	—	—
Partington, Carl	1	—	—	—	—
Peacham, Gary	13 + 6	10	—	—	40
Peters, Barry	12	1	—	—	4
Pickavance, Ian	13 + 6	3	—	—	12
Pucill, Andy	31 + 1	3	—	1	13
Rabbitt, Jason	1	—	—	—	—
Ranson, Scott	31	15	—	—	60
Ratu, Emon	2 + 2	1	—	—	4
Ropati, Joe	21 + 2	4	—	—	16
Scott, Terry	13	7	—	—	28
Skeech, Ian	2 + 1	—	—	—	—
Snape, Steve	27 + 1	5	—	1	21
Street, Tim	12 + 2	4	—	—	16
Subritzky, Peter	11	2	—	1	9
Topping, Steve	2 + 1	—	2	1	5
Tupaea, Shane	30 + 1	6	—	—	24
Wilkinson, Chris	7	2	21	1	51

TOTALS:
40 players ... 96 79 14 556

1990-91 MATCH ANALYSIS

Date	Competition	H/A	Opponent	Rlt	Score	Tries	Goals	Attendance	Referee
26.8.90	LC(1)	A	Leigh	L	6-26	Street	Johnson	—	—
9.9.90	SD	H	Whitehaven	W	40-10	Scott (2), Snape, Tupaea, Ranson, Ropati, Peacham	Johnson (6)	1138	Cross
16.9.90	SD	H	Bramley	W	34-19	Kerr (2), Scott, Johnson, Edwards	Johnson (7)	1110	Steele
23.9.90	SD	H	Keighley	W	22-16	Hancock, Street, Tupaea, Ranson	Johnson (3)	1271	Carter
30.9.90	SD	A	Nottingham C.	W	35-27	Street, Edwards, Morrison, Peacham, Tupaea	Johnson (7), Ashall (dg)	—	—
7.10.90	SD	H	Halifax	L	13-20	Morrison, Ranson	Johnson (2), Snape (dg)	4003	Asquith
14.10.90	SD	A	Dewsbury	W	18-4	Street, Peacham, Edwards	Johnson (3)	—	—
21.10.90	SD	H	Carlisle	W	22-10	Tupaea, Snape, Edwards, Ashall	Johnson (2), Ashall (dg), Pucill (dg)	1457	Smith
4.11.90	SD	A	Whitehaven	W	24-16	Ranson (2), Scott, Snape, Peacham	Mellor, Ashall	—	—
11.11.90	SD	H	Dewsbury	W	13-6	Ranson, Melling, Snape	Ashall (dg)	1462	Holgate
18.11.90	SD	H	Fulham	W	13-4	Edwards, Ropati	Topping (2, 1dg)	1238	Asquith
25.11.90	SD	A	Leigh	W	20-12	Edwards, Ropati, Griffiths	Ashall (3, 2dg)	—	—
2.12.90	RT(1)	H	St. Helens	L	7-31	Ashall	Ashall (1, 1dg)	3385	Smith
16.12.90	SD	H	Hunslet	W	22-10	Pucill, Ranson, Allen, Subritzky	Ashall (3)	1252	Kershaw
1.1.91	SD	A	Salford	L	0-13	—	—	—	—
6.1.91	SD	H	Ryedale-York	W	12-6	Ranson, Scott	Ashall (1, 2dg)	1600	Tidball
9.1.91	SD	H	Trafford B.	W	12-10	Scott, Edwards	Johnson (2)	881	Cross
20.1.91	SD	A	Huddersfield	W	21-12	Edwards, Scott, Ranson, Tupaea	Johnson (2, 1dg)	—	—
27.1.91	SD	H	Nottingham C.	W	16-4	Ranson, Peacham, Johnson	Johnson (2)	1133	Carter
3.2.91	SD	A	Fulham	L	10-26	Peacham (2)	Johnson	—	—
10.2.91	CC(1)	H[1]	St Helens	L	8-18	Pickavance (2)	—	2922	Allatt
17.2.91	SD	A	Carlisle	W	32-11	Ranson (4), Peacham, Ropati	Johnson (4)	—	—
24.2.91	SD	A	Ryedale-York	D	12-12	McNicol, Peacham	Johnson (2)	—	—
3.3.91	SD	H	Leigh	W	7-6	Pickavance	Daintith, Subritzky (dg)	1901	Cross
17.3.91	SD	A	Bramley	W	17-10	Edwards, Subritzky	Wilkinson (4, 1dg)	—	—
24.3.91	SD	A	Hunslet	W	16-12	Frodsham (2), Edwards	Wilkinson (2)	—	—
29.3.91	SD	A[2]	Trafford B.	W	16-10	Pucill, Edwards	Wilkinson (4)	—	—
1.4.91	SD	H	Salford	D	10-10	Morrison, Ratu	Wilkinson	4102	Holdsworth
4.4.91	SD	A	Halifax	L	14-42	Ashall, Pucill, Boucher	Johnson	—	—
7.4.91	SD	A	Keighley	L	10-14	Griffiths, Snape	Wilkinson	—	—
14.4.91	SD	H	Huddersfield	W	42-18	Wilkinson (2), Frodsham (2), Tupaea, Ranson, Leyland	Wilkinson (7)	1769	Holgate
21.4.91	SDP(1)	H	Workington T.	L	12-19	Peacham, Peters	Wilkinson (2)	1690	Carter

[1] at Man City FC   [2] at Widnes

TRAFFORD BOROUGH

Ground:	Moss Lane, Altrincham (061-928-1045)
Colours:	Blue and crimson
First Season:	1954-55 as Blackpool Borough; changing to Springfield Borough in 1987-88; Chorley Borough in 1988-89; and Trafford Borough from 1989-90
Nickname:	Griffins
Chairman:	Fred Wood
Secretary:	Alan Sherratt
Coach:	Mike Peers (Aug 1987-May 1991) Norman Turley (June 1991-)
Honours:	**Regal Trophy** Beaten finalists, 1976-77
Records:	Attendance: 7,614 v. Castleford (RL Cup) 14 Mar, 1964. There was an attendance of 21,000 in an RL Cup-tie against Leigh on Blackpool FC ground on 9 Mar, 1957

Season
Goals: 98 by M. Smith, 1987-88
Tries: 30 by T. Frodsham, 1985-86
Points: 201 by P. Fearis, 1957-58

Match
Goals: 11 by N. Turley v. Carlisle, 26 Apr, 1984;
Tries: 4 by T. Wilkshire v. Bradford N, 14 Jan, 1961;
J. Stockley v. Doncaster, 1 Apr, 1984
T. Frodsham v. Bridgend, 14 Apr, 1985 and v. Mansfield M., 30 Nov, 1986
Points: 27 by N. Turley v. Carlisle, 26 Apr, 1984
Highest score: 56-2 v. Runcorn H., 1988-89
Highest against: 77-8 v. Wigan, 1963-64

1990-91 PLAYERS' SUMMARY

	App	Tries	Goals	Dr	Pts
Abram, Darren	5	1	—	—	4
Bamber, Simon	7 + 1	—	—	—	—
Bent, P.	0 + 1	—	—	—	—
Bigg, Paul	19 + 1	4	—	—	16
Brown, Darren	7	7	—	—	28
Brown, David	4 + 4	—	—	—	—
Connor, Steve	29	10	—	—	40
Eccles, Cliff	9 + 1	3	—	—	12
Farrell, Lee	1	—	—	—	—
Flannery, Steve	19 + 1	2	—	—	8
Galbraith, Stuart	3 + 1	3	—	—	12
Garner, Steve	25	6	—	—	24
Greaves, Alan	2 + 7	—	—	—	—
Green, Andy	17 + 3	1	—	—	4
Gregory, Paul	3 + 2	—	—	—	—
Griffiths, Steve	1 + 3	1	—	—	4
Herbert, Steve	8 + 4	1	—	—	4
Hilton, Peter	1	—	—	—	—
Hough, Mick	4 + 4	—	—	—	—
Hudson, Mark	5 + 6	—	—	—	—
Iddon, Tim	17 + 6	6	—	—	24
Jones, Ken	30	10	18	2	78
Litz, Terry	0 + 2	—	—	—	—
Lowrie, Jason	16	1	—	—	4
McCarthy, Darren	2 + 1	—	—	—	—
Maloney, David	4 + 1	—	—	—	—
Mavin, Steve	7	7	—	—	28
Meadows, Mark	23 + 1	3	—	—	12
Nuttall, Nick	5	—	—	—	—
Platt, Billy	13	5	—	5	25
Ramsey, Neville	15 + 1	3	—	—	12
Reynolds, Paul	26	8	—	—	32
Rippon, Andy	14 + 5	2	1	—	10
Slater, Neil	2 + 1	—	—	—	—
Smith, Graham	1	—	—	—	—
Stewart, Mike	26	7	—	—	28
Sumner, Richard	8	—	—	—	—
Thompson, Courtney	4	1	—	—	4
Tickle, Steve	26 + 1	1	69	1	143
Toomata, Mike	4 + 3	—	—	—	—
Webb, Vinny	4 + 2	—	—	—	—
TOTALS:					
41 players		93	88	8	556

Andy Rippon, two tries in 19 Trafford Borough appearances.

1990-91 MATCH ANALYSIS

Date	Com-petition	H/A	Opponent	Rlt	Score	Tries	Goals	Atten-dance	Referee
26.8.90	LC(1)	A	St. Helens	L	24-56	Garner (2), Abram, Eccles	Tickle (4)	—	—
9.9.90	SD	H	Runcorn H.	W	20-12	Eccles (2), Stewart	Tickle (4)	358	Ollerton
16.9.90	SD	H	Nottingham C.	W	42-4	Mavin (2), Brown, Jones, Stewart, Connor, Iddon	Tickle (7)	341	Campbell
26.9.90	SD	A	Hunslet	L	10-17	Meadows, Mavin	Rippon	—	—
30.9.90	SD	H	Workington T.	W	32-8	Iddon (2), Brown (2), Meadows, Reynolds	Jones (4)	508	Campbell
7.10.90	SD	A	Huddersfield	W	28-12	Mavin (2), Green, Reynolds, Brown, Connor	Tickle (2)	—	—
14.10.90	SD	H	Hunslet	W	48-26	Brown (3), Connor, Meadows, Jones, Galbraith, Stewart, Mavin	Tickle (6)	705	Carter
21.10.90	SD	A	Batley	L	2-10	—	Tickle	—	—
30.10.90	SD	A	Salford	L	12-38	Connor, Mavin	Tickle (2)	—	—
4.11.90	SD	H	Fulham	L	27-28	Galbraith (2), Lowrie, Jones	Tickle (5), Jones (dg)	503	K. Morris
11.11.90	SD	A	Doncaster	L	14-19	Bigg (2)	Tickle (3)	—	—
18.11.90	SD	A	Barrow	L	6-10	Herbert	Tickle	—	—
25.11.90	SD	A	Workington T.	L	6-36	Jones	Tickle	—	—
2.12.90	RT(1)	H	Doncaster	D	10-10	Connor	Tickle (3)	409	Steele
5.12.90	Replay	A	Doncaster	L	7-19	Garner	Tickle, Jones (dg)	—	—
20.12.90	SD	H	Batley	W	20-8	Jones (2), Stewart, Rippon	Jones (2)	405	R. Connolly
1.1.91	SD	A	Chorley	L	8-9	Jones	Tickle (2)	—	—
6.1.91	SD	A	Fulham	L	6-13	—	Tickle (3)	—	—
9.1.91	SD	A	Swinton	L	10-12	Connor, Ramsey	Tickle	—	—
20.1.91	SD	A	Runcorn H.	W	10-6	—	Tickle (4), Platt (2dg)	—	—
3.2.91	SD	H	Doncaster	L	25-29	Reynolds (2), Tickle, Platt, Griffiths	Tickle (2), Platt (dg)	362	Campbell
17.2.91	CC(1)	A	Wakefield T.	L	7-18	Ramsey	Tickle, Platt (dg)	—	—
24.2.91	SD	H	Huddersfield	W	23-22	Flannery, Ramsey, Jones, Stewart	Tickle (3), Platt (dg)	471	Crashley
3.3.91	SD	H	Halifax	L	8-39	Platt	Tickle (2)	2284	Whitelam
10.3.91	SD	H	Barrow	L	20-27	Reynolds (2), Jones	Tickle (4)	177	C. Morris
17.3.91	SD	A	Nottingham C.	W	48-12	Stewart (2), Iddon (2), Reynolds (2), Garner, Connor	Jones (8)	—	—
24.3.91	SD	H	Carlisle	L	14-52	Bigg, Flannery, Garner	Jones	291	Holgate
29.3.91	SD	H[1]	Swinton	L	10-16	Garner	Tickle (3)	836	R. Connolly
1.4.91	SD	H	Chorley	W	21-19	Connor (2), Platt, Iddon	Tickle (2, 1dg)	200	Campbell
4.4.91	SD	A	Carlisle	L	0-28	—	—	—	—
7.4.91	SD	A	Halifax	L	26-66	Bigg, Connor, Platt, Rippon, Thompson	Jones (3)	—	—
10.4.91	SD	H	Salford	L	12-40	Platt, Jones	Tickle (2)	1500	Campbell

[1] at Widnes

WAKEFIELD TRINITY

Ground:	Belle Vue (0924-372445)
Colours:	Red, white and blue
First Season:	1895-96
Nickname:	Dreadnoughts
Chairman:	Rodney Walker
General Manager:	Neil Cadigan
Coach:	David Topliss (May 1987-)
Honours:	**Championship** Winners, 1966-67, 1967-68

Beaten finalists, 1959-60, 1961-62
Division Two Champions, 1903-04
Challenge Cup Winners, 1908-09, 1945-46, 1959-60, 1961-62, 1962-63
Beaten finalists, 1913-14, 1967-68, 1978-79
Yorkshire League Winners, 1909-10, 1910-11, 1945-46, 1958-59, 1959-60, 1961-62, 1965-66
Yorkshire Cup Winners, 1910-11, 1924-25, 1946-47, 1947-48, 1951-52, 1956-57, 1960-61, 1961-62, 1964-65
Beaten finalists, 1926-27, 1932-33, 1934-35, 1936-37, 1939-40, 1945-46, 1958-59, 1973-74, 1974-75, 1990-91
Regal Trophy Beaten finalists, 1971-72

Ged Byrne, eight tries in 29 appearances for Wakefield Trinity.

Records: Attendance: 37,906 Leeds v. Huddersfield (RL Cup SF) 21 Mar, 1936
Home: 28,254 v. Wigan (RL Cup) 24 Mar, 1962
Season
Goals: 163 by N. Fox, 1961-62
Tries: 38 by F. Smith, 1959-60, D. Smith, 1973-74
Points: 407 by N. Fox, 1961-62
Match
Goals: 12 by N. Fox v. Batley, 26 Aug, 1967 and v. Workington T., 19 Sep, 1970; B. Ward v. Hunslet, 6 Feb, 1971
Tries: 7 by F. Smith v. Keighley, 25 Apr, 1959; K. Slater v. Hunslet, 6 Feb, 1971
Points: 33 by N. Fox v. Batley, 26 Aug, 1967
Highest score: 78-9 v. Batley, 1967-68
Highest against: 72-6 v. Wigan, 1986-87

1990-91 PLAYERS' SUMMARY

	App	Tries	Goals	Dr	Pts
Bell, Nigel	31 + 3	3	—	—	12
Byrne, Ged	29	8	—	—	32
Carter, Darren	1 + 1	—	—	—	—
Colbeck, Mark	2	—	—	—	—
Conway, Billy	11 + 5	1	—	—	4
Conway, Mark	34	6	70	2	166
Du Toit, Nick	16 + 7	2	—	—	8
Eden, Phil	9 + 6	3	—	—	12
Glancy, John	25	2	—	—	8
Goddard, Richard	1 + 2	—	—	—	—
Harcombe, Kevin	9	2	31	—	70
Hirst, John	0 + 1	—	—	—	—
Jones, David	35	4	—	—	16
Jowitt, Ian	1	—	—	—	—
Kelly, Andy	13 + 3	2	—	—	8
Lazenby, Tracy	12 + 8	2	1	3	13
Mason, Andy	35	16	—	—	64
Morris, Lynton	3 + 7	—	—	—	—
Mortimer, Chris	22 + 2	2	—	—	8
Perry, Chris	19 + 5	6	—	—	24
Potts, Steve	2	—	—	—	—
Price, Gary	33 + 1	7	—	—	28
Shelford, Adrian	28	2	—	—	8
Slater, Richard	17 + 15	3	—	—	12
Spencer, Gary	15 + 1	—	—	—	—
Thompson, John	31	1	—	—	4
Walker, Andy	2	—	—	—	—
Wilson, Andy	32 + 2	14	—	—	56
Wright, Nigel	0 + 2	—	—	—	—
TOTALS:					
29 players		86	102	5	553

1990-91 MATCH ANALYSIS

Date	Competition	H/A	Opponent	Rlt	Score	Tries	Goals	Attendance	Referee
26.8.90	YC(1)	H	Hunslet	W	28-18	Price, Harcombe, Slater, Perry, M. Conway	Harcombe (4)	3150	Whitelam
2.9.90	YC(2)	H	Halifax	W	26-17	M. Conway, Thompson, Price, Kelly	Harcombe (5)	6492	Holdsworth
9.9.90	SBC	H	Rochdale H.	W	42-6	Mason (2), Eden (2), Price, Bell, Wilson	Harcombe (7)	4034	Smith
12.9.90	YC(SF)	H	Dewsbury	W	25-2	Perry, Wilson, Bell, Mason	Harcombe (4), Lazenby (dg)	5640	Tennant
16.9.90	SBC	H	Oldham	W	17-12	Harcombe, Eden	Harcombe (4), Lazenby (dg)	5643	C. Morris
23.9.90	YC(F)	Leeds Castleford		L	8-11	Mason	Harcombe (2)	(12,420)	Smith
26.9.90	SBC	A	Sheffield E.	L	6-34	Perry	M. Conway	—	—
30.9.90	SBC	A	Hull K.R.	W	18-12	Mason, Shelford, Price	Harcombe (3)	—	—
10.10.90	Tour	H	Australia	L	18-36	Du Toit, Mason, Wilson	M. Conway (3)	7724	Allatt
14.10.90	SBC	A	Castleford	L	12-42	Kelly, Byrne	Harcombe (2)	—	—
21.10.90	SBC	H	Widnes	L	6-16	Wilson	M. Conway	5811	Kershaw
4.11.90	SBC	H	Hull	W	22-6	Mason (2), Byrne, Wilson	M. Conway (3)	6901	Smith
11.11.90	SBC	A	Warrington	W	18-10	Byrne, Mason	M. Conway (4, 2dg)	—	—
18.11.90	RT(P)	A	Carlisle	W	28-10	M. Conway, Mason, Glancy, Jones	M. Conway (6)	—	—
27.11.90	SBC	H	Wigan	W	14-12	Price, Byrne	M. Conway (3)	6225	Kendrew
2.12.90	RT(1)	H	Hunslet	W	40-8	Mason (2), Price, Wilson, Jones, Slater	M. Conway (8)	3531	Ollerton
9.12.90	RT(2)	H	Castleford	L	4-20	Shelford	—	7031	Smith
26.12.90	SBC	A	Featherstone R.	L	8-14	Byrne	M. Conway (2)	—	—
30.12.90	SBC	H	Featherstone R.	L	8-16	M. Conway	M. Conway (2)	6929	Burke
6.1.91	SBC	A	St. Helens	L	14-36	Wilson (2), Perry	M. Conway	—	—
17.1.91	SBC	H	Warrington	D	12-12	Mason	M. Conway (4)	3023	Ollerton
20.1.91	SBC	A	Oldham	L	22-26	Byrne (?), Du Toit, Wilson	M. Conway (3)	—	—
27.1.91	SBC	H	Castleford	L	8-12	W. Conway	M. Conway (2)	5619	Whitfield
3.2.91	SBC	A	Widnes	L	6-34	Mortimer	M. Conway	—	—
17.2.91	CC(1)	H	Trafford B.	W	18-7	Jones, Wilson, M. Conway	M. Conway (3)	2551	C. Morris
23.2.91	CC(2)	A	St. Helens	L	2-16	—	M. Conway	—	—
3.3.91	SBC	A	Wigan	L	8-16	Wilson	M. Conway (2)	—	—
6.3.91	SBC	H	Sheffield E.	W	12-4	M. Conway, Byrne	M. Conway (2)	3639	Gilmour
10.3.91	SBC	H	Hull K.R.	W	26-6	Jones, Wilson, Mortimer, Perry, Mason	M. Conway (3)	3702	Kershaw
13.3.91	SBC	A	Bradford N.	L	10-12	Mason	M. Conway (3)	—	—
17.3.91	SBC	A	Hull	W	14-6	Glancy, Slater	M. Conway (3)	—	—
24.3.91	SBC	H	Bradford N.	L	6-16	Mason	M. Conway	5182	Holdsworth
29.3.91	SBC	A	Leeds	L	0-7	—	—	—	—
1.4.91	SBC	H	Leeds	D	14-14	Bell, Lazenby	M. Conway (3)	6241	Burke
7.4.91	SBC	H	St. Helens	L	8-22	Perry	M. Conway (2)	4650	Smith
10.4.91	SBC	A	Rochdale H.	W	25-6	Wilson (2), Lazenby, Price	M. Conway (3), Lazenby (1, 1dg)	—	—

WARRINGTON

Ground: Wilderspool (0925-35338)
Colours: Primrose and blue
First Season: 1895-96
Nickname: Wire
Chairman: Peter Higham
General
  Manager: Ron Close
Coach: Brian Johnson (Nov 1988-)
Honours: **Championship** Winners, 1947-48,
1953-54, 1954-55
Beaten finalists, 1925-26, 1934-35,
1936-37, 1948-49, 1950-51, 1960-61
League Leaders Trophy Winners,
1972-73
Club Championship (Merit Table)
Winners, 1973-74
Challenge Cup Winners, 1904-05,
1906-07, 1949-50, 1953-54, 1973-74
Beaten finalists, 1900-01, 1903-04,
1912-13, 1927-28, 1932-33, 1935-36,
1974-75, 1989-90
Lancashire League Winners,
1937-38, 1947-48, 1948-49, 1950-51,
1953-54, 1954-55, 1955-56, 1967-68
Lancashire Cup Winners, 1921-22,
1929-30, 1932-33, 1937-38, 1959-60,
1965-66, 1980-81, 1982-83, 1989-90
Beaten finalists, 1906-07, 1948-49,
1950-51, 1967-68, 1985-86, 1987-88
Regal Trophy Winners, 1973-74,
1977-78, 1980-81, 1990-91
Beaten finalists, 1978-79, 1986-87
Premiership Trophy Winners,
1985-86
Beaten finalists, 1976-77, 1986-87
Captain Morgan Trophy Winners,
1973-74
BBC2 Floodlit Trophy Beaten
finalists, 1974-75
Records: Attendance: 35,000 Wigan v. Leigh
(Lancs. Cup Final) 29 Oct, 1949
Home: 34,304 v. Wigan (League)
22 Jan, 1949

Season
Goals: 170 by S. Hesford, 1978-79
Tries: 66 by B. Bevan, 1952-53
Points: 363 by H. Bath, 1952-53
Match
Goals: 14 by H. Palin v. Liverpool
C., 13 Sep, 1950
Tries: 7 by B. Bevan v. Leigh,
29 Mar, 1948 and v. Bramley,
22 Apr, 1953
Points: 33 by G. Thomas v. St.
Helens, 12 Apr, 1909
Highest score: 78-3 v. St. Helens,
1908-09
Highest against: 68-14 v. Hunslet,
1927-28

1990-91 PLAYERS' SUMMARY

	App	Tries	Goals	Dr	Pts
Bateman, Alan	28 + 1	9	—	—	36
Bishop, Paul	10	4	8	—	32
Burke, Tony	11 + 3	—	—	—	—
Chambers, Gary	13 + 5	—	—	—	—
Crompton, Martin	3 + 10	5	—	—	20
Cullen, Paul	28 + 2	2	—	—	8
Darbyshire, Paul	6 + 6	—	—	—	—
Drummond, Des	37	9	—	—	36
Duffy, Don	5 + 3	—	—	—	—
Elliott, David	0 + 1	—	—	—	—
Ellis, Kevin	29 + 2	11	—	—	44
Forster, Mark	15	6	—	—	24
Gregory, Mike	7 + 1	1	—	—	4
Harmon, Neil	32	6	—	—	24
Jackson, Bob	17	1	—	—	4
Kenyon, Neil	1	—	—	—	—
Lyon, David	36	8	73	—	178
McGinty, Billy	31 + 1	4	—	—	16
Mann, Duane	37 + 1	7	—	—	28
Mercer, Gary	35 + 1	7	3	—	34
Myler, Robert	2	—	—	—	—
O'Sullivan, Chris	28	3	—	2	14
Phillips, Rowland	4 + 8	—	—	—	—
Richards, Basil	1 + 4	1	—	—	4
Rudd, Chris	29 + 1	9	11	—	58
Sanderson, Gary	6 + 1	—	—	—	—
Sumner, Phil	7 + 2	—	—	—	—
Tees, Gary	6 + 5	—	—	—	—
Thomas, Mark	5 + 7	1	—	—	4
Thorniley, Tony	21 + 2	8	—	—	32
Thursfield, John	1	—	—	—	—
Turner, Robert	12 + 5	1	19	—	42
Williamson, Paul	4 + 3	1	—	—	4
TOTALS:					
33 players		104	114	2	646

1990-91 MATCH ANALYSIS

Date	Com-petition	H/A	Opponent	Rlt	Score	Tries	Goals	Atten-dance	Referee
26.8.90	LC(1)	H	Chorley	W	36-8	Harmon (2), Lyon, Mercer, Thorniley, Bishop	Lyon (6)	3143	J. Connolly
2.9.90	LC(2)	A	Carlisle	W	28-7	Crompton (2), Bishop, Mercer	Bishop (4), Turner (2)	—	—
9.9.90	SBC	H	Castleford	W	30-12	Rudd (2), Drummond, Crompton, Thorniley	Lyon (5)	5597	C. Morris
12.9.90	LC(SF)	A	Widnes	L	4-20	—	Turner (2)	—	—
16.9.90	SBC	A	Hull K.R.	L	14-20	Rudd, Harmon, Jackson	Turner	—	—
23.9.90	SBC	H	Leeds	L	10-22	McGinty	Lyon (2), Bishop	6647	Whitelam
30.9.90	SBC	A	Sheffield E.	W	20 18	Bishop, Mann, Rudd	Bishop (3), Lyon	—	—
7.10.90	SBC	H	Rochdale H.	W	26-9	Mercer (2), Lyon, Crompton, Bishop	Lyon (3)	5124	Kershaw
13.10.90	SBC	H	Hull	L	2-3	—	Lyon	4499	Smith
20.10.90	SBC	A	Oldham	L	2-4	—	Lyon	—	—
31.10.90	Tour	H	Australia	L	6-26	Thorniley	Lyon	10,200	Carter
4.11.90	SBC	A	Bradford N.	L	16-25	Lyon, Rudd, Mann	Rudd (2)	—	—
11.11.90	SBC	H	Wakefield T.	L	10-18	Ellis, Cullen	Turner	4920	Holdsworth
18.11.90	SBC	A	Hull	L	8-17	Ellis	Turner (2)	—	—
25.11.90	SBC	H	Sheffield E.	W	30-8	Thorniley (2), Bateman, McGinty, Gregory, Mercer	Turner (2), Mercer	3943	Holdsworth
2.12.90	RT(1)	H	Runcorn H.	W	33-7	Bateman (4), McGinty, Harmon	Turner (3), Mercer, O'Sullivan (dg)	2712	Holgate
9.12.90	RT(2)	H	Leigh	W	11-6	Ellis, McGinty	Mercer, O'Sullivan (dg)	3588	Whitfield
16.12.90	RT(3)	H	St. Helens	W	18-12	Lyon, O'Sullivan, Ellis	Rudd (3)	7390	Galtress
19.12.90	SBC	A	Castleford	L	18-22	O'Sullivan, Bateman, Williamson	Turner (3)	—	—
26.12.90	SBC	H	Widnes	L	2-6	—	Rudd	8401	Smith
29.12.90	RT(SF)	Wigan	Widnes	W	8-4	Rudd	Rudd (2)	(7874)	Holdsworth
1.1.91	SBC	A	Wigan	L	14-6	Forster, Richards, Mann	Rudd	—	—
6.1.91	SBC	H	Hull K.R.	W	30-12	Forster (2), Lyon, Mercer, Ellis, Drummond	Turner (3)	1600	Gilmour
12.1.91	RT(F)	Leeds	Bradford N.	W	12-2	Thomas	Lyon (4)	(11,154)	Smith
17.1.91	SBC	A	Wakefield T.	D	12-12	Drummond, O'Sullivan	Lyon (2)	—	—
20.1.91	SBC	H	Featherstone R.	W	16-10	Lyon, Rudd	Lyon (4)	5348	J. Connolly
27.1.91	CC(P)	H	Huddersfield	W	22-4	Turner, Ellis, Crompton	Lyon (5)	3554	Allatt
30.1.91	SBC	A	Leeds	D	20-20	Rudd, Ellis, Drummond	Lyon (4)	—	—
3.2.91	SBC	H	Bradford N.	L	12-13	Drummond	Lyon (4)	5236	Ollerton
17.2.91	CC(1)	A	Ryedale-York	W	8-1	Lyon, Mann	—	—	—
24.2.91	CC(2)	A	Keighley	W	42-10	Drummond (3), Mercer, Forster, Ellis, Thorniley	Lyon (7)	—	—
27.2.91	SBC	A	Rochdale H.	W	18-10	Rudd, Cullen	Lyon (5)	—	—
3.3.91	SBC	H	St. Helens	W	34-20	Mann, Forster, Lyon, Drummond, Ellis	Lyon (7)	7033	Holdsworth
9.3.91	CC(3)	H	Widnes	L	14-26	Bateman, Thorniley	Lyon (3)	8637	Smith
14.3.91	SBC	A	Featherstone R.	L	8-22	Harmon	Lyon (2)	—	—
20.3.91	SBC	A	Widnes	L	6-25	—	Lyon (3)	—	—
26.3.91	SBC	H	Wigan	L	8-26	Mann	Lyon (2)	8437	Whitfield
7.4.91	SBC	H	Oldham	W	22-14	Bateman (2), Ellis, Forster, Mann	Lyon	6849	Holdsworth
14.4.91	SBC	A	St. Helens	L	16-62	Ellis, Thorniley, Harmon	Rudd (2)	—	—

93

WHITEHAVEN

Ground:	Recreation Ground (0946-692915)
Colours:	Chocolate, blue and gold
First Season:	1948-49
Nickname:	Haven
Chairman:	Keith Irving
Secretary:	Keith Nelson
Coach:	Norman Turley (June 1990-Apr 1991)
	Jackie Davidson (June 1991-)
Records:	Attendance: 18,500 v. Wakefield T. (RL Cup) 19 Mar, 1960

Season

Goals: 141 by J. McKeown, 1956-57

Tries: 29 by W. Smith, 1956-57

Points: 291 by J. McKeown, 1956-57

Match

Goals: 11 by W. Holliday v. Hunslet, 31 Mar, 1962

Tries: 6 by V. Gribbin v. Doncaster, 18 Nov, 1984

Points: 25 by W. Holliday v. Hunslet, 31 Mar, 1962

Highest score: 72-6 v. Fulham, 1986-87

Highest against: 92-10 v. Hull K.R., 1989-90

1990-91 PLAYERS' SUMMARY

	App	Tries	Goals	Dr	Pts
Amor, Martin	2 + 3	1	—	—	4
Bailey, Sam	0 + 2	—	—	—	—
Beckwith, Mark	10	—	—	—	—
Blaney, Ged	14 + 1	5	—	—	20
Branthwaite, Steve	4 + 1	—	—	—	—
Brown, Dave	4 + 1	1	—	—	4
Burney, Phil	1 + 2	—	—	—	—
Burney, Steve	2	—	—	—	—
Burns, David	0 + 2	—	—	—	—
Cameron, Graham	26	2	5	2	20
Camroux, Peter	16 + 2	6	—	—	24
Davidson, Alan	3 + 2	—	—	—	—
D'Leny, Tony	11	—	—	—	—
Fisher, Billy	28	4	—	—	16
Fryer, Stephen	6 + 3	—	—	—	—
Gaffney, Mike	4	—	—	—	—
Gribbin, Vince	18	14	—	—	56
Hetherington, Gary	14 + 1	—	—	—	—
Hewer, Gary	2	—	—	—	—
Horo, Shane	30	15	—	—	60
Howse, Steve	16	2	—	—	8
Kendall, Dave	5	—	—	—	—
Lofthouse, Norman	5 + 7	1	2	—	8
Lupton, Graham	2	—	—	—	—
McCartney, Duncan	13	—	—	—	—
McFarlane, Gary	17	7	—	—	28
Maguire, Steve	13	3	1	1	15
Mounsey, Gary	29	2	—	—	8
Pollard, Damien	3	1	—	—	4
Pugsley, Stuart	24	1	—	—	4
Rae, Neil	4 + 3	1	—	—	4
Rea, Steve	1 + 4	1	—	—	4
Richardson, Willie	28 + 2	2	64	—	136
Routledge, John	28	7	—	—	28
Ryan, Mark	5 + 9	—	—	1	1
Short, Tom	6 + 3	—	—	—	—
Solarie, Tony	6	1	—	—	4
Toomata, Mike	6	—	—	—	—
Turley, Norman	10 + 9	1	—	2	6
TOTALS:					
39 players		78	72	6	462

Vince Gribbin, 14 tries in 18 appearances.

Gary Mounsey, an appearance tally of 29 games for Whitehaven scoring two tries.

1990-91 MATCH ANALYSIS

Date	Com-petition	H/A	Opponent	Rlt	Score	Tries	Goals	Atten-dance	Referee
26.8.90	LC(1)	H	Widnes	L	6-70	Routledge	Richardson	4054	Burke
9.9.90	SD	A	Swinton	L	10-40	Horo, Howse	Richardson	—	—
12.9.90	SD	H	Halifax	W	16-8	Blaney, Horo	Richardson (4)	1510	Steele
16.9.90	SD	H	Huddersfield	W	11-8	Richardson, Blaney	Richardson, Turley (dg)	1206	Asquith
23.9.90	SD	A	Fulham	W	30-8	Horo (2), McFarlane, Howse	Richardson (6), Cameron (2dg)	—	—
30.9.90	SD	H	Barrow	W	22-15	Lofthouse, McFarlane, Horo	Richardson (5)	1903	Ollerton
7.10.90	SD	A	Chorley	W	19-4	Fisher, McFarlane, Horo	Richardson (3), Turley (dg)	—	—
14.10.90	SD	H	Doncaster	L	6-10	McFarlane	Richardson	1203	Kendrew
4.11.90	SD	H	Swinton	L	16-24	Camroux, Blaney, McFarlane	Richardson (2)	1174	Whitelam
11.11.90	SD	A	Batley	L	16-26	Horo, Routledge, Cameron	Richardson (2)	—	—
18.11.90	SD	H	Hunslet	W	12-7	Horo, Brown	Lofthouse (2)	802	Tidball
25.11.90	SD	A	Salford	L	6-40	Pugsley	Richardson	—	—
2.12.90	RT(1)	H	Wigan	L	6-24	Horo	Richardson	3459	Crashley
16.12.90	SD	H	Salford	L	12-38	Blaney, McFarlane, Routledge	—	1093	Ollerton
23.12.90	SD	A	Huddersfield	L	18-52	Gribbin, Horo, Mounsey	Cameron (3)	—	—
30.12.90	SD	A	Carlisle	W	14-10	Solarie, Amor	Richardson (3)	—	—
3.1.91	SD	H	Workington T.	L	6-29	Camroux	Richardson	2006	Allatt
6.1.91	SD	A	Hunslet	L	8-17	Routledge, Gribbin	—	—	—
20.1.91	SD	A	Nottingham C.	W	28-14	Horo (2), Routledge, Gribbin, Cameron, McFarlane	Cameron (2)	—	—
23.1.91	SD	H	Nottingham C.	W	20-10	Fisher, Gribbin, Mounsey	Richardson (4)	553	R. Connolly
27.1.91	SD	H	Runcorn H.	W	22-14	Camroux (3), Rae	Richardson (3)	377	Crashley
17.2.91	CC(1)	A	Nottingham C.	W	26-10	Horo, Maguire, Camroux, Turley, Gribbin	Richardson (3)	—	—
24.2.91	CC(2)	A	Halifax	L	12-46	Gribbin (3)	—	—	—
27.2.91	SD	H	Batley	L	2-18	—	Richardson	427	C. Morris
3.3.91	SD	A	Doncaster	L	0-36	—	—	—	—
6.3.91	SD	A	Halifax	L	6-56	Horo	Richardson	—	—
10.3.91	SD	H	Chorley	W	21-16	Gribbin (2), Fisher	Richardson (4), Ryan (dg)	447	Whitelam
17.3.91	SD	A	Runcorn H.	W	30-16	Maguire, Richardson, Fisher, Rae, Blaney	Richardson (5)	—	—
24.3.91	SD	H	Fulham	L	16-20	Routledge, Maguire	Richardson (4)	635	Tidball
29.3.91	SD	A	Workington T.	W	17-12	Horo, Gribbin	Richardson (3), Maguire (1, 1dg)	—	—
7.4.91	SD	A	Barrow	L	16-26	Pollard, Gribbin, Routledge	Richardson (2)	—	—
14.4.91	SD	H	Carlisle	L	12-18	Gribbin (2)	Richardson (2)	1156	Cross

WIDNES

Ground:	Naughton Park (051-495-2250)
Colours:	Black and white
First Season:	1895-96
Nickname:	Chemics
Chairman:	Ray Owen
General Manager:	John Stringer
Coach:	Doug Laughton (Jan 1986-May 1991)
	Frank Myler (June 1991-)

Honours: **Division One** Champions, 1977-78, 1987-88, 1988-89
Championship Beaten finalists, 1935-36
Challenge Cup Winners, 1929-30, 1936-37, 1963-64, 1974-75, 1978-79, 1980-81, 1983-84
Beaten finalists, 1933-34, 1949-50, 1975-76, 1976-77, 1981-82
Lancashire League Winners, 1919-20
Lancashire Cup Winners, 1945-46, 1974-75, 1975-76, 1976-77, 1978-79, 1979-80, 1990-91
Beaten finalists, 1928-29, 1939-40, 1955-56, 1971-72, 1981-82, 1983-84
Regal Trophy Winners, 1975-76, 1978-79
Beaten finalists, 1974-75, 1977-78, 1979-80, 1983-84, 1988-89
Premiership Winners, 1979-80, 1981-82, 1982-83, 1987-88, 1988-89, 1989-90
Beaten finalists, 1977-78, 1990-91
BBC2 Floodlit Trophy Winners, 1978-79
Beaten finalists, 1972-73, 1973-74
Western Division Championship Beaten finalists, 1962-63
Charity Shield Winners, 1988-89, 1989-90, 1990-91
World Club Challenge Winners, 1989-90

Records: Attendance: 24,205 v. St. Helens (RL Cup) 16 Feb, 1961
Season
Goals: 140 by M. Burke, 1978-79
Tries: 58 by M. Offiah, 1988-89
Points: 342 by J. Davies, 1990-91

Match
Goals: 11 by R. Whitfield v. Oldham, 28 Oct, 1965
Tries: 5 by E. Cunningham v. Doncaster, 15 Feb, 1981; J. Basnett v. Hunslet, 17 Oct, 1981 and v. Hull K.R., 2 Nov, 1986; D. Hulme v. Dewsbury, 30 Nov, 1986; A. Currier v. Featherstone R., 25 Sep, 1988; M. Offiah v. Warrington, 15 Mar, 1989
Points: 34 by A. Currier v. Featherstone R., 25 Sep, 1988; J. Davies v. Whitehaven, 26 Aug, 1990
Highest score: 82-0 v. Dewsbury, 1986-87
Highest against: 60-5 v. Oldham, 1927-28

1990-91 PLAYERS' SUMMARY

	App		Tries	Goals	Dr	Pts
Ashurst, Chris	10	+ 2	1	—	—	4
Atcheson, Paul	3		1	—	—	4
Currier, Andy	40	+ 1	23	28	—	148
Critchley, Jason	0	+ 3	—	—	—	—
Davidson, Paul	1	+ 2	—	—	—	—
Davies, Jonathan	32	+ 2	30	110	2	342
Devereux, John	37		23	3	—	98
Dowd, Barry	6	+ 2	—	—	—	—
Eyres, Andy	1		2	—	—	8
Eyres, Richie	32	+ 2	7	—	—	28
Faimalo, Esene	19	+ 5	2	—	—	8
Grima, Joe	32	+ 7	1	—	—	4
Holliday, Les	22	+ 2	1	2	—	8
Howard, Harvey	6	+ 5	—	—	—	—
Hulme, David	38	+ 1	14	—	—	56
Hulme, Paul	27	+ 3	1	—	—	4
Koloto, Emosi	37	+ 1	6	—	—	24
Lia, Ben	2		2	—	—	8
McCurrie, Steve	9	+ 4	2	—	1	9
McKenzie, Phil	41		6	—	—	24
Moriarty, Paul	0	+ 3	—	—	—	—
Myler, Tony	28		6	—	—	24
Offiah, Martin	37		41	—	—	164
Smith, David	6	+ 4	2	—	—	8
Sorensen, Kurt	26	+ 8	2	—	—	8
Spruce, Stuart	11	+ 13	3	—	—	12
Tait, Alan	28		12	—	—	48
Wright, Darren	26	+ 6	9	—	—	36
Wynne, Steve	2	+ 3	3	—	—	12

TOTALS:
29 players .... 200 | 143 | 3 | 1,089

1990-91 MATCH ANALYSIS

Date	Competition	H/A	Opponent	Rlt	Score	Tries	Goals	Attendance	Referee
19.8.90	CS	Swansea FC	Wigan	W	24-8	Davies (3), Devereux, Offiah	Davies (2)	(11,178)	C. Morris
26.8.90	LC(1)	A	Whitehaven	W	70-6	Davies (4), Offiah (3), Tait (2), D. Hulme, Wright, Currier, Myler	Davies (9)	—	—
2.9.90	LC(2)	H	Wigan	W	24-22	Davies, Offiah, Devereux	Davies (6)	14,035	Allatt
9.9.90	SBC	A	Bradford N.	W	14-10	Wright (2)	Davies (3)	—	—
12.9.90	LC(SF)	H	Warrington	W	20-4	Myler, Wright, Tait	Davies (4)	12,028	Burke
16.9.90	SBC	H	Featherstone R.	W	41-14	Devereux (2), A. Eyres (2), Currier, Wright, Ashurst	Davies (6), McCurrie (dg)	6566	Crashley
23.9.90	SBC	A	Hull	L	6-32	Tait	Davies	—	—
29.9.90	LC(F)	Wigan	Salford	W	24-18	Currier, Myler, Smith, Offiah	Davies (4)	(7485)	Burke
2.10.90	SBC	H	Oldham	W	24-16	Devereux, Currier, Tait, Offiah	Davies (4)	7361	Kershaw
5.10.90	SBC	H	Castleford	W	46-4	Offiah (3), D. Hulme (2), Myler, Currier, McKenzie, Holliday	Davies (5)	4185	Burke
14.10.90	SBC	A	Hull K.R.	L	20-22	Myler (2), Davies, Devereux	Davies (2)	—	—
21.10.90	SBC	A	Wakefield T.	W	16-6	Davies (2), Koloto	Davies (2)	—	—
3.11.90	SBC	H	Leeds	W	26-8	Offiah, Devereux, Koloto, D. Hulme, Sorensen	Davies (3)	6163	Holdsworth
18.11.90	Tour	H	Australia	L	8-15	Davies	Davies (2)	14,666	Kendrew
25.11.90	SBC	A	Oldham	W	24-18	Davies (2), Wright, Offiah, Devereux	Davies (2)	—	—
1.12.90	RT(1)	H	Hull	W	24-16	Devereux (2), Davies, Offiah, D. Hulme	Davies (2)	4940	Kershaw
8.12.90	RT(2)	H	Leeds	W	22-6	Currier (2), D. Hulme, Offiah	Davies (3)	3465	Galtress
16.12.90	RT(3)	H	Batley	W	56-6	Offiah (4), Currier (3), Davies, Atcheson, Faimalo, Tait	Davies (6)	6656	Burke
19.12.90	SBC	H	Hull K.R.	W	28-8	Offiah (4), Currier	Davies (4)	5344	Burke
26.12.90	SBC	A	Warrington	W	6-2	D. Hulme	Currier	—	—
29.12.90	RT(SF)	Wigan	Warrington	L	4-8	Offiah	—	7874	Holdsworth
1.1.91	SBC	H	St. Helens	W	14-8	Offiah, Smith, Devereux	Devereux	10,494	Kershaw
6.1.91	SBC	A	Castleford	L	10-20	R. Eyres (2)	Holliday	—	—
19.1.91	SBC	H	Wigan	L	14-22	Offiah (2), Spruce	Holliday	7365	C. Morris
30.1.91	SBC	A	Rochdale H.	W	60-6	R. Eyres (2), Lia (2), Devereux (2), Currier, Faimalo, D. Hulme, Tait	Currier (8)	—	—
3.2.91	SBC	H	Wakefield T.	W	34-6	Offiah (3), McKenzie, D. Hulme, Devereux, Spruce	Currier (3)	6310	Smith
10.2.91	CC(1)	A	Doncaster	W	30-4	Devereux (2), Currier, Tait, McKenzie	Currier (3), Devereux (2)	—	—
17.2.91	SBC	A	Leeds	W	38-0	Currier (3), Offiah, Grima, Spruce, Devereux	Currier (5)	—	—
24.2.91	CC(2)	A	Barrow	W	28-4	Offiah (2), Tait (2), D. Hulme, R. Eyres	Currier (2)	—	—
27.2.91	SBC	H	Hull	W	28-2	Tait (2), Offiah, Devereux, Sorensen	Currier (4)	8404	Kershaw
3.3.91	SBC	H	Sheffield E.	L	14-23	Davies (2), McKenzie	Currier	6041	Galtress
9.3.91	CC(3)	A	Warrington	W	26-14	D. Hulme, Koloto, Offiah, Currier	Davies (5)	—	—
17.3.91	SBC	H	Bradford N.	W	32-14	Davies (4), Wright, D. Hulme, Offiah	Davies (2)	7282	Kershaw

(continued on page 104)

WIGAN

Ground: Central Park (0942-31321)
Colours: Cherry and white
First Season: 1895-96
Nickname: Riversiders
Chairman: Maurice Lindsay
Secretary: Mary Charnock
Coach: John Monie (Sep 1989-)
Honours: **Championship** Winners, 1908-09, 1921-22, 1925-26, 1933-34, 1945-46, 1946-47, 1949-50, 1951-52, 1959-60
Beaten finalists, 1909-10, 1910-11, 1911-12, 1912-13, 1923-24, 1970-71
League Leaders Trophy Winners, 1970-71
Division One Champions, 1986-87, 1989-90, 1990-91
Challenge Cup Winners, 1923-24, 1928-29, 1947-48, 1950-51, 1957-58, 1958-59, 1964-65, 1984-85, 1987-88, 1988-89, 1989-90, 1990-91
Beaten finalists, 1910-11, 1919-20, 1943-44, 1945-46, 1960-61, 1962-63, 1965-66, 1969-70, 1983-84
Lancashire League Winners, 1901-02, 1908-09, 1910-11, 1911-12, 1912-13, 1913-14, 1914-15, 1920-21, 1922-23, 1923-24, 1925-26, 1945-46, 1946-47, 1949-50, 1951-52, 1958-59, 1961-62, 1969-70
Lancashire War League Winners, 1940-41
Lancashire Cup Winners, 1905-06, 1908-09, 1909-10, 1912-13, 1922-23, 1928-29, 1938-39, 1946-47, 1947-48, 1948-49, 1949-50, 1950-51, 1951-52, 1966-67, 1971-72, 1973-74, 1985-86, 1986-87, 1987-88, 1988-89
Beaten finalists, 1913-14, 1914-15, 1925-26, 1927-28, 1930-31, 1934-35, 1935-36, 1936-37, 1945-46, 1953-54, 1957-58, 1977-78, 1980-81, 1984-85
Regal Trophy Winners, 1982-83, 1985-86, 1986-87, 1988-89, 1989-90
Premiership Winners, 1986-87
BBC2 Floodlit Trophy Winners, 1968-69. Beaten finalists, 1969-70
Charity Shield Winners, 1985-86, 1987-88. Beaten finalists, 1988-89, 1989-90, 1990-91

World Club Challenge Winners, 1987-88
War League Championship Winners, 1943-44
Beaten finalists, 1940-41
Records: Attendance: 47,747 v. St. Helens (League) 27 Mar, 1959
Season
Goals: 176 by F. Griffiths, 1958-59
Tries: 62 by J. Ring, 1925-26
Points: 394 by F. Griffiths, 1958-59
Match
Goals: 22 by J. Sullivan v. Flimby & Fothergill, 14 Feb, 1925
Tries: 7 by J. Ring v. Flimby & Fothergill, 14 Feb, 1925; v. Salford, 13 Apr, 1925 and v. Pemberton R., 12 Feb, 1927; G. Ratcliffe v. Liverpool S., 23 Aug, 1947; W. Boston v. Dewsbury, 20 Aug, 1955 and v. Salford, 30 Apr. 1962; G. Vigo v. St. Helens, 21 Aug, 1976
Points: 44 by J. Sullivan v. Flimby & Fothergill, 14 Feb, 1925
Highest score: 116-0 v. Flimby & Fothergill, 1924-25
Highest against: 58-3 v. Leeds, 1972-73

1990-91 PLAYERS' SUMMARY

	App	Tries	Goals	Dr	Pts
Bell, Dean	36 + 1	11	—	—	44
Betts, Denis	37 + 2	12	—	—	48
Blakely, Steve	0 + 1	1	—	—	4
Botica, Frano	30	18	126	—	324
Bridge, Russ	1	—	—	—	—
Byrne, Ged	3 + 1	—	—	—	—
Clarke, Phil	11 + 8	1	—	—	4
Dermott, Martin	29 + 1	6	—	—	24
Edwards, Shaun	33 + 1	16	1	—	66
Forshaw, Mike	2 + 10	1	—	—	4
Gartland, Paul	1	—	—	—	—
Gildart, Ian	8 + 14	1	—	—	4
Gilfillan, John	1	—	—	—	—
Goodway, Andy	19 + 8	11	—	—	44
Goulding, Bobby	12 + 6	3	5	3	25
Gregory, Andy	29 + 1	4	—	1	17
Hampson, Steve	32	2	12	—	32
Hanley, Ellery	33	29	—	1	117
Iro, Kevin	27	16	—	—	64
Lucas, Ian	30 + 1	1	—	—	4
Lydon, Joe	21 + 3	11	21	—	86
Marshall, Dave	4 + 3	—	—	—	—
Myers, Dave	32 + 4	19	—	—	76
O'Donnell, Augustine	1	—	—	—	—
Platt, Andy	32	1	—	—	4
Preston, Mark	7 + 1	2	—	—	8
Skerrett, Kelvin	27 + 2	3	—	—	12
Stazicker, Ged	5 + 6	1	—	—	4
Tyrer, Sean	1 + 2	—	—	3	6
Wane, Shaun	1	—	—	—	—
West, Graeme	2	1	—	—	4
TOTALS: 31 players		171	168	5	1,025

1990-91 MATCH ANALYSIS

Date	Competition	H/A	Opponent	Rlt	Score	Tries	Goals	Attendance	Referee
19.8.90	CS	Swansea FC	Widnes	L	8-24	Botica	Botica (2)	(11,178)	C. Morris
26.8.90	LC(1)	H	Barrow	W	70-8	Edwards (4), Bell (2), Dermott (2), Forshaw, Betts, Botica, Hampson, Goodway	Botica(8), Lydon	8377	Campbell
2.9.90	LC(2)	A	Widnes	L	22-24	Gregory, Bell, Goodway	Lydon (5)	—	—
9.9.90	SBC	H	Sheffield E.	D	18-18	Goulding, Myers, Goodway	Goulding (2), Lydon	10,903	Crashley
16.9.90	SBC	A	Castleford	W	38-18	Botica (2), Myers (2), Iro, Edwards, Betts	Botica (4), Goulding	—	—
23.9.90	SBC	H	Rochdale H.	W	24-2	Bell (2), Botica, Lydon	Botica (2), Goulding (2)	11,248	Campbell
30.9.90	SBC	A	Bradford N.	L	30-31	Myers, Lydon, Edwards, Dermott, Betts	Lydon (3), Botica (2)	—	—
7.10.90	SBC	A	Hull	L	4-24	Skerrett	—	—	—
14.10.90	Tour	H	Australia	L	6-34	Edwards	Lydon	24,814	C. Morris
4.11.90	SBC	H	Oldham	W	38-15	Myers (2), Preston, Lydon, Gregory, Hanley, Hampson	Hampson (3), Lydon (2)	13,917	Tennant
13.11.90	SBC	A	Hull K.R.	W	36-6	Hanley (2), Goodway, Betts, Lydon, Edwards	Lydon (5), Hampson	—	—
17.11.90	SBC	H	Featherstone R.	W	24-4	Hanley (2), Edwards, Lydon, Goulding	Hampson (2)	7539	Kershaw
27.11.90	SBC	A	Wakefield T.	L	12-14	Goodway (2)	Lydon (2)	—	—
2.12.90	RT(1)	A	Whitehaven	W	24-6	Bell (2), Iro, Platt	Hampson (4)	—	—
9.12.90	RT(2)	H	Keighley	W	36-16	Iro (3), Hanley (2), Goodway	Botica (6)	5955	Burke
15.12.90	RT(3)	H	Bradford N.	L	6-12	Goodway	Botica	5285	Holdsworth
23.12.90	SBC	H	Leeds	W	22-16	Hanley, Botica, Betts, Goulding	Botica (3)	14,784	Holdsworth
26.12.90	SBC	A	St. Helens	W	28-15	Botica, Edwards, Iro, Myers, Hanley	Botica (4)	—	—
1.1.91	SBC	H	Warrington	L	6-14	Bell	Botica	15,916	Carter
6.1.91	SBC	A	Sheffield E.	W	46-4	Edwards (2), Hanley (2), Iro, Lydon, Botica, Betts	Botica (3), Hampson (2), Lydon, Edwards	—	—
19.1.91	SBC	A	Widnes	W	22-14	Hanley (3)	Botica (5)	—	—
2.2.91	SBC	H	Hull K.R.	W	34-4	Lydon (2), Hanley, Iro, Myers	Botica (7)	7340	Burke
12.2.91	CC(1)	A	Castleford	W	28-4	Botica (2), Iro, Edwards, Myers	Botica (4)	—	—
24.2.91	CC(2)	A	Rochdale H.	W	72-4	Hanley (6), Botica, Bell, Betts, Lucas, Edwards, Myers	Botica (12)	—	—
3.3.91	SBC	H	Wakefield T.	W	16-8	Preston, Myers, Hanley	Botica (2)	11,618	Carter
10.3.91	CC(3)	H	Bradford N.	W	32-2	Dermott, Botica, Gregory, Iro, Bell	Botica (6)	17,734	Holdsworth
13.3.91	SBC	H	Hull	W	34-12	Botica (3), Lydon (2), Betts	Botica (5)	15,239	Galtress
17.3.91	SBC	A	Rochdale H.	W	44-16	Stazicker, Myers, Hanley, Iro, Gregory, Bell, Goodway	Botica (8)	—	—
23.3.91	CC(SF)	Bolton	Oldham	W	30-16	Edwards, Hanley, Goodway, Iro, Botica	Botica (5)	(19,057)	Smith
26.3.91	SBC	A	Warrington	W	26-8	Hanley (2), Lydon, Myers	Botica (5)	—	—
29.3.91	SBC	A	Featherstone R.	W	24-16	Iro (2), Hanley (2)	Botica (4)	—	—
1.4.91	SBC	A	Oldham	W	10-4	Betts	Botica (3)	—	—
4.4.91	SBC	H	St. Helens	W	28-14	Myers (2), Skerrett, Dermott	Botica (6)	17,580	Carter

(continued on page 104)

WORKINGTON TOWN

Ground:	Derwent Park (0900-603609)
Colours:	Blue and white
First Season:	1945-46
Nickname:	Town
Chairman:	Kevan Gorge
Secretary:	John Bell
Coach:	Ray Ashton (June 1990-)

Honours: **Championship** Winners, 1950-51
Beaten finalists, 1957-58
Challenge Cup Winners, 1951-52
Beaten finalists, 1954-55, 1957-58
Lancashire Cup Winners, 1977-78
Beaten finalists, 1976-77, 1978-79, 1979-80
Western Division Championship Winners, 1962-63

Records: Attendance: 17,741 v. Wigan (RL Cup) 3 Mar, 1965. There was a crowd of 20,403 at Borough Park for a RL Cup-tie v. St. Helens on 8 Mar, 1952

Season
Goals: 186 by L. Hopkins, 1981-82
Tries: 49 by J. Lawrenson, 1951-52
Points: 438 by L. Hopkins, 1981-82

Match
Goals: 11 by I. MacCorquodale v. Blackpool B., 6 Jan, 1973
Tries: 7 by I. Southward v. Blackpool B., 17 Sep, 1955
Points: 33 by I. Southward v. Blackpool B., 17 Sep, 1955
Highest score: 62-15 v. Hunslet, 1963-64
Highest against: 68-0 at Wigan, 1986-87

1990-91 PLAYERS' SUMMARY

	App	Tries	Goals	Dr	Pts
Ainsworth, Gary	17 + 2	8	—	—	32
Armstrong, Colin	31	4	25	4	70
Armstrong, Malcolm	7 + 2	—	—	—	—
Ashton, Ray	29 + 5	5	—	13	33
Beattie, John	0 + 1	—	—	—	—
Burgess, Glen	4 + 1	—	—	—	—
Charlton, Jason	4 + 2	1	—	—	4
Chick, Stuart	5	—	—	—	—
Falcon, Colin	20	6	—	—	24
Graham, John	1 + 1	—	—	—	—
Kerr, Ken	22	9	—	—	36
Kitchin, Wayne	9 + 2	5	3	—	26
Lowden, David	34	8	14	2	62
McGuirk, Gary	8 + 9	2	—	—	8
McLean, Ian	30	10	6	—	52
McMullen, Alan	34 + 2	—	—	—	—
Oglanby, Martin	19 + 8	4	—	—	16
Penrice, Paul	21 + 7	7	—	—	28
Riley, Peter	16 + 2	1	—	—	4
Rooney, Neil	24 + 5	6	—	—	24
Roskell, Mark	19 + 4	1	—	—	4
Scott, Ian	17 + 6	2	—	—	8
Simpson, Colin	3	—	1	—	2
Smith, Gary	19 + 1	1	—	—	4
Stansfield, Ivan	13	—	—	—	—
Sullivan, Joe	4 + 2	—	—	—	—
Tubman, Keith	1 + 1	—	—	—	—
Tuimavave, Paddy	16 + 1	10	—	1	41
Wear, Steve	21	6	42	4	112
Wilkes, Mark	6	3	—	—	12
Williams, Dean	14 + 2	—	—	—	—

TOTALS:
31 players		99	91	24	602

Player-coach Ray Ashton, 33 points in a 34-match debut season for Workington Town.

1990-91 MATCH ANALYSIS

Date	Competition	H/A	Opponent	Rlt	Score	Tries	Goals	Attendance	Referee
26.8.90	LC(1)	A	Carlisle	L	18-38	Kitchin (2), Ashton	Kitchin (3)	—	—
9.9.90	SD	H	Fulham	W	9-4	Oglanby	Lowden (2), Ashton (dg)	771	J. Connolly
16.9.90	SD	A	Salford	L	8-30	Falcon	Lowden (2)	—	—
23.9.90	SD	H	Dewsbury	W	15-9	Penrice, McLean, McGuirk	Ashton (3dg)	728	K. Morris
30.9.90	SD	A	Trafford B.	L	8-32	Rooney	Lowden, McLean	—	—
5.10.90	SD	H	Carlisle	L	8-13	Oglanby, Falcon	—	1839	Holgate
14.10.90	SD	A	Nottingham C.	W	23-12	McLean, Roskell, Penrice, Falcon	McLean (3), Ashton (dg)	—	—
21.10.90	SD	H	Keighley	W	42-0	Wilkes (2), Lowden, Rooney, McGuirk, Charlton, Wear	Wear (5), McLean (2)	804	Allatt
4.11.90	SD	A	Huddersfield	D	16-16	Penrice, Wear	Wear (3), Ashton (2dg)	—	—
11.11.90	SD	H	Halifax	W	24-16	Oglanby, Lowden, Wilkes, Rooney	Lowden (2), Armstrong (2)	1351	C. Morris
18.11.90	SD	A	Ryedale-York	L	0-22	—	—	—	—
25.11.90	SD	H	Trafford B.	W	36-6	Tuimavave (3), Kerr, McLean, Ashton, Rooney	Lowden (4)	755	Burke
2.12.90	RT(1)	A	Bradford N.	L	11-12	McLean, Falcon	Lowden, Ashton (dg)	—	—
16.12.90	SD	A	Dewsbury	L	6-7	Ashton	Lowden	—	—
23.12.90	SD	H	Hunslet	W	22-12	Kerr, Wear, McLean	Armstrong (5)	864	Campbell
3.1.91	SD	A	Whitehaven	W	29-6	Kerr (2), Scott, Lowden, Armstrong	Armstrong (4, 1dg)	—	—
6.1.91	SD	H	Leigh	W	10-3	Kitchin	Armstrong (1, 2dg), Ashton (dg), Tuimavave (dg)	1583	C. Morris
20.1.91	SD	H	Bramley	W	52-9	Kerr (2), Tuimavave (2), Rooney, Scott, Lowden, Penrice, Ainsworth, Kitchin	Armstrong (6)	1001	Carter
27.1.91	CC(P)	A	Carlisle	W	9-8	McLean	Armstrong (2), Wear (dg)	—	—
30.1.91	SD	A	Leigh	L	12-18	Armstrong, Ashton, Ainsworth	—	—	—
3.2.91	SD	H	Huddersfield	W	28-17	Tuimavave (2), Falcon (2), Ainsworth	Armstrong (2), Lowden, Ashton (2dg)	1148	McCallum (Aus)
17.2.91	CC(1)	H	Hull K.R.	W	18-12	Lowden, Armstrong, Tuimavave	Wear (3)	3380	Galtress
24.2.91	CC(2)	H	Oldham	L	15-20	McLean, Tuimavave	Wear (3), Lowden (dg)	5549	Holdsworth
3.3.91	SD	H	Nottingham C.	W	38-4	Ainsworth (3), Kitchin, McLean, Kerr	Wear (7)	1169	K. Morris
7.3.91	SD	A	Keighley	W	15-10	Tuimavave, Wear	Wear (3, 1dg)	—	—
10.3.91	SD	A	Fulham	W	7-6	Penrice	Simpson, Lowden (dg)	—	—
17.3.91	SD	H	Salford	W	7-0	Kerr	Wear (1, 1dg)	2743	Tennant
24.3.91	SD	A	Halifax	L	14-22	Oglanby, Ashton, Lowden	Wear	—	—
29.3.91	SD	H	Whitehaven	L	12-17	Armstrong	Wear (4)	3233	Whitelam
1.4.91	SD	A	Carlisle	W	12-5	Rooney, Ainsworth	Wear (2)	—	—
4.4.91	SD	A	Bramley	W	18-6	Wear, Riley, McLean	Armstrong (2), Wear	—	—
7.4.91	SD	H	Ryedale-York	W	12-6	Lowden, Kerr	Armstrong (1, 1dg), Aston (dg)	1978	Ollerton
14.4.91	SD	A	Hunslet	L	14-15	Lowden, Wear	Wear (3)	—	—
21.4.91	SDP(1)	A	Swinton	W	19-12	Ainsworth, Smith, Penrice	Wear (3), Ashton (dg)	—	—
5.5.91	SDP(SF)	A	Salford	D	9-9	McLean	Wear (2, 1dg)	—	—
7.5.91	SDP(SF) Replay	H	Salford	L	6-26	Penrice	Wear	5500	Tennant

Paul Lyman, 11 tries in 25 appearances in 1990-91 for Hull K.R.

Mark Conway, a 1990-91 tally of 166 points in 34 appearances for Wakefield Trinity.

HALIFAX MATCH ANALYSIS (continued)

Date	Competition	H/A	Opponent	Rlt	Score	Tries	Goals	Attendance	Referee
10.3.91	CC(3)	H	St. Helens	L	16-24	Keebles, Ramshaw, Brown	Brown (2)	9672	Whitfield
13.3.91	SD	H	Barrow	W	48-10	Austin (2), Ramshaw (2), Platt, Bell, Irvine, Brown, Silva	Platt (6)	3343	Campbell
17.3.91	SD	A	Chorley	W	22-13	Wood, Austin, George, Ramshaw, Sharp	Platt	—	—
20.3.91	SD	A	Doncaster	L	6-12	Ramshaw	Brown	—	—
24.3.91	SD	H	Workington T.	W	22-14	Sharp (2), Milner, Wilson	Brown (3)	5322	Carter
1.4.91	SD	A	Dewsbury	W	26-0	Hutchinson (2), Irvine, Austin, Ramshaw	Brown (3)	—	—
4.4.91	SD	H	Swinton	W	42-14	Austin (3), Wood (2), Bell, Scott, Hutchinson	Smith (4), Wood	5338	Tennant
7.4.91	SD	H	Trafford B.	W	66-26	Austin (6), Wood (2), Hill (2), Sharp, McCallion	Silva (9)	3909	J. Connolly
10.4.91	SD	H	Leigh	W	24-18	Brown (2), Smith, Wood	Smith (4)	4487	C. Morris
21.4.91	SDP(1)	H	Fulham	W	42-24	Wood (4), Sharp, Lyons, Wilson, Ramshaw	Platt (3), Smith (2)	4385	Galtress
5.5.91	SDP(SF)	H	Leigh	W	32-8	Austin (2), Smith (2), Brown, Wilson	Silva (4)	5885	Holdsworth
12.5.91	SDP(F)	Man U. FC	Salford	L	20-27	Southernwood, Wilson, Hill, Wood	Platt (2)	(—)	Galtress

SALFORD MATCH ANALYSIS (continued)

Date	Competition	H/A	Opponent	Rlt	Score	Tries	Goals	Attendance	Referee
17.3.91	SD	A	Workington T.	L	0-7	—	—	—	—
21.3.91	SD	H	Batley	W	32-14	Hadley, Williams, Gibson, O'Loughlin, Fell	Kerry (6)	1643	Holgate
24.3.91	SD	A	Bramley	W	27-18	Gibson (2), Birkett, Kerry	Kerry (5), Cassidy (dg)	—	—
29.3.91	SD	H	Leigh	W	18-11	Cassidy, Birkett, Hadley	Kerry (3)	3122	Smith
1.4.91	SD	A	Swinton	D	10-10	Birkett, O'Loughlin	Kerry	—	—
10.4.91	SD	A	Trafford B.	W	40-12	Fell (2), Hadley (2), Worrall, Bentley, Dean	Kerry (6)	—	—
14.4.91	SD	H	Keighley	W	30-0	Hadley (3), Blease, Worrall	Kerry (5)	2274	Steele
21.4.91	SDP(1)	H	Carlisle	W	26-12	O'Neill (2), Hadley, Gibson	Kerry (5)	1697	C. Morris
5.5.91	SDP(SF)	H	Workington T.	D	9-9	Hadley	Kerry (2), Lee (dg)	4291	Tennant
7.5.91	SDP(SF) Replay	A	Workington T.	W	26-6	Birkett (2), Kerry, Evans, Hadley	Kerry (2, 1dg), Lee (dg)	—	—
12.5.91	SDP(F)	Man U. FC	Halifax	W	27-20	Kerry (2), Evans, Gilfillan	Kerry (4, 1dg), Cassidy (dg), Lee (dg)	(—)	Galtress

WIDNES MATCH ANALYSIS (continued)

Date	Com-petition	H/A	Opponent	Rlt	Score	Tries	Goals	Atten-dance	Referee
20.3.91	SBC	H	Warrington	W	25-6	Currier (2), Davies, Offiah	Davies (4, 1dg)	8165	J. Connolly
24.3.91	SBC	A	Featherstone R.	W	27-22	Wynne (2), Davies, R. Eyres, Koloto	Davies (3, 1dg)	—	—
30.3.91	CC(SF)	Wigan	St. Helens	L	2-19	—	Davies	(16,109)	Holdsworth
1.4.91	SBC	A	St. Helens	W	20-12	McCurrie, D. Hulme, Wynne	Davies (4)	—	—
6.4.91	SBC	A	Sheffield E.	W	18-13	Davies, Offiah	Davies (5)	—	—
9.4.91	SBC	A	Wigan	L	6-26	Davies	Davies	—	—
14.4.91	SBC	H	Rochdale H.	W	44-20	Davies, D. Hulme, P. Hulme, Currier, McKenzie, Koloto, Offiah, Devereux	Davies (6)	4634	Tennant
21.4.91	PT(1)	H	Bradford N.	W	46-10	Davies (2), Currier (2), Wright (2), Koloto, Devereux, McKenzie	Davies (5)	5419	Holdsworth
5.5.91	PT(SF)	H	Featherstone R.	W	42-28	Devereux (3), Offiah (2), Davies, McCurrie, Currier	Davies (4), Currier	8358	Smith
12.5.91	PT(F)	Man U. FC	Hull	L	4-14	Offiah	—	(42,043)	Holdsworth

WIGAN MATCH ANALYSIS (continued)

Date	Com-petition	H/A	Opponent	Rlt	Score	Tries	Goals	Atten-dance	Referee
7.4.91	SBC	H	Castleford	W	24-4	Myers (2), Hanley, West	Botica (4)	13,948	Kershaw
9.4.91	SBC	H	Widnes	W	26-6	Botica, Edwards, Betts, Clarke	Botica (5)	29,763	Tennant
11.4.91	SBC	H	Bradford N.	D	18-18	Betts, Skerrett	Botica (5)	19,112	Allatt
13.4.91	SBC	A	Leeds	W	20-8	Goodway, Dermott, Betts	Botica (2), Goulding (3dg), Hanley (dg)	—	—
21.4.91	PT(1)	H	Featherstone R.	L	26-31	Iro (2), Myers, Blakely, Gildart	Tyrer (3)	9046	Whitfield
27.4.91	CC(F)	Wem-bley	St. Helens	W	13-8	Myers, Botica	Botica (2), Gregory (dg)	(75,532)	Smith

Salford scrum half Steve Kerry, top goals and points
scorer for 1990-91.

RECORDS

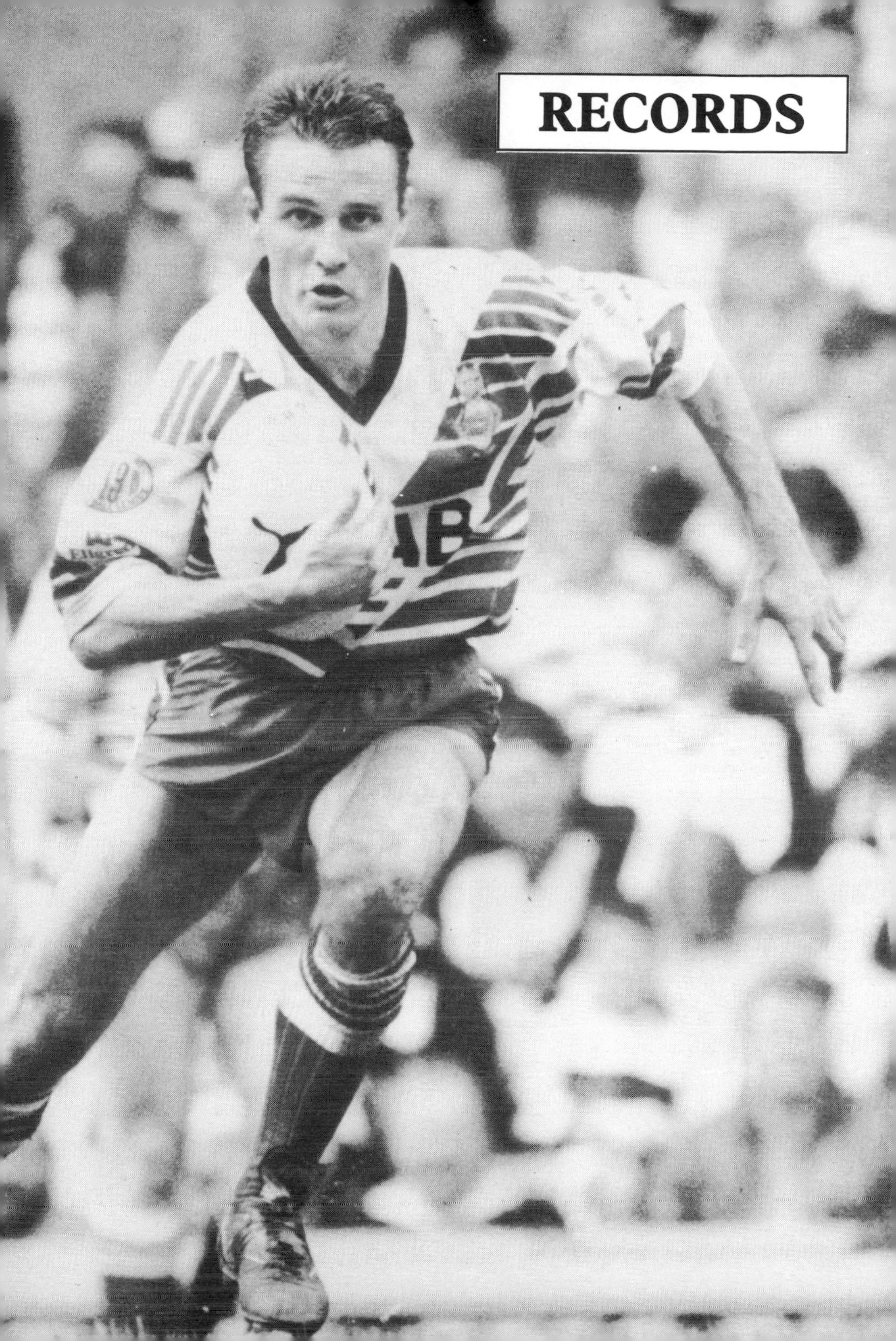

LEADING SCORERS FOR 1990-91

TOP TEN TRIES

1. Martin Offiah (Widnes) 49
2. Greg Austin (Halifax)................................ 47
3. Martin Wood (Halifax).............................. 31
   Adrian Hadley (Salford)............................ 31
5. Jonathan Davies (Widnes).......................... 30
6. Ellery Hanley (Wigan).............................. 29
7. Les Quirk (St. Helens).............................. 26
   Allan Hunte (St. Helens) 26
9. Garry Schofield (Leeds) 25
10. Graham Steadman (Castleford) 23
    Andy Currier (Widnes)............................. 23
    John Devereux 23

● Others with 20 or more: Anthony Sullivan (Hull K.R.) 22; David Fell (Salford) 21; Steve Kerry (Salford), David Myers (Wigan), Owen Simpson (Featherstone R.) 20.

TOP TEN GOALS
(Including drop goals)

1. Steve Kerry (Salford)............................... 177
2. Frano Botica (Wigan) 126
3. Paul Eastwood (Hull) 119
4. Jonathan Davies (Widnes) 112
5. Simon Irving (Leeds)................................ 99
6. Graham Sullivan (Ryedale-York) 94
7. Paul Loughlin (St. Helens) 94
8. Alan Platt (Halifax)................................. 91
9. Barry Vickers (Carlisle) 88
10. Tim Lumb (Hunslet)................................ 85

A top ten try chart placing for Graham Steadman.

TOP FIVE DROP GOALS

1. Ray Ashton (Workington T.) 13
   Dean Carroll (Doncaster)............................. 13
3. Mark Lee (Salford) 10
4. Billy Platt (Trafford B.) 8
   Paul Topping (Leigh) 8
   Barry Ashall (Swinton)................................ 8

TOP FIVE POINTS

		T	G	DG	Pts
1.	Steve Kerry (Salford)........	20	170	7	427
2.	Jonathan Davies (Widnes)..	30	110	2	342
3.	Frano Botica (Wigan)........	18	126	0	324
4.	Paul Eastwood (Hull)........	14	119	0	294
5.	Simon Irving (Leeds)	11	99	0	242

Key:
SBC .... Stones Bitter Championship
SD............... Second Division
PT .... Premiership Trophy
SDP............ Second Division Premiership
LC............... Lancashire Cup
YC............... Yorkshire Cup
RT .... Regal Trophy
CC.............. Challenge Cup
CS .... Charity Shield
NA .... Non-appearance

OUTSTANDING SCORING FEATS IN 1990-91

INDIVIDUAL

Most tries in a match:
6 by Greg Austin (Hull K.R.) v.
    *Nottingham C. .... YC
    Greg Austin (Halifax) v. Trafford B........... SD
    Ellery Hanley (Wigan) at Rochdale H. CC
5 by Anthony Sullivan (Hull K.R.) v.
    *Nottingham C. .... YC
    Martin Offiah (Britain) v. France .... Test
*Away tie played at Doncaster

Most goals in a match:
14 by Colin Armstrong (Hull K.R.) v.
    *Nottingham C. .... YC
13 by Alan Platt (Halifax) v. Runcorn H. .... SD
12 by Frano Botica (Wigan) at Rochdale H........ CC
11 by Greg Pearce (Fulham) v. Runcorn H. LC
10 by Steve Kerry (Salford) v. Barrow .... SD
    Simon Irving (Leeds) v. Rochdale H. .... SBC
    Graham Steadman (Castleford)
    at Rochdale H. .... SBC
*Away tie played at Doncaster

Most points in a match:

34 by Jonathan Davies (Widnes) at Whitehaven .. LC
32 by Graham Steadman (Castleford)
   at Rochdale H. .... SBC
30 by Alan Platt (Halifax) v. Runcorn H. .... SD
   Norman Barrow (Runcorn H.) v. Keighley SD

TEAM

Highest score:

Nottingham C. 6 v. Hull K.R. 100* .... YC
*Away tie played at Doncaster.
● There was a total of 40 matches in which a team scored
50 points or more, compared with 52 in the previous
season. The other 60-plus scores were:

Home:
Halifax 82 v. Runcorn H. 8 .... SD
Salford 76 v. Barrow 10 .... SD
Wigan 70 v. Barrow 8 LC
Leigh 66 v. Chorley 5 .... RT
Halifax 66 v. Trafford B. 26 .... SD
Dewsbury 64 v. Nottingham C. 0 .... SD
Leeds 64 v. Rochdale H. 4 .... SBC
Sheffield E. 62 v. Hull K.R. 16 .... SBC
St. Helens 62 v. Warrington 16 .... SBC
Great Britain 60 v. France 4 .... Test

Away:
Rochdale H. 12 v. Castleford 76 .... SBC
Rochdale H. 4 v. Wigan 72 CC
Whitehaven 6 v. Widnes 70 LC
Runcorn H. 0 v. Halifax 62 .... SD
Rochdale H. 6 v. Widnes 60 .... SBC

Highest score by losing team:

St. Helens 54 v. Featherstone R. 38 .... SBC
● There was a total of 54 matches in which a team scored
20 points or more and lost, compared with 61 the
previous season.

High-scoring draws:

Hull K.R. 26 v. St. Helens 26 .... SBC
Leeds 20 v. Warrington 20 .... SBC
● Two matches the previous season also produced draws
in which both teams scored 20 points or more.

● **From the start of the 1983-84 season, the value of a
try was raised from three points to four. It was decided
officially that records for most points in a match,
season or career would subsequently include the four-
point try and that no attempt would be made to adjust
existing records featuring the three-point try.**
● Substitute appearances do not count towards
players' full appearance records.
● Points and appearances in abandoned matches are
included in records, except in League matches which
are replayed. Although the abandoned League match
points and appearances are included in players' overall
totals they do not count towards League records.

RECORD-BREAKING FEATS 1990-91

JONATHAN DAVIES of Widnes scored a club record
342 points in a season, including a record-equalling 34 in
a match.

JOHN WOODS of Leigh finished with a club points
career record of 2,272.

MARTIN OFFIAH of Widnes scored a Great Britain
record of five tries in a Test match and raced to the
fastest century of Division One tries.

GREG AUSTIN of Halifax equalled the Division Two
record of six tries in a match.

TIM LUMB of Hunslet scored a club record 28 points
in a match.

DEAN CARROLL of Doncaster equalled the club
record of nine goals in a match.

NORMAN BARROW of Runcorn Highfield scored a
club record 30 points in a match.

GREG PEARCE of Fulham equalled club records of 11
goals and 22 points.

COLIN ARMSTRONG of Hull K.R. equalled the club
record of 14 goals in a match.

HULL KINGSTON ROVERS' 100-6 John Smiths
Yorkshire Cup win over Nottingham City at Doncaster
produced several records including a club record score.

HALIFAX scored a club record 82-8 victory, over
Runcorn Highfield.

DONCASTER ran up a club record score with a 58-2
defeat of Bramley.

CASTLEFORD scored a Division One record away
score with a 76-12 win at Rochdale Hornets.

RUNCORN HIGHFIELD suffered a record run of 75
matches without a win, including 61 successive defeats.

GREAT BRITAIN ran up their highest score with a 60-4
defeat of France.

NEW RECORDS IN DETAIL . . .

JONATHAN DAVIES of Widnes scored a club record
342 points in a season, including a record 34 in a match.
The utility back's total for the season was made up of 30
tries and 112 goals, including two drop goals. Mick
Burke held the previous record with 316 points from 140
goals and 12 three-point tries in 1978-79, playing wing,
stand off and centre.
   Davies passed the record with 18 points in Widnes's
46-10 Stones Bitter Premiership first round home defeat
of Bradford Northern on 21 April.
   Playing centre, the Welshman equalled Widnes's
match record with 34 points in the 70-6 Greenalls

Lancashire Cup first round win at Whitehaven on 26 August, scoring nine goals and four tries. He shares the record with centre Andy Currier, who scored five tries and seven goals in a 58-2 Division One home defeat of Featherstone Rovers on 25 September 1988.

His record-breaking season went as follows:

		T	G	Pts
Wigan (CS)	(1)*	3	2	16
Whitehaven (LC)	(A)	4	9	34
Wigan (LC)	(H)	1	6	16
Bradford N.	(A)	0	3	6
Warrington (LC)	(H)	0	4	8
Featherstone R.	(H)	0	6	12
Hull	(A)	0	1	2
Salford (LC)	(2)*	0	4	8
Oldham	(H)	0	4	8
Castleford	(H)	0	5	10
Hull K.R.	(A)	1	2	8
Wakefield T.	(A)	2	2	12
Leeds	(H)	0	3	6
Australia	(H)	1	2	8
Oldham	(A)	2	2	12
Hull (RT)	(H)	1	2	8
Leeds (RT)	(H)	0	3	6
Batley (RT)	(H)	1	6	16
Hull K.R.	(H)	0	4	8
Warrington	(A)	NA		
Warrington (RT)	(2)*	NA		
St. Helens	(H)	NA		
Castleford	(A)	NA		
Wigan	(H)	NA		
Rochdale H.	(A)	NA		
Wakefield T.	(H)	NA		
Doncaster (CC)	(A)	NA		
Leeds	(A)	NA		
Barrow (CC)	(A)	0	0	0
Hull	(H)	0	0	0
Sheffield E.	(H)	2	0	8
Warrington (CC)	(A)	0	5	10
Bradford N.	(H)	4	2	20
Warrington	(H)	1	5(1)	13
Featherstone R.	(A)	1	4(1)	11
St. Helens (CC)	(2)*	0	1	2
St. Helens	(A)	0	4	8
Sheffield E.	(A)	1	5	14
Wigan	(A)	1	1	6
Rochdale H.	(H)	1	6	16
Bradford N. (PT)	(H)	2	5	18
Featherstone R. (PT)	(H)	1	4	12
Hull (PT)	(3)*	0	0	0

*(1) At Swansea
(2) At Wigan
(3) At Manchester U. FC

Totals
34 appearances ... 30 112(2) 342
() drop goals included in total.

JOHN WOODS notched up a Leigh career record of 2,272 points before retiring during the season. His total was made up of 143 tries and 904 goals, including 11 drop goals. The previous record of 2,194 was set by former full back Jim Ledgard from 1948 to 1958 with 36 tries and 1,043 goals.

Woods returned to Leigh at the start of the season, after leaving in 1985 for spells with Bradford Northern, Warrington and Rochdale Hornets, needing only 23 points to beat the record. He broke the record with the first of three goals in a 16-6 Division Two home defeat by Halifax on 16 September.

Woods first signed for Leigh in December 1975 and made a tryscoring debut on the wing at home to Barrow in an 18-8 Division One victory on 5 September 1976.

He also holds the Leigh record for most points in a match, with 38 from 13 goals and four tries in a 62-15 home defeat of Blackpool Borough on 11 September 1977 which remains a Division Two record.

Woods still holds the Division One records for most points in a season with 295 for Leigh in 1983-84; most career points, 2,130; and most career goals, 854. Mainly a stand off, the former Test player also played several matches at full back and centre. His season-by-season totals for Leigh are as follows:

	T	G	Pts
1976-77	5	90(2)	193
1977-78	16	140	328
1978-79	10	86(1)	201
1979-80	22	82(2)	228
1980-81	14	86(1)	213
1981-82	18	147(1)	347
1982-83	12	49(1)	133
1983-84	27	124(1)	355
1984-85	11	66(2)	174
1990-91	8	34	100
Totals	**143**	**904(11)**	**2,272**

MARTIN OFFIAH of Widnes raced to the fastest century of Division One tries and scored a Great Britain record of five tries in a Test match.

Offiah reached his century in his 70th Division One match with the first of three tries in a 46-4 home defeat of Castleford on 6 October. No other player has scored a century of Division One tries in fewer than 100 matches, the previous record being Keith Fielding's 100 tries in 108 matches for Salford. The former Test winger reached a century early in his fifth season after signing for Salford from Moseley RU club.

Offiah has been the top scorer of Divison One tries in each season since he left Rosslyn Park RU club before the start of the 1987-88 season. His total of 120 Division One tries is made up as follows:

	App	Tries
1987-88	25	33
1988-89	25	37

Jonathan Davies, new holder of the Widnes record for points in a season.

1989-90	**18**	**28**
1990-91	**23**	**22**
Totals.................	**91**	**120**

Offiah broke the Great Britain Test match record with five tries in the 60-4 home defeat of France at Leeds on 16 February. The previous record of four was shared by Jim Leytham (Wigan) v. Australia in 1910; Billy Boston (Wigan) v. New Zealand in 1954; Alex Murphy (St. Helens) v. France in 1959 and Garry Schofield (Hull) v. New Zealand in 1985.

GREG AUSTIN of Halifax equalled the Division Two match record with six tries in a 66-26 home defeat of Trafford Borough on 7 April. The centre shares the record with wingers Ged Dunn (Hull K.R.) v. New Hunslet on 2 February 1975 and David Kettlestring (Ryedale-York) at Keighley on 11 March 1990.

TIM LUMB of Hunslet scored a club record 28 points in a match with eight goals and three tries in a 52-12 Division Two home defeat of Runcorn Highfield on 7 October. The scrum half beat the record of 27 set by full back Billy Langton with 12 goals and a try in a 63-7 league victory at Keighley on 18 August 1959.

DEAN CARROLL of Doncaster equalled the club record of nine goals in a match at home to Bramley in a Division Two match on 6 January. He shares the record with David Towle, who kicked nine in a 33-14 league win at York on 9 September 1967.

NORMAN BARROW of Runcorn Highfield scored a club record 30 points in a 54-16 Division Two home win over Keighley on 31 March. The centre's total was made up of nine goals and three tries. Centre Terry Rose had set the record with 24 points, scoring eight goals and two tries in a 41-4 home defeat of Workington Town on 4 October 1987.

GREG PEARCE of Fulham equalled two club records with 11 goals and 22 points in a 50-0 Lancashire Cup first round home defeat of Runcorn Highfield on 26 August. He shares the goals record with Steve Guyett who included a drop goal in the 61-22 Division Two home defeat of Huddersfield on 23 October 1988. The points record is shared with Alan Platt, who scored two tries and seven goals in a 43-20 Division Two home win over Mansfield Marksman on 10 May 1986.

COLIN ARMSTRONG of Hull Kingston Rovers equalled a club record with 14 goals in a 100-6 Yorkshire Cup preliminary round away win over Nottingham City played at Doncaster on 19 August. It was the prop's last full appearance for Rovers before being transferred to

Hunslet half back Tim Lumb, scorer of a club record 28 points in a match.

Workington Town. He shares the record with Mike Fletcher, who kicked 14 goals in a 92-10 Division Two home defeat of Whitehaven on 18 March 1990; and Alf Carmichael's feat in a 70-13 league home defeat of Merthyr Tydfil on 8 October 1910.

HULL KINGSTON ROVERS' 100-6 away defeat of Nottingham City at Doncaster in the Yorkshire Cup preliminary round on 19 August produced the following records:

● A club record score and winning margin, beating the 92-10 Division Two home defeat of Whitehaven on 18 March 1990. Rovers scored 18 tries against Nottingham, compared with 16 against Whitehaven.
● It was Nottingham's biggest defeat, beating the 14-try 76-6 Division Two loss at Leigh in City's Mansfield Marksman days on 13 October 1985.
● It was the highest score and winning margin in a Yorkshire Cup-tie, beating Castleford's 17-try 94-12 first round home defeat of Huddersfield on 18 September 1988.
● It was the biggest win by an away side or on a neutral ground. Nottingham's home tie had been switched to Doncaster's Tattersfield because their own Harvey Hadden Stadium was not available.

HALIFAX scored a club record 82-8 victory over Runcorn Highfield in a Division Two home game on 14 October. The 14-try victory beat the 76-8 Yorkshire Cup first round win at Hunslet on 27 August 1972 when they scored 16 tries.

DONCASTER ran up a club record score with a 58-2 Division Two home defeat of Bramley on 6 January. Their previous highest scores were both 50-6 Division Two victories, at home to Keighley on 22 March 1987 and at Nottingham City on 26 December 1989. They scored nine tries each time compared with 10 against Bramley.

CASTLEFORD gained a Division One record away score with a 76-12 win at Rochdale Hornets on 3 March. It beat Wigan's 72-6 win at Wakefield Trinity on 29 March 1987.

RUNCORN HIGHFIELD suffered a record run of 75 matches without a win, including a record 61 successive defeats. After winning 20-12 at home to Fulham on 30 October 1988, Runcorn did not win again until beating Dewsbury 9-2 at home on 3 March 1991. The run included two draws and was made up of a record 67 league matches and eight cup ties. They lost all 31 matches in 1989-90.

GREAT BRITAIN ran up their highest score and widest margin victory with a 60-4 defeat of France at Leeds in the second British Coal Test on 16 February. It beat the 53-19 World Cup win over New Zealand at Pau, France, on 4 November 1972 and the 52-4 defeat of France at Leeds on 24 January 1987.

MILESTONES . . .

ELLERY HANLEY scored his 300th career try and became the first to make 200 Division One touchdowns. The Wigan loose forward's 300th career try came with the first of two in a 46-4 Division One win at Sheffield Eagles on 6 January. At the end of the season his total stood at 319 made up of 189 for Wigan, 90 for Bradford Northern and 40 in representative matches, including 18 for Great Britain in Tests.

Hanley scored his 200th Division One try with two in Wigan's 26-8 win at Warrington on 26 March. He now leads with 203, having scored 131 for Wigan and 72 for Bradford.

Hanley holds the record for Division One tries in a season with 44 for Wigan in 1986-87, having set the previous best with 40 for Bradford in 1984-85. His total of 63 tries in all matches in 1986-87 is still a record for a non-winger, playing loose forward, stand off and centre that season.

Five tries against Bradford on 1 March 1987 is a Division One record for a forward. But his best feat was six tries in a Silk Cut Challenge Cup tie at Rochdale Hornets on 24 February 1991. He has scored three tries or more in 26 matches, including seven four-try feats and 17 hat-tricks.

Hanley turned professional as a 17-year-old with Bradford on 2 June 1978 from Corpus Christi, Leeds. He made his debut as a substitute, scoring a try in the 30-18 home league defeat of Rochdale on 26 November 1978. He was then absent for a period and did not make his full debut until 16 August 1981 when he scored a try in the centre in a 33-5 Yorkshire Cup first round win at Halifax.

Wigan signed him in a then world record £150,000 deal on 16 September 1985. They paid a then record £85,000 plus the transfer of Phil Ford and Steve Donlan. He made his Wigan debut in the centre in a 32-10 home Division One victory over Widnes on 22 September 1985. After playing as a centre or stand off, Hanley switched to loose forward in February 1987.

His season-by-season totals are as follows:
( ) Division One tries included in total.

Bradford Northern

1978-79	1 (1)	
1979-80	Did not play	
1980-81	Did not play	
1981-82	15 (12)	
1982-83	10 (8)	
1983-84	12 (11)	+1 GB Under-24
1984-85	52 (40)	+2 GB, 1 England

Wigan

1985-86	35 (22)	+2 GB, 1 Yorks.
1986-87	59 (44)	+3 GB, 1 Yorks.
1987-88	31 (22)	+4 GB, 1 Yorks.
1988-89	25 (18)	+3 GB*, 1 Yorks.
1989-90	10 (5)	
1990-91	29 (20)	

Totals
Bradford N. 90 (72)
Wigan 189 (131)
Great Britain ..... 19★
1984 Tour......... 8   Not inc. 4 in Tests
1988 Tour......... 7   Not inc. 1 in Test
GB Under-24s.... 1
England............ 1
Yorkshire.......... 4

GRAND TOTAL........ **319 (203)**
★Including one try against a World XIII which is not
classed as a Test match.

MARTIN OFFIAH of Widnes scored the 200th try of
his career with the first of three in a 34-6 Division One
home defeat of Wakefield Trinity on 3 February. He also
raced to the fastest century of Division One tries during
the season (see *Records in Detail*). Offiah's career total at
the end of the season stood at 219, made up of 181 for
Widnes and 38 in representative matches, including 19 in
Test matches for Great Britain.

The former Rosslyn Park RU winger has finished at
the top of the try chart in all four seasons since he
switched codes at the start of 1987-88. Australian Albert
Rosenfeld of Huddersfield holds the record with five
successive seasons at the top from 1910-11, while Welsh
winger Johnny Ring of Wigan was also top in four
successive seasons from 1922-23.

Offiah holds the Widnes record for most tries in a
season with 58 in 1988-89, having set the target with 42
in the previous season. He also shares the club record of
five in a match against Warrington on 15 March 1989 and
scored a Great Britain Test match record of five against
France at Leeds on 16 February 1991. Offiah has scored
four tries in a match eight times and has a total of 24 hat-
tricks.

He made his debut for Widnes at home to Halifax on
30 August 1987 when he failed to score in a Division One
match. His total of tries is made up as follows:

Widnes
1987-88 42   +1 GB,
                                  1 RL Chairman's XIII
1988-89 58   +2 GB★
1989-90 40   +5 GB
1990-91 41   +8 GB

Totals
Widnes.................... 181
Britain .... 20★
1988 tour 17   Not inc. 2 in Tests
1990 tour................. 0   Not inc. 2 in Tests
RL Chairman's XIII ... 1

GRAND TOTAL...... **219**
★Including one try against a World XIII which is not
classed as a Test match.

*Widnes flier Martin Offiah, who passed the career
200-try landmark in February 1991.*

GARRY SCHOFIELD of Leeds scored the 200th try of his career with the second of three touchdowns for the Great Britain tourists in the 40-18 defeat of Southern Zone at Port Moresby, Papua New Guinea on 20 May 1990. At the end of the season Schofield's total was 230 tries made up of 82 for Leeds, 107 for Hull and 41 in representative matches, including 25 for Britain in Test matches. Schofield has scored four tries in a match six times plus six other hat-tricks.

A former Hunslet Parkside Junior, Schofield signed for Hull soon after captaining the Great Britain youth squad to New Zealand in 1983. He made his professional debut in a 22-22 Division One home draw against Warrington on 21 August 1983. Hull transferred Schofield to Leeds for a then world record £155,000, scoring two debut tries for his home town club in a 29-25 defeat by Auckland on 25 October 1987. Schofield's season-by-season totals are as follows:

Hull

1983-84	37	+1 GB Under 21
1984-85	23	
1985-86	15	+5 GB
1986-87	32	+5 GB

Leeds

1987-88	22	+3 GB
1988-89	20	+1 GB★, 1 Yorks
1989-90	20	+1 Yorks
1990-91	20	+5 GB

Totals

Hull	107	
Leeds	82	
Britain	26★	
1984 tour	5	Not inc. 2 in Tests
1988 tour	3	Not inc. 2 in Tests
1990 tour	4	Not inc. 3 in Tests
GB Under-24s	1	
Yorkshire	2	

GRAND TOTAL...... 230

★Including one try against a World XIII which is not classed as a Test match.

JOHN JOYNER scored the 200th try of his career in Castleford's 19-14 home defeat by Rochdale Hornets in the Regal Trophy third round on 16 December. The former Test centre added only one more try before the end of the season and his total is made up of 184 for Castleford plus 17 in representative matches, including two for Great Britain in Test matches.

Joyner made his debut for Castleford on the wing in an 18-0 home league victory over Bramley on 1 September 1972. The following season he equalled a club record with five tries in an 88-5 Player's No. 6 Trophy first round defeat of Millom amateurs on 16 September 1973. He was still on the wing then but soon settled at centre where he gained Test honours before moving to stand off and loose forward in later years. Joyner has also scored four tries in a match and one other hat-trick. His most prolific season was 1978-79 when he scored 18 in all matches. He has never finished in the top ten. His season by season totals are as follows:

Castleford

1972-73	3	
1973-74	13	
1974-75	15	
1975-76	12	
1976-77	11	+ 1 Yorks
1977-78	15	
1978-79	16	+1 Yorks, 1 GB Under-24s
1979-80	15	+1 England
1980-81	8	+1 England
1981-82	8	+4 Yorks
1982-83	10	+1 GB
1983-84	14	
1984-85	9	
1985-86	6	
1986-87	13	
1987-88	3	
1988-89	7	
1989-90	3	
1990-91	3	

Totals

Castleford	184	
Britain	2	
1979 tour	5	Not inc. 1 in Tests
1984 tour	1	
1988 tour	0	
England	2	
Under-24s	1	
Yorkshire	6	

GRAND TOTAL...... 201

WILF GEORGE scored the 100th try of his career with two in Halifax's 26-17 Yorkshire Cup second round defeat at Wakefield Trinity on 2 September. The winger's total at the end of the season was 113 with 75 for Halifax, 32 for Huddersfield and six for Widnes.

George made his senior debut for Huddersfield as a substitute on 8 April 1981 when he scored one try in a 30-13 Division Two defeat at York. His first full appearance was in a 34-7 Yorkshire Cup first round defeat at Hull K.R. on 14 August 1981. After five years he was transferred to Widnes but stayed less than a season after making his debut in a 33-10 Division One victory at Hull on 1 September 1985.

George played his first match for Halifax away to Oldham at the town's soccer ground on 16 February 1986 when they won a Division One game 19-14. He has scored six hat-tricks including four tries a match three times, and has finished in the top ten once, when he was 10th with 24 in 1989-90.

His season-by-season totals are as follows:

Huddersfield

1980-81	1
1981-82	11
1982-83	6
1983-84	12
1984-85	2

Widnes

1985-86	6

Halifax

1985-86	2
1986-87	15
1987-88	15
1988-89	4
1989-90	24
1990-91	15

Totals

Huddersfield	32
Widnes	6
Halifax	75

GRAND TOTAL...... 113

DAVID PLANGE scored the 100th try of his career with the last of three in Castleford's 28-19 Division One home defeat of Oldham on 18 November. The winger ended the season with 104 made up of 98 for Castleford, five for Doncaster and one for Great Britain.

He made his senior professional debut as a trialist centre for Doncaster on 13 March 1983 when they lost 32-18 to Rochdale Hornets in a Division Two home game. Plange moved to Castleford and made his debut on the wing in a 30-12 Division One home defeat of St. Helens on 27 January 1985. He has scored six hat-tricks, including one four-try feat, but has never finished in the top ten. His season-by-season totals are as follows:

Doncaster

1982-83	0
1983-84	2
1984-85	3

Castleford

1984-85	4	
1985-86	17	
1986-87	21	
1987-88	13	+1 GB
1988-89	10	
1989-90	17	
1990-91	16	

Totals

Doncaster	5
Castleford	98
Britain	1

GRAND TOTAL...... 104

GREG AUSTIN of Halifax scored the 100th try of his British career with the first of three for them against Fulham in a Silk Cut Challenge Cup first round 46-6 home victory on 17 February. The Australian centre's total at the end of the season was 121, with 40 for Halifax, 45 for Hull K.R., 25 for Salford and 11 for Rochdale Hornets.

Austin equalled the Division Two match record with six for Halifax in a 66-26 home defeat of Trafford Borough on 7 April. Before moving to Halifax, Austin had scored six tries for Hull K.R. in the first match of the season against Nottingham City in a Yorkshire Cup-tie at Doncaster. He has also scored four tries in a match twice and four other hat-tricks.

Austin began his British career with Rochdale Hornets, making a substitute debut in a 52-13 Division Two home defeat of Doncaster on 22 September 1985. His full debut followed seven days later when he scored a try in a 25-16 league victory at Keighley. He moved to Salford the next season and scored two goals on his debut at Wigan on 31 August 1986 in a 42-12 Division One defeat.

Austin had two seasons at Salford, returned to Australia for a year and then signed for Hull Kingston Rovers, for whom he made a two-try debut in a 54-12 Yorkshire Cup first-round victory on 17 September 1989. He stayed at Rovers for just over a season, when they released him from their overseas quota to make way for New Zealand international forward James Goulding.

Halifax snapped up Austin and he made another tryscoring debut at Bramley in a 56-8 Division Two win on 23 September 1990. Austin has finished second in the try charts in the last two seasons with totals of 38 and 47. His career total of 121 is made up as follows:

Rochdale H.

1985-86	11

Salford

1986-87	17
1987-88	8

Hull K.R.

1989-90	38
1990-91	7

Halifax

1990-91	40

Totals

Rochdale H.	11
Salford	25
Hull K.R.	45
Halifax	40

GRAND TOTAL...... 121

Century of career tries for threequarter Andy Mason.

ANDY MASON scored the 100th try of his career with Wakefield Trinity's only touchdown in a 16-6 Division One home defeat by Bradford Northern on 13 March. The centre did not add to his total, which is made up of 61 for Wakefield, 32 for Bramley, five for Leeds and two for Yorkshire.

Although Mason gained England Rugby League honours as a schoolboy he was with Roundhay RU club when he signed for Bramley in January 1985. He made his debut for them as a centre when they lost 19-12 at Batley on 3 February 1985.

Leeds signed him in a player plus cash deal worth about £60,000, which was then a record for both clubs, and he made his debut with a try on the wing in a 32-10 Division One win at Hull on 2 November 1986. Mason played only 17 matches for Leeds before being involved in the most remarkable player-exchange deal of all time. He joined Wakefield Trinity along with Mark Conway, Phil Fox and Keith Rayne, while Gary Spencer and John Lyons signed for Leeds. The deal was estimated at £120,000. Mason made a two-try debut for Trinity in the centre when they beat Carlisle 56-8 in a Division Two home match on 30 August 1987.

He has scored three hat-tricks and his season-by-season totals are as follows:

Bramley

1984-85	10	
1985-86	16	+2 Yorks.
1986-87	6	

Leeds

1986-87	5

Wakefield Trinity

1987-88	14
1988-89	14
1989-90	17
1990-91	16

Totals

Bramley	32
Leeds	5
Wakefield T.	61
Yorkshire	2

GRAND TOTAL 100

Full back Chris Johnson, who scored his 500th goal in January 1991.

CHRIS JOHNSON of Swinton scored the 500th goal of his career with the second of two in a 12-10 Division Two home defeat of Trafford Borough on 9 January. He finished the season with 513 goals made up of 46, including one drop goal, for Swinton and 467 for Leigh, including 13 drop goals. Johnson still holds the Leigh record for most goals in a season with 173, including two drop goals, in 1985-86 when he topped the goals chart. He was seventh, with 86, the following season and fourth in 1988-89 with 117. His best match tally is 14 for Leigh against Keighley in a 92-2 Division Two home win on 30 April 1986. He has also kicked 10 goals in a match twice.

Johnson made his senior debut for Leigh in the centre on 12 February 1984 when they lost 16-10 at St. Helens in an RL Challenge Cup first round game. He was transferred to Swinton and made his debut at his old club's ground on 26 August 1990 when he kicked a goal in a 26-6 Lancashire Cup first round defeat. Johnson did not take over as Leigh's goalkicker until his third season and since then his season-by-season totals have been as follows:

Leigh

1985-86	173 (2)
1986-87	86 (2)
1987-88	41 (6)
1988-89	117 (3)
1989-90	50

Swinton

1990-91	46 (1)

Totals

Leigh	467 (13)
Swinton	46 (1)

GRAND TOTAL 513 (14)

() Drop goals included in total.

PAUL DIXON of Leeds scored the 100th try of his career with the first of three in a 64-4 Division One home defeat of Rochdale Hornets on 11 November. The Test forward finished the season with 104 tries made up of 30 for Huddersfield, 52 for Halifax, one for Oldham, 17 for Leeds and four in representative matches including one in a Test for Great Britain.

A former Underbank, Huddersfield, amateur, Dixon made his senior professional debut for Huddersfield as an unnamed second row trialist and scored a try in a 22-19 Division Two defeat at Cardiff City on 3 May 1982. Dixon had a brief spell on loan to Oldham in 1984-85 before signing for Halifax in 1985. He scored the only try on his debut for Halifax when they drew 12-12 at home to Oldham in a Division One home match on 1 September 1985.

Leeds signed Dixon in an exchange deal reckoned to be worth about £140,000, with Paul Medley and John Lyons moving to Halifax. He made his debut for Leeds in a 15-6 Division One defeat at St. Helens on 8 January 1988. Dixon has scored only one hat-trick and his season-by-season totals are as follows:

Huddersfield

1981-82	1
1982-83	8
1983-84	14
1984-85	7

Oldham

1984-85	1

Halifax

1985-86	13
1986-87	14
1987-88	17
1988-89	8

Leeds

1988-89	1
1989-90	6
1990-91	10 +1 GB

Totals

Huddersfield	30
Oldham	1
Halifax	52
Leeds	17
Britain	1
1988 Tour	1
1990 Tour	2
GRAND TOTAL	**104**

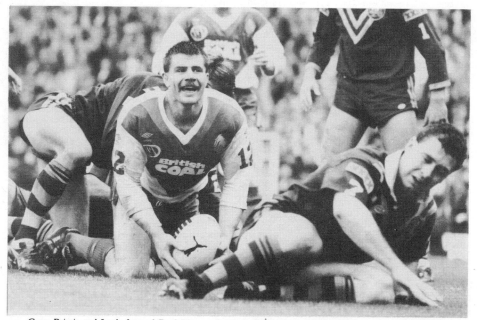

Great Britain and Leeds forward Paul Dixon, who crashed through the 100-try barrier in November 1990.

LEADING SCORERS 1895-1973

	TRIES	GOALS	POINTS
1895-96	Hurst (Oldham) 28	Lorimer (Manningham) 35	Cooper (Bradford)...........106
			Lorimer (Manningham)...106
1896-97	Hannah (Hunslet)............19	Goldthorpe (Hunslet) 26	Rigg (Halifax) 112
		Sharpe (Liversedge) 26	
1897-98	Hoskins (Salford) 30	Goldthorpe (Hunslet) 66	Goldthorpe (Hunslet)......135
1898-99	Williams (Oldham) 39	Goldthorpe (Hunslet) 67	Jaques (Hull) 169
1899-00	Williams (Oldham) 36	Cooper (Bradford) 39	Williams (Oldham).........108
1900-01	Williams (Oldham) 47	Goldthorpe (Hunslet) 44	Williams (Oldham).........141
1901-02	Wilson (Broughton R.) 38	James (Broughton R.) 75	Lomas (Salford)..............172
1902-03	Evans (Leeds).................27	Goldthorpe (Hunslet) 48	Davies (Batley)..............136
1903-04	Hogg (Broughton R.) 34	Lomas (Salford) 66	Lomas (Salford)..............222
1904-05	Dechan (Bradford)...........31	Ferguson (Oldham)..........50	Lomas (Salford)..............146
1905-06	Leytham (Wigan) 40	Ferguson (Oldham)..........49	Leytham (Wigan)............160
1906-07	Eccles (Halifax)..............41	Lomas (Salford) 86	Lomas (Salford)..............280
1907-08	Leytham (Wigan) 44	Goldthorpe (Hunslet)......101	Goldthorpe (Hunslet)......217
1908-09	Miller (Wigan)................49	Lomas (Salford) 88	Lomas (Salford)..............272
	Williams (Halifax) 49		
1909-10	Leytham (Wigan) 48	Carmichael (Hull K.R.) 78	Leytham (Wigan)...........232
1910-11	Kitchen (Huddersfield).....40	Carmichael (Hull K.R.)...129	Carmichael (Hull K.R.)...261
	Rosenfeld (Huddersfield) ..40		
	Miller (Wigan)................40		
1911-12	Rosenfeld (Huddersfield) ..78	Carmichael (Hull K.R.)...127	Carmichael (Hull K.R.)...254
1912-13	Rosenfeld (Huddersfield) ..56	Carmichael (Hull K.R.) 93	Thomas (Wigan)............198
1913-14	Rosenfeld (Huddersfield) ..80	Holland (Huddersfield) ...131	Holland (Huddersfield) ...268
1914-15	Rosenfeld (Huddersfield) ..56	Gronow (Huddersfield) ...136	Gronow (Huddersfield) ...284
● Competitive matches suspended during war years			
1918-19	Francis (Hull)..................25	Kennedy (Hull) 54	Kennedy (Hull)..............135
1919-20	Moorhouse (Huddersfield).39	Gronow (Huddersfield) ...148	Gronow (Huddersfield) ...332
1920-21	Stone (Hull) 41	Kennedy (Hull) 108	Kennedy (Hull)..............264
1921-22	Farrar (Oldham) 49	Sullivan (Wigan)............100	Farrar (Oldham) 213
1922-23	Ring (Wigan) 41	Sullivan (Wigan)............161	Sullivan (Wigan)............349
1923-24	Ring (Wigan) 49	Sullivan (Wigan)............158	Sullivan (Wigan)............319
1924-25	Ring (Wigan) 54	Sullivan (Wigan)............138	Sullivan (Wigan)............282
1925-26	Ring (Wigan) 63	Sullivan (Wigan)............131	Sullivan (Wigan)............274
1926-27	Ellaby (St. Helens)..........55	Sullivan (Wigan)............149	Sullivan (Wigan)............322
1927-28	Ellaby (St. Helens) 37	Thompson (Leeds).........106	Thompson (Leeds)..........233
1928-29	Brown (Wigan) 44	Sullivan (Wigan)............107	Sullivan (Wigan)............226
	Mills (Huddersfield).........44		
1929-30	Ellaby (St. Helens) 39	Thompson (Leeds).........111	Thompson (Leeds).........243
1930-31	Harris, E. (Leeds)...........58	Sullivan (Wigan)............133	Sullivan (Wigan)............278
1931-32	Mills (Huddersfield).........50	Sullivan (Wigan)............117	Sullivan (Wigan)............249
1932-33	Harris, E. (Leeds)...........57	Sullivan (Wigan)............146	Sullivan (Wigan)............307
1933-34	Brown (Salford) 45	Sullivan (Wigan)............193	Sullivan (Wigan)............404

	TRIES	GOALS	POINTS
1934-35	Morley (Wigan) 49	Sullivan (Wigan)............165	Sullivan (Wigan)............348
1935-36	Harris, E. (Leeds)...........63	Sullivan (Wigan)............117	Sullivan (Wigan)............246
1936-37	Harris, E. (Leeds)...........40	Sullivan (Wigan)............120	Sullivan (Wigan)............258
1937-38	Harris, E. (Leeds)...........45	Sullivan (Wigan)............135	Sullivan (Wigan)............285
1938-39	Markham (Huddersfield)...39	Sullivan (Wigan)............124	Risman (Salford)............267

● For the next six seasons emergency war-time competitions resulted in a reduction of matches and players were allowed to 'guest' for other clubs

	TRIES	GOALS	POINTS
1939-40	Batten (Hunslet) 38	Hodgson (Swinton)..........98	Hodgson (Swinton) 208
1940-41	Walters (Bradford N.)......32	Lockwood (Halifax) 70	Belshaw (Warrington) 174
1941-42	Francis (Barrow) 30	Lockwood (Halifax) 91	Lockwood (Halifax)........185
1942-43	Batten (Hunslet) 24	Lockwood (Halifax) 65	Lockwood (Halifax)........136
1943-44	Lawrenson (Wigan) 21	Horne (Barrow) 57	Horne (Barrow) 144
1944-45	Batten (Bradford N.)........41	Stott (Wakefield T.).........51	Stott (Wakefield T.) 129

● Normal peace-time rugby resumed

	TRIES	GOALS	POINTS
1945-46	Batten (Bradford N.)........35	Ledgard (Dewsbury)........89	Bawden (Huddersfield) ...239
1946-47	Bevan (Warrington) 48	Miller (Hull).................103	Bawden (Huddersfield) ...243
1947-48	Bevan (Warrington) 57	Ward (Wigan)................141	Ward (Wigan) 312
1948-49	Cooper (Huddersfield)......60	Ward (Wigan)................155	Ward (Wigan) 361
1949-50	Nordgren (Wigan) 57	Gee (Wigan) 133	Palin (Warrington) 290
		Palin (Warrington) 133	
1950-51	Bevan (Warrington) 68	Cook (Leeds) 155	Cook (Leeds) 332
1951-52	Cooper (Huddersfield)......71	Ledgard (Leigh) 142	Horne (Barrow)..............313
1952-53	Bevan (Warrington) 72	Bath (Warrington)..........170	Bath (Warrington)..........379
1953-54	Bevan (Warrington) 67	Metcalfe (St. Helens)......153	Metcalfe (St. Helens)......369
		Bath (Warrington)..........153	
1954-55	Cooper (Huddersfield)......66	Ledgard (Leigh) 178	Ledgard (Leigh) 374
1955-56	McLean (Bradford N.) 61	Ledgard (Leigh) 155	Bath (Warrington)..........344
1956-57	Boston (Wigan)...............60	Jones (Leeds).................194	Jones (Leeds).................496
1957-58	Sullivan (Wigan)..............50	Ganley (Oldham) 219	Ganley (Oldham) 453
1958-59	Vollenhoven (St. Helens) ..62	Ganley (Oldham) 190	Griffiths (Wigan) 394
1959-60	Vollenhoven (St. Helens) ..54	Rhodes (St. Helens) 171	Fox (Wakefield T.) 453
		Fox (Wakefield T.) 171	
1960-61	Vollenhoven (St. Helens) ..59	Rhodes (St. Helens) 145	Rhodes (St. Helens) 338
1961-62	Boston (Wigan)...............51	Fox (Wakefield T.) 183	Fox (Wakefield T.) 456
1962-63	Glastonbury (Work'ton T.)41	Coslett (St. Helens)........156	Coslett (St. Helens)........321
1963-64	Stopford (Swinton) 45	Coslett (St. Helens)........138	Fox (Wakefield T.) 313
1964-65	Lake (Wigan)..................40	Kellett (Hull K.R.) 150	Killeen (St. Helens)........360
1965-66	Killeen (St. Helens).........32	Killeen (St. Helens)........120	Killeen (St. Helens)........336
	Lake (Wigan) 32		
1966-67	Young (Hull K.R.)...........34	Risman (Leeds) 163	Killeen (St. Helens)........353
	Howe (Castleford) 34		
1967-68	Millward (Hull K.R.).......38	Risman (Leeds) 154	Risman (Leeds) 332
1968-69	Francis (Wigan) 40	Risman (Leeds) 165	Risman (Leeds) 345
1969-70	Atkinson (Leeds).............38	Tyrer (Wigan)................167	Tyrer (Wigan)................385
1970-71	Haigh (Leeds) 40	Coslett (St. Helens)........183	Coslett (St. Helens)........375
1971-72	Atkinson (Leeds).............36	Coslett (St. Helens)........214	Watkins (Salford)...........473
	Lamb (Bradford N.) 36		
1972-73	Atkinson (Leeds).............39	Watkins (Salford)...........221	Watkins (Salford)...........493

LEADING SCORERS 1973-90

TRIES

1973-74

Fielding (Salford)	49
Mathias (St. Helens)	40
D. Smith (Wakefield T.)	38
Eckersley (St. Helens)	26
Fleay (Swinton)	26
Jones (St. Helens)	25
Wilson (St. Helens)	25
Watkins (Salford)	24
Atkinson (Leeds)	23
Lamb (Bradford N.)	22
A. Smith (Leeds)	22
Bevan (Warrington)	22
Ayres (Wigan)	22

1974-75

Dunn (Hull K.R.)	42
Fielding (Salford)	35
Bevan (Warrington)	31
A. Smith (Leeds)	30
Millward (Hull K.R.)	30
Atkinson (Leeds)	29
Richards (Salford)	28
Sullivan (Hull K.R.)	28
Mathias (St. Helens)	27
Dyl (Leeds)	26

1975-76

Richards (Salford)	37
Fielding (Salford)	33
Jones (St. Helens)	31
Briggs (Leigh)	27
D. Smith (Wakefield T.)	26
Burton (Castleford)	25
Clark (Hull)	23
Wright (Workington T.)	22
Barends (York)	21
Boxall (Hull)	21
Holmes (Leeds)	21
Mathias (St. Helens)	21
Butler (Salford)	21

1976-77

Wright (Widnes)	31
Burton (Castleford)	29
D. Smith (Leeds)	28
Fielding (Salford)	27
Dunn (Hull K.R.)	26
Cunningham (St. Helens)	26
Topliss (Wakefield T.)	24
Richards (Salford)	23
Mathias (St. Helens)	23
Barends (York)	22

1977-78

Wright (Widnes)	33
Fielding (Salford)	31
Cunningham (St. Helens)	30
Bevan (Warrington)	30
Fenton (Castleford)	30
Vigo (Wigan)	29
Glynn (St. Helens)	28
D. Smith (Leeds)	28
T. Morgan (York)	27
Burton (Castleford)	27

1978-79

Hartley (Hull K.R.)	35
Wright (Widnes)	28
Barends (Bradford N.)	25
Lowe (Hull K.R.)	25
Prendiville (Hull)	25
Fielding (Salford)	24
D. Redfearn (Bradford N.)	23
Mathias (St. Helens)	22
Bray (Hull)	21
O'Loughlin (Wigan)	21
Sullivan (Hull K.R.)	21

1979-80

Fielding (Salford)	30
Hubbard (Hull K.R.)	30
Munro (Oldham)	29
Ball (Barrow)	27
Bentley (Widnes)	27
Glynn (St. Helens)	27
Mathias (St. Helens)	27
Bevan (Warrington)	26
D. Redfearn (Bradford N.)	26
D. Smith (Leeds)	24

1980-81

Crossley (York)	35
Richardson (Castleford)	28
Hubbard (Hull K.R.)	25
Hartley (Hull K.R.)	23
McDermott (York)	23
Slater (Huddersfield)	23
Drummond (Leigh)	20
Ball (Barrow)	19
Bevan (Warrington)	19
Cramp (Huddersfield)	19
Hyde (Castleford)	19
Ramsdale (Wigan)	19

1981-82

Jones (Workington T.)	31
Drummond (Leigh)	26
Basnett (Widnes)	26
Ashton (Oldham)	26
Morgan (Carlisle)	25

Hartley (Hull K.R.)..23
Hopkins (Workington T.)...............................23
Day (Hull)...23
Evans (Hull)..22
D. Hobbs (Featherstone R.)..........................21
Moll (Keighley)...21

1982-83
Eccles (Warrington).......................................37
Evans (Hull)..28
Crossley (Fulham)..27
David (Cardiff C.)...26
Topliss (Hull)..24
M'Barki (Fulham)..23
Hyde (Castleford) 22
McDermott (York)...22
Leuluai (Hull)..21
Phil Ford (Warrington)...................................20
Clark (Hull K.R.)...20

1983-84
Schofield (Hull)...38
Lydon (Widnes)...28
King (Hunslet)...28
Woods (Leigh)...27
Basnett (Widnes)...26
Gibson (Batley) 26
Herbert (Barrow)...25
Steadman (York)..25
Prohm (Hull K.R.)...25
Clark (Hull K.R.)...24

1984-85
Hanley (Bradford N.) 55
Prohm (Hull K.R.)...45
Gill (Wigan) 34
Ledger (St. Helens)..30
Meninga (St. Helens)......................................28
Gibbin (Whitehaven)......................................27
Gibson (Batley) 26
G. Peacham (Carlisle) 25
Byrne (Salford)..25
Evans (Hull) 24
Ferguson (Wigan) 24

1985-86
Halliwell (Leigh)..49
Hanley (Wigan)..38
Lister (Bramley)..34
Henderson (Leigh)...31
Frodsham (Blackpool B.)................................30
Fox (Leigh)...29
Williams (Barrow)..27
Garrity (Runcorn H.) 24
Gibson (Leeds)..23
Beck (Workington T.) 23

1986-87
Hanley (Wigan)..63
Schofield (Hull)...37
Gill (Wigan) 32
Bate (Swinton) 31
Ford (Bradford N.)...30
Henderson (Leigh)...27
Edwards (Wigan)...26
Johnson (Warrington) 25
Lydon (Wigan)...24
Dunn (Rochdale H.) 23
Ledger (St. Helens)..23
McCormack (St. Helens) 23

1987-88
Offiah (Widnes)...44
Hanley (Wigan)..36
Schofield (Leeds)...25
Gibson (Leeds)..24
Goodway (Wigan) 23
Pape (Carlisle)...23
Edwards (Wigan)...21
Foy (Oldham)..21
Smith (Featherstone R.) 21
Bibb (Featherstone R.) 20
M. Conway (Wakefield T.)...............................20
Elia (St. Helens)..20
Quirk (St. Helens)..20

1988-89
Offiah (Widnes)...60
Ledger (Leigh)...34
Bate (Swinton)...32
Hanley (Wigan)..29
Lister (Bramley)...28
Powell (Sheffield E.)......................................28
Lewis (Bramley)..26
Quirk (St. Helens)..24
Anderson (Castleford).....................................24
Burns (Barrow)..24

1989-90
Offiah (Widnes)...45
Austin (Hull K.R.) 38
Sullivan (Hull K.R.) 35
Preston (Wigan) 33
Cordle (Bradford N.).......................................32
Larder (Castleford)...29
P. Lord (Oldham)...29
Edwards (Wigan)...26
Goodway (Wigan) 26
Cogger (Oldham)..24
Ellis (Castleford)...24
George (Halifax)..24
M. Lord (Rochdale H.) 24
Simpson (Keighley)...24

GOALS
(including drop goals)

1973-74

Watkins (Salford)	183
Whitehead (Warrington)	168
Jefferson (Keighley)	165
Coslett (St. Helens)	134
Mumby (Bradford N.)	131
Dutton (Widnes)	129
Lloyd (Castleford)	121
Quinn (York)	112
Fiddler (Leigh)	111
Holliday (Rochdale H.)	107

1974-75

Fox (Hull K.R.)	146
Coslett (St. Helens)	129
Dutton (Widnes)	122
Lloyd (Castleford)	112
Quinn (York)	112
Hartley (Huddersfield)	110
MacCorquodale (Workington T.)	107
Marshall (Leeds)	107
Mumby (Bradford N.)	96
Fiddler (Salford, Leigh)	85

1975-76

Watkins (Salford)	175
Pimblett (St. Helens)	149
Lloyd (Castleford)	149
Dutton (Widnes)	148
Fairbairn (Wigan)	146
Stacey (Leigh)	137
MacCorquodale (Workington T.)	130
Fox (Hull K.R., York)	102
Marshall (Leeds)	101
Gaitley (New Hunslet)	100

1976-77

Lloyd (Castleford)	163
Quinn (Featherstone R.)	152
Pimblett (St. Helens)	152
Hesford (Warrington)	132
MacCorquodale (Workington T.)	128
Watkins (Salford)	125
Stephenson (Dewsbury)	106
Fairbairn (Wigan)	105
Dutton (Widnes)	97
Woods (Leigh)	90

1977-78

Pimblett (St. Helens)	178
Hesford (Warrington)	158
Woods (Leigh)	149
MacCorquodale (Workington T.)	138
Woods (Widnes)	122
Watkins (Salford)	110
Mumby (Bradford N.)	107
Lloyd (Castleford)	104
Fox (Bradford N.)	95
Oulton (Leeds)	80

1978-79

Lloyd (Hull)	172
Hesford (Warrington)	170
Burke (Widnes)	140
MacCorquodale (Workington T.)	114
Pimblett (St. Helens)	105
Beale (Keighley)	96
Woods (Leigh)	96
Birts (Halifax)	86
Fairbairn (Wigan)	86
Norton (Castleford)	82

1979-80

Quinn (Featherstone R.)	163
Hubbard (Hull K.R.)	138
Rule (Salford)	134
Hesford (Warrington)	128
Burke (Widnes)	127
Ball (Barrow)	119
Diamond (Wakefield T.)	116
Fitzsimons (Oldham)	108
Parrish (Hunslet)	98
Birts (Halifax)	97

1980-81

Hesford (Warrington)	147
Quinn (Featherstone R.)	123
Diamond (Wakefield T.)	112
Burke (Widnes)	110
Hubbard (Hull K.R.)	109
Ball (Barrow)	104
Birts (Halifax)	100
Beale (Keighley)	97
Parrish (Oldham)	95
Fairbairn (Wigan)	94

1981-82

Hopkins (Workington T.)	190
Fairbairn (Hull K.R.)	168
Parrish (Oldham)	164
Woods (Leigh)	158
Rule (Salford)	130
Dick (Leeds)	125
Quinn (Featherstone R.)	120
Agar (Halifax)	119
Crooks (Hull)	118
Hesford (Warrington)	116

1982-83

Diamond (Fulham)	136
Fitzsimons (Hunslet)	121
Crooks (Hull)	120
R. Beardmore (Castleford)	117
Hesford (Warrington)	113
Fenwick (Cardiff C.)	111
Jones (Swinton)	110
Whitfield (Wigan)	104
Kilner (Bramley)	104
Quinn (Featherstone R.)	98

1983-84

Hesford (Warrington)	142
R. Beardmore (Castleford)	142
Hallett (Cardiff C.)	140
Fitzsimons (Hunslet)	131
Woods (Leigh)	124
Whitfield (Wigan)	122
Ball (Barrow)	104
Parrish (Oldham)	101
Agar (Halifax)	94
Tickle (Barrow)	91

1984-85

Day (St. Helens)	157
Fairbairn (Hull K.R.)	141
Wood (Runcorn H.)	126
Steadman (York)	122
Griffiths (Salford)	118
Parrish (Oldham)	117
Schofield (Hull)	105
Creasser (Leeds)	102
Agar (Halifax)	87
Jones (Swinton)	87

1985-86

C. Johnson (Leigh)	173
Stephenson (Wigan)	128
Noble (Doncaster)	118
Harcombe (Rochdale H.)	115
Kilner (Bramley)	110
Dorahy (Hull K.R.)	101
Woods (Bradford N.)	98
Creasser (Leeds)	84
Carroll (Carlisle)	83
Smith (Workington T.)	83

1986-87

Loughlin (St. Helens)	190
Bishop (Warrington)	117
Noble (Doncaster)	114
Whitfield (Halifax)	109
Platt (Hunslet)	102
Topping (Swinton)	100
C. Johnson (Leigh)	86
Ketteridge (Castleford)	80
Wood (Rochdale H.)	80
Quinn (Featherstone R.)	77

1987-88

Woods (Warrington)	152
Quinn (Featherstone R.)	128
Harcombe (Wakefield T.)	116
Loughlin (St. Helens)	114
Pearce (Hull)	111
Smith (Springfield B.)	98
Stephenson (Leeds)	95
M. Fletcher (Hull K.R.)	94
Hobbs (Bradford N.)	83
Jones (Salford)	79

1988-89

Aston (Sheffield E.)	148
Ketteridge (Castleford)	129
Hobbs (Bradford N.)	118
C. Johnson (Leigh)	117
Marwood (Barrow)	115
Loughlin (St. Helens)	113
Noble (Doncaster)	110
Woods (Warrington)	107
Currier (Widnes)	107
Turner (Rochdale H.)	104

1989-90

M. Fletcher (Hull K.R.)	199
Loughlin (St. Helens)	145
Platt (Oldham)	126
Maskill (Leeds)	114
M. Conway (Wakefield T.)	107
Hobbs (Bradford N.)	104
Eastwood (Hull)	101
Aston (Sheffield E.)	99
Davies (Widnes)	98
Turner (Rochdale H.)	98

DROP GOALS

1974-75	Seabourne (Bradford N.)	10
1975-76	Hancock (Hull)	10
1976-77	N. Stephenson (Dewsbury)	16
1977-78	Fiddler (Bramley, Leigh)	10
1978-79	Turley (Blackpool B.)	18
1979-80	Dean (Hunslet)	18
1980-81	Walker (Whitehaven)	22
1981-82	Agar (Halifax)	17
	Donlan (Leigh)	17
1982-83	Pinner (St. Helens)	13
1983-84	Hallett (Cardiff C.)	29
1984-85	Wood (Runcorn H.)	28
1985-86	Bishop (Warrington)	13
1986-87	Platt (Mansfield M.)	18
1987-88	W. Parker (Hull K.R.)	15
1988-89	Pearce (Hull)	16
1989-90	Harkin (Bradford N.)	12

POINTS

Year	Player	Points
1973-74	Watkins (Salford)	438
1974-75	Fox (Hull K.R.)	333
1975-76	Watkins (Salford)	385
1976-77	Lloyd (Castleford)	341
1977-78	Pimblett (St. Helens)	381
1978-79	Lloyd (Hull)	373
1979-80	Quinn (Featherstone R.)	375
1980-81	Hesford (Warrington)	310
1981-82	Hopkins (Workington T.)	446
1982-83	Diamond (Fulham)	308
1983-84	Woods (Leigh)	355
1984-85	Day (St. Helens)	362
1985-86	C. Johnson (Leigh)	400
1986-87	Loughlin (St. Helens)	424
1987-88	Woods (Warrington)	351
1988-89	Aston (Sheffield E.)	307
1989-90	M. Fletcher (Hull K.R.)	450

ALL-TIME RECORDS

Most goals in a match:
22 by Jim Sullivan (Wigan) v. Flimby & Fothergill (Challenge Cup), 14th February 1925

Most goals in a season:
DAVID WATKINS holds the record for most goals in a season with 221 — all for Salford — in 1972-73. Watkins played and scored a goal in every match that season as follows:

1972

Date		Opponent		
Aug.	19	Leeds	(H)	5
	23	Featherstone R.	(A)	3
	26	Whitehaven	(A)	4
	28	Swinton	(H)	1
Sept.	1	Oldham	(LC) (H)	10
	9	Leeds	(A)	2
	15	Rochdale H.	(LC) (H)	11
	17	Leigh	(A)	6
	24	Barrow	(JP) (A)	4
	29	Huyton	(H)	10
Oct.	3	Oldham	(FT) (A)	4
	6	Wigan	(LC) (A)	4
	8	Blackpool B.	(A)	5
	13	Blackpool B.	(H)	8
	21	Swinton	(LCF)	5
Nov.	5	Huyton	(A)	8
	10	Rochdale H.	(H)	6
	17	Warrington	(A)	4
	19	New Zealand	(H)	10
	24	Dewsbury	(JP) (H)	4
	26	Workington T.	(H)	6
Dec.	1	Barrow	(H)	9
	10	Bradford N.	(JP) (H)	9
	13	Oldham	(A)	4
	15	Leigh	(H)	3
	24	Bradford N.	(A)	5

Date		Opponent		
	26	Workington T.	(A)	3
	30	Hull K.R.	(JP) (A)	5
1973				
Jan.	3	Bradford N.	(H)	6
	7	Rochdale H.	(A)	2
	12	Featherstone R.	(H)	4
	28	Featherstone R.	(RL Cup) (A)	4
Feb.	2	Whitehaven	(H)	4
	11	Barrow	(A)	5
	23	St. Helens	(H)	3
Mar.	7	Widnes	(A)	3
	9	Dewsbury	(H)	3
	16	St. Helens	(A)	2
	24	Leeds	(JP Final)	2
	30	Warrington	(H)	1
Apr.	6	Widnes	(H)	4
	13	Oldham	(H)	3
	15	Dewsbury	(A)	3
	17	Wigan	(A)	3
	20	Swinton	(A)	7
	23	Wigan	(H)	3
	29	Rochdale H.	(top 16) (H)	2

	App	Gls
League	34	147
Lancs Cup	4	30
John Player	5	24
Tour match	1	10
RL Cup	1	4
Floodlit Cup	1	4
Top 16	1	2
Totals	**47**	**221**

Fastest goals century:
Three players share the record of scoring the fastest 100 goals from the start of a season in terms of number of matches played. They are Bernard Ganley, David Watkins and Steve Quinn, who achieved the century in 18 matches.

Ganley reached 100 goals on 16 November 1957, after playing 17 matches for Oldham and one for Great Britain.

Watkins scored his 100th goal on 17 November 1972, all for Salford.

Quinn scored his 100th goal on 16 December 1979, all for Featherstone Rovers.

Most goals in a career:
JIM SULLIVAN holds the record for most goals in a career with 2,867 between 1921-22 and 1945-46. He scored a century of goals in every season after leaving Welsh Rugby Union for Wigan until the War interrupted the 1939-40 campaign. The Test full back played all of his club rugby for Wigan apart from War-time appearances with Bradford Northern, Dewsbury and Keighley.

Sullivan's total includes 441 in representative matches, including three tours of Australasia. These figures are accepted by the Record Keepers' Club following research by James Carter and Malcolm Bentley.

Most one-point drop goals in a match:
5 by Danny Wilson (Swinton) v. Hunslet (John Player
Special), 6 November 1983.
Peter Wood (Runcorn H.) v.Batley, 21 October 1984.
Paul Bishop (Warrington) at Wigan (Premiership
semi-final), 11 May 1986.

Most one-point drop goals in a season:
29 by Lyn Hallett (Cardiff C.)......................1983-84

Most one-point drop goals in a career:
96 by Norman Turley (Warrington, Runcorn H.,
Swinton, Blackpool B., Rochdale H., Barrow,
Workington T., Trafford B.,
Whitehaven).....................................1974-91

Most tries in a match:
11 by George West (Hull K.R.) v Brookland Rovers
Challenge Cup ....4 March 1905

Most tries in a career:
BRIAN BEVAN holds the record for most tries in a career
with 796 between 1946 and 1964. His season-by-season
record is:

1946-47	48
1947-48	57
1948-49	56
1949-50	33
1950-51	68
1951-52	51
1952-53	72
1953-54	67
1954-55	63
1955-56	57
1956-57	17
1957-58	46
1958-59	54
1959-60	40
1960-61	35
1961-62	15
1962-63	10
1963-64	 7

Totals
Warrington 740
Blackpool Borough...17
Other Nationalities...26
Other representative
matches 13
Grand Total **796**

The Australian winger played his first game for
Warrington on 17 November 1945 and his last on 23 April
1962 before having two seasons at Blackpool Borough.
His last match for Borough was on 22 February, 1964.

Most tries in a season:
ALBERT ROSENFELD holds the record for most tries
in a season with 80 — all for Huddersfield — in 1913-14.

Rosenfeld's match-by-match record:

1913

Sept.	6	York......................................(A)	4
	8	Warrington ....(H)	2
	13	Leeds ....(H)	5
	20	Halifax ....(A)	1
	27	Batley ....(A)	0
Oct.	4	Oldham..................................(H)	2
	11	Rochdale H.............................(A)	0
	18	Bramley ....(YC) (H)	2
	25	Dewsbury ....(A)	4
Nov.	1	Halifax..........................(YC) (A)	2
	8	Wigan ....(A)	1
	15	Dewsbury ....(YC) (H)	3
	19	Bradford N.............................(H)	3
	22	Leeds ....(A)	3
	29	Bradford N...........(Halifax, YCF)	1
Dec.	3	Halifax.................................(H)	3
	6	Hunslet ....(A)	2
	13	Rochdale H..............................(H)	3
	20	Hull K.R. ....(A)	2
	25	Hull ....(A)	1
	26	Wakefield T............................(H)	3
	27	Hunslet ....(H)	0

1914

Jan.	1	St. Helens...............................(A)	0
	3	Warrington ....(A)	0
	10	York ....(H)	3
	17	Keighley................................(A)	2
	24	Dewsbury ....(H)	1
	31	Batley ....(H)	0
Feb.	7	Oldham ....(A)	0
	14	Bramley ....(H)	5
	21	Wigan ....(H)	3
	28	Swinton Park R..........(RL Cup) (H)	7
Mar.	7	Wakefield T.............................(A)	2
	14	Hull K.R. ....(RL Cup) (A)	2
	18	Bramley..................................(A)	3
	21	Widnes ....(RL Cup) (H)	0
	25	Keighley ....(H)	3
	28	Hull K.R. ....(H)	1
	30	Bradford N. ....(A)	1
Apr.	4	Hull................(Leeds, RL Cup SF)	0
	11	Hull ....(H) did not play	
	13	St. Helens ....(H)	0
	20	Hull ....(Play-off) (H) did not play	
	25	Salford ..(Leeds, Championship final)	0

	App	Tries
League	33	63
Yorks Cup....................................	4	8
RL Cup.......................................	4	9
Play Off.....................................	1	0
Totals	**42**	**80**

Most points in a season:

LEWIS JONES holds the record for most points in a season with 496 from 194 goals and 36 tries for Leeds and representative teams in 1956-57.

Jones' match-by-match record:

For Leeds

1956

			Gls	Tries	Pts
Aug. 17	Halifax	(H)	3	0	6
22	Bradford N.	(A)	11	3	31
25	Wigan	(A)	4	0	8
27	Featherstone R.	(H)	4	1	11
Sept. 1	Wakefield	(YC) (A)	3	1	9
8	Dewsbury	(A)	6	0	12
15	Warrington	(H)	7	0	14
22	Huddersfield	(A)	3	0	6
29	York	(H)	6	0	12
Oct. 6	Batley	(A)	4	2	14
13	Australia	(H)	Did not play		
20	Hull K.R.	(A)	Did not play		
27	Wigan	(H)	2	0	4
Nov. 3	Hunslet	(A)	1	0	2
10	Barrow	(H)	3	2	12
17	Halifax	(A)	4	0	8
24	Keighley	(H)	3	3	15
Dec. 1	Barrow	(A)	4	0	8
8	Bramley	(A)	5	0	10
15	Doncaster	(H)	1	2	8
22	Bradford N (abandoned)	(H)	1	1	5
25	Batley	(H)	8	1	19
29	Keighley	(A)	3	0	6
1957					
Jan. 5	Hull	(H)	5	2	16
12	Warrington	(A)	0	3	9
19	St. Helens	(H)	5	1	13
26	Doncaster	(A)	Did not play		
Feb. 2	Huddersfield	(H)	6	0	12
9	Wigan	(RL Cup) (H)	2	1	7
16	York	(A)	7	1	17
23	Warrington	(RL Cup) (H)	5	1	13
27	Castleford	(H)	4	1	11
Mar. 9	Halifax	(RL Cup) (A)	5	0	10
16	Wakefield T.	(H)	5	1	13
20	Bradford N	(H)	5	1	13
23	Hull	(A)	2	0	4
30	Whitehaven (Odsal, RL Cup SF)		1	0	2
Apr. 3	Wakefield T.	(A)	3	0	6
6	St. Helens	(A)	0	0	0
12	Hull K.R.	(H)	Did not play		
13	Dewsbury	(H)	6	2	18
19	Hunslet	(H)	5	2	16
20	Featherstone R.	(A)	2	0	4
22	Castleford	(A)	2	0	4
23	Bramley	(H)	7	1	17
May 4	Oldham	(Play-off) (A)	3	0	6
11	Barrow (Wembley, RL Cup final)		0	0	0

Representative matches

For Great Britain:

Jan. 26	France	(at Leeds)	9	1	21
Mar. 3	France	(at Toulouse)	5	1	13
Apr. 10	France	(at St. Helens)	7	1	17

For The Rest:

Oct. 3	Britain XIII	(at Bradford)	4	0	8

For RL XIII:

Oct. 29	Australia	(Leigh)	3	0	6

	App	Gls	Tries	Pts
League	36	147	30	384
RL Cup	5	13	2	32
Yorks Cup	1	3	1	9
Play-off	1	3	0	6
Representative	5	28	3	65
Totals	**48**	**194**	**36**	**496**

Most points in a match:

53 (11t, 10g) by George West (Hull K.R.) v. Brookland Rovers (RL Cup) ....4 March, 1905

Most points in a career:

NEIL FOX holds the record for most points in a career with 6,220 between 1956 and 1979. This total does not include points scored during a spell of club rugby in New Zealand.

Fox was a month short of his 17th birthday when he made his debut for Wakefield Trinity on 10 April, 1956. Apart from a brief time at Bradford Northern Fox had 19 seasons at Wakefield before moving to a succession of clubs in later years.

After a long career as an international centre Fox moved into the forwards and played his last professional match for Bradford in their opening fixture of the 1979-80 season, on 19 August. That match enabled him to join the elite few who have played first team rugby at 40 years of age.

Fox's season-by-season tally is as follows:

	Gls	Tries	Pts
1955-56	6	0	12
1956-57	54	10	138
1957-58	124	32	344
1958-59	148	28	380
1959-60	171	37	453
1960-61	94	20	248
1961-62	183	30	456
1962 Tour			
Australasia	85	19	227
South Africa	19	4	50
1962-63	125	14	292
1963-64	125	21	313
1964-65	121	13	281
1965-66	98	11	229
1966-67	144	16	336
1967-68	98	18	250
1968-69	95	9	217
1969-70	17	5	49
1970-71	110	12	256
1971-72	84	6	186
1972-73	138	8	300
1973-74	62	8	148
1974-75	146(1)	14	333

1975-76	102(1)	4	215
1976-77	79(1)	6	175
1977-78	95(1)	9	216
1978-79	50	4	112
1979-80	2	0	4

A breakdown of Fox's club and representative totals is as follows:

	App	Gls	Tries	Pts
Wakefield T.	574	1,836	272	4,488
Bradford N.	70	85(1)	12	205
Hull K.R.	59	212(2)	16	470
York	13	42	2	90
Bramley	23	73	6	164
Huddersfield	21	73(1)	5	160
Club Totals	**760**	**2,321(4)**	**313**	**5,577**
				(cont)
Yorkshire	17	60	9	147
Britain v. Australia	8	26	3	61
New Zealand.	4	11	1	25
France	17	56	10	142
Other representative games including tour	22	101	22	268
Representative Totals.	**68**	**254**	**45**	**643**
Grand Totals	**828**	**2,575(4)**	**358**	**6,220**

( ) Figures in brackets are one point drop goals included in total.

Score-a-match:

The following players have appeared and scored in all of their club's matches in one season:

Jim Hoey (Widnes) 1932-33
Billy Langton (Hunslet) 1958-59
Stuart Ferguson (Leigh) 1970-71
David Watkins (Salford)..............................1972-73
David Watkins (Salford)..............................1973-74
John Woods (Leigh)...................................1977-78
Steve Quinn (Featherstone R.) 1979-80
Mick Parrish (Hunslet) 1979-80
John Gorton (Swinton)...............................1980-81
Mick Parrish (Oldham) 1981-82
Peter Wood (Runcorn H.) 1984-85
David Noble (Doncaster).............................1986-87
Mark Aston (Sheffield E.) 1988-89
Mike Fletcher (Hull K.R.) 1989-90

Longest scoring run:

DAVID WATKINS holds the record for the longest scoring run, playing and scoring in 92 consecutive matches for Salford from 19 August 1972 to 25 April 1974. He totalled 403 goals, 41 tries and 929 points.

Longest run of appearances:

KEITH ELWELL holds the record for the longest run of appearances with one club with a total of 239 for Widnes. The consecutive run started at Wembley in the 1977 Challenge Cup final against Leeds on 7 May, and ended after he played in a Lancashire Cup-tie at home to St. Helens on 5 September 1982. He was dropped for the match at Featherstone Rovers a week later. Although he went on as a substitute the record refers to full appearances only.

Elwell played as a substitute in the next match and then made a full appearance before his run of all appearances ended at 242.

Highest score:
Huddersfield 119 v. Swinton Park 2 (RL Cup)
.......28 February 1914

Most points in all matches in a season:
1,436 by Leigh from 43 matches in 1985-86 as follows:
34 Division Two matches 1,156
2 Lancashire Cup 54
4 John Player Special Trophy 161
3 RL Challenge Cup 65

Most League points in a season:
1,156 by Leigh from 34 Division Two matches in 1985-86.

Longest winning run:
29 by Wigan from February to October 1987, as follows:
20 Division One, 3 Premiership, 4 Lancashire Cup, 1 Charity Shield and 1 World Club Challenge.

Longest unbeaten run:
38 Cup and League matches by Huddersfield in 1914-15, including two draws. After the interruption by the First World War Huddersfield won their next five competitive matches — 4 Yorkshire Cup ties in 1918-19 and the opening league match of 1919-20.

Longest winning run in the League:
31 matches by Wigan. Last 8 matches of 1969-70 and first 23 of 1970-71.
● In 1978-79 Hull won all of their 26 Division Two matches, the only time a club has won all its league matches in one season.

Longest losing run:
61 Cup and League matches by Runcorn Highfield from January 1989 to February 1991. Made up of 55 Division Two, 2 Challenge Cup, 2 Regal Trophy and 2 Lancashire Cup.

Longest run without a win:
75 Cup and League matches by Runcorn Highfield from October 1988 to March 1991. Made up of 67 Division Two, 3 Challenge Cup, 3 Regal Trophy and 2 Lancashire Cup.

Longest League losing run and run without a win:
Included in the above.

● Only two teams have lost all their matches in a season: Liverpool City and Runcorn Highfield.
In 1906-07 Liverpool City lost all 30 of their league matches. Liverpool also lost their two cup ties and dropped out after only one season. They did manage a home league draw against Bramley, but when they were unable to fulfil a return fixture the match was expunged from league records.
In 1989-90 Runcorn Highfield lost all 28 of their league matches, plus three cup ties.

Hull skipper Greg Mackey and hooker Lee Jackson (right) celebrate receipt of the 1991 Stones Bitter Premiership Trophy.

CUPS

RUGBY LEAGUE CHALLENGE CUP

1991 Final

The coveted Lance Todd Trophy was awarded to second row man Denis Betts as weary Wigan beat arch-rivals St. Helens 13-8 in an unspectacular Silk Cut Challenge Cup final. The Riversiders' own choice as Man of the Match was a non-player, club doctor Ansar Zaman.

The plastic surgeon administered a revolutionary nerve-blocking injection to Ellery Hanley's torn thigh muscle to enable the inspirational skipper to pass an unprecedented fitness check on the Wembley turf only an hour before kick off. Six other pain-killing injections were given to Wigan's walking wounded, half backs Shaun Edwards and Andy Gregory, packmen Martin Dermott, Andy Platt and Phil Clarke, plus centre Kevin Iro, making his last appearance before joining Sydney club Manly.

Winger Joe Lydon was ruled out on the eve of the final with a hamstring injury, while prop Kelvin Skerrett was suspended. After clinching the Stones Bitter Championship and a place at Wembley in a strength-sapping end-of-season programme of 10 matches in 33 days, coach John Monie described his second successive double-winning side as 'held together by needles and sticking plaster'.

While Wigan had to overcome weariness and injuries, St. Helens suffered a dose of dropsy, continual mishandling marring the first quarter as Wigan opened a 12-0 lead inside 12 minutes. In a final destined for the record books rather than the sporting memory, Gregory struck a strategic drop goal seven minutes after the break before Saints fought their way back into the game to put some excitement into a showpiece occasion to be remembered for commitment rather than entertainment.

Wigan's professionalism was sufficient to hold on to the lead and the Silk Cut Challenge Cup, extending the Wembley record of wins to 11 in a record 17th appearance under the twin towers. The Riversiders stretched the record number of successive final victories to four, while equalling the record successive appearances at any venue. Their second Wembley triumph over neighbours St. Helens in three years was their 20th consecutive Challenge Cup-tie win, with Shaun Edwards the only player to appear in all of them, dating back to the start of the 1987-88 campaign.

Captain Hanley suffered the hamstring injury two weeks earlier in Wigan's title-clinching success at Leeds, being confined to a London clinic for the fortnight. The dramatic Wembley fitness test was his first run since coming off at Headingley. He was never more than an organiser and inspiration. That he was lacking match fitness was typified when he gave up the chase as Bernard Dwyer almost produced a try for Saints when the hooter sounded for half-time. Hanley stayed the course and climbed the Wembley steps to become the first skipper to lift the Challenge Cup in three successive seasons, in doing so equalling the total of three Wembley victories as captain by Derek Turner, Eric Ashton and Alex Murphy.

Wigan were at their best in the opening stages before the fixture-crammed last month of the league took its toll. Lance Todd Trophy winner Betts epitomised Wigan's display in that opening burst. The young forward, ever-present in all Wigan's 39 matches, plus four for Great Britain, was full of running in the first 25 minutes when his magnificent break set up Botica's try. But little was seen of him in the second half, which included a 10-minute spell on the wing, and he handled the ball only four times.

Scrum half Gregory ran him closest in the Press voting, although it was probably the quietest of his record-equalling seven

Wembley final appearances, extending the most wins record to six to add to the drawn final in 1982. His main contributions were two energy-saving touchfinding kicks and a 35-yard drop goal that opened up a vital 13-0 lead.

Debutant David Myers, the 11th-hour replacement for Lydon, made the most of his limited chances on the right wing, stepping inside neatly to touch down after seven minutes. On the left flank, Frano Botica, joining an elite band of former New Zealand All Blacks to grace Wembley, finished strongly to get the second try five minutes later before adding a superb touchline goal.

With Alan Hunte scoring St. Helens' only try, all three match touchdowns went to wingers despite play being generally confined to the packs and half backs. Hunte's try came in the 61st minute and, with Bishop adding the goal and a penalty 10 minutes later, the Saints might have made it even closer had their inability to hold possession not continued to the end.

Second row pair John Harrison — the tallest-ever player at Wembley at 6ft 7in — and Kiwi import George Mann led the Saints' forward barrage. Harrison drove in harder and more often than any other packman.

Behind the St. Helens six, scrum half Bishop was at least equal to opposite number Gregory. He found three touch kicks and landed two excellent goals to inspire the fightback in the last quarter. His most promising break was halted by a blatant obstruction by Wigan's Steve Hampson after a kick ahead, a foul which earned the full-back a 10-minute spell in the sin bin.

Although Wigan carried injuries into the final, St. Helens suffered badly during the action. The only two survivors from their Wembley defeats of 1987 and 1989, Phil Veivers and Paul Loughlin, both left the field with concussion. Veivers missed most of the match after being knocked out in the incident

that led to Wigan's lucky first try, returning late on in the loose forward role. Loughlin was kept off in the second half and Dwyer suffered an horrific ear wound in the closing stages.

The bravery of the finalists was reflected in the blood-stained jerseys, bruised faces and bodies at the medal presentation ceremony. Both dressing rooms resembled casualty wards after the match, with coach Monie providing the final diagnosis for his Cup and League winning outfit. 'No side should have to go through again what we have experienced in the past six weeks. This is a very special team.'

Wigan's Ellery Hanley becomes the first skipper to receive the Challenge Cup at three successive Wembley finals.

SILK CUT CHALLENGE CUP FINAL

27 April   **Wembley**

WIGAN 13		**ST. HELENS 8**
Steve Hampson	1.	Phil Veivers
David Myers	2.	Alan Hunte
Kevin Iro	3.	Tea Ropati
Dean Bell	4.	Paul Loughlin
Frano Botica	5.	Les Quirk
Shaun Edwards	6.	Jonathan Griffiths
Andy Gregory	7.	Paul Bishop
Ian Lucas	8.	Jonathan Neill
Martin Dermott	9.	Bernard Dwyer
Andy Platt	10.	Kevin Ward
Denis Betts	11.	John Harrison
Phil Clarke	12.	George Mann
Ellery Hanley, Capt.	13.	Shane Cooper, Capt.
Bobby Goulding	14.	Gary Connolly
Andy Goodway	15.	Paul Groves

T: Myers, Botica
G: Botica (2), Gregory (dg)
Substitutions:
Goodway for Clarke (22 min.)
Goulding for Dermott (60 min.)
Half-time: 12-0
Referee: Jim Smith (Halifax)

T: Hunte
G: Bishop (2)
Substitutions:
Connolly for Veivers (8 min.)
Groves for Neill (26 min.)
Attendance: 75,532
Receipts: £1,610,447

Scorechart

Minute	Score	Wigan	St. Helens
5:	Botica (P)	2	0
7:	Myers (T)	6	0
12:	Botica (T)		
	Botica (G)	12	0
47:	Gregory (DG)	13	0
61:	Hunte (T)		
	Bishop (G)	13	6
71:	Bishop (P)	13	8
	Scrums	10	8
	Penalties	7	9

*St. Helens tryscorer Alan Hunte, with goalscorer
Paul Bishop in support.*

1991 Round by Round

The shock result of the six-tie preliminary round was relegation-haunted Sheffield Eagles' 19-6 disposal of Championship title-chasers Hull at the Don Valley Stadium. Man of the Match Mark Aston kicked five goals and Daryl Powell a drop goal as the Eagles led 11-6 before celebrating victory with two tries in the last five minutes. Second Division Huddersfield restricted Warrington to three tries in a 22-4 defeat at Wilderspool, only Wire scrum half Kevin Ellis shining in a dour contest. Carlisle led 8-0 at half-time at home to Workington Town, who crowned a second half revival with a Stephen Wear drop goal to snatch a 9-8 victory. The three amateur clubs fell to professional outfits, Leigh East putting up the best performance to First Division Bradford Northern, going down 24-12 at Leigh but providing the Silk Cut Award winner in Steve Grimshaw before superior fitness told. Cumbria Cup winners Hensingham entertained Dewsbury at Workington, Simon Knox taking the Man of the Match award while Dewsbury clinched a 24-7 victory with 18 points in 11 minutes straight after the interval. Second Division leaders Salford displayed too much pace and power for Yorkshire Cup winners Cutsyke, from Castleford, who went down 44-4 at the Willows.

The staging of the first round was severely disrupted by heavy snow. Second Division promotion candidates Swinton hired Manchester City FC's heated pitch to entertain St. Helens and led 8-4 at the break, after which the Saints ran in three tries in seven minutes for an 18-8 success. Leeds played hosts to Dewsbury on the heated Headingley pitch and were rewarded with a 40-20 victory, scoring eight tries to Dewsbury's three. More than 200 volunteers helped clear Doncaster's Tattersfield for the visit of Widnes, who opened with two tries and two goals inside 15 minutes on the way to a 30-4 victory. Castle-

ford's battle to stage the attractive home tie with Wigan was rewarded with a 28-4 defeat, the Riversiders cruising 22-0 at the break, Frano Botica collecting a tally of 16 points.

Runcorn Highfield held out for half an hour at Keighley before Man of the Match Jeff Butterfield opened the scoring with a 33rd minute try, the home side amassing seven tries in a 36-4 victory. In-form Second Division side Workington Town produced the shock of the round with an 18-12 home success over First Division Hull K.R., who led 8-0 before former Rovers forward Colin Armstrong inspired a comeback to 12-12 and New Zealander Paddy Tuimavave touched down in the corner. Barrow entertained Hunslet a week after going down 52-4 at Elland Road. Coach Steve Norton was sacked and they bounced back under new coach Paul Kavanagh to record a 13-8 success. Nottingham City led 10-4 at the interval at home to Whitehaven before the Cumbrians, marshalled by two-try player-coach Norman Turley, rallied with four second-half touchdowns for a 26-10 victory.

Second Division Ryedale-York led 1990 Wembley runners-up Warrington 1-0 on the hour at the Ryedale Stadium before Wire full back David Lyon scored the only try of a tense encounter to clinch an 8-1 success. Halifax beat Fulham 46-6 at Thrum Hall with centre Greg Austin registering a hat-trick of tries and Alan Platt contributing 18 points with a try and seven goals. Test forward Karl Fairbank was outstanding in Bradford Northern's nine-try, 50-4 defeat of Leigh at Bradford City FC. Second Division Bramley were level 6-6 with First Division Oldham at the interval before the home side conceded six second-half tries and had Peter Lister sent off for tripping as they went down 38-6.

Sheffield Eagles built a 19-0 lead before visitors Featherstone Rovers rallied with tries from Tim Sharp and Martin Pearson. The 19-12 triumph was marred by the dismissal of home winger David Nelson and

Featherstone forward Brendan Tuuta in a late brawl. Second Division Trafford Borough trailed only 12-7 at Wakefield Trinity before home scrum half Mark Conway scored a try and goal for an unconvincing 18-7 victory. Chorley took the lead at Rochdale with a Steve Hankney try before the Hornets hit back with Stuart Galbraith and Mark Nixon tries on the way to a 14-10 success. Brave Batley trailed only 18-14 at Salford before the Red Devils pulled away in the second half for a 36-14 win, Batley's Sonny Whakarau taking the Silk Cut Award.

In the second round, Second Division pacesetters Salford pulled off the shock result with a 19-16 success at Sheffield, who led 8-6 after 23 minutes. Big-spending Leeds took a four-day break at Blackpool but could not turn the tide at Bradford, who won 5-0 with a Darrall Shelford try and John Pendlebury drop goal. Alan Hunte and John Harrison scored the tries in St. Helens' 16-2 home success over Wakefield Trinity, who extended their poor form to only one win in 10 matches. First round giant-killers Workington Town trailed 14-2 at half-time to First Division visitors Oldham, pulling back to lead 15-14 on the hour before Charlie McAlister created the winning try for Ronnie Duane and a final scoreline of 20-15 to Oldham.

After prop forward Brendan Hill had opened the scoring for Halifax in the third minute, visitors Whitehaven threatened a shock with two tries from Vince Gribbin before the Thrum Hallers settled down to run up a 46-12 victory. Silk Cut Award winner Des Drummond played a captain's role for Warrington with a hat-trick of tries in the 42-10 success at Keighley. Bottom of the table Rochdale Hornets received a 72-4 hammering at home from Silk Cut Challenge Cup holders Wigan, Ellery Hanley amassing six tries and Botica contributing a try and 12 goals. Widnes struggled at Second Division Barrow, clinching a 28-4 victory with three tries in the last quarter, two from Alan Tait and a second for Test winger Martin Offiah.

In the third round, Jonathan Davies returned to the Widnes ranks after injury to demoralise hosts Warrington with five goals and a host of pinpoint touch kicks. The Chemics gained revenge for their earlier Regal Trophy semi-final defeat by the Wire with a 26-14 success, inspired by Man of the Match Esene Faimalo. Wigan continued their trek on the well-worn path to Wembley by disposing of injury-hit Bradford Northern 32-2 at Central Park, Andy Gregory gaining the Silk Cut Award, while Botica added a try and six goals. Seven-try Oldham sent unbeaten Second Division leaders Salford crashing to a 40-3 defeat at Watersheddings, captain Mike Ford earning Man of the Match rating. St. Helens made it an all West of the Pennines semi-final line-up by registering a 24-16 victory at Halifax, Welshman Jonathan Griffiths having a hand in three of the Saints' four tries.

Wigan reached Wembley for the fourth successive year with a 30-16 defeat of relegation-doomed Oldham at Burnden Park, Bolton. The Riversiders led 24-0 shortly after half-time with half backs Shaun Edwards and Andy Gregory masterminding the romp, the latter being awarded the Silk Cut Award. Oldham rallied to score three tries to one in the last half hour, although Wigan could be excused for having their hectic Championship final programme on their minds. Underdogs St. Helens rewrote the form book a week later at Wigan, defeating League-Cup double hopefuls Widnes 19-2. Saints set up a revenge meeting with derby rivals Wigan, who beat them 27-0 at Wembley in 1989, with a tremendous pack display headed by George Mann and Kevin Ward. Stand off Griffiths took full advantage to score two tries and earn the Silk Cut Award as lacklustre Widnes failed to find their top-of-the-table form.

1991 PRIZES

Round	Per Team	Total
Preliminary	12 × £2,250	£27,000
First	16 × £2,250	£36,000
Second	8 × £3,500	£28,000
Third	4 × £5,500	£22,000
Semi-Finals	2 × £9,000	£18,000
Runners-up	1 × £17,000	£17,000
Winners	1 × £32,000	£32,000
	Total Prize Money	£180,000
	Capital Development Fund	£120,000
	Grand Total	£300,000

1991 RESULTS

Preliminary Round

Carlisle	8	Workington T.	9
Hensingham	7	Dewsbury	24
(at Workington)			
Leigh East	12	Bradford N.	24
(at Leigh)			
Salford	44	Cutsyke	4
Sheffield E.	19	Hull	6
Warrington	22	Huddersfield	4

First Round

Barrow	13	Hunslet	8
Bradford N.	50	Leigh	4
(at Bradford City FC)			
Bramley	6	Oldham	38
Castleford	4	Wigan	28
Doncaster	4	Widnes	30
Halifax	46	Fulham	6
Keighley	36	Runcorn H.	4
Leeds	40	Dewsbury	20
Nottingham C.	10	Whitehaven	26
Rochdale H.	14	Chorley	10
Ryedale-York	1	Warrington	8
Salford	36	Batley	14
Sheffield E.	19	Featherstone R.	12
Swinton	8	St. Helens	18
(at Manchester City FC)			
Wakefield T.	18	Trafford B.	7
Workington T.	18	Hull K.R.	12

Second Round

Barrow	4	Widnes	28
Bradford N.	5	Leeds	0
Halifax	46	Whitehaven	12
Keighley	10	Warrington	42
Rochdale H.	4	Wigan	72
St. Helens	16	Wakefield T.	2
Sheffield E.	16	Salford	19
Workington T.	15	Oldham	20

Third Round

Halifax	16	St. Helens	24
Oldham	40	Salford	3
Warrington	14	Widnes	26
Wigan	32	Bradford N.	2

Semi-Finals

Wigan	30	Oldham	16
(at Bolton FC)			
St. Helens	19	Widnes	2
(at Wigan)			

Final

Wigan	13	St. Helens	8
(at Wembley)			

Wigan centre Dean Bell, a commanding figure at Wembley.

Welshman Jonathan Griffiths, a Wembley debut in the beaten St. Helens side.

St. Helens scrum half Paul Bishop grapples with Wigan packman Andy Goodway as Bernard Dwyer moves in to add support.

Wigan skipper Ellery Hanley falls to a twin tackle by Saints Kevin Ward (right) and John Harrison.

CHALLENGE CUP ROLL OF HONOUR

Year	Winners		Runners-up		Venue	Attendance	Receipts
1897	Batley	10	St. Helens	3	Leeds	13,492	£624.17.7
1898	Batley	7	Bradford	0	Leeds	27,941	£1,586.3.0
1899	Oldham	19	Hunslet	9	Manchester	15,763	£946.16.0
1900	Swinton	16	Salford	8	Manchester	17,864	£1,100.0.0
1901	Batley	6	Warrington	0	Leeds	29,563	£1,644.16.0
1902	Broughton R.	25	Salford	0	Rochdale	15,006	£846.11.0
1903	Halifax	7	Salford	0	Leeds	32,507	£1,834.8.6
1904	Halifax	8	Warrington	3	Salford	17,041	£936.5.6
1905	Warrington	6	Hull K.R.	0	Leeds	19,638	£1,271.18.0
1906	Bradford	5	Salford	0	Leeds	15,834	£920.0.0
1907	Warrington	17	Oldham	3	Broughton	18,500	£1,010.0.0
1908	Hunslet	14	Hull	0	Huddersfield	18,000	£903.0.0
1909	Wakefield T.	17	Hull	0	Leeds	23,587	£1,490.0.0
1910	Leeds	7	Hull	7	Huddersfield	19,413	£1,102.0.0
Replay	Leeds	26	Hull	12	Huddersfield	11,608	£657.0.0
1911	Broughton R.	4	Wigan	0	Salford	8,000	£376.0.0
1912	Dewsbury	8	Oldham	5	Leeds	15,271	£853.0.0
1913	Huddersfield	9	Warrington	5	Leeds	22,754	£1,446.9.6
1914	Hull	6	Wakefield T.	0	Halifax	19,000	£1,035.5.0
1915	Huddersfield	37	St. Helens	3	Oldham	8,000	£472.0.0
1920	Huddersfield	21	Wigan	10	Leeds	14,000	£1,936.0.0
1921	Leigh	13	Halifax	0	Broughton	25,000	£2,700.0.0
1922	Rochdale H.	10	Hull	9	Leeds	32,596	£2,964.0.0
1923	Leeds	28	Hull	3	Wakefield	29,335	£2,390.0.0
1924	Wigan	21	Oldham	4	Rochdale	41,831	£3,712.0.0
1925	Oldham	16	Hull K.R.	3	Leeds	28,335	£2,879.0.0
1926	Swinton	9	Oldham	3	Rochdale	27,000	£2,551.0.0
1927	Oldham	26	Swinton	7	Wigan	33,448	£3,170.0.0
1928	Swinton	5	Warrington	3	Wigan	33,909	£3,158.1.11
1929	Wigan	13	Dewsbury	2	Wembley	41,500	£5,614.0.0
1930	Widnes	10	St. Helens	3	Wembley	36,544	£3,102.0.0
1931	Halifax	22	York	8	Wembley	40,368	£3,908.0.0
1932	Leeds	11	Swinton	8	Wigan	29,000	£2,479.0.0
1933	Huddersfield	21	Warrington	17	Wembley	41,874	£6,465.0.0
1934	Hunslet	11	Widnes	5	Wembley	41,280	£6,686.0.0
1935	Castleford	11	Huddersfield	8	Wembley	39,000	£5,533.0.0
1936	Leeds	18	Warrington	2	Wembley	51,250	£7,070.0.0
1937	Widnes	18	Keighley	5	Wembley	47,699	£6,704.0.0
1938	Salford	7	Barrow	4	Wembley	51,243	£7,174.0.0
1939	Halifax	20	Salford	3	Wembley	55,453	£7,681.0.0
1940	*No competition*						
1941	Leeds	19	Halifax	2	Bradford	28,500	£1,703.0.0
1942	Leeds	15	Halifax	10	Bradford	15,250	£1,276.0.0
1943	Dewsbury	16	Leeds	9	Dewsbury	10,470	£823.0.0
	Dewsbury	0	Leeds	6	Leeds	16,000	£1,521.0.0
	Dewsbury won on aggregate 16-15						
1944	Bradford	0	Wigan	3	Wigan	22,000	£1,640.0.0
	Bradford	8	Wigan	0	Bradford	30,000	£2,200.0.0
	Bradford won on aggregate 8-3						
1945	Huddersfield	7	Bradford N.	4	Huddersfield	9,041	£1,184.3.7
	Huddersfield	6	Bradford N.	5	Bradford	17,500	£2,050.0.0
	Huddersfield won on aggregate 13-9						

Year	Winners		Runners-up		Venue	Attendance	Receipts
1946	Wakefield T.	13	Wigan	12	Wembley	54,730	£12,013.13.6
1947	Bradford N.	8	Leeds	4	Wembley	77,605	£17,434.5.0
1948	Wigan	8	Bradford N.	3	Wembley	91,465	£21,121.9.9
1949	Bradford N.	12	Halifax	0	Wembley	*95,050	£21,930.5.0
1950	Warrington	19	Widnes	0	Wembley	94,249	£24,782.13.0
1951	Wigan	10	Barrow	0	Wembley	94,262	£24,797.19.0
1952	Workington T.	18	Featherstone R.	10	Wembley	72,093	£22,374.2.0
1953	Huddersfield	15	St. Helens	10	Wembley	89,588	£30,865.12.3
1954	Warrington	4	Halifax	4	Wembley	81,841	£29,706.7.3
Replay	Warrington	8	Halifax	4	Bradford	102,569	£18,623.7.0
1955	Barrow	21	Workington T.	12	Wembley	66,513	£27,453.16.0
1956	St. Helens	13	Halifax	2	Wembley	79,341	£29,424.7.6
1957	Leeds	9	Barrow	7	Wembley	76,318	£32,671.14.3
1958	Wigan	13	Workington T.	9	Wembley	66,109	£33,175.17.6
1959	Wigan	30	Hull	13	Wembley	79,811	£35,718.19.9
1960	Wakefield T.	38	Hull	5	Wembley	79,773	£35,754.16.0
1961	St. Helens	12	Wigan	6	Wembley	94,672	£38,479.11.9
1962	Wakefield T.	12	Huddersfield	6	Wembley	81,263	£33,390.18.4
1963	Wakefield T.	25	Wigan	10	Wembley	84,492	£44,521.17.0
1964	Widnes	13	Hull K.R.	5	Wembley	84,488	£44,840.19.0
1965	Wigan	20	Hunslet	16	Wembley	89,016	£48,080.4.0
1966	St. Helens	21	Wigan	2	Wembley	*98,536	£50,409.0.0
1967	Featherstone R.	17	Barrow	12	Wembley	76,290	£53,465.14.0
1968	Leeds	11	Wakefield T.	10	Wembley	87,100	£56,171.16.6
1969	Castleford	11	Salford	6	Wembley	*97,939	£58,848.1.0
1970	Castleford	7	Wigan	2	Wembley	95,255	£89,262.2.0
1971	Leigh	24	Leeds	7	Wembley	85,514	£84,452.15
1972	St. Helens	16	Leeds	13	Wembley	89,495	£86,114.30
1973	Featherstone R.	33	Bradford N.	14	Wembley	72,395	£125,826.40
1974	Warrington	24	Featherstone R	9	Wembley	77,400	£132,021.05
1975	Widnes	14	Warrington	7	Wembley	85,098	£140,684.45
1976	St. Helens	20	Widnes	5	Wembley	89,982	£190,129.40
1977	Leeds	16	Widnes	7	Wembley	80,871	£241,488.00
1978	Leeds	14	St. Helens	12	Wembley	*96,000	£330,575.00
1979	Widnes	12	Wakefield T.	3	Wembley	94,218	£383,157.00
1980	Hull K.R.	10	Hull	5	Wembley	*95,000	£448,202.90
1981	Widnes	18	Hull K.R.	9	Wembley	92,496	£591,117.00
1982	Hull	14	Widnes	14	Wembley	92,147	£684,500.00
Replay	Hull	18	Widnes	9	Elland Rd., L'ds	41,171	£180,525.00
1983	Featherstone R.	14	Hull	12	Wembley	84,969	£655,510.00
1984	Widnes	19	Wigan	6	Wembley	80,116	£686,171.00
1985	Wigan	28	Hull	24	Wembley	*97,801	£760,322.00
1986	Castleford	15	Hull K.R.	14	Wembley	82,134	£806,676.00
1987	Halifax	19	St. Helens	18	Wembley	91,267	£1,009,206.00
1988	Wigan	32	Halifax	12	Wembley	*94,273	£1,102,247.00
1989	Wigan	27	St. Helens	0	Wembley	*78,000	£1,121,293.00
1990	Wigan	36	Warrington	14	Wembley	*77,729	£1,360,000.00
1991	Wigan	13	St. Helens	8	Wembley	75,532	£1,610,447.00

*Indicates a capacity attendance, the limit being fixed annually taking into account variable factors.

RUGBY LEAGUE CHALLENGE CUP ....
A REVIEW
1968-69
Castleford 11 Edwards; Briggs, Howe (1t),
Thomas, Lowndes; Hardisty (1t), Hepworth (1t);
Hartley, C. Dickinson, J. Ward, Redfearn (1g),
Lockwood, Reilly
Salford 6 K. Gwilliam; Burgess, Whitehead,
Hesketh, Jackson; Watkins, Brennan; Ogden,
Dickens, Bott, Coulman, Dixon, Hill (3g)
Referee: D.S. Brown (Preston)
1969-70
Castleford 7 Edwards; Briggs, Thomas, Stenton,
Lowndes (1t); Hardisty (Hargrave), Hepworth;
Hartley, C. Dickinson, Redfearn (2g), Kirkbride,
Lockwood, Reilly
Wigan 2 Tyrer (1g) (C. Hill); Jones, Francis,
Rowe, Kevin O'Loughlin; D. Hill, Parr;
Ashcroft, Burdell, Hogan, Ashurst, D. Robinson,
Laughton
Referee: G.F. Lindop (Wakefield)
1970-71
Leigh 24 Eckersley (1t, 1g); Ferguson (5g),
Dorrington (1t), Collins, Walsh; A. Barrow,
Murphy (2g) (L. Chisnall); Watts, Ashcroft,
Fiddler (1g), Grimes, Clarkson, Smethurst
Leeds 7 Holmes (2g); Langley, Hynes, Cowan
(Dyl), Atkinson; Wainwright (1t), Seabourne;
J. Burke, Fisher, Barnard, Hick, Haigh, Ramsey
Referee: W.H. Thompson (Huddersfield)
1971-72
St. Helens 16 G. Pimblett; L. Jones (1t), Benyon,
Walsh, Wilson; K. Kelly, Heaton; Rees (1t),
Greenall, J. Stephens, Mantle, E. Chisnall,
Coslett (5g)
Leeds 13 Holmes; Alan Smith, Hynes (Langley),
Dyl, Atkinson; Hardisty, Hepworth; Clawson
(5g), Fisher, Ramsey, Cookson (1t), Haigh, Batten
Referee: E. Lawrinson (Warrington)
1972-73
Featherstone R. 33 C. Kellett (8g); Coventry,
M. Smith (1t) (Hartley) (1t), Newlove (2t),
K. Kellett; Mason, Nash (1g); Tonks, Bridges,
Farrar (1t), Rhodes (Hollis), Thompson, Stone
Bradford N. 14 Tees (4g); Lamb, Stockwell,
Watson, D. Redfearn (1t); Blacker (Treasure),
Seabourne; Hogan, Dunn, Earl (Long), Joyce,
W. Pattinson, Fearnley (1t)
Referee: M.J. Naughton (Widnes)
1973-74
Warrington 24 Whitehead (7g); M. Philbin,
Noonan, Whittle, Bevan; Murphy (2g) (Pickup),
Gordon; D. Chisnall, Ashcroft (1t), Brady
(Wanbon), Wright, Nicholas (1t), B. Philbin
Featherstone R. 9 Box (3g); Dyas, M. Smith,
Hartley, Bray; Newlove (1t), Nash; Tonks,
Bridges, Harris, Rhodes (Busfield), Thompson
(Stone), Bell *Referee:* S. Shepherd (Oldham)

1974-75
Widnes 14 Dutton (5g, 1dg); A. Prescott, George,
Aspey, Anderson; Hughes, Bowden; Mills (1t),
Elwell, Sheridan, Foran, Adams, Laughton
Warrington 7 Whitehead (2g); M. Philbin,
Noonan, Reynolds (W. Briggs), Bevan (1t);
Whittle, Gordon; D. Chisnall, Ashcroft, Wanbon,
Conroy, Martyn (Nicholas), B. Philbin
Referee: P. Geraghty (York)
1975-76
St. Helens 20 G. Pimblett (3g, 2dg); L. Jones,
Cunningham (1t), Noonan, Mathias; Benyon
(Glynn 2t), Heaton (1t); Mantle (James),
A. Karalius, Coslett, Nicholls, E. Chisnall, Hull
Widnes 5 Dutton (2g); A. Prescott (D. O'Neill),
Hughes, George, Jenkins; Eckersley, Bowden;
Nelson, Elwell (1dg), Wood, Foran (Sheridan),
Adams, Laughton
Referee: R. Moore (Wakefield)
1976-77
Leeds 16 Murrell; Alan Smith (D. Smith),
Hague, Dyl (1t), Atkinson (1t); Holmes,
Dick (1t, 3g, 1dg); Harrison, Ward, Pitchford,
Eccles, Cookson, Fearnley (Dickinson)
Widnes 7 Dutton (2g); S. Wright (George),
Aspey (1t), Eckersley, D. O'Neill; Hughes,
Bowden; Ramsey, Elwell, Mills, Dearden
(Foran), Adams, Laughton
Referee: V. Moss (Manchester)
1977-78
Leeds 14 Oulton (1g); D. Smith (1t), Hague, Dyl,
Atkinson (1t); Holmes (1dg), J. Sanderson (Dick);
Harrison (Dickinson), Ward (2dg), Pitchford,
Cookson (1t), Eccles, Crane
St. Helens 12 G. Pimblett (3g), L. Jones,
Noonan, Glynn, Mathias; Francis (1t),
K. Gwilliam; D. Chisnall, Liptrot (1t), James,
Nicholls, Cunningham, Pinner
Referee: W.H. Thompson (Huddersfield)
1978-79
Widnes 12 Eckersley (1dg); S. Wright (1t),
Aspey, George (Hull), Burke (2g); Hughes (1t),
Bowden; Mills, Elwell (1dg), Shaw, Adams,
Dearden (M. O'Neill), Laughton
Wakefield T. 3 Sheard; Fletcher (1t), K. Smith,
Diamond, Juliff; Topliss, Lampkowski; Burke,
McCurrie, Skerrett, Ashurst, Keith Rayne, Idle
Referee: J.E. Jackson (Pudsey)
1979-80
Hull K.R. 10 Hall; Hubbard (3g, 1t) (Hogan),
M. Smith, Hartley, Sullivan; Millward (1dg),
Agar; Holdstock, Watkinson, Lockwood, Lowe,
Rose (Millington), Casey
Hull 5 Woods; Bray, Walters, Wilby (1t),
Prendiville; Newlove (Hancock), Pickerill;
Tindall, Wileman, Stone (Farrar), Birdsall,
Lloyd (1g), Norton
Referee: G.F. Lindop (Wakefield)

1980-81
Widnes 18 Burke (4g, 1t); S. Wright, George (1t),
Cunningham (J. Myler), Bentley; Hughes,
Gregory (1t); M. O'Neill (Shaw), Elwell,
Lockwood, L. Gorley, E. Prescott, Adams (1dg)
Hull K.R. 9 Hall; Hubbard (3g), M. Smith,
Hogan, Muscroft; Hartley, Harkin; Holdstock
(Millington), Watkinson, Crooks (Proctor), Lowe,
Burton (1t), Casey
Referee: D.G. Kershaw (Easingwold)
1981-82
Hull 14 Kemble; O'Hara (1t), Day, S. Evans,
Prendiville; Topliss, Harkin; Skerrett, Wileman,
Stone, Crane (Crooks), Lloyd (4g), Norton (1t)
Widnes 14 Burke (1g), (A. Myler); S. Wright (1t),
Keiron O'Loughlin, Cunningham (2t), Basnett;
Hughes, Gregory (1g); M. O'Neill, Elwell (1dg),
Lockwood (S. O'Neill), L. Gorley, E. Prescott,
Adams
Referee: G.F. Lindop (Wakefield)
Replay
Hull 18 Kemble (1t); Sullivan, Leuluai, S. Evans,
Prendiville; Topliss (2t), Dean; Tindall, Duke,
Stone, Skerrett, Crooks (1t, 3g), Norton (Crane)
Widnes 9 Burke (3g); S. Wright (1t), Keiron
O'Loughlin, Cunningham, Basnett; Hughes,
Gregory; M. O'Neill, Elwell, Lockwood,
L. Gorley, E. Prescott, Adams
Referee: G.F. Lindop (Wakefield)
1982-83
Featherstone R. 14 N. Barker; Marsden,
Quinn (4g), Gilbert (Lyman), K. Kellett;
A. Banks, Hudson; Gibbins, Handscombe,
Hankins, D. Hobbs (2t), Slatter (Siddall), Smith
Hull 12 Kemble; O'Hara, S. Evans, Leuluai (1t),
Prendiville; Topliss, Harkin (Day), (Crane);
Skerrett, Bridges, Stone, Rose, Crooks (1t, 3g),
Norton
Referee: M.R. Whitfield (Widnes)
1983-84
Widnes 19 Burke (3g); S. Wright, Hughes
(D. Hulme), Lydon (2t), Basnett;
Keiron O'Loughlin (1t), Gregory; S. O'Neill
(1dg), Elwell, K. Tamati, L. Gorley, M. O'Neill
(Whitfield), Adams
Wigan 6 Edwards; Ramsdale, Stephenson,
Whitfield (1g), (Elvin), Gill; Cannon, Stephens;
Hemsley (1t), H. Tamati, Case (Juliff), West,
Scott, Pendlebury
Referee: W.H. Thompson (Huddersfield)
1984-85
Wigan 28 Edwards (1t); Ferguson (2t),
Stephenson (1g), Donlan, Gill (1t, 3g);
Kenny (1t), M. Ford; Courtney, Kiss, Case
(Campbell), West, Dunn, Potter

Hull 24 Kemble; James (1t), S. Evans (1t),
Leuluai (2t), O'Hara (Schofield); Ah Kuoi,
Sterling; Crooks (2g), Patrick, Puckering
(Divorty 1t), Muggleton, Rose, Norton
Referee: R. Campbell (Widnes)
1985-86
Castleford 15 Lord (Roockley); Plange,
Marchant (1t), Hyde, Sandy (1t); Joyner,
R. Beardmore (1t, 1dg); Ward, K. Beardmore
(Horton), Johnson, England, Ketteridge (1g),
French
Hull K.R. 14 Fairbairn; Clark, M. Smith,
Prohm (2t), Laws; Dorahy (1g), Harkin; P.
Johnston, Watkinson, Ema, Kelly (G. Smith),
Des Harrison (Lydiat 1t), Miller
Referee: R. Whitfield (Widnes)
1986-87
Halifax 19 Eadie (1t); Wilson, Whitfield (3g),
Rix, George (1t); C. Anderson (Juliff), Stephens;
Beevers (James), McCallion (1t), Neller, Dixon,
Scott, Pendlebury (1dg)
St. Helens 18 Veivers; Ledger, Loughlin (1t, 3g),
Elia (1t), McCormack; Clark, Holding; Burke,
Liptrot, Fieldhouse, Platt, Haggerty (Round 1t),
Arkwright
Referee: J. Holdsworth (Kippax)
1987-88
Wigan 32 Lydon (1t, 1g); T. Iro (1t), K. Iro (2t),
Bell (1t), Gill (1t); Edwards (Byrne), Gregory
(1g); Case, Kiss, Shelford, Goodway, Potter
(Wane), Hanley (1t)
Halifax 12 Eadie; Meredith, T. Anderson (1t),
Wilkinson, Whitfield (2g); Grogan, Robinson
(Fairbank); James (1t), McCallion, Neller,
Holliday (Scott), Dixon, Pendlebury
Referee: G. F. Lindop (Wakefield)
1988-89
Wigan 27 Hampson (1t); T. Iro, K. Iro (2t),
Bell, Lydon (3g); Edwards, Gregory (1t, 1dg);
Lucas, Kiss (Betts), Shelford, Platt, Potter
(Goodway), Hanley (1t)
St. Helens 0 Connolly; O'Connor, Veivers,
Loughlin (Bloor), Quirk; Cooper, Holding;
Burke, Groves, Forber, Dwyer (Evans),
Haggerty, Vautin
Referee: R. Tennant (Castleford)
1989-90
Wigan 36 Hampson; Lydon (6g), K. Iro (2t),
Bell, Preston (2t) (Gildart); Edwards, Gregory;
Shelford, Dermott (Goulding), Platt, Betts (1t),
Goodway, Hanley (1t)
Warrington 14 Lyon (1t); Drummond, Mercer,
Darbyshire (1g), Forster; Crompton, Bishop (2g)
(McGinty); Burke, D. Mann, Harmon, Jackson
(Thomas), Sanderson, Gregory (1t)
Referee: J. Holdsworth (Kippax)

THE LANCE TODD TROPHY

The Lance Todd Trophy is presented to the Man of the Match in the Rugby League Challenge Cup Final, the decision being reached by a ballot of members of the Rugby League Writers' Association present at the game.

Lance Todd made his name in Britain as a player with Wigan and as manager of Salford. His untimely death in a road accident on the return journey from a game at Oldham was commemorated by the introduction of the Lance Todd Trophy.

The award was instituted by Australian-born Harry Sunderland, Warrington director Bob Anderton and Yorkshire journalist John Bapty.

Around 1950, the Red Devils' Association at Salford, comprising players and officials who had worked with Todd, raised sufficient funds to provide a trophy and replica for each winner.

Len Killeen, of St. Helens, is the only winger to earn the title; Hull's Tommy Harris the only hooker; and Ray Ashby and Brian Gabbitas the only players to share the honour.

Following the 1954 replay, it was decided by the Red Devils that in future the trophy would be awarded for the Wembley game. In 1954, Gerry Helme had received the trophy for his performance in the Odsal replay. In the 1982 replay at Elland Road, Leeds, the Man of the Match award went to Hull skipper David Topliss, the Lance Todd Trophy having been awarded to Eddie Cunningham, of Widnes, in the drawn Wembley tie.

In 1990 Andy Gregory, of Wigan, became the first player to win the trophy twice at Wembley, having also won it two years earlier.

The Lance Todd Trophy Roll of Honour

Year	Winner	Team	Position
1946	Billy Stott	Wakefield Trinity (v Wigan)	Centre
1947	Willie Davies	Bradford Northern (v Leeds)	Stand off
1948	Frank Whitcombe	Bradford Northern (v Wigan)	Prop
1949	Ernest Ward	Bradford Northern (v Halifax)	Centre
1950	Gerry Helme	Warrington (v Widnes)	Scrum half
1951	Cec Mountford	Wigan (v Barrow)	Stand off
1952	Billy Ivison	Workington T. (v Featherstone R.)	Loose forward
1953	Peter Ramsden	Huddersfield (v St. Helens)	Stand off
1954	Gerry Helme	Warrington (v Halifax)	Scrum half
1955	Jack Grundy	Barrow (v Workington Town)	Second row
1956	Alan Prescott	St. Helens (v Halifax)	Prop
1957	Jeff Stevenson	Leeds (v Barrow)	Scrum half
1958	Rees Thomas	Wigan (v Workington Town)	Scrum half
1959	Brian McTigue	Wigan (v Hull)	Second row
1960	Tommy Harris	Hull (v Wakefield Trinity)	Hooker
1961	Dick Huddart	St. Helens (v Wigan)	Second row
1962	Neil Fox	Wakefield Trinity (v Huddersfield)	Centre
1963	Harold Poynton	Wakefield Trinity (v Wigan)	Stand off
1964	Frank Collier	Widnes (v Hull K.R.)	Prop
1965	Ray Ashby	Wigan	Full back
	Brian Gabbitas	Hunslet	Stand off
1966	Len Killeen	St. Helens (v Wigan)	Winger

1967	Carl Dooler	Featherstone Rovers (v Barrow)	Scrum half
1968	Don Fox	Wakefield Trinity (v Leeds)	Prop
1969	Malcolm Reilly	Castleford (v Salford)	Loose forward
1970	Bill Kirkbride	Castleford (v Wigan)	Second row
1971	Alex Murphy	Leigh (v Leeds)	Scrum half
1972	Kel Coslett	St. Helens (v Leeds)	Loose forward
1973	Steve Nash	Featherstone R. (v Bradford N.)	Scrum half
1974	Derek Whitehead	Warrington (v Featherstone Rovers)	Full back
1975	Ray Dutton	Widnes (v Warrington)	Full back
1976	Geoff Pimblett	St. Helens (v Widnes)	Full back
1977	Steve Pitchford	Leeds (v Widnes)	Prop
1978	George Nicholls	St. Helens (v Leeds)	Second row
1979	David Topliss	Wakefield Trinity (v Widnes)	Stand off
1980	Brian Lockwood	Hull K.R. (v Hull)	Prop
1981	Mick Burke	Widnes (v Hull K.R.)	Full back
1982	Eddie Cunningham	Widnes (v Hull)	Centre
1983	David Hobbs	Featherstone Rovers (v Hull)	Second row
1984	Joe Lydon	Widnes (v Wigan)	Centre
1985	Brett Kenny	Wigan (v Hull)	Stand off
1986	Bob Beardmore	Castleford (v Hull K.R.)	Scrum half
1987	Graham Eadie	Halifax (v St. Helens)	Full back
1988	Andy Gregory	Wigan (v Halifax)	Scrum half
1989	Ellery Hanley	Wigan (v St. Helens)	Loose forward
1990	Andy Gregory	Wigan (v Warrington)	Scrum half
1991	Denis Betts	Wigan (v St. Helens)	Second row

Coach John Monie and skipper Ellery Hanley lead the Wigan celebrations for a record fourth successive victory at Wembley.

CHALLENGE CUP RECORDS

ALL ROUNDS

TEAM

Highest score:
Huddersfield 119 v. *Swinton Park 2. 1914

INDIVIDUAL

Most goals in a match:
22 by Jim Sullivan (Wigan) v. *Flimby and Fothergill
. . . . 1925

Most tries in a match:
11 by George West (Hull K.R.) v. *Brookland Rovers
. . . . 1905

Most points in a match:
53 (11t,10g) by George West (Hull K.R.) as above.

*Amateur teams

FINAL RECORDS

TEAM

Most wins: 12 by Wigan

Most finals: 21 by Wigan

Highest score:
Wakefield T. 38 v. Hull 5. 1960

Widest margin:
Huddersfield 37 v. St. Helens 3. 1915

Biggest attendance:
102,569 Warrington v. Halifax (Replay) at Bradford
. . . . 1954

INDIVIDUAL

Most goals:
8 by Cyril Kellett (Featherstone R.) v. Bradford N.
. . . . 1973

Most tries:
3 by Bob Wilson (Broughton R.) v. Salford. 1902
Stan Moorhouse (Huddersfield) v. Warrington. 1913
Tom Holliday (Oldham) v. Swinton. 1927

Most points:
20 (7g,2t) by Neil Fox (Wakefield T.) v. Hull. . . 1960

WEMBLEY FACTS

WIGAN have made a record 17 appearances at Wembley and won there a record 11 times, including a record four successive appearances from 1988.

A RECORD 10 overseas players trod the Wembley turf in 1985. Hull fielded six — a record for one club. The Airlie Birds sextet were Australians Peter Sterling and John Muggleton, plus New Zealanders Gary Kemble, James Leuluai, Dane O'Hara and Fred Ah Kuoi. Wigan added Australians John Ferguson and Brett Kenny together with New Zealanders Graeme West and Danny Campbell, who went on as substitute. South African Nick Du Toit was substitute back but did not play.

THE 1985 aggregates of 10 tries and 52 points were both record totals for a Challenge Cup final with Hull's 24 points the most by a losing side. There were also 10 tries in the 1915 final when Huddersfield beat St. Helens 37-3, which is the widest margin. Wakefield Trinity ran up the highest Cup final score when they beat Hull 38-5 in 1960.

WORLD RECORD receipts of £1,610,447 were taken at the 1991 Final between Wigan and St. Helens from a crowd of 75,532.

ANDY GREGORY holds the record for most Cup-winning appearances at Wembley with six. The scrum half has never been on a losing side at the stadium, having also been in the Widnes side that drew with Hull in 1982 before losing the replay at Elland Road, Leeds.
   Gregory's winning appearances were with Widnes (1981, 1984) and Wigan (1988, 1989, 1990, 1991).

THE Widnes trio of Eric Hughes, Keith Elwell and Mick Adams, plus Andy Gregory (see above) hold the record for most appearances at Wembley...seven. They earned winners' medals in 1975, 1979, 1981 and 1984, plus the drawn final of 1982. They were on the losing side in 1976 and 1977.

ERIC ASHTON captained a record six teams at Wembley — Wigan in 1958, 1959, 1961, 1963, 1965 and 1966. His record of three wins (in 1958, 1959, 1965) is shared with Derek Turner (Wakefield Trinity 1960, 1962, 1963), Alex Murphy (St. Helens 1966, Leigh 1971 and Warrington 1974) and Ellery Hanley (Wigan 1989, 1990, 1991), this being the only three successive wins.

THE YOUNGEST player to appear in a Wembley Cup final was Shaun Edwards who was 17 years, 6 months and 19 days when he played full back for Wigan against Widnes in 1984. He was also the youngest captain at Wembley, leading Wigan to success in the 1988 final against Halifax at the age of 21 years, 6 months and 14 days.

ALEX MURPHY has been a record six times to Wembley as a coach. He was a winner as player-coach with Leigh (1971) and Warrington (1974), but losing each time when confined to the bench with Warrington (1975), Wigan (1984) and St. Helens (1987 and 1989). Murphy also went twice solely as a player, with St. Helens in 1961 and 1966.

MOST WINS as a coach at Wembley is three, by Jim Sullivan (Wigan 1948, 1951 and St. Helens 1956), Joe Egan (Wigan 1958, 1959 and Widnes 1964) and Ken Traill (Wakefield T. 1960, 1962 and 1963).

THE OLDEST player at Wembley was Gus Risman, who at 41 years 29 days led Workington Town to victory over Featherstone Rovers in 1952. He played full back.

THE TALLEST player at Wembley was St. Helens second row man John Harrison who appeared in the 1991 final against Wigan. He measured 6ft. 7in.

SCHOOLBOYS who have appeared in an Under-11 curtain-raiser at Wembley and gone on to play in the major final at the stadium are Joe Lydon, David Hulme, Mike Ford, Neil Puckering, David Plange, Denis Betts and Bobby Goulding. Lydon became the first to achieve the feat with Widnes in the 1984 final against Wigan, followed by teammate Hulme who went on as a 72nd minute substitute. Both had played in the first schoolboys' curtain-raiser in 1975 — Lydon for Wigan, and Hulme for Widnes.

CYRIL KELLETT holds the record for most goals in a Challenge Cup final with his eight for Featherstone Rovers in 1973.
In the most remarkable exhibition of kicking seen at Wembley, the veteran full back was successful with every one of his attempts as Bradford Northern crashed 33-14.
Nine years earlier he scored only one for Hull Kingston Rovers in the 13-5 defeat by Widnes.

NEIL FOX — the record aggregate points scorer of all time — piled up the most points in a Challenge Cup final in 1960. His 20 points helped Wakefield Trinity to a 38-5 defeat of Hull. Fox's points came from two tries and seven goals.
His three drop goals for Trinity in the 12-6 victory over Huddersfield two years later was another extraordinary feat in the days when the drop goal was a rarity.

NO player has scored a hat-trick of tries at Wembley, the feat being achieved only three times in the preceding era.
The last to do it was Oldham winger Tom Holliday in the 26-7 defeat of Swinton in 1927.
Bob Wilson, the Broughton Rangers centre and captain,

was the first to score three tries, in the 25-0 victory over Salford in 1902.
In between, Stan Moorhouse's three-try feat accounted for all of Huddersfield's points when they beat Warrington 9-5 in 1913. Moorhouse was winger to Harold Wagstaff, recognised as the greatest centre of all time.

MANY great players have gone through an entire career without achieving their ambition of playing at Wembley. Hull's Mike Smith achieved it in his first senior game.
Smith made one of the most remarkable debuts in sporting history when he played in the second row of an injury-hit Boulevard side against Wakefield Trinity in 1960.
In contrast, Freddie Miller signed for Hull in 1932 and did not play at Wembley until 1952…two years after joining Featherstone Rovers.

A NOTABLE Wembley captain was Gus Risman who led two clubs to victory…14 years apart.
He was captain of Salford when they beat Barrow in 1938. At 41, he led Workington Town to their triumph over Featherstone Rovers in 1952.

PROBABLY the unluckiest Challenge Cup finalist was Dai Davies who appeared in four finals and was on the losing side each time. Three of those occasions were at Wembley with different clubs. He was a loser with Warrington (1933), Huddersfield (1935) and Keighley (1937). Before the Wembley era he was also in Warrington's beaten team of 1928.
Steve Norton played at Wembley four times and was never on the winning side. He was in the beaten Hull teams of 1980, 1983 and 1985 in addition to playing in the 1982 drawn final. In 1970 he was a non-playing substitute for Castleford who won the Cup.
Bill Ramsey was on the losing side in four Wembley finals but gained a winners' medal with Leeds in 1968. He picked up losers' medals with Hunslet (1965), Leeds (1971 and 1972) and Widnes (1977).

A TOTAL of 14 current clubs have yet to play at Wembley …Batley, Bramley, Carlisle, Chorley, Doncaster, Fulham, Nottingham City, Oldham, Rochdale Hornets, Runcorn Highfield, Sheffield Eagles, Swinton, Trafford Borough and Whitehaven.
Fate seems to be against Swinton and Oldham. In the five years preceding the move to Wembley, one or the other appeared in the final, twice meeting each other. Oldham played in a record four successive finals in that period. Swinton's run of three finals ended when the first Wembley took place in 1929. They got through to the final three years later …only for it to be played at Wigan!

WEMBLEY ERA SEMI-FINALS

It is generally felt that it is better to have played at Wembley and lost than never to have played there at all. This makes the semi-final stage of the RL Challenge Cup almost as important as the final with no consolation for the losers.

Of the 14 current clubs who have never appeared at Wembley four have been beaten semi-finalists. They are Oldham (six times), Swinton, Rochdale Hornets (twice) and Whitehaven.

Probably the unluckiest are Oldham. They have reached the penultimate stage six times without being able to realise their ambition. Oldham almost made it in 1964. After drawing 5-5 with Hull K.R. they were winning 17-14 in extra time of the replay when bad light stopped play and they were beaten in the third game.

Swinton did win a semi-final in 1932 but the final that year was switched from Wembley to Wigan!

There have been three occasions when Yorkshire has provided all four semi-finalists in one year — in 1962, 1973 and 1983. Four times have all four semi-finalists come from west of the Pennines — in 1930, 1989, 1990

and 1991.

Until 1962 the two semi-finals were always played on the same Saturday, but with four Yorkshire clubs competing for the first time it was decided to play one mid-week. Both matches were played at Odsal Stadium, Bradford. The first was on a Wednesday evening — without floodlights — when 43,625 saw Wakefield Trinity beat Featherstone Rovers and on the following Saturday there were 31,423 to see Huddersfield beat Hull K.R.

The following year both semi-finals were again played on the same Saturday, but since then they have been staged on different Saturdays.

Some semi-final facts during the Wembley era are:

Biggest attendance: 69,898 Warrington v. Leeds at Bradford in 1950

Biggest aggregate: 104,453 in 1939 (Only other six-figure aggregate was 102,080 in 1951)

Record receipts: £177,161 St. Helens v. Wigan at Old Trafford, Manchester in 1990

Lowest attendance: 7,971 Featherstone R. v. Leigh at Leeds in 1974

Highest score and widest margin:
Wigan 34 v. Salford 4 in 1988

CHALLENGE CUP SEMI-FINALS

Year	Winners		Runners-up		Venue	Attendance	Receipts
1929	Dewsbury	9	Castleford	3	Huddersfield	25,000	£1,562
	Wigan	7	St. Helens Recs.	7	Swinton	31,000	£2,209
Replay	Wigan	13	St. Helens Recs.	12	Leigh	21,940	£1,437
1930	Widnes	10	Barrow	3	Warrington	25,500	£1,630
	St. Helens	5	Wigan	5	Swinton	37,169	£2,666
Replay	St. Helens	22	Wigan	10	Leigh	24,000	£1,657
1931	Halifax	11	St. Helens	2	Rochdale	21,674	£1,498
	York	15	Warrington	5	Leeds	32,419	£2,329
1932	Leeds	2	Halifax	2	Huddersfield	31,818	£2,456
Replay	Leeds	9	Halifax	2	Wakefield	21,000	£1,417
	Swinton	7	Wakefield T.	4	Rochdale	21,273	£1,369
●	*Final was played at Wigan, not Wembley*						
1933	Huddersfield	30	Leeds	8	Wakefield	36,359	£2,299
	Warrington	11	St. Helens	5	Swinton	30,373	£2,055
1934	Hunslet	12	Huddersfield	7	Wakefield	27,450	£1,797
	Widnes	7	Oldham	4	Swinton	17,577	£1,050

Year	Winners		Runners-up		Venue	Attendance	Receipts
1935	Castleford	11	Barrow	5	Swinton	24,469	£1,534
	Huddersfield	21	Hull	5	Leeds	37,111	£2,753
1936	Leeds	10	Huddersfield	5	Wakefield	37,906	£2,456
	Warrington	7	Salford	2	Wigan	41,538	£2,796
1937	Keighley	0	Wakefield T.	0	Leeds	39,998	£2,793
Replay	Keighley	5	Wakefield T.	3	Huddersfield	14,400	£1,052
	Widnes	13	Wigan	9	Warrington	29,260	£1,972
1938	Barrow	4	Halifax	2	Huddersfield	31,384	£2,431
	Salford	6	Swinton	0	Belle Vue, Manchester	31,664	£2,396
1939	Halifax	10	Leeds	4	Bradford	64,453	£3,645
	Salford	11	Wigan	2	Rochdale	40,000	£2,154

● *During the war the semi-finals were two-legged and the finals were not played at Wembley*

Year	Winners		Runners-up		Venue	Attendance	Receipts
1946	Wakefield T.	7	Hunslet	3	Leeds	33,000	£4,991
	Wigan	12	Widnes	5	Swinton	36,976	£4,746
1947	Bradford N.	11	Warrington	7	Swinton	33,474	£4,946
	Leeds	21	Wakefield T.	0	Huddersfield	35,136	£6,339
1948	Bradford N.	14	Hunslet	7	Leeds	38,125	£7,437
	Wigan	11	Rochdale H.	0	Swinton	26,004	£4,206
1949	Bradford N.	10	Barrow	0	Swinton	26,572	£4,646
	Halifax	11	Huddersfield	10	Bradford	61,875	£8,638
1950	Warrington	16	Leeds	4	Bradford	69,898	£9,861
	Widnes	8	Bradford N.	0	Wigan	25,390	£3,936
1951	Barrow	14	Leeds	14	Bradford	57,459	£8,248
Replay	Barrow	28	Leeds	13	Huddersfield	31,078	£5,098
	Wigan	3	Warrington	2	Swinton	44,621	£7,358
1952	Featherstone R.	6	Leigh	2	Leeds	35,621	£6,494
	Workington T.	5	Barrow	2	Wigan	31,206	£4,782
1953	Huddersfield	7	Wigan	0	Bradford	58,722	£10,519
	St. Helens	9	Warrington	3	Swinton	38,059	£7,768
1954	Halifax	18	Hunslet	3	Bradford	46,961	£8,243
	Warrington	8	Leeds	4	Swinton	36,993	£7,596
1955	Barrow	9	Hunslet	6	Wigan	25,493	£4,671
	Workington T.	13	Featherstone R.	2	Leeds	33,499	£7,305
1956	Halifax	11	Wigan	10	Bradford	51,889	£9,054
	St. Helens	5	Barrow	5	Swinton	38,897	£7,793
Replay	St. Helens	10	Barrow	5	Wigan	44,731	£7,750
1957	Barrow	2	Leigh	2	Wigan	34,628	£6,340
Replay	Barrow	15	Leigh	10	Swinton	28,081	£5,695
	Leeds	10	Whitehaven	9	Bradford	49,094	£8,987
1958	Wigan	5	Rochdale H.	3	Swinton	28,597	£6,354
	Workington T.	8	Featherstone R.	2	Bradford	31,517	£6,325
1959	Wigan	5	Leigh	0	Swinton	27,906	£6,068
	Hull	15	Featherstone R.	5	Bradford	52,131	£9,776
1960	Wakefield T.	11	Featherstone R.	2	Bradford	55,935	£10,390
	Hull	12	Oldham	9	Swinton	27,545	£6,093
1961	St. Helens	26	Hull	9	Bradford	42,935	£9,231
	Wigan	19	Halifax	10	Swinton	35,118	£7,557
1962	Wakefield T.	9	Featherstone R.	0	Bradford	43,625	£8,496
	Huddersfield	6	Hull K.R.	0	Bradford	31,423	£6,685

Year	Winners		Runners-up		Venue	Attendance	Receipts
1963	Wakefield T.	5	Warrington	2	Swinton	15,565	£3,530
	Wigan	18	Hull K.R.	4	Leeds	21,420	£6,029
1964	Widnes	7	Castleford	7	Swinton	25,603	£5,541
Replay	Widnes	7	Castleford	5	Wakefield	28,739	£5,313
	Hull K.R.	5	Oldham	5	Leeds	28,823	£7,411
Replay	Hull K.R.	14	Oldham	17	Swinton	27,209	£5,929

● *Score after 80 minutes was 14-14, then bad light caused match to be abandoned after 12 minutes of extra time with Oldham winning 17-14*

Second Replay	Hull K.R.	12	Oldham	2	Huddersfield	28,732	£6,183
1965	Wigan	25	Swinton	10	St. Helens	26,658	£6,384
	Hunslet	8	Wakefield T.	0	Leeds	21,262	£6,090
1966	St. Helens	12	Dewsbury	5	Swinton	13,046	£3,102
	Wigan	7	Leeds	2	Huddersfield	22,758	£5,971
1967	Featherstone R.	16	Leeds	8	Huddersfield	20,052	£6,276
	Barrow	14	Dewsbury	9	Swinton	13,744	£4,560
1968	Leeds	25	Wigan	4	Swinton	30,058	£9,845
	Wakefield T.	0	Huddersfield	0	Bradford	21,569	£6,196
Replay	Wakefield T.	15	Huddersfield	10	Leeds	20,983	£6,425
1969	Castleford	16	Wakefield T.	10	Leeds	21,497	£8,477
	Salford	15	Warrington	8	Wigan	20,600	£7,738
1970	Castleford	6	St. Helens	3	Swinton	18,913	£7,171
	Wigan	19	Hull K.R.	8	Leeds	18,495	£7,862
1971	Leeds	19	Castleford	8	Bradford	24,464	£9,120
	Leigh	10	Huddersfield	4	Wigan	14,875	£5,670
1972	St. Helens	10	Warrington	10	Wigan	19,300	£8,250
Replay	St. Helens	10	Warrington	6	Wigan	32,380	£12,604
	Leeds	16	Halifax	3	Bradford	16,680	£6,851
1973	Featherstone R.	17	Castleford	3	Leeds	15,369	£9,454
	Bradford N.	23	Dewsbury	7	Leeds	14,028	£9,221
1974	Warrington	17	Dewsbury	7	Wigan	11,789	£6,821
	Featherstone R.	21	Leigh	14	Leeds	7,971	£4,461
1975	Widnes	13	Wakefield T.	7	Bradford	9,155	£5,856
	Warrington	11	Leeds	4	Wigan	13,168	£9,581
1976	Widnes	15	Featherstone R.	9	Swinton	13,019	£9,078
	St. Helens	5	Keighley	4	Huddersfield	9,829	£6,113
1977	Leeds	7	St. Helens	2	Wigan	12,974	£11,379
	Widnes	14	Hull K.R.	5	Leeds	17,053	£16,068
1978	Leeds	14	Featherstone R.	9	Bradford	12,824	£11,322
	St. Helens	12	Warrington	8	Wigan	16,167	£13,960
1979	Widnes	14	Bradford N.	11	Swinton	14,324	£16,363
	Wakefield T.	9	St. Helens	7	Leeds	12,393	£14,195
1980	Hull K.R.	20	Halifax	7	Leeds	17,910	£31,650
	Hull	10	Widnes	5	Swinton	18,347	£29,415
1981	Widnes	17	Warrington	9	Wigan	12,624	£20,673
	Hull K.R.	22	St. Helens	5	Leeds	17,073	£30,616
1982	Hull	15	Castleford	11	Leeds	21,207	£41,867
	Widnes	11	Leeds	8	Swinton	13,075	£25,796
1983	Featherstone R.	11	Bradford N.	6	Leeds	10,784	£22,579
	Hull	14	Castleford	7	Elland Rd., L'ds	26,031	£65,498
1984	Wigan	14	York	8	Elland Rd., L'ds	17,156	£52,888
	Widnes	15	Leeds	4	Swinton	14,046	£37,183

Year	Winners		Runners-up		Venue	Attendance	Receipts
1985	Wigan	18	Hull K.R.	11	Elland Rd., L'ds	19,275	£70,192
	Hull	10	Castleford	10	Leeds	20,982	£64,163
Replay	Hull	22	Castleford	16	Leeds	20,968	£65,005
1986	Castleford	18	Oldham	7	Wigan	12,430	£38,296
	Hull K.R.	24	Leeds	24	Elland Rd., L'ds	23,866	£83,757
Replay	Hull K.R.	17	Leeds	0	Elland Rd., L'ds	32,485	£113,345
1987	St. Helens	14	Leigh	8	Wigan	13,105	£48,627
	Halifax	12	Widnes	8	Leeds	16,064	£61,260
1988	Wigan	34	Salford	4	Bolton W. FC	20,783	£95,876
	Halifax	0	Hull	0	Leeds	20,534	£82,026
Replay	Halifax	4	Hull	3	Elland Rd., L'ds	25,117	£113,679
1989	St. Helens	16	Widnes	14	Wigan	17,119	£70,411
	Wigan	13	Warrington	6	Man. C. FC	26,529	£144,056
1990	Wigan	20	St. Helens	14	Man. U. FC	26,489	£177,161
	Warrington	10	Oldham	6	Wigan	15,631	£80,500
1991	Wigan	30	Oldham	16	Bolton W. FC	19,057	£116,937
	St. Helens	19	Widnes	2	Wigan	16,109	£81,342

NON-LEAGUE CLUBS IN THE CHALLENGE CUP

AMATEUR clubs were invited to compete in the 1986 Rugby League Challenge Cup after a five-year break. The League asked for two of the three county cup competition winners to enter the preliminary round.

The League later decided that from 1987 the Silk Cut Challenge Cup campaign would feature 38 teams, amateur clubs joining the professionals for a preliminary round of six ties.

In the early years of the Northern Union Challenge Cup — as it was then called — the line between professional and amateur was less clearly defined.

A variety of Leagues also make it difficult to set non-League clubs apart. Fifty-six clubs appeared in the inaugurating first round of 1897 and four others received byes. The complications continued until 1904 when the League format settled down and non-League clubs had to qualify for the first round.

Between 1904 and 1907 there was a preliminary round of up to 14 ties involving mostly non-league clubs. In 1906-07 SAVILLE GREEN beat Bramley 10-0, and NEWINGTON ROVERS drew 3-3 and 13-13 with York before losing 14-5.

Not since 1909 when BEVERLEY beat Ebbw Vale 7-2 has a senior team been knocked out by a non-League club although amateur teams twice had victories in the two-leg era of 1946-54.

NON-LEAGUE CLUB VICTORIES OVER SENIOR CLUBS SINCE 1904
(Excluding preliminary rounds before 1908)
Non-League Clubs in Capitals

1905-06
*FEATHERSTONE ROVERS 23 v. Widnes 2
(second round)

1907-08
WHITEHAVEN RECREATION 13 v. St. Helens 8
(Lost 33-5 at Merthyr Tydfil in second round)

1908-09
BEVERLEY 7 v. Ebbw Vale 2
(Lost 53-2 at Halifax in second round)

1945-46
SHARLSTON 12 v. Workington Town 7
(1st leg) (Workington Town won 2nd leg 16-2)

1947-48
RISEHOW and GILLHEAD 10 v. Keighley 2 (2nd leg)
(Keighley won 1st leg 11-0)

*FEATHERSTONE ROVERS are the only non-League club to appear in the third round when they lost 3-0 at Keighley. In the first round they beat BROOKLAND ROVERS 16-5.

There have been seven drawn clashes, with the professional club winning through each time. The last draw was in 1986-87 when KELLS drew 4-4 with Fulham at Whitehaven. Fulham won the replay 22-14 at Chiswick.

There have been several other instances of non-League clubs meeting in the first round. The last occasion was in 1960 when WALNEY CENTRAL beat LOCK LANE 10-5 before losing at Oldham 55-4 in the second round.

In 1964 THAMES BOARD MILLS received a bye when Bradford Northern disbanded, but lost 48-8 at Blackpool Borough in the second round.

CHALLENGE CUP PROGRESS CHART
A 20-year review ....

Key: W — Winners. F — Beaten finalists. SF — Semi-final. P — Preliminary round.

	1990-91	1989-90	1988-89	1987-88	1986-87	1985-86	1984-85	1983-84	1982-83	1981-82	1980-81	1979-80	1978-79	1977-78	1976-77	1975-76	1974-75	1973-74	1972-73	1971-72
BARROW	2	1	2	1	2	2	P	1	2	2	1	2	3	1	2	1	1	1	1	2
BATLEY	1	1	1	1	1	1	1	1	1	2	1	1	1	1	1	1	1	1	1	1
BRADFORD N.	3	3	2	1	2	3	3	3	SF	3	1	3	SF	3	3	2	3	3	F	2
BRAMLEY	1	1	P	P	1	2	3	1	1	1	1	1	2	1	1	1	1	2	1	3
CARLISLE	P	1	2	1	2	1	1	P	1	1										
CASTLEFORD	1	P	2	1	1	W	SF	3	SF	SF	2	2	3	3	3	1	1	1	SF	2
CHORLEY	1	1																		
DEWSBURY	1	2	1	1	1	1	1	1	1	1	2	1	2	1	3	1	1	SF	SF	1
DONCASTER	1	P	1	3	1	2	P	2	1	1	1	1	1	1	1	2	1	1	1	1
FEATHERSTONE R.	1	1	3	2	1	1	P	1	W	P	3	1	1	SF	2	SF	1	F	W	2
FULHAM	1	2	1	1	1	1	1	2	2	2	1									
HALIFAX	3	1	1	F	W	1	2	1	2	3	2	SF	1	1	1	1	1	1	1	SF
HUDDERSFIELD	P	P	1	P	1	1	1	1	1	1	1	2	3	3	1	1	1	1	1	2
HULL	P	2	1	SF	3	1	F	2	F	W	2	F	3	2	2	1	2	1	2	2
HULL K.R.	1	1	3	3	3	F	SF	3	1	2	F	W	2	1	SF	2	3	2	2	1
HUNSLET	1	1	P	1	2	1	3	2	3	1	1	1	1	2	1	2	3	1	2	1
KEIGHLEY	2	2	2	2	2	1	1	1	1	1	2	1	2	1	1	SF	1	1	1	1
LEEDS	2	P	3	2	3	SF	1	SF	2	SF	1	2	1	W	W	3	SF	3	1	F
LEIGH	1	1	1	1	SF	3	2	1	1	3	2	1	2	1	3	2	SF	2	2	
NOTTINGHAM C.	1	1	1	2	2	P	1													
OLDHAM	SF	SF	3	1	2	SF	1	2	1	2	3	2	2	1	3	3	1	3	1	
ROCHDALE H.	2	2	1	2	1	2	2	1	1	2	1	2	2	1	2	1	2	2	2	1
RUNCORN H.	1	1	1	1	1	1	2	1	2	1	1	1	1	1	1	1	1	2	1	1
RYEDALE-YORK	1	1	1	1	P	2	1	SF	1	1	2	2	1	1	2	2	1	1	3	
ST. HELENS	F	SF	F	3	F	2	1	3	3	1	SF	2	SF	F	SF	W	2	3	2	W
SALFORD	3	2	1	SF	1	1	2	1	2	1	3	3	1	2	2	2	2	1	1	
SHEFFIELD E.	2	2	2	2	1	1	1													
SWINTON	1	1	1	1	P	P	1	P	2	1	1	1	2	1	1	2	1	1	2	3
TRAFFORD B.	1	2	2	2	1	2	1	1	1	1	1	1	1	1	1	1	1	1	1	1
WAKEFIELD T.	2	3	2	1	2	1	2	2	2	3	3	3	F	2	2	1	SF	1	3	3
WARRINGTON	3	F	SF	2	1	2	2	2	3	1	SF	3	1	SF	1	3	F	W	3	SF
WHITEHAVEN	2	3	1	P	3	1	1	1	1	1	1	1	1	1	1	1	1	1	1	1
WIDNES	SF	3	SF	3	SF	3	3	W	1	F	W	SF	W	3	F	F	W	2	2	1
WIGAN	W	W	W	W	1	3	W	F	1	2	1	1	2	2	2	2	3	3	2	
WORKINGTON T.	2	1	P	1	P	1	2	2	3	2	2	1	1	2	3	2	2	2	2	1

REGAL TROPHY

1990-91 Final

With Widnes and Wigan having dominated finals for the past five years, this meeting of Bradford Northern and Warrington was given 'new faces' billing. The big match performances of the star-studded Lancashire duo proved to be a formidable act to follow.

The lowest final crowd for seven years witnessed a colourless contest with the only try coming in the last minute. Mark Thomas, a 41st minute substitute, slipped through following smart combined play by half back partners Australian Chris O'Sullivan and Welshman Kevin Ellis.

O'Sullivan's experience in the Sydney Premiership had helped Wales B international Ellis make rapid progress since his switch from the 15-a-side code the previous May and together they gave Warrington a vital edge outside the scrum.

By contrast, Northern's half backs were both from Rugby Union, needing an experienced Rugby League partner to fulfil early promise. A failure to spread the ball wide meant the tryscoring potential of Great Britain winger Gerald Cordle was wasted and the powerful Welshman did not receive his first running chance until the 67th minute.

Having refound their form to dispose of Widnes and St. Helens on the way to the Headingley final, Warrington were equally negative and generally lacked creativity. The devastating finishing power of rightwing combination Drummond and Welshman Allan Bateman was ignored and the first final of 1991 dragged on in a dour forward battle.

That should have suited the respected Northern pack, even lacking the suspended Test forward Karl Fairbank, but they were more than matched by a Wire forward unit lacking three or four first-choice players. Any one of the Warrington six could have taken the Man of the Match award and been no more of a debatable choice than Billy McGinty, who won the £250 prize cheque with a solid, workmanlike second row performance.

Skipper John Pendlebury was Bradford's only contender for the individual honour with the loose forward providing the occasional distributive touch that was lacking among their backs. With the game developing into a front line battle it was surprising that Northern did not call on the services of barnstorming substitute Craig Richard to add his considerable power to the barrage.

Only Medley looked capable of breaking down the Wire rearguard, producing the best solo effort of the lack-lustre game when the former Test man broke three tackles in a tremendous first-half run.

That break was halted by a marvellous tackle by Wire full back David Lyon, whose all-round performance and four vital goals made him a leading candidate for the Man of the Match award. A bravery award might have been equally appropriate as the 1990 replacement tourist had been discharged from hospital only a few days earlier with an eye injury that had ruled him out earlier in the week. A major incentive had been the golden opportunity to use the prestigious occasion as a personal showcase to impress the watching Great Britain coach Malcolm Reilly.

Despite play being confined mostly to the forwards, there was only one foul in a penalty count of 7-6 to Bradford, Warrington taking the scrums 11-10.

REGAL TROPHY FINAL

12 January   Leeds

WARRINGTON 12   **BRADFORD NORTHERN 2**

Warrington		Bradford Northern
David Lyon	1.	Ian Wilkinson
Des Drummond, Capt.	2.	Gerald Cordle
Allan Bateman	3.	Darrall Shelford
Tony Thorniley	4.	Roger Simpson
Mark Forster	5.	Tony Marchant
Chris O'Sullivan	6.	Neil Summers
Kevin Ellis	7.	Brett Iti
Neil Harmon	8.	David Hobbs
Duane Mann	9.	Brian Noble
Gary Chambers	10.	John Hamer
Gary Mercer	11.	Paul Medley
Billy McGinty	12.	David Croft
Paul Cullen	13.	John Pendlebury, Capt.
Mark Thomas	14.	Phil Hellewell
Rowland Phillips	15.	Craig Richards

T: Thomas   G: Hobbs
G: Lyon (4)   Substitution:
Substitutions: Hellewell for Marchant (41 min.)
Thomas for Chambers (41 min.)   Referee: Jim Smith (Halifax)
Phillips for Harmon (79 min.)   Attendance: 11,154
Half-time: 4-2

Warrington captain Des Drummond shows off the Regal Trophy, flanked by David Lyon.

1990-91 Round by Round

In the six-tie preliminary round, amateurs Saddleworth made progress by beating fellow non-professionals Egremont 35-18, Saddleworth's John Fleming being sent off. National League Champions Dudley Hill entertained Second Division Dewsbury, who recorded a 24-18 victory over the Bradford-based amateurs for whom Dave Savage tallied 14 points with a try and five goals. Sheffield Eagles extended a run of six successive league defeats with an exit from the Regal Trophy, visitors Bradford Northern winning 12-8, although the Eagles provided the Man of the Match in prop forward Hugh Waddell. Second Division pacesetters Halifax came down to earth with a 58-6 defeat at Leeds, centre Simon Irving contributing a try and nine goals, skipper Garry Schofield scoring two tries and creating three more. Wakefield Trinity built a 16-0 first-half lead at Carlisle before the Cumbrians pulled back to 16-10, Trinity's David Jones and Mark Conway scoring tries after Carlisle's Tony Catton had been sent off 10 minutes from the end to register a 28-10 success. Doncaster came back twice to clinch a 14-12 success over visitors Ryedale-York, winger Darren Price sealing victory with a late try.

In the first round, top of the table Hull travelled to second-placed Widnes and took a shock 10-0 lead after 15 minutes before the Chemics' Welsh connection paid off, winger John Devereux grabbing two touchdowns before the try of the match from Jonathan Davies to seal a 24-16 Widnes triumph. Bradford Northern scraped home 12-11 for an undeserved victory over Second Division Workington Town, the Cumbrian visitors taking the lead five minutes from time with a Ray Ashton drop goal. The player-coach then conceded a penalty at a play-the-ball and Northern skipper John Pendlebury kicked the match-winning goal. Leeds and Hull K.R. served up a 48-point thriller, each side taking the lead three times and scoring four tries, home skipper Schofield clinching victory with a try 11 minutes from the end for a 26-22 Headingley triumph. Holders Wigan travelled to Whitehaven for a 24-6 hard-earned success, leading 10-0 at the break and adding 12 points in the last three minutes.

Featherstone Rovers enjoyed a comfortable 54-16 victory at lowly Barrow, leading 16-0 after only 22 minutes and being well served by centres Ikram Butt and Man of the Match Terry Manning. Dewsbury led three times at Bramley before the Villagers finished strongly in the last quarter for a flattering 30-16 scoreline, having been level 16-16 on the hour. Fulham led 2-0 at half-time at home to Castleford, who pulled away 14-8 with tries for Graham Steadman and Steve Larder. Keighley snatched a 15-13 win at Huddersfield with four minutes to go, Paul Moses kicking a penalty goal for ball stealing, Fartowner Stuart Cocker missed a last ditch penalty goal attempt to force a replay.

Leigh rattled up their current biggest score of the season with a 66-5 hammering of Chorley, who had player-coach Bob Eccles and Mark Edwards sent off midway through the second half. Ian Jeffrey and Mick Round scored hat-tricks of tries while scrum half Bob Beardmore landed nine goals. Batley took 34 minutes to open their account at Nottingham City before going on to win 35-6, Man of the Match Steve Parrish hitting six goals from eight attempts. After four successive league defeats, Oldham returned to winning ways with a 26-6 home success over Salford to avenge an earlier Lancashire Cup defeat. St. Helens recovered from conceding a try to scrum half Barry Ashall to run in five of their own in a 31-7 victory at Swinton, despite being reduced to 11 men with the dismissal of Paul Forber and the sin-binning of Stuart Evans.

First Division strugglers Rochdale Hornets disposed of amateur neighbours Saddleworth 30-10, scoring six tries to two. Wakefield Trinity scored 20 points in each half in the 40-8 triumph over visitors Hunslet, Man of the Match Mark Conway hitting eight goals from nine attempts. Centre Allan Bateman grabbed four tries in Warrington's 33-7 home victory over Runcorn Highfield, who trailed only 6-1 at the break having taken the lead with a Billy Platt drop goal. Doncaster led with eight minutes remaining at Trafford Borough, home winger Steve Connor crashing over at the corner to level the scores at 10-10. In the replay at Tattersfield, Doncaster won 19-7, the scores being level 3-3 at the break with early second half tries from Carl Hall and substitute Dick Jasiewicz setting up victory.

In the second round, Second Division Batley produced the shock result with a 20-16 success over First Division Oldham on a snow-covered Mount Pleasant pitch. Player-coach Keith Rayne notched his hat-trick of tries in the last move of a thrilling match to seal victory, Oldham having lost loose forward John Cogger on the stroke of half-time for inciting the crowd with a V-sign. Widnes disposed of Leeds 22-6 at Naughton Park, the Yorkshiremen having taken a five-minute lead with a Phil Ford try. The Chemics did not take command until the second half, the visitors being hampered by the sending off of Paul Dixon, and John Bentley being sent to the sin bin. Inconsistent Castleford went to Wakefield to secure a comfortable 20-4 victory to end Trinity's run of five successive victories, Steadman taking the Man of the Match award. Crisis club Leigh rallied on the field to pressurise Warrington, who held on for an 11-6 home victory, Leigh being hit by the disallowing of a Round try from a Paul Topping crosskick.

Gallant Keighley scored three tries in the 36-16 defeat at Wigan, who had hooker Martin Dermott sent off and were contained by the visitors in the second half after leading 28-10 at the break. St. Helens disposed of Featherstone Rovers at Post Office Road more comfortably than the 33-16 scoreline suggested, Paul Loughlin kicking only two goals from seven attempts. Player-coach Hobbs came on as second-half substitute to inspire Bradford Northern to a 28-0 victory over Second Division Bramley at Odsal, creating two tries for Welsh winger Gerald Cordle and hitting two touchline goals to spoil Barry Johnson's last match as coach of Bramley. Rochdale Hornets achieved their first away win of the season with a 14-10 success at Doncaster, who had won their last seven home matches, Hornets hooker Martin Hall collecting two tries.

In the third round, bottom of the table Rochdale Hornets — with only one Championship win — pulled off a giant-killing act with a 19-14 triumph at Castleford. With the Wheldon Road side leading 14-12 Hornets full back Colin Whitfield earned his Man of the Match rating by scoring the match-winning try in the 54th minute. Warrington led 14-6 at home to St. Helens before the visitors pulled back with a Mark Bailey try and a Loughlin goal, David Lyon deciding the tie 18-12 with a try four minutes from the end. Wigan's bid for a hat-trick of Regal Trophy successes was ended by Bradford Northern, 12-6 victors at Central Park. Northern notched tries through skipper Pendlebury and Paul Medley, Wigan's sole touchdown coming from Andy Goodway. Buoyant Batley came down to earth with a 56-6 hammering at Widnes, who ran in 11 tries, four to Martin Offiah and a hat-trick for Andy Currier, Batley's best player being Sonny Whakarau.

In the semi-finals, giant-killers Rochdale Hornets travelled to Headingley to meet Bradford Northern in front of the lowest crowd — 3,788 — since neutral semi-finals were introduced in 1979. Northern reached their first Regal Trophy final since 1980 with an unimpressive 13-2 success, with tries from Karl Fairbank and Darrall Shelford, the Man of the Match award going to Hornets centre Darren Abram. A week later at Wigan, injury-ridden Warrington pulled off the third major shock of the tournament by defeating in-form Widnes 8-4. Lacking nine players, the Wire lost Neil Harmon and Bateman during the pulsating game and went behind 4-2 to a controversial Offiah touchdown with only seven minutes left. Extra time looked likely when centre Chris Rudd equalised with a penalty goal, only for skipper Des Drummond and Kiwi Gary Mercer to combine to send Rudd over for the match-winning try in the dying seconds.

1990-91 RESULTS

Preliminary Round

Carlisle	10	Wakefield T.	28
Doncaster	14	Ryedale-York	12
Dudley Hill	18	Dewsbury	24
Leeds	58	Halifax	6
Saddleworth R.	35	Egremont R.	18
Sheffield E.	8	Bradford N.	12

First Round

Barrow	16	Featherstone R.	54
Bradford N.	12	Workington T.	11
Bramley	30	Dewsbury	16
Fulham	8	Castleford	14
Huddersfield	13	Keighley	15
Leeds	26	Hull K.R.	22
Leigh	66	Chorley	5
Nottingham C.	6	Batley	35
Oldham	26	Salford	6
Rochdale H.	30	Saddleworth R.	10
Swinton	7	St. Helens	31
Trafford B.	10	Doncaster	10
Wakefield T.	40	Hunslet	8
Warrington	33	Runcorn H.	7

Whitehaven	6	Wigan	24
Widnes	24	Hull	16

Replay

Doncaster	19	Trafford B.	7

Second Round

Batley	20	Oldham	16
Bradford N.	28	Bramley	0
Doncaster	10	Rochdale H.	14
Featherstone R.	16	St. Helens	33
Wakefield T.	4	Castleford	20
Warrington	11	Leigh	6
Widnes	22	Leeds	6
Wigan	36	Keighley	16

Third Round

Castleford	14	Rochdale H.	19
Warrington	18	St. Helens	12
Widnes	56	Batley	6
Wigan	6	Bradford N.	12

Semi-Finals

Rochdale H. (at Leeds)	2	Bradford N.	13
Warrington (at Wigan)	8	Widnes	4

Final

Warrington (at Leeds)	12	Bradford N.	2

1990-91 PRIZES

Round		Per Team	Total
Preliminary	12 ×	£2,000	£24,000
First	16 ×	£2,000	£32,000
Second	8 ×	£3,250	£26,000
Third	4 ×	£5,000	£20,000
Semi-Finals	2 ×	£8,500	£17,000
Runners-up	1 ×	£16,000	£16,000
Winners	1 ×	£30,000	£30,000

Total Prize Money	£165,000
Capital Development Fund	£110,000
Grand Total	£275,000

REGAL TROPHY ROLL OF HONOUR

Season	Winners		Runners-up		Venue	Attendance	Receipts
1971-72	Halifax	22	Wakefield T.	11	Bradford	7,975	£2,545
1972-73	Leeds	12	Salford	7	Huddersfield	10,102	£4,563
1973-74	Warrington	27	Rochdale H.	16	Wigan	9,347	£4,380
1974-75	Bradford N.	3	Widnes	2	Warrington	5,935	£3,305
1975-76	Widnes	19	Hull	13	Leeds	9,035	£6,275
1976-77	Castleford	25	Blackpool B.	15	Salford	4,512	£2,919
1977-78	Warrington	9	Widnes	4	St. Helens	10,258	£8,429
1978-79	Widnes	16	Warrington	4	St. Helens	10,743	£11,709
1979-80	Bradford N.	6	Widnes	0	Leeds	9,909	£11,560
1980-81	Warrington	12	Barrow	5	Wigan	12,820	£21,020
1981-82	Hull	12	Hull K.R.	4	Leeds	25,245	£42,987
1982-83	Wigan	15	Leeds	4	Elland Rd, Leeds	19,553	£49,027
1983-84	Leeds	18	Widnes	10	Wigan	9,510	£19,824
1984-85	Hull K.R.	12	Hull	0	Hull City FC	25,326	£69,555
1985-86	Wigan	11	Hull K.R.	8	Elland Rd, Leeds	17,573	£66,714
1986-87	Wigan	18	Warrington	4	Bolton W. FC	21,144	£86,041
1987-88	St. Helens	15	Leeds	14	Wigan	16,669	£62,232
1988-89	Wigan	12	Widnes	6	Bolton W. FC	20,709	£94,874
1989-90	Wigan	24	Halifax	12	Leeds	17,810	£73,688
1990-91	Warrington	12	Bradford N.	2	Leeds	11,154	£57,652

REGAL TROPHY FINAL ....
A REVIEW
1971-72
Halifax 22 Hepworth; Rayner, Davies (1t), Willicombe (1t), Kelly (1t); Burton (5g), Baker (Sanderson); Dewhirst, Hawksley, Callon (1t), (Reeves), Fogerty, J. Martin, Halmshaw
Wakefield T. 11 Wraith (Ward); Slater (1t), Marston, Hegarty, Major; Topliss (1t), Harkin; Jeanes, Morgan, Lyons, Harrison (Spencer), Valentine (1t), N. Fox (1g)
Referee: S. Shepherd (Oldham)
1972-73
Leeds 12 Holmes (1g); Alan Smith, Hynes, Dyl, Atkinson (2t); Hardisty, Hepworth; Clawson (2g) (Ward), Fisher (Pickup), Jeanes, Haigh, Cookson, Eccles
Salford 7 Charlton; Colloby, Watkins (2g), Hesketh, Richards; Gill (P. Ward), Banner; Ramshaw, J. Ward, Mackay, Grice (Davies), Kirkbride, Dixon (1t)
Referee: W.H. Thompson (Huddersfield)
1973-74
Warrington 27 Whitehead (6g, 1t); M. Philbin, Noonan (2t), Reynolds (Pickup), Bevan (1t); Whittle, Gordon; D. Chisnall, (Nicholas 1t), Ashcroft, Brady, Wright, Wanbon, B. Philbin
Rochdale H. 16 Crellin; Brelsford (2t), Brophy

(1t), Taylor (1t), Aspinall; Butler (Wood), Gartland; Holliday (2g), Harris, Whitehead, Fogerty, Sheffield, Halmshaw
Referee: D.G. Kershaw (York)
1974-75
Bradford N. 3 Carlton (1t); Francis, Ward, Gant, D. Redfearn; Blacker, Seabourne; Earl, Jarvis, Jackson, Joyce, Trotter, Fearnley
Widnes 2 Dutton (1g); A. Prescott, D. O'Neill, Aspey, Anderson; Hughes, Bowden; Mills, Elwell, Sheridan, Adams, Blackwood, Laughton
Referee: G.F. Lindop (Wakefield)
1975-76
Widnes 19 Dutton (3g); A. Prescott, George, Aspey, Jenkins (2t); Hughes, Bowden (1t, 1dg); Mills, Elwell, Wood, Foran, Sheridan, Adams (1t)
Hull 13 Stephenson; A. Macklin, Clark, Portz, Hunter (1t); Hancock, Foulkes (Davidson); Ramsey, Flanagan, Wardell, Boxall (2g), Walker, Crane (2t)
Referee: J.V. Moss (Manchester)
1976-77
Castleford 25 Wraith (1t); Fenton, Joyner (1t), P. Johnson (1t), Briggs; Burton (1t), Stephens (1t); Khan, Spurr, A. Dickinson, Reilly, Lloyd (5g), S. Norton

154

Blackpool B 15 Reynolds; Robinson, Heritage, Machen (1t), Pitman (Lamb); Marsh, Newall; Hamilton, Allen (1t), Egan (3g, 1t), Gamble, Groves (Hurst), M. Pattinson
Referee: M. J. Naughton (Widnes)
1977-78
Warrington 9 Finnegan; Hesford (3g), Benyon, Wilson, Bevan (1t); K. Kelly, Gordon; Lester, Dalgreen, Nicholas, Martyn, B. Philbin, Potter
Widnes 4 Eckersley; Wright, Aspey, George, Woods (2g); Hughes, Bowden; Ramsey, Elwell, Shaw (Dearden), Adams, Hull, Laughton
Referee: W.H. Thompson (Huddersfield)
1978-79
Widnes 16 Eckersley; Wright (1t), Aspey, Hughes, Burke (3g); Moran, Bowden; Mills, Elwell (2dg), Shaw, Dearden, Hull (1t), Adams (2dg)
Warrington 4 Finnegan; M. Kelly, Hesford (2g), Benyon, Sutton; K. Kelly, (Hunter), Gordon; Lester, Waller, Nicholas, Case, Martyn, A. Gwilliam
Referee: G.F. Lindop (Wakefield)
1979-80
Bradford N. 6 Mumby (1g); Barends, D. Redfearn, D. Parker (1t), Gant; Stephenson (1dg), A. Redfearn; Thompson, Bridges, Forsyth (I. Van Bellen), Grayshon, G. Van Bellen (Ferres), Casey
Widnes 0 Eckersley; Wright, Aspey, George, Burke; Hughes, Bowden; Hogan (Mills), Elwell, Shaw, L. Gorley, Hull, Adams
Referee: W.H. Thompson (Huddersfield)
1980-81
Warrington 12 Hesford (2g, 2dg); Thackray, I. Duane, Bevan (2t), M. Kelly; K. Kelly, A. Gwilliam; Courtney, Waller, Case, Martyn, Potter, Hunter (Eccles)
Barrow 5 Elliott; McConnell, French, Ball (1g), Wainwright; Mason (1t), Cairns; D. Chisnall, Allen (Szymala), Flynn, K. James, Kirkby, Hadley
Referee: W.H. Thompson (Huddersfield)
1981-82
Hull 12 Banks; O'Hara, Harrison, Leuluai, Prendiville; Day, Dean (1dg) (K. Harkin); Skerrett, Wileman (1t), Stone, Crane, L. Crooks (4g), Norton
Hull K.R. 4 Fairbairn (2g); Hubbard, M. Smith, Hogan, Muscroft; Hartley, P. Harkin (Burton); Holdstock (Millington), Watkinson, S. Crooks, Lowe, Casey, Hall
Referee: G.F. Lindop (Wakefield)
1982-83
Wigan 15 Williams; Ramsdale, Stephenson, Whitfield (4g, 1dg), Gill (1t) (Juliff 1t); M. Foy, Fairhurst; Shaw, Kiss, Campbell, West (Case), Scott, Pendlebury

Leeds 4 Hague; Campbell, Wilkinson, Dyl, Andy Smith; Holmes, Dick (2g); Dickinson, Ward, Burke, Sykes, W. Heron, D. Heron
Referee: R. Campbell (Widnes)
1983-84
Leeds 18 Wilkinson; Prendiville, Creasser (5g), D. Bell, Andy Smith; Holmes (1t), Dick (1t); Keith Rayne, Ward (Squire), Kevin Rayne, Moorby, Laurie, Webb
Widnes 10 Burke (1g); Wright, Keiron O'Loughlin, Lydon (1t), Linton (1t); Hughes, Gregory; S. O'Neill, Elwell, K. Tamati, L. Gorley, Whitfield, Adams
Referee: W.H. Thompson (Huddersfield)
1984-85
Hull K.R. 12 Fairbairn; Clark (1t), Robinson, Prohm (1t), Laws; M. Smith, Harkin; Broadhurst, Watkinson, Ema, Burton, Hogan (1t), Miller
Hull 0 Kemble (Schofield); S. Evans, Ah Kuoi, Leuluai, O'Hara; Topliss, Sterling; Edmonds (Dannatt), Patrick, Rose, L. Crooks, Proctor, Divorty
Referee: S. Wall (Leigh)
1985-86
Wigan 11 Hampson; Mordt, Stephenson (1g), Hanley, Gill (Edwards); Ella, M. Ford (1t); Dowling (1dg), Kiss, Wane (1t), West, Goodway, Potter (Du Toit)
Hull K.R. 8 Lydiat (1t); Clark, M. Smith, Dorahy, Laws (1t); G. Smith, Harkin; P. Johnston (Robinson), Watkinson, Ema, Burton, Kelly, Miller
Referee: J. Holdsworth (Kippax)
1986-87
Wigan 18 Hampson; Stephenson, Lydon, Bell (1t), Gill (2t, 1g); Hanley, Edwards; West, Dermott, Case, Roberts, Potter, Goodway (1t)
Warrington 4 Johnson; Meadows, Cullen, Ropati, Forster (1t); K. Kelly, Peters (Duane); Boyd, K. Tamati (Rathbone), Jackson, Sanderson, Roberts, M. Gregory
Referee: J. Holdsworth (Kippax)
1987-88
St. Helens 15 Veivers; Tanner, Loughlin (2t, 3g), Elia, Quirk; Cooper, Holding (1dg); Burke, Groves, Souto (Evans), Forber, Haggerty, Platt
Leeds 14 Gurr; Morris, Schofield, Jackson (1t), Basnett (Gibson); Creasser (1t, 3g), Ashton; Tunks, Maskill, Kevin Rayne (Fairbank), Powell, Medley, D. Heron
Referee: G.F. Lindop (Wakefield)
1988-89
Wigan 12 Hampson; Bell, K. Iro (1t), Lydon (2g) (Gregory); T. Iro; Byrne, Edwards; Shelford (Goodway), Dermott, Wane, Betts, Potter, Hanley (1t)

155

Widnes 6 Tait; Thackray, Currier (1g), Wright (1t), Offiah; T. Myler, D. Hulme; Sorensen, McKenzie, Grima, M. O'Neill, Koloto (P. Hulme), Eyres
Referee: J. Holdsworth (Kippax)
1989-90
Wigan 24 Lydon (2g); Marshall, K. Iro, Bell, Preston; Edwards (1t), A. Gregory; Lucas (Wane), Dermott, Platt, Betts, Gildart (Goodway, 1t), Hanley (3t)
Halifax 12 Whitfield (Smith) (Scott); Riddlesden, Anderson, Hetherington, George; Dorahy, Lyons; Hill (1t), McCallion, Johnston, Bell, Milner, Holliday (4g)
Referee: D.G. Kershaw (Easingwold)

REGAL TROPHY MAN OF THE MATCH

Season	Winner	Team	Position
1971-72	Bruce Burton	Halifax (v. Wakefield T.)	Stand off
1972-73	Keith Hepworth	Leeds (v. Salford)	Scrum half
1973-74	Kevin Ashcroft	Warrington (v. Rochdale H.)	Hooker
1974-75	Barry Seabourne	Bradford N. (v. Widnes)	Scrum half
1975-76	Reg Bowden	Widnes (v. Hull)	Scrum half
1976-77	Gary Stephens	Castleford	Scrum half
	Howard Allen	Blackpool B.	Hooker
1977-78	Steve Hesford	Warrington (v. Widnes)	Winger
1978-79	David Eckersley	Widnes (v. Warrington)	Full back
1979-80	Len Casey	Bradford N. (v. Widnes)	Loose forward
1980-81	Tommy Martyn	Warrington (v. Barrow)	Second row
1981-82	Trevor Skerrett	Hull (v. Hull K.R.)	Prop
1982-83	Martin Foy	Wigan (v. Leeds)	Stand off
1983-84	Mark Laurie	Leeds (v. Widnes)	Second row
1984-85	Paul Harkin	Hull K.R. (v. Hull)	Scrum half
1985-86	Paul Harkin	Hull K.R. (v. Wigan)	Scrum half
1986-87	Andy Goodway	Wigan (v. Warrington)	Loose forward
1987-88	Paul Loughlin	St. Helens (v. Leeds)	Centre
1988-89	Ellery Hanley	Wigan (v. Widnes)	Loose forward
1989-90	Ellery Hanley	Wigan (v. Halifax)	Loose forward
1990-91	Billy McGinty	Warrington (v. Bradford N.)	Second row

REGAL TROPHY RECORDS

ALL ROUNDS

TEAM
Highest score: Wigan 92 v. Runcorn H. 2 (1988-89)
Biggest attendance: 25,326 Hull v. Hull K.R.
(at Hull C. FC)....... Final 1984-85

INDIVIDUAL
Most tries: 6 by Vince Gribbin (Whitehaven) v. Doncaster 1984-85
*Most goals: 17 by Sammy Lloyd (Castleford)
*Most points: 43 (17g,3t) by Sammy Lloyd (Castleford)
*The above records were achieved in the Castleford v. Millom first round tie in 1973-74.

REGAL TROPHY FINAL RECORDS

Most final appearances: 7 by Widnes
Most wins: 5 by Wigan
Most tries: 3 by Ellery Hanley (Wigan) v. Halifax
.... 1989-90
Most goals: 6 by Derek Whitehead (Warrington) v. Rochdale H............................. 1973-74
Most points: 15 (6g,1t) by Derek Whitehead (Warrington) v. Rochdale H........................ 1973-74
Highest score: Warrington 27 v. Rochdale H. 16 1973-74
Widest margin win: Wigan 18 v. Warrington 4 1986-87
Biggest attendance: 25,326 Hull v. Hull K.R.
(at Hull C. FC)............... 1984-85
Biggest receipts: £94,874 Widnes v. Wigan
(at Bolton W. FC)............... 1988-89

●*BEFORE 1977-78 the competition was known as the Player's No. 6 Trophy, then the John Player Trophy. In 1983-84 it became the John Player Special Trophy, renamed the Regal Trophy in 1989-90. It was not until 1979-80 that semi-finals were played at neutral venues.*

NON-LEAGUE CLUBS IN THE REGAL TROPHY

Amateur clubs have entered the Regal tournament in every season apart from a period between 1981 and 1984. Two figured in the first round up to 1979-80 and one the following season. They were then left out from 1981-82

because the number of professional clubs had grown beyond the mathematically suitable 32.

But the amateurs returned in 1984-85 with two clubs joining the professionals in a small preliminary round, the number being increased to three in 1989-90.

The fate of the amateurs has varied from the record 88-5 hammering Millom received at Castleford to victories by Cawoods and Myson over Halifax and Batley respectively.

The full list of amateur clubs' results — all first round matches except where stated (P) Preliminary (2) Second Round — is:

Season							Attendance
1971-72		Wigan	33	v	Ace Amateurs (Hull)	9	2,678
		Thames Board Mill (Warr.)	7	v	Huddersfield	27	1,175
1972-73		Bramley	26	v	Pilkington Recs. (St. Helens)	5	616
		Dewsbury	22	v	Dewsbury Celtic	4	1,897
1973-74		Whitehaven	26	v	Dewsbury Celtic	3	1,276
		Castleford	88	v	Millom (Cumbria)	5	1,031
1974-75		Whitehaven	32	v	Lock Lane (Castleford)	6	537
		Doncaster	15	v	Kippax White Swan	6	453
1975-76		Salford	57	v	Mayfield (Rochdale)	3	3,449
		Barrow	16	v	Pilkington Recs. (St. Helens)	9	612
1976-77		Halifax	24	v	Ovenden (Halifax)	4	3,680
		Salford	39	v	Ace Amateurs (Hull)	15	3,037
1977-78		N.D.L.B. (Hull)	4	v	New Hunslet	18	3,845
		Halifax	8	v	Cawoods (Hull)	9	1,168
	(2)	Wakefield T.	31	v	Cawoods (Hull)	7	3,380
1978-79		Leigh Miners Welfare	9	v	Halifax	21	1,621
		Milford (Leeds)	5	v	Dewsbury	38	3,129
1979-80		Pilkington Recs. (St. Helens)	9	v	Wigan	18	6,707
		Blackpool B.	6	v	West Hull	3	555
1980-81		Castleford	30	v	Pilkington Recs. (St. Helens)	17	2,823
1984-85	(P)	Myson (Hull)	2	v	Dewsbury	8	1,572
	(P)	Keighley	24	v	Dudley Hill (Bradford)	10	1,570
1985-86	(P)	Keighley	24	v	Jubilee (Featherstone)	6	1,007
	(P)	West Hull	10	v	Castleford	24	2,500
1986-87	(P)	Batley	2	v	Myson (Hull)	8	687
	(P)	Millom (Cumbria)	4	v	Wakefield T.	18	2,000
		Myson (Hull)	11	v	Swinton	18	1,648
1987-88	(P)	Featherstone R.	34	v	Thatto Heath (St. Helens)	16	1,045
	(P)	Heworth (York)	5	v	Swinton	32	1,063
1988-89	(P)	Wigan St. Patricks	36	v	Elland (Halifax)	2	2,510
		Sheffield E.	80	v	Wigan St. Patricks	8	621
1989-90	(P)	Batley	28	v	West Hull	14	844
	(P)	Crosfields (Warrington)	14	v	Workington T.	19	942
	(P)	Kells (Whitehaven)	2	v	Doncaster	28	2,127
1990-91	(P)	Dudley Hill (Bradford)	18	v	Dewsbury	24	970
	(P)	Saddleworth (Oldham)	35	v	Egremont (Cumbria)	18	900
		Rochdale H.	30	v	Saddleworth (Oldham)	10	2,434

REGAL TROPHY PROGRESS CHART

Key: W — Winners. F — Beaten finalists. SF — Semi-final. P — Preliminary round.

	1990-91	1989-90	1988-89	1987-88	1986-87	1985-86	1984-85	1983-84	1982-83	1981-82	1980-81	1979-80	1978-79	1977-78	1976-77	1975-76	1974-75	1973-74	1972-73	1971-72
BARROW	1	1	1	1	3	2	1	2	3	3	F	1	1	1	1	2	1	1	1	3
BATLEY	3	1	1	2	P	1	1	P	1	1	1	1	1	1	1	2	1	1	2	1
BRADFORD N.	F	2	SF	1	3	2	2	1	3	2	1	W	SF	SF	2	1	W	1	3	1
BRAMLEY	2	1	2	P	1	1	3	*	1	1	1	2	1	1	2	1	2	SF	2	2
CARLISLE	P	1	1	1	2	P	P	2	2	2										
CASTLEFORD	3	SF	2	2	2	1	2	1	1	2	SF	3	3	2	W	SF	1	2	1	2
CHORLEY	1	1																		
DEWSBURY	1	2	1	2	1	1	3	1	1	1	1	1	2	1	1	1	1	3	2	1
DONCASTER	2	1	2	1	2	2	1	1	1	1	1	1	1	1	1	1	2	1	1	1
FEATHERSTONE R.	2	3	1	1	2	P	2	3	1	2	2	2	2	3	2	1	1	1	2	1
FULHAM	1	1	P	P	1	1	1	1	1	1	2									
HALIFAX	P	F	2	2	2	1	SF	1	1	1	3	1	2	1	2	1	1	2	1	W
HUDDERSFIELD	1	2	1	1	P	1	1	1	2	2	2	1	1	3	1	3	1	1	2	2
HULL	1	1	2	3	SF	3	F	2	2	W	SF	1	2	1	3	F	1	1	3	3
HULL K.R.	1	1	3	2	1	F	W	2	3	F	2	1	SF	1	1	3	SF	1	SF	2
HUNSLET	1	2	P	1	1	2	P	1	1	1	2	1	1	2	1	2	1	1	1	1
KEIGHLEY	2	1	1	1	2	1	2	1	2	1	2	3	2	1	1	2	3	1	2	1
LEEDS	2	3	1	F	1	1	SF	W	F	3	1	2	1	1	3	2	3	3	W	SF
LEIGH	2	1	3	2	3	SF	1	SF	2	1	3	3	3	3	SF	2	1	2	2	1
NOTTINGHAM C.	1	1	1	2	1	1	1													
OLDHAM	2	3	1	SF	1	2	2	1	1	SF	1	1	1	2	2	2	2	1	1	1
ROCHDALE H.	SF	1	2	1	1	1	2	1	2	1	1	1	1	1	1	1	1	F	1	2
RUNCORN H.	1	1	1	1	1	1	2	2	P	1	1	1	1	1	1	1	2	1	1	1
RYEDALE-YORK	P	P	1	1	P	3	1	1	2	1	2	2	1	1	3	1	2	2	2	2
ST. HELENS	3	SF	SF	W	3	SF	3	SF	2	1	1	2	2	2	2	3	1	SF	SF	SF
SALFORD	1	2	1	3	1	2	1	2	3	3	2	SF	2	2	2	SF	3	2	F	1
SHEFFIELD E.	P	3	2	1	2	1	1													
SWINTON	1	2	1	2	1	1	3	1	SF	1	1	1	1	1	1	3	1	3	1	1
TRAFFORD B.	1	1	2	3	2	1	1	2	P	2	2	1	1	F	1	1	1	1	3	1
WAKEFIELD T.	2	P	3	2	2	2	P	1	1	1	1	SF	3	SF	1	2	2	3	2	F
WARRINGTON	W	P	3	3	F	3	1	2	SF	2	W	3	F	W	1	1	3	W	1	1
WHITEHAVEN	1	2	1	1	1	1	2	P	1	1	3	1	1	1	1	1	SF	2	1	2
WIDNES	SF	2	F	1	SF	3	3	F	SF	3	3	F	W	F	SF	W	F	1	3	1
WIGAN	3	W	W	SF	W	W	2	3	W	1	1	2	2	3	2	2	2	2	1	3
WORKINGTON T.	1	1	P	1	1	1	1	1	1	2	1	3	2	2	3	3	1	2	1	1

*Bramley withdrew from the Trophy while in liquidation, opponents Hull K.R. receiving a bye.

PREMIERSHIP TROPHY

1991 Final

Underdogs Hull pulled off a shock three tries to one victory over hot favourites Widnes in the Stones Bitter Premiership final to bring a major trophy to Yorkshire for the first time in four years.

A record Premiership crowd of 42,043, paying a record £384,300, saw the Airlie Birds halt Widnes's attempt to win the trophy for a fourth successive season as half backs Greg Mackey and Patrick Entat took control behind a dominant pack.

Hull's Australian coach Noel Cleal had spent 20 hours analysing video tapes of the Chemics and his homework paid dividends with Hull's first cup haul since 1984. The base of forward supremacy, established by the front row of Karl Harrison, Lee Jackson and Andy Dannatt, was built upon by the craft of the half backs.

Skipper Mackey was irrepressible to earn the coveted Harry Sunderland Trophy as Man of the Match. The Australian stand off dictated play from the first whistle, spraying out passes, putting in kicks and constantly probing for openings. He mesmerised Widnes to set up Hull's first try as he pointed skywards for an up and under after the fifth tackle, then suddenly switched the ball away for enterprising full back Richard Gay to crash through for a 13th minute touchdown.

The early shock affected a Widnes side seeking a 12th consecutive Premiership tie victory but already disrupted by the revelation of a transfer demand from star winger Martin Offiah and accurate speculation of coach Doug Laughton's impending move to Leeds.

Capitalising on a forward barrage, Hull stretched their lead in the 27th minute, French scrum half Entat teasing his way through grasping defenders as he searched for support on the right flank. British Test winger Eastwood provided it and burrowed infield before arcing back towards his wing where second row man Russ Walker took over to crash through for the touchdown.

Widnes, who, as Championship runners-up, finished one place ahead of Hull in the final league table, were 8-0 down and it could have been more before half-time as the Boulevarders continued to outplay them.

The Chemics threatened to claw their way back into the game on the hour as Test winger Offiah scored his 49th try of the season, confirming a fourth successive campaign as top tryscorer, the first Englishman to perform the feat.

Hull wavered, but regrouped and then hit back in stunning fashion. With 10 minutes to go, substitute centre Gary Nolan, a 48th minute replacement for the injured Australian Damien McGarry, scored the clinching try to maintain a remarkable track record. The 24-year-old back had been playing amateur Rugby League only six weeks earlier and was making only his fourth appearance for the first team, coming on as substitute three times and scoring on each occasion.

His Old Trafford touchdown came out of nothing. Mackey slipped Nolan the ball a few yards from the line, the novice hurling himself forward and somehow reaching one arm through tangled bodies to plant the ball over the line. As the army of Hull fans erupted, Eastwood remained calm to bang over the goal from near touch to put the contest out of Widnes's reach.

Hull's defence was equally impressive. They swarmed all over the Widnes star backs so that newly-crowned Stones Bitter First Division Player of the Year, Jonathan Davies, and colleagues rarely got a running chance.

Hull deservedly collected the Stones Bitter Premiership Trophy for the first time at the fifth attempt as Widnes added Old Trafford disappointment to non-fulfilment of their Championship and Challenge Cup ambitions.

STONES BITTER PREMIERSHIP FINAL

12 May   **Old Trafford, Manchester**

HULL   14   **WIDNES 4**

Richard Gay	1.	Alan Tait
Paul Eastwood	2.	John Devereux
Damien McGarry	3.	Andy Currier
Brad Webb	4.	Jonathan Davies, Capt.
Neil Turner	5.	Martin Offiah
Greg Mackey, Capt.	6.	Barry Dowd
Patrick Entat	7.	David Hulme
Karl Harrison	8.	Kurt Sorensen
Lee Jackson	9.	Phil McKenzie
Andy Dannatt	10.	Joe Grima
Ian Marlow	11.	Paul Hulme
Russ Walker	12.	Emosi Koloto
Jon Sharp	13.	Steve McCurrie
Gary Nolan	14.	Darren Wright
Dean Busby	15.	Harvey Howard

T: Gay, Walker, Nolan
G: Eastwood
Substitutions:
Nolan for McGarry (48 min.)
Busby for Marlow (61 min.)
Half-time: 8-0
Referee: John Holdsworth (Kippax)

T: Offiah
Substitutions:
Howard for Koloto (28 min.)
Wright for McKenzie (40 min.)
Attendance: 42,043
Receipts: £384,300

1991 Round by Round

Leeds captain Garry Schofield crowned a magnificent display by forcing his way over between the posts for a last-minute try to snatch a dramatic 24-20 first-round victory at Castleford. Earlier, Schofield had raced 70 yards for a spectacular interception try, only for referee Jim Smith to controversially rule a knock on, the skipper's objections earning a spell in the sin bin. Rampant Widnes inflicted a nine-try, 46-10 defeat on Bradford Northern, Jonathan Davies claiming two tries and five goals to establish a club points-in-a-season record. Champions Wigan rested 11 of their Wembley line-up and came unstuck with a 31-26 home defeat by Featherstone Rovers, inspired by skipper Deryck Fox and registering their first win at Central Park since 1965. Wembley-bound St. Helens created enough first-half chances to secure victory at Hull, but the superb home defence paved the way for a second-half comeback highlighted by three tries in 11 minutes as Hull won 28-12.

In the semi-finals, Hull clinched a 10-7 victory a minute from time when it looked as though Leeds' superb defence was to earn them their first Premiership final appearance for 12 years. Substitute Gary Nolan, brought on four minutes earlier for only his third first-team match, touched the ball for the first time to score by snatching it from the grasp of Leeds full back John Gallagher after a pin-point up and under from Greg Mackey. Winger John Devereux grabbed a hat-trick of tries as Widnes demolished Featherstone Rovers 42-28 at Naughton Park.

1991 Results

First Round

Castleford	20	Leeds	24
Hull	28	St. Helens	12
Widnes	46	Bradford N.	10
Wigan	26	Featherstone R.	31

Semi-Finals

Hull	10	Leeds	7
Widnes	42	Featherstone R.	28

Final

Hull	14	Widnes	4

(at Old Trafford, Manchester)

1991 Prizes

Winners: £17,000
Runners-up: £6,750

Hull hooker Lee Jackson, a key figure in the 1991 Old Trafford final.

History

With the reintroduction of two divisions in 1973-74 there was no longer a need for a play-off to decide the championship.

However, it was decided to continue the tradition of an end-of-season play-off, the winners to receive the newly instituted Premiership Trophy.

In the first season of the Premiership, 1974-75, the top 12 Division One clubs and the top four from Division Two went into a first round draw, the luck of the draw operating through to the final, played on a neutral venue.

The following season the play-off was reduced to the top eight clubs in the First Division, the ties being decided on a merit basis i.e. 1st v. 8th, 2nd v. 7th etc. At the semi-final stage the highest placed clubs had the option of when to play at home in the two-legged tie.

In 1978-79 the two-leg system was suspended because of fixture congestion and the higher placed clubs had home advantage right through to the neutrally staged final.

Two legs returned the following season, but were finally abolished from 1980-81.

A Second Division Premiership tournament was introduced for the first time in 1986-87, Manchester United's Old Trafford being selected as a new fixed venue for a doubleheader final.

PREMIERSHIP ROLL OF HONOUR

Year	Winners		Runners-up		Venue	Attendance	Receipts
1975	Leeds	26	St. Helens	11	Wigan	14,531	£7,795
1976	St. Helens	15	Salford	2	Swinton	18,082	£13,138
1977	St. Helens	32	Warrington	20	Swinton	11,178	£11,626
1978	Bradford N.	17	Widnes	8	Swinton	16,813	£18,677
1979	Leeds	24	Bradford N.	2	Huddersfield	19,486	£21,291
1980	Widnes	19	Bradford N.	5	Swinton	10,215	£13,665
1981	Hull K.R.	11	Hull	7	Leeds	29,448	£47,529
1982	Widnes	23	Hull	8	Leeds	12,100	£23,749
1983	Widnes	22	Hull	10	Leeds	17,813	£34,145
1984	Hull K.R.	18	Castleford	10	Leeds	12,515	£31,769
1985	St. Helens	36	Hull K.R.	16	Elland Rd, Leeds	15,518	£46,950
1986	Warrington	38	Halifax	10	Elland Rd, Leeds	13,683	£50,879
1987	Wigan	8	Warrington	0	Old Trafford, Man'r	38,756	£165,166
1988	Widnes	38	St. Helens	14	Old Trafford, Man'r	35,252	£202,616
1989	Widnes	18	Hull	10	Old Trafford, Man'r	40,194	£264,242
1990	Widnes	28	Bradford N.	6	Old Trafford, Man'r	40,796	£273,877
1991	Hull	14	Widnes	4	Old Trafford, Man'r	42,043	£384,300

PREMIERSHIP FINAL . . . . A REVIEW

1974-75
Leeds 26 Holmes (2g) (Marshall 3g); Alan Smith
(1t), Hynes (1t, 1dg) (Eccles), Dyl, Atkinson
(2t), Mason (1t), Hepworth; Dickinson, Ward,
Pitchford, Cookson, Batten, Haigh
St. Helens 11 G. Pimblett; L. Jones (1t),
Wilson, Hull, Mathias (1t); Walsh, Heaton (1t);
Warlow (Cunningham), A. Karalius, Mantle
(K. Gwilliam), E. Chisnall, Nicholls, Coslett (1g)
Referee: W.H. Thompson (Huddersfield)
1975-76
St. Helens 15 G. Pimblett (3g); L. Jones, Glynn
(1t), Noonan, Mathias; Benyon, Heaton
(K. Gwilliam); Mantle, A. Karalius (1t), James,
Nicholls, E. Chisnall (1t), Coslett
Salford 2 Watkins (2dg); Fielding, Richards,
Hesketh, Graham; Butler, Nash; Coulman,
Raistrick, Sheffield, Knighton (Turnbull),
Dixon, E. Prescott
Referee: M. J. Naughton (Widnes)
1976-77
St. Helens 32 G. Pimblett (7g, 1t); L. Jones,
Benyon (1t), Cunningham (1t), Mathias (1t),
Glynn (Ashton); K. Gwilliam (1t); D. Chisnall,
Liptrot, James (1t), Nicholls (A. Karalius),
E. Chisnall, Pinner
Warrington 20 Finnegan; Curling, Bevan
(Cunliffe), Hesford (4g), M. Kelly; A. Gwilliam
(1t), Gordon (1t); Weavill (1t), Price, Case,
Martyn (Peers), Lester, B. Philbin (1t)
Referee: G.F. Lindop (Wakefield)
1977-78
Bradford N. 17 Mumby (2g); Barends (1t),
Roe (1t), Austin, D. Redfearn (1t); Wolford (1dg),
A. Redfearn; I. Van Bellen (Fox), Raistrick,
Thompson, Joyce (Forsyth), Trotter, Haigh (1t)
Widnes 8 Eckersley; Wright, Hughes, Aspey (2t),
Woods (1g); Gill, Bowden; Mills, Elwell, Shaw
(Ramsey) (George), Adams, Hull, Laughton
Referee: J.E. Jackson (Pudsey)
1978-79
Leeds 24 Hague; Alan Smith (1t), D. Smith (1t),
Dyl (Fletcher), Atkinson; Dick (7g, 1dg),
J. Sanderson; Harrison, Ward (1t), Pitchford,
Joyce, Eccles (Adams), Cookson
Bradford N. 2 Mumby; D. Parker, Okulicz,
Gant, Spencer; Ferres (1g), A. Redfearn;
Thompson, Bridges, Forsyth (I. Van Bellen),
Trotter (Mordue), Grayshon, Casey
Referee: W.H. Thompson (Huddersfield)

1979-80
Widnes 19 Burke (1g); Wright (1t), George,
Aspey (1t), Bentley (1t); Eckersley (1dg),
Bowden; Shaw, Elwell (1t, 1dg), M. O'Neill,
L. Gorley (1t), Hull (Hogan), Adams
Bradford N. 5 Mumby (1g); MacLean (Ferres),
D. Redfearn (1t), D. Parker, Gant; Stephenson,
A. Redfearn; Thompson, Bridges, Forsyth,
Clarkson (G. Van Bellen), Grayshon, Hale
Referee: W.H. Thompson (Huddersfield)
1980-81
Hull K.R. 11 Proctor; Hubbard (1g), M. Smith
(1t), Hogan (1t), Muscroft; Hartley (1t), Harkin;
Holdstock, Watkinson, Millington, Lowe, Casey,
Hall (Burton)
Hull 7 Woods (2g); Peacham, Elliott, Wilby,
Prendiville; Banks, Dean; Tindall, Wileman,
Stone, Skerrett (Madley), Crane (1t), Norton
Referee: J. Holdsworth (Leeds)
1981-82
Widnes 23 Burke (4g, 1t); Wright (1t), Kieron
O'Loughlin, Cunningham (A. Myler), Basnett
(1t); Hughes (1t), Gregory; M. O'Neill, Elwell,
Lockwood (Whitfield), L. Gorley, E. Prescott,
Adams (1t)
Hull 8 Kemble; O'Hara (Day), Leuluai,
S. Evans, Prendiville; Topliss, Harkin; Tindall,
Wileman (Lloyd), Stone, Skerrett, Crooks
(1t, 2g, 1dg), Norton
Referee: S. Wall (Leigh)
1982-83
Widnes 22 Burke; Linton, Hughes, Lydon (5g),
Basnett (2t); A. Myler (1t), Gregory (1t) (Hulme);
M. O'Neill, Elwell, L. Gorley, Whitfield
(S. O'Neill), Prescott, Adams
Hull 10 Kemble; O'Hara (1t), Day (Solal),
Leuluai, S. Evans; Topliss (1t), Dean; Skerrett,
Bridges, Stone, Rose, Crooks (2g), Norton
(Crane)
Referee: F. Lindop (Wakefield)
1983-84
Hull K.R. 18 Fairbairn; Clark, M. Smith (1t),
Prohm (1t), Laws (1t), Dorahy (1t, 1g), Harkin;
Holdstock, Rudd, Millington (Robinson),
Burton (Lydiat), Broadhurst, Hall
Castleford 10 Roockley; Coen, Marchant, Hyde,
Kear (1t); Robinson, R. Beardmore (3g); Ward,
Horton, Connell, Crampton, Atkins, Joyner
Referee: R. Campbell (Widnes)
1984-85
St. Helens 36 Veivers (1t); Ledger (2t), Peters,
Meninga (2t) (Allen), Day (4g); Arkwright,
Holding; Burke (Forber), Ainsworth (1t),
P. Gorley, Platt, Haggerty, Pinner (1t)

Hull K.R. 16 Fairbairn (1t, 2g); Clark, Robinson (1t), Prohm, Laws (1t); M. Smith, G. Smith (Harkin); Broadhurst, Watkinson, Ema (Lydiat), Kelly, Hogan, Hall
Referee: S. Wall (Leigh)
1985-86
Warrington 38 Paul Ford (Johnson 1t); Forster (1t), Cullen, R. Duane, Carbert; Bishop (1t, 5g), A. Gregory; Boyd (2t), Tamati (1t), Jackson (1t), Sanderson (McGinty), Roberts, M. Gregory
Halifax 10 Whitfield (3g) (Smith); Riddlesden, T. Anderson, C. Anderson (1t), Wilson; Crossley, Stephens; Scott, McCallion, Robinson, Juliff, James (Bond), Dixon
Referee: F. Lindop (Wakefield)
1986-87
Wigan 8 Hampson; Gill (1g), Stephenson (1g), Bell, Lydon (1t) (Russell); Edwards, Gregory; Case, Kiss, Wane (West), Goodway, Potter, Hanley
Warrington 0 Johnson; Drummond, Ropati, B. Peters, Forster; Cullen, Bishop; Tamati, Roberts (Eccles), Jackson, Humphries (M. Gregory), Sanderson, Duane
Referee: K. Allatt (Southport)
1987-88
Widnes 38 Platt (1g); Thackray (Tait, 1t), Currier (4g), Wright (2t), Offiah; Dowd, D. Hulme (2t), Sorensen (1t), McKenzie (1t), Grima (S. O'Neill), M. O'Neill, P. Hulme, R. Eyres
St. Helens 14 Loughlin (3g); Ledger (1t), Tanner, Elia, Quirk; Bailey, Holding; Burke, Groves, Evans (Dwyer), Forber, Fieldhouse (Allen), Haggerty (1t)
Referee: J. Holdsworth (Kippax)
1988-89
Widnes 18 Tait; Davies (3g), Currier (1t) (Pyke), Wright (1t), Offiah (1t); D. Hulme (A. Myler), P. Hulme; Sorensen, McKenzie, Grima, M. O'Neill, Koloto, R. Eyres
Hull 10 Fletcher; Eastwood, Blacker, Price (Wilby), O'Hara; Pearce (3g), Windley (Nolan); Dannatt, Jackson, S. Crooks, Welham (1t), Sharp, Divorty
Referee: J. Holdsworth (Kippax)
1989-90
Widnes 28 Tait (2t); Davies (4g), Currier (2t), Wright, Offiah; D. Hulme, P. Hulme; Sorensen (A. Myler), McKenzie, M. O'Neill, Koloto (Grima), Eyres, Holliday (1t)
Bradford N. 6 Wilkinson; Cordle, McGowan (Cooper), Marchant (1t), Francis; Simpson, Harkin; Skerrett, Noble (Richards), Hobbs, Medley, Fairbank, Mumby (1g)
Referee: C. Morris (Huddersfield)

Hull skipper Greg Mackey with the 1991 Harry Sunderland Trophy.

THE HARRY SUNDERLAND TROPHY

The trophy, in memory of the famous Queenslander, a former Australian Tour Manager, broadcaster and journalist, is presented to the Man of the Match in the end of season Championship or Premiership final.

The award is donated and judged by the Rugby League Writers' Association and is sponsored by Stones Bitter.

Year	Winner	Team	Position
1965	Terry Fogerty	Halifax (v. St. Helens)	Second row
1966	Albert Halsall	St. Helens (v. Halifax)	Prop
1967	Ray Owen	Wakefield T. (v. St. Helens)	Scrum half
1968	Gary Cooper	Wakefield T. (v. Hull K.R.)	Full back
1969	Bev Risman	Leeds (v. Castleford)	Full back
1970	Frank Myler	St. Helens (v. Leeds)	Stand off
1971	Bill Ashurst	Wigan (v. St. Helens)	Second row
1972	Terry Clawson	Leeds (v. St. Helens)	Prop
1973	Mick Stephenson	Dewsbury (v. Leeds)	Hooker
1974	Barry Philbin	Warrington (v. St. Helens)	Loose forward
1975	Mel Mason	Leeds (v. St. Helens)	Stand off
1976	George Nicholls	St. Helens (v. Salford)	Second row
1977	Geoff Pimblett	St. Helens (v. Warrington)	Full back
1978	Bob Haigh	Bradford N. (v. Widnes)	Loose forward
1979	Kevin Dick	Leeds (v. Bradford N.)	Stand off
1980	Mal Aspey	Widnes (v. Bradford N.)	Centre
1981	Len Casey	Hull K.R. (v. Hull)	Second row
1982	Mick Burke	Widnes (v. Hull)	Full back
1983	Tony Myler	Widnes (v. Hull)	Stand off
1984	John Dorahy	Hull K.R. (v. Castleford)	Stand off
1985	Harry Pinner	St. Helens (v. Hull K.R.)	Loose forward
1986	Les Boyd	Warrington (v. Halifax)	Prop
1987	Joe Lydon	Wigan (v. Warrington)	Winger
1988	David Hulme	Widnes (v. St. Helens)	Scrum half
1989	Alan Tait	Widnes (v. Hull)	Full back
1990	Alan Tait	Widnes (v. Bradford N.)	Full back
1991	Greg Mackey	Hull (v. Widnes)	Stand off

PREMIERSHIP RECORDS   First staged 1975

ALL ROUNDS

TEAM

Highest score: Hull K.R. 54 v. Leeds 0 1984
(Also widest margin)
Biggest attendance: 42,043 Hull v. Widnes
.........Final at Old Trafford 1991

INDIVIDUAL

Most goals:
9 by Andy Gregory (Widnes) v. Leeds...Round 1 1982
Most points:
22 (7g, 2t) by John Dorahy (Hull K.R.) v. Leeds
.............Round 1 1984

Most tries:
4 by David Hall (Hull K.R.) v. Castleford
.............Round 1 1983
4 by Phil Ford (Wigan) v. Hull...........Round 1 1985
4 by Ellery Hanley (Wigan) v. Hull K.R.
.............Round 1 1986

PREMIERSHIP FINAL

TEAM

Most appearances: 8 by Widnes
Most wins: 6 by Widnes
Highest score:
Warrington 38 v. Halifax 10 (widest margin).......1986
Widnes 38 v. St. Helens 14 1988
Biggest attendance:
42,043 Hull v. Widnes
(at Old Trafford, Man'r) 1991

INDIVIDUAL

Most tries:
No player has scored 3 or more
Most goals:
8 by Kevin Dick (Leeds) v. Bradford N.............1979
Most points: 17 (7g, 1t) by Geoff Pimblett (St. Helens)
v. Warrington..........1977

SECOND DIVISION
PREMIERSHIP TROPHY

1991 Final

Halifax threw away the Stones Bitter Second Division Premiership Trophy with two costly errors in the last 15 minutes of a fluctuating final.

The Yorkshiremen were leading 16-14 when scrum half Roy Southernwood lost the ball, Salford opposite number Steve Kerry collecting possession and moving the ball out for winger Tex Evans to score in the corner. Kerry, the League's top goalscorer added the touchline goal, hooker Mark Lee knocking over a drop goal to open a 21-16 lead.

Halifax always looked likely to regain supremacy until they made another blunder inside their own 25-yard zone. Full back Steve Smith and loose forward Mick Keebles got into a tangle clearing their line for substitute Mike Dean to pounce on the loose ball and send former Wigan centre John Gilfillan romping to the posts.

Former Preston Grasshopper RU half back Kerry added his fourth goal to a drop goal and two tries to take the Tom Bergin Trophy as Man of the Match.

The Thrum Hall men made a brave attempt to salvage something from the late shambles and Martin Wood went in for a 76th minute try to claim third spot in the League's top try chart.

But the drama of yet another entertaining Second Division showpiece was marred by serious skirmishes at the start and finish of the Old Trafford encounter. The season's first meeting of the two sides, due to the fixture formula, was settling down when fighting broke out during which Kerry kicked a grounded Halifax player. Bradford referee Brian Galtress awarded a penalty to restart play.

The match official was again lenient when the match finished in an unseemly brawl. The melee continued after the final hooter, but Galtress elected not to dismiss anyone, although the League later charged Peter Brown with bringing the game into disrepute and ordered Halifax skipper Brendan Hill, plus Salford's Ian Sherratt, to appear before the Disciplinary Committee.

Salford opened the scoring after 14 minutes, when enterprising Australian full back Steve Gibson broke brilliantly to send Kerry racing in for his first try. The Red Devils held the lead for 18 minutes until ex-Castleford half back Southernwood levelled the scores by scampering over after flashing a quick dummy pass.

Two drop goals in two minutes from half backs Frank Cassidy and Kerry edged Salford back in front again, but Halifax took a 10-6 half-time lead when Hill blasted in off an astute pass from New Zealand Test forward Brown, substitute Alan Platt adding the simple goal.

Six minutes after the interval, Kerry grabbed eight points to wipe out the lead as the number seven repeated his supporting role to another Gibson break, added the goal and then a penalty.

Halifax's response six minutes later was magnificent. Having piled on the pressure, their centres split Salford wide open with a devastating attack from halfway. Australian Greg Austin, bidding for the Stones Bitter top scoring award of £25 a try, made the initial break before linking with former Leeds utility back Warren Wilson, who cut inside sharply to finish off in style behind the posts. Platt added the goal for a 16-14 lead which should have been the springboard to success. Instead the White Rose men cracked under enforced errors.

Salford became the second club to complete a Second Division Championship-Premiership double in the five-year history of the top-eight competition, Oldham having performed the feat in 1988.

SECOND DIVISION PREMIERSHIP FINAL

12 May   Old Trafford, Manchester

SALFORD 27		HALIFAX 20
Steve Gibson	1.	Steve Smith
Tex Evans	2.	Martin Wood
John Gilfillan	3.	Warren Wilson
Martin Birkett	4.	Greg Austin
Adrian Hadley	5.	Matthew Silva
Frank Cassidy	6.	John Lyons
Steve Kerry	7.	Roy Southernwood
Mick Worrall	8.	Brendan Hill, Capt.
Mark Lee	9.	Jason Ramshaw
Shane Hansen	10.	Peter Bell
Arthur Bradshaw	11.	Peter Brown
Ian Blease, Capt.	12.	Richard Milner
Andy Burgess	13.	Mick Keebles
Mike Dean	14.	Alan Platt
Ian Sherratt	15.	Mick Scott

T: Kerry (2), Evans, Gilfillan
G: Kerry (4,1dg), Cassidy (dg), Lee (dg)
Substitutions:
Sherratt for Bradshaw (40 min.)
Dean for Hadley (51 min.)
Referee: Brian Galtress (Bradford)

T: Southernwood, Hill, Wilson, Wood
G: Platt (2)
Substitutions:
Platt for Silva (25 min.)
Scott for Bell (72 min.)
Half-time: 6-10

1991 Round by Round

Sixth-placed Workington Town provided the shock of the first round with a well deserved 19-12 victory at promoted Swinton, the Cumbrians scoring 17 points without reply in a barnstorming second-half rally of three tries, two goals and a drop goal. Winger Martin Wood grabbed four tries as Halifax gained a comfortable 42-24 success over visitors Fulham, the Yorkshiremen never looking convincing, especially after the 22nd minute loss of injured skipper Brendan Hill. Ryedale-York lost home advantage due to the unavailability of their dual-purpose athletic stadium, then lost the tie 11-6 to Leigh at Scarborough FC's McCain Stadium. Leigh acclimatised to the seaside surroundings with a 10-0 lead, although Ryedale-York pulled back to trail 10-6 at the interval. Salford winger Steve O'Neill collected two excellent tries as the Champions gained a 26-12 home victory over Carlisle, the visitors being inspired by Kiwi half back Clayton Friend.

In the semi-finals, table-toppers Salford were held to a 9-9 draw at home to Workington Town, a drop goal by half back Stephen Wear four minutes from time earning the Cumbrians a replay. Two days later at Derwent Park, Salford wore down Town's resistance and registered a comfortable 26-6 victory. Halifax cruised to a 32-8 home success over Leigh, centre Greg Austin and full back Steve Smith each collecting two tries.

Salford's rampaging former Test forward Mick Worrall tears into the Halifax defence.

Old Trafford joy for 1991 Second Division Premiership Trophy victors, Salford.

Results

First Round

Halifax	42	Fulham	24
Ryedale-York	6	Leigh	11

(at Scarborough FC)

Salford	26	Carlisle	12
Swinton	12	Workington T.	19

Semi-Finals

Halifax	32	Leigh	8
Salford	9	Workington T.	9

Replay

Workington T.	6	Salford	26

Final

Salford	27	Halifax	20

(at Old Trafford, Manchester)

1991 Prizes

Winners:	£9,000
Runners-up:	£3,500

SECOND DIVISION PREMIERSHIP. . . . A REVIEW

1986-87

Swinton 27 Viller; Bate (1t), Topping (Ratcliffe), Brown, Rippon (3g); Snape, Lee (1t); Grima (1t), Ainsworth (1t), Muller, Derbyshire (1t), M. Holliday (Allen), L. Holliday (1dg)

Hunslet 10 Kay; Tate, Penola, Irvine, Wilson; Coates, King; Sykes, Gibson (Senior), Bateman (2t), Platt (1g) (Mason), Bowden, Jennings
Referee: J. McDonald (Wigan)

1987-88
Oldham 28 Burke (Irving); Round, D. Foy (2t), McAlister (4g), Meadows (1t); Walsh (1t), Ford; Sherratt (Warnecke), Sanderson, Waddell, Hawkyard, Graham, Flanagan (1t)
Featherstone R. 26 Quinn (5g); Bannister (1t), Sykes (1t), Banks, Marsh (Crossley); Steadman (2t), Fox; Siddall (Bastian), K. Bell, Harrison, Hughes, Smith, Lyman
Referee: R. Whitfield (Widnes)

1988-89
Sheffield E. 43 Gamson; Cartwright, Dickinson, Powell (3t), Young; Aston (1t, 7g, 1dg), Close (Evans); Broadbent (1t), Cook (1t), Van Bellen, Nickle, Fleming (McDermott, 1t), Smiles
Swinton 18 Topping; Ranson (1t), Viller (Maloney), Snape, Bate; Frodsham (1t), Hewitt; Mooney, Melling (1t), S. O'Neill, Ainsworth, Allen (1t) (Horrocks), J. Myler (3g)
Referee: R. Whitfield (Widnes)
1989-90
Oldham 30 Platt (1g) (Martyn, 1t); Irving (1t), Hyde (2g), Henderson (1t), Lord (1t); Clark, Ford (1t); Casey (Newton), Ruane (1t), Fieldhouse, Round, McAlister, Russell
Hull K.R. 29 Lightfoot; Clark (1t), M. Fletcher (4g), Austin, Sullivan; Parker (2t, 1dg), Bishop (Irvine); Niebling, Rudd, Ema, D. Harrison (1t) (Armstrong), Thompson, Lyman (1t)
Referee: R. Whitfield (Widnes)

SECOND DIVISION PREMIERSHIP ROLL OF HONOUR

Year	Winners		Runners-up		Venue
1987	Swinton	27	Hunslet	10	Old Trafford, Manchester
1988	Oldham	28	Featherstone R.	26	Old Trafford, Manchester
1989	Sheffield E	43	Swinton	18	Old Trafford, Manchester
1990	Oldham	30	Hull K.R.	29	Old Trafford, Manchester
1991	Salford	27	Halifax	20	Old Trafford, Manchester

THE TOM BERGIN TROPHY

The trophy, in honour of the President of the Rugby League Writers' Association and former Editor of the *Salford City Reporter*, is presented to the Man of the Match in the end of season Second Division Premiership final. The award is donated and judged by the Association and sponsored by Stones Bitter.

Year	Winner	Team	Position
1987	Gary Ainsworth	Swinton (v. Hunslet)	Hooker
1988	Des Foy	Oldham (v. Featherstone R.)	Centre
1989	Mark Aston	Sheffield E. (v. Swinton)	Stand off
1990	Mike Ford	Oldham (v. Hull K.R.)	Scrum half
1991	Steve Kerry	Salford (v. Halifax)	Scrum half

LANCASHIRE CUP

1990 Final

Second Division giant-killers Salford came within 12 minutes of toppling cup kings Widnes in the Greenalls Lancashire Cup final at Wigan. Having disposed of First Division outfits Rochdale Hornets, Oldham and St. Helens on the way to their second county final in three years, the Red Devils held an 18-12 lead inside the last quarter of an hour.

Late tries from substitute forward David Smith and Great Britain winger Martin Offiah sunk the Second Division club's hopes of adding cup glory to their current unbeaten run in the league.

But Salford, who had won only four and drawn one of their previous season's relegation campaign, had graduated with honours from a testing examination and deserved at least a replay in midweek.

Salford arrived at Central Park bidding to become only the second Division Two side to lift the Lancashire Cup and faced a Widnes outfit packed with nine Test players. But it was only in the final stages that they were overwhelmed.

The Red Devils refused to be overawed either by the occasion or by the star-studded opposition. It was the Salford ranks which produced the outstanding individual performances, Widnes providing just 10 minutes of top-class fare, enough to clinch the trophy and a prize cheque for £6,000.

Salford stand off David Fell was voted Man of the Match, skipper Ian Blease worked non-stop in the second row and new Kiwi capture Shane Hansen made a tremendous impact after coming on as a 31st minute substitute for Chris Whiteley.

Great Britain tourist Jonathan Davies opened the scoring after 10 minutes with a penalty goal when Blease was caught offside.

But a blunder by fellow Test man Alan Tait gifted Salford centre Peter Williams — the Red Devils' sole Great Britain representative — with a shock touchdown four minutes later. When Andy Burgess kicked for the corner, the ball eluded winger Darren Wright, and full back Tait came racing over to cover. Needing only to prod the ball into touch, the ex-Scotland RU star missed completely and Williams picked up to score.

Two tries in four minutes were a double hammer-blow to Salford. First, Fell's over-ambitious pass went straight to Widnes centre Andy Currier, who had a clear run from halfway to the corner, Davies missing the kick. Then, with Salford's Arthur Bradshaw in the sin bin, Widnes took advantage of the extra man, Currier slipping the ball out of the tackle to skipper Tony Myler who strolled in by the posts, Davies adding the goal to open up a 12-4 lead.

Even the most partisan Salford fan in the 7,485 crowd must have feared a landslide, but scrum half Steve Kerry pulled back two points when Kurt Sorensen was penalised for a foul on opposite number Ian Sherratt.

Hansen's introduction added a new dimension to the Red Devils' attack and his powerful drive set up the position for Blease to crash over for a try, Kerry's goal levelling the scores at 12-12 at the break.

Never-say-die Salford regained the lead in the 52nd minute with a 70-yard try which deserved to be the match-winner. Centre Williams collected his own chip kick and sent winger Adrian Hadley away with Fell backing up superbly for a brilliant try to which Kerry added the goal.

But Kerry's third goal-miss minutes later, which would have opened an eight-point gap, proved to be costly. Kiwi Test forward Sorensen fed Smith to cross near the posts, before a try six minutes from time from Offiah finally broke Salford's hearts, Davies adding both goals.

GREENALLS LANCASHIRE CUP FINAL

29 September   Wigan

WIDNES 24		SALFORD 18
Alan Tait	1.	Steve Gibson
Darren Wright	2.	Tex Evans
Andy Currier	3.	Martin Birkett
Jonathan Davies	4.	Peter Williams
Martin Offiah	5.	Adrian Hadley
Tony Myler, Capt.	6.	David Fell
David Hulme	7.	Steve Kerry
Kurt Sorensen	8.	Ian Sherratt
Phil McKenzie	9.	Mark Lee
Chris Ashurst	10.	Chris Whiteley
Richard Eyres	11.	Arthur Bradshaw
Emosi Koloto	12.	Ian Blease, Capt.
Les Holliday	13.	Andy Burgess
John Devereux	14.	Frank Cassidy
David Smith	15.	Shane Hansen

T: Currier, Myler, Smith, Offiah
G: Davies (4)
Substitutions:
Smith for Ashurst (31 min.)
Half-time: 12-12
Referee: Alan Burke (Oldham)

T: Williams, Blease, Fell
G: Kerry (3)
Substitutions:
Hansen for Whiteley (31 min.)
Cassidy for Kerry (72 min.)
Attendance: 7,485

1990 Round by Round

In the preliminary round, newly-promoted Rochdale Hornets entertained freshly relegated Salford, the visitors running in seven top-class tries in a convincing 41-12 victory.

In a high-scoring first round, holders Warrington disposed of Second Division Chorley 36-8 after leading 10-0 at the break, prop forward Neil Harmon scoring two tries and David Lyon tallying 16 points, visiting player-coach Bob Eccles grabbing a try on his return to Wilderspool. Widnes travelled to Whitehaven to inflict a 70-6 hammering, Welshman Jonathan Davies amassing a club record-equalling 34 points with four tries and nine goals, Martin Offiah contributing a hat-trick of tries. Wigan also hit the 70-mark at home to Barrow, who scored eight points in reply. Central Park stand off Shaun Edwards marked his first full match since receiving facial injuries at Wembley the

previous May by grabbing four tries. St. Helens shared an 80-point bonanza with visitors Trafford Borough, Saints running out 56-24 victors after Borough had trailed by only 10 points at the interval. St. Helens touched down 10 times, only Mark Bailey more than once, Paul Loughlin adding eight goals.

In an all-Second Division encounter, Fulham beat Runcorn Highfield 50-0 at the Crystal Palace Sports Centre, Fulham racing in for seven tries, Greg Pearce contributing club records of 11 goals and 22 points. In a Cumbrian derby, home club Carlisle built a 34-6 half-time lead before Workington Town rallied to take the second half honours, the final score being 38-18. Kevin Pape scored two of Carlisle's six tries, while Town's Wayne Kitchin notched a brace of touchdowns and three goals. Having led by only 10-6 at the break, Leigh pulled clear for a five-try 26-6 victory over Swinton at Hilton Park, Swinton's points coming from ex-Leigh captures — a Tim Street try and a Chris Johnson goal. Salford beat newly-promoted Oldham 27-24 in a Willows thriller. Having trailed 20-8, Oldham, beaten finalists a year earlier, took the lead for the first time after 63 minutes, Salford's Andy Burgess snatching the vital winning try.

Second Division giant-killers Salford took their third First Division scalp in the shock result of the second round, a 21-7 victory over St. Helens at the Willows. Ex-Saints hooker Mark Lee inspired the Red Devils with a drop goal to break a 6-6 deadlock, Salford scoring four tries to one. At Naughton Park, Great Britain tourist Davies saved Widnes with only four minutes left. Man of the Match Andy Gregory had put visitors Wigan ahead with a glorious solo try, converted by Joe Lydon, when Davies plunged over for an equalising try, adding the goal for a 24-22 victory. Warrington continued their defence of the trophy by beating Carlisle at Gillford Park by 28-7, the Second Division outfit proving tough opposition until the dismissal of Kiwi Test scrum half Clayton Friend after 34 minutes. The score was 4-4 at the interval, after which the Wire ran in four tries, two to half back Martin Crompton. Leigh reached their first Lancashire Cup semi-final for six years with a 40-8 rout of Fulham at Hilton Park, two tries from veteran John Woods edging him within 11 points of the club career record of 2,194 set by Jim Ledgard.

In the semi-finals, Widnes met Warrington at Naughton Park to record a 20-4 victory to reach the final for the first time in seven years. Man of the Match Emosi Koloto created two of the Chemics' three tries after the visitors had led 4-2 at half-time. In an all-Second Division tie, Salford beat Leigh 16-7 at the Willows as Leigh bid for their third Lancashire Cup final under coach Alex Murphy. Salford's Ian Sherratt destroyed their hopes by twice creating tries for ex-Orrell RU back David Fell, the second after Leigh had pulled back to 10-7 with a Mike Round try.

Widnes skipper Tony Myler holds aloft the Greenalls Lancashire Cup, the Chemics' first county trophy triumph for 11 years.

171

1990 RESULTS

Preliminary Round

Rochdale H.	12	Salford	41

First Round

Carlisle	38	Workington T.	18
Fulham	50	Runcorn H.	0
Leigh	26	Swinton	6
St. Helens	56	Trafford B.	24
Salford	27	Oldham	24
Warrington	36	Chorley	8
Whitehaven	6	Widnes	70
Wigan	70	Barrow	8

Second Round

Carlisle	7	Warrington	28
Leigh	40	Fulham	8
Salford	21	St. Helens	7
Widnes	24	Wigan	22

Semi-Finals

Salford	16	Leigh	7
Widnes	20	Warrington	4

Final

Widnes	24	Salford	18
(at Wigan)			

LANCASHIRE CUP ROLL OF HONOUR

Season	Winners		Runners-up		Venue	Attendance	Receipts
1905-06	Wigan	0	Leigh	0	Broughton	16,000	£400
(replay)	Wigan	8	Leigh	0	Broughton	10,000	£200
1906-07	Broughton R.	15	Warrington	6	Wigan	14,048	£392
1907-08	Oldham	16	Broughton R.	9	Rochdale	14,000	£340
1908-09	Wigan	10	Oldham	9	Broughton	20,000	£600
1909-10	Wigan	22	Leigh	5	Broughton	14,000	£296
1910-11	Oldham	4	Swinton	3	Broughton	14,000	£418
1911-12	Rochdale H.	12	Oldham	5	Broughton	20,000	£630
1912-13	Wigan	21	Rochdale H.	5	Salford	6,000	£200
1913-14	Oldham	5	Wigan	0	Broughton	18,000	£610
1914-15	Rochdale H.	3	Wigan	2	Salford	4,000	£475
1915-16 to 1917-18 *Competition suspended*							
1918-19	Rochdale H.	22	Oldham	0	Salford	18,617	£1,365
1919-20	Oldham	7	Rochdale H.	0	Salford	19,000	£1,615
1920-21	Broughton R.	6	Leigh	3	Salford	25,000	£1,800
1921-22	Warrington	7	Oldham	5	Broughton	18,000	£1,200
1922-23	Wigan	20	Leigh	2	Salford	15,000	£1,200
1923-24	St. Helens Recs.	17	Swinton	0	Wigan	25,656	£1,450
1924-25	Oldham	10	St. Helens Recs.	0	Salford	15,000	£1,116
1925-26	Swinton	15	Wigan	11	Broughton	17,000	£1,115
1926-27	St. Helens	10	St. Helens Recs.	2	Warrington	19,439	£1,192
1927-28	Swinton	5	Wigan	2	Oldham	22,000	£1,275
1928-29	Wigan	5	Widnes	4	Warrington	19,000	£1,150
1929-30	Warrington	15	Salford	2	Wigan	21,012	£1,250
1930-31	St. Helens Recs.	18	Wigan	3	Swinton	16,710	£1,030
1931-32	Salford	10	Swinton	8	Broughton	26,471	£1,654
1932-33	Warrington	10	St. Helens	9	Wigan	28,500	£1,675
1933-34	Oldham	12	St. Helens Recs.	0	Swinton	9,085	£516
1934-35	Salford	21	Wigan	12	Swinton	33,544	£2,191
1935-36	Salford	15	Wigan	7	Warrington	16,500	£950
1936-37	Salford	5	Wigan	2	Warrington	17,500	£1,160
1937-38	Warrington	8	Barrow	4	Wigan	14,000	£800

Season	Winners		Runners-up		Venue	Attendance	Receipts
1938-39	Wigan	10	Salford	7	Swinton	27,940	£1,708
1939-40*	Swinton	5	Widnes	4	Widnes	5,500	£269
	Swinton	16	Widnes	11	Swinton	9,000	£446
	Swinton won on aggregate 21-15						
1940-41 to 1944-45 *Competition suspended during war-time*							
1945-46	Widnes	7	Wigan	3	Warrington	28,184	£2,600
1946-47	Wigan	9	Belle Vue R.	3	Swinton	21,618	£2,658
1947-48	Wigan	10	Belle Vue R.	7	Warrington	23,110	£3,043
1948-49	Wigan	14	Warrington	8	Swinton	39,015	£5,518
1949-50	Wigan	20	Leigh	7	Warrington	35,000	£4,751
1950-51	Wigan	28	Warrington	5	Swinton	42,541	£6,222
1951-52	Wigan	14	Leigh	6	Swinton	33,230	£5,432
1952-53	Leigh	22	St. Helens	5	Swinton	34,785	£5,793
1953-54	St. Helens	16	Wigan	8	Swinton	42,793	£6,918
1954-55	Barrow	12	Oldham	2	Swinton	25,204	£4,603
1955-56	Leigh	26	Widnes	9	Wigan	26,507	£4,090
1956-57	Oldham	10	St. Helens	3	Wigan	39,544	£6,274
1957-58	Oldham	13	Wigan	8	Swinton	42,497	£6,918
1958-59	Oldham	12	St. Helens	2	Swinton	38,780	£6,933
1959-60	Warrington	5	St. Helens	4	Wigan	39,237	£6,424
1960-61	St. Helens	15	Swinton	9	Wigan	31,755	£5,337
1961-62	St. Helens	25	Swinton	9	Wigan	30,000	£4,850
1962-63	St. Helens	7	Swinton	4	Wigan	23,523	£4,122
1963-64	St. Helens	15	Leigh	4	Swinton	21,231	£3,857
1964-65	St. Helens	12	Swinton	4	Wigan	17,383	£3,393
1965-66	Warrington	16	Rochdale H.	5	St. Helens	21,360	£3,800
1966-67	Wigan	16	Oldham	13	Swinton	14,193	£3,558
1967-68	St. Helens	2	Warrington	2	Wigan	16,897	£3,886
(replay)	St. Helens	13	Warrington	10	Swinton	7,577	£2,485
1968-69	St. Helens	30	Oldham	2	Wigan	17,008	£4,644
1969-70	Swinton	11	Leigh	2	Wigan	13,532	£3,651
1970-71	Leigh	7	St. Helens	4	Swinton	10,776	£3,136
1971-72	Wigan	15	Widnes	8	St. Helens	6,970	£2,204
1972-73	Salford	25	Swinton	11	Warrington	6,865	£3,321
1973-74	Wigan	19	Salford	9	Warrington	8,012	£2,750
1974-75	Widnes	6	Salford	2	Wigan	7,403	£2,833
1975-76	Widnes	16	Salford	7	Wigan	7,566	£3,880
1976-77	Widnes	16	Workington T.	11	Wigan	8,498	£6,414
1977-78	Workington T.	16	Wigan	13	Warrington	9,548	£5,038
1978-79	Widnes	15	Workington T.	13	Wigan	10,020	£6,261
1979-80	Widnes	11	Workington T.	0	Salford	6,887	£7,100
1980-81	Warrington	26	Wigan	10	St. Helens	6,442	£8,629
1981-82	Leigh	8	Widnes	3	Wigan	9,011	£14,029
1982-83	Warrington	16	St. Helens	0	Wigan	6,462	£11,732
1983-84	Barrow	12	Widnes	8	Wigan	7,007	£13,160
1984-85	St. Helens	26	Wigan	18	Wigan	26,074	£62,139
1985-86	Wigan	34	Warrington	8	St. Helens	19,202	£56,030
1986-87	Wigan	27	Oldham	6	St. Helens	20,180	£60,329
1987-88	Wigan	28	Warrington	16	St. Helens	20,237	£67,339
1988-89	Wigan	22	Salford	17	St. Helens	19,154	£71,879
1989-90	Warrington	24	Oldham	16	St. Helens	9,990	£41,804
1990-91	Widnes	24	Salford	18	Wigan	7,485	£36,867

*Emergency War-time competition

LANCASHIRE CUP FINAL .... A REVIEW

1968-69
St. Helens 30 Rhodes; F. Wilson (2t), Benyon, Myler, Williams (1t); Whittle, Bishop (1t); Warlow, Sayer, Watson, Rees (1t), E. Chisnall (1t) Coslett (6g)
Oldham 2 Murphy; Elliott, Larder, McCormack, Whitehead; Briggs (1g), Canning; K. Wilson, Taylor, Fletcher (Maders), Irving, McCourt, Hughes
Referee: W.H. Thompson (Huddersfield)

1969-70
Swinton 11 Gowers; Gomersall, Fleet, Buckley, M. Philbin (1t); Davies, Kenny (4g); Bate, D. Clarke, Mackay, Holliday, Smith, Robinson
Leigh 2 Grainey; Tickle, Warburton, Collins, Stringer (Brown); Eckersley, Murphy (1g); D. Chisnall, Ashcroft, Watts, Welding, Lyon, Fiddler
Referee: E. Clay (Leeds)

1970-71
Leigh 7 Ferguson (2g); Tickle (Canning), L. Chisnall, Collins, Walsh; Eckersley (1t), Murphy; D. Chisnall, Ashcroft, Watts, Grimes, Clarkson, Mooney
St. Helens 4 F. Barrow; L. Jones, Benyon, Walsh, Wilson; Myler, Whittle; Halsall, A. Karalius, Rees (Prescott), Mantle, E. Chisnall, Coslett (2g)
Referee: W.H. Thompson (Huddersfield)

1971-72
Wigan 15 Tyrer (3g); Eastham (1t), Francis (1t), Fuller, Wright (Gandy); D. Hill, Ayres (1t); Ashcroft, Clarke, Fletcher, Ashurst, Kevin O'Loughlin, Laughton
Widnes 8 Dutton; Brown, McLoughlin, Aspey (1g), Gaydon (1t); D. O'Neill (1t), Bowden; Warlow, Foran, Doughty, Kirwan, Walsh (Lowe), Nicholls
Referee: W.H. Thompson (Huddersfield)

1972-73
Salford 25 Charlton (1t); Eastham (1t), Watkins (1t, 5g), Hesketh, Richards (1t); Gill, Banner (1t); Mackay, Walker, Ward, Whitehead, Dixon, Prescott
Swinton 11 Jackson; Fleay (1t), Cooke, Buckley, Gomersall; Kenny (1g) (M. Philbin), Gowers (3g); Halsall, Evans, Bate, R. Smith (Holliday), Hoyle, W. Pattinson
Referee: W.H. Thompson (Huddersfield)

1973-74
Wigan 19 Francis; Vigo, D. Hill, Keiron O'Loughlin (2t), Wright (1t); Cassidy, Ayres (1g); Smethurst, Clarke, Gray (4g), Irving, D. Robinson, Cunningham

Salford 9 Charlton; Fielding, Watkins (1t, 3g), Hesketh, Holland; Gill, Banner; Mackay, Walker, Davies (Grice), Dixon, Kear (Knighton), E. Prescott
Referee: W.H. Thompson (Huddersfield)

1974-75
Widnes 6 Dutton (1g); George (1t), D. O'Neill, Aspey, A. Prescott; Hughes (1dg), Bowden; Mills, Elwell, J. Stephens, Adams, Blackwood, Laughton
Salford 2 Charlton; Fielding (1g), Dixon, Graham, Richards; Taylor, Banner; Mackay, Devlin, Grice, Knighton, Coulman, E. Prescott
Referee: G.F. Lindop (Wakefield)

1975-76
Widnes 16 Dutton (3g, 1dg); A. Prescott (1t), George (1t), Aspey (1t), Jenkins; Hughes, Bowden; Mills, Elwell, Nelson, Foran, Fitzpatrick (Sheridan), Adams
Salford 7 Watkins (2g); Fielding, Butler, Hesketh, Richards (1t); Gill, Nash; Fiddler, Hawksley, Dixon (Mackay), Turnbull, Knighton, E. Prescott
Referee: W.H. Thompson (Huddersfield)

1976-77
Widnes 16 Dutton (4g, 1dg); Wright (1t), Aspey, George (1t), A. Prescott; Eckersley, Bowden (1dg); Ramsey, Elwell, Nelson, Dearden, Adams, Laughton
Workington T. 11 Charlton; Collister, Wilkins (1t), Wright, MacCorquodale (4g); Lauder, Walker; Mills, Banks, Calvin, Bowman, L. Gorley, W. Pattinson (P. Gorley)
Referee: W.H. Thompson (Huddersfield)

1977-78
Workington T. 16 Charlton (Atkinson); Collister, Risman, Wright (1t), MacCorquodale (4g); Wilkins (1t), Walker (2dg); Watts, Banks, Bowman, L. Gorley, W. Pattinson, P. Gorley
Wigan 13 Swann; Vigo, Davies (Burke 1g), Willicombe (1t), Hornby; Taylor, Nulty (1t, 1g); Hogan, Aspinall, Irving, Ashurst (1t), Blackwood, Melling (Regan)
Referee: W.H. Thompson (Huddersfield)

1978-79
Widnes 15 Eckersley; Wright (1t), Aspey, George, Burke (3g); Hughes, Bowden; Mills, Elwell, Shaw, Adams, Dearden (Hull), Laughton (2t)
Workington T. 13 Charlton; Collister, Risman, Wilkins (1t), MacCorquodale (1t, 2g), McMillan, Walker; Beverley, Banks, Bowman, Blackwood, P. Gorley, W. Pattinson (L. Gorley 1t)
Referee: W.H. Thompson (Huddersfield)

1979-80
Widnes 11 Eckersley; Wright, Aspey, Hughes (George), Burke (2g); Moran (1t), Bowden; Hogan, Elwell (1dg), Shaw, L. Gorley, Dearden, Adams (1t)
Workington T. 0 Charlton; MacCorquodale, Maughan, Thompson, Beck; Rudd, Walker (Roper); Beverley, Banks, Wallbanks (Varty), W. Pattinson, Lewis, Dobie
Referee: W.H. Thompson (Huddersfield)
1980-81
Warrington 26 Finnegan; Thackray (1t), I. Duane, Bevan (1t), Hesford (7g, 1t); K. Kelly, A. Gwilliam; Courtney, Waller, Case, Martyn (1t), Eccles (Potter), Hunter
Wigan 10 Fairbairn (1t, 2g); Ramsdale (1t), Willicombe, Davies, Hornby; M. Foy, Bolton (Coyle); Breheny, Pendlebury (M. Smith), S. O'Neill, Melling, Clough, Hollingsworth
Referee: D. G. Kershaw (York)
1981-82
Leigh 8 Hogan; Drummond, Bilsbury (1t), Donlan (1dg), Worgan; Woods (2g), Green; Wilkinson, Tabern, Cooke, Martyn (Platt), Clarkson, McTigue
Widnes 3 Burke; George, Hughes, Cunningham, Bentley (1t); Moran, Gregory; M. O'Neill, Elwell, Lockwood, L. Gorley, E. Prescott, Adams
Referee: W.H. Thompson (Huddersfield)
1982-83
Warrington 16 Hesford (2g); Fellows (1t), R. Duane, Bevan, M. Kelly (1t); Cullen, K. Kelly (1t); Courtney, Webb, Cooke (D. Chisnall), Eccles (1t), Fieldhouse, Gregory
St. Helens 0 Parkes (Smith); Ledger, Arkwright, Haggerty, Litherland; Peters, Holding; James, Liptrot, Bottell (Mathias), Moorby, P. Gorley, Pinner
Referee: J. Holdsworth (Leeds)
1983-84
Barrow 12 Tickle (1dg); Moore, Whittle, Ball (3g, 1dg), Milby; McConnell (1t), Cairns; Hodkinson, Wall, McJennett, Herbert, Szymala, Mossop
Widnes 8 Burke; Lydon (1t, 2g), Hughes, Keiron O'Loughlin, Basnett; A. Myler, Gregory; S. O'Neill, Elwell, K. Tamati, Whitfield, E. Prescott, Adams
Referee: K. Allatt (Southport)
1984-85
St. Helens 26 Veivers (Haggerty 1t); Ledger, Allen, Meninga (2t), Day (1t, 5g); Arkwright, Holding; Burke, Liptrot, P. Gorley, Platt, Round, Pinner

Wigan 18 Edwards; Ferguson, Stephenson, Whitfield (3g), Gill (1t) (Pendlebury); Cannon, Fairhurst; Courtney, Kiss (1t), Case, West (1t), Wane, Potter
Referee: R. Campbell (Widnes)
1985-86
Wigan 34 Edwards (1t); Henley-Smith (Hampson), Stephenson (7g), Hanley (1t), Whitfield; Ella (2t), M. Ford; Dowling, Kiss (1t), Wane (Case), Du Toit, Goodway, Potter
Warrington 8 Johnson (1t); Carbert (2g), Cullen, Blake (Forster), Thackray; Kelly, A. Gregory; Eccles, Webb, Jackson, Boyd (Tamati), M. Gregory, Rathbone
Referee: J. Holdsworth (Kippax)
1986-87
Wigan 27 Edwards (2t); Lydon (1t, 1dg), Stephenson, Bell, Gill (5g); Hanley, M. Ford (1t); West, Dermott, Case, Roberts (Louw), Potter, Goodway
Oldham 6 M'Barki; Sherman, Bridge (1t), Warnecke, Taylor; Topliss, Kirwan; Clark, Flanagan, Hobbs (1g), Nadiole, Worrall, Raper (Hawkyard)
Referee: J.E. Smith (Halifax)
1987-88
Wigan 28 Hampson; Russell, Stephenson (1g) (Bell), Lydon (5g), Gill (1t); Edwards, A. Gregory; Case, Kiss, Wane (West, 1t), Goodway, Potter, Hanley (2t)
Warrington 16 Johnson; Drummond, Forster (2t), Peters, Carbert; Woods (2g), Holden; K. Tamati, Webb (Harmon), Humphries, Sanderson, Roberts, M. Gregory (1t)
Referee: G.F. Lindop (Wakefield)
1988-89
Wigan 22 Hampson; T. Iro, K. Iro (2t, 3g), Bell (1t), Lydon (Byrne); Edwards, Gregory; Lucas (Betts), Dermott, Shelford (1t), Platt, Goodway, Hanley
Salford 17 Williams (Blease); Evans (1t). Bentley (1t), Jones, Hadley; Shaw, Cairns; Herbert (1t), Moran, Brown (2g), Gormley, M. Worrall (1dg), Horo (McTigue)
Referee: K. Allatt (Southport)
1989-90
Warrington 24 Lyon (Darbyshire); Drummond, J. Ropati (1t), Thorniley, Forster (1t); Turner (4g), Mackey; Burke, Roskell, Molloy, Jackson (2t), Sanderson (Duane), M. Gregory
Oldham 16 Platt (1g) (Russell); Robinson (1t), Hyde (1g), Irving (1t), Lord (1t); Clark, M. Ford; Casey (J. Fairbank), A. Ruane, Fieldhouse, Allen, Newton, Cogger
Referee: R. Tennant (Castleford)

MAN OF THE MATCH AWARDS

An award for the adjudged man of the match in the Lancashire Cup final was first presented in 1974-75. For four years the award was sponsored by the *Rugby Leaguer* newspaper. From 1978-85 the trophy was presented by Burtonwood Brewery, then from 1986 by Greenall Whitley, as part of their sponsorship of the Lancashire Cup. Under the auspices of the *Rugby Leaguer*, the choice was made by the Editor, while the breweries invited a panel of the Press to make the decision.

Season	Winner	Team	Position
1974-75	Mike Coulman	Salford (v. Widnes)	Second row
1975-76	Mick George	Widnes (v. Salford)	Centre
1976-77	David Eckersley	Widnes (v. Workington T.)	Stand off
1977-78	Arnold Walker	Workington T. (v. Wigan)	Scrum half
1978-79	Arnold Walker	Workington T. (v. Widnes)	Scrum half
1979-80	Mick Adams	Widnes (v. Workington T.)	Loose forward
1980-81	Tony Waller	Warrington (v. Wigan)	Hooker
1981-82	Ray Tabern	Leigh (v. Widnes)	Hooker
1982-83	Steve Hesford	Warrington (v. St. Helens)	Full back
1983-84	David Cairns	Barrow (v. Widnes)	Scrum half
1984-85	Mal Meninga	St. Helens (v. Wigan)	Centre
1985-86	Steve Ella	Wigan (v. Warrington)	Stand off
1986-87	Mike Ford	Wigan (v. Oldham)	Scrum half
1987-88	Shaun Edwards	Wigan (v. Warrington)	Stand off
1988-89	Paul Shaw	Salford (v. Wigan)	Stand off
1989-90	Bob Jackson	Warrington (v. Oldham)	Second row
1990-91	David Fell	Salford (v. Widnes)	Stand off

LANCASHIRE CUP FINAL RECORDS

TEAM

Most appearances: 34 by Wigan
Most wins: 20 by Wigan
Highest score: Wigan 34 v. Warrington 8 1985
Widest margin: St. Helens 30 v. Oldham 2 1968
Biggest attendance:
42,793 St. Helens v. Wigan (at Swinton) 1953

INDIVIDUAL

Most tries:
4 by Brian Nordgren (Wigan) v. Leigh 1949
Most goals:
7 by Jim Ledgard (Leigh) v. Widnes 1955
      Steve Hesford (Warrington) v. Wigan 1980
      David Stephenson (Wigan) v. Warrington .. 1985
Most points:
17 (7g, 1t) by Steve Hesford (Warrington) v. Wigan
         1980

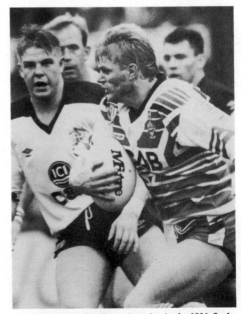

Salford winger Tex Evans in action in the 1991 final at Wigan.

YORKSHIRE CUP

1990 Final

Castleford's Test winger David Plange marked his first match of the season with a disputed match-winning touchdown and a vital try-saving tackle in the John Smiths Yorkshire Cup final victory over neighbours Wakefield Trinity at Elland Road, Leeds.

The defensive act came first to prevent underdogs Trinity extending their lead to a probable 10 points in the 43rd minute. The Dreadnoughts were ahead 8-4 when county centre Andy Mason looked to be a certain scorer as he headed for the posts, until Plange cut in to bring him down with a magnificent tackle.

Lee Crooks, bidding to impress the Great Britain management, reduced the lead with a penalty goal a few minutes later and was in the build-up that led to Plange's crucial 63rd minute try.

After Neil Battye and St. John Ellis had run strongly down the right, Castleford switched the ball swiftly to the left, Great Britain Under-21 hooker Graham Southernwood producing the final pass for Plange to charge for the corner. Disconsolate Trinity defenders claimed the winger had made a double movement, although coach David Topliss later agreed with referee Jim Smith's decision.

A last-second drop goal by Neil Roebuck capped Castleford's victory and the Glassblowers greeted the hooter with as much relief as jubilation.

Consolation for battling Trinity was the White Rose Trophy for the Man of the Match which was awarded to Tracy Lazenby, the former Hull K.R. and Hull utility man setting up Mason for his side's only try and putting him through for a near miss.

Lazenby's try-making break after only five minutes was a brilliant piece of stand-off play, as he carved a wide arc from a scrum near halfway before linking with Mason, who had

the extra pace to go clear to the line. A touchline goal by full back Kevin Harcombe sent Trinity's hopes soaring in their first county cup final for 16 years.

Castleford, making their seventh county final appearance in 10 seasons, were facing the distinct prospect of continuing their losing run at Elland Road, having been defeated in their previous three Yorkshire Cup finals and a 1983 Challenge Cup semi-final. Newly-signed scrum half Gary Atkins, recruited from Ryedale-York, dummied his way over for a Castleford try four minutes later, but the favourites were already looking unsettled.

Coach Topliss had predicted an upset if free-flowing Castleford could be held for the opening quarter. His charges did better than that as Harcombe added a penalty goal while the rearguard held watertight to take an 8-4 lead at the interval.

The Belle Vue outfit continued to thwart Castleford's much-vaunted attack, but were unable to offer much in reply, apart from some neat touches from Lazenby, who moved into the second row after Australian Chris Perry replaced Andy Kelly in the 55th minute.

New Zealand Test prop Adrian Shelford produced a succession of hefty charges as Wakefield took the midfield route, while his opposite number Crooks adopted a more subtle approach with several cleverly concealed passes out of the tackle. Castleford's Dean Sampson gained in power during the last half-hour, when substitute Keith England also made an immediate impact, though the usually all-action Australian second row man Jeff Hardy had one of his quietest matches.

A 13-6 penalty count in Wakefield's favour added to Castleford's frustration and though they edged the scrums 8-6 — Trinity hooker Billy Conway retiring after 38 minutes with a suspected fractured cheekbone — Great Britain tourist Graham Steadman was more of a threat than a danger at stand off.

JOHN SMITHS YORKSHIRE CUP FINAL

23 September   **Elland Road, Leeds**

CASTLEFORD 11		WAKEFIELD TRINITY 8
Steve Larder	1.	Kevin Harcombe
St. John Ellis	2.	David Jones
Shaun Irwin	3.	Andy Mason
Grant Anderson	4.	Phil Eden
David Plange	5.	Andy Wilson
Graham Steadman	6.	Tracy Lazenby
Gary Atkins	7.	Mark Conway
Lee Crooks, Capt.	8.	Adrian Shelford
Graham Southernwood	9.	Billy Conway
Dean Sampson	10.	John Thompson
Neil Battye	11.	Andy Kelly, Capt.
Jeff Hardy	12.	Gary Price
Neil Roebuck	13.	Nigel Bell
Keith England	14.	Chris Perry
Martin Ketteridge	15.	Richard Slater

T: Atkins, Plange
G: Crooks, Roebuck (dg)
Substitutions:
England for Atkins (49 min.)
Ketteridge for Battye (77 min.)
Half-time: 4-8
Attendance: 12,420

T: Mason
G: Harcombe (2)
Substitutions:
Slater for B. Conway (38 min.)
Perry for Kelly (55 min.)
Referee: Jim Smith (Halifax)

1990 Round by Round

In the two-tie preliminary round, newly-promoted Hull K.R. visited Nottingham City in a tie at Doncaster and ran up 100 points with only six in reply. The century was a Rovers club record score, including 18 tries, six to Greg Austin and five to Anthony Sullivan. Colin Armstrong hit a club record 14 goals. Holders Bradford Northern did not take the lead against visitors Sheffield Eagles until the 47th minute, when the Eagles were still smarting from a disallowed try just before half-time which would have put them 14-2 in front. Instead, Sonny Nickle was sin-binned.

The first round was highlighted by the first-class debut for Leeds of former New Zealand RU All Black John Gallagher, but visitors Bradford Northern spoiled the celebrations by winning 24-16 after trailing 16-8. Northern scored 16 points in the last 17 minutes, boosted by the performances of ex-Leeds players Paul Medley and Mark Wilson. Former Hull prop Lee Crooks returned to the Boulevard to star in Castleford's 10-6 victory and help his own bid to regain a Great Britain role. Crooks created the opening try for Giles Boothroyd, St. John Ellis adding a second before Crooks hit a 40-yard penalty goal. Australian centre Brad Webb came on to score a debutant try for Hull, Paul Eastwood's goal setting up a thrilling finish. Trailing 16-6 at half time, Keighley came back at Dewsbury to trail only 16-14 before tries in the last six minutes for Paul Durnin and Andy Dickinson made it safe for the Crown Flatt side at 26-14. After being fortunate to go in at the break level at six-apiece, home side Batley staged a second-half transformation to dispose of Huddersfield 17-10, a Simon Wilson drop goal securing victory.

Debt-ridden Halifax put their off-field

problems behind them by inflicting Doncaster's heaviest home defeat for six years, their seven-try 40-4 victory being highlighted by a Colin Atkinson hat-trick. In the first-ever live broadcast by British Aerospace, Ryedale-York went down 10-0 to Hull K.R., with tries by Sullivan and centre Graeme Hallas, who added a goal. Having taken time to settle against Second Division visitors Bramley, Featherstone Rovers strolled through by 36-4, debutants Leo Casey and Ikram Butt showing up well in a home side inspired by half back Tim Sharp and skipper Deryck Fox. A try from livewire half back Tim Lumb put Second Division Hunslet ahead of hosts Wakefield Trinity 18-14 three minutes after the interval but Trinity rallied with three touchdowns to secure a 28-18 success.

In the second round, Bradford Northern were forced to switch their home tie with Castleford from Odsal to Bradford City's Valley Parade soccer ground because of a speedway meeting. Castleford looked more at home as they ran in six superb tries in a 42-12 victory, building a 16-2 lead inside just 15 minutes and being well in command before Northern hooker Brian Noble was sent off in the 63rd minute. Featherstone Rovers, beaten finalists 12 months earlier, were disposed of 31-22 by visitors Hull K.R. in a Post Office Road thriller. The Robins staged a tremendous comeback after trailing by 15 points early in the second half, three tries taking them into the lead for the first time before a Terry Manning try put the Colliers back in front 22-19, the Humbersiders snatching two more touchdowns to secure victory. Wakefield Trinity reached the semi-finals for the first time in seven years with a hard-fought 26-17 success at home to Halifax, who opened the scoring with a John Lyons drop goal and an Alan Platt penalty goal. Man of the Match Mark Conway scored a try, converted by Kevin Harcombe, for a lead which they never

surrendered. In a Heavy Woollen derby, Dewsbury disposed of Batley 18-8 at Crown Flatt to reach the semi-finals for the first time in 11 years. Man of the Match Paul Shuttleworth regained his own chip kick to put Dewsbury 16-2 ahead early in the second half, Batley gaining a consolation try from Mark Fortis.

In the semi-finals, Castleford reached their seventh final in 10 years, with two decisive tries in a five-minute spell setting them up for an emphatic 29-6 home success over Hull K.R., running in five tries to one. Wakefield Trinity recovered from a shaky start to qualify for their first Yorkshire Cup final for 16 years, Dewsbury opening the scoring after only a minute with a Nathan Graham penalty goal before Trinity found their rhythm to run in four tries without reply in a 25-2 victory.

1990 RESULTS

Preliminary Round

Bradford N.	20	Sheffield E.	12
Nottingham City	6	Hull K.R.	100
(at Doncaster)			

First Round

Batley	17	Huddersfield	10
Dewsbury	26	Keighley	14
Doncaster	4	Halifax	40
Featherstone R.	36	Bramley	4
Hull	6	Castleford	10
Leeds	16	Bradford N.	24
Ryedale-York	0	Hull K.R.	10
Wakefield T.	28	Hunslet	18

Second Round

Bradford N.	12	Castleford	42
(at Bradford C. FC)			
Dewsbury	18	Batley	8
Featherstone R.	22	Hull K.R.	31
Wakefield T.	26	Halifax	17

Semi-Finals

Castleford	29	Hull K.R.	6
Wakefield T.	25	Dewsbury	2

Final

Castleford	11	Wakefield T.	8
(at Elland Road, Leeds)			

YORKSHIRE CUP ROLL OF HONOUR

Year	Winners		Runners-up		Venue	Attendance	Receipts
1905-06	Hunslet	13	Halifax	3	Bradford P.A.	18,500	£465
1906-07	Bradford	8	Hull K.R.	5	Wakefield	10,500	£286
1907-08	Hunslet	17	Halifax	0	Leeds	15,000	£397
1908-09	Halifax	9	Hunslet	5	Wakefield	13,000	£356
1909-10	Huddersfield	21	Batley	0	Leeds	22,000	£778
1910-11	Wakefield T.	8	Huddersfield	2	Leeds	19,000	£696
1911-12	Huddersfield	22	Hull K.R.	10	Wakefield	20,000	£700
1912-13	Batley	17	Hull	3	Leeds	16,000	£523
1913-14	Huddersfield	19	Bradford N.	3	Halifax	12,000	£430
1914-15	Huddersfield	31	Hull	0	Leeds	12,000	£422
1918-19	Huddersfield	14	Dewsbury	8	Leeds	21,500	£1,309
1919-20	Huddersfield	24	Leeds	5	Halifax	24,935	£2,096
1920-21	Hull K.R.	2	Hull	0	Leeds	20,000	£1,926
1921-22	Leeds	11	Dewsbury	3	Halifax	20,000	£1,650
1922-23	York	5	Batley	0	Leeds	33,719	£2,414
1923-24	Hull	10	Huddersfield	4	Leeds	23,300	£1,728
1924-25	Wakefield T.	9	Batley	8	Leeds	25,546	£1,912
1925-26	Dewsbury	2	Huddersfield	0	Wakefield	12,616	£718
1926-27	Huddersfield	10	Wakefield T.	3	Leeds	11,300	£853
1927-28	Dewsbury	8	Hull	2	Leeds	21,700	£1,466
1928-29	Leeds	5	Featherstone R.	0	Wakefield	13,000	£838
1929-30	Hull K.R.	13	Hunslet	7	Leeds	11,000	£687
1930-31	Leeds	10	Huddersfield	2	Halifax	17,812	£1,405
1931-32	Huddersfield	4	Hunslet	2	Leeds	27,000	£1,764
1932-33	Leeds	8	Wakefield T.	0	Huddersfield	17,685	£1,183
1933-34	York	10	Hull K.R.	4	Leeds	22,000	£1,480
1934-35	Leeds	5	Wakefield T.	5	Dewsbury	22,598	£1,529
Replay	Leeds	2	Wakefield T.	2	Huddersfield	10,300	£745
Replay	Leeds	13	Wakefield T.	0	Hunslet	19,304	£1,327
1935-36	Leeds	3	York	0	Halifax	14,616	£1,113
1936-37	York	9	Wakefield T.	2	Leeds	19,000	£1,294
1937-38	Leeds	14	Huddersfield	8	Wakefield	22,000	£1,508
1938-39	Huddersfield	18	Hull	10	Bradford	28,714	£1,534
1939-40	Featherstone R.	12	Wakefield T.	9	Bradford	7,077	£403
1940-41	Bradford N.	15	Dewsbury	5	Huddersfield	13,316	£939
1941-42	Bradford N.	24	Halifax	0	Huddersfield	5,989	£635
1942-43	Dewsbury	7	Huddersfield	0	Dewsbury	11,000	£680
	Huddersfield	2	Dewsbury	0	Huddersfield	6,252	£618
	Dewsbury won on aggregate 7-2						
1943-44	Bradford N.	5	Keighley	2	Bradford	10,251	£757
	Keighley	5	Bradford N.	5	Keighley	8,993	£694
	Bradford N. won on aggregate 10-7						
1944-45	Hunslet	3	Halifax	12	Hunslet	11,213	£744
	Halifax	2	Hunslet	0	Halifax	9,800	£745
	Halifax won on aggregate 14-3						

Year	Winners		Runners-up		Venue	Attendance	Receipts
1945-46	Bradford N.	5	Wakefield T.	2	Halifax	24,292	£1,934
1946-47	Wakefield T.	10	Hull	0	Leeds	34,300	£3,718
1947-48	Wakefield T.	7	Leeds	7	Huddersfield	24,344	£3,461
Replay	Wakefield T.	8	Leeds	7	Bradford	32,000	£3,251
1948-49	Bradford N.	18	Castleford	9	Leeds	31,393	£5,053
1949-50	Bradford N.	11	Huddersfield	4	Leeds	36,000	£6,365
1950-51	Huddersfield	16	Castleford	3	Leeds	28,906	£5,152
1951-52	Wakefield T.	17	Keighley	3	Huddersfield	25,495	£3,347
1952-53	Huddersfield	18	Batley	8	Leeds	14,705	£2,471
1953-54	Bradford N.	7	Hull	2	Leeds	22,147	£3,833
1954-55	Halifax	22	Hull	14	Leeds	25,949	£4,638
1955-56	Halifax	10	Hull	10	Leeds	23,520	£4,385
Replay	Halifax	7	Hull	0	Bradford	14,000	£2,439
1956-57	Wakefield T.	23	Hunslet	5	Leeds	30,942	£5,609
1957-58	Huddersfield	15	York	8	Leeds	22,531	£4,123
1958-59	Leeds	24	Wakefield T.	20	Bradford	26,927	£3,833
1959-60	Featherstone R.	15	Hull	14	Leeds	23,983	£4,156
1960-61	Wakefield T.	16	Huddersfield	10	Leeds	17,456	£2,937
1961-62	Wakefield T.	19	Leeds	9	Bradford	16,329	£2,864
1962-63	Hunslet	12	Hull K.R.	2	Leeds	22,742	£4,514
1963-64	Halifax	10	Featherstone R.	0	Wakefield	13,238	£2,471
1964-65	Wakefield T.	18	Leeds	2	Huddersfield	13,527	£2,707
1965-66	Bradford N.	17	Hunslet	8	Leeds	17,522	£4,359
1966-67	Hull K.R.	25	Featherstone R.	12	Leeds	13,241	£3,482
1967-68	Hull K.R.	8	Hull	7	Leeds	16,729	£5,515
1968-69	Leeds	22	Castleford	11	Wakefield	12,573	£3,746
1969-70	Hull	12	Featherstone R.	9	Leeds	11,089	£3,419
1970-71	Leeds	23	Featherstone R.	7	Bradford	6,753	£1,879
1971-72	Hull K.R.	11	Castleford	7	Wakefield	5,536	£1,589
1972-73	Leeds	36	Dewsbury	9	Bradford	7,806	£2,659
1973-74	Leeds	7	Wakefield T.	2	Leeds	7,621	£3,728
1974-75	Hull K.R.	16	Wakefield T.	13	Leeds	5,823	£3,090
1975-76	Leeds	15	Hull K.R.	11	Leeds	5,743	£3,617
1976-77	Leeds	16	Featherstone R.	12	Leeds	7,645	£5,198
1977-78	Castleford	17	Featherstone R.	7	Leeds	6,318	£4,528
1978-79	Bradford N.	18	York	8	Leeds	10,429	£9,188
1979-80	Leeds	15	Halifax	6	Leeds	9,137	£9,999
1980-81	Leeds	8	Hull K.R.	7	Huddersfield	9,751	£15,578
1981-82	Castleford	10	Bradford N.	5	Leeds	5,852	£10,359
1982-83	Hull	18	Bradford N.	7	Leeds	11,755	£21,950
1983-84	Hull	13	Castleford	2	Elland Rd, Leeds	14,049	£33,572
1984-85	Hull	29	Hull K.R.	12	Hull C. FC	25,237	£68,639
1985-86	Hull K.R.	22	Castleford	18	Leeds	12,686	£36,327
1986-87	Castleford	31	Hull	24	Leeds	11,132	£31,888
1987-88	Bradford N.	12	Castleford	12	Leeds	10,947	£40,283
Replay	Bradford N.	11	Castleford	2	Elland Rd, Leeds	8,175	£30,732
1988-89	Leeds	33	Castleford	12	Elland Rd, Leeds	22,968	£76,658
1989-90	Bradford N.	20	Featherstone R.	14	Leeds	12,607	£50,775
1990-91	Castleford	11	Wakefield T.	8	Elland Rd, Leeds	12,420	£61,432

YORKSHIRE CUP FINAL .... A REVIEW
1969-70
Hull 12 Owbridge; Sullivan (1t), Gemmell, Maloney (2g), A. Macklin; Hancock, Davidson; Harrison, McGlone, J. Macklin (1t), Kirchin, Forster, Brown (1g)
Featherstone R. 9 C. Kellett (3g); Newlove, Jordan, M. Smith, Hartley (T. Hudson); D. Kellett, Nash (1t); Tonks, Farrar, Lyons, A. Morgan, Thompson, Smales
Referee: R.L. Thomas (Oldham)
1970-71
Leeds 23 Holmes; Alan Smith (2t), Hynes (4g), Cowan, Atkinson (1t); Wainwright (Langley), Shoebottom; J. Burke, Dunn (1t), Cookson, Ramsey (1t), Haigh, Batten
Featherstone R. 7 M. Kellett (2g); M. Smith, Cotton, Newlove, Hartley (1t); Harding (Coventry), Hudson; Windmill, D. Morgan, Lyons, Rhodes, Thompson, Farrar
Referee: D.S. Brown (Preston)
1971-72
Hull K.R. 11 Markham; Stephenson, Coupland, Kirkpatrick, Longstaff (1t); Millward (4g), Daley; Wiley, Flanagan, Millington, Wallis, Palmer (Cooper), Brown
Castleford 7 Edwards; Foster (1t), S. Norton, Worsley, Lowndes; Hargrave, Stephens; Hartley, Miller, I. Van Bellen (Ackroyd 2g), A. Dickinson, Lockwood, Blakeway
Referee: A. Givvons (Oldham)
1972-73
Leeds 36 Holmes (3t); Alan Smith, Hynes (1g), Dyl (2t), Atkinson (1t); Hardisty (1t), Hepworth (Langley); Clawson (5g) (Fisher), Ward, Ramsey, Cookson, Eccles (1t), Batten
Dewsbury 9 Rushton; Ashcroft (1t), Childe, Day, Yoward; Agar (3g), A. Bates; Bell (Beverley), M. Stephenson, Lowe, Grayshon, J. Bates (Lee), Hankins
Referee: M.J. Naughton (Widnes)
1973-74
Leeds 7 Holmes; Langley (1t) (Marshall 1g), Hynes (1g), Dyl, Atkinson; Hardisty, Hepworth; Jeanes (Ramsey), Ward, Clarkson, Eccles, Cookson, Batten
Wakefield T. 2 Wraith (Sheard); D. Smith, Crook (1g), Hegarty, B. Parker; Topliss, Bonnar; Valentine, Morgan, Bratt, Knowles (Ballantyne), Endersby, Holmes
Referee: M.J. Naughton (Widnes)
1974-75
Hull K.R. 16 Smithies; Sullivan (Dunn lt), Watson (2t), Coupland, Kirkpatrick (1t); Millward, Stephenson; Millington, Heslop, Rose, Wallis, N. Fox (2g) (Madley), Brown

Wakefield T. 13 Sheard; D. Smith (1t), Crook (2g), Hegarty (1t), Archer; Topliss, Bonnar; Ballantyne, Handscombe, Bratt (1t), Skerrett, A. Tonks (Goodwin), (Holmes), Morgan
Referee: M.J. Naughton (Widnes)
1975-76
Leeds 15 Marshall; Alan Smith, Hague, Dyl (1t), Atkinson; Holmes (4g, 1dg), Hynes; Harrison, Payne, Pitchford, (Dickinson), Eccles, Batten, Cookson (1t)
Hull K.R. 11 Wallace; Dunn, A. Burwell, Watson, Sullivan (1t); Turner, Millward (1dg); Millington, Dickinson, Lyons, Rose, N. Fox (2g, 1t), Hughes (Holdstock)
Referee: J.V. Moss (Manchester)
1976-77
Leeds 16 Marshall (2g); Hague, Hynes, Dyl (2t), D. Smith; Holmes, Banner; Dickinson, Ward, Pitchford, Eccles (1t), Burton, Cookson (1t)
Featherstone R. 12 Box; Bray (1t), Coventry, Quinn (3g), K. Kellett; Newlove, Fennell; Gibbins, Bridges, Farrar, Stone, P. Smith (1t), Bell (Spells)
Referee: M.J. Naughton (Widnes)
1977-78
Castleford 17 Wraith; Richardson, Joyner, P. Johnson, Fenton; Burton (2t, 1dg), Pickerill (Stephens); Fisher (Woodall), Spurr, Weston, Huddlestone, Reilly, Lloyd (5g)
Featherstone R. 7 Marsden; Evans, Gilbert, Quinn (1g) (N. Tuffs), K. Kellett; Newlove, Butler; Townend (1g), Bridges, Farrar, Gibbins, Stone (P. Smith 1t), Bell
Referee: M.J. Naughton (Widnes)
1978-79
Bradford N. 18 Mumby; Barends, Gant (1t), D. Parker (1t), D. Redfearn; Slater (Wolford), A. Redfearn (1t); Thompson, Fisher, Forsyth (Joyce), Fox (3g), Trotter, Haigh (1t)
York 8 G. Smith (1t); T. Morgan, Day (Crossley), Foster, Nicholson; Banks (2g), Harkin; Dunkerley, Wileman, Harris, Rhodes, Hollis (1dg) (Ramshaw), Cooper
Referee: M.J. Naughton (Widnes)
1979-80
Leeds 15 Hague; Alan Smith (2t), D. Smith (1t), Dyl, Atkinson; Holmes (J. Sanderson), Dick (3g); Dickinson, Ward, Pitchford, Eccles, D. Heron (Adams), Cookson
Halifax 6 Birts (3g); Howard (Snee), Garrod, Cholmondeley, Waites; Blacker, Langton; Jarvis (Callon), Raistrick, Wood, Scott, Sharp, Busfield
Referee: M.J. Naughton (Widnes)

1980-81
Leeds 8 Hague; Alan Smith (1t), D. Smith,
Atkinson, Oulton; Holmes, Dick (2g, 1dg);
Harrison, Ward, Pitchford, Eccles, Cookson
(Carroll), D. Heron
Hull K.R. 7 Robinson; McHugh (1t),
M. Smith, Hogan (2g), Youngman; Hall,
Harkin; Holdstock, Price, Crooks (Rose),
Lowe, Casey, Crane
Referee: R. Campbell (Widnes)
1981-82
Castleford 10 Claughton; Richardson, Fenton,
Hyde (1t), Morris; Joyner (1t), R. Beardmore;
Hardy (P. Norton), Spurr, B. Johnson, Finch
(2g), Ward, Timson
Bradford N. 5 Mumby; Barends, Hale,
A. Parker (1t), Gant; Hanley (1g), A. Redfearn;
Grayshon, Noble, Sanderson (D. Redfearn),
G. Van Bellen (Jasiewicz), Idle, Rathbone
Referee: M.R. Whitfield (Widnes)
1982-83
Hull 18 Kemble; S. Evans (1t), Day, Leuluai,
Prendiville (1t); Topliss, Harkin; Skerrett,
Bridges, Stone, Rose (2t), L. Crooks (2g, 2dg),
Crane (Norton)
Bradford N. 7 Mumby; Barends, Gant,
A. Parker, Pullen (Smith); Whiteman (1t),
Carroll (1g, 2dg); Grayshon, Noble, G. Van
Bellen (Sanderson), Idle, Jasiewicz, Hale
Referee: S. Wall (Leigh)
1983-84
Hull 13 Kemble; Solal, Schofield, Leuluai,
O'Hara (1t); Topliss, Dean; Edmonds,
Wileman, Skerrett, Proctor (1t), L. Crooks,
Crane (1t, 1dg)
Castleford 2 Coen; Fenton, Marchant, Hyde
(Orum), Kear; Joyner, R. Beardmore (1g);
Connell, Horton, Reilly, Timson, James,
England
Referee: W.H. Thompson (Huddersfield)
1984-85
Hull 29 Kemble (2t); Leuluai, Schofield (4g,
1dg), S. Evans (1t), O'Hara; Ah Kuoi,
Sterling; Edmonds, Patrick, L. Crooks (1t),
Norton (1t), Proctor, Divorty (Rose)
Hull K.R. 12 Fairbairn (1t); Clark, Robinson
(1t), Prohm, Laws; M. Smith, Harkin (Rudd);
Broadhurst, Watkinson, Ema (Hartley),
Burton, Kelly, Hall (1t)
Referee: G.F. Lindop (Wakefield)
1985-86
Hull K.R. 22 Fairbairn (Lydiat); Clark (1t),
Dorahy (5g), Prohm, Laws; G. Smith, Harkin;
Des Harrison, Watkinson, Ema, Burton, Hogan
(Kelly), Miller (2t)
Castleford 18 Lord; Plange, Marchant (2t),
Hyde, Spears; Diamond (1g), R. Beardmore

(1t, 2g); Ward, K. Beardmore, B. Johnson,
England, Ketteridge, Joyner
Referee: R. Campbell (Widnes)
1986-87
Castleford 31 Scott; Plange, Marchant, Johns,
Hyde (Lord); Joyner, R. Beardmore (1dg);
Ward (1t), K. Beardmore (2t), B. Johnson,
Ketteridge (1t, 5g), Atkins (1t) (Shillito),
England
Hull 24 Kemble; Brand (2t), Schofield, O'Hara
(2t), Eastwood; Ah Kuoi, Windley; Brown
(Puckering), S. Patrick, Dannatt, Norton
(Divorty), L. Crooks (4g), Sharp
Referee: J. McDonald (Wigan)
1987-88
Bradford N. 12 Mercer; Ford, McGowan,
Simpson, Francis; Mumby (2g), Harkin;
Grayshon (Hobbs 2g), Noble, Hill, Skerrett,
Fairbank (1t), Holmes (Roebuck)
Castleford 12 Roockley; Plange (1t), Marchant,
Beattie, Hyde; Joyner, R. Southernwood;
Shillito (R. Beardmore), K. Beardmore
(Sampson), Ward, Ketteridge (2g), Fifita,
Lindner (1t)
Referee: K. Allatt (Southport)
Replay
Bradford N. 11 Mumby; Ford, McGowan,
Mercer, Simpson; Stewart, Harkin; Hobbs (1g,
1dg), Noble, Hill (1t), Skerrett, Fairbank,
Heron (1t)
Castleford 2 Roockley; Plange, Marchant,
Beattie, Hyde; R. Southernwood, R.
Beardmore; Ward, Hill, Fifita (Sampson),
Ketteridge (1g), England (Boothroyd), Joyner
Referee: K. Allatt (Southport)
1988-89
Leeds 33 Spencer; Ettingshausen, Schofield
(2t, 1dg), Stephenson (6g), Gibson (2t);
C. Lyons, Ashton; Crooks, Maskill, Waddell
(Backo), Powell, Brooke-Cowden (Medley, 1t),
Heron
Castleford 12 Belcher; Plange, Marchant,
Boothroyd (1t), Chapman (Roockley)
(Sampson); Anderson, R. Beardmore; Ward,
K. Beardmore, England, Ketteridge (2g),
Gibbs, Joyner (1t)
Referee: R. Whitfield (Widnes)
1989-90
Bradford N. 20 Wilkinson; Cordle (2t),
McGowan, Simpson, Francis; Henjak
(Mumby), Harkin (2t); Skerrett, Barraclough,
Hamer (Medley), Hobbs (2g), Fairbank,
Pendlebury
Featherstone R. 14 Bibb; Drummond,
I. Ropati (1t), Newlove, Banks; Smales, Fox
(3g); Grayshon, Clark, G. Bell (Dakin), Price,
Booth (Fisher), Smith (1t)
Referee: R. Whitfield (Widnes)

THE WHITE ROSE TROPHY

First awarded in 1966, the trophy is presented to the adjudged man of the match in the Yorkshire Cup final.

Donated by the late T.E. Smith, of York, the award is organised by the Yorkshire Federation of Rugby League Supporters' Clubs and judged by a panel of the Press.

The trophy is not awarded in replays, although Bradford Northern's Brendan Hill was named Man of the Match in the second game against Castleford in 1987.

Season	Winner	Team	Position
1966-67	Cyril Kellett	Hull K.R. (v. Featherstone R.)	Full back
1967-68	Chris Davidson	Hull (v. Hull K.R.)	Scrum half
1968-69	Barry Seabourne	Leeds (v. Castleford)	Scrum half
1969-70	Joe Brown	Hull (v. Featherstone R.)	Loose forward
1970-71	Syd Hynes	Leeds (v. Featherstone R.)	Centre
1971-72	Ian Markham	Hull K.R. (v. Castleford)	Full back
1972-73	John Holmes	Leeds (v. Dewsbury)	Full back
1973-74	Keith Hepworth	Leeds (v. Wakefield T.)	Scrum half
1974-75	Roger Millward	Hull K.R. (v. Wakefield T.)	Stand off
1975-76	Neil Fox	Hull K.R. (v. Leeds)	Second row
1976-77	Les Dyl	Leeds (v. Featherstone R.)	Centre
1977-78	Bruce Burton	Castleford (v. Featherstone R.)	Stand off
1978-79	Bob Haigh	Bradford N. (v. York)	Loose forward
1979-80	Alan Smith	Leeds (v. Halifax)	Winger
1980-81	Kevin Dick	Leeds (v. Hull K.R.)	Scrum half
1981-82	Barry Johnson	Castleford (v. Bradford N.)	Prop
1982-83	Keith Mumby	Bradford N. (v. Hull)	Full back
1983-84	Mick Crane	Hull (v. Castleford)	Loose forward
1984-85	Peter Sterling	Hull (v. Hull K.R.)	Scrum half
1985-86	Gavin Miller	Hull K.R. (v. Castleford)	Loose forward
1986-87	Kevin Beardmore	Castleford (v. Hull)	Hooker
1987-88	Paul Harkin	Bradford N. (v. Castleford)	Scrum half
1988-89	Cliff Lyons	Leeds (v. Castleford)	Stand off
1989-90	Paul Harkin	Bradford N. (v Featherstone R.)	Scrum half
1990-91	Tracy Lazenby	Wakefield T. (v. Castleford)	Stand off

YORKSHIRE CUP FINAL RECORDS

TEAM
Most appearances: 21 Leeds
Most wins: 17 Leeds
Highest score: Leeds 36 v. Dewsbury 9............ 1972
Widest margin win: Huddersfield 31 v. Hull 0... 1914
Biggest attendance:
36,000 Bradford N. v. Huddersfield (at Leeds).. 1949

INDIVIDUAL
Most tries:
4 by Stan Moorhouse (Huddersfield) v. Leeds.... 1919
Most goals:
6 by David Stephenson (Leeds) v. Castleford..... 1988
Most points:
14 (5g, 1t) by Martin Ketteridge (Castleford)
v. Hull 1986

Yorkshire Cup-winning hero for Castleford, tryscoring wingman David Plange.

1990 CHARITY SHIELD

Jonathan Davies, the former idol of Welsh Rugby Union, made a triumphant return to the land of his fathers to inspire Widnes to a third successive CIS Insurance Charity Shield victory over Wigan.

Davies notched his first-ever Rugby League hat-trick of tries as the Chemics brushed aside an injury-hit Wigan outfit as Rugby League made its debut at Swansea City's Vetch Field soccer ground. Despite day-long torrential rain, the 13-a-side code's return to South Wales attracted a commendable crowd of 11,178, two-thirds of whom were from the Principality, paying £53,705.

Wigan had qualified for the Swansea showpiece as winners of both the Stones Bitter Championship and the Silk Cut Challenge Cup — the first double since the Charity Shield was introduced in 1985 — the League deciding that their opponents should be the Stones Bitter Premiership victors, Widnes beating Bradford Northern in the Old Trafford final to qualify.

The stage was set for Rugby League to show off its new-style brand of football after a six-year absence from the valleys. Davies could not have written a better script than his Man-of-the-Match, 16-point performance. There was no disputing his top-of-the-bill status, even if skipper Tony Myler, David Hulme and Emosi Koloto played high-quality supporting roles.

While Davies, who was denied further points by twice hitting the post with shots at goal, was the shining light, Wigan were a shadow of their best, with seven internationals absent through injury — including skipper Ellery Hanley — and an eighth, Shaun Edwards, on substitute duty. The Riversiders displayed enthusiasm which kept them in the game for the first quarter, but once the Widnes pack exposed their frailty, the result was never in doubt.

While the intention was to put Rugby League in the showcase, all 32 points in this sixth Charity Shield encounter were scored by Rugby Union converts. The tries came from the Davies hat-trick, fellow Welshman John Devereux, ex-Rosslyn Park winger Martin Offiah and former New Zealand All Black Frano Botica. Davies added five goals, Botica two.

Wigan's only reward for a bright opening spell was a penalty goal from Botica, making his professional debut. But two tries in nine minutes shortly before the interval put Widnes in control.

Myler fashioned the first for Davies, the top goalscorer and points-scorer on the summer tour Down Under, using Offiah as a decoy to score in the corner. A fine pass from Currier, having returned from an unhappy summer stint with Sydney club Balmain, sent Devereux over on the opposite flank.

Within seven minutes of the second half starting, Tongan Koloto burst through and lured two defenders before sending Great Britain winger Offiah over. Then came two further touchdowns for Davies, the centre-piece of the South Wales pre-publicity.

The first came in the 52nd minute when Edwards's kick to the Widnes 25-yard zone bounced out to Davies who raced 80 yards. His third, and best, score came on the hour when he took Kurt Sorensen's pass before bursting past Wigan debutants Kelvin Skerrett and David Myers from 30 yards.

The only blackspots for a Widnes side maintaining an unbeaten Charity Shield record on their third consecutive appearance were a broken thumb sustained by Paul Hulme and a sin bin dismissal for brother David, for dissent 10 minutes from time. Wigan's Bobby Goulding was also sent to the sin bin for the same offence.

Davies duly collected the Jack Bentley Memorial Trophy as the Man of the Match, while skipper Myler picked up the CIS Insurance Charity Shield and a winners' cheque for £10,000.

CIS INSURANCE CHARITY SHIELD

19 August   **Vetch Field, Swansea**

WIDNES 24		**WIGAN 8**
Alan Tait	1.	John Gilfillan
John Devereux	2.	David Myers
Andy Currier	3.	Dean Bell, Capt.
Jonathan Davies	4.	Ged Byrne
Martin Offiah	5.	Mark Preston
Tony Myler, Capt.	6.	Frano Botica
David Hulme	7.	Bobby Goulding
Chris Ashurst	8.	Kelvin Skerrett
Phil McKenzie	9.	Russell Bridge
Joe Grima	10.	Shaun Wane
Paul Hulme	11.	Ian Gildart
Emosi Koloto	12.	Andy Platt
Les Holliday	13.	Denis Betts
Darren Wright	14.	Shaun Edwards
Kurt Sorensen	15.	Michael Forshaw

T: Davies (3), Devereux, Offiah
G: Davies (2)
Substitutions:
Sorensen for P. Hulme (20 min.)
Wright for Ashurst (59 min.)
Half-time: 10-2
Referee: Colin Morris (Huddersfield)

T: Botica
G: Botica (2)
Substitutions:
Forshaw for Gildart (22 min.)
Edwards for Botica (41 min.)
Attendance: 11,178

A clash of substitutes at Swansea as Widnes packman Kurt Sorensen is met by Wigan's Michael Forshaw, aided by the grounded Denis Betts.

CHARITY SHIELD ROLL OF HONOUR

Year	Winners		Runners-up		Venue	Attendance
1985-86	Wigan	34	Hull K.R.	6	Isle of Man	4,066
1986-87	Halifax	9	Castleford	8	Isle of Man	3,276
1987-88	Wigan	44	Halifax	12	Isle of Man	4,804
1988-89	Widnes	20	Wigan	14	Isle of Man	5,044
1989-90	Widnes	27	Wigan	22	Liverpool FC	17,263
1990-91	Widnes	24	Wigan	8	Swansea C. FC	11,178

CHARITY SHIELD .... A REVIEW

1985-86

Wigan 34 Hampson; P. Ford, Stephenson (7g), Donlan (2t), Gill (2t); Edwards, M. Ford (1t); Courtney (Mayo), Kiss, Campbell, West (Lucas), Du Toit, Wane
Hull K.R. 6 Fairbairn (Lydiat 1g); Clark (1t), Robinson, Prohm, Laws; M. Smith, G. Smith; Des Harrison, Watkinson, Ema, Kelly (Rudd), Burton, Hogan
Referee: R. Campbell (Widnes)

1986-87

Halifax 9 Smith (Wilson); Riddlesden, Whitfield (1t), Hague (1dg), George (1t); C. Anderson, Stephens; Dickinson, McCallion, Juliff, Scott (James), Bell, Dixon
Castleford 8 Roockley; Plange, Lord (1t), Irwin (R. Southernwood), Spears; Joyner (Fletcher), R. Beardmore; Ward, K. Beardmore, Johnson, Ketteridge (2g), Mountain, England
Referee: G. F. Lindop (Wakefield)

1987-88

Wigan 44 Hampson (2t); Stephenson (8g), Byrne (Russell), Bell (2t), Gill (1t); Edwards (2t), Gregory; West, Kiss, Case, Gildart (Wane), Potter, Goodway

Halifax 12 Eadie (2g); Taylor, Wilson, T. Anderson, George; Simpson (Juliff, 1t), Stephens; Dickinson, Pendlebury, Beevers, James, Scott (Bell), Dixon (1t)
Referee: J. Holdsworth (Kippax)

1988-89

Widnes 20 Tait; Thackray, Currier (4g), Wright (1t), Offiah (1t); Dowd, D. Hulme; Sorensen, McKenzie (1t), Grima (Pyke), M. O'Neill, P. Hulme, Eyres
Wigan 14 Hampson; Gill, Lydon (1t, 1g), Bell, Preston (Lucas); Byrne, Gregory; Shelford (Betts), Kiss, Case, T. Iro (2t), Wane, Goodway
Referee: R. Tennant (Castleford)

1989-90

Widnes 27 Tait (dg); Kebbie (1t), Davies (1t, 5g), Wright, Offiah (1t); T. Myler, D. Hulme (1t); Sorensen, P. Hulme, Grima (Pyke), M. O'Neill, Koloto, Eyres
Wigan 22 Hampson; Bell (Gilfillan), K. Iro (1t), Lydon (1t, 5g), Preston; Byrne, Gregory; Lucas, Kiss, Platt (1t) (Stazicker), Betts, Gildart, Goodway
Referee: J. Holdsworth (Kippax)

MAN OF THE MATCH AWARDS

Season	Winner	Team	Position
1985-86	Shaun Edwards	Wigan (v. Hull K.R.)	Stand off
1986-87	Chris Anderson	Halifax (v. Castleford)	Stand off
1987-88	Shaun Edwards	Wigan (v. Halifax)	Stand off
1988-89	Phil McKenzie	Widnes (v. Wigan)	Hooker
1989-90	Denis Betts	Wigan (v. Widnes)	Second row
1990-91	Jonathan Davies	Widnes (v. Wigan)	Centre

● From 1987 it became the Jack Bentley Trophy in memory of the former Daily Express Rugby League journalist.

BBC-2 FLOODLIT TROPHY

The BBC-2 Floodlit Trophy competition was launched in 1965. Eight clubs competed in the first year and the total had grown to 22 by 1980 when the competition was abolished as part of the BBC's financial cut-backs.

For 15 years the matches became a regular television feature on Tuesday evenings throughout the early winter months.

Although the format changed slightly over the years, it was basically a knockout competition on the lines of the Challenge Cup.

In 1966 the Floodlit Competition was used to introduce the limited tackle rule, then four tackles, which proved such a great success it was adopted in all other matches before the end of the year.

BBC-2 FLOODLIT TROPHY FINALS
(Only the 1967, at Leeds, and 1972, at Wigan, finals were played on neutral grounds)

Season	Winners		Runners-up		Venue	Attendance	Receipts
1965-66	Castleford	4	St. Helens	0	St. Helens	11,510	£1,548
1966-67	Castleford	7	Swinton	2	Castleford	8,986	£1,692
1967-68	Castleford	8	Leigh	5	Leeds	9,716	£2,099
1968-69	Wigan	7	St. Helens	4	Wigan	13,479	£3,291
1969-70	Leigh	11	Wigan	6	Wigan	12,312	£2,854
1970-71	Leeds	9	St. Helens	5	Leeds	7,612	£2,189
1971-72	St. Helens	8	Rochdale H.	2	St. Helens	9,300	£2,493
1972-73	Leigh	5	Widnes	0	Wigan	4,691	£1,391
1973-74	Bramley	15	Widnes	7	Widnes	4,422	£1,538
1974-75	Salford	0	Warrington	0	Salford	4,473	£1,913
Replay	Salford	10	Warrington	5	Warrington	5,778	£2,434
1975-76	St. Helens	22	Dewsbury	2	St. Helens	3,858	£1,747
1976-77	Castleford	12	Leigh	4	Leigh	5,402	£2,793
1977-78	Hull K.R.	26	St. Helens	11	Hull K.R.	10,099	£6,586
1978-79	Widnes	13	St. Helens	7	St. Helens	10,250	£7,017
1979-80	Hull	13	Hull K.R.	3	Hull	18,500	£16,605

BBC2 FLOODLIT TROPHY . . . . A REVIEW
1965-66
Castleford 4 Edwards; C. Battye, M. Battye, Willett (2g), Briggs; Hardisty, Millward; Terry, J. Ward, C. Dickinson, Bryant, Taylor, Small
St. Helens 0 F. Barrow; Vollenhoven, Wood, Benyon, Killeen; Murphy, Prosser; French, Dagnall, Watson, Hicks, Mantle, Laughton
Referee: L. Gant (Wakefield)
1966-67
Castleford 7 Edwards; Howe, Stenton, Willett (1g), Austin (1t); Hardisty, Hepworth (1g); Hartley, C. Dickinson, McCartney, Bryant, Small, Walker
Swinton 2 Gowers; Whitehead (1g), Gomersall, Buckley, Davies; Fleet, G. Williams; Halliwell, D. Clarke, Scott (Cummings), Rees, Simpson, Robinson
Referee: J. Manley (Warrington)
1967-68
Castleford 8 Edwards; Harris, Thomas, Stenton, Willett (4g); Hardisty, Hepworth; Hartley, J. Ward, Walton, Bryant (C. Dickinson), Redfearn, Reilly

Leigh 5 Grainey; Tickle (1t), Lewis, Collins, Walsh; Entwistle, A. Murphy; Whitworth, Ashcroft, Major, Welding, M. Murphy, Gilfedder (1g)
Referee: G.F. Lindop (Wakefield)
1968-69
Wigan 7 Tyrer (2g); Francis, Ashton, Ashurst, Rowe; C. Hill (1t), Jackson; J. Stephens, Clarke, Mills, Fogerty (Lyon), Kevin O'Loughlin, Laughton
St. Helens 4 Williams; Wilson, Benyon, Myler, Wills; Whittle, Bishop; Warlow, Sayer, Watson, Mantle, Hogan, Coslett (2g)
Referee: E. Clay (Leeds)
1969-70
Leigh 11 Ferguson (3g) (Lewis); Tickle (1t), Dorrington, Collins, Walsh; Eckersley, Murphy (1g); D. Chisnall, Ashcroft, Watts, Welding, Grimes, Lyon
Wigan 6 C. Hill; Wright, Francis (2g), Rowe, Kevin O'Loughlin; D. Hill (1g), Jackson; J. Stephens, Clarke, Ashcroft, Ashurst, Mills, Laughton
Referee: W.H. Thompson (Huddersfield)

1970-71
Leeds 9 Holmes (2g); Alan Smith, Hynes (1t, 1g), Cowan, Atkinson; Wainwright, Shoebottom; J. Burke, Fisher, Barnard, Haigh, Ramsey, Batten
St. Helens 5 F. Barrow; L. Jones (1t), Benyon, Walsh, Wilson; Whittle, Heaton; Rees, A. Karalius, E. Chisnall, Mantle, E. Prescott, Coslett (1g)
Referee: E. Lawrinson (Warrington)
1971-72
St. Helens 8 G. Pimblett; L. Jones, Benyon, Walsh, Wilson; Kelly, Heaton; Rees, A. Karalius, E. Chisnall, E. Prescott, Mantle, Coslett (4g)
Rochdale H. 2 Chamberlain (1g); Brelsford, Crellin, Taylor, Glover; Myler, Gartland; Birchall, P. Clarke, Brown, Welding, Sheffield (Hodkinson), Delooze
Referee: E. Clay (Leeds)
1972-73
Leigh 5 Hogan; Lawson (1t) (Lester), Atkin, Collins, Stacey; A. Barrow, Sayer (Ryding); Grimes, D. Clarke, Fletcher, Fiddler (1g), F. Barrow, Martyn
Widnes 0 Dutton; A. Prescott, Aspey, Blackwood, McDonnell; Lowe, Ashton; Mills, Elwell, Warlow, Foran, Sheridan, Nicholls
Referee: G.F. Lindop (Wakefield)
1973-74
Bramley 15 Keegan; Goodchild (1t), Bollon, Hughes, Austin (1t); T. Briggs, Ward (1g) (Ashman); D. Briggs, Firth, Cheshire, D. Sampson (1t), Idle, Wolford (2g)
Widnes 7 Dutton (2g); D. O'Neill, Hughes, Aspey, Macko (1t); Warburton, Bowden; Hogan, Elwell, Nelson, Sheridan, Blackwood (Foran) Laughton
Referee: D. G. Kershaw (York)
1974-75
Salford 0 Charlton; Fielding, Hesketh, Graham, Richards; Brophy (Taylor), Banner; Coulman, Devlin, Grice, Knighton, Dixon, E. Prescott
Warrington 0 Whitehead; Sutton, Cunliffe (Lowe), Whittle, Bevan; Briggs, Gordon; D. Chisnall, Ashcroft, Wright, Gaskell, Conroy, B. Philbin (Jewitt)
Referee: W.H. Thompson (Huddersfield)
Replay
Salford 10 Stead; Fielding (1t), Watkins (2g), Hesketh, Richards (1t); Gill, Banner; Grice, Walker, Mackay, Dixon, Knighton, E. Prescott

Warrington 5 Cunliffe; Whitehead (1g), Pickup, Whittle, Bevan (1t); Noonan (Briggs), Gordon; D. Chisnall, Ashcroft, Wanbon, Conroy, Nicholas (Brady), B. Philbin
Referee: W.H. Thompson (Huddersfield)
1975-76
St. Helens 22 G. Pimblett (2g); L. Jones, Benyon (1t), Hull (1t), Mathias (2t); Wilson (1t), Heaton (1dg); Mantle, A. Karalius, James, Nicholls, E. Chisnall, Coslett (1g)
Dewsbury 2 Langley; Hegarty, Chalkley, Simpson, Mitchell; N. Stephenson (1g) (Lee), A. Bates; Beverley, Price, Hankins, Halloran (Artis), Bell, Grayshon
Referee: W.H. Thompson (Huddersfield)
1976-77
Castleford 12 Wraith; Fenton, Joyner, P. Johnson, Walsh (1t); Burton (1t), Stephens; Khan, Spurr, A. Dickinson, Reilly, Lloyd (3g), S. Norton
Leigh 4 Hogan; A. Prescott, Stacey, Woods, Walsh (1t); Taylor, Sayer; D. Chisnall, Ashcroft (1dg), Fletcher, Macko, Grimes, Boyd
Referee: J.E. Jackson (Pudsey)
1977-78
Hull K.R. 26 Hall (4g); Dunn (2t), M. Smith (1t), Watson, Sullivan (1t); Hartley (1t), Millward; Millington, Watkinson, Cunningham (Hughes), Lowe, Rose (1t), Casey
St. Helens 11 G. Pimblett (Platt); L. Jones (Courtney), Noonan, Cunningham (1t), Glynn (2t, 1g); Francis, K. Gwilliam; D. Chisnall, Liptrot, James, Hope, A. Karalius, Pinner
Referee: M. J. Naughton (Widnes)
1978-79
Widnes 13 Eckersley; Wright (2t), Hughes, Aspey, P. Shaw; Burke (2g, 1t), Bowden; Hogan, Elwell, Mills, Adams, Dearden, Laughton
St. Helens 7 G. Pimblett (2g), L. Jones, Glynn, Cunningham, Mathias; Francis, Holding; D. Chisnall (1t), Liptrot, James, Nicholls, Knighton (E. Chisnall), Pinner
Referee: J. McDonald (Wigan)
1979-80
Hull 13 Woods; Bray, G. Evans (1t), Coupland, Dennison (1t, 2g); Newlove, Hepworth; Tindall, Wileman, Farrar, Stone, Boxall (Birdsall 1t), Norton
Hull K.R. 3 Robinson; Hubbard (1t), M. Smith, Watson, Sullivan; Hall, Agar; Holdstock, Tyreman, Lockwood, Clarkson (Hartley), Lowe, Hogan (Millington)
Referee: W.H. Thompson (Huddersfield)

CAPTAIN MORGAN TROPHY

This sponsored competition, with a winners' prize of £3,000, lasted only one season. Entry was restricted to the 16 clubs who won their Yorkshire and Lancashire Cup first round ties. The Lancashire contingent was made up to eight by including the side which lost their first round county Cup-tie by the narrowest margin. The first round of the Captain Morgan Trophy was zoned with clubs being drawn against those in their own county. The remainder of the competition was integrated. The final was on a neutral ground as follows:

1973-74	Warrington	4	Featherstone R.	0	Salford	5,259	£2,265

1973-74

Warrington 4 Whitehead (2g); M. Philbin, Noonan, Reynolds (Pickup), Bevan; Whittle, Gordon; D. Chisnall, Ashcroft, Brady, Wanbon (Price), Wright, Mather

Featherstone R. 0 Box; Coventry, M. Smith, Hartley, Bray; Mason, Wood; Tonks, Bridges, Harris, Gibbins (Stone), Rhodes, Bell
Referee: G.F. Lindop (Wakefield)

Wigan skipper Ellery Hanley hoists the 1990-91 Stones Bitter Championship Trophy after the 20-8 defeat of Leeds at Headingley.

LEAGUE

1990-91 CHAMPIONSHIP

Battle-worn Wigan retained their Stones Bitter Championship crown after achieving what coach John Monie described as 'Mission Impossible'. The resilient Riversiders proved worthy of the title Champions by blasting through an end-of-season league fixture pile-up undefeated to capture the record £44,000 Stones Bitter prize cheque and going on to complete a Cup and League title double for a record second successive season.

The Championship was retained despite playing their last eight matches in 19 days, including four in the final week. They had begun the year in fifth position but were unbeaten in their last 14 matches, including a draw.

Monie's men not only bore the fixture burden of a game every three days but also swept through majestically with an average of 22 points a match during the eight game period.

Wigan's triumph was the culmination of a four-horse race for the Championship Trophy. Unfancied Hull took pole position on the third weekend of the new campaign, topping the pile until 17 February when Widnes took over. The Airlie Birds, under Australian mentor Brian Smith until his departure in early January for former club St. George in Sydney, and then under fellow countryman Noel Cleal, took advantage of first stage departures from the John Smiths Yorkshire Cup, the Regal Trophy and the Silk Cut Challenge Cup to maintain their surprise challenge for the title.

Seeking their third Stones Bitter success in four seasons, Widnes gave way to Castleford, who had gained league momentum having been knocked off the Wembley trail at the first attempt by Wigan. On 10 March the top four of the Championship was: Castleford with 30 points from 21 matches, followed by Widnes and Hull with 28 from 19, while Wigan were trailing with 23 from only 16

matches. At this stage the Riversiders were electing not to play rearranged league fixtures around their Challenge Cup and international commitments, thus adding to their end-of-season workload.

April opened with Widnes and Wigan in the driving seat, passengers Hull and Castleford poised to take advantage of any sign of battle fatigue. After the Easter Monday games Widnes were at the top of the table with 36 points from 23 matches, Wigan three points behind but with two games in hand.

Politics entered the hurdle chase at this stage, with Wigan failing in a bid to have the season extended by three days, the League ruling that it would be unfair to all the other clubs who had fitted their fixtures into the hectic schedule. The Board of Directors took over the end-of-season fixture formulation and ruled that Wigan's final week would comprise home matches against Castleford on the Sunday, Bradford Northern on Tuesday, Widnes on Thursday and a trip to Leeds on the Saturday.

Wigan chairman Maurice Lindsay subsequently persuaded his fellow RL Board members that the meeting with Widnes would be the virtual title decider and should be staged on the Tuesday to ensure that both clubs were carrying the same burden after the weekend fixtures. Widnes's weekend commitment was a Saturday afternoon meeting at Sheffield for Granada Television, while Wigan entertained Castleford in a Sunday evening BSB televised game. The Board of Directors endorsed the switch as 'fair', Widnes failing with an appeal.

The Central Park clash of the giants attracted a lock-out attendance of 29,763, a new First Division record gate. Victory for Widnes would have meant that they only had to dispose of bottom-of-the-table Rochdale Hornets at home on the Sunday to lift the trophy. Determined Wigan wrecked their hopes by producing a five star show to score four tries to one in a 26-6 victory. The Riversiders then needed two points from their two remaining matches to retain the title.

Two days later, nearly 20,000 expectant fans again packed Central Park for the visit of Bradford Northern, who turned out to be party poopers by powering their way into an 18-2 lead shortly after half-time. Wigan rallied under the supreme leadership of skipper Ellery Hanley, to pull level at 18-18, failing to break the deadlock with two Frano Botica drop goal attempts.

The title showdown moved into Yorkshire on the Saturday. A Leeds success would mean that Widnes knew how many points they needed to score to beat wooden spooners Rochdale at Naughton Park, Wigan holding a 56 points difference advantage before the Headingley game.

Once again, Wigan dug deep into their reserves of resourcefulness. Shaun Edwards, Steve Hampson, Martin Dermott and Andy Platt turned out with the aid of pain-killing injections, Kelvin Skerrett started his four-match suspension and the inspirational Andy Gregory was ruled out by injury, as was Joe Lydon. As Hanley had to leave the fray with a leg injury, weakened Wigan found a new saviour in the almost forgotten Test hero Bobby Goulding, who took over Gregory's number seven jersey to mastermind a 20-8 triumph, highlighted by his three drop goals. Wigan had lifted the Stones Bitter title in true champion style.

It was equally tough at the bottom of the table. Rochdale Hornets, shock promotion successes the previous season, always seemed doomed to an immediate return to the lower reaches, despite battling to the semi-finals of the Regal Trophy. Their one victory equalled the lowest Division One points tally and they finished with a Division One record-equalling run of 20 successive defeats.

But the other two relegation spots were fiercely contested. Sheffield Eagles' fairytale rise to stardom came to an abrupt end when their attractive style of football brought only seven wins and a draw. Oldham also made an immediate return to the Second Division, although they were in line to become the first club to go down and reach Wembley in the same season until Wigan beat them in the Silk Cut Challenge Cup semi-final at Bolton.

Warrington, Wakefield Trinity and Hull K.R. also suffered relegation blues, coach Roger Millward ending a 25-year career at Craven Park with his worst defeat during an otherwise golden era — 62-16 at Sheffield.

In the Second Division, Salford dropped only three points in their 28-match campaign, the Red Devils' one defeat being at revitalised Workington Town 7-0, a month away from the end of the season. Kevin Tamati's charges heralded the best defensive record in the division, but the top points-scorers were runners-up Halifax, who returned to winning ways under new coach Peter Roe, previously in charge of amateur champions Dudley Hill. Swinton, despite an injury-ridden season, clinched the third promotion place.

The challenge of much-fancied Leigh fell away as the club became embroiled in a financial crisis which saw the Hilton Park outfit put in the hands of an administrator at the end of the season. Unrated Workington appointed former Oldham and Leeds scrum half Ray Ashton as coach at the start of the season, his influence taking the Cumbrians to sixth place in the table and Ashton to the Stones Bitter Man of Steel Awards as a nominee for the title of Coach of the Year.

But the most newsworthy feat belonged to Runcorn Highfield, who ended a record run of 75 cup and league matches without a win by defeating Dewsbury 9-2 at home at the start of March. Runcorn's run included a record 55 successive league defeats and 67 without a win.

FINAL TABLES 1990-91

STONES BITTER CHAMPIONSHIP

	P.	W.	D.	L.	Dr.	FOR Gls.	Trs.	Pts.	Dr.	AGAINST Gls.	Trs.	Pts.	Pts.
Wigan	26	20	2	4	4	108	108	652	3	53	51	313	42
Widnes	26	20	0	6	3	82	117	635	6	63	52	340	40
Hull	26	17	0	9	3	85	85	513	1	59	62	367	34
Castleford	26	17	0	9	2	88	100	578	2	62	79	442	34
Leeds	26	14	2	10	4	99	100	602	6	75	73	448	30
St. Helens	26	14	1	11	4	96	108	628	9	90	86	533	29
Bradford N.	26	13	1	12	8	59	77	434	4	84	80	492	27
Featherstone R.	26	12	1	13	3	83	91	533	2	97	99	592	25
Warrington	26	10	2	14	0	70	66	404	10	75	69	436	22
Wakefield T.	26	10	2	14	4	66	55	356	5	56	73	409	22
Hull K.R.	26	9	3	14	2	81	72	452	1	75	116	615	21
Oldham	26	10	0	16	9	80	78	481	4	93	93	562	20
Sheffield E.	26	7	2	17	7	76	75	459	3	96	97	583	16
Rochdale H.	26	1	0	25	5	42	57	317	2	137	159	912	2

Corals pre-season betting for the 1990-91 Championship: 5-4 Wigan; 11-4 Widnes; 3-1 Leeds; 14-1 St. Helens; 20-1 Bradford N., Hull; 25-1 Warrington, Castleford; 33-1 Hull K.R.; 50-1 Wakefield T.; 100-1 Featherstone R., Oldham; 200-1 Rochdale H., Sheffield E.

SECOND DIVISION

	P.	W.	D.	L.	Dr.	FOR Gls.	Trs.	Pts.	Dr.	AGAINST Gls.	Trs.	Pts.	Pts.
Salford	28	26	1	1	12	130	146	856	3	38	35	219	53
Halifax	28	24	0	4	1	116	177	941	3	54	50	311	48
Swinton	28	21	2	5	13	75	90	523	6	56	63	370	44
Ryedale-York	28	20	2	6	7	90	93	559	12	53	44	294	42
Leigh	28	18	1	9	6	104	121	698	12	64	58	372	37
Workington T.	28	18	1	9	19	73	83	497	11	56	50	323	37
Fulham	28	17	2	9	2	82	71	450	10	64	50	338	36
Carlisle	28	16	2	10	7	101	101	613	13	58	74	425	34
Doncaster	28	16	0	12	11	76	86	507	10	66	73	434	32
Hunslet	28	13	2	13	9	79	88	519	6	74	71	438	28
Huddersfield	28	13	1	14	5	78	83	493	11	73	80	477	27
Whitehaven	28	13	0	15	6	67	68	412	8	92	100	592	26
Keighley	28	12	0	16	4	68	79	456	6	97	97	588	24
Dewsbury	28	10	1	17	14	60	69	410	7	62	81	455	21
Trafford B.	28	10	0	18	6	79	86	508	12	99	102	618	20
Batley	28	10	0	18	7	49	58	337	6	64	83	466	20
Barrow	28	8	2	18	5	71	67	415	5	104	123	705	18
Chorley	28	7	1	20	10	63	63	388	7	107	125	721	15
Bramley	28	7	1	20	9	69	58	379	2	116	123	726	15
Runcorn H.	28	3	1	24	5	61	56	351	7	108	139	779	7
Nottingham C.	28	2	0	26	6	51	44	284	7	137	166	945	4

Corals pre-season betting for the 1990-91 Second Division Championship: 4-5 Leigh; 5-2 Salford; 8-1 Halifax, Ryedale-York; 14-1 Swinton; 16-1 Barrow; 33-1 Huddersfield, Doncaster; 40-1 Dewsbury; 50-1 Batley; 66-1 Hunslet, Fulham; 100-1 Carlisle, Trafford B., Bramley; 200-1 Keighley, Chorley, Whitehaven; 250-1 Workington T.; 300-1 Nottingham C., Runcorn H.

Wigan's powerhouse prop, Test man Andy Platt.

Salford's New Zealand import Shane Hansen.

TWO DIVISION CHAMPIONSHIP ROLL OF HONOUR

	FIRST DIVISION	SECOND DIVISION
1902-03	Halifax	Keighley
1903-04	Bradford	Wakefield Trinity
1904-05	Oldham	Dewsbury
1962-63	Swinton	Hunslet
1963-64	Swinton	Oldham
1973-74	Salford	Bradford Northern
1974-75	St. Helens	Huddersfield
1975-76	Salford	Barrow
1976-77	Featherstone Rovers	Hull
1977-78	Widnes	Leigh
1978-79	Hull Kingston Rovers	Hull
1979-80	Bradford Northern	Featherstone Rovers
1980-81	Bradford Northern	York
1981-82	Leigh	Oldham
1982-83	Hull	Fulham
1983-84	Hull Kingston Rovers	Barrow
1984-85	Hull Kingston Rovers	Swinton
1985-86	Halifax	Leigh
1986-87	Wigan	Hunslet
1987-88	Widnes	Oldham
1988-89	Widnes	Leigh
1989-90	Wigan	Hull Kingston Rovers
1990-91	Wigan	Salford

THE UPS AND DOWNS OF TWO DIVISION FOOTBALL
Since re-introduction of two divisions in 1973-74.

● Figure in brackets indicates position in division.

	RELEGATED	PROMOTED
1973-74	Oldham (13) Hull K.R. (14) Leigh (15) Whitehaven (16)	Bradford Northern (1) York (2) Keighley (3) Halifax (4)
1974-75	York (13) Bramley (14) Rochdale Hornets (15) Halifax (16)	Huddersfield (1) Hull K.R. (2) Oldham (3) Swinton (4)

1975-76	Dewsbury (13) Keighley (14) Huddersfield (15) Swinton (16)	Barrow (1) Rochdale Hornets (2) Workington T. (3) Leigh (4)
1976-77	Rochdale Hornets (13) Leigh (14) Barrow (15) Oldham (16)	Hull (1) Dewsbury (2) Bramley (3) New Hunslet (4)
1977-78	Hull (13) New Hunslet (14) Bramley (15) Dewsbury (16)	Leigh (1) Barrow (2) Rochdale Hornets (3) Huddersfield (4)
1978-79	Barrow (13) Featherstone Rovers (14) Rochdale Hornets (15) Huddersfield (16)	Hull (1) New Hunslet (2) York (3) Blackpool Borough (4)
1979-80	Wigan (13) Hunslet (14) York (15) Blackpool Borough (16)	Featherstone Rovers (1) Halifax (2) Oldham (3) Barrow (4)
1980-81	Halifax (13) Salford (14) Workington T. (15) Oldham (16)	York (1) Wigan (2) Fulham (3) Whitehaven (4)
1981-82	Fulham (13) Wakefield T. (14) York (15) Whitehaven (16)	Oldham (1) Carlisle (2) Workington T. (3) Halifax (4)
1982-83	Barrow (13) Workington T. (14) Halifax (15) Carlisle (16)	Fulham (1) Wakefield T. (2) Salford (3) Whitehaven (4)
1983-84	Fulham (13) Wakefield T. (14) Salford (15) Whitehaven (16)	Barrow (1) Workington T. (2) Hunslet (3) Halifax (4)
1984-85	Barrow (13) Leigh (14) Hunslet (15) Workington T. (16)	Swinton (1) Salford (2) York (3) Dewsbury (4)
1985-86	York (14) Swinton (15) Dewsbury (16)	Leigh (1) Barrow (2) Wakefield T. (3)
1986-87	Oldham (13) Featherstone Rovers (14) Barrow (15) Wakefield T. (16)	Hunslet (1) Swinton (2)

1987-88	Leigh (12) Swinton (13) Hunslet (14)	Oldham (1) Featherstone Rovers (2) Wakefield T. (3)
1988-89	Oldham (12) Halifax (13) Hull K.R. (14)	Leigh (1) Barrow (2) Sheffield E. (3)
1989-90	Leigh (12) Salford (13) Barrow (14)	Hull K.R. (1) Rochdale Hornets (2) Oldham (3)
1990-91	Oldham (12) Sheffield E. (13) Rochdale Hornets (14)	Salford (1) Halifax (2) Swinton (3)

Salford captain Ian Blease holds aloft the 1990-91 Stones Bitter Second Division Championship Bowl.

FIRST DIVISION RECORDS
Since reintroduction in 1973

INDIVIDUAL

Match records

Most tries:
6 Shane Cooper (St. Helens) v. Hull Feb 17, 1988

Most goals: 13 Geoff Pimblett (St. Helens) v. Bramley Mar 5, 1978

Most points: 38 (11g, 4t) Bob Beardmore (Castleford) v. Barrow Mar 22, 1987

Season records

Most tries: 44 Ellery Hanley (Wigan) 1986-87
Most goals: 130 Steve Hesford (Warrington) 1978-79
Most points: 295 (101g, 1dg, 23t) John Woods (Leigh) 1983-84

TEAM

Highest score and widest margin: Leeds 90 v. Barrow 0 Feb 11, 1990

Highest away score: Rochdale H. 12 v. Castleford 76 Mar 3, 1991

Widest away margin: Wakefield T. 6 v. Wigan 72 Mar 29, 1987; Barrow 0 v. Wigan 66 Oct 1, 1989

Most points by losing team: Hunslet 40 v. Barrow 41 Sep 9, 1984

Scoreless draw: Wigan 0 v. Castleford 0 Jan 26, 1974

Highest score draw: Hunslet 32 v. Swinton 32 Sep 20, 1987

Best opening sequence: 13 wins then a draw by Widnes 1981-82

Longest winning run: 25 by St. Helens Won last 13 of 1985-86 and first 12 of 1986-87 (Also longest unbeaten run.)

Longest losing run: 20 by Whitehaven 1983-84; Rochdale H. 1990-91

Longest run without a win: 23, including 3 draws, by Whitehaven 1981-82 (Also worst opening sequence)

Biggest attendance: 29,763 Wigan v. Widnes Apr 9, 1991

100 Division One career tries
203 Ellery Hanley (Bradford N., Wigan)
165 Keith Fielding (Salford)
144 David Smith (Wakefield T., Leeds, Bradford N.)
139 Stuart Wright (Wigan, Widnes)
136 Roy Mathias (St. Helens)
134 Garry Schofield (Hull, Leeds)
132 John Joyner (Castleford)
131 Phil Ford (Warrington, Wigan, Bradford N., Leeds)
130 John Bevan (Warrington)
126 Steve Hartley (Hull K.R.)
126 David Topliss (Wakefield T., Hull, Oldham)
125 John Woods (Leigh, Bradford N., Warrington)
122 Maurice Richards (Salford)
122 Steve Evans (Featherstone R., Hull, Wakefield T., Bradford N.)
120 Des Drummond (Leigh, Warrington)
120 Martin Offiah (Widnes)
113 David Redfearn (Bradford N.)

107 Henderson Gill (Bradford N., Wigan)
106 Neil Holding (St. Helens, Rochdale H.)
106 Gary Hyde (Castleford, Oldham)
103 Keiron O'Loughlin (Wigan, Workington T., Widnes, Salford)

Top four Division One career goals
854 John Woods (Leigh, Bradford N., Warrington)
845 Steve Hesford (Warrington)
818 Steve Quinn (Featherstone R.)
811 George Fairbairn (Wigan, Hull K.R.)

Top four Division One career points
2,130 John Woods (Leigh, Bradford N., Warrington)
1,814 George Fairbairn (Wigan, Hull K.R.)
1,768 Steve Quinn (Featherstone R.)
1,756 Steve Hesford (Warrington)

20 Division One tries in a season

1973-74	36	Keith Fielding (Salford)
	29	Roy Mathias (St. Helens)
	21	David Smith (Wakefield T.)
1974-75	21	Maurice Richards (Salford)
	21	Roy Mathias (St. Helens)
1975-76	26	Maurice Richards (Salford)
	20	David Smith (Wakefield T.)
1976-77	22	David Topliss (Wakefield T.)
	21	Keith Fielding (Salford)
	21	Ged Dunn (Hull K.R.)
	20	David Smith (Leeds)
	20	Stuart Wright (Widnes)
1977-78	26	Keith Fielding (Salford)
	25	Steve Fenton (Castleford)
	24	Stuart Wright (Widnes)
	20	David Smith (Leeds)
	20	Bruce Burton (Castleford)
	20	John Bevan (Warrington)
1978-79	28	Steve Hartley (Hull K.R.)
1979-80	24	Keith Fielding (Salford)
	21	Roy Mathias (St. Helens)
	21	Steve Hubbard (Hull K.R.)
	20	David Smith (Leeds)
1980-81	20	Steve Hubbard (Hull K.R.)
1981-82		David Hobbs (Featherstone R.) was top scorer with 19 tries.
1982-83	22	Bob Eccles (Warrington)
	20	Steve Evans (Hull)
1983-84	28	Garry Schofield (Hull)
	23	John Woods (Leigh)
	20	James Leuluai (Hull)
1984-85	40	Ellery Hanley (Bradford N.)
	34	Gary Prohm (Hull K.R.)
	23	Henderson Gill (Wigan)
	22	Barry Ledger (St. Helens)
	22	Mal Meninga (St. Helens)
1985-86	22	Ellery Hanley (Wigan)
1986-87	44	Ellery Hanley (Wigan)
	24	Phil Ford (Bradford N.)
	24	Henderson Gill (Wigan)
	23	Garry Schofield (Hull)
	21	John Henderson (Leigh)
1987-88	33	Martin Offiah (Widnes)
	22	Ellery Hanley (Wigan)
1988-89	37	Martin Offiah (Widnes)
	20	Grant Anderson (Castleford)

1989-90	28	Martin Offiah (Widnes)
	25	Mark Preston (Wigan)
	20	Steve Larder (Castleford)
1990-91	22	Martin Offiah (Widnes)
	22	Les Quirk (St. Helens)
	20	Ellery Hanley (Wigan)

Top Division One goalscorers

1973-74	126	David Watkins (Salford)
1974-75	96	Sammy Lloyd (Castleford)
1975-76	118	Sammy Lloyd (Castleford)
1976-77	113	Steve Quinn (Featherstone R.)
1977-78	116	Steve Hesford (Warrington)
1978-79	130	Steve Hesford (Warrington)
1979-80	104	Steve Hubbard (Hull K.R.)
1980-81	96	Steve Diamond (Wakefield T.)
1981-82	110	Steve Quinn (Featherstone R.)
		John Woods (Leigh)
1982-83	105	Bob Beardmore (Castleford)
1983-84	106	Steve Hesford (Warrington)
1984-85	114	Sean Day (St. Helens)
1985-86	85	David Stephenson (Wigan)
1986-87	120	Paul Loughlin (St. Helens)
1987-88	95	John Woods (Warrington)
1988-89	95	David Hobbs (Bradford N.)
1989-90	96	Paul Loughlin (St. Helens)
1990-91	85	Paul Eastwood (Hull)

Top Division One pointscorer 1990-91
214 (85g, 11t) Paul Eastwood (Hull)

SECOND DIVISION RECORDS
Since reintroduction in 1973

INDIVIDUAL

Match records

Most tries: 6 Ged Dunn (Hull K.R.) v. New Hunslet Feb 2, 1975; David Kettlestring (Ryedale-York) at Keighley Mar 11, 1990; Greg Austin (Halifax) v. Trafford B. Apr 7, 1991

Most goals: 15 Mick Stacey (Leigh) v. Doncaster Mar 28, 1976

Most points: 38 (13g, 4t) John Woods (Leigh) v. Blackpool B. Sep 11, 1977

Season records

Most tries: 48 Steve Halliwell (Leigh) 1985-86

Most goals: 167 Mike Fletcher (Hull K.R.) 1989-90

Most points: 395 (163g, 3dg, 22t) Lynn Hopkins (Workington T.) 1981-82

TEAM

Highest score: Leigh 92 v. Keighley 2 Apr 30, 1986; Hull K.R. 92 v. Whitehaven 10 Mar 18, 1990; Rochdale H. 92 v. Runcorn H. 0 Nov 5, 1989 (Also widest margin)

Highest away: Runcorn H. 2 v. Leigh 88 Jan 15, 1989 (Also widest margin)

Most points by losing team:
Dewsbury 36 v. Rochdale H. 34 Oct 9, 1988; Oldham 50 v. Keighley 34 Nov 12, 1989

Highest score draw: Huddersfield B. 32 v. Keighley 32 Apr 17, 1986

Scoreless draw: Dewsbury 0 v. Rochdale H. 0. Jan 30, 1983

Longest winning run: 30 by Leigh in 1985-86. Hull won all 26 matches in 1978-79

Longest losing run: 55 by Runcorn H. (9 in 1988-89, all 28 in 1989-90 and 18 in 1990-91)

Longest run without a win: 67, inc 2 draws, by Runcorn H. (19 in 1988-89, all 28 in 1989-90 and 20 in 1990-91)

Biggest attendance: 12,424 Hull v. New Hunslet May 18, 1979

1990-91 Top Division Two scorers

Most tries: 33 Greg Austin (Halifax)

Most goals: 130 Steve Kerry (Salford)

Most points: 312 (126g, 4dg, 14t) Steve Kerry (Salford)

NB. Division One and Two records do not include scores in abandoned matches that were replayed.

Hull winger Paul Eastwood, top Division One points-scorer in 1990-91 with a tally of 214.

TWO DIVISION SCORING

The following tables show the scoring totals for each two-division season:

DIVISION ONE

Season	Matches each club played	Goals	1-Point drop goals	Tries	Pts
1973-74	30	1,508	—	1,295	6,901
1974-75	30	1,334	48	1,261	6,499
1975-76	30	1,498	53	1,331	7,042
1976-77	30[1]	1,435	91	1,423	7,230
1977-78	30[2]	1,402	99	1,443	7,232
1978-79	30	1,367	119	1,448	7,197
1979-80	30	1,389	131	1,349	6,956
1980-81	30	1,439	147	1,342	7,051
1981-82	30	1,486	132	1,354	7,166
1982-83	30	1,369	64	1,386	6,960
1983-84	30	1,472	108	1,479	8,968
1984-85	30	1,464	84	1,595	9,392
1985-86	30	1,296	80	1,435	8,412
1986-87	30	1,412	90	1,607	9,342
1987-88	26	1,070	75	1,170	6,895
1988-89	26	1,107	80	1,154	6,910
1989-90	26	1,198	80	1,295	7,656
1990-91	26	1,115	58	1,189	7,044

[1] Salford & Leeds played 29 matches — their final match was abandoned and not replayed. This match was expunged from league records.
[2] Featherstone R. & Bradford N. played 29 matches — their final match was cancelled following Featherstone's strike.

DIVISION TWO

Season	Matches each club played	Goals	1-Point drop goals	Tries	Pts
1973-74	26	1,054	—	955	4,973
1974-75	26	992	36	919	4,777
1975-76	26	1,034	49	963	5,006
1976-77	26	942	78	1,046	5,100
1977-78	26	976	86	1,020	5,098
1978-79	26	971	114	972	4,972
1979-80	26	1,046	106	1,069	5,405
1980-81	28	1,133	123	1,220	6,049
1981-82	32	1,636	152	1,589	8,189
1982-83	32	1,510	103	1,648	8,067
1983-84	34	1,782	254	1,897	11,406
1984-85	28[1]	1,542	226	1,666	9,974
1985-86	34	1,722	130	2,021	11,658
1986-87	28[1]	1,323	112	1,496	8,742
1987-88	28[2]	1,443	125	1,543	9,183
1988-89	28[1]	1,644	162	1,784	10,586
1989-90	28[3]	1,747	130	1,965	11,484
1990-91	28[3]	1,642	164	1,787	10,596

[1] The 20 clubs played 28 matches each.
[2] The 18 clubs played 28 matches each.
[3] The 21 clubs played 28 matches each.

Half back Frank Cassidy, a Second Division Championship medal in his first full season with Salford.

EIGHTEEN-SEASON TABLE

Widnes continue as the most successful Division One club since the reintroduction of two divisions in 1973 in terms of most points gained. The three times champions head an 18-season table with 696 points from 524 matches.

Although St. Helens have won the title just once, in 1974-75, they are the only club to have finished in the top eight throughout the 18 seasons. In addition to St. Helens, only Widnes, Leeds, Warrington and Castleford have remained in Division One.

Three clubs have spent the entire 18 seasons in Division Two — Batley, Doncaster and Runcorn Highfield.

Bradford Northern, Hull and Leigh were all Division Two champions who went on to win the Division One title a few years after being promoted, while Hull Kingston Rovers, Halifax and Wigan are other former lower grade clubs who later won the major championship.

The highest place gained by a newly-promoted club is third by Hull in 1979-80 after winning the Division Two title with a 100 per cent record the previous season.

Division One champions who were relegated a few seasons after winning the Division One title were Salford, Featherstone Rovers, Leigh, Halifax and Hull K.R.

The records of the five clubs who have appeared in Division One throughout the 18 seasons are as follows:

Castleford's John Joyner has featured in all 18 seasons of the First Division.

	P.	W.	D.	L.	F.	A.	Pts
1. Widnes	524	338	20	166	9,831	6,742	696
2. St. Helens	524	331	20	173	10,990	7,431	682
3. Leeds	523	304	21	198	9,947	7,759	629
4. Warrington	524	283	20	221	8,850	7,621	586
5. Castleford	524	272	25	227	9,935	8,434	569

● Although Wigan and Bradford Northern have had only 17 seasons in Division One their points totals exceed some of the above. Three times champions Wigan have totalled 626 and Bradford, twice champions, have totalled 569.

CHAMPIONSHIP PLAY-OFFS

Following the breakaway from the English Rugby Union, 22 clubs formed the Northern Rugby Football League. Each club played 42 matches and Manningham won the first Championship as league leaders in 1895-96.

This format was then abandoned and replaced by the Yorkshire Senior and Lancashire Senior Combination leagues until 1901-02 when 14 clubs broke away to form the Northern Rugby League with Broughton Rangers winning the first Championship.

The following season two divisions were formed with the Division One title going to Halifax (1902-03), Bradford (1903-04), who won a play-off against Salford 5-0 at Halifax after both teams tied with 52 points, and Oldham (1904-05).

In 1905-06 the two divisions were merged with Leigh taking the Championship as league leaders. They won the title on a percentage basis as the 31 clubs did not play the same number of matches. The following season the top four play-off was introduced as a fairer means of deciding the title.

The top club played the fourth-placed, the second meeting the third, with the higher club having home advantage. The final was staged at a neutral venue.

It was not until 1930-31 that all clubs played the same number of league matches, but not all against each other, the top four play-off being a necessity until the reintroduction of two divisions in 1962-63.

This spell of two division football lasted only two seasons and the restoration of the Championship table brought about the introduction of a top-16 play-off, this format continuing until the reappearance of two divisions in 1973-74.

Since then the Championship Trophy has been awarded to the leaders of the First Division, with the Second Division champions receiving a silver bowl.

Slalom Lager launched a three-year sponsorship deal of the Championship and the Premiership in 1980-81 in a £215,000 package, extending the deal for another three years from 1983-84 for £270,000. From 1986-87, the sponsorship was taken over by brewers Bass, under the Stones Bitter banner, in a new £400,000 three-year deal, renewed for a further three years from 1989-90 for £750,000.

CHAMPIONSHIP PLAY-OFF FINALS

Season	Winners		Runners-up		Venue	Attendance	Receipts
Top Four Play-Offs							
1906-07	Halifax	18	Oldham	3	Huddersfield	13,200	£722
1907-08	Hunslet	7	Oldham	7	Salford	14,000	£690
Replay	Hunslet	12	Oldham	2	Wakefield	14,054	£800
1908-09	Wigan	7	Oldham	3	Salford	12,000	£630
1909-10	Oldham	13	Wigan	7	Broughton	10,850	£520
1910-11	Oldham	20	Wigan	7	Broughton	15,543	£717
1911-12	Huddersfield	13	Wigan	5	Halifax	15,000	£591
1912-13	Huddersfield	29	Wigan	2	Wakefield	17,000	£914
1913-14	Salford	5	Huddersfield	3	Leeds	8,091	£474
1914-15	Huddersfield	35	Leeds	2	Wakefield	14,000	£750
COMPETITION SUSPENDED DURING WAR TIME							
1919-20	Hull	3	Huddersfield	2	Leeds	12,900	£1,615
1920-21	Hull	16	Hull K.R.	14	Leeds	10,000	£1,320
1921-22	Wigan	13	Oldham	2	Broughton	26,000	£1,825
1922-23	Hull K.R.	15	Huddersfield	5	Leeds	14,000	£1,370
1923-24	Batley	13	Wigan	7	Broughton	13,729	£968
1924-25	Hull K.R.	9	Swinton	5	Rochdale	21,580	£1,504
1925-26	Wigan	22	Warrington	10	St. Helens	20,000	£1,100
1926-27	Swinton	13	St. Helens Recs.	8	Warrington	24,432	£1,803
1927-28	Swinton	11	Featherstone R.	0	Oldham	15,451	£1,136
1928-29	Huddersfield	2	Leeds	0	Halifax	25,604	£2,028
1929-30	Huddersfield	2	Leeds	2	Wakefield	32,095	£2,111
Replay	Huddersfield	10	Leeds	0	Halifax	18,563	£1,319
1930-31	Swinton	14	Leeds	7	Wigan	31,000	£2,100
1931-32	St. Helens	9	Huddersfield	5	Wakefield	19,386	£943
1932-33	Salford	15	Swinton	5	Wigan	18,000	£1,053
1933-34	Wigan	15	Salford	3	Warrington	31,564	£2,114
1934-35	Swinton	14	Warrington	3	Wigan	27,700	£1,710
1935-36	Hull	21	Widnes	2	Huddersfield	17,276	£1,208

Season	Winners		Runners-up		Venue	Attendance	Receipts
1936-37	Salford	13	Warrington	11	Wigan	31,500	£2,000
1937-38	Hunslet	8	Leeds	2	Elland Rd., Leeds	54,112	£3,572
1938-39	Salford	8	Castleford	6	Man. C. FC	69,504	£4,301

WAR-TIME EMERGENCY PLAY-OFFS

For the first two seasons the Yorkshire League and Lancashire League champions met in a two-leg final as follows:

1939-40	Swinton	13	Bradford N.	21	Swinton	4,800	£237
	Bradford N.	16	Swinton	9	Bradford	11,721	£570

Bradford N. won 37-22 on aggregate

1940-41	Wigan	6	Bradford N.	17	Wigan	11,245	£640
	Bradford N.	28	Wigan	9	Bradford	20,205	£1,148

Bradford N. won 45-15 on aggregate

For the remainder of the War the top four in the War League played-off as follows:

1941-42	Dewsbury	13	Bradford N.	0	Leeds	18,000	£1,121
1942-43	Dewsbury	11	Halifax	3	Dewsbury	7,000	£400
	Halifax	13	Dewsbury	22	Halifax	9,700	£683

Dewsbury won 33-16 on aggregate but the Championship was declared null and void because they had played an ineligible player

1943-44	Wigan	13	Dewsbury	9	Wigan	14,000	£915
	Dewsbury	5	Wigan	12	Dewsbury	9,000	£700

Wigan won 25-14 on aggregate

1944-45	Halifax	9	Bradford N.	2	Halifax	9,426	£955
	Bradford N.	24	Halifax	11	Bradford	16,000	£1,850

Bradford N. won 26-20 on aggregate

1945-46	Wigan	13	Huddersfield	4	Man. C. FC	67,136	£8,387
1946-47	Wigan	13	Dewsbury	4	Man. C. FC	40,599	£5,895
1947-48	Warrington	15	Bradford N.	5	Man. C. FC	69,143	£9,792
1948-49	Huddersfield	13	Warrington	12	Man. C. FC	75,194	£11,073
1949-50	Wigan	20	Huddersfield	2	Man. C. FC	65,065	£11,500
1950-51	Workington T.	26	Warrington	11	Man. C. FC	61,618	£10,993
1951-52	Wigan	13	Bradford N.	6	Huddersfield Town FC	48,684	£8,215
1952-53	St. Helens	24	Halifax	14	Man. C. FC	51,083	£11,503
1953-54	Warrington	8	Halifax	7	Man. C. FC	36,519	£9,076
1954-55	Warrington	7	Oldham	3	Man. C. FC	49,434	£11,516
1955-56	Hull	10	Halifax	9	Man. C. FC	36,675	£9,179
1956-57	Oldham	15	Hull	14	Bradford	62,199	£12,054
1957-58	Hull	20	Workington T.	3	Bradford	57,699	£11,149
1958-59	St. Helens	44	Hunslet	22	Bradford	52,560	£10,146
1959-60	Wigan	27	Wakefield T.	3	Bradford	83,190	£14,482
1960-61	Leeds	25	Warrington	10	Bradford	52,177	£10,475
1961-62	Huddersfield	14	Wakefield T.	5	Bradford	37,451	£7,979

TWO DIVISIONS 1962-63 and 1963-64

Top Sixteen Play-Offs

1964-65	Halifax	15	St. Helens	7	Swinton	20,786	£6,141
1965-66	St. Helens	35	Halifax	12	Swinton	30,634	£8,750
1966-67	Wakefield T.	7	St. Helens	7	Leeds	20,161	£6,702
Replay	Wakefield T.	21	St. Helens	9	Swinton	33,537	£9,800
1967-68	Wakefield T.	17	Hull K.R.	10	Leeds	22,586	£7,697
1968-69	Leeds	16	Castleford	14	Bradford	28,442	£10,130
1969-70	St. Helens	24	Leeds	12	Bradford	26,358	£9,791
1970-71	St. Helens	16	Wigan	12	Swinton	21,745	£10,200
1971-72	Leeds	9	St. Helens	5	Swinton	24,055	£9,513
1972-73	Dewsbury	22	Leeds	13	Bradford	18,889	£9,479

CHAMPIONSHIP FINAL . . . . A 10-YEAR REVIEW

1961-62 HUDDERSFIELD 14 Dyson (4g); Breen, Deighton, Booth, Wicks (1t); Davies, Smales (1t); Slevin, Close, Noble, Kilroy, Bowman, Ramsden
WAKEFIELD T. 5 Round; F. Smith, Skene, N. Fox (1t, 1g), Hirst; Poynton, Holliday; Wilkinson, Kosanovic, Firth, Briggs, Vines, Turner
Referee: N. T. Railton (Wigan)

TWO DIVISIONS — NO PLAY-OFFS 1963 and 1964

1964-65 HALIFAX 15 James (3g); Jackson (1t), Burnett (2t), Kellett, Freeman; Robinson, Daley; Roberts, Harrison, Scroby, Fogerty, Dixon, Renilson
ST. HELENS 7 F. Barrow; Harvey, Vollenhoven, Northey, Killeen (1t, 2g); Murphy, Smith; Tembey (Warlow), Dagnall, Watson, French, Mantle, Laughton
Referee: D. S. Brown (Dewsbury)

1965-66 ST. HELENS 35 F. Barrow; A. Barrow (1t), Murphy (1g), Benyon, Killeen (3t, 6g); Harvey; Bishop; Halsall (3t), Sayer, Watson, French, Warlow (Hitchen), Mantle
HALIFAX 12 Cooper (3g); Jones, Burnett, Dixon, Freeman; Robinson, Baker (1t); Roberts, Harrison, Scroby, Ramshaw (Duffy), Fogerty (1t), Renilson
Referee: J. Manley (Warrington)

1966-67 WAKEFIELD T. 7 Cooper; Hirst, Brooke, N. Fox (2g), Coetzer; Poynton, Owen (1t); Bath, Prior, Campbell, Clarkson, Haigh, D. Fox
ST. HELENS 7 F. Barrow; Vollenhoven, A. Barrow, Smith, Killeen (2g); Douglas, Bishop; Warlow, Sayer, Watson (1t), French, Hogan (Robinson), Mantle
Referee: G. Philpott (Leeds)

Replay: WAKEFIELD T. 21 Cooper; Hirst (1t), Brooke (2t), N. Fox (3g), Coetzer; Poynton (1t), Owen (1t); Bath, Prior, Campbell, Clarkson, Haigh, D. Fox
ST. HELENS 9 F. Barrow; Vollenhoven (1t), A. Barrow, Smith, Killeen (2g); Douglas, Bishop (1g); Warlow, Sayer, Watson, French, Hogan, Mantle
Referee: J. Manley (Warrington)

1967-68 WAKEFIELD T. 17 G. Cooper; Coetzer, Brooke, N. Fox (1t, 2g), Batty; Poynton (1g), Owen (1t); Jeanes (1t), Shepherd, D. Fox (1g), Haigh, McLeod, Hawley
HULL K.R. 10 Wainwright; C. Young, Moore (1t), A. Burwell, Longstaff (1t); Millward (2g), C. Cooper; L. Foster, Flanagan, Mennell, Lowe, Major, F. Foster
Referee: D. S. Brown (Preston)

1968-69 LEEDS 16 Risman (4g); Cowan (1t), Hynes, Watson, Atkinson (1t); Shoebottom, Seabourne (Langley); Clark (Hick), Crosby, K. Eyre, Joyce, Ramsey (1g), Batten
CASTLEFORD 14 Edwards; Briggs, Howe, Thomas, Lowndes; Hardisty (1t, 1g), Hepworth; Hartley, C. Dickinson (1t), J. Ward, Redfearn (3g), Lockwood, Reilly (Fox)
Referee: W. H. Thompson (Huddersfield)

1969-70 ST. HELENS 24 F. Barrow; L. Jones, Benyon, Walsh (1t, 2g), E. Prescott (2t), Myler, Heaton; Halsall, Sayer (1t), Watson, Mantle, E. Chisnall, Coslett (4g)
LEEDS 12 Holmes (3g); Alan Smith (1t), Hynes, Cowan (1t), Atkinson; Shoebottom, Seabourne; J. Burke, Crosby, A. Eyre, Ramsey (Hick), Eccles, Batten
Referee: W. H. Thompson (Huddersfield)

1970-71 ST. HELENS 16 Pimblett; L. Jones, Benyon (1t), Walsh, Blackwood (1t); Whittle, Heaton; J. Stephens, A. Karalius, Rees (Wanbon), Mantle, E. Chisnall, Coslett (5g)
WIGAN 12 Tyrer (1g); Kevin O'Loughlin; Francis, Rowe, Wright; D. Hill, Ayres, Hogan, Clarke, Fletcher, Ashurst (1t, 2g), Robinson (1t) (Cunningham), Laughton
Referee: E. Lawrinson (Warrington)

1971-72 LEEDS 9 Holmes (Hick); Alan Smith, Langley, Dyl, Atkinson (1t); Hardisty, Barham; Clawson (3g), Ward, Fisher (Pickup), Cookson, Eccles, Batten
ST. HELENS 5 Pimblett; L. Jones (Whittle), Benyon, Walsh (1g), Wilson; Kelly, Heaton; Rees, Greenall (1t), J. Stephens, Mantle, E. Chisnall, Coslett
Referee: S. Shepherd (Oldham)

1972-73 DEWSBURY 22 Rushton; Ashcroft, Clark, N. Stephenson (5g, 1t), Day; Agar (1t), A. Bates; Beverley (Taylor), M. Stephenson (2t), Lowe, Grayshon, J. Bates, Whittington
LEEDS 13 Holmes; Alan Smith, Hynes (1g), Dyl (1t), Atkinson; Hardisty, Hepworth; Clawson (1g), Fisher (Ward), Clarkson (Langley), Cookson (1t), Eccles (1t), Haigh
Referee: H. G. Hunt (Prestbury)

LEAGUE LEADERS TROPHY

While the top 16 play-off decided the Championship between 1964 and 1973 it was decided to honour the top club in the league table with a League Leaders Trophy. The winners were:

1964-65 St. Helens
1965-66 St. Helens
1966-67 Leeds
1967-68 Leeds
1968-69 Leeds
1969-70 Leeds
1970-71 Wigan
1971-72 Leeds
1972-73 Warrington

CLUB CHAMPIONSHIP (Merit Table)

With the reintroduction of two divisions, a complicated merit table and Division Two preliminary rounds system produced a 16-club play-off with the Club Championship finalists as follows:

Season	Winners		Runners-up		Venue	Attendance	Receipts
1973-74	Warrington	13	St. Helens	12	Wigan	18,040	£10,032

This format lasted just one season and was replaced by the Premiership.

CLUB CHAMPIONSHIP FINAL . . . . A REVIEW

1973-74 WARRINGTON 13 Whitehead (2g); M. Philbin (1t), Noonan (1t), Pickup (Lowe), Bevan; Whittle, A. Murphy; D. Chisnall, Ashcroft, Brady (1t), Wanbon (Gaskell), Mather, B. Philbin

ST. HELENS 12 Pimblett; Brown, Wills, Wilson (2t), Mathias; Eckersley, Heaton; Mantle, Liptrot, M. Murphy, E. Chisnall (Warlow), Nicholls, Coslett (3g)
Referee: P. Geraghty (York)

PREMIERSHIP

With the further reintroduction of two divisions in 1973-74, it was declared that the title of Champions would be awarded to the leaders of the First Division.

However, it was also decided to continue the tradition of an end-of-season play-off, the winners to receive the newly instituted Premiership Trophy.

*For full details of the Premiership Trophy see the CUPS section.

David Eckersley, stand off for 1974 Club Championship runners-up St. Helens.

COUNTY LEAGUE

In the early seasons of the code the Lancashire Senior and Yorkshire Senior Competitions, not to be confused with the later reserve leagues, were major leagues. The winners were:

	Lancashire SC	Yorkshire SC
1895-96	Runcorn	Manningham
1896-97	Broughton Rangers	Brighouse Rangers
1897-98	Oldham	Hunslet
1898-99	Broughton Rangers	Batley
1899-00	Runcorn	Bradford
1900-01	Oldham	Bradford
1901-02	Wigan	Leeds

With the introduction of two divisions in 1902-03, the county league competitions were scrapped until they reappeared as the Lancashire League and Yorkshire League in 1907-08. Clubs from the same county played each other home and away to decide the titles. These games were included in the main championship table along with inter-county fixtures. The county leagues continued until 1970, with the exception of war-time interruptions and two seasons when regional leagues with play-offs operated during the 1960s two division era. They were then abolished when a more integrated fixture formula meant clubs did not play all others from the same county, this system later being replaced by the present two division structure.

LEAGUE LEADERS .... A REVIEW

The following is a list of the League leaders since the formation of the Northern Union, with the exception of the three eras of two-division football. From 1896 to 1901, the League was divided into a Lancashire Senior Competition and a Yorkshire Senior Competition, winners of both leagues being listed for those seasons.

From 1905 to 1930 not all the clubs played each other, the League being determined on a percentage basis.

LSC — Lancashire Senior Competition
LL — Lancashire League
YSC — Yorkshire Senior Competition
YL — Yorkshire League
WEL — War Emergency League
* Two points deducted for breach of professional rules
† Decided on a percentage basis after Belle Vue Rangers withdrew shortly before the start of the season.

		P.	W.	D.	L.	F.	A.	Pts.	
1895-96	Manningham	42	33	0	9	367	158	66	
1896-97	Broughton R.	26	19	5	2	201	52	43	LSC
	Brighouse R.	30	22	4	4	213	68	48	YSC
1897-98	Oldham	26	23	1	2	295	94	47	LSC
	Hunslet	30	22	4	4	327	117	48	YSC
1898-99	Broughton R.	26	21	0	5	277	74	42	LSC
	Batley	30	23	2	5	279	75	48	YSC
1899-00	Runcorn	26	22	2	2	232	33	46	LSC
	Bradford	30	24	2	4	324	98	50	YSC
1900-01	Oldham	26	22	1	3	301	67	45	LSC
	Bradford	30	26	1	3	387	100	51*	YSC
1901-02	Broughton R.	26	21	1	4	285	112	43	
1902-05	Two Divisions								
1905-06	Leigh	30	23	2	5	245	130	48	80.00%
1906-07	Halifax	34	27	2	5	649	229	56	82.35%
1907-08	Oldham	32	28	2	2	396	121	58	90.62%
1908-09	Wigan	32	28	0	4	706	207	56	87.50%
1909-10	Oldham	34	29	2	3	604	184	60	88.23%
1910-11	Wigan	34	28	1	5	650	205	57	83.82%
1911-12	Huddersfield	36	31	1	4	996	238	63	87.50%
1912-13	Huddersfield	32	28	0	4	732	217	56	87.50%
1913-14	Huddersfield	34	28	2	4	830	258	58	85.29%
1914-15	Huddersfield	34	28	4	2	888	235	60	88.24%
1915-18	Competitive matches suspended during First World War								
1918-19	Rochdale H.	12	9	0	3	92	52	18	75.00% LL
	Hull	16	13	0	3	392	131	26	81.25% YL
1919-20	Huddersfield	34	29	0	5	759	215	58	85.29%
1920-21	Hull K.R.	32	24	1	7	432	233	49	76.56%
1921-22	Oldham	36	29	1	6	521	201	59	81.94%
1922-23	Hull	36	30	0	6	587	304	60	83.33%
1923-24	Wigan	38	31	0	7	824	228	62	81.57%
1924-25	Swinton	36	30	0	6	499	224	60	83.33%
1925-26	Wigan	38	29	3	6	641	310	61	80.26%
1926-27	St. Helens R.	38	29	3	6	544	235	61	80.26%
1927-28	Swinton	36	27	3	6	439	189	57	79.16%

		P.	W.	D.	L.	F.	A.	Pts.	
1928-29	Huddersfield	38	26	4	8	476	291	56	73.68%
1929-30	St. Helens	40	27	1	12	549	295	55	68.75%
1930-31	Swinton	38	31	2	5	504	156	64	
1931-32	Huddersfield	38	30	1	7	636	368	61	
1932-33	Salford	38	31	2	5	751	165	64	
1933-34	Salford	38	31	1	6	715	281	63	
1934-35	Swinton	38	30	1	7	468	175	61	
1935-36	Hull	38	30	1	7	607	306	61	
1936-37	Salford	38	29	3	6	529	196	61	
1937-38	Hunslet	36	25	3	8	459	301	53	
1938-39	Salford	40	30	3	7	551	191	63	
1939-40	Swinton	22	17	0	5	378	158	34	WEL LL
	Bradford N.	28	21	0	7	574	302	42	WEL YL
1940-41	Wigan	16	15	1	0	297	71	31	WEL LL
	Bradford N.	25	23	1	1	469	126	47	WEL YL
1941-42	Dewsbury	24	19	1	4	431	172	39	81.25% WEL
1942-43	Wigan	16	13	0	3	301	142	26	81.25% WEL
1943-44	Wakefield T.	22	19	0	3	359	97	38	86.36% WEL
1944-45	Bradford N.	20	17	0	3	337	69	34	85.00% WEL
1945-46	Wigan	36	29	2	5	783	219	60	
1946-47	Wigan	36	29	1	6	567	196	59	
1947-48	Wigan	36	31	1	4	776	258	63	
1948-49	Warrington	36	31	0	5	728	247	62	
1949-50	Wigan	36	31	1	4	853	320	63	
1950-51	Warrington	36	30	0	6	738	250	60	
1951-52	Bradford N.	36	28	1	7	758	326	57	
1952-53	St. Helens	36	32	2	2	769	273	66	
1953-54	Halifax	36	30	2	4	538	219	62	
1954-55	Warrington	36	29	2	5	718	321	60	
1955-56	Warrington	34	27	1	6	712	349	55	80.88% †
1956-57	Oldham	38	33	0	5	893	365	66	
1957-58	Oldham	38	33	1	4	803	415	67	
1958-59	St. Helens	38	31	1	6	1,005	450	63	
1959-60	St. Helens	38	34	1	3	947	343	69	
1960-61	Leeds	36	30	0	6	620	258	60	
1961-62	Wigan	36	32	1	3	885	283	65	
1962-64	Two Divisions								
1964-65	St. Helens	34	28	0	6	621	226	56	
1965-66	St. Helens	34	28	1	5	521	275	57	
1966-67	Leeds	34	29	0	5	704	373	58	
1967-68	Leeds	34	28	0	6	720	271	56	
1968-69	Leeds	34	29	2	3	775	358	60	
1969-70	Leeds	34	30	0	4	674	314	60	
1970-71	Wigan	34	30	0	4	662	308	60	
1971-72	Leeds	34	28	2	4	750	325	58	
1972-73	Warrington	34	27	2	5	816	400	56	

Appointed Hull coach in September 1990, Noel Cleal enjoys his first trophy success in the 1991 Stones Bitter Premiership final.

COACHES

Between June 1990 and end of May 1991 a total of 17 clubs made first team coaching changes, some more than once. Eleven new coaches had their first British senior appointments bringing the total of coaches since the start of the 1974-75 season to 232.

This chapter is a compilation of those appointments, featuring a club-by-club coaches register, an index, plus a detailed dossier of the 1990-91 coaches.

CLUB-BY-CLUB REGISTER

The following is a list of coaches each club has had since the start of the 1974-75 season.

BARROW

Frank Foster	May 73 - Apr. 83
Tommy Dawes	May 83 - Feb. 85
Tommy Bishop	Feb. 85 - Apr. 85
Ivor Kelland	May 85 - Feb. 87
Dennis Jackson	Feb. 87 - Nov. 87
Rod Reddy	Nov. 87 - Nov. 89
Dennis Jackson	Nov. 89 - Apr. 90
Steve Norton	May 90 - Feb. 91
Paul Kavanagh	Feb. 91 -

BATLEY

Don Fox	Nov. 72 - Oct. 74
Alan Hepworth	Nov. 74 - Apr. 75
Dave Cox	May 75 - June 75
Trevor Walker	June 75 - June 77
Albert Fearnley	June 77 - Oct. 77
Dave Stockwell	Oct. 77 - June 79
*Tommy Smales	June 79 - Oct. 81
Trevor Lowe	Oct. 81 - May 82
Terry Crook	June 82 - Nov. 84
George Pieniazek	Nov. 84 - Nov. 85
Brian Lockwood	Nov. 85 - May 87
Paul Daley	July 87 - Apr. 90
Keith Rayne	May 90 - Apr. 91

Ex-forward

BRADFORD NORTHERN

Ian Brooke	Jan. 73 - Sept. 75
Roy Francis	Oct. 75 - Apr. 77
Peter Fox	Apr. 77 - May 85
Barry Seabourne	May 85 - Sep. 89
Ron Willey	Oct. 89 - Mar. 90
David Hobbs	Mar. 90 -

BRAMLEY

Arthur Keegan	May 73 - Sept. 76
Peter Fox	Sept. 76 - Apr. 77
*Tommy Smales	May 77 - Dec. 77
Les Pearce	Jan. 78 - Oct. 78
Don Robinson	Oct. 78 - May 79
Dave Stockwell	June 79 - June 80
Keith Hepworth	June 80 - May 82
Maurice Bamford	May 82 - Oct. 83
Peter Jarvis	Oct. 83 - Apr. 85
Ken Loxton	Apr. 85 - Dec. 85
Allan Agar	Dec. 85 - Apr. 87
Chris Forster	June 87 - Nov. 87
Tony Fisher	Nov. 87 - Feb. 89
Barry Johnson	Mar. 89 - Dec. 90
John Kear	Dec. 90 - Jan. 91
Roy Dickinson	Jan. 91 -

Ex-forward

CARLISLE

Allan Agar	May 81 - June 82
Mick Morgan	July 82 - Feb. 83
John Atkinson	Feb. 83 - Feb. 86
Alan Kellett	Feb. 86 - May 86
Roy Lester	June 86 - Nov. 88
Tommy Dawes	Dec. 88 - Jan. 90
Cameron Bell	Feb. 90 -

CASTLEFORD

Dave Cox	Apr. 74 - Nov. 74
*Malcolm Reilly	Dec. 74 - May 87
Dave Sampson	May 87 - Apr. 88
Darryl Van de Velde	July 88 -

Shortly after his appointment Reilly returned to Australia to fulfil his contract before resuming at Castleford early the next season.

CHORLEY

Stan Gittins	June 89 - Apr. 90
Bob Eccles	May 90 -

DEWSBURY

Maurice Bamford	June 74 - Oct. 74
Alan Hardisty	Oct. 74 - June 75
Dave Cox	June 75 - July 77
Ron Hill	July 77 - Dec. 77
Lewis Jones	Dec. 77 - Apr. 78
Jeff Grayshon	May 78 - Oct. 78
Alan Lockwood	Oct. 78 - Oct. 80
Bernard Watson	Oct. 80 - Oct. 82
Ray Abbey	Nov. 82 - Apr. 83
*Tommy Smales	May 83 - Feb. 84
Jack Addy	Feb. 84 - Jan. 87
Dave Busfield	Jan. 87 - Apr. 87
Terry Crook	Apr. 87 - Dec. 88
Maurice Bamford	Dec. 88 - Dec. 90
Jack Addy	Dec. 90 -

*Ex-forward

DONCASTER

Ted Strawbridge	Feb. 73 - Apr. 75
Derek Edwards	July 75 - Nov. 76
Don Robson	Nov. 76 - Sept. 77
Trevor Lowe	Sept. 77 - Apr. 79
*Tommy Smales	Feb. 78 - Apr. 79
Billy Yates	Apr. 79 - May 80
Don Vines	Sept. 79 - Jan. 80
Bill Kenny	June 80 - May 81
Alan Rhodes	Aug. 81 - Mar. 83
Clive Sullivan	Mar. 83 - May 84
John Sheridan	June 84 - Nov. 87
Graham Heptinstall	Nov. 87 - Jan. 88
John Sheridan	Jan. 88 - Apr. 89
Dave Sampson	May 89 -

*Ex-forward, who shared the coaching post with Trevor Lowe for just over a year.

FEATHERSTONE ROVERS

*Tommy Smales	July 74 - Sept. 74
Keith Goulding	Sept. 74 - Jan. 76
†Tommy Smales	Feb. 76 - May 76
Keith Cotton	June 76 - Dec. 77
Keith Goulding	Dec. 77 - May 78

Terry Clawson	July 78 - Nov. 78
†Tommy Smales	Nov. 78 - Apr. 79
Paul Daley	May 79 - Jan. 81
Vince Farrar	Feb. 81 - Nov. 82
Allan Agar	Dec. 82 - Oct. 85
George Pieniazek	Nov. 85 - Nov. 86
Paul Daley	Nov. 86 - Apr. 87
Peter Fox	May 87 -

*Ex-forward
†Ex-scrum half

FULHAM

Reg Bowden	July 80 - June 84
Roy Lester	June 84 - Apr. 86
Bill Goodwin	Apr. 86 - May 88
*Bev Risman	May 88 - Feb. 89
Phil Sullivan	Feb. 89 - Mar. 89
Bill Goodwin	Mar. 89 - Apr 89
Ross Strudwick	June 89 -

*Team manager

HALIFAX

Derek Hallas	Aug. 74 - Oct. 74
Les Pearce	Oct. 74 - Apr. 76
Alan Kellett	May 76 - Apr. 77
Jim Crellin	June 77 - Oct. 77
Harry Fox	Oct. 77 - Feb. 78
Maurice Bamford	Feb. 78 - May 80
Mick Blacker	June 80 - June 82
Ken Roberts	June 82 - Sept. 82
Colin Dixon	Sept. 82 - Nov. 84
Chris Anderson	Nov. 84 - May 88
Graham Eadie	May 88 - Aug 88
Ross Strudwick	Aug. 88 - Feb. 89
Alan Hardisty	Feb. 89 - Apr. 89
John Dorahy	June 89 - Aug. 90
Peter Roe	Aug. 90 - May 91
Roger Millward	May 91 -

HUDDERSFIELD

Brian Smith	Jan. 73 - Mar. 76
Keith Goulding	Mar. 76 - Dec. 76
Bob Tomlinson	Jan. 77 - May 77
Neil Fox	June 77 - Feb. 78
*Roy Francis	-
Keith Goulding	May 78 - July 79

Roger Millward, who left Hull K.R. in May 1991 after a 25-year career as player and coach.

Ian Brooke	July 79 - Mar. 80
Maurice Bamford	May 80 - May 81
Les Sheard	June 81 - Nov. 82
Dave Mortimer	Nov. 82 - Aug. 83
Mel Bedford	Aug. 83 - Nov. 83
Brian Lockwood	Nov. 83 - Feb. 85
Chris Forster	Feb. 85 - Dec. 86
Jack Addy	Jan. 87 - Mar. 88
Allen Jones ⎫ Neil Whittaker ⎭	Mar. 88 - Nov. 88
Nigel Stephenson	Nov. 88 - Mar. 90
Barry Seabourne	Mar. 90 - Feb. 91
Mick Blacker ⎫ Francis Jarvis ⎭	Feb. 91 -

Although Roy Francis was appointed he was unable to take over and Dave Heppleston stood in until the next appointment.

HULL

David Doyle-Davidson	May 74 - Dec. 77
Arthur Bunting	Jan. 78 - Dec. 85
Kenny Foulkes	Dec. 85 - May 86
Len Casey	June 86 - Mar. 88
Tony Dean ⎫ Keith Hepworth ⎭	Mar. 88 - Apr. 88
*Brian Smith	July 88 - Jan. 91
*Noel Cleal	Sept. 90 -

Joint coaches Sept. 90 - Jan 91.

212

HULL KINGSTON ROVERS

Arthur Bunting	Feb. 72 - Nov. 75
Harry Poole	Dec. 75 - Mar. 77
Roger Millward	Mar. 77 - May 91
George Fairbairn	May 91 -

HUNSLET

Paul Daley	Apr. 74 - Aug. 78
Bill Ramsey	Aug. 78 - Dec. 79
Drew Broatch	Dec. 79 - Apr. 81
Paul Daley	Apr. 81 - Nov. 85
*Peter Jarvis	Nov. 85 - Apr. 88
*David Ward	July 86 - Apr. 88
Nigel Stephenson	Jun. 88 - Oct. 88
Jack Austin ⎫ John Wolford ⎭	Oct. 88 - Jan. 89
David Ward	Jan. 89 - May 89
Graeme Jennings	Sept. 89 - Apr. 90
Paul Daley	May 90 -

Joint coaches from July 1986.

KEIGHLEY

Alan Kellett	Jan. 73 - May 75
Roy Sabine	Aug. 75 - Oct. 77
Barry Seabourne	Nov. 77 - Mar. 79
Albert Fearnley (Mgr)	Apr. 79 - Aug. 79
Alan Kellett	Apr. 79 - Apr. 80
Albert Fearnley	May 80 - Feb. 81
Bakary Diabira	Feb. 81 - Sept. 82
Lee Greenwood	Sept. 82 - Oct. 83
Geoff Peggs	Nov. 83 - Sept. 85
Peter Roe	Sept. 85 - July 86
Colin Dixon	July 86 - June 89
Les Coulter	July 86 - Apr. 90
Tony Fisher	June 90 -

LEEDS

Roy Francis	June 74 - May 75
Syd Hynes	June 75 - Apr. 81
Robin Dewhurst	June 81 - Oct. 83
Maurice Bamford	Nov. 83 - Feb. 85
Malcolm Clift	Feb. 85 - May 85
Peter Fox	May 85 - Dec. 86
Maurice Bamford	Dec. 86 - Apr. 88
Malcolm Reilly	Aug. 88 - Sept. 89
David Ward	Sept. 89 - May 91
Doug Laughton	May 91 -

LEIGH

Eddie Cheetham	May 74 - Mar. 75
Kevin Ashcroft	June 75 - Jan. 77
Bill Kindon	Jan. 77 - Apr. 77
John Mantle	Apr. 77 - Nov. 78
Tom Grainey	Nov. 78 - Dec. 80
*Alex Murphy	Nov. 80 - June 82
*Colin Clarke	June 82 - Dec. 82
Peter Smethurst	Dec. 82 - Apr. 83
Tommy Bishop	June 83 - June 84
John Woods	June 84 - May 85
Alex Murphy	Feb. 85 - Nov. 85
Tommy Dickens	Nov. 85 - Dec. 86
Billy Benyon	Dec. 86 - Mar. 90
Alex Murphy	Mar. 90 -

From Dec. 80 to June 82 Clarke was officially appointed coach and Murphy manager

NOTTINGHAM CITY

Mick Blacker	May 84 - Oct. 85
Bill Kirkbride	Nov. 85 - Mar. 86
Steve Dennison	Apr. 86 - Dec. 86
Jim Crellin	Dec. 86 - June 88
Billy Platt	July 88 - Dec. 88
Steve Nash	Dec. 88 - Feb. 89
Lee Greenwood	Feb. 89 - Mar. 90
Mel Wibberley	Mar. 90 - Feb. 91
Arnold Hema	Feb. 91 -

OLDHAM

Jim Challinor	Aug. 74 - Dec. 76
Terry Ramshaw	Jan. 77 - Feb. 77
Dave Cox	July 77 - Dec. 78
Graham Starkey (Mgr)	Jan. 79 - May 81
Bill Francis	June 79 - Dec. 80
Frank Myler	May 81 - Apr. 83
Peter Smethurst	Apr. 83 - Feb. 84
Frank Barrow	Feb. 84 - Feb. 84
Brian Gartland	Mar. 84 - June 84
Frank Myler	June 84 - Apr. 87
*Eric Fitzsimons	June 87 - Nov. 88
*Mal Graham	June 87 - Apr. 88
Tony Barrow	Nov. 88 - Jan. 91
John Fieldhouse	Jan. 91 - Apr. 91
Peter Tunks	Apr. 91 -

Joint coaches June 87 - Apr. 88

ROCHDALE HORNETS

Frank Myler	May 71 - Oct. 74
Graham Starkey	Oct. 74 - Nov. 75
Henry Delooze	Nov. 75 - Nov. 76
Kel Coslett	Nov. 76 - Aug. 79
Paul Longstaff	Sept. 79 - May 81
Terry Fogerty	May 81 - Jan. 82
Dick Bonser	Jan. 82 - May 82
Bill Kirkbride	June 82 - Sept. 84
Charlie Birdsall	Sept. 84 - Apr. 86
Eric Fitzsimons	June 86 - June 87
Eric Hughes	June 87 - June 88
Jim Crellin	June 88 - June 89
Allan Agar	July 89 - Jan. 91
Neil Holding	Jan. 91 - Apr. 91
Stan Gittins	Apr. 91 -

RUNCORN HIGHFIELD

Terry Gorman	Aug. 74 - May 77
Geoff Fletcher	Aug. 77 - June 86
Frank Wilson	July 86 - Nov. 86
Arthur Daley } Paul Woods }	Nov. 86 - Apr. 87
Bill Ashurst	Apr. 87 - Jan. 89
John Cogger	Jan. 89 - Feb. 89
Geoff Fletcher	Feb. 89 - Apr. 89
Dave Chisnall	June 89 - Oct. 90
Alan Bishop	Oct. 90 -

RYEDALE-YORK

Keith Goulding	Nov. 73 - Sept. 74
Gary Cooper	Dec. 74 - Sept. 76
Mal Dixon	Sept. 76 - Dec. 78
Paul Daley	Jan. 79 - May 79
David Doyle-Davidson	July 79 - July 80
Bill Kirkbride	Aug. 80 - Apr. 82
Alan Hardisty	May 82 - Jan. 83
Phil Lowe	Mar. 83 - Mar. 87
Danny Sheehan	Mar. 87 - Apr. 88
Gary Stephens	Apr. 88 -

ST. HELENS

Eric Ashton	May 74 - May 80
Kel Coslett	June 80 - May 82
Billy Benyon	May 82 - Nov. 85
Alex Murphy	Nov. 85 - Jan. 90
Mike McClennan	Feb. 90 -

SALFORD

Les Bettinson	Dec. 73 - Mar. 77
Colin Dixon	Mar. 77 - Jan. 78
Stan McCormick	Feb. 78 - Mar. 78
Alex Murphy	May 78 - Nov. 80
Kevin Ashcroft	Nov. 80 - Mar. 82
Alan McInnes	Mar. 82 - May 82
Malcolm Aspey	May 82 - Oct. 83
Mike Coulman	Oct. 83 - May 84
Kevin Ashcroft	May 84 - Oct. 89
Kevin Tamati	Oct. 89 -

SCARBOROUGH PIRATES

Len Casey	Feb.91 -

SHEFFIELD EAGLES

Alan Rhodes	Apr. 84 - May 86
Gary Hetherington	July 86 -

SWINTON

Austin Rhodes	June 74 - Nov. 75
Bob Fleet	Nov. 75 - Nov. 76
John Stopford	Nov. 76 - Apr. 77
Terry Gorman	June 77 - Nov. 78
Ken Halliwell	Nov. 78 - Dec. 79
Frank Myler	Jan. 80 - May 81
Tom Grainey	May 81 - Oct. 83
Jim Crellin	Nov. 83 - May 86
Bill Holliday } Mike Peers }	June 86 - Oct. 87
Frank Barrow	Oct. 87 - June 89
Jim Crellin	July 89 -

TRAFFORD BOROUGH

Tommy Blakeley	Aug. 74 - Apr. 76
Jim Crellin	May 76 - Mar. 77
Joe Egan Jnr.	Mar. 77 - Oct 77
Albert Fearnley (Mgr)	Nov. 77 - Apr. 79
Bakary Diabira	Nov. 78 - June 79
Graham Rees	June 79 - Mar. 80
Geoff Lyon	July 80 - Aug. 81
Bob Irving	Aug. 81 - Feb. 82
John Mantle	Feb. 82 - Mar. 82
Tommy Dickens	Mar. 82 - Nov. 85
*Stan Gittins	Nov. 85 - June 88
*Mike Peers	June 88 -

Joint coaches Aug. 87 - June 88

WAKEFIELD TRINITY

Peter Fox	June 74 - May 76
Geoff Gunney	June 76 - Nov. 76
Brian Lockwood	Nov. 76 - Jan. 78
Ian Brooke	Jan. 78 - Jan. 79
Bill Kirkbride	Jan. 79 - Apr. 80
Ray Batten	Apr. 80 - May 81
Bill Ashurst	June 81 - Apr. 82
Ray Batten	May 82 - July 83
Derek Turner	July 83 - Feb. 84
Bob Haigh	Feb. 84 - May 84
Geoff Wraith	May 84 - Oct. 84
David Lamming	Oct. 84 - Apr. 85
Len Casey	Apr. 85 - June 86
Tony Dean	June 86 - Dec. 86
Trevor Bailey	Dec. 86 - Apr. 87
David Topliss	May 87 -

WARRINGTON

Alex Murphy	May 71 - May 78
Billy Benyon	June 78 - Mar. 82
Kevin Ashcroft	Mar. 82 - May 84
Reg Bowden	June 84 - Mar. 86
Tony Barrow	Mar. 86 - Nov. 88
Brian Johnson	Nov. 88 -

WHITEHAVEN

Jeff Bawden	May 72 - May 75
Ike Southward	Aug. 75 - June 76
Bill Smith	Aug. 76 - Oct. 78
Ray Dutton	Oct. 78 - Oct. 79
Phil Kitchin	Oct. 79 - Jan. 82
Arnold Walker	Jan. 82 - May 82
Tommy Dawes	June 82 - May 83
Frank Foster	June 83 - June 85
Phil Kitchin	June 85 - Oct. 87
John McFarlane	Oct. 87 - May 88
Barry Smith	July 88 - Sept 89
Eric Fitzsimons	Oct. 89 - Mar. 90
Norman Turley	June 90 - Apr. 91
Jackie Davidson	May 91 -

WIDNES

Vince Karalius	Jan. 72 - May 75
Frank Myler	May 75 - May 78
Doug Laughton	May 78 - Mar. 83
Harry Dawson ⎫ Colin Tyrer ⎭	Mar. 83 - May 83
*Vince Karalius ⎫ Harry Dawson ⎭	May 83 - May 84
Eric Hughes	June 84 - Jan. 86
Doug Laughton	Jan. 86 - May 91

Dawson quit as coach in March 1984 with Karalius continuing as team manager.

WIGAN

Ted Toohey	May 74 - Jan. 75
Joe Coan	Jan. 75 - Sept. 76
Vince Karalius	Sept. 76 - Sept. 79
Kel Coslett	Oct. 79 - Apr. 80
George Fairbairn	Apr. 80 - May 81
Maurice Bamford	May 81 - May 82
Alex Murphy	June 82 - Aug. 84
Colin Clarke ⎫ Alan McInnes ⎭	Aug. 84 - May 86
Graham Lowe	Aug. 86 - June 89
John Monie	Sept. 89 -

WORKINGTON TOWN

Ike Southward	Aug. 73 - June 75
Paul Charlton	June 75 - June 76
Ike Southward	June 76 - Feb. 78
Sol Roper	Feb. 78 - Apr. 80
Keith Irving	Aug. 80 - Oct. 80
Tommy Bishop	Nov. 80 - June 82
Paul Charlton	July 82 - Dec. 82
Dave Cox	Mar. 83 - Mar. 83
Harry Archer/Bill Smith	May 83 - June 84
Bill Smith	June 84 - Apr. 85
Jackie Davidson	Apr. 85 - Jan. 86
Keith Davies	Feb. 86 - Mar. 87
Norman Turley	Mar. 87 - Apr. 88
Maurice Bamford	July 88 - Dec. 88
Phil Kitchin	Dec. 88 - May 90
Ray Ashton	June 90 -

REPRESENTATIVE REGISTER

The following is a list of international and county coaches since 1974-75.

GREAT BRITAIN

Jim Challinor	Dec. 71 - Aug. 74 (Inc. tours)
David Watkins	1977 World Championship
Peter Fox	1978
Eric Ashton	1979 tour
Johnny Whiteley	Aug. 80 - Nov. 82
Frank Myler	Dec. 82 - Aug. 84 (Inc. tour)
Maurice Bamford	Oct. 84 - Dec. 86
Malcolm Reilly	Jan. 87 - (Inc. tours)

ENGLAND

Alex Murphy	Jan. 75 - Nov. 75 (Inc. World Championship tour)
Peter Fox	1976-77
Frank Myler	1977-78
Eric Ashton	1978-79 & 1979-80
Johnny Whiteley	1980-81 & 1981-82
Reg Parker (Mgr)	1984-85

Frank Myler, former coach of Great Britain and England.

WALES

Les Pearce	Jan. 75 - Nov. 75
	(Inc. World Championship tour)
David Watkins Bill Francis }	1976-77
Kel Coslett Bill Francis }	1977-78
Kel Coslett	1978-79 to 1981-82
David Watkins	1982-83, 1984-85

GREAT BRITAIN UNDER-24s
Johnny Whiteley	1976-82
Frank Myler	1983-84

GREAT BRITAIN UNDER-21s
Maurice Bamford	Oct. 84 - Dec. 86
Malcolm Reilly	1986-87, 1987-88, 1989-90
David Topliss	1988-89
Phil Larder	1990-91

CUMBRIA
Ike Southward	1975-76
Frank Foster	1976-77 & 1977-78
Sol Roper	1978-79
Frank Foster	1979-80
Phil Kitchin	1980-81 to 1981-82
Frank Foster	1982-83
Jackie Davidson	1985-86
Phil Kitchin	1986-87 to 1990-91

LANCASHIRE
Alex Murphy	1973-74 to 1977-78
Eric Ashton	1978-79 to 1979-80
Tom Grainey	1980-81 to 1981-82
Doug Laughton	1982-83
Alex Murphy	1985-86 to 1987-88
Doug Laughton	1988-89 to 1989-90

YORKSHIRE
Johnny Whiteley	1970-71 to 1979-80
Arthur Keegan	1980-81
Johnny Whiteley	1981-82 to 1982-83
Peter Fox	1985-86 to 1989-90

OTHER NATIONALITIES
Dave Cox	1974-75 to 1975-76

INDEX OF COACHES

The following is an index of the 232 coaches who have held first team coaching posts since the start of the 1974-75 season with the alphabetical listing of British clubs they coached in this period.

Ray Abbey (Dewsbury)
Jack Addy (Dewsbury, Huddersfield B.)
Allan Agar (Bramley, Carlisle, Featherstone R., Rochdale H.)
Dave Alred (Bridgend)
Chris Anderson (Halifax)
Harry Archer (Workington T.)
Kevin Ashcroft (Leigh, Salford, Warrington)
Eric Ashton (St. Helens)
Ray Ashton (Workington T.)
Bill Ashurst (Runcorn H., Wakefield T.)
Mal Aspey (Salford)
Jack Austin (Hunslet)
John Atkinson (Carlisle)

Trevor Bailey (Wakefield T.)
Maurice Bamford (Bramley, Dewsbury, Halifax, Huddersfield, Leeds, Wigan, Workington T.)
Frank Barrow (Oldham, Swinton)
Tony Barrow (Oldham, Warrington)
Ray Batten (Wakefield T.)
Jeff Bawden (Whitehaven)
Mel Bedford (Huddersfield)
Cameron Bell (Carlisle)
Billy Benyon (Leigh, St. Helens, Warrington)
Les Bettinson (Salford)
Charlie Birdsall (Rochdale H.)
Alan Bishop (Runcorn H.)
Tommy Bishop (Barrow, Leigh, Workington T.)
Mick Blacker (Halifax, Huddersfield, Mansfield M.)
Tommy Blakeley (Blackpool B.)
Dick Bonser (Rochdale H.)
Reg Bowden (Fulham, Warrington)
Drew Broatch (Hunslet)
Ian Brooke (Bradford N., Huddersfield, Wakefield T.)
Arthur Bunting (Hull, Hull K.R.)
Dave Busfield (Dewsbury)

Len Casey (Hull, Scarborough P., Wakefield T.)
Jim Challinor (Oldham)
Paul Charlton (Workington T.)
Eddie Cheetham (Leigh)
Dave Chisnall (Runcorn H.)
Colin Clarke (Leigh, Wigan)

Terry Clawson (Featherstone R.)
Noel Cleal (Hull)
Malcolm Clift (Leeds)
Joe Coan (Wigan)
John Cogger (Runcorn H.)
Gary Cooper (York)
Kel Coslett (Rochdale H., St. Helens, Wigan)
Keith Cotton (Featherstone R.)
Mike Coulman (Salford)
Les Coulter (Keighley)
Dave Cox (Batley, Castleford, Dewsbury, Huyton, Oldham, Workington T.)
Jim Crellin (Blackpool B., Halifax, Mansfield M., Rochdale H., Swinton)
Terry Crook (Batley, Dewsbury)

Arthur Daley (Runcorn H.)
Paul Daley (Batley, Featherstone R., Hunslet, York)
Jackie Davidson (Whitehaven, Workington T.)
Keith Davies (Workington T.)
Tommy Dawes (Barrow, Carlisle, Whitehaven)
Harry Dawson (Widnes)
Tony Dean (Hull, Wakefield T.)
Henry Delooze (Rochdale H.)
Steve Dennison (Mansfield M.)
Robin Dewhurst (Leeds)
Bakary Diabira (Blackpool B., Keighley)
Tommy Dickens (Blackpool B., Leigh)
Roy Dickinson (Bramley)
Colin Dixon (Halifax, Keighley, Salford)
Mal Dixon (York)
John Dorahy (Halifax)
David Doyle-Davidson (Hull, York)
Ray Dutton (Whitehaven)

Graham Eadie (Halifax)
Bob Eccles (Chorley)
Derek Edwards (Doncaster)
Joe Egan Jnr. (Blackpool B.)

George Fairbairn (Hull K.R., Wigan)
Vince Farrar (Featherstone R.)
Albert Fearnley (Batley, Blackpool B., Keighley)
John Fieldhouse (Oldham)
Tony Fisher (Bramley, Keighley)
Eric Fitzsimons (Oldham, Rochdale H., Whitehaven)
Bob Fleet (Swinton)
Geoff Fletcher (Huyton, Runcorn H.)
Terry Fogerty (Rochdale H.)
Chris Forster (Bramley, Huddersfield B.)
Frank Foster (Barrow, Whitehaven)

Kenny Foulkes (Hull)
Don Fox (Batley)
Harry Fox (Halifax)
Neil Fox (Huddersfield)
Peter Fox (Bradford N., Bramley, Featherstone R., Leeds, Wakefield T.)
Bill Francis (Oldham)
Roy Francis (Bradford N., Huddersfield, Leeds)

Brian Gartland (Oldham)
Stan Gittins (Blackpool B., Chorley, Rochdale H., Springfield B.)
Bill Goodwin (Fulham, Kent Invicta)
Terry Gorman (Huyton, Swinton)
Keith Goulding (Featherstone R., Huddersfield, York)
Mal Graham (Oldham)
Tom Grainey (Leigh, Swinton)
Jeff Grayshon (Dewsbury)
Lee Greenwood (Keighley, Mansfield M./ Nottingham C.)
Geoff Gunney (Wakefield T.)

Bob Haigh (Wakefield T.)
Derek Hallas (Halifax)
Ken Halliwell (Swinton)
Alan Hardisty (Dewsbury, Halifax, York)
Arnold Hema (Nottingham C.)
Graham Heptinstall (Doncaster)
Alan Hepworth (Batley)
Keith Hepworth (Bramley, Hull)
Gary Hetherington (Sheffield E.)
Ron Hill (Dewsbury)
David Hobbs (Bradford N.)
Neil Holding (Rochdale H.)
Bill Holliday (Swinton)
Eric Hughes (Rochdale H., Widnes)
Syd Hynes (Leeds)

Bob Irving (Blackpool B.)
Keith Irving (Workington T.)

Dennis Jackson (Barrow)
Francis Jarvis (Huddersfield)
Peter Jarvis (Bramley, Hunslet)
Graeme Jennings (Hunslet)
Barry Johnson (Bramley)
Brian Johnson (Warrington)
Allen Jones (Huddersfield B.)
Lewis Jones (Dewsbury)

Vince Karalius (Widnes, Wigan)
Paul Kavanagh (Barrow)

John Kear (Bramley)
Arthur Keegan (Bramley)
Ivor Kelland (Barrow)
Alan Kellett (Carlisle, Halifax, Keighley)
Bill Kenny (Doncaster)
Bill Kindon (Leigh)
Bill Kirkbride (Mansfield M., Rochdale H.,
   Wakefield T., York)
Phil Kitchin (Whitehaven, Workington T.)

Dave Lamming (Wakefield T.)
Steve Lane (Kent Invicta)
Doug Laughton (Leeds, Widnes)
Roy Lester (Carlisle, Fulham)
Alan Lockwood (Dewsbury)
Brian Lockwood (Batley, Huddersfield,
   Wakefield T.)
Paul Longstaff (Rochdale H.)
Graham Lowe (Wigan)
Phil Lowe (York)
Trevor Lowe (Batley, Doncaster)
Ken Loxton (Bramley)
Geoff Lyon (Blackpool B.)

Mike McClennan (St. Helens)
Stan McCormick (Salford)
John McFarlane (Whitehaven)
Alan McInnes (Salford, Wigan)
John Mantle (Blackpool B., Cardiff C., Leigh)
Roger Millward (Halifax, Hull K.R.)
John Monie (Wigan)
Mick Morgan (Carlisle)
David Mortimer (Huddersfield)
Alex Murphy (Leigh, St. Helens, Salford,
   Warrington, Wigan)
Frank Myler (Oldham, Rochdale H., Swinton,
   Widnes)

Steve Nash (Mansfield M.)
Steve Norton (Barrow)

Les Pearce (Bramley, Halifax)
Mike Peers (Chorley B./Trafford B., Swinton)
Geoff Peggs (Keighley)
George Pieniazek (Batley, Featherstone R.)
Billy Platt (Mansfield M.)
Harry Poole (Hull K.R.)

Bill Ramsey (Hunslet)
Terry Ramshaw (Oldham)
Keith Rayne (Batley)
Rod Reddy (Barrow)
Graham Rees (Blackpool B.)

Malcolm Reilly (Castleford)
Alan Rhodes (Doncaster, Sheffield E.)
Austin Rhodes (Swinton)
Bev Risman (Fulham)
Ken Roberts (Halifax)
Don Robinson (Bramley)
Don Robson (Doncaster)
Peter Roe (Halifax, Keighley)
Sol Roper (Workington T.)

Roy Sabine (Keighley)
Dave Sampson (Castleford, Doncaster)
Barry Seabourne (Bradford N., Huddersfield,
   Keighley)
Les Sheard (Huddersfield)
Danny Sheehan (York)
John Sheridan (Doncaster)
Tommy Smales [Scrum half] (Featherstone R.)
Tommy Smales [Forward] (Batley, Bramley,
   Dewsbury, Doncaster, Featherstone R.)
Peter Smethurst (Leigh, Oldham)
Barry Smith (Whitehaven)
Bill Smith (Whitehaven, Workington T.)
Brian Smith (Huddersfield)
Brian Smith [Australian] (Hull)
Ike Southward (Whitehaven, Workington T.)
Graham Starkey (Oldham, Rochdale H.)
Gary Stephens (York)
Nigel Stephenson (Huddersfield, Hunslet)
Dave Stockwell (Batley, Bramley)
John Stopford (Swinton)
Ted Strawbridge (Doncaster)
Ross Strudwick (Fulham, Halifax)
Clive Sullivan (Doncaster, Hull)
Phil Sullivan (Fulham)

Kevin Tamati (Salford)
Bob Tomlinson (Huddersfield)
Ted Toohey (Wigan)
David Topliss (Wakefield T.)
Peter Tunks (Oldham)
Norman Turley (Whitehaven, Workington T.)
Derek Turner (Wakefield T.)
Colin Tyrer (Widnes)

Darryl Van de Velde (Castleford)
Don Vines (Doncaster)

Arnold Walker (Whitehaven)
Trevor Walker (Batley)
David Ward (Hunslet, Leeds)
John Warlow (Bridgend)

David Watkins (Cardiff C.)
Bernard Watson (Dewsbury)
Neil Whittaker (Huddersfield B.)
Mel Wibberley (Nottingham C.)
Ron Willey (Bradford N.)
Frank Wilson (Runcorn H.)
John Wolford (Hunslet)
Jeff Woods (Bridgend)
John Woods (Leigh)
Paul Woods (Runcorn H.)
Geoff Wraith (Wakefield T.)

Billy Yates (Doncaster)

DOSSIER OF 1990-91 COACHES

The following is a dossier of the British coaching and playing careers of coaches holding first team posts from June 1990 to the end of May 1991.
Overseas details are not included.
● BF — beaten finalist.

JACK ADDY

Dewsbury:	Feb. 84 - Jan. 87 (Promotion)
Huddersfield B:	Jan. 87 - Mar. 88
Dewsbury:	Dec. 90 -

Played for: Dewsbury

ALLAN AGAR

Carlisle:	May 81 - June 82 (Promotion)
Featherstone R.:	Dec. 82 - Oct. 85
	(RL Cup winners)
Bramley:	Dec. 85 - Apr. 87
Rochdale H.:	July 89 - Jan. 91 (Promotion)

Played for: Featherstone R., Dewsbury, New Hunslet, Hull K.R., Wakefield T., Carlisle, Bramley

RAY ASHTON

Workington T.:	June 90 -

Played for: Oldham, Leeds, Workington T.

MAURICE BAMFORD

Dewsbury:	Aug. - Oct. 74
Halifax:	Feb. 78 - May 80
	(Yorks. Cup BF, Promotion)
Huddersfield:	May 80 - May 81
Wigan:	May 81 - May 82
Bramley:	May 82 - Oct. 83
Leeds:	Nov. 83 - Feb. 85
	(John Player winners)
Leeds:	Dec. 86 - Apr. 88
	(John Player BF)
Workington T:	July 88 - Dec. 88
Dewsbury:	Dec. 88 - Dec. 90
Great Britain &	
Under-21s:	Oct. 84 - Dec. 86

Played for: Dewsbury, Batley

TONY BARROW

Warrington:	Mar. 86 - Nov. 88 (Premier winners and BF, John Player BF, Lancs. Cup BF)
Oldham:	Nov. 88 - Jan. 91 (Promotion, Lancs. Cup BF, Div. 2 Premier winners)

Played for: St. Helens, Leigh

CAMERON BELL (New Zealander)

Carlisle:	Feb. 90 -

ALAN BISHOP

Runcorn H:	Oct. 90 -

Played for: Huyton

MICK BLACKER

Halifax:	June 80 - June 82 (Promotion)
Mansfield M.:	May 84 - Oct. 85
Huddersfield:	Feb. 91 -

Played for: Bradford N., Halifax, Warrington, Mansfield M.

LEN CASEY

Wakefield T.:	Apr. 85 - June 86 (Promotion)
Hull:	June 86 - Mar. 88 (Yorks. Cup BF)
Scarborough P.:	Feb. 91 -

Played for: Hull, Hull K.R., Bradford N., Wakefield T.

DAVE CHISNALL
Runcorn H.: June 89 - Oct. 90
Played for: Leigh, Warrington, Swinton,
St. Helens, Barrow, Keighley, Mansfield M.,
Rochdale H.

NOEL CLEAL (Australian)
Hull: Sep. 90 - (Premier winners)
Played for: Widnes, Hull

JIM CRELLIN
Blackpool B.: May 76 - Mar. 77
(John Player BF)
Halifax: June 77 - Oct. 77
Swinton: Nov. 83 - May 86 (Div. 2
champs)
Mansfield M.: Dec. 86 - June 88
Rochdale H: June 88 - June 89
Swinton: July 89 - (Promotion)
Played for: Workington T., Oldham, Rochdale H.

PAUL DALEY
New Hunslet: Apr. 74 - Aug. 78 (Promotion)
York: Jan. 79 - May 79 (Promotion)
Featherstone R.: May 79 - Jan. 81 (Div. 2
champs)
Hunslet: Apr. 81 - Nov. 85 (Promotion)
Featherstone R.: Nov. 86 - Apr. 87
Batley: July 87 - Apr. 90
Hunslet: May 90 -
Played for: Halifax, Bradford N., Hull K.R.,
Hunslet

JACKIE DAVIDSON
Workington T.: Apr. 85 - Jan. 86
Whitehaven: May 91 -
Cumbria: 1985-86
Played for: Whitehaven

ROY DICKINSON
Bramley: Jan. 91 -
Played for: Leeds, Halifax, Bramley

JOHN DORAHY (Australian)
Halifax: June 89 - Aug. 90 (Regal BF)
Played for: Leigh, Hull K.R., Halifax

BOB ECCLES
Chorley: May 90 -
Played for: Warrington, Springfield B./Chorley B./
Trafford B.

GEORGE FAIRBAIRN
Wigan: Apr. 80 - May 81 (Promotion)
Hull K.R.: May 91 -
Played for: Wigan, Hull K.R.

JOHN FIELDHOUSE
Oldham: Jan. 91 - Apr. 91
Played for: Warrington, St. Helens, Oldham

TONY FISHER
Bramley: Nov. 87 - Feb. 89
Keighley: June 90 -
Played for: Bradford N., Leeds, Castleford

PETER FOX
Featherstone R.: Jan. 71 - May 74
(RL Cup winners & BF)
Wakefield T.: June 74 - May 76
(Yorks. Cup BF)
Bramley: Sep. 76 - Apr. 77 (Promotion)
Bradford N.: Apr. 77 - May 85 (Div. 1
champs (2), Yorks. Cup winners
and BF (2), Premier winners
and BF (2), John Player winners)
Leeds: May 85 - Dec. 86
Featherstone R.: May 87 - (Promotion, Div. 2
Premier BF, Yorks. Cup BF)
England: 1977 (2 matches)
Great Britain: 1978 (3 Tests v. Australia)
Yorkshire: 1985-86 to 1989-90
Played for: Featherstone R., Batley, Hull K.R.,
Wakefield T.

STAN GITTINS
Blackpool B./
Springfield B.: Nov. 85 - June 88
Chorley: June 89 - Apr. 90
Rochdale H.: Apr. 91 -
Played for: Batley, Swinton, Chorley

ARNOLD HEMA (New Zealander)
Nottingham C.: Feb. 91 -
Played for: Nottingham C.

GARY HETHERINGTON
Sheffield E.: July 86 - (Promotion, Div. 2
Premier winners)
Played for: York, Leeds, Kent I., Sheffield E.

DAVID HOBBS
Bradford N.: Mar. 90 - (Premier BF,
Regal BF)
Played for: Featherstone R., Oldham, Bradford N.

NEIL HOLDING
Rochdale H.:   Jan. 91 - Apr. 91
Played for: St. Helens, Rochdale H.

FRANCIS JARVIS
Huddersfield: Feb. 91 -
Played for: Bradford N., Featherstone R., Hunslet, Halifax

BARRY JOHNSON
Bramley: Mar. 89 - Dec. 90
Played for: Castleford, Bramley

BRIAN JOHNSON (Australian)
Warrington: Nov. 88 - (Lancs. Cup Winners, RL Cup BF, Regal winners)
Played for: Warrington

PAUL KAVANAGH
Barrow: Feb. 91 -
Played for: Barrow, Workington T.

JOHN KEAR
Bramley: Dec. 90 - Jan. 91
Played for: Castleford

PHIL KITCHIN
Whitehaven: Oct.79 - Jan. 82 (Promotion)
Whitehaven: June 85 - Oct. 87
Workington T.:   Dec. 88 - May 90
Cumbria: 1980-81, 1981-82, 1986-87, 1987-88, 1989-90, 1990-91
Played for: Whitehaven, Workington T.

DOUG LAUGHTON
Widnes: May 78 - Mar. 83 (RL Cup winners (2) and BF, Lancs. Cup winners (2) and BF, John Player winners and BF, Premier winners (2), Floodlit Trophy winners)
Widnes: Jan. 86 - May 91 (Div. 1 champs (2), Premier winners (3) and BF, Charity Shield winners (3), John Player BF, Lancs. Cup winners)
Leeds: May 91 -
Lancashire: 1982-83, 1988-89, 1989-90
Played for: Wigan, St. Helens, Widnes

MIKE McCLENNAN (New Zealander)
St. Helens   Feb. 90 - (RL Cup BF)

ROGER MILLWARD
Hull K.R.:   Mar. 77 - May 91 (Div. 1 champs (3), RL Cup winners and BF (2), John Player winners and BF (2), Premier winners (2) and BF, Yorks. Cup winners and BF (2), Floodlit Trophy winners and BF, Charity Shield BF, Div. 2 champs, Div. 2 Premier BF)
Halifax: May 91 -
Played for: Castleford, Hull K.R.

JOHN MONIE (Australian)
Wigan: Sep. 89 - (Div 1 champs (2), RL Cup winners (2), Regal winners, Charity Shield BF)

ALEX MURPHY
Leigh: Nov. 66 - May 71 (RL Cup winners, Lancs. Cup winners and BF, Floodlit Trophy winners and BF)
Warrington: May 71 - May 78 (League Leaders, Club Merit winners, RL Cup winners and BF, John Player winners (2), Floodlit Trophy BF, Capt. Morgan winners, Premier BF)
Salford: May 78 - Nov. 80
Leigh: Nov. 80 - June 82 (Div. 1 champs, Lancs. Cup winners)
Wigan: June 82 - Aug. 84 (John Player winners, RL Cup BF)
Leigh: Feb. 85 - Nov. 85
St. Helens: Nov. 85 - Jan. 90 (RL Cup BF (2), John Player winners, Premier BF)
Leigh: Mar. 90 -
Lancashire: 1973-74 to 1977-78 Champions (2); 1985-86 to 1987-88
England: 1975 (including World Championship (European Champions))
Played for: St. Helens, Leigh, Warrington

STEVE NORTON
Barrow: May 90 - Feb. 91
Played for: Castleford, Hull, Wakefield T.

MIKE PEERS
Swinton: June 86 - Oct. 87 (Promotion,
                Div. 2 Premier winners)
Springfield B./
Chorley B./
Trafford B.:   Aug. 87 -
Played for: Warrington, Swinton

KEITH RAYNE
Batley: May 90 - Apr. 91
Played for: Wakefield T., Leeds, Batley

PETER ROE
Keighley: Sep. 85 - July 86
Halifax: Aug. 90 - May 91 (Promotion
                Div 2, Premier BF)
Played for: Keighley, Bradford N., York, Hunslet

BARRY SEABOURNE
Keighley: Nov. 77 - Mar. 79
Bradford N.:   May 85 - Sep. 89 (Yorks. Cup
                winners)
Huddersfield: Mar. 90 - Feb. 91
Played for: Leeds, Bradford N., Keighley

BRIAN SMITH (Australian)
Hull: July 88 - Jan. 91 (Premier BF)

GARY STEPHENS
York: Apr. 88 -
Played for: Castleford, Wigan, Leigh, Halifax,
Leeds, York

ROSS STRUDWICK (Australian)
Halifax: Aug. 88 - Feb. 89
Fulham: June 89 -

KEVIN TAMATI (New Zealander)
Salford: Oct. 89 -(Lancs. Cup BF, Div.
                2 champs, Premier winners)
Played for: Widnes, Warrington

DAVID TOPLISS
Wakefield T.:   May 87 - (Promotion, Yorks.
                Cup BF)
Under-21s: 1988-89
Played for: Wakefield T., Hull, Oldham

PETER TUNKS (Australian)
Oldham: Apr. 91 -
Played for: Leeds, Salford, Sheffield E.

NORMAN TURLEY
Workington T.: Mar. 87 - Apr. 88
Whitehaven: June 90 - Apr. 91
Played for: Warrington, Rochdale H.,
Blackpool B., Trafford B., Swinton, Runcorn H.,
Barrow, Workington T., Whitehaven

DARRYL VAN DE VELDE (Australian)
Castleford: July 88 - (Yorks. Cup winners
                and BF)

DAVID WARD
Hunslet: July 86 - Apr. 88 (Div. 2
                champs, Div. 2 Premier BF)
Hunslet: Jan. 89 - May 89
Leeds: Sep. 89 - May 91
Played for: Leeds, Workington T.

MEL WIBBERLEY
Nottingham C.: Mar. 90 - Feb. 91
Non-professional player

Forward Roy Heni on 1987 Kumul tour duty in Britain.

KUMULS

KUMULS

PAPUA NEW GUINEA TESTS

The following is a list of Test matches involving Papua New Guinea since they became full members of the International Board in November 1978. * Denotes also World Cup.

14 Oct. 1979	v. France	L	9-16	Albi
28 Oct. 1979	v. France	L	2-15	Carcassonne
23 Aug. 1981	v. France	D	13-13	Port Moresby
25 Jul. 1982	v. New Zealand	L	5-56	Port Moresby
2 Oct. 1982	v. Australia	L	2-38	Port Moresby
2 Oct. 1983	v. New Zealand	L	20-60	Auckland
5 Aug. 1984	v. Great Britain	L	20-38	Mount Hagen
10 Aug. 1986	v. New Zealand	L	26-36	Goroka
*17 Aug. 1986	v. New Zealand	W	24-22	Port Moresby
* 4 Oct. 1986	v. Australia	L	12-62	Port Moresby
12 Jul. 1987	v. New Zealand	L	22-36	Port Moresby
*24 Oct. 1987	v. Great Britain	L	0-42	Wigan
*15 Nov. 1987	v. France	L	4-21	Carcassonne
*22 May 1988	v. Great Britain	L	22-42	Port Moresby
*10 Jul. 1988	v. New Zealand	L	14-66	Auckland
*20 Jul. 1988	v. Australia	L	8-70	Wagga Wagga
27 May 1990	v. Great Britain	W	20-18	Goroka
* 2 Jun. 1990	v. Great Britain	L	8-40	Port Moresby
5 Aug. 1990	v. New Zealand	L	4-36	Goroka
*11 Aug. 1990	v. New Zealand	L	10-18	Port Moresby

SUMMARY	P	W	D	L	F	A
Great Britain	5	1	0	4	70	180
Australia	3	0	0	3	22	170
France	4	0	1	3	28	65
New Zealand	8	1	0	7	125	330

Other International matches

6 Jul. 1975	v. England	L	12-40	Port Moresby
6 May 1977	v. France	W	37-6	Port Moresby
30 Jul. 1978	v. New Zealand	L	20-31	Port Moresby

PAPUA NEW GUINEA TEAMS

The following is a compendium of Papua New Guinea Test and World Cup teams since being granted full International Board status in November 1978.

Key: *, Captain; t, try; g, goal; dg, drop goal; (WC), World Cup

1979 France
Albi: 14 Oct
Lost 9-16
Kuveu
*Sapu
Kombinari 3g
Tinemau
Kapani 1t
Joseph
Kila, P
Gau
Geni
Koki
Bangkoma
Monama
Wanimara
Subs: Sirosi
    Giheno

1979 France
Carcassonne: 28 Oct
Lost 2-15
Kuveu
Kapani
Akis
Aope
Tinemau
Joseph
Kila, P. 1g
Gomfa
Gau
Koki
*Sapu
Wanimara
Karava

1981 France
Port Moresby: 23 Aug
Drew 13-13
Kuveu, 1t
Kapani, 1t
Tinemau 1t
Limi
Akis
*Wagambi
Haili 2g
Koki
Paiyesi
Gau
Waketsi
Bangkoma
Aope
Subs: Ralda
    Yip

1982 New Zealand
Port Moresby: 25 July
Lost 5-56
Kuveu
Rero 1t
Pilokos
Peter
Sasama
Joseph
Kila, P. 1g
Gau
Tenakanai
Ralda
Taumaku
Wanimara
*Wagambi
Subs: Tep
    Katsir

1982 Australia
Port Moresby: 2 Oct
Lost 2-38
Kuveu 1g
Rero
Segeyaro
Yip
Timi
*Joseph
Kabavas
Gau
Asotau
Tep
Taumaku
Tete
Loitive
Subs: Matmillo, F.
    Togili

1983 New Zealand
Auckland: 2 Oct
Lost 20-60
Kitimun 1t
Nil
Noifa
Katsir
Waluka
Segeyaro 1t
Kila, P. 3g
Tep
Ario 1t
Koki
Gau
*Loitive
Togili
Subs: Taumaku 1g
    Heni

1984 Great Britain
Mount Hagen: 5 Aug
Lost 20-38
Kitimun
Karai
Noifa 1t
Numapo 2g
Tolik 1t
Gebob
Kila, P.
*Tep
Asorifa
Jakis 1t
Kubak
Loitive
Taumaku 1t
Subs: Peter
    Wek

1986 New Zealand
Goroka: 10 Aug
Lost 26-36
Kuveu
Katsir
Atoi 1t
Numapo
Tivelit
Haili 1t
Gebob
Tep 1t
Heni
Ako
Loitive
Waketsi 1t
Taumaku
Subs: Peng
    Kovae 5g

1986 New Zealand (Also WC)
Port Moresby: 17 Aug
Won 24-22
Kovae 4g
Katsir
Atoi 1t
Numapo
Kerekere
Haili 2t
*Kila, T.
Tep
Heni
Lomutopa
Ako 1t
Waketsi
Taumaku
Subs: Saea
    Andy

1986 Australia (Also WC)
Port Moresby: 4 Oct
Lost 12-62
Kovae 2g
Katsir
Atoi
Numapo 2t
Kerekere
Haili
*Kila, T.
Tep
Heni
Lomutopa
Ako
Waketsi
Taumaku
Subs: Saea
     Andy

1987 New Zealand
Port Moresby: 12 July
Lost 22-36
Peter
Kerekere
Kovae 1t, 3g
*Numapo 2t
Kapia
Haili
Kila, T.
Tep
Heni 1t
Lomutopa
Waketsi
Taumaku
Kouoru, G.
Subs: Saea
     Kombra

1987 Great Britain (Also WC)
Wigan: 24 Oct
Lost 0-42
Kovae
Saea
Atoi
*Numapo
Krewanty
Haili
Kila, T.
Tep
Heni
Lomutopa
Kombra
Waketsi
Taumaku
Subs: Kitimun
     Gaius

1987 France (Also WC)
Carcassonne: 15 Nov
Lost 4-21
Kovae 1t
Krewanty
Atoi
Morea
Saea
*Numapo
Kila, T.
Ako
Heni
Lomutopa
Waketsi
Taumaku
Kouoru, G.
Subs: Haili
     Kombra

1988 Great Britain (Also WC)
Port Moresby: 22 May
Lost 22-42
Kovae 2t
Saea
Morea
*Numapo 3g
Krewanty 1t
Haili
Kila, T.
Rop 1t
Matmillo, M.
Bom
Kombra
Evei
Kouoru, H.
Subs: Rombuk
     Lapan

1988 New Zealand (Also WC)
Auckland: 10 July
Lost 14-66
Kovae 1t
Krewanty
*Numapo 3g
Atoi
Morea
Haili
Kila. T
Bom
Matmillo, M. 1t
Ben-Moide
Evei
Kombra
Kouoru, G.
Sub: Kouoru, H.

1988 Australia (Also WC)
Wagga Wagga: 20 July
Lost 8-70
Wanega
Krewanty
Kovae
*Numapo 2g
Morea 1t
Atoi
Haili
Rombuk
Matmillo, M.
Ben-Moide
Kombra
Evei
Gispe
Subs: Karara
     Kuno

1990 Great Britain
Goroka: 27 May
Won 20-18
Wanega
Krewanty
Boge
Numapo 5g, 1dg
Morea
Haru 1t, 1dg
Ongugo
Ako
Matmillo, M.
Evei 1t
Gispe
*Taumaku
Angara
Subs: Arigae
     Kool

1990 Great Britain (Also WC)
Port Moresby: 2 June
Lost 8-40
Wanega
Krewanty
Boge
Numapo 2g
Morea
Haru
Ongugo 1t
Lomutopa
Matmillo, M.
Evei
Gispe
*Taumaku
Angara
Subs: Tiri
     Itam

1990 New Zealand
Goroka: 5 Aug
Lost 4-36
Wanega
Krewanty
Boge
*Numapo
Waine
Haru
Ongugo
Ako
Matmillo, M.
Evei
Angara
Tiri
Elara 1t
Subs: Morea, Soga
      Paglipari, Kuno

1990 New Zealand (Also WC)
Port Moresby: 11 Aug
Lost 10-18
Wanega
Krewanty
Boge
*Numapo 1g
Haru
Soga 1t
Ongugo
Ako
Matmillo, M.
Evei
Angara
Paglipari
Elara
Subs: Waine 1t
      Tiri

Bal Numapo, holder of four Kumul scoring records.

Papuan second row man Mathias Kombra fends off a Featherstone Rovers defender in the opening tour fixture of 1987.

PAPUA NEW GUINEA REGISTER

The following is an index of players who have appeared for Papua New Guinea or toured since the country became full members of the International Board in November 1978. Tours to Britain also included France.

Appearances refer to Test matches only. Substitute appearances are in lower case letters and are included even when a player may not have played, as official information from Papua New Guinea does not differentiate.

Key: B, Britain; A, Australia; F, France; NZ, New Zealand.

AIYA, O.
Tours: NZ 1983
AKIS, P.
Appearances: 1979 F; 1981 F
Tours: Britain 1979
AKO, R.
Appearances: 1986 NZ2, A; 1987 F; 1990 B, NZ2
Tours: Britain 1987
ANDY, N.
Appearances: 1986 nz,a
ANGARA, M.
Appearances: 1990 B2, NZ2
AOPE, H.
Appearances: 1979 F; 1981 F
Tours: Britain 1979
ARIGAE, G.
Appearances: 1990 b
ARIO, K.
Appearances: 1983 NZ
Tours: NZ 1983
ASORIFA, F.
Appearances: 1984 B
ASOTAU, O.
Appearances: 1982 A
ATOI, L.
Appearances: 1986 NZ2,A; 1987 B, F; 1988 NZ,A
Tours: Britain 1987; NZA 1988

BANGKOMA, N.
Appearances: 1979 F; 1981 F
Tours: 1979 Britain
BEN-MOIDE, D.
Appearances: 1988 NZ,A
Tours: NZA 1988
BOGE, P.
Appearances: 1990 B2, NZ2

BOM, Y.
Appearances: 1988 B,NZ
Tours: NZA 1988

ELARA, M.
Appearances: 1990 NZ2
EVEI, T.
Appearances: 1988 B,NZ,A; 1990 B2, NZ2
Tours: NZA 1988

GAUIS, D.
Appearances: 1987 b
Tours: Britain 1987
GAU, T.
Appearances: 1979 F2; 1981 F; 1982 NZ,A; 1983 NZ
Tours: NZ 1983
GEBOB, G.
Appearances: 1984 B; 1986 NZ
GENI, L.
Appearances: 1979 F
Tours: Britain 1979
GIHENO, F.
Appearances: 1979 f
Tours: Britain 1979
GISPE, J.
Appearances: 1988 A; 1990 B2
Tours: Britain 1987; NZA 1988
GOMIA, J.
Appearances: 1979 F
Tours: Britain 1979

HAILI, D.
Appearances: 1981 F; 1986 NZ2,A; 1987 NZ,B,f; 1988 B,NZ,A
Tours: Britain 1987; NZA 1988
HARU, S.
Appearances: 1990 B2, NZ2
HENI, R.
Appearances: 1983 nz, 1986 NZ2,A; 1987 NZ,B,F
Tours: NZ 1983; Britain 1987

IPU, M.
Tours: Britain 1987
ITAM, C.
Appearances: 1990 b

JAKIS, R.
Appearances: 1984 B
JOSEPH, J.
Appearances: 1979 F2, 1982 NZ,A
Tours: Britain 1979; NZ 1983

KABAVAS, A.
Appearances: 1982 A
KAETA, S.
Tours: NZA 1988

KAMIAK, E.
Tours: Britain 1987
KAPANI, V.
Appearances: 1979 F2; 1981 F
Tours: Britain 1979
KAPIA, J.
Appearances: 1987 NZ
Tours: Britain 1987
KARAI, N.
Appearances: 1984 B
KARARA, S.
Appearances: 1988 a
Tours: NZA 1988
KARAVA, V.
Appearances: 1979 F
Tours: Britain 1979
KATSIR, J.
Appearances: 1982 nz; 1983 NZ; 1986 NZ2,A
Tours: NZ 1983
KELLY, J.
Tours: NZ 1983
KEREKERE, M.
Appearances: 1986 NZ,A; 1987 NZ
KILA, P.
Appearances: 1979 F2; 1982 NZ; 1983 NZ; 1984 B
Tours: Britain 1979; NZ 1983
KILA, T.
Appearances: 1986 NZ,A; 1987 NZ,B,F; 1988 B, NZ
Tours: Britain 1987; NZA 1988
KIMIA, S.
Tours: NZ 1983
KITIMUN, M.
Appearances: 1983 NZ, 1984 B; 1987 b
Tours: NZ 1983; Britain 1987
KOKI, D.
Appearances: 1979, F2; 1981 F; 1983 NZ
Tours: Britain 1979; NZ 1983
KOMBINARI, P.
Appearances: 1979 F
Tours: Britain 1979
KOMBRA, M.
Appearances: 1987 nz,B,F; 1988 B,NZ,A
Tours: Britain 1987; NZA 1988
KOOL, H.
Appearances: 1990 b
KOUORU, G.
Appearances: 1987 NZ,F; 1988 NZ
Tours: Britain 1987; NZA 1988
KOUORU, H.
Appearances: 1988 B,nz
Tours: NZA 1988
KOVAE, D.
Appearances: 1986 nz,NZ,A; 1987 NZ,B,F;
    1988 B, NZ
Tours: Britain 1987; NZA 1988
KREWANTY, A.
Appearances: 1987 B,F; 1988 B,NZ,A; 1990 B2,NZ2
Tours: Britain 1987; NZA 1988

KUBAK, R.
Appearances: 1984 B
KUNO, A.
Appearances: 1988 a; 1990 nz
Tours: NZA 1988
KUVEU, K.
Appearances: 1979 F2; 1981 F; 1982 NZ2,A; 1986 NZ
Tours: Britain 1979

LAIWA, D.
Tours: Britain 1979
LAPAN, N.
Appearances: 1988 b
Tours: Britain 1987; NZA 1988
LIMI, A.
Appearances: 1981 F
Tours: Britain 1979
LOITIVE, R.
Appearances: 1982 A; 1983 NZ; 1984 B; 1986 NZ
Tours: NZ 1983
LOMUTOPA, A.
Appearances: 1986 A,NZ; 1987 NZ,B,F; 1990 B
Tours: Britain 1987

MATMILLO, F.
Appearances: 1982 a
Tours: NZ 1983
MATMILLO, M.
Appearances: 1988 B,NZ,A; 1990 B2,NZ2
Tours: Britain 1987, NZA 1988
MINADI, L.
Tours: NZ 1983
MONAMA, P.
Appearances: 1979 F
Tours: Britain 1979
MOREA, M.
Appearances: 1987 F; 1988 B,NZ,A; 1990 B2,nz
Tours: Britain 1987, NZA 1988
MOU, C.
Tours: Britain 1987

NGALA, L.
Tours: NZ 1983
NIL, K.
Appearances: 1983 NZ
Tours: NZ 1983
NOIFA, D.
Appearances: 1983 NZ; 1984 B
Tours: NZ 1983
NUMAPO, B.
Appearances: 1984 B; 1986 NZ2,A; 1987 NZ,B,F;
    1988 B,NZ,A; 1990,B2,NZ2
Tours: Britain 1987; NZA 1988

ONGUGO, G.
Appearances: 1990 B2, NZ2

PAGLIPARI, K.
Appearances: 1990 nzNZ
PAIYESI, H.
Appearances: 1981 F
PENG, P.
Appearances: 1986 nz
PETER, J.
Appearances: 1982 NZ; 1984 b; 1987 NZ
PILOKOS, Y.
Appearances: 1982 NZ
POSU, K.
Tours: Britain 1979

RALDA, P.
Appearances: 1981 f; 1987 NZ
RERO, A.
Appearances: 1982 NZ,A
ROMBUK, T.
Appearances: 1988 b,A
Tours: Britain 1987, NZA 1988
ROP, I.
Appearances: 1988 B
Tours: NZA 1988

SAEA, K.
Appearances: 1986 nz,a; 1987 nz,B,F; 1988 B
Tours: Britain 1987
SAPU, S.
Appearances: 1979 F2
Tours: 1979
SASAMA, S.
Appearances: 1982 NZ
SEGEYARO, I.
Appearances: 1982 A; 1983 NZ
Tours: NZ 1983
SIROSI, C.
Appearances: 1979 f
Tours: Britain 1979
SOGA, O.
Appearances: 1990 nzNZ
SOM, R.
Tours: Britain 1979

TAMTU, D.
Tours: Britain 1979
TAUMAKU, A.
Appearances: 1982 NZ,A; 1983 nz; 1984 B; 1986 NZ;
      1987 NZ,B,F; 1990 B2
Tours: NZ 1983; Britain 1987
TENAKANAI, J.
Appearances: 1982 NZ

TEP, J.
Appearances: 1982 nz,A; 1983 NZ; 1984 B; 1986
      NZ2,A; 1987 NZ,B
Tours: NZ 1983; Britain 1987
TETE, L.
Appearances: 1982 A
TIMI, D.
Appearances: 1982 A
TINEMAU, D.
Appearances: 1979 F2; 1981 F
Tours: Britain 1979
TIRI, M.
Appearances: 1990 b,NZnz
TIVELIT, A
Appearances: 1986 NZ
Tours: NZA 1988
TOGILI, E.
Appearances: 1982 a; 1983 NZ
Tours: NZ 1983
TOLIK, B.
Appearances: 1984 B
TORE, M.
Tours: Britain 1979

WAGAMBI, J.
Appearances: 1981 F; 1982 NZ
Tours: NZ 1983
WAINE, G.
Appearances: 1990 NZnz
WAKETSI, B.
Appearances: 1981 F; 1986 NZ,A; 1987 NZ,B,F
Tours: Britain 1987
WALUKA, W.
Appearances: 1983 NZ
Tours: NZ 1983
WANEGA, I.
Appearances: 1988 A; 1990 B2, NZ2
Tours: NZA 1988
WANIMARA, J.
Appearances: 1979 F2; 1982 NZ
Tours: Britain 1979
WARTABAR, J.
Tours: Britain 1979
WEK, P.
Appearances: 1984 b
WEMAS, S.
Tours: NZ 1983

YIP, J.
Appearances: 1981 f; 1982 A

Papuan loose forward Arebo Taumaku and prop Ati Lomutopa converge on British stand off Shaun Edwards in the 1987 Test at Wigan.

Kumul prop Joe Tep pursues British back row forward Paul Medley in the 1987 Test encounter.

PAPUA NEW GUINEA TOUR OF GREAT BRITAIN

1987 TOUR

MATCH RESULTS

Featherstone R.	won	22-16	3,315
Lancashire (St. Helens)	**drew**	**22-22**	**4,202**
Swinton	lost	6-13	2,132
Cumbria (Whitehaven)	**lost**	**4-22**	**3,750**
BRITAIN (Wigan)	**lost**	**0-42**	**9,121**
Yorkshire (Leeds)	**lost**	**4-28**	**1,908**
Fulham	won	12-4	1,216

● The Kumuls also beat a British Amateur Rugby League Association XIII at Thrum Hall, Halifax, 20-16, before a 2,700 crowd, but this is not included in tour records.

SUMMARY

Played 7   Won 2   Drew 1   Lost 4

For
Tries 14   Goals 7   Points 70

Against
Tries 29   Goals 15   Drop goals 1   Points 147

Lost Test series 1-0

Kumul winger Arnold Krewanty

TOUR PARTY

Managers: Tau Peruka and Miller Ovasuru
Coach: Barry Wilson
Captain: Bal Numapo

	App	Tries	Gls	Pts
Bobby Ako	1+2	1	0	4
Lauta Atoi	6	1	0	4
David Gaius	4+1	0	1	2
Joe Gispe	2	0	0	0
Darius Haili	4+1	2	0	8
Roy Heni	4	0	1	2
Mark Ipu	2+1	0	0	0
Elias Kamiak	2	0	0	0
James Kapia	2	0	0	0
Tony Kila	5	0	0	0
Mathias Kitimun	4+1	1	0	4
Mathias Kombra	4	1	0	4
Gideon Kouoru	4	0	0	0
Dairi Kovae	4+2	0	0	0
Arnold Krewanty	6	1	0	4
Ngala Lapan	2+1	0	0	0
Ati Lomutopa	5	0	0	0
Michael Matmillo	2	0	0	0
Mea Morea	3	0	0	0
Clement Mou	1+2	1	0	4
Bal Numapo	4	1	5	14
Thomas Rombuk	1+2	1	0	4
Kepi Saea	6	3	0	12
Arebo Taumaku	4	0	0	0
Joe Tep	3+1	0	0	0
Bernard Waketsi	6	1	0	4

MEMO

First match on October 11, last match on November 1.

The first Kumul tour of the British professional scene began in great style with an opening victory over Featherstone Rovers followed by a draw against Lancashire. But their lack of experience resulted in four successive defeats before they finished as they began — with a victory — at Fulham.

Based at Harrogate, the tourists experienced difficulties with the language, diet and lack of funds, but they coped well enough to ensure a return visit.

It proved to be a friendly tour on and off the field with no Papuan or opponent sent off or sin-binned.

PAPUA NEW GUINEA TOURS

1979 to Britain and France

● The three-match tour in Britain was against amateur opposition.

P. Akis
H. Aope
N. Bangkoma
L. Geni
F. Giheno
Z. Gomia
J. Joseph
V. Kapani
V. Karava
P. Kila
D. Koki
P. Kombinari
K. Kuveu
D. Laiwa
A. Limi
P. Monama
K. Posu
S. Sapu
C. Sirosi
R. Som
D. Tamtu
D. Tinemau
M. Tore
J. Wanimara
J. Wartabar

Managers: R. Cutmore and T. Lavutul

Coach: U. Sabumei. Captain: S. Sapu

SUMMARY	P	W	D	L	F	A
In France	7	2	0	5	81	89

Lost Test series 2-0

	P	W	D	L	F	A
In Britain	3	1	0	2	52	56

BRITISH TOUR RESULTS

St. Helens lost 17-19
Britain (at Hull) lost 12-28
Cumbria (at Barrow) won 23-9

MEMO
The Kumuls made a good impression in France but disappointed in Britain. They were well beaten by Great Britain amateurs 28-12 at the Boulevard, Hull, before a crowd of 2,651.

1983 to New Zealand

O. Aiya
K. Ario
T. Gau
R. Heni
J. Joseph
J. Katsir
J. Kelly
P. Kila
S. Kimia
M. Kitimun
D. Koki
R. Loitive
F. Matmillo
L. Minadi
L. Ngala
K. Nil
D. Noifa
I. Segeyaro
A. Taumaku
J. Tep
E. Togili
J. Wagamhi
W. Waluka
S. Wemas

Managers: J. Keviame and H. Arek
Coach: U. Sabumei
Captain: L. Ngala

SUMMARY	P	W	D	L	F	A
	7	4	0	3	234	213

Lost Test

MEMO
Despite a 60-20 hammering in the Test against New Zealand and 56-32 defeat against the Maoris, the Kumuls regarded this as a successful tour. Their victories included a 62-16 win over Wellington.

Poka Kila was top scorer on tour with 40 points from 16 goals and two tries. Hugh McGahan of New Zealand scored a Test record six tries in the match at Carlaw Park, Auckland.

1988 to New Zealand and Australia

L. Atoi
D. Ben-Moide
Y. Bom
T. Evei
J. Gispe
D. Haili
S. Kaeta
S. Karara
T. Kila
M. Kombra
G. Kouoru
H. Kouoru
D. Kovae
A. Krewanty
A. Kuno
N. Lapan
M. Matmillo
M. Morea
B. Numapo
T. Rombuk
I. Rop
A. Tivelit
I. Wanega

Managers: Stanley Pil and Tau Peruka
Coach: Skerry Palanga
Captain: Bal Numapo

SUMMARY	P	W	D	L	F	A
In New Zealand	4	3	0	1	168	92
In Australia	4	1	0	3	54	136

Lost Test in each country

MEMO

Despite being hammered 66-14 by New Zealand and 70-8 by Australia, the tourists gave a good account of themselves. They won all three other matches in New Zealand, scoring 58 points against both Midlands Region and Northland.

Dairi Kovae, who was registered with North Sydney, was available only for the Test Matches.

RECORDS IN TEST AND WORLD CUP MATCHES

For Papua New Guinea

Highest score: Lost 26-36 v. New Zealand, at Goroka, 10 August 1986
Most tries in a match: No player has scored 3 or more
Most goals in a match: 6 by Bal Numapo v. Great Britain, at Goroka, 27 May, 1990
Most points in a match: 11(5g,1dg) by Bal Numapo v. Great Britain, at Goroka, 27 May 1990
Biggest attendance: 15,000 v. New Zealand, at Port Moresby, 17 August 1986, and Port Moresby, 12 July 1987; v. Australia, at Port Moresby, 4 October, 1986

Against Papua New Guinea

Highest score: 70-8 v. Australia, at Wagga Wagga, 20 July 1988 (also widest margin)
Most tries in a match: 6 by Hugh McGahan (New Zealand) at Auckland, 2 October, 1983
Most goals in a match: 9 by Gordon Smith (New Zealand), at Port Moresby, 25 July, 1982; Peter Brown (New Zealand), at Auckland, 10 July, 1988
Most points in a match: 30(4t,7g) by Michael O'Connor (Australia), at Wagga Wagga, 20 July, 1988

Career records

Most career appearances: 14 by Bal Numapo (1984-)
Most career tries: 5 by Dairi Kovae (1986-)
Most career goals: 19 (inc. 1dg) by Bal Numapo (1984-)
Most career points: 53(4t,18g,1dg) by Bal Numapo (1984-)

Carl Gibson, voted by his colleagues as 1990 best tourist.

1990 LIONS

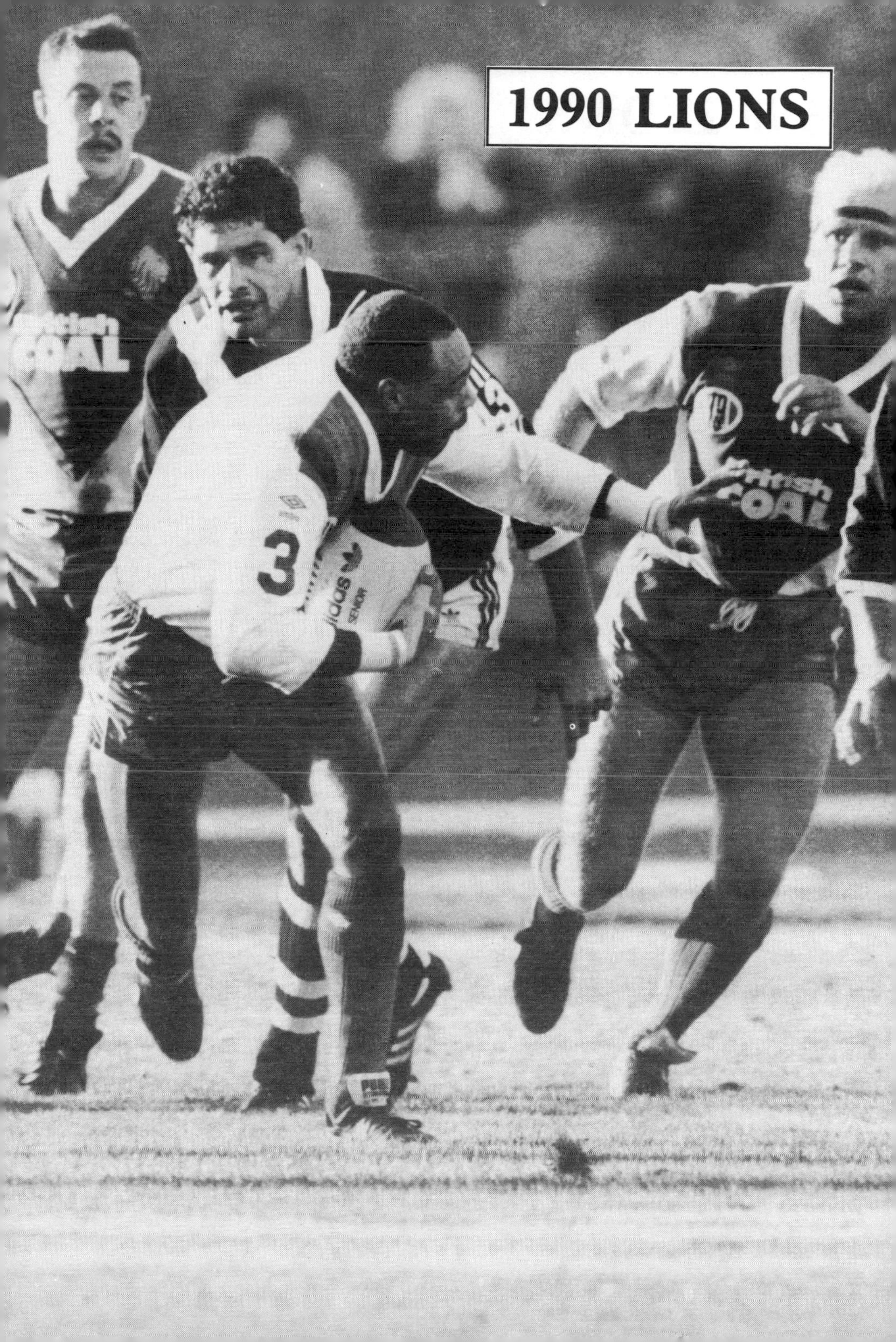

1990 LIONS

1990 TOUR REVIEW

Branded no-hopers on departure, the 1990 Lions tourists to Papua New Guinea and New Zealand — with an average age of under 23 — returned home as Test heroes, having recorded the first series win Down Under since 1979. Superbly led by third-choice skipper Mike Gregory, the 28-man squad, devastated by withdrawals and injury, battled to register a 2-1 British Coal Test triumph in New Zealand against all the odds. But the tourists also conceded a few unwanted records.

Great Britain's tour jinx — a continuation of the ill-fortune of 1988 — commenced immediately after the announcement of the party. Six original choices withdrew — Wigan's Ellery Hanley, Andy Platt and Shaun Edwards, plus Paul Loughlin (St. Helens) because of injury, and Les Holliday (Widnes) and Wigan's Steve Hampson, for personal reasons. Hanley was first-choice skipper, with Edwards lined up to be named as his replacement. Wigan had begun with a record 10 selected to tour, but in the end only six went.

In came pre-departure replacements Karl Fairbank and Roger Simpson (Bradford Northern), Chris Bibb (Featherstone Rovers), Gary Price (Wakefield Trinity), Daryl Powell (Sheffield Eagles) and Paul Dixon (Leeds). In addition, Hull K.R. winger Anthony Sullivan was called up to cover for Widnes flier Martin Offiah, who was bidding to overcome a painful toe injury and fly out in time for the New Zealand Test series. Wigan's Joe Lydon, troubled by an ankle injury, underwent surgery five days before departure, putting back his out-going until the four-day break in Cairns.

Serious injuries continued to plague the Lions on tour. Sullivan was sent home after tearing a hamstring in training 48 hours after arriving in Papua New Guinea without playing a game. Widnes Welsh Rugby Union recruit John Devereux flew out to take his place. Bradford's Kelvin Skerrett was sent to Sydney for treatment on his injured knee after playing only 50 minutes of the opening fixture in Port Moresby, returning to duty for the eighth game, against Auckland.

After only four appearances, two of them in the Papuan Tests, Widnes full back Alan Tait was sent home, five weeks into the tour, with a groin injury, Warrington's David Lyon being called up for the first time. Shortly after, Castleford stand off Graham Steadman, who had never produced the form to justify his record £170,000 price-tag, was flown home with a nagging knee injury, a replacement not being sought.

Britain's youngest-ever touring party were bonded together by adversity, the resultant team-spirit inspiring the Lion's first Test series triumph Down Under in 11 years. The first quarter of the opening Kiwi Test, in the Rugby Union stronghold of Palmerston North, was exactly what the pundits had gloomily predicted — New Zealand producing powerful, flowing football to lead 10-4.

The Lions, well led by Gregory and inspired by the brilliance of vice-captain Garry Schofield in his new stand off role, then successfully operated team manager Malcolm Reilly's simple gameplan, which was to be their hallmark throughout the series.

A magnificent 11-10 victory was followed two weeks later by a more impressive 16-14 success in Auckland — by three tries to one — to clinch the series. The controversial decision to fly out Offiah solely for the Kiwi series, at a cost of over £1,000 per match, was fully justified by his brilliant touchdown which secured victory in the second Test.

Ironically, it was Offiah who carried the blame for losing the third encounter — and two vital World Cup points — at Christchurch a week later. After just three minutes Offiah only had to touch down under the posts to give the gallant Lions a lead which would probably have sunk the Kiwis and secured a Test whitewash. With 180 tries already to his credit in only three seasons in the professional ranks, Offiah spilled the ball a foot from the ground and the Kiwis counted their blessings and went on to win 21-18.

The Kiwi Test series was the undoubted highlight of the 10-week trip which was otherwise riddled with negative elements. The weakened party suffered a trio of un-wanted playing records. The 1990 Lions became the first Great Britain team to suffer defeat at the hands of Papua New Guinea, going down 20-18 in the first Test in Goroka. On the New Zealand leg, Canterbury recorded a victory over a Great Britain side for the first time in their 70-year history, while Wellington's success was a first over an overseas touring team in their 76 years.

The total of four defeats also equalled the worst record by the Lions in New Zealand.

Off the field, Britain's fortunes were also ill-starred. Tour Director Maurice Lindsay was very critical of the New Zealand League's planning and staging of the 10-match visit. The wide-ranging travel costs could never be balanced against the poor gate returns from a tour itinerary which featured unattractive midweek afternoon kick-offs and speculative venues, several in Rugby Union heartland. A high level of media attention was never translated into match attendance, none of the 10 fixtures attracting a five-figure gate and two of them being returned at less than 1,000.

Accordingly, the first-ever combined tour of Papua New Guinea and New Zealand was destined to become the last. Pre-tour budgets of an £80,000 loss proved to be con-servative. The 15-match tour registered a total loss of £309,131, which was cushioned by the first-ever inclusion of sponsorship money reducing the official deficit to £136,631.

Ironically, the International Board, meeting in the week of the second Kiwi Test, decided to revert to traditional four-year cycles with Britain resuming their Papua-Australia-New Zealand format in 1992.

Controversy hit the tour when Wigan scrum half Bobby Goulding — the youngest-ever British Lion at 18 years 4 months — was arrested for allegedly assaulting two men in an Auckland restaurant in the early hours. He was subsequently ordered by the local magistrates to hand over £500, £175 going to each of the men involved and the remainder to charity, although it was ruled that the charge would not count as a criminal record. Goulding was later found guilty by the League's Board of Directors of bringing the game into disrepute and warned as to his future conduct.

On the positive front, the tour was a personal triumph for a handful of players. Captain Gregory, who had led Britain to their 2-1 series win over New Zealand the previous autumn, was an inspirational figurehead who defied a painful Achilles' injury to lead by example, especially in the Test arena.

Former Welsh Rugby Union skipper Jonathan Davies confirmed his graduation to star status in the 13-a-side code by earning selection for all five Tests and becoming the top goalscorer and points-scorer on the tour with tallies of 34 and 92 respectively in 11 appearances.

Leeds threequarter Carl Gibson was chosen by his colleagues to receive the award from the British Lions Association to com-memorate the best all-round contribution to the tour, on and off the field. The ex-Batley centre made the most full appearances with 11, although clubmate Roy Powell made most appearances with 14, being a playing substitute on seven occasions.

While Gibson received the best tourist accolade, there was no doubting the player of the tour. Leeds skipper Schofield dominated the playing scene, being the mainspring of the tremendous Kiwi series triumph. After scoring a hat-trick — which included his 200th career try — in the opening tour fixture against Southern Zone in his traditional centre position, Schofield was given the troublesome stand off role in the first Test against Papua New Guinea and served up his worst-ever performance in a Great Britain jersey to shoulder much of the blame for the shock defeat.

The ex-Hull star then went on to fully justify Reilly's confidence in his filling the number six jersey, having spent only half the previous season serving Leeds in that stand off role. Schofield displayed a showcase of skills as the ill-fated tour took an upturn, scoring in each of the four remaining Tests,

including the winning drop goal in the first Kiwi victory. More importantly, he was the key figure in Britain's tactical gameplan, providing the vital pivot which was to spoil New Zealand coach Bob Bailey's induction in Test football.

While these established Test stars were the pride of the Lions, a host of the cubs took the golden opportunity to lay foundations for future Great Britain selection. Goulding established himself as first choice scrum half throughout the tour despite his youngest-ever tag; Shaun Irwin, Daryl Powell and Fairbank added to their meagre Test cap tallies; while Test debuts were given to Paul Eastwood, Lee Jackson, Martin Dermott, Chris Bibb and Phil Clarke, as well as Davies and Goulding.

TOUR RESULTS

Date	Result	Score	Opposition	Venue	Attendance
In Papua New Guinea					
May 20	W	40-18	Southern Zone	Port Moresby	5,066
23	W	24-10	Northern/Highland Zones	Lae	2,550
27	L	18-20	PAPUA NEW GUINEA	Goroka	11,598
30	W	50-4	Islands Zone	Rabaul	3,558
June 2	W	40-8	PAPUA NEW GUINEA*	Port Moresby	5,969
In New Zealand					
10	W	23-22	President's XIII	Napier	3,163
13	L	10-18	Canterbury Select	Christchurch	1,338
17	L	13-24	Auckland	Auckland	7,614
20	W	22-10	Kiwi Colts	Huntly	972
24	W	11-10	NEW ZEALAND	Palmerston North	8,073
27	L	22-30	Wellington	Wellington	845
July 1	W	20-12	NZ Maoris	Rotorua	3,184
4	W	24-0	Taranaki Invitation	New Plymouth	2,675
8	W	16-14	NEW ZEALAND	Auckland	7,843
15	L	18-21	NEW ZEALAND*	Christchurch	3,133

*World Cup-rated

TOUR SUMMARY

	P	W	D	L	T	G	Dr	Pts	T	G	Dr	Pts
						FOR				AGAINST		
In Papua New Guinea	5	4	0	1	31	24	0	172	7	15	2	60
In New Zealand	10	6	0	4	30	28	3	179	24	32	1	161
Tour totals	15	10	0	5	61	52	3	351	31	47	3	221

TEST SUMMARY

	P	W	D	L	T	G	Dr	Pts	T	G	Dr	Pts
						FOR				AGAINST		
In Papua New Guinea	2	1	0	1	10	9	0	58	3	7	2	28
In New Zealand	3	2	0	1	8	6	1	45	5	12	1	45
Test totals	5	3	0	2	18	15	1	103	8	19	3	73

TOUR RECORDS

Biggest attendance: 11,598, first PNG Test at Goroka

Highest score and widest margin: 50-4 v. Islands Zone

Highest score against: Lost to Wellington 30-22

Widest margin defeat: Lost to Auckland 24-13

Most tries in a match: 3 by Garry Schofield v. Southern Zone; 3 by Paul Eastwood v. Kiwi Colts

Most goals in a match: 6 by Jonathan Davies
  v. Southern Zone
  v. PNG, second Test

Most points in a match: 16 by Jonathan Davies v. Southern Zone

Most tries on tour: 9 by Paul Eastwood

Most goals on tour: 34 by Jonathan Davies

Most points on tour: 92 by Jonathan Davies

Most appearances: 14 (including seven as substitute) by Roy Powell

Most full appearances: 11 by Carl Gibson

Sin bin: Bobby Goulding v. Auckland; David Bishop v. Kiwi Colts; Shaun Irwin v. Wellington; Bobby Goulding and Garry Schofield v. New Zealand (third Test)

Opponents' sin bin: Andrew Kuno (Northern/Highlands); Stuart Galbraith (Auckland); Tony Tuimavave (Kiwi Colts); Dave O'Sullivan and Barry Harvey (Wellington); Darrell Williams (New Zealand, third Test)

Player of the tour, vice-captain Garry Schofield.

239

TOUR MANAGEMENT

Manager: Maurice Lindsay
Coach: Malcolm Reilly
Assistant Coach: Phil Larder
Doctor: Forbes Mackenzie
Physiotherapist: David Fevre

TOUR PARTY

Player	Club	IN PAPUA NEW GUINEA					IN NEW ZEALAND					TOUR TOTALS				
		App	Sub	T	G	Pts	App	Sub	T	G	Pts	App	Sub	T	G	Pts
BETTS, Denis	Wigan	3	1	2	—	8	6	—	2	—	8	9	1	4	—	16
BIBB, Chris	Featherstone R.	3	—	1	—	4	5	2	—	—	—	8	2	1	—	4
BISHOP, David	Hull K.R.	1	—	—	—	—	7	1	1	—	4	8	1	1	—	4
CLARKE, Phil	Wigan	3	—	3	15	42	7	—	3	19	50	10	—	6	34	92
DAVIES, Jonathan	Widnes	2	1	—	—	—	7	—	1	(1)	5	10	1	1	(1)	5
DERMOTT, Martin	Wigan	1	—	—	—	—	6	—	2	—	8	7	—	2	—	8
† DEVEREUX, John	Widnes	3	—	2	—	8	4	3	—	—	—	5	3	2	—	8
DIXON, Paul	Leeds	3	—	2	—	8	4	3	—	—	—	5	3	2	—	8
EASTWOOD, Paul	Hull	5	—	5	9	38	5	—	4	9	34	10	—	9	18	72
ENGLAND, Keith	Castleford	3	—	—	—	—	6	—	2	—	8	9	—	2	—	8
FAIRBANK, Karl	Bradford N.	2	1	—	—	—	4	—	2	—	8	6	1	2	—	8
FOX, Deryck	Featherstone R.	2	2	—	—	—	5	—	2	—	8	7	2	2	—	8
GIBSON, Carl	Leeds	5	—	4	—	16	6	1	2	—	8	11	1	6	—	24
GOULDING, Bobby	Wigan	3	—	2	—	8	5	1	—	(1)	1	8	1	2	(1)	9
GREGORY, Mike	Warrington	3	—	—	—	—	5	—	1	—	4	8	—	1	—	4
IRWIN, Shaun	Castleford	2	1	—	—	—	4	2	—	—	—	6	3	—	—	—
JACKSON, Lee	Hull	3	—	—	—	—	4	—	1	—	4	7	—	1	—	4
LUCAS, Ian	Wigan	2	—	—	—	—	4	1	—	—	—	6	1	—	—	—
● LYDON, Joe	Wigan	—	—	—	—	—	5	1	2	—	8	5	1	2	—	8
† LYON, David	Warrington	—	—	—	—	—	2	—	2	—	8	2	—	2	—	8
● OFFIAH, Martin	Widnes	—	—	—	—	—	4	—	2	—	8	4	—	2	—	8
POWELL, Daryl	Sheffield E.	3	2	—	—	—	6	5	1	—	4	9	7	1	—	4
POWELL, Roy	Leeds	1	1	1	—	4	3	1	—	—	—	4	2	1	—	4
PRICE, Gary	Wakefield T.	3	—	4	—	16	6	1	3	(1)	13	9	1	7	(1)	29
SCHOFIELD, Garry	Leeds	2	—	2	—	8	3	—	1	—	4	5	—	3	—	12
SIMPSON, Roger	Bradford N.	1	2	—	—	—	3	1	1	—	4	5	1	1	—	4
SKERRETT, Kelvin	Bradford N.[1]	1	—	—	—	—	4	—	1	—	4	5	—	1	—	4
SMALES, Ian	Featherstone R.	1	2	—	—	—	4	—	1	—	4	5	2	1	—	4
* STEADMAN, Graham	Castleford	1	1	1	—	—	2	—	1	—	4	3	1	1	—	4
* SULLIVAN, Anthony	Hull K.R.	—	—	—	—	—	1	1	1	—	—	3	1	1	—	—
* TAIT, Alan	Widnes	2	—	—	—	—	1	1	1	—	4	3	1	1	—	4

● Joined tour party late, Lydon in Cairns (4 June), Offiah in Auckland (15 June)
* Sent home injured, Sullivan (22 May), Tait (21 June), Steadman (26 June)
† Arrived as replacement, Devereux (28 May), Lyon (24 June)
(1) Indicates drop goal
1 Agreed terms with Wigan on 24 June being registered as a Wigan player on 13 August.

1990 British Lions, left to right, Back Row: Graham Steadman, Ian Lucas, Denis Betts, Karl Fairbank, Joe Lydon, Roy Powell, Kelvin Skerrett, Gary Price, Martin Offiah, Paul Dixon, Daryl Powell. Middle Row: David Ferre (Physiotherapist), Forbes Mackenzie (Doctor), David Bishop, Jonathan Davies, Keith England, Chris Bibb, Paul Eastwood, Shaun Irwin, Ian Smales, Lee Jackson, Phil Clarke, Phil Larder (Assistant Coach). Front Row: Martin Dermott, Bobby Goulding, Carl Gibson, Maurice Lindsay (Manager), Mike Gregory (Captain), Malcolm Reilly (Coach), Garry Schofield (Vice-Captain), Deryck Fox, Alan Tait.

MATCH BY MATCH

20 May

Port Moresby

SOUTHERN ZONE	**18**
GREAT BRITAIN	**40**

1. Bibb (D. Powell, 30 min.)
2. Eastwood
3. Schofield
4. Davies
5. Gibson
6. Steadman
7. Goulding (Fox, Half-time)
8. Skerrett (Smales, 50 min.)
9. Dermott (R. Powell, Half-time)
10. England
11. Fairbank
12. Betts
13. Gregory, Capt.

T: Schofield (3), Eastwood (2), Davies, Gibson
G: Davies (6)

Southern Zone:
Sevesoa; P. Lae, Bagme (Barlia), Bilbaesi, Wazineso; Waldiat (Daipo), Vaieke; Ngaffin, Igo, W. Lae, Kaupa (Kolant), Tia (Bre), Ganiga, Capt.

T: Igo, Lae, Ganiga
G: Lae (3)

Half-time: 0-26

Referee: Graham Anui
Attendance: 5,066

Wearing a Great Britain jersey for the first time, ex-Wales Rugby Union skipper Davies contributed 16 points in searing heat. Playing in the centre, Davies scored a superb try, played a key part in three others and kicked six goals from nine attempts.

Tour vice-captain Schofield also played a starring role, grabbing a hat-trick of tries in an incredible eight-minute spell midway through the first half, which included the 200th of his career.

The first scores of the 15-match tour came from a 40-yard penalty goal from Davies before Hull winger Eastwood zipped in for the opening touchdown. British team boss Reilly welcomed the seven-try victory but lamented the concession of 18 points, including three tries.

23 May

Lae

NORTHERN/HIGHLAND	
ZONES	**10**
GREAT BRITAIN	**24**

1. Bibb (Davies, 74 min.)
2. Eastwood
3. Gibson (Steadman, Half-time)
4. Irwin
5. Simpson
6. D. Powell
7. Fox, Capt.
8. Lucas
9. Jackson
10. Dixon (Smales, 61 min.)
11. R. Powell (Price, Half-time)
12. Clarke
13. Bishop

T: Bibb, Dixon, Simpson, Davies
G: Eastwood (4)

Northern/Highland Zones:
Peni (Hoffman); Tofi, Sigepal, Sinemau, Mivin (Bina); Sambu, Lapan; Seeto (Wale), Gul, Lomutopa, Markham (Kuno), Kombra, Capt., Elara

T: Elara
G: Sambu (3)

Half-time: 8-8

Referee: Aiwa Olni
Attendance: 2,550

Britain recorded their second successive victory, but it was the off-field activities which dominated the afternoon. A violent clash between police and rioting supporters cast an ugly shadow over the tourists' four tries to one triumph, after the combined side had held Britain to an 8-8 half-time scoreline.

Fans unable to enter the packed Lae stadium resorted to throwing stones and bottles, the police replying with a barrage of tear gas. At the height of the crowd trouble, the British tour management rescued local female staff in the turnstile booths .... plus the receipts!

On the field, Britain's young tourists survived fears of a second-half collapse in the heat by scoring three tries and two goals with only a goal in reply, skipper Fox leading the side well in his bid to clinch the scrum half Test role. Jackson and Dixon in the front row were also impressive.

FIRST TEST v. PAPUA NEW GUINEA

Papua New Guinea celebrated their first-ever victory over Great Britain, by a two-point margin, in a high altitude encounter at Goroka in what will be known as the 'Tear Gas Test'. New Zealand referee Dennis Hale stopped play after just 14 minutes as police fired rifle shots and tear gas cannisters into an hysterical mob of stone-throwing fans locked out of the Danny Leahy Oval.

The Test was held up for three minutes as tear gas drifted across the field, the unsettled British side immediately conceding a try to level the scores at 6-6. Shots and tear gas continued to be fired throughout the match as armed police patrolled the perimeter to keep order among the 2,000 fans locked out.

At the post-match inquest, British team manager Malcolm Reilly acknowledged that the stoppage had been disruptive to concentration but put most blame on a number of uninspiring individual performances.

The 20-18 Papuan triumph was only their second at Test level in their 10-year history, having pulled off a shock victory over New Zealand four years earlier. Previously, Britain had won all three Test encounters, two in Papua New Guinea, never scoring less than 38 points.

One of the crucially disappointing performances of the afternoon came from Leeds skipper Garry Schofield, making his first Test appearance in the stand off role for his 22nd cap. His dramatic loss of form hampered the tactical structure of the British game, especially in the strength-sapping high altitude conditions. Little went right for the tour vice-captain, and his mistakes multiplied the harder he tried to get himself going.

Britain opened in confident style, a fine five-man move ending with Widnes full back Alan Tait sending Hull winger Paul Eastwood in for a try, brilliantly converted by fellow Test debutant Jonathan Davies. Straight after the tear gas disruption, the Papuans opened their account with a try from prop forward Tuiyo Evei, centre Bal Numapo adding the goal.

Welshman Davies restored Britain's lead with a penalty goal, equality being re-established by drop goals from Numapo and stand off Stanley Haru.

With Britain struggling to find any sort of rhythm, Papua New Guinea took the lead for the first time when Haru raced in for a try, Numapo again adding the goal. The Papuans began to sense victory when former skipper Numapo contributed two penalty goals to open up an 18-8 scoreline.

Centre Davies pulled the Lions back into contention with a superbly taken try in the corner before a controversial decision wrecked the visitors' hopes of a comeback. New Zealand referee Hale awarded the tourists a penalty, only for local touch judge Aiwa Dini to run on to persuade him the kick should go the other way. Numapo obliged by converting the penalty into two points for a 20-12 margin.

Debutant scrum half Bobby Goulding chipped over the cover and regathered for a superb try, converted by Davies, but it was too late to prevent the Papuans recording their first triumph over the Lions.

It was generally accepted that any other result, even with the off-field distractions, would have been unjust, despite Britain scoring three tries to two. Papua New Guinea played with more passion and a greater will to win.

FIRST TEST
27 May
Goroka

PAPUA NEW GUINEA 20   GREAT BRITAIN 18

Ipisa Wanega	1.	Alan Tait
Arnold Krewanty	2.	Paul Eastwood
Phillip Boge	3.	Daryl Powell
Bal Numapo	4.	Jonathan Davies
Mea Morea	5.	Carl Gibson
Stanley Haru	6.	Garry Schofield
Gigmai Ongugo	7.	Bobby Goulding
Bobby Ako	8.	Roy Powell
Michael Matmillo	9.	Lee Jackson
Tuiyo Evei	10.	Paul Dixon
Joe Gispe	11.	Denis Betts
Arebo Taumaku, Capt	12.	Karl Fairbank
Michael Angara	13.	Mike Gregory, Capt.
Chris Itam	14.	Deryck Fox
Hoah Kool	15.	Phil Clarke
Goro Arigai	16.	Shaun Irwin
Max Tiri	17.	Keith England

T: Evei, Haru
G: Numapo (5, 1dg), Haru (dg)
Substitutions:
Arigai for Ako (45 min.)
Kool for Boge (52 min.)
Half-time: 14-8
Referee: Dennis Hale (New Zealand)
Attendance: 11,598

T: Eastwood, Davies, Goulding
G: Davies (3)
Substitutions:
Irwin for D. Powell (38 min.)
England for Fairbank (50 min.)

Scorechart

Minute	Score	PNG	GB
12:	Eastwood (T)		
	Davies (G)	0	6
18:	Evei (T)		
	Numapo (G)	6	6
27:	Davies (PG)	6	8
30:	Numapo (DG)	7	8
36:	Haru (DG)	8	8
38:	Haru (T)		
	Numapo (G)	14	8
46:	Numapo (PG)	16	8
60:	Numapo (PG)	18	8
64:	Davies (T)	18	12
71:	Numapo (PG)	20	12
79:	Goulding (T)		
	Davies (G)	20	18

30 May

Rabaul

ISLANDS ZONE   4
GREAT BRITAIN   50

1. Bibb
2. Eastwood
3. Gibson
4. Irwin (Betts, 60 min.)
5. Devereux
6. Simpson
7. Fox, Capt.
8. Lucas
9. Dermott (Fairbank, 33 min.)
10. England (R. Powell, 30 min.)
11. Smales
12. Price
13. Clarke

T: Devereux (2), Fox (2), Betts (2), Simpson, Gibson, Price, Eastwood
G: Eastwood (5)

Islands Zone:
Eremas; Tivilet, Levi, Joseph (Lavat), Sabat; Ngatia (Wallace), Hennessey; Peter, Walia, Akumai, Dambui (Maninga), Teine, Capt., Umapi

G: Eremas (2)

Half-time: 4-20

Referee: Moses Tolingling
Attendance: 3,558

Hull winger Paul Eastwood, scorer of five tries and nine goals on the Papuan leg of the tour.

Tear gas riots again disrupted play for the third successive tour match, the action at the tiny, picturesque Queen Elizabeth Stadium being halted for a quarter of an hour after 23 minutes.

The worst of the tear gas attacks, launched to prevent gatecrashers, caused fans inside the stadium to break down fences to flee the stinging gas. A policeman was later arrested for sparking the chaos by prematurely firing a gas cannister.

On the field, Britain also ran riot with a 10-try display spearheaded by captain Fox and tour replacement Devereux, who both touched down twice. Powerful bursts by Roy Powell and Smales proved too much for the Islands Zone, who contributed only two goals. Wigan's 19-year-old loose forward Clarke put himself in contention for a Test substitute role.

SECOND TEST v.
PAPUA NEW GUINEA

Great Britain's determination to wipe out the shock first Test defeat a week earlier was reflected in a seven tries to one triumph in Port Moresby, earning two valuable World Cup points. The second Test was virtually over as a contest at half-time, with the Lions leading 20-0 and well on their way to restoring prestige and confidence after the Goroka humiliation.

Britain pack workhorses Keith England — recalled to the Test arena — and Paul Dixon were the heroes of the 40-8 victory, achieved in soaring 100-degree heat. Dixon, moved back to the second row to make room for prop England, was the only packman to score a try, other scorers including Leeds clubmates Carl Gibson, who touched down twice, and Garry Schofield.

That Schofield try sealed a return to characteristic form after a disappointing display in the first Test shock defeat. The touchdown was the most spectacular of the afternoon, a curving gallop through the opposition from the halfway line, while the stand off had a hand in four other tries.

Jonathan Davies continued his Rugby League education, kicking six goals from eight attempts, including a towering touchline goal that drifted in after seeming to be heading for oblivion.

The recall of England for his sixth cap confirmed a no-nonsense approach by team manager Malcolm Reilly, the Papuan pack never rekindling the fire of Goroka. The Castleford packman was well supported by Dixon and captain Mike Gregory, who withdrew with an ankle injury in the 57th minute, allowing Wigan loose forward Phil Clarke to make his Test debut.

Hull hooker Lee Jackson was also a lively customer until he was forced off with stomach cramps after 37 minutes, Bobby Goulding moving to hooker with Deryck Fox coming on to play his traditional scrum half role.

By then, Britain were already 20-0 up, with tries from Paul Eastwood, Goulding and Dixon, plus four goals from Davies. Aware of the danger of flagging in the sapping heat of the Lloyd Robson Oval, the Lions came out roaring at the start of the second half and ran in three tries in a five-minute spell through Gibson, Daryl Powell and Schofield.

Papua New Guinea gained consolation through a try from scrum half Gigmai Ongugo, but Britain had the last word with Gibson's second touchdown putting the strained Lions in the right mood for a four-day break in Cairns before the 10-match tour of New Zealand.

Complementing the seven-try triumph was the fact that the second Test was played before a Port Moresby crowd bereft of riot police, rifle shots and tear gas cannisters.

Packman Paul Dixon, scorer of a 37th minute try in the Port Moresby Test.

SECOND TEST (World Cup-rated)

2 June   Port Moresby

PAPUA NEW GUINEA 8   **GREAT BRITAIN 40**

Ipisa Wanega	1.	Alan Tait
Arnold Krewanty	2.	Paul Eastwood
Phillip Boge	3.	Jonathan Davies
Bal Numapo	4.	Daryl Powell
Mea Morea	5.	Carl Gibson
Stanley Haru	6.	Garry Schofield
Gigmai Ongugo	7.	Bobby Goulding
Ati Lomutopa	8.	Ray Powell
Michael Matmillo	9.	Lee Jackson
Tuiyo Evei	10.	Keith England
Joe Gispe	11.	Denis Betts
Arebo Taumaku, Capt	12.	Paul Dixon
Michael Angara	13.	Mike Gregory, Capt.
Chris Itam	14.	Deryck Fox
Hoah Kool	15.	Karl Fairbank
Goro Arigai	16.	Shaun Irwin
Max Tiri	17.	Phil Clarke

T: Ongugo
G: Numapo (2)
Substitutions:
Tiri for Lomutopa (45 min.)
Itam for Morea (55 min.)
Half-time 0-20
Referee: Dennis Hale (New Zealand)
Attendance: 5,969

T: Gibson (2), Eastwood,
Goulding, Dixon, D. Powell,
Schofield
G: Davies (6)
Substitutions:
Fox for Jackson (37 min.)
Clarke for Gregory (57 min.)

Scorechart

Minute	Score	PNG	GB
6:	Eastwood (T)		
	Davies (G)	0	6
24:	Goulding (T)		
	Davies (G)	0	12
33:	Davies (PG)	0	14
37:	Dixon (T)		
	Davies (G)	0	20
42:	Numapo (PG)	2	20
54:	Gibson (T)	2	24
57:	D. Powell (T)	2	28
59:	Schofield (T)		
	Davies (G)	2	34
62:	Ongugo (T)		
	Numapo (G)	8	34
73:	Gibson (T)		
	Davies (G)	8	40

10 June

Napier

PRESIDENT'S XIII	22
GREAT BRITAIN	23

1. Bibb
2. Devereux
3. D. Powell
4. Davies
5. Gibson
6. Schofield, Capt.
7. Goulding
8. Lucas
9. Dermott
10. England (R. Powell, 54 min.)
11. Betts
12. Dixon
13. Clarke (Bishop, 64 min.)

T: Gibson, Dermott, Davies
G: Davies (5), Dermott (dg)

President's XIII:

M. Edwards; W. Mann, M. Nixon, P. Tuimavave, Panapa; Clark (K. Shelford), Galbraith; A. Shelford, P. Ropati, G. Mann, Tagaloa, Leota (Faimalo), Kuiti, Capt.

T: Nixon (2), Panapa, Tuimavave
G: Edwards (3)

Half-time: 12-16

Referee: Jim Stokes
Attendance: 3,163

Wigan hooker Dermott dropped a goal four minutes from time to clinch a one-point victory for Britain at Napier's McLean Park, staging a Rugby League tour fixture for the first time in its 70-year history. Dermott struck the ball on the turn from 18 yards to give the Lions a morale-boosting start to a demanding six-week tour of New Zealand.

The home side were hardly strangers to the tourists, all but one of the starting 13 having played in England, 10 on club duty. With Kiwi Test jerseys at stake, the President's XIII enjoyed the greater share of possession and generally supported and moved the ball to better effect.

But the Lions were inspired by big-hearted Wigan prop Lucas, who overcame formidable pack opposition to gain valuable yardage. Davies continued to make his mark, particularly on the scoring front with a further five goals and a try to take his tally to 56 points in five appearances.

13 June

Addington Showgrounds, Christchurch

CANTERBURY SELECT	18
GREAT BRITAIN	10

1. Tait
2. Eastwood
3. Irwin
4. Lydon
5. Simpson
6. Steadman
7. Fox, Capt.
8. Lucas (R. Powell, 37 min.)
9. Jackson
10. Fairbank (Gregory, 61 min.)
11. Smales
12. Price
13. Bishop

T: Bishop, Tait
G: Eastwood

Canterbury Select XIII:

Hall; Taewa, Dorreen, Rodger, Kaisa; M. Nixon, Whittaker; Cowan, Wallace, Capt., Simanu (Angell), Leck, Culley, L. Edwards (Setu)

T: Dorreen, Whittaker, Leck

G: Culley (3)

Half-time: 4-0

Referee: Dennis Hale
Attendance: 1,338

Canterbury's first-ever victory over a British touring side sent coach Reilly back to the drawing board. The Christchurch fixture had been intended to be a stage for Castleford's Steadman to stake a claim for the troublesome Test role at stand off and for Wigan prop Lucas to further his graduation to a full international cap. It was not to be.

Reilly described the British performance as 'abysmal' with only Hull K.R.'s Bishop making an impression in just his second tour appearance, having been hit by injury and dental problems. Canterbury had built an 18-0 lead before Bishop scored his try after a 35-yard run from the base of the scrum, slipping two tackles on the way.

However, it was too late and a more respectable scoreline was achieved only after the final hooter had blown as a high crossfield kick from Lydon — making his first appearance on the tour — eventually reached Tait, Eastwood adding the goal.

Ironically, history-making Canterbury featured just five players with British club experience and even then only in the more humble ranks of Rochdale Hornets, Swinton, Carlisle, Doncaster and Chorley Borough.

17 June

Carlaw Park, Auckland

AUCKLAND	24
GREAT BRITAIN	13

1. Bibb
2. Gibson
3. Lydon (Tait, Half-time)
4. Schofield
5. Davies
6. Steadman
7. Goulding
8. Skerrett (Dixon, 46 min.)
9. Dermott
10. England
11. Betts
12. R. Powell
13. Gregory, Capt.

T: Skerrett, Steadman
G: Davies (2), Goulding (dg)

Auckland:
P. Tuimavave; Patton, Panapa, I. Ropati, W. Mann; McClennan, Capt., Galbraith; Brown, P. Ropati, Solomona (Leota), Nikau, Tagaloa, T. Tuimavave.

T: Panapa (2), Patton, Nikau
G: Brown (4)

Half-time: 12-12

Referee: Keith Blackler
Attendance: 7,614

Two tries in the last 18 minutes gave Auckland a fifth victory against Great Britain in their last six meetings. The 'fourth Test' was marred by ugly first-half scenes including three brawls.

A quagmire of a Carlaw Park pitch was not conducive to open football, and it took an exceptional try from centre Panapa to clinch success for the Auckland outfit.

Coach Reilly found plenty to enthuse about in defeat, particularly the form of packmen Roy Powell, Betts and England. The loss of injury worries Lydon and Skerrett around half-time handicapped Britain after raised fists disrupted concentration earlier. It was not until the third outburst, shortly before the break — when Galbraith appeared to hit Lydon, who missed the second period with a bruised jaw — that referee Blackler took disciplinary action, the Kiwi half back being sent to the sin bin.

20 June

Huntly

KIWI COLTS	10
GREAT BRITAIN	22

1. Simpson (Price, 22 min)
2. Eastwood
3. Irwin
4. D. Powell
5. Devereux
6. Davies
7. Fox, Capt.
8. R. Powell
9. Jackson
10. Fairbank
11. Clarke
12. Smales
13. Bishop

T: Eastwood (3), Clarke
G: Davies (3)

Kiwi Colts:
Nahu (Rodger), Hall, I. Ropati, Patton, Taewa; K. Shelford, Galbraith; Lomax, Fisher, Simcott (Pongia), Tagaloa, L. Edwards, T. Tuimavave, Capt.

T: I. Ropati, Fisher
G: K. Shelford

Half-time: 6-2

Referee: Jim Stokes
Attendance: 972

A second-half hat-trick of tries by Hull winger Eastwood highlighted an impressive Great Britain fightback after the Lions had trailed 6-2. The Airlie Bird provided perfect finishing to complete two powerful breaks by centre partner Irwin and a brilliant 40-yard run by Davies.

Although Britain included only three of their squad preparing for the first British Coal Test, the victory was a morale-booster for the whole party after two successive defeats. A depressing hat-trick of defeats seemed to be on the way as they fumbled through an awkward first 40 minutes in wet, miserable conditions against an eager under-24 side.

Trailing 6-2, the Lions lost full back Simpson with a dislocated finger and were relying heavily on Daryl Powell and Fairbank before ripping into the Colts with four tries in 20 minutes in a devastating second-half spell.

Davies, playing at stand off in a bid to clinch the Test role, fared favourably against former Kiwi Test man Kelly Shelford, the only full international in the Colts side, although the British line-up also contained a host of under-24s.

FIRST TEST v. NEW ZEALAND

Garry Schofield, villain of the shock first Test defeat in Papua New Guinea, was hailed as the hero of this dramatic one-point against-the-odds triumph. The beleaguered British toppled pre-match favourites New Zealand 11-10, a 57th minute drop goal by tour vice-captain Schofield tipping the scales.

The Leeds skipper also had a hand in both of Britain's tries as he fully justified team manager Reilly's decision to stand by him, despite his early disappointing form. Even the ultra-loyal Reilly admitted he had wavered a little before handing Schofield the key stand off role, but was full of praise for him after Britain's victory ended a run of five successive Test defeats in New Zealand stretching back to 1979.

Britain fell behind twice in the first half and trailed 10-4 after 21 minutes, but Schofield led them back each time to finish the first half level at 10-10 before banging over the winning drop goal from 25 yards.

New Zealand, under new coach Bob Bailey, had pledged to play open football and shot into the lead inside three minutes when Sam Panapa touched down. Schofield made his first strike seven minutes later, slipping a tackle 25 yards out to send in Jonathan Davies.

Peter Brown's penalty edged the Kiwis back in front and they went further ahead when Kevin Iro crashed over in the corner. New Zealand were well in command at that stage before Schofield struck again in the 34th minute. He began a three-pronged Leeds attack, unleashing Paul Dixon on a strong run which led to Carl Gibson taking over to dash in for the equalising try.

Although that finished the tryscoring, Schofield remained the dominant figure, adding six raking touch-finding kicks and being the top tackling back with 18. It was not a faultless display, but errors were inevitable as he was so totally involved.

With New Zealand winning the scrums 15-10 and penalties going 9-4 in their favour, the Kiwis were in possession a valuable 10 minutes more than Britain. But a tremendous defensive display kept the home side out for the last hour. Dixon led the way with 37 tackles, followed by skipper Mike Gregory's 30.

One long second-half siege by New Zealand ended when Martin Offiah, playing his first match of the tour after battling with an ankle injury, dashed in for an interception near his own line, and was well on the way to the other end when he was recalled for offside amid British protests. Gibson was also unlucky with an interception as he failed to hold the ball after going clear.

New Zealand had most of the luck, particularly with their second try when a clearance kick by Brown deflected off a British player to set up the 60-yard five-man tryscoring move.

That seemed to give the Kiwis the impression tries would come easily and, after their impressive opening, much of their directness went out of their play. They had plenty of chances to win by goal kicks, but Brown succeeded with only one from five attempts.

Dean Clark was their most dangerous back early on, while Tawera Nikau and skipper Hugh McGahan threatened up front, but Britain's backs-against-the-wall spirit proved too much.

FIRST TEST

24 June   Palmerston North

NEW ZEALAND 10   **GREAT BRITAIN 11**

Darrell Williams	1.	Chris Bibb
Tony Iro	2.	Jonathan Davies
Kevin Iro	3.	Joe Lydon
Tony Kemp	4.	Carl Gibson
Sam Panapa	5.	Martin Offiah
Dean Clark	6.	Garry Schofield
Gary Freeman	7.	Bobby Goulding
Peter Brown	8.	Kelvin Skerrett
Duane Mann	9.	Martin Dermott
Brent Todd	10.	Keith England
Tawera Nikau	11.	Denis Betts
Mark Horo	12.	Paul Dixon
Hugh McGahan, Capt.	13.	Mike Gregory, Capt.
Mark Nixon	14.	Deryck Fox
Morvin Edwards	15.	Ian Lucas
Dean Lonergan	16.	Daryl Powell
George Mann	17.	Roy Powell

T: Panapa, K. Iro   T: Davies, Gibson
G: Brown   G: Davies, Schofield (dg)
Substitutions: Substitutions:
G. Mann for Todd (60 min.)   R. Powell for Skerrett (46 min.)
Edwards for T. Iro (69 min.)   D. Powell for Lydon (62 min.)
Half-time: 10-10
Referee: Dennis Manson (Australia)
Attendance: 8,073

Scorechart

Minute	Score	NZ	GB
3:	Panapa (T)	4	0
10:	Davies (T)	4	4
18:	Brown (PG)	6	4
21:	K. Iro (T)	10	4
34:	Gibson (T)		
	Davies (G)	10	10
57:	Schofield (DG)	10	11
	Scrums	15	10
	Penalties	9	4

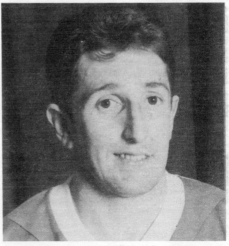

A first Kiwi Test try and goal for Jonathan Davies, the top goal and points scorer of the Lions tour.

27 June

Wellington

WELLINGTON	30
GREAT BRITAIN	22

1. Lyon
2. Eastwood
3. Irwin
4. D. Powell
5. Devereux
6. Davies
7. Fox, Capt.
8. Lucas (Bishop, 60 min.)
9. Jackson
10. Fairbank
11. Smales (Dixon, 40 min.)
12. Price
13. Clarke

T: Fairbank, Smales, Davies, Lyon
G: Davies (3)

Wellington:
P. Edwards; Molemau, Ewe, M. Edwards, Capt., Aramoana; Gilbert, G. Tangira; Lomax, Harvey, Piva (Whakarau), O'Sullivan, Faimalo, Kuiti

T: Molemau, Aramoana, M. Edwards, G. Tangira
G: Gilbert (7)

Half-time: 8-22

Referee: Neville Kesha
Attendance: 845

Great Britain again rewrote the record books in defeat, by becoming the first-ever international side to lose to Wellington. Ironically, the unwanted breakthrough came at a saturated Basin Reserve after a good first-half performance saw the tourists establish a 22-8 half-time lead.

Tries from Fairbank and Smales helped open a 12-2 margin and, even allowing for the concession of a soft try, the Lions played some admirable rugby in difficult conditions, adding tries from stand off Davies and full back Lyon, making his tour debut after being flown in as a replacement for the injured Tait.

Wellington, fired up at half-time by coach Howie Tamati, the former Wigan hooker, soon sensed that they could snatch an unlikely and historic victory. Three goals from Gilbert and a try from Kiwi Test squad member Morvin Edwards brought them back to 22-18, before Tangira ran on to a grubber kick from what Britain claimed was an offside position. The final mistake in a second-half catalogue of errors came in the last minute when winger Aramoana was presented with an interception try.

1 July

Rotorua

NEW ZEALAND MAORIS	12
GREAT BRITAIN	20

1. Bibb
2. Eastwood
3. Gibson (Lydon, Half-time)
4. D. Powell
5. Offiah
6. Schofield
7. Fox
8. R. Powell
9. Dermott (Goulding, 16 min.)
10. England
11. Betts
12. Dixon
13. Gregory, Capt.

T: Schofield, Betts, Eastwood
G: Eastwood (4)

New Zealand Maoris:
M. Edwards; Hoppe, Nahu, Watson, Aramoana; K. Shelford, Capt., G. Tangira; Lomax, Harvey, Lowrie (Harris), Nikau, Kuiti, Ramsey

T: G. Tangira, Aramoana
G: M. Edwards (2)

Half-time: 8-2

Referee: Des O'Sullivan
Attendance: 3,184

Inspired by skipper Gregory and vice-captain Schofield, Britain got the morale-boosting victory they desperately needed. Kingpin Gregory finished in pain with a recurrence of his Achilles' tendon injury, while Schofield was a tryscorer as well as playmaker.

Hull winger Eastwood put in a strong claim for a second Test spot, taking his tour points tally to 66 in nine games with four goals from five attempts and a last minute try after a 60-yard break from a scrum by Gregory.

With a strong wind at their backs, Britain controlled the second half for long periods but they had to wait until the final 10 minutes before translating their authority into points. Lydon's high kick 10 minutes from time was to prove the game's decisive factor. As the Maori full back succumbed to pressure, Fox collected the spilled ball to feed Schofield who sent out a sweetly timed pass for Betts to touch down, Eastwood's last-ditch try leaving a scoreline which did not flatter the tourists.

Denis Betts, a tryscorer against the Maoris at Rotorua.

4 July

New Plymouth

TARANAKI INVITATION	**0**
GREAT BRITAIN	**24**

1. Bibb
2. Eastwood
3. Irwin
4. Lyon
5. Devereux
6. Simpson
7. Fox, Capt.
8. Lucas (R. Powell, 37 min.)
9. Smales
10. Fairbank
11. Price
12. Clarke
13. Bishop (Dermott, 50 min.)

T: Simpson, Lyon, Fairbank, Irwin
G: Eastwood (4)

Taranaki Invitation XIII:
Tumoana; W. Tangira, Gwiazdzinski, Watson,
B. Nixon; Smith, G. Tangira; Piva, Mason (Martin),
Katene, McAllister, Kitto (Jackson), Harvey

Half-time: 0-8

Referee: Dennis Hale
Attendance: 2,675

Relishing the heavy going, Great Britain produced one of their best displays of the tour, the final margin of four tries without reply being an accurate reflection of their superiority in farcical conditions against an experienced Taranaki side.

Heavy rain left large areas of the pitch under water and the match could have been postponed. Handling mistakes were inevitable, but Britain cut theirs to a minimum, employed a suitable kicking game and fully deserved their ovation from a 2,000-plus crowd who braved the driving rain.

A Simpson try and two Eastwood goals were scant reward for the tourists' first-half superiority, but their fitness told in the last quarter. Picking up a loose ball, Price ran across the home defence to send in Lyon; substitute Roy Powell powered through to set up Fairbank; then Fox's pass created the touchdown for Irwin. Two further goals from Eastwood completed the comprehensive Lions victory.

Assistant coach Larder was in full charge for the first time as coach Reilly stayed with the Test squad in Auckland.

SECOND TEST v. NEW ZEALAND

Martin Offiah's controversial late inclusion in the British Coal tour party was costed at more than £1,000 a match. The Widnes flier repaid the bill by finishing off a spectacular 75-yard attack to snatch a 16-14 victory for Great Britain — and with it the Test series — seven minutes from time.

It was the first touchdown of the tour for Offiah and the record-breaking winger showed he had not lost the scoring touch as he high-stepped away from a desperate cover tackle inches from the touchline at the end of his triumphant 40-yard sprint. The build-up was as good as the outcome, with Kelvin Skerrett bumping his way through in his own 25-yard zone before slipping a neat pass to Garry Schofield, who linked with Daryl Powell to launch Offiah.

New Zealand, clear pre-series favourites, were beaten more emphatically than the scoreline suggests. Britain scored three tries to one and only five penalty goals from ex-All Black Matthew Ridge kept the Kiwis in the hunt. Ridge, gaining Test selection after only four club games, was not as impressive as the scoring sheet would suggest. His goals were all from easy positions and he missed two from reasonable distances.

Seven of Ridge's goal attempts came from an overall penalty count of 14-3 in New Zealand's favour and though skipper Mike Gregory, an inspiring captain, often questioned the decisions of Australian referee Bill Harrigan, his players refused to be put off their game.

Schofield's part in Britain's match-winning try was almost inevitable, as he was also responsible for the other two in a repeat of his first Kiwi Test display when he carved out both touchdowns. The Lions had defended for almost the whole of the first 33 minutes and were trailing 4-0 when the Leeds skipper made his first spellbinding move, opening the Kiwi defence with a dummy and going straight between the posts. Davies added the goal to give Britain a brief 6-4 lead before Ridge equalised with his third penalty goal just before the interval and then edged New Zealand in front with another in the 50th minute.

Then Schofield worked his magic again, slipping effortlessly out of two tackles and sending in Denis Betts, Davies's goal putting the Lions four points ahead. On the hour, Mark Horo juggled with Tawera Nikau's pass to grab an equalising try in the corner and, although Ridge missed the resultant goal, the Manly full back was on target with a subsequent penalty.

With Britain nattering over refereeing decisions, Offiah was blatantly held back as he tried to support a break by Betts. Justice was done when the Widnes winger was given just enough room to escape for his match-winning try.

Hull hooker Lee Jackson contributed his usual tremendous workrate, probing in attack, making 27 tackles and winning the scrums 10-8 in an impressive display. Paul Dixon headed the tackle count with 29, despite being substituted for the last 14 minutes, while Skerrett completed his first 80 minutes on tour with 25 tackles and a barrage of forward rushes.

Having dominated both Tests territorially, New Zealand failed miserably to push home their advantage, although Hugh McGahan was again an inspirational capitain. Victory gave Britain their first overseas Test series triumph since 1979 — a credit to the indomitable team spirit established by manager Malcolm Reilly.

SECOND TEST

8 July   **Mount Smart Stadium, Auckland**

NEW ZEALAND 14		GREAT BRITAIN 16
Matthew Ridge	1.	Joe Lydon
Sam Panapa	2.	Jonathan Davies
Kevin Iro	3.	Daryl Powell
Darrell Williams	4.	Carl Gibson
Tony Iro	5.	Martin Offiah
Dean Clark	6.	Garry Schofield
Gary Freeman	7.	Bobby Goulding
Peter Brown	8.	Kelvin Skerrett
Duane Mann	9.	Lee Jackson
Brent Todd	10.	Keith England
Tawera Nikau	11.	Denis Betts
Mark Horo	12.	Paul Dixon
Hugh McGahan, Capt.	13.	Mike Gregory, Capt.
Morvin Edwards	14.	Deryck Fox
Tony Kemp	15.	Roy Powell
George Mann	16.	Shaun Irwin
Dean Lonergan	17.	Karl Fairbank

T: Horo
G: Ridge (5)
Substitutions:
Kemp for Clark (76 min.)
Lonergan for Todd (76 min.)
Half-time: 6-6
Referee: Bill Harrigan (Australia)
Attendance: 7,843

T: Schofield, Betts, Offiah
G: Davies (2)
Substitutions:
Irwin for Gibson (59 min.)
R. Powell for Dixon (67 min.)

Scorechart

Minute	Score	NZ	GB
7:	Ridge (PG)	2	0
13:	Ridge (PG)	4	0
33:	Schofield (T)		
	Davies (G)	4	6
39:	Ridge (PG)	6	6
50:	Ridge (PG)	8	6
55:	Betts (T)		
	Davies (G)	8	12
60:	Horo (T)	12	12
66:	Ridge (PG)	14	12
73:	Offiah (T)	14	16
	Scrums	8	10
	Penalties	14	3

Match-winning tryscorer Martin Offiah.

THIRD TEST v. NEW ZEALAND

New Zealand's former All Black Matthew Ridge justified his rapid call-up to Test Rugby League by caning Great Britain with six of the best to ruin the Lions' chances of making a clean sweep of the British Coal Test series. Britain scored three tries to two, but in a faultless display Ridge never missed a shot at goal, including four penalties.

Ridge's kicking apart, Britain should still have won this World Cup-rated third Test. In comparison to the rest of his award-winning career in the 13-a-side code, the role of culprit fell to record-breaking winger Martin Offiah.

Within three minutes, the Widnes flier was given the simple opportunity to finish off a splendid 75-yard move engineered by Wigan scrum half Bobby Goulding, but lost the ball as he attempted to make a one-handed touchdown between the posts. After becoming a hero by scoring the match-winning try in the second Test, Offiah's blunder would have shamed a schoolboy! Even a well-taken try in the 75th minute could not cover Offiah's embarrassment and he suffered in the silence in the dressing room afterwards.

It did not make it any easier that Tony Kemp, twice a servant with Doncaster, also threw away a tryscoring chance for New Zealand when he lost the ball plunging for the line in the 67th minute. That was due in no small measure to Garry Schofield's desperate diving tackle on his opposite number.

That tackle was just one part of another outstanding performance at stand off which confirmed Schofield as the man of the series. Having had a major role in all five of Britain's tries in the first two Tests, the Leeds captain scored the first and set up the second. His 12th minute touchdown was a brilliant solo effort as he sent the defence the wrong way with a big dummy and foiled them again with a little one on his 35-yard dash for the line.

That edged Britain 4-2 ahead, but they had

slipped to 20-6 down before Schofield carved out the second try after 59 minutes, a strong break leading to Daryl Powell sending in Roy Powell near the posts. Davies added the simple goal and then one from the touchline, after Offiah's try, to leave Britain only two points behind, but a last second drop goal by Kiwi skipper Hugh McGahan clinched New Zealand's victory.

Tawera Nikau was undoubtedly the outstanding Kiwi player of the series, highlighting another impressive second row performance by scoring their second try after Kemp had powered in for the first to help them to an 18-6 interval lead.

Despite being beaten by penalty goals, the overall penalty count was 10-9 to the Lions, who also won the scrums 8-3. Three players were sent to the sin bin, Britain's Bobby Goulding and Kiwi Darren Williams for foul play and Schofield for holding down in the tackle. Keith England topped the British tackle count with 32.

Third Test hooker Martin Dermott.

THIRD TEST (World Cup-rated)

15 July   **Queen Elizabeth Park, Christchurch**

NEW ZEALAND 21		**GREAT BRITAIN 18**
Matthew Ridge	1.	Joe Lydon
Sam Panapa	2.	Jonathan Davies
Kevin Iro	3.	Carl Gibson
Darrell Williams	4.	Daryl Powell
Tony Iro	5.	Martin Offiah
Tony Kemp	6.	Garry Schofield
Gary Freeman	7.	Bobby Goulding
Peter Brown	8.	Kelvin Skerrett
Duane Mann	9.	Martin Dermott
Brent Todd	10.	Keith England
Tawera Nikau	11.	Denis Betts
Mark Horo	12.	Roy Powell
Hugh McGahan, Capt.	13.	Mike Gregory, Capt.
Morvin Edwards	14.	Deryck Fox
Dean Clark	15.	Shaun Irwin
George Mann	16.	Paul Dixon
Dean Lonergan	17.	Karl Fairbank

T: Kemp, Nikau   T: Schofield, R. Powell, Offiah
G: Ridge (6), McGahan (dg)   G: Davies (3)
Substitutions: Substitutions:
Edwards for K. Iro (45 min.)   Irwin for Gibson (Half-time)
Lonergan for Todd (56 min.)   Dixon for Skerrett (Half-time)
Half-time: 18-6
Referee: Bill Harrigan (Australia)   Attendance: 3,133

Scorechart

Minute	Score	NZ	GB
6:	Ridge (PG)	2	0
12:	Schofield (T)	2	4
19:	Davies (PG)	2	6
22:	Kemp (T)		
	Ridge (G)	8	6
25:	Ridge (PG)	10	6
28:	Ridge (PG)	12	6
36:	Nikau (T)		
	Ridge (G)	18	6
55:	Ridge (PG)	20	6
59:	R. Powell (T)		
	Davies (G)	20	12
75:	Offiah (T)		
	Davies (G)	20	18
79:	McGahan (DG)	21	18
	Scrums	3	8
	Penalties	9	10

Roy Powell, scored his only try of the tour in the last match.

Highly praised 1990 British Lions skipper Mike Gregory in action in the third Test in Christchurch.

Australian tour vice-captain Benny Elias, Man of the Match in the second British Coal Test victory at Old Trafford, Manchester.

1990 KANGAROOS

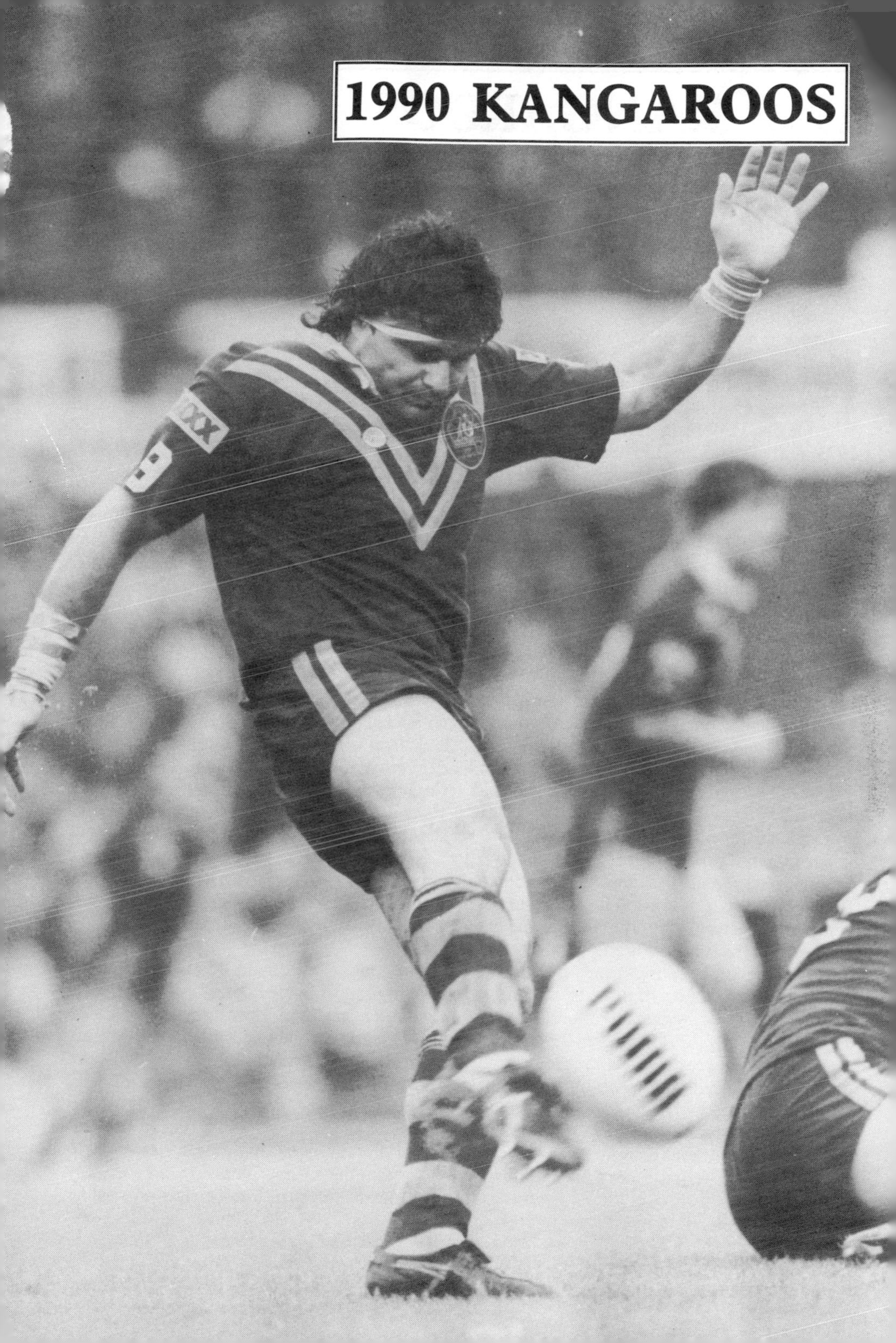

1990 KANGAROOS

1990 TOUR REVIEW

The bold, imaginative idea to hire Wembley Stadium for the first British Coal Test rekindled the Ashes and set the 1990 Anglo-Australian series alight.

The Rugby Football League's adventurous decision to stage the opening Test encounter outside of the North caused widespread controversy. Two previous Tests at Wembley had flopped, with gates of 9,874 in 1973 and 13,946 in 1963. But the latest experiment was a roaring success .... on and off the field. A record British Test crowd of 54,569 paying a Rugby League Test world record £560,000 witnessed a well-deserved, emotional 19-12 victory for a Great Britain side written off as underdogs and fuelled only by self-belief.

Great Britain entered the Wembley arena to the strains of *Land of Hope and Glory* led by the Philharmonia Chorus and left to a long drawn-out standing ovation. Australia had lost their Invincibles tag carried through the 1982 and 1986 tours, Britain having proved that their 26-12 success in Sydney in July 1988 — their last meeting — was not a one-off.

The League had stated that the Wembley venue was selected because the game's top international event deserved the nation's finest sporting stadium. The mixture of venue and victory gave Rugby League its highest-ever national awareness, attracting massive television ratings and media exposure, breaking a host of records including:

● A record Test aggregate attendance of 133,684, beating the 114,883 in 1948.

● World record receipts for the three-match Test series, breaking the seven-figure barrier for the first time with a total of £1,180,000.

● A record British Test crowd of 54,569 at Wembley for the first encounter, beating the 50,583 at the 1986 first Test at Old Trafford, Manchester.

● A record average crowd for a tour of Britain of 19,995 at the 13 matches, beating the 16,732 at 27 matches in 1948.

● Record Kangaroo tour share of £570,000, made up of £380,000 from the gates, £70,000 from television and £120,000 Castlemaine XXXX sponsorship.

The choice of Wembley proved to be a major advantage in the British hope for further Test glory, the 1988 Sydney triumph being followed by the home and away Test series successes over New Zealand.

A near-capacity 46,615 crowd at Manchester United's ground paid £381,000 to witness probably the most dramatic ending to a Test match, a 10-10 draw looming as the game entered the final minute. A 70-yard run by Australian scrum half Ricky Stuart set up the match-winning try for skipper Mal Meninga with just 20 seconds on the official timekeeper's watch.

The third British Coal Test at Elland Road, Leeds, was already a 32,500 sell-out with receipts of £239,000. The Australians had learnt their lessons well and British danger men skipper Ellery Hanley and Garry Schofield were blotted out as the Kangaroos ran in three tries in a 14-0 series-clinching victory.

Meninga was again a tryscorer to become only the second Australian to touch down in each match of a series in Britain, winger Ken Irvine achieving the notable feat 27 years earlier.

The convincing Elland Road success, after making eight changes for the Old Trafford encounter, restored the Kangaroos' world standing and earned two valuable World Cup points, while retaining their 31-year unbeaten Test series record in Britain.

The harrowing Wembley defeat was to be the 17th Kangaroos' only defeat on the 13-match tour, equalling the shortest-ever. It was Australia's first defeat in any British tour fixture since the second Test reversal at

Bradford in 1978, a run of 37 consecutive victories.

Elsewhere the 1990 tourists carried all before them, with notable high scoring triumphs over Championship title contenders Hull and Wigan, the biggest club gate of 24,814 being attracted to Central Park. Other 30-plus scores were run up against St. Helens, Wakefield Trinity, Cumbria and Halifax, while Widnes came closest to a club victory with a 15-8 scoreline at Naughton Park.

Despite ground safety restrictions forcing limited all-ticket crowds at the likes of Hull, Wakefield, Castleford, Warrington and Halifax, the 1990 tour aggregate of 259,938 was the biggest since 22 matches drew 286,729 in 1963.

The Kangaroos were slightly subdued on the scoring front compared with the Invincibles of 1982 and 1986. Although bagging a creditable 68 tries, one of the blackspots of the tour was poor goalkicking with only 37 goals and one drop goal. Andrew Ettingshausen topped their tryscoring chart with 11, including hat-tricks in his first two outings. Utility back Greg Alexander led the goalscorers with 21, including the best match tally of six. Skipper Meninga was top points-scorer with 58 from seven tries and 15 goals.

Meninga and Ettingshausen made most full appearances, with nine each, while Alexander played in 12 matches including six as substitute, missing only the second British Coal Test when he was a non-playing substitute.

As always, the tour saw the emergence of new Test talent and in-form travellers, with coach Bobby Fulton transforming the side en route to Ashes glory. Keeping faith with the Test side which had beaten France and New Zealand during the summer, the Warrington-born coach reacted to the trauma of defeat at Wembley by making eight changes for the pressure meeting at Old Trafford. Out went early tour favourites Michael Hancock, Allan Langer, Kerrod Walters, Martin Bella and John Cartwright. In came Dale Shearer, debutant Cliff Lyons, the irrepressible Benny Elias, Glenn Lazarus and hard-working Brad Mackay, with ex-Wallaby Stuart moving to his regular scrum half spot. The newcomers all proved to be winners.

Britain were less adventurous in their selections. After the wholehearted success of Wembley — particularly the controversial choices of Paul Eastwood, Carl Gibson, Daryl Powell and Karl Harrison — coach Malcolm Reilly drafted in only fit-again Andy Platt and Paul Loughlin, as a substitute, for the second Test. Eastwood, a 14-point hero at Wembley, became the villain, missing vital goalkicks, one after Loughlin's score-levelling 70th minute try, when hindsight decreed that Loughlin himself should have been the marksman.

Reilly stayed loyal for the decider at Leeds, potential match-winner Jonathan Davies — the choice of the people — only being drafted in as substitute, although he took part for 71 minutes, being largely ineffective against the well-oiled Australian machine.

British Coal again presented £250 Man of the Match awards in each Test, the winners being Hanley at Wembley, Elias at Old Trafford and Stuart at Elland Road. The British Coal Men of the Series, selected by each team management, were British skipper Hanley and Australian back row forward Bob Lindner.

Meninga crowned a memorable year — having been named Adidas Golden Boot winner as best International player, Premiership Trophy-winning captain and Kangaroo skipper — by being named as BBC TV Overseas Sports Personality of the Year.

BRITISH TOUR RESULTS

Date		Result	Score	Opposition	Venue	Attendance
Oct	7	W	34-4	St. Helens	St. Helens	15,219
	10	W	36-18	Wakefield T.	Wakefield	7,724
	14	W	34-6	Wigan	Wigan	24,814
	17	W	42-10	Cumbria	Workington	6,750
	21	W	22-10	Leeds	Leeds	16,037
	27	L	12-19	GREAT BRITAIN	Wembley, London	54,569
	31	W	26-6	Warrington	Warrington	10,200
Nov	4	W	28-8	Castleford	Castleford	9,033
	6	W	36-18	Halifax	Halifax	8,730
	10	W	14-10	GREAT BRITAIN	Old Trafford, Man'r	46,615
	14	W	34-4	Hull	Hull	13,081
	18	W	15-8	Widnes	Widnes	14,666
	24	W	14-0	GREAT BRITAIN*	Elland Road, Leeds	32,500

*World Cup-rated

BRITISH TOUR SUMMARY

				FOR				AGAINST			
P	W	D	L	T	G	Dr	Pts	T	G	Dr	Pts
13	12	0	1	68	37	1	347	21	17	3	121

BRITISH TEST SUMMARY

				FOR				AGAINST			
P	W	D	L	T	G	Dr	Pts	T	G	Dr	Pts
3	2	0	1	8	4	0	40	5	4	1	29

BRITISH TOUR RECORDS

Biggest attendance: 54,569, first Test at Wembley

Highest score and widest margin: 42-10 v. Cumbria

Highest score against: Lost to Great Britain 19-12

Most tries in a match: 3 by Andrew Ettingshausen v. St. Helens and Wigan; Dale Shearer v. Cumbria

Most goals in a match:
6 by Greg Alexander v. Wakefield T.

Most points in match: 12 by Andrew Ettingshausen v. St. Helens and Wigan; Greg Alexander v. Wakefield Trinity and Halifax; Dale Shearer v. Cumbria; Mal Meninga v. Castleford

Most tries on tour: 11 by Andrew Ettingshausen

Most goals on tour: 21 by Greg Alexander

Most points on tour: 58 by Mal Meninga

Most appearances: 12 (including six as substitute) by Greg Alexander

Most full appearances: 9 by Andrew Ettingshausen and Mal Meninga

Sent off: Mark Carroll, Ricky Stuart and David Gillespie, all v. Wakefield T.

Sin bin: Dale Shearer v. Wakefield T. and Castleford; Des Hasler v. Wakefield T.; Mark McGaw v. Leeds; Glenn Lazarus v. Warrington; Mark Sargent v. Halifax; Allan Langer v. Halifax; Cliff Lyons v. Widnes; Steve Roach v. Widnes and Great Britain, third Test.

Opponent sent off: John Thompson (Wakefield T.)

Opponents' sin bin: Billy Conway (Wakefield T.); Mike Gregory (Warrington); Ben Beevers (Halifax)

FRENCH TOUR RESULTS

Date	Result	Score	Opposition	Venue	Attendance
Nov 27	W	46-18	**French President's XIII**	Paris	3,000

T: Alexander (2), Fittler (2), Johns, Hasler, Kevin Walters, Langer, Sargent
G: Alexander (3), Shearer, Sargent

29	W	78-6	**France B**	Lyon	2,000

T: Alexander (5), Belcher (2), Fittler (2), Langer, Sargent, Geyer, Carroll
G: Alexander (13)

Dec 2	W	60-4	**FRANCE**	Avignon	3,329

France: Roses; Bouzer, Bienes, Bret, Pons; Fraisse (1t), Entat (capt); Titeux, Valero, Calvo, Divet, Verdes, Moliner. Subs: Marginet, Bouscayrol, Tisseyre. Lope (not used)
Australia: Belcher (2t); Ettinghausen (2t); Meninga (1g) (Capt), Daley, Shearer (1t); Lyons, Stuart; Roach, Elias, Lazarus (1t), Sironen (1t), Gillespie (1t), Mackay. Subs: Alexander (3t, 7g), Sargent, Geyer, Hasler (all played)
Referee: John Holdsworth (England)

5	W	38-9	**Roussillon**	Carcassonne	1,000

T: Fittler (2), Alexander, Shearer, Ettinghausen, Langer, Cartwright, Sargent
G: Alexander (3)

9	W	34-10	**FRANCE (World Cup-rated)**	Perpignan	3,428

France: Fraisse; Pons (1t), Bret, Delaunay, Bouzer; Moliner, Entat (1t) (capt); Tisseyre (1g), Valero, Buttignol, Divet, Lope, Verdes. Subs: Bienes, Marginet. Rimeriz, Titeux (not used)
Australia: Belcher; Alexander (1t, 3g), Meninga (1t) (capt), Shearer (1t), Ettinghausen (1t); Lyons, Stuart; Roach (1t), Elias, Lazarus, Sironen, Lindner, Mackay (2t). Subs: Johns, Sargent, Hasler, Gillespie. (all played)
Referee: John Holdsworth (England)

FRENCH TOUR SUMMARY

				FOR				AGAINST			
P	W	D	L	T	G	Dr	Pts	T	G	Dr	Pts
5	5	0	0	48	32	0	256	8	7	1	47

TOUR PARTY

Managers: Keith Barnes and Les Stokes
Coach: Bob Fulton
Medical Officer: Nathan Gibbs
Trainers: Shaun McRae, John Lewis and Brian Hollis

Player	Club	IN BRITAIN					IN FRANCE					IN TOTAL				
		App	Sub	T	G	Pts	App	Sub	T	G	Pts	App	Sub	T	G	Pts
ALEXANDER, Greg	Penrith	6	6	2	21	50	4	1	12	29	106	10	7	14	50	156
BELCHER, Gary	Canberra	8	—	2	2(1)	11	3	—	4	—	16	11	—	6	2(1)	27
BELLA, Martin	Manly-Warringah	5	3	1	—	4	3	—	1	—	4	8	3	2	—	8
CARROLL, Mark	South Sydney	2	1	1	—	4	3	—	—	—	—	5	1	1	—	4
CARTWRIGHT, John	Penrith	5	2	—	—	—	1	—	1	—	4	6	2	1	—	4
DALEY, Laurie	Canberra	5	1	—	—	—	1	—	—	—	—	6	1	—	—	—
ELIAS, Ben	Balmain	7	1	2	—	8	2	—	—	—	—	9	1	2	—	8
ETTINGSHAUSEN, Andrew	Cronulla	9	—	11	—	44	3	—	4	—	16	12	—	15	—	60
FITTLER, Brad	Penrith	5	1	2	—	8	3	—	6	—	24	8	1	8	—	32
GEYER, Mark	Penrith	4	1	3	—	12	3	1	1	—	4	7	2	4	—	16
GILLESPIE, David	Canterbury-Bankstown	5	3	—	—	—	3	1	1	—	4	8	4	1	—	4
HANCOCK, Michael	Brisbane Broncos	5	1	4	—	16	—	—	—	—	—	5	1	4	—	16
HASLER, Des	Manly-Warringah	4	4	2	—	8	3	2	1	—	4	7	6	3	—	12
JOHNS, Chris	Brisbane Broncos	5	2	3	—	12	3	1	1	—	4	8	3	4	—	16
LANGER, Allan	Brisbane Broncos	7	1	1	—	4	3	—	3	—	12	10	1	4	—	16
LAZARUS, Glenn	Canberra	6	5	1	—	4	2	—	1	—	4	8	5	2	—	8
LINDNER, Bob	Western Suburbs	8	1	2	—	8	1	—	—	—	—	9	1	2	—	8
LYONS, Cliff	Manly-Warringah	6	—	3	—	12	2	—	—	—	—	8	—	3	—	12
McGAW, Mark	Cronulla	5	1	1	—	4	2	—	2	—	8	7	1	3	—	12
MACKAY, Brad	St. George	7	3	2	—	8	2	—	2	—	8	9	3	4	—	16
MENINGA, Mal	Canberra	9	—	7	15	58	2	1	1	1	6	11	1	8	16	64
ROACH, Steve	Balmain	8	1	1	—	4	2	—	1	—	4	10	1	2	—	8
SARGENT, Mark	Newcastle	5	1	3	—	12	3	2	3	—	14	8	3	6	—	26
SHEARER, Dale	Brisbane Broncos	8	1	6	—	24	4	—	3	1	14	12	1	9	1	38
SIRONEN, Paul	Balmain	8	—	2	—	8	2	—	1	—	4	10	—	3	—	12
STUART, Ricky	Canberra	6	1	1	—	4	2	—	—	—	—	8	1	1	—	4
WALTERS, Kerrod	Brisbane Broncos	6	2	2	—	8	2	—	—	—	—	8	2	2	—	8
WALTERS, Kevin	Brisbane Broncos	5	—	4	—	16	3	—	1	—	4	8	—	5	—	20

( ) Drop goal included in total

The 1990 Kangaroos, left to right: Back Row: Roach, Ettingshausen, McGaw, Cartwright, Geyer, Carroll, Sironen, Bella, Alexander, Hasler, Hancock. Middle Row: Lewis, Hollis, Lyons, Gillespie, Daley, Kevin Walters, Stuart, Shearer, Mackay, Sargent, Lazarus, Gibbs, McRae. Front Row: Kerrod Walters, Langer, Johns, Stokes, Elias, Fulton, Meninga, Barnes, Belcher, Lindner, Fittler.

MATCH BY MATCH

7 October

ST. HELENS   **4**
AUSTRALIA   **34**

1. Belcher
2. Ettingshausen
3. Meninga, Capt.
4. McGaw
5. Hancock (Johns, 67 min.)
6. Daley
7. Langer (Alexander, 70 min.)
8. Roach (Lazarus, 66 min.)
9. Kerrod Walters
10. Bella
11. Cartwright
12. Sironen
13. Lindner (Mackay, 66 min.)

T: Ettingshausen (3), Meninga (2), Kerrod Walters, Roach, Hancock
G: Meninga

St. Helens:
Connolly; Hunte, Ropati, Veivers, Quirk; Griffiths (Bailey), Cooper; Neil (Haggerty), Groves, Ward, Forber (Connor), Harrison (Mann), Dwyer

T: Quirk

Half-time: 0-22

Referee: John Holdsworth (Kippax)
Attendance: 15,219

Australia spoilt St. Helens' ground centenary celebrations by inflicting an eight tries to one hammering in the opening tour fixture to give notice of their intention to extend a two-tour unbeaten record.

Ironically, it was Knowsley Road's favourite son — Kangaroo skipper Mal Meninga — who opened the scoring with a try after only three minutes. The ex-Saint added another touchdown but could not find his form with the boot, hitting only one successful shot from six attempts, Alexander and Daley also missing once.

Former Leeds utility back Ettingshausen notched a hat-trick of tries, while superb all-round performances were served up by Belcher, centre McGaw, scrum half Langer and second row pair Cartwright and Sironen.

As well as the off-target goalkicking, the Kangaroos were perturbed by a 20-11 penalty deficit with most offences being for offside or play-the-ball transgressions.

10 October

WAKEFIELD T.   **18**
AUSTRALIA   **36**

1. Alexander
2. Johns
3. Fittler
4. Kevin Walters (Hasler, 60 min.)
5. Shearer
6. Lyons (McGaw, 59 min.)
7. Stuart
8. Lazarus
9. Elias, Capt.
10. Sargent (Geyer, 62 min.)
11. Gillespie
12. Carroll
13. Mackay

T: Sargent, Johns, Kevin Walters, Lazarus, Fittler, Stuart
G: Alexander (6)

Wakefield T.:
Perry (Slater); Jones, Byrne, Eden (Wilson), Mason; Lazenby, M. Conway; Shelford, Thompson, Bell, Kelly (B. Conway), Du Toit (Morris), Price

T: Du Toit, Mason, Wilson
G: M. Conway (3)

Half-time: 8-24

Referee: Kevin Allatt (Southport)
Attendance: 7,724

Four players, including three Australians, were sent off and another three sent to the sin bin in an ill-tempered affair in Wakefield's first Kangaroo tour fixture since 1973.

The tourists were already down to 10 men when it was learnt after the match that second row forward Gillespie had been dismissed on the final whistle for dissent. Two of the sin-binned trio were also Australians as Southport referee Allatt struggled to keep control, receiving a post-match blasting from Kangaroo coach Fulton.

At the following day's judiciary, Gillespie, for dissent, and Stuart, allegedly punching, were found not guilty, while Carroll and Trinity's Thompson — sent off together for fighting at a scrum — each received sending-off-sufficient verdicts. Kangaroos Hasler and Shearer, plus Trinity's Billy Conway were sent to the sin bin, the overall penalty count being 26-7 to Trinity.

The Kangaroo second string outfit always looked too strong for Trinity, who contributed three top-class tries, county threequarter Mason scoring one and creating another for Wilson.

14 October

WIGAN   6
AUSTRALIA   34

1. Belcher (Alexander, 78 min.)
2. Ettingshausen
3. Meninga, Capt.
4. McGaw
5. Hancock
6. Daley
7. Langer (Stuart, 62 min.)
8. Roach
9. Kerrod Walters
10. Bella (Lazarus, 41 min.)
11. Cartwright
12. Sironen (Mackay, 48 min.)
13. Lindner

T: Ettingshausen (3), Belcher, Hancock, Langer, Mackay
G: Meninga (3)

Wigan:
Hampson; Myers (Preston), Iro (Goulding), Lydon, Marshall; Edwards, Gregory (Gildart); Lucas (Forshaw), Dermott, Skerrett, Betts, Goodway, Hanley

T: Edwards
G: Lydon

Half-time: 6-20

Referee: Colin Morris (Huddersfield)
Attendance: 24,814

Cliff Lyons, a graduate from the Emus second string side to a Test debut at Old Trafford.

Fielding six current Test squad members and four players who toured Down Under during the summer, Wigan's hopes of becoming the first British side to beat the Kangaroos since 1978 turned to humiliation. The near-25,000 crowd were stunned into near silence as the tourists ran in seven tries, winger Ettingshausen collecting a hat-trick in his second successive outing.

The Riversiders' consolation reply was a penalty try awarded to stand off Edwards, Lydon adding the goal, to open the scoring after seven minutes. After that, Wigan's challenge began to wane and once the rolling waves of green and gold breached the home defence the tries flooded in, four in the last 15 minutes of the first half. Australia's 35th consecutive victory in Britain could have been by a greater margin but for the continuing poor goalkicking, skipper Meninga hitting the target only three times.

Watching Great Britain coach Malcolm Reilly agonised at the awesome Kangaroo performance by the likely first Test line-up and the lack-lustre displays of Lion candidates Edwards, Hampson, Gregory and Hanley, who started impressively before fizzling out.

17 October
Workington

CUMBRIA	**10**
AUSTRALIA	**42**

1. Alexander
2. Shearer
3. Lyons
4. Fittler
5. Johns
6. Kevin Walters
7. Stuart (Mackay, 48 min.)
8. Gillespie (Lazarus, 61 min.)
9. Elias, Capt.
10. Sargent
11. Geyer
12. Carroll (Lindner, 61 min.)
13. Hasler

T: Shearer (3), Lyons (2), Carroll, Geyer, Elias
G: Alexander (5)

Cumbria:
Vickers (Carlisle); Rudd (Warrington), Fisher (Whitehaven), Rooney (Workington T.), Richardson (Whitehaven); Cameron (Whitehaven), D. Marwood (Barrow); Armstrong (Hull K.R.), Mounsey (Whitehaven), Howse (Whitehaven), G. Kendall (Barrow), Riley (Workington T.), Walker (Hull). Substitutions: Chambers (Warrington) for Riley, Neil (St. Helens) for G. Kendall, Penrice (Workington T.) for Rudd, Lofthouse (Whitehaven) for Vickers.

T: Richardson
G: Vickers, Cameron, Marwood (2dg)

Half-time: 4-16

Referee: Jim Smith (Halifax)
Attendance: 6,750

Celebrating the launch of Workington Town's floodlights, Australia ran in eight tries with second row Geyer proving to be the leading light on his first full appearance in the green and gold jersey. Having recovered from tonsilitis, Geyer paved the way for the first two touchdowns with astute ball handling and added the first try of the second half which triggered 20 minutes of rapid-fire scoring.

The game never matched the brightness of the new lights, the constant drizzle and the largely Second Division opposition providing a dampener. The conditions did not make for articulate football, but Alexander was outstanding at full back, winger Shearer collected a hat-trick of tries, while fellow second-stringers Sargent, Hasler and Carroll all showed up well.

21 October

LEEDS	**10**
AUSTRALIA	**22**

1. Belcher
2. Ettingshausen
3. Meninga, Capt.
4. McGaw (Gillespie, 41 min.)
5. Hancock
6. Daley
7. Langer (Alexander, 78 min.)
8. Roach (Lazarus, 72 min.)
9. Kerrod Walters (Elias, 41 min.)
10. Bella
11. Sironen
12. Lindner
13. Mackay

T: Sironen (2), Lindner, Meninga
G: Meninga (3)

Leeds:
Gallagher; Ford, Irving, Gibson (Creasser), Fawcett; Schofield, Harkin (Delaney); Molloy (Divorty), Gunn, Powell (Young), Dixon, Heugh, Kuiti

T: Gallagher, Dixon
G: Irving

Half-time: 10-6

Referee: Ray Tennant (Castleford)
Attendance: 16,037

Determined Leeds gave Britain's hopes a massive boost six days before the opening Test at Wembley, the Australians continuing their all-conquering run with one of the hardest earned of their 37 successive wins.

Leeds led 10-0 inside 18 minutes, were still four points ahead at half-time and did not fall behind until the 49th minute. Leeds skipper Schofield justified his claim to the Great Britain stand off spot, matching Kangaroo number six Daley for power and holding the edge in creativity as he carved out both Loiner touchdowns.

The Kangaroos clawed their way back, scoring 22 points without ever being able to relax. The giant second row Sironen pulled them back with their first two tries, loose forward Lindner adding a third before their backline got in on the act, full back Belcher creating a try for skipper Meninga.

Dixon's grafting Man of the Match display augured well for Test selection, while ex-All Black Gallagher, a tryscorer, staked a claim for future consideration.

Inspirational 1990 Kangaroo skipper Mal Meninga, BBC TV's prestigious Overseas Personality of the Year.

FIRST TEST

The stage was the world famous Wembley. The audience was a British Test record crowd of 54,569. The drama which unfolded was an emotional 19-12 victory for Great Britain to pull down the curtain on Australia's 12-year winning run on British soil. And the star of the show was British skipper Ellery Hanley, who shunned the spotlight in the build-up and then took centre stage to dominate a tense, pulsating contest.

Britain's shock victory, following on from their memorable 26-12 success in Sydney in July 1988, captured the imagination of an international television audience of millions and set the British Coal series alight, after Kangaroo whitewashes of 1982 and 1986.

Fresh from summer triumphs over France and New Zealand, plus a five-match victorious opening tour sequence — including the scalps of giants Wigan, Leeds and St. Helens — Australia arrived in London full of confidence. But only coach Bobby Fulton had performed under the twin towers and the magic of Wembley worked its spell on a Great Britain side written off as underdogs.

Australia's dominance during the '80s had sprung from half back — Wally Lewis and Peter Sterling were able to direct operations with world-class skills and leadership. Their absence from the Anglo-Aussie arena coincided with Britain's Garry Schofield confirming his new status as the world's most dominant stand off and field marshall, dictating everything in midfield, partner Andy Gregory bossing the scrum zone to extend his unbeaten run at Wembley to seven appearances.

Hanley proved once again that he was the man for the big occasion, delivering the goods when it most mattered. Overshadowed in the personality stakes by Kangaroo captain Mal Meninga, Hanley reclaimed the international limelight by casting aside his year-long injury hoodoo to re-emerge as the game's supreme talent, adding latent kicking skills to set up

Britain's first two tries and walk away with the British Coal Man of the Match award.

After a tryless first half of almost unbearable tension, Hanley broke the 2-2 deadlock with an incomparable blast of black action. Piston-driven legs smashed him into the open near halfway, then a delicate kick over Australian full back Gary Belcher was regathered in graceful style before the Wigan skipper was crashed down inches from the line. A quick play-the-ball and Sheffield Eagles centre Daryl Powell sent Paul Eastwood burrowing through for the 44th minute touchdown.

Meninga made a magnificent captain's reply with a powerful try to level the scores eight minutes later, only for Hanley to shatter the Kangaroos' defence again with a bomb of a kick. It came homing down near the posts where it bounced off Belcher for the neglected Martin Offiah to come from nowhere to score with a rare touch of the ball.

Hull winger Eastwood added the goal to make it 12-6, before Schofield coolly popped over a drop goal to open up a vital seven-point gap in true Lewis fashion. Still the Australians threatened to extend their 37-match winning run in Britain as giant centre Mark McGaw pounded 50 yards through four tackles to score one of the best solo tries seen at Wembley, while Meninga's goal reduced the margin to one point with 15 minutes left.

The game was well and truly in the balance, crying out for one act of destiny. British vice-captain Schofield stepped up to ensure a famous win with a majestic piece of football. Yet another kick broke up Australia's regimental defence as Schofield chipped the ball over the front line, regathered in full stride and linked with Daryl Powell for Eastwood to take the last, long pass for his second touchdown, adding a 78th minute penalty goal for a 14-point haul on his first home Test appearance.

Australian loose forward Bob Lindner was the pick of a stunned, dejected Australian outfit.

FIRST BRITISH COAL TEST

27 October   Wembley, London

GREAT BRITAIN 19		AUSTRALIA 12
Steve Hampson (Wigan)	1.	Gary Belcher
Paul Eastwood (Hull)	2.	Andrew Ettingshausen
Daryl Powell (Sheffield E.)	3.	Mal Meninga, Capt.
Carl Gibson (Leeds)	4.	Mark McGaw
Martin Offiah (Widnes)	5.	Michael Hancock
Garry Schofield (Leeds)	6.	Ricky Stuart
Andy Gregory (Wigan)	7.	Allan Langer
Karl Harrison (Hull)	8.	Steve Roach
Lee Jackson (Hull)	9.	Kerrod Walters
Paul Dixon (Leeds)	10.	Martin Bella
Denis Betts (Wigan)	11.	Paul Sironen
Roy Powell (Leeds)	12.	John Cartwright
Ellery Hanley (Wigan), Capt.	13.	Bob Lindner
Shaun Edwards (Wigan)	14.	Greg Alexander
Kevin Ward (St. Helens)	15.	Des Hasler
David Hulme (Widnes)	16.	Dale Shearer
Karl Fairbank (Bradford N.)	17.	Glenn Lazarus

T: Eastwood (2), Offiah
G: Eastwood (3), Schofield (dg)
Substitutions:
Ward for R. Powell (45 min.)
Fairbank for Harrison (72 min.)
Half-time: 2-2
Referee: Alain Sablayrolles (France)
Attendance: 54,569

T: Meninga, McGaw
G: Meninga (2)
Substitutions:
Lazarus for Bella (72 min.)
Hasler for Cartwright (72 min.)
Alexander for Langer (79 min.)
Shearer for Hancock (79 min.)

Scorechart

Minute	Score	GB	Aus
22:	Eastwood (PG)	2	0
37:	Meninga (PG)	2	2
44:	Eastwood (T)	6	2
52:	Meninga (T)	6	6
57:	Offiah (T)		
	Eastwood (G)	12	6
63:	Schofield (DG)	13	6
66:	McGaw (T)		
	Meninga (G)	13	12
71:	Eastwood (T)	17	12
78:	Eastwood (PG)	19	12
	Scrums	5	6
	Penalties	17	7

Mark McGaw, scorer of one of the best solo tries at Wembley.

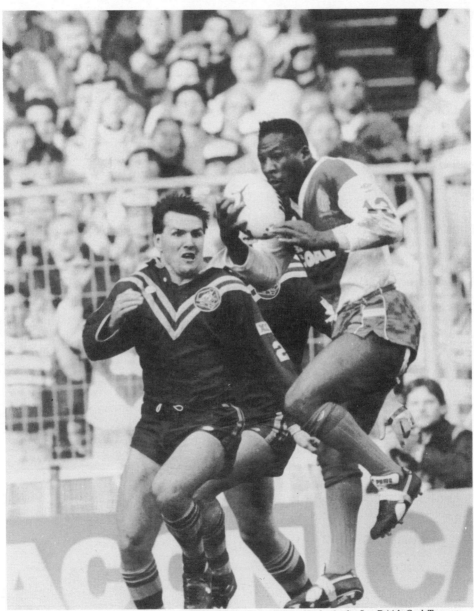

Australian winger Michael Hancock sizes up Great Britain skipper Ellery Hanley in the first British Coal Test at Wembley.

A triple Kangaroo tackle on British packman Paul Dixon by Ricky Stuart (left), Mal Meninga (below) and Andrew Ettingshausen.

31 October

WARRINGTON	6
AUSTRALIA	26

1. Alexander
2. Shearer
3. Meninga, Capt.
4. Kevin Walters
5. Johns
6. Fittler
7. Hasler (Hancock, 74 min.)
8. Lazarus
9. Elias
10. Sargent
11. Gillespie (Cartwright, 41 min.)
12. Geyer
13. Mackay

T: Mackay, Sargent, Geyer, Fittler, Hancock
G: Alexander (3)

Warrington:
Lyon; Drummond, Thorniley, Bateman, Williamson (Rudd); O'Sullivan, Ellis; Burke, Mann, Harmon (McGinty), Jackson (Darbyshire), Gregory, Cullen (Thomas)

T: Thorniley
G: Lyon

Half-time: 4-14

Referee: Dave Carter (Widnes)
Attendance: 10,200

Kangaroo coach Fulton put second Test places up for grabs following the shock Wembley defeat and his Emus side responded against a highly competitive Warrington outfit. Two tries in the final three minutes presented a distorted scoreline which did not reflect the tightly fought Wilderspool contest.

Tour vice-captain Elias gave the most notable Test hint with a display which was decisive and industrious on a rain-sodden pitch, playing a significant part in three of his side's five tries. Props Lazarus and Sargent were dominant upfront, though Fittler's move to stand off was unproductive.

British eyes were concentrated on summer tour skipper Gregory, returning to the Warrington ranks for his first full club game since the previous April's Wembley final and playing with a special harness on his injured finger. Gregory enjoyed a stiff workout and would have played all the match but for being sent to the sin bin for disputing a try.

4 November

CASTLEFORD	8
AUSTRALIA	28

1. Belcher
2. Ettingshausen
3. Meninga, Capt.
4. McGaw (Alexander, 24 min.)
5. Shearer
6. Lyons
7. Stuart (Langer, 75 min.)
8. Roach (Cartwright, 71 min.)
9. Elias
10. Lazarus (Bella, 22 min.)
11. Sironen
12. Lindner
13. Mackay

T: Ettingshausen (2), Meninga, Shearer, Lindner
G: Meninga (4)

Castleford:
Ellis; Larder (Fletcher), Irwin, Anderson, Plange; Steadman, French; Crooks (Clarke), Beardmore (Roebuck), Sampson, England, Hardy, Joyner (Ketteridge)

T: Plange
G: Crooks, Steadman

Half-time: 2-18

Referee: Gerry Kershaw (Easingwold)
Attendance: 9,033

Australian Test centre McGaw was ruled out of the rest of the tour with torn knee ligaments in an unimpressive victory. McGaw suffered a 21st minute collision with colleague Lazarus, who needed 17 stitches in a head wound yet still hoped for a second Test spot.

Lazarus was one of five selection candidates who did enough to sustain their Test hopes, though the ordinary team performance did little to restore the Kangaroos' dented confidence. Scrum half Stuart sparked off the moves for both Ettingshausen tries, which began and finished the Australian scoring. Elias was energetic as well as winning the scrums 6-5, while loose forward Mackay was the most impressive packman. Shearer and Lyons were less obvious in the five-try victory.

Castleford never looked likely to repeat their feat of being the last Yorkshire side to beat Australia in 1967. They were 18-2 down at half time and 22 points behind before scoring their first try after 66 minutes, veteran Joyner contributing some vintage touches.

6 November

| HALIFAX | 18 |
| AUSTRALIA | 36 |

1. Alexander
2. Shearer
3. Johns
4. Kevin Walters
5. Hancock
6. Fittler
7. Langer
8. Gillespie
9. Kerrod Walters
10. Sargent
11. Geyer
12. Cartwright (Bella, 76 min.)
13. Hasler

T: Johns (2), Geyer, Sargent, Alexander, Kevin Walters, Hancock
G: Alexander (4)

Halifax:
Smith; Hutchinson, Elia, Austin, George; Wood, Southernwood; Hill, McCallion (Ramshaw), Fairbank (Beevers), Platt (Mitchell), Scott (Milner), Keebles

T: Hutchinson (2), Austin, George
G: Smith

Half-time: 0-32

Referee: Brian Galtress (Bradford)
Attendance: 8,730

Trailing 32-6 at the interval, Second Division Halifax rocked the Australians with a storming second-half comeback. While never likely to catch up the Kangaroos, the Thrum Hall side had the consolation of equalling the best club score of the tour.

At the break it seemed a question of how many tries the Kangaroos would register, but they managed only one more, while revitalised Halifax raced in for a further three, all from the wings. Sin bins were imposed on Australian prop Sargent after only four minutes, colleague Langer and home substitute Beevers going off in the final 10 minutes.

Amid the Australians' first-half scoring blitz, Halifax had the satisfaction of scoring one of the best tries of the night, ironically by Australian centre Austin. The first of winger Hutchinson's two tries in the 58th minute signalled Halifax's fightback, the home side finishing stronger with Hutchinson and George completing the evening's scoring.

Balmain second row man Paul Sironen, one of the successes of the 1990 tour.

SECOND TEST

Valiant Great Britain came within 20 seconds of a deserved draw which would have ended 31 years of Australian Test series dominance on British soil.

With the scores balanced at 10-10, the re-shaped Australians set off on an 80-yard charge to protect their international supremacy. Ricky Stuart, restored to his normal scrum half role, sold a dummy to British hooker Lee Jackson and galloped down the right flank to set up skipper Mal Meninga for the last minute touchdown, probably the most dramatic match-winning try in Test history.

The devastated home camp duly noted that Meninga had pushed opposite number Carl Gibson out of the way before receiving the final try-making pass. But it was generally accepted that Australia's superior teamwork, after eight changes from the shell-shocked Wembley line-up, had produced three breathtaking tries, regaining much of the flair missing since the early tour games.

All the eight changes were for the better, though none made more impact than the return of tour vice-captain Benny Elias. The Balmain, Lebanese-born hooker produced an extraordinary workrate to be a clear winner of the British Coal Man of the Match award. Second top Kangaroo defender with 36 tackles, Elias contributed a series of penetrating dashes from acting half back, touch-finding kicks and an even share of scrum possession to add a new dimension to the Kangaroo attack.

Stuart's switch back to the number seven jersey also added to the smoother running of the Australian gameplan, while Cliff Lyons proved why he should have been given the vacant stand off jersey for the opening Test encounter at Wembley. Both were involved in the build-up to Australia's first two marvellous tries. The opening touchdown after 24 minutes was a long-distance strike by winger Dale Shearer, one of the recalled troop.

The second try was of 1982 and 1986 Invincible vintage, after a Paul Eastwood penalty goal and Paul Dixon 52nd minute try had clawed Britain into a 6-4 lead. Four minutes after the Leeds back row forward had powered his way over, the pressurised Kangaroos pulled apart the British defence with a 12-pass move before Andrew Ettingshausen kicked inside from the right wing for Lyons to touch down with his third involvement in the stunning move.

The loss of Widnes winger Martin Offiah in the 45th minute with a knee injury was to have a double effect on the last 10 minutes of a thrilling encounter in front of a near-capacity 46,615 Old Trafford crowd.

While the presence of Offiah always promised a flash of individual brilliance to take Britain to an Ashes success for the first time in 20 years, it was his replacement, Paul Loughlin, who used his telescopic reach to intercept a pass from Stuart to gallop 50 yards for a score-levelling try in the 70th minute.

But it was the absence of Offiah's undoubted speed which allowed Stuart to make amends and embark on his 70-yard dash down Britain's left flank to set up the nerve-tingling match-winner in the dying seconds.

The British camp were also left to lament the failure to convert Loughlin's try. Eastwood, who had missed from a similar angle after Dixon's touchdown, offered the goalkick to Loughlin, who declined. The Airlie Bird missed again and was inconsolable in the dressing room after being hailed as a 14-point hero at Wembley two weeks earlier.

Skipper Ellery Hanley epitomised the British effort, giving his all without being able to climb the heights of Wembley. It reflected the improvement in the Australian performance that Hanley had more to do in defence, leading the way with 35 tackles ahead of Andy Platt, back on Test duty after missing the summer tour and the Wembley Test through injury. For Australia, Bob Lindner made another massive contribution with 40 tackles.

276

SECOND BRITISH COAL TEST

10 November   **Old Trafford, Manchester**

GREAT BRITAIN 10		AUSTRALIA 14
Steve Hampson (Wigan)	1.	Gary Belcher
Paul Eastwood (Hull)	2.	Andrew Ettingshausen
Daryl Powell (Sheffield E.)	3.	Mal Meninga, Capt.
Carl Gibson (Leeds)	4.	Laurie Daley
Martin Offiah (Widnes)	5.	Dale Shearer
Garry Schofield (Leeds)	6.	Cliff Lyons
Andy Gregory (Wigan)	7.	Ricky Stuart
Karl Harrison (Hull)	8.	Steve Roach
Lee Jackson (Hull).	9.	Ben Elias
Andy Platt (Wigan)	10.	Glenn Lazarus
Denis Betts (Wigan)	11.	Paul Sironen
Paul Dixon (Leeds)	12.	Bob Lindner
Ellery Hanley (Wigan), Capt.	13.	Brad Mackay
David Hulme (Widnes)	14.	Greg Alexander
Kevin Ward (St. Helens)	15.	Des Hasler
Paul Loughlin (St. Helens)	16.	Mark Sargent
Roy Powell (Leeds)	17.	John Cartwright

T: Dixon, Loughlin

G: Eastwood

Substitutions:

Loughlin for Offiah (45 min.)

Ward for Harrison (51 min.)

Attendance: 46,615

T: Shearer, Lyons, Meninga

G: Meninga

Half-time: 4-2

Referee: Alain Sablayrolles
(France)

Scorechart

Minute	Score		GB	Aus
24:	Shearer (T)		0	4
32:	Eastwood (PG)		2	4
52:	Dixon (T)		6	4
56:	Lyons (T)			
	Meninga (G)		6	10
70:	Loughlin (T)		10	10
79:	Meninga (T)		10	14
		Scrums	6	6
		Penalties	12	8

Dale Shearer, a tryscorer on his recall to Test football.

14 November

HULL 4
AUSTRALIA 34

1. Alexander
2. Johns
3. Fittler
4. Ettingshausen
5. Hasler
6. Kevin Walters
7. Langer
8. Bella
9. Kerrod Walters
10. Sargent
11. Geyer
12. Cartwright (Carroll, 50 min.)
13. Gillespie

T: Hasler (2), Ettingshausen (2), Kevin Walters (2), Kerrod Walters
G: Alexander (3)

Hull:

Gay; Eastwood, Nolan, Webb (Blacker), Turner; Mackey, Entat; Marlow, L. Jackson, Dannatt (Windley), McNamara (Dixon), Walker (A. Jackson), Sharp

T: Turner

Half-time: 4-20

Referee: Dave Campbell (St. Helens)
Attendance: 13,081

Top-of-the-table Hull were no match for Australia's second string who produced their best midweek performance of the tour to secure a comfortable seven-try victory.

The only fireworks offered by a disappointing Hull side were the pre-match display to celebrate the opening of their new Threepenny Stand. The Kangaroos provided the spectacle on the field even though they fielded only one of the Test team which beat Great Britain the previous Saturday.

Test discards Langer and Kerrod Walters led the Emus in style, half-back twin Kevin Walters serving up his best display of the tour. Prop Sargent and back row Geyer again staked claims for promotion as Hull were made to look anything but league leaders.

The Airlie Birds were saved from further humiliation by the superb defence of full back Gay, while prop Marlow, in his first season, took their Man of the Match award.

18 November

WIDNES 8
AUSTRALIA 15

1. Belcher
2. Alexander
3. Meninga, Capt.
4. Shearer (Johns, 41 min.)
5. Ettingshausen
6. Lyons
7. Langer
8. Roach (Bella, 73 min.)
9. Elias
10. Lazarus
11. Sironen (Gillespie, 41 min.)
12. Lindner
13. Mackay (Hasler, 73 min.)

T: Belcher, Shearer, Alexander
G: Belcher (1, 1dg)

Widnes:

Davies; Devereux, Currier, Wright, Howard; Myler, D. Hulme; Sorensen, McKenzie, Grima (Faimalo), Koloto, Eyres (P. Hulme), Holliday

T: Davies

G: Davies (2)

Half-time: 0-10

Referee: John Kendrew (Castleford)
Attendance: 14,666

The 1990 Kangaroos completed the 10-match club section of their tour undefeated with a hard-earned victory over Widnes to make it a third successive trip in which they had beaten all opposition outside the Test arena.

Coach Fulton alleged gouging incidents, Test second row Sironen suffering a scratched eyeball to make him doubtful for the third and deciding British Coal Test.

The Australians led 10-0 at half-time, pressing home two tryscoring chances in superb style before emphasising their win with a third spectacular effort holding off a powerful Widnes recovery. Kangaroos Lyons and Roach were sent to the sin bin in separate incidents late in the first half.

Widnes full back Davies, enhancing his chances of a Test recall, scored all his side's points in a second half rally led by veteran Kiwi prop forward Sorensen, but the Chemics were thwarted by a 50-yard move begun by Meninga and finished by Alexander.

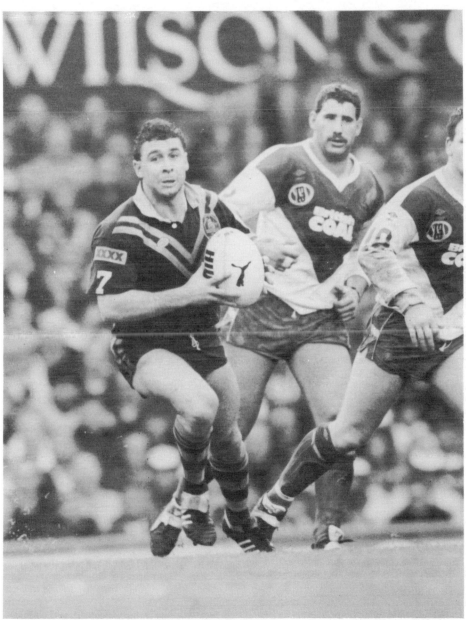

Kangaroo half back Ricky Stuart, Test stand off at Wembley before reverting to his traditional scrum half role.

THIRD TEST

In the aftermath of the shock Test defeat at Wembley, the major lament was the absence of half-back dictators Wally Lewis and Peter Sterling. Five weeks later, the toast was to a new match-winning combination, Cliff Lyons and Ricky Stuart. The 1990 rookies dominated a Test match just as much as their legendary predecessors ever did to inspire Australia to retain the Ashes, held since 1973, and to stretch their unbeaten Test series run in Britain to 31 years.

Brought together for the first time after the Wembley setback, Lyons and Stuart played a major role in levelling the series at Old Trafford before methodically taking Britain apart in this third and deciding British Coal Test at Elland Road, Leeds. Stuart's long, precision passes and the short, sharp dashes of Lyons was half-back play at its brilliant best, earning Australia another two World Cup points to maintain their 100 per cent record after four qualifying Tests. The two combined to create Australia's clinching try in the 50th minute after Andrew Ettingshausen had squeezed in at the corner from a floated Stuart pass inside eight minutes, while injured British centre Carl Gibson was off the field and substitute Jonathan Davies was waiting for permission to come on.

The second-half clincher came when Lyons shot on to Stuart's 20-yard pass to slip easily through a gap and then flip a high inside ball for Mal Meninga to charge for the posts. The vital touchdown enabled the Kangaroo skipper to become only the second Australian to score a try in each match of a series in Britain, winger Ken Irvine achieving the feat 27 years ago.

The half backs were rivals for the British Coal Man of the Match award, Stuart taking the prize though his partner could easily have shared the award as Lyons was a match for him in attack and made twice as many tackles, with 22. Together, they completely outplayed British duo Garry Schofield and Andy Gregory, who announced his retirement from international football after what was probably one of his most ineffective displays in a Test.

The British management were faced with three sources of criticism in the pre-match build-up, none of which materialised. Claims for the selection of ex-Welsh Rugby Union skipper Davies subsided with his making little impact in the centre after coming on after nine minutes. Concern over Paul Eastwood's poor goalkicking form was equally unnecessary, as Britain were not given even one shot at goal by the miserly tourists. Whether Martin Offiah was fully fit after injuring his knee in the second Test was also idle conjecture as the game's number one match-winner was again left entirely to his own devices.

British captain Ellery Hanley again set a magnificent example, though rarely can one player have been so well marked, being the target for a barrage of body-jarring tackles, particularly from the outstanding Paul Sironen. Hanley's opposite number, Brad Mackay, was on patrol watch to amass Australia's top tackle count of 40, followed by hooker Benny Elias, who needed pain-killing tablets at half-time for suspected broken ribs, only to score the final try nine minutes from the end.

Britain's front row bore the brunt of their defensive workload, headed by Andy Platt's 46 tackles, hooker Lee Jackson 44 and Karl Harrison 35. The home side's tackling all-round was sound until the later stages, on a miserable day when the incessant rain washed away any hopes of the sides producing a third classic encounter.

A capacity 32,500 Elland Road crowd created a new record aggregate attendance for a Test series in Britain. Ironically, the revitalised British effort resulted in their being nilled for only the second time in a home Test against any country, the previous occasion being the only scoreless draw, against Australia in 1930.

THIRD BRITISH COAL TEST (World Cup-rated)

24 November   **Elland Road, Leeds**

GREAT BRITAIN   0   AUSTRALIA   14

Steve Hampson (Wigan)	1.	Gary Belcher
Paul Eastwood (Hull)	2.	Andrew Ettingshausen
Daryl Powell (Sheffield E.)	3.	Mal Meninga, Capt.
Carl Gibson (Leeds)	4.	Laurie Daley
Martin Offiah (Widnes)	5.	Dale Shearer
Garry Schofield (Leeds)	6.	Cliff Lyons
Andy Gregory (Wigan)	7.	Ricky Stuart
Karl Harrison (Hull)	8.	Steve Roach
Lee Jackson (Hull)	9.	Ben Elias
Andy Platt (Wigan)	10.	Glenn Lazarus
Denis Betts (Wigan)	11.	Paul Sironen
Paul Dixon (Leeds)	12.	Bob Lindner
Ellery Hanley (Wigan), Capt.	13.	Brad Mackay
David Hulme (Widnes)	14.	Greg Alexander
Mike Gregory (Warrington)	15.	Des Hasler
Jonathan Davies (Widnes)	16.	Mark Sargent
Roy Powell (Leeds)	17.	Dave Gillespie

Substitutions:
Davies for Gibson (9 min.)
M. Gregory for Dixon (55 min.)
R. Powell for Harrison (72 min.)
Half-time: 0-4
Referee: Alain Sablayrolles (France)
Attendance: 32,500

T: Ettingshausen, Meninga, Elias
G: Meninga
Substitutions:
Alexander for Shearer (76 min.)
Hasler for Mackay (76 min.)
Sargent for Lazarus (76 min.)
Gillespie for Sironen (76 min.)

Scorechart

Minute	Score	GB	Aus
8:	Ettingshausen (T)	0	4
50:	Meninga (T)		
	Meninga (G)	0	10
71:	Elias (T)	0	14
	Scrums	10	11
	Penalties	12	11

Winger Andrew Ettingshausen, opening tryscorer.

Prop forward Mark Sargent, in action against Hull, graduated to the substitute bench for the second and third British Coal Tests.

Hull K.R. forward Phil Lowe, a tryscorer for Manly in their victorious 1976 Sydney Premiership Final.

DOWN UNDER

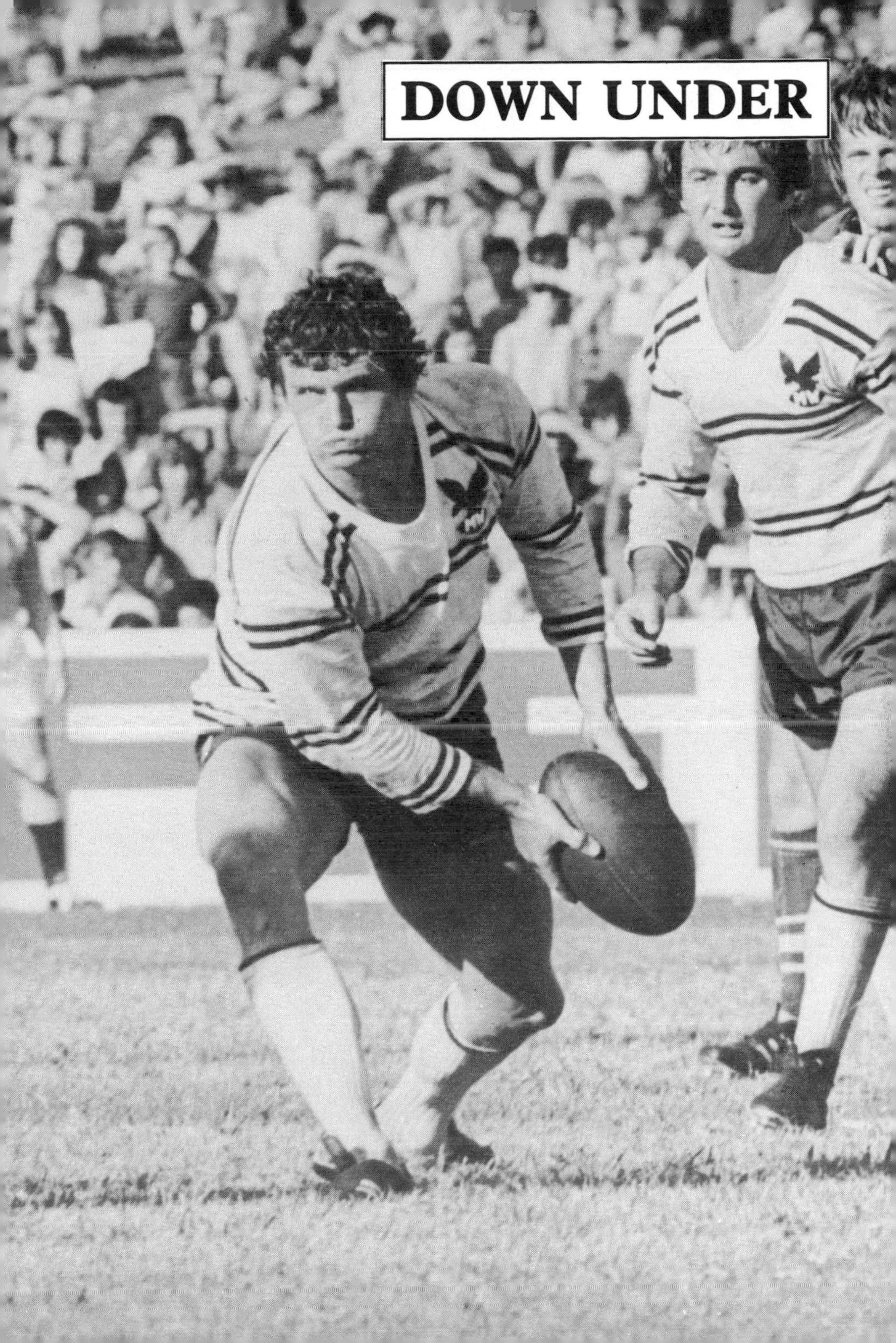

DOWN UNDER

WINFIELD CUP
1990 Sydney Premiership Grand Final

For the first time since 1986 no British players appeared in the Grand Final as Canberra retained the Winfield Cup by beating Penrith 18-14 at the Sydney Football Stadium. It was the first time Australia's major final had been contested by teams who were both from well outside the centre of Sydney.

League leaders Canberra went into the final as favourites despite having been beaten 30-12 by third-place Penrith in a dramatic semi-final which went into extra time after 80 minutes had produced a 12-12 scoreline.

Canberra scrum half Ricky Stuart won the Clive Churchill Medal as Man of the Match with a commanding game in which his superb touch-kicking kept Penrith pinned in their own quarter for long periods. Stuart also had a hand in Canberra's first two tries in a performance which clinched a place on the Kangaroos tour of Britain for the former Rugby Union international.

With both teams scoring three tries, it was Mal Meninga's three goals that made the difference, as Canberra's captain made sure of lifting the trophy for a second successive year.

Penrith were appearing in their first final, 23 years after entering the competition, while Canberra made it three finals in only nine years of existence.

A continuing increase in capacity resulted in the Sydney Football Stadium attracting a record full house — 41,535 — for a third successive season since the new ground replaced Sydney Cricket Ground as the final venue.

WINFIELD CUP GRAND FINAL
Sydney Football Stadium

23 September 1990

CANBERRA 18		PENRITH 14
Gary Belcher	1.	David Greene
Paul Martin	2.	Alan McIndoe
Mal Meninga, Capt.	3.	Brad Fittler
Laurie Daley	4.	Col Bentley
John Ferguson	5.	Paul Smith
Chris O'Sullivan	6.	Brad Izzard
Ricky Stuart	7.	Greg Alexander
Brent Todd	8.	Paul Clarke
Steve Walters	9.	Royce Simmons, Capt
Glenn Lazarus	10.	Barry Walker
Nigel Gaffey	11.	Mark Geyer
Gary Coyne	12.	John Cartwright
Dean Lance	13.	Chris Mortimer

T: Ferguson, Daley, Wood
G: Meninga (3)
Substitutions:
Matthew Wood for Gaffey
Phil Carey for Martin
David Woods for Coyne
Craig Bellamy for O'Sullivan
Coach: Tim Sheens
Half-time: 12-6
Referee: Bill Harrigan

T: Fittler, Smith, Alexander
G: Alexander
Substitutions:
Steve Carter for Bentley
Joe Vitanza for Walker
Coach: Phil Gould
Clive Churchill Medal for Man of the Match:
Ricky Stuart (Canberra)
Scrums: 4-11
Penalties: 7-4
Attendance: 41,535

1990 WINFIELD CUP

	P.	W.	D.	L.	F.	A.	Pts
Canberra	22	16	1	5	532	245	33
Brisbane Broncos	22	16	1	5	478	278	33
Penrith	22	15	1	6	415	286	31
Manly-Warringah	22	15	0	7	395	255	30
Balmain	22	14	0	8	432	284	28
Newcastle	22	13	2	7	344	305	28
Canterbury-Bankstown	22	12	1	9	354	291	25
Parramatta	22	12	1	9	387	347	25
Illawarra	22	11	1	10	366	361	23
Cronulla-Sutherland	22	11	0	11	370	359	22
North Sydney	22	10	0	12	322	298	20
St. George	22	8	0	14	371	399	16
Western Suburbs	22	6	1	15	323	433	13
Eastern Suburbs	22	6	1	15	283	547	13
Gold Coast	22	4	0	18	233	567	8
South Sydney	22	2	0	20	302	652	4

WINFIELD CUP PLAY-OFF
Fifth place play off
Balmain 12 v. Newcastle 4
Minor preliminary semi-final
Manly 16 v. Balmain 0
Major preliminary semi-final
Penrith 26 v. Brisbane Broncos 16
Minor semi-final
Brisbane Broncos 12 v. Manly 4
Major semi-final
Penrith 30 v. Canberra 12 (After extra time)
Preliminary final
Canberra 32 v. Brisbane Broncos 4
Grand Final
Canberra 18 v. Penrith 14

● All matches played at the
Sydney Football Stadium except for
the fifth place play-off at the
Parramatta Stadium.

LEADING SCORERS
● Not including play-offs

Tries
15 Willy Carne (Brisbane Broncos)
 Ashley Gordon (Newcastle)
 Mal Meninga (Canberra)
Goals (inc. drop goals)
62 Mal Meninga (Canberra)
Points
184 Mal Meninga (Canberra)

*Penrith centre Brad Fittler, a tryscorer in the 1990
Winfield Cup Grand Final.*

BRITISH PLAYERS IN GRAND FINALS

British players who have appeared in the Sydney Grand Final are:

Dick Huddart (St. George) 1966 winners, 1 try
Dave Bolton (Balmain) 1966 losers; 1969 winners, 2 drop goals
Mervyn Hicks (Canterbury) 1967 losers
Ken Batty (St. George) 1971 losers
Malcolm Reilly (Manly) 1972 winners, 1973 winners
Tommy Bishop (Cronulla) 1973 losers
Bob Wear (Cronulla) 1973 losers
Cliff Watson (Cronulla) 1973 losers
Brian Lockwood (Canterbury) 1974 losers
Gary Stephens (Manly) 1976 winners
Steve Norton (Manly) 1976 winners
Phil Lowe (Manly) 1976 winners, 1 try
Kevin Ward (Manly) 1987 winners
Ellery Hanley (Balmain) 1988 losers
Andy Currier (Balmain) 1989 losers, 3 goals
Shaun Edwards (Balmain) 1989 losers, sub

Apart from Hicks, Wear and Currier, all the above also appeared in a Challenge Cup final at Wembley. In addition Len Killeen, the South African winger who began his league career with St. Helens, also played at Wembley and got a Grand Final winners' medal with Balmain in 1969 when he kicked two goals.

Australians who have achieved the big double since the Grand Final became mandatory in 1954 are: Chris Anderson, Harry Bath, Graham Eadie, John Ferguson, Kerry Hemsley, Brett Kenny, John Muggleton, Peter Sterling, Michael O'Connor and Paul Vautin.

There were a record four British players in the 1973 Grand Final. Reilly got a winners' medal with Manly, while Bishop, Watson and Wear were in the beaten Cronulla side.

Three British players — Stephens, Norton and Lowe — were also in the Manly side which won the final in 1976.

Ellery Hanley was the first player to appear in both major finals in the same year. In 1988 he led Wigan to success at Wembley and four months later was in Balmain's beaten Grand Final team.

Shaun Edwards is the only other player to play in both finals in the same year. He was stand off when Wigan beat St. Helens at Wembley in 1989 and made a late substitute appearance for Balmain when they were beaten by Canberra at Sydney.

Widnes centre Andy Currier, the top British points scorer in the 1990 Winfield Cup Sydney Premiership.

BRITISH PLAYERS IN 1990 WINFIELD CUP SYDNEY PREMIERSHIP

The British Lions' tour of Papua New Guinea and New Zealand restricted the opportunities for Britain's best players to play in the Winfield Cup competition in 1990. After a record total of 14 British players appeared in the Sydney Premiership the previous year only five played in 1990 and none made more than five full appearances.

Widnes centre Andy Currier was the only player to appear for a second successive season. After making a big impact in 1989, when he played in the Grand Final, Currier's second spell with Balmain amounted to only six matches.

British players records in the 1990 Winfield Cup, including play-off matches:

	App	T	G	Pts
Andy Currier (Widnes-Balmain)	5 + 1	—	15	30
Gary Divorty (Leeds-Gold Coast)	5	—	—	—
Steve McGowan (Bradford N-North Sydney)	3 + 3	1	—	4
Dean Sampson (Castleford-Gold Coast)	5 + 3	—	—	—
Darren Wright (Widnes-North Sydney)	0 + 2	—	—	—

STATE OF ORIGIN

The State of Origin matches between New South Wales and Queensland began in 1980 and are now established as a major part of the Australian Rugby League scene.

Their introduction revived interest in the inter-state matches which had been dominated by New South Wales, who had won the last 15 matches by mainly wide margins. Under the old system players appeared for the state in which they were playing club rugby at the time and this gave a big advantage to New South Wales because many of Queensland's best players were with Sydney clubs.

But in State of Origin matches players appear for the state in which they first played senior rugby and this has resulted in the matches becoming more fiercely and evenly fought before increased attendances.

NEW SOUTH WALES v. QUEENSLAND RESULTS
State of Origin only.

Date	Winner	Score	Venue	Attendance
8 July 1980	Queensland	20 - 10	Brisbane	31,000
28 July 1981	Queensland	22 - 15	Brisbane	25,613
1 June 1982	New South Wales	20 - 16	Brisbane	27,326
8 June 1982	Queensland	11 - 7	Brisbane	19,435
22 June 1982	Queensland	10 - 5	Sydney	20,242
7 June 1983	Queensland	24 - 12	Brisbane	29,412
21 June 1983	New South Wales	10 - 6	Sydney	21,620
28 June 1983	Queensland	43 - 22	Brisbane	26,084
29 May 1984	Queensland	29 - 12	Brisbane	33,662
19 June 1984	Queensland	14 - 2	Sydney	29,088
17 July 1984	New South Wales	22 - 12	Brisbane	16,599
28 May 1985	New South Wales	18 - 2	Brisbane	33,011
11 June 1985	New South Wales	21 - 14	Sydney	39,068
23 July 1985	Queensland	20 - 6	Brisbane	18,825
27 May 1986	New South Wales	22 - 16	Brisbane	33,000
10 June 1986	New South Wales	24 - 20	Sydney	40,707
1 July 1986	New South Wales	18 - 16	Brisbane	21,097
2 June 1987	New South Wales	20 - 16	Brisbane	33,411
16 June 1987	Queensland	12 - 6	Sydney	42,048
15 July 1987	Queensland	10 - 8	Brisbane	33,000
*6 Aug. 1987	New South Wales	30 - 18	California	12,349
17 May 1988	Queensland	26 - 18	Sydney	26,441
31 May 1988	Queensland	16 - 6	Brisbane	31,817
21 June 1988	Queensland	38 - 22	Sydney	16,910
23 May 1989	Queensland	36 - 6	Brisbane	33,000
14 June 1989	Queensland	16 - 12	Sydney	40,000
28 June 1989	Queensland	36 - 16	Brisbane	33,000
9 May 1990	New South Wales	8 - 0	Sydney	41,235
30 May 1990	New South Wales	12 - 6	Melbourne	25,800
13 June 1990	Queensland	14 - 10	Brisbane	31,000

SUMMARY
New South Wales won 12; Queensland won 18.
Since it became a three-match series in 1982 Queensland have won six series to New South Wales' three.
*Not part of 1987 series.

ENGLISH REFEREES
English referees who have taken charge of State of Origin matches are: Billy Thompson on 8 July 1980 and Robin Whitfield on 28 June 1983.

1990 STATE OF ORIGIN MATCHES

*Denotes captain

9 May
Sydney
New South Wales 8
Ettingshausen (Cronulla)
Wishart (Illawarra)
O'Connor (Manly) 2g
McGaw (Cronulla) 1t
Walford (St. George)
Daley (Canberra)
Stuart (Canberra)
Roach (Balmain)
*Elias (Balmain)
Roberts (Manly)
Gillespie (Canterbury)
McGuire (Balmain)
Clyde (Canberra)
Subs: G. Lyons (Souths)
    Toovey (Manly)
    Lazarus (Canberra)
    Sironen (Balmain)

30 May
Melbourne
New South Wales 12
Ettingshausen (Cronulla)
Wishart (Illawarra) 2g
Mackay (St. George) 1t
McGaw (Cronulla)
G. Lyons (Souths)
Hasler (Manly)
Stuart (Canberra) 1t
Roach (Balmain)
*Elias (Balmain)
Roberts (Manly)
Gillespie (Canterbury)
McGuire (Balmain)
Clyde (Canberra)
Subs: Farrar (Canterbury)
    Fittler (Penrith)
    Lazarus (Canberra)
    Sironen (Balmain)

13 June
Brisbane
New South Wales 10
Ettingshausen (Cronulla)
Wishart (Illawarra) 1g
O'Connor (Manly)
McGaw (Cronulla) 1t
G. Lyons (Souths)
Mackay (St. George)
Stuart (Canberra)
Lazarus (Canberra) 1t
*Elias (Balmain)
Roberts (Manly)
Gillespie (Canterbury)
McGuire (Balmain)
Clyde (Canberra)
Subs: Farrar (Canterbury)
    Alexander (Penrith)
    Sargent (Newcastle)
    Sironen (Balmain)

Queensland 0
Belcher (Canberra)
McIndoe (Penrith)
Shearer (Brisbane B.)
Meninga (Canberra)
Kiss (Norths)
Hagan (Newcastle)
Langer (Brisbane B.)
Bella (Manly)
S. Walters (Canberra)
Stains (Cronulla)
*Vautin (Easts)
Fullerton-Smith (St. George)
Lindner (Wests)
Subs: M. Coyne (St. George)
    G. Coyne (Canberra)
    Kevin Walters (Brisbane B.)
    Gillmeister (Easts)
Referee: David Manson
Man of the Match: Elias

Queensland 6
Belcher (Canberra)
McIndoe (Penrith)
Shearer (Brisbane B.)
Meninga (Canberra) 1g
Kiss (Norths) 1t
*Lewis (Brisbane B.)
Langer (Brisbane B.)
Bella (Manly)
Kerrod Walters (Brisbane B.)
Backo (Brisbane B.)
Stains (Cronulla)
G. Coyne (Canberra)
Lindner (Wests)
Subs: M. Coyne (St. George)
    Gillmeister (Easts)
    Gee (Brisbane B.)

Referee: Greg McCallum
Man of the Match: Stuart

Queensland 14
Belcher (Canberra) 1t, 2g
McIndoe (Penrith)
Shearer (Brisbane B.)
P. Jackson (Brisbane B.)
Carne (Brisbane B.)
*Lewis (Brisbane B.) 1g
Langer (Brisbane B.)
Bella (Manly)
Kerrod Walters (Brisbane B.)
Backo (Brisbane B.)
Gillmeister (Easts)
G. Coyne (Canberra)
Lindner (Wests)
Subs: Kevin Walters (Brisbane B.)
    Gee (Brisbane B.)
    Hagan (Newcastle)
    S. Jackson (Wests) 1t
Referee: David Manson
Man of the Match: Lindner

NEW SOUTH WALES v. QUEENSLAND RECORDS
State of Origin only

NEW SOUTH WALES
Highest score: 30-18 at California, 6 August 1987
Widest margin: 18-2 at Brisbane, 28 May 1985
Most full appearances: 17 by Garry Jack (Balmain)
Most tries in a match: 3 by Chris Anderson (Canterbury), 28 June 1983
Most goals in a match: No player has kicked more than five
Most points in a match: 18 (2t, 5g) Michael O'Connor (Manly), 28 May 1985
Biggest home attendance: 42,048, 16 June 1987

QUEENSLAND

Highest score:	43-22 at Brisbane, 28 June 1983
Widest margin:	36-6 at Brisbane, 23 May 1989
Most full appearances:	28 by Wally Lewis (Fortitude Valley, Wynnum Manly, Brisbane Broncos)
Most tries in a match:	3 by Kerry Boustead (Manly), 29 May 1984
Most goals in a match:	7 by Mal Meninga (Souths, B), 8 July 1980
Most points in a match:	16 (2t, 4g) by Mal Meninga (Canberra), 23 May 1989 and Dale Shearer (Manly), 28 June 1989
Biggest home attendance:	33,662, 29 May 1984

Coaches:

New South Wales:	Ted Glossop (1980, 1981, 1983); Frank Stanton (1982, 1984); Terry Fearnley (1985); Ron Willey (1986, 1987); John Peard (1988); Jack Gibson (1989, 1990)
Queensland:	John McDonald (1980); Arthur Beetson (1981, 1982, 1983, 1984, 1989, 1990); Des Morris (1985); Wayne Bennett (1986, 1987, 1988)

QUEENSLAND REGISTER

The following is a register of players who have appeared for Queensland in the State of Origin series plus the match against New South Wales in the United States of America, up to and including 1990. + indicates number of matches played as a substitute. B-Brisbane, S-Sydney.

ASTILL, Bruce (+1) Souths, B

BACKER, Brad (3) Easts, B
BACKO, Sam (7) Canberra 3; Brisbane Broncos 4
BEETSON, Arthur (1) Parramatta
BELCHER, Gary (15) Canberra
BELLA, Martin (11) Norths, S 8; Manly 3
BOUSTEAD, Kerry (6) Easts, S 3; Manly 3
BRENNAN, Mitch (4) Souths, S 3; Redcliffe 1
BROHMAN, Darryl (2) Penrith
BROWN, Dave (9+1) Manly 5+1; Easts, S 4
BUTLER, Terry (1) Wynnum Manly

CARNE, Willy (1) Brisbane B.
CARR, Norm (2) Wests, B
CLOSE, Chris (9) Manly 7; Redcliffe 2
CONESCU, Greg (20) Norths, B 4; Redcliffe 10; Gladstone Brothers 3; Brisbane Broncos 3
COYNE, Gary (2+4) Canberra
COYNE, Mark (+2) St. George
CURRIE, Tony (8+3) Wests, B +1; Redcliffe +1; Canterbury 5+1; Brisbane Broncos 3

DOWLING, Greg (11) Wynnum Manly 7; Norths, B 4
DOWLING, John (3) St. George

FRENCH, Brett (1+3) Wynnum Manly; Norths S +3
FRENCH, Ian (3+6) Wynnum Manly 2+3; Norths, S 1+3
FULLERTON-SMITH, Wally (12) Redcliffe 8; St. George 4

GEE, Andrew (+1) Brisbane B.
GILLMEISTER, Trevor (5+5) Easts, S

HAGAN, Michael (2+3) Newcastle
HANCOCK, Michael (3) Brisbane Broncos
HANCOCK, Rohan (5) Easts, B 1; Toowoomba Wattles 4
HENRICK, Ross (2) Norths, B 1; Fortitude Valley 1
HEUGH, Cavill (2+1) Easts, B

JACKSON, Peter (8+2) Canberra 7; Souths, B +1; Brisbane Broncos 1+1
JACKSON, Steve (+1) Wests, S
JONES, Gavin (3) Norths, S

KELLAWAY, Bob (+1) Souths, B
KHAN, Paul (4) Easts, B 3; Cronulla 1
KILROY, Joe (2) Brisbane Broncos
KISS, Les (4) Norths, S

LANG, John (1) Easts, S
LANGER, Allan (12) Ipswich 4, Brisbane Broncos 8
LEWIS, Wally (28) Wynnum Manly 13; Fortitude Valley 8; Brisbane Broncos 7
LINDNER, Bob (17) Souths, B 1; Wynnum Manly 5; Parramatta 6; Gold Coast 2; Wests, S 3

McCABE, Paul (5) Easts, S 1; Manly 4
McINDOE, Alan (9) Illawarra 3; Penrith 6
MENINGA, Mal (20) Souths, B 13; Canberra 7
MILES, Gene (19) Wynnum Manly 14; Brisbane Broncos 5
MORRIS, Rod (4) Balmain 2; Wynnum Manly 2
MURRAY, Mark (14) Fortitude Valley 3, Redcliffe 11

NIEBLING, Bryan (9) Fortitude Valley 3; Redcliffe 6

OLIPHANT, Greg (1) Balmain

PHELAN, Chris (2) Souths, B 1; Parramatta 1

QUINN, Graham (1) St. George

REDDY, Rod (1) St. George
RIBOT, John (8) Manly 5; Redcliffe 3

SCOTT, Colin (16+1) Wynnum Manly 15+1; Easts, B 1
SHEARER, Dale (14+2) Manly 11+2; Brisbane B. 3
SMITH, Allan (1) Norths, S
SMITH, Gary (+1) Brothers
STACEY, Steve (2) Easts, B
STAINS, Danny (4) Cronulla

TESSMAN, Brad (4+1) Souths, B 3; Easts, S 1+1
TRONC, Scott (+1) Wests, S

VAUTIN, Paul (20+1) Manly 19+1; Easts 1

WALKER, Bruce (1) Manly
WALTERS, Kerrod (5) Brisbane Broncos
WALTERS, Kevin (+3) Canberra +1; Brisbane B. +2
WALTERS, Steve (1) Canberra

NEW SOUTH WALES REGISTER

The following is a register of players who have appeared for New South Wales in the State of Origin series plus the match against Queensland in the United States of America, up to and including 1990. + indicates number of matches played as a substitute. B-Brisbane, S-Sydney.

ALEXANDER, Greg (2 + 2) Penrith
ANDERSON, Chris (4) Canterbury
AYLIFFE, Royce (1 + 2) Easts, S

BLAKE, Phil (+1) Souths, S
BOWDEN, Steve (1) Newtown
BOYD, Les (3) Manly
BOYLE, David (2 + 2) Souths, S
BRENTNALL, Greg (4) Canterbury
BROOKS, David (1) Balmain
BROWN, Ray (1 + 2) Manly
BUGDEN, Geoff (2) Parramatta

CARTWRIGHT, John (1 + 2) Penrith
CLEAL, Noel (11 + 1) Manly
CLYDE, Bradley (5) Canberra
CONLON, Ross (3) Canterbury
COOPER, Bob (1) Wests, S
COVENEY, John (2) Canterbury
CRONIN, Mick (6) Parramatta

DALEY, Laurie (3) Canberra
DALEY, Phil (3) Manly
DAVIDSON, Les (5) Souths, S
DOCKING, Jonathan (2) Cronulla
DUKE, Phillip (1) Moree
DUNN, Paul (2 + 1) Canterbury

EADIE, Graham (1) Manly
EDGE, Steve (1) Parramatta
ELIAS, Ben (8) Balmain
ELLA, Steve (3 + 4) Parramatta
ETTINGSHAUSEN, Andrew (10 + 1) Cronulla

FAHEY, Terry (2) Easts, S
FARRAR, Andrew (5 + 2) Canterbury
FENECH, Mario (2) Souths, S
FERGUSON, John (8) Easts, S 3; Canberra 5
FIELD, Paul (2) Cootamundra
FITTLER, Brad (+1) Penrith
FLORIMO, Greg (+1) Norths, S
FOLKES, Steve (8 + 1) Canterbury

GERARD, Geoff (2) Manly
GEYER, Mark (1) Penrith
GILLESPIE, David (3 + 3) Canterbury
GROTHE, Eric (9) Parramatta
GURR, Marty (2) Easts, S

HAMBLY, Gary (1) Souths, S
HANSON, Steve (1) Norths, S
HASLER, Des (5 + 4) Manly
HASTINGS, Kevin (+1) Easts, S
HETHERINGTON, Brian (1 + 1) Illawarra
HILDITCH, Ron (1) Parramatta
HUNT, Neil (2) Parramatta

IZZARD, Brad (2 + 1) Penrith

JACK, Garry (17) Balmain
JARVIS, Pat (6 + 2) St. George (4 + 2), Canterbury 2
JENSEN, Barry (1) Newtown
JOHNS, Chris (3) Brisbane Broncos
JOHNSTON, Brian (8) St. George

JOHNSTON, Lindsey (2) Norths, S
JURD, Stan (1 + 1) Parramatta

KELLY, Peter (2) Penrith
KENNY, Brett (16 + 1) Parramatta
KRILICH, Max (5) Manly

LAMB, Terry (4 + 3) Canterbury 3 + 3, Wests, S 1
LANGMACK, Paul (3 + 1) Canterbury
LAZARUS, Glenn (1 + 3) Canberra
LEIS, Jim (1) Wests, S
LYONS, Cliff (4) Manly
LYONS, Graham (2 + 1) Souths, S

McGAW, Mark (9 + 1) Cronulla
McGUIRE, Bruce (5) Balmain
MACKAY, Brad (3) St. George
McKINNON, Don (1) Norths, S
MATTERSON, Terry, (+1) Brisbane Broncos
MELROSE, Tony (1) Souths, S
MERLO, Paul (1) Wests, S
MILLER, Gavin (5) Cronulla
MORRIS, Steve (2) St. George
MORTIMER, Chris (8 + 1) Canterbury 7, Penrith 1 + 1
MORTIMER, Steve (8) Canterbury
MUGGLETON, John (2) Parramatta

NISZCOTT, Ziggy (2) Souths, S

O'CONNOR, Michael (16) St. George 6, Manly 10

PEARCE, Wayne (15) Balmain
POTTER, Michael (+1) Canterbury
PRICE, Ray (8) Parramatta

RAMPLING, Tony (2 + 1) Souths, S
RAUDONIKIS, Tom (1) Newtown
ROACH, Steve (14) Balmain
ROBERTS, Ian (3) Manly
ROGERS, Steve (4) Cronulla

SARGENT, Mark (+1) Newcastle
SIGSWORTH, Phil (3) Newtown 2, Manly 1
SIMMONS, Royce (10) Penrith
SIRONEN, Paul (1 + 3) Balmain
STERLING, Peter (13) Parramatta
STONE, Robert (+1) St. George
STUART, Ricky (3) Canberra

THOMPSON, Alan (5 + 1) Manly
TOOVEY, Geoff (+1) Manly
TREWHELLA, David (1 + 1) Easts, S
TUNKS, Peter (7 + 1), Souths 1, Canterbury 6 + 1

WALFORD, Ricky (1) St. George
WALSH, Chris (1) St. George
WILSON, Alan (+2) Cronulla
WISHART, Rod (3) Illawarra
WRIGHT, Rex (1) N. Newcastle
WYNN, Graeme (1) St. George
WYNN, Peter (4) Parramatta

YOUNG, Craig (4 + 1) St. George

FRANCE TOUR OF AUSTRALIA 1990

Date	Result	Score	Opposition	Venue	Attendance
10 June	W	16-8	**Western Australia** T: Pons, Dumas, Delaunay G: Dumas 2	Perth	5,265
14 June	W	16-9	**Queensland Country** T: Moliner (2), Dumas G: Dumas (2)	Cairns	5,000
16 June	L	16-22	**Queensland Selection** T: Fraisse, Entat, Moliner G: Dumas 2	Rockhampton	4,500
20 June	L	10-26	**North Coast Division** T: Chamorin, Pons G: Dumas	Wauchope	3,500
24 June	W	32-20	**Western Division** T: Pons (2), Divet (2), Marquet, Chamorin G: Tisseyre (4)	Bathurst	1,500
27 June	L	2-34	**AUSTRALIA**	Parkes	12,384

Australia:
Belcher (1g); O'Connor, Meninga (Capt, 1t), McGaw (2t), Shearer (1t); Daley (1t), Langer; Bella, Kerrod Walters, Roach, Sironen, Gillespie, Mackay (3t). Subs: Ettingshausen, Carroll (both played)
France:
Castel, Ratier (Capt), Ganriou, Delaunay, Pons; Dumas (1g), Entat; Rabot, Lope, Buttignol, Cabestany, Divet, Valero. Sub: Ruiz
Referee: Graham Ainui (Papua New Guinea)

TOUR SUMMARY

P	W	L	F	A
6	3	3	92	119

TOUR REGISTER
Captain: Hugues Ratier
Coach: Jacques Jorda
Managers: Robert Cousty and Louis Bonnery

Player	Club	App	Sub	T	G	Pts
AILLERES, Pierre	Toulouse	2	1	—	—	—
ALESINA, Adolphe	Pamiers	1	2	—	—	—
BUTTIGNOL, Thierry	Avignon	4	—	—	—	—
CABESTANY, Didier	St. Esteve	4	1	—	—	—
CASTEL, Eric	Albi	3	1	—	—	—
CHAMORIN, Pierre	St. Esteve	4	—	2	—	8
DELAUNAY, Guy	Catalan X111	5	—	1	—	4
DIVET, Daniel	Carcassonne	4	1	2	—	8
DUMAS, Gilles	St. Gaudens	4	1	2	8	24
ENTAT, Patrick	Avignon	6	—	1	—	4
FAGES, Pascal	Pia	—	1	—	—	—
FRAISSE, David	Carcassonne	2	—	1	—	4

GESTAS, Philippe	St. Gaudens	2	1	—	—	—
LOPE, Francis	Toulouse	3	1	—	—	—
MARQUET, Jean-Paul	Limoux	2	—	1	—	4
MOLINER, Jacques	Pamiers	3	1	3	—	12
PIREDDA, Christian	Avignon	1	1	—	—	—
PONS, Cyrille	St. Gaudens	5	1	4	—	16
RABOT, Jean-Luc	Villeneuve	4	2	—	—	—
RATIER, Hugues	Lezignan	5	—	—	—	—
RUIZ, Jean	St. Esteve	2	3	—	—	—
SAUMITOU, J. Bernard	Villeneuve	5	—	—	—	—
SOKOLOW, Philippe	Carcassonne	1	1	—	—	—
TISSEYRE, Marc	Pamiers	2	—	—	4	8
VALERO, Thierry	Lezignan	4	2	—	—	—
TOTALS				17	12	92

OTHER TEST MATCHES DOWN UNDER IN 1990

Date		**Venue**	**Attendance**
5 August	**PAPUA NEW GUINEA 4 NEW ZEALAND 36**	Goroka	12,000

Papua New Guinea: Wanega; Krewanty, Boge, Numapo (Capt), Waine; Haru, Ongugo; Ako, M. Matmillo, Evei, Angara, Tiri, Elara (1t). Subs: Morea, Soga, Paglipari, Kuno (all played).

New Zealand: M. Edwards (2g); Panapa (1t), Watson, Tuimavave, T. Iro (1t); Kemp (1t), Freeman (Capt); Brown (1t, 2g), D. Mann (1t), Todd, Nikau, Kuiti, M. Horo. Subs: Nixon, G. Mann, Lonergan (2t).
Referee: Bill Harrigan (Australia).

11 August	**PAPUA NEW GUINEA 10 NEW ZEALAND 18**	Port Moresby	10,000

Papua New Guinea: Wanega; Krewanty, Boge, Numapo (Capt, 1g), Haru; Soga (1t), Ongugo; Ako, M. Matmillo, Evei, Angara, Paglipari, Elara. Subs: Waine (1t), Tiri.

New Zealand: Ridge (3g); Panapa (1t), Watson, (1t), Tuimavave, T. Iro; Nixon, Freeman (Capt); Brown, D. Mann, Todd, Nikau, Lonergan (1t), Kuiti. Subs: M. Edwards, Patton, G. Mann, Leota (all played).
Referee: Bill Harrigan (Australia).

19 August	**NEW ZEALAND 6 AUSTRALIA 24**	Wellington	25,000

New Zealand: Ridge (1g); M. Edwards, Williams, Watson, Panapa (1t); K. Shelford, Freeman; Todd, D. Mann, Brown, Nikau, Lonergan, McGahan (Capt). Non-playing subs: Tuimavave, Nixon, M. Horo, G. Mann.

Australia: Belcher; Hancock (1t), Meninga (Capt, 4g), McGaw (1t), Shearer; Daley, Langer (1t); Bella, Kerrod Walters, Roach, Roberts, Sironen, Lindner. Subs: Ettingshausen, Hasler, Mackay (1t), Lazarus (all played).
Referee: Robin Whitfield (England)

Mick Sullivan, scorer of most tries for Great Britain.

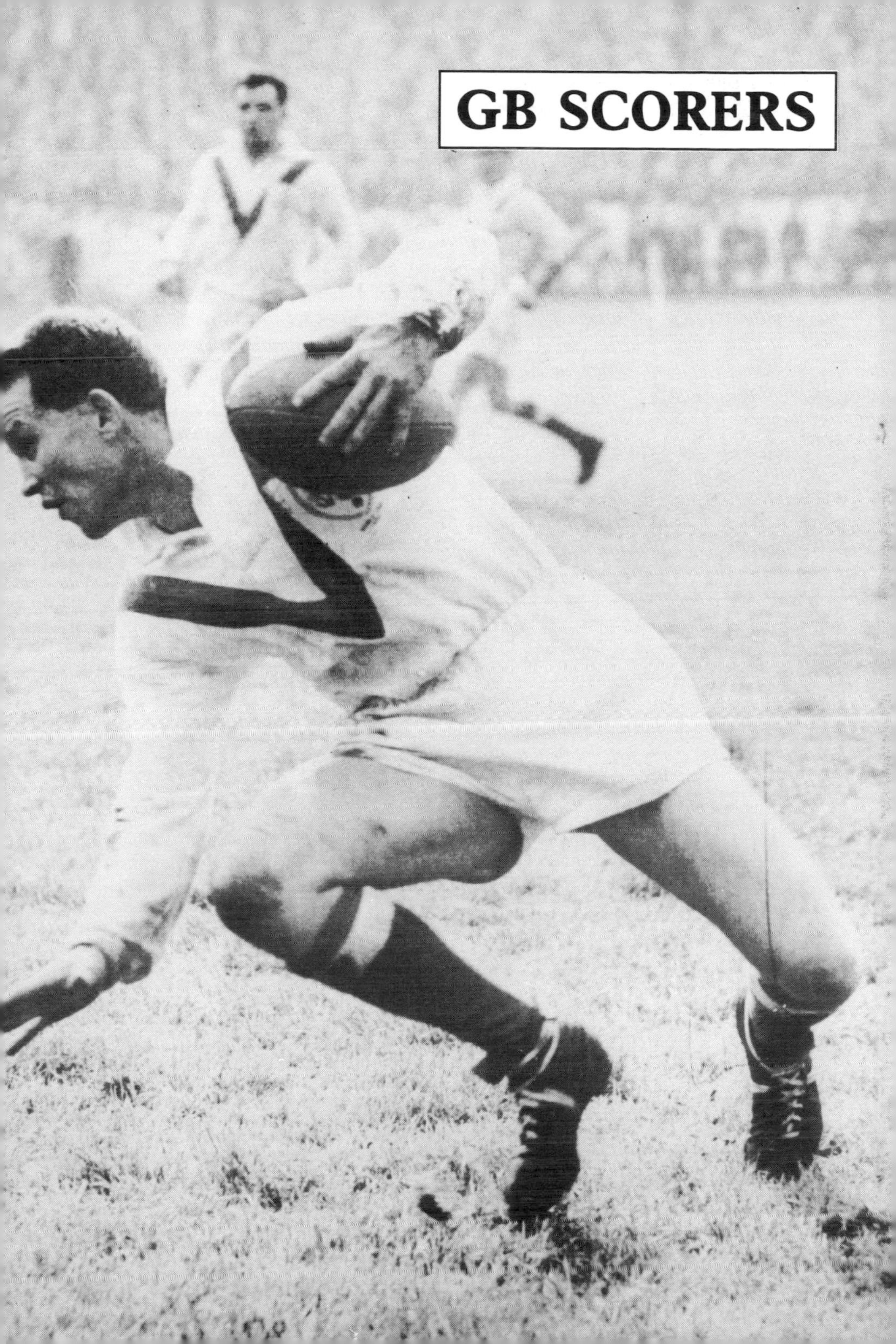
GB SCORERS

GB SCORERS

GREAT BRITAIN SCORERS

Featured for the first time in *Rothmans Rugby League Yearbook* is a record of Great Britain leading scorers of tries, goals and points, in a career and for an individual match. The statistics refer to Great Britain duty in Test and World Cup matches.

Centre Neil Fox, scorer of most goals and points for Great Britain.

Winger Billy Boston, third top Great Britain tryscorer.

MOST TRIES IN CAREER

*41 Mick Sullivan (Huddersfield, Wigan,
    St. Helens, York)............................... 1954-63
25 Garry Schofield (Hull, Leeds)................. 1984-
24 Billy Boston (Wigan)........................... 1954-63
19 Martin Offiah (Widnes)........................ 1988-
18 Ellery Hanley (Bradford N., Wigan)....... 1984-
17 Roger Millward (Cas'd, Hull K.R.)........ 1966-78
16 Alex Murphy (St. Helens, Warrington).... 1958-71
14 Eric Ashton (Wigan)............................ 1957-63
14 Neil Fox (Wakefield T.)........................ 1959-69
13 Clive Sullivan (Hull)............................. 1967-73
12 John Atkinson (Leeds).......................... 1968-80
10 Shaun Edwards (Wigan)........................ 1985-
10 Jim Leytham (Wigan)............................ 1907-10
*Mick Sullivan also scored two tries for Great Britain against France before the matches were given Test status.
● Most tries by a forward is eight by Derek Turner (Oldham, Wakefield T.) 1956-62; and Phil Lowe (Hull K.R.) 1970-78.

MOST GOALS IN CAREER

93 Neil Fox (Wakefield T.)......................... 1959-69
66 Lewis Jones (Leeds)............................... 1954-57
64 Jim Sullivan (Wigan)............................ 1924-33
53 Eric Fraser (Warrington)....................... 1958-61
44 George Fairbairn (Wigan, Hull K.R.)....... 1977-82
29 Paul Loughlin (St. Helens).................... 1988-
26 Joe Lydon (Widnes, Wigan)................... 1983-
25 Terry Clawson
    (Featherstone R., Leeds, Oldham).......... 1962-74
22 Ray Dutton (Widnes)............................ 1970
22 John Holmes (Leeds)............................ 1971-82
22 Ernest Ward (Bradford N.)..................... 1946-52
21 Mick Burke (Widnes)............................ 1980-86
21 Ken Gowers (Swinton).......................... 1962-66

MOST POINTS IN CAREER

228 Neil Fox (Wakefield T.)........................ 1959-69
147 Lewis Jones (Leeds)............................. 1954-57
128 Jim Sullivan (Wigan)........................... 1924-33
123 Mick Sullivan (Huddersfield, Wigan,
    St. Helens, York)............................... 1954-63
122 Garry Schofield (Hull, Leeds)............... 1984-
109 Eric Fraser (Warrington)...................... 1958-61
 91 George Fairbairn (Wigan, Hull K.R.)..... 1977-82
 81 Roger Millward (Castleford, Hull K.R.).. 1966-78
 76 Martin Offiah (Widnes)........................ 1988-
 75 Joe Lydon (Widnes, Wigan)................. 1983-

Back row forward Derek Turner, joint top tryscoring Great Britain packman.

Classic centre Ernest Ward, 22 Great Britain goals between 1946 and 1952.

Alex Murphy dives over for one of his 16 Great Britain tries.

MOST TRIES IN A MATCH

5 by Martin Offiah (Widnes) v. France at Leeds
16 February, 1991
4 by Jim Leytham (Wigan) v. Australia at Brisbane
2 July, 1910
Billy Boston (Wigan) v. New Zealand at Auckland
24 July, 1954
Alex Murphy (St. Helens) v. France at Leeds
14 March, 1959
Garry Schofield (Hull) v. New Zealand at Wigan
2 November, 1985
3 by Bill Jukes (Hunslet) v. Australia at Sydney
18 June, 1910
Bert Avery (Oldham) v. New Zealand at Auckland
30 July, 1910
Billy Stone (Hull) v. New Zealand at Auckland
31 July, 1920
Jonty Parkin (Wakefield T.) v. New Zealand at
Auckland 31 July, 1920
Charlie Carr (Barrow) v. New Zealand at Leeds
15 January, 1927
Stan Smith (Leeds) v. Australia at Sydney
16 July, 1932
Arthur Bassett (Halifax) v. Australia at Brisbane
6 July, 1946
George Wilson (Workington T.) v. New Zealand at
Bradford 6 October, 1951
Mick Sullivan (Huddersfield) v. New Zealand at
Bradford 12 November, 1955
Dave Bolton (Wigan) v. France at Wigan
23 November, 1957
Mick Sullivan (Wigan) v. Australia at Sydney
19 July, 1958
Mick Sullivan (Wigan) v. New Zealand at
Auckland 9 August, 1958
Mick Sullivan (Wigan) v. France at Leeds
14 March, 1959
Clive Sullivan (Hull) v. New Zealand at Sydney
(World Cup) 8 June, 1968
Bill Burgess (Barrow) v. France at St. Helens
30 November, 1968
Keith Fielding (Salford) v. France at Grenoble
20 January, 1974
Henderson Gill (Wigan) v. France at Hull
6 December, 1981
Garry Schofield (Leeds) v. France at Leeds
16 February, 1991

● Bill Jukes and Bert Avery are the only forwards to have
scored hat-tricks for Great Britain, both on tour in 1910.

Half back Dave Bolton, scorer of a hat-trick against France in 1957.

Second row man Phil Lowe, joint top tryscoring forward for Great Britain.

MOST GOALS IN A MATCH

10 by Lewis Jones (Leeds) v. Australia at Brisbane
    3 July, 1954
    Bernard Ganley (Oldham) v. France at Wigan
    23 November, 1957
    John Holmes (Leeds) v. New Zealand at Pau
    (World Cup) 4 November, 1972

9 by Lewis Jones (Leeds) v. France at Leeds
    26 January, 1957
    Neil Fox (Wakefield T.) v. France at Wigan
    3 April, 1963
    Neil Fox (Wakefield T.) v. France at Leigh
    18 March, 1964

8 by Eric Fraser (Warrington) v. Australia at Sydney
    19 July, 1958
    David Creasser (Leeds) v. France at Leeds
    1 March, 1985
    Joe Lydon (Wigan) v. France at Leeds
    24 January, 1987
    Paul Eastwood (Hull) v. France at Leeds
    16 February, 1991

7 by Lewis Jones (Leeds) v. France at St. Helens
    10 April, 1957
    Eric Fraser (Warrington) v. New Zealand at
    Auckland 9 August, 1958
    Eric Fraser (Warrington) v. France at Leeds
    14 March, 1959
    Neil Fox (Wakefield T.) v. New Zealand at
    Swinton 4 November, 1961
    Neil Fox (Wakefield T.) v. France at Swinton
    23 January, 1965
    Bev Risman (Leeds) v. New Zealand at Sydney
    (World Cup) 8 June, 1968
    Roger Millward (Hull K.R.) v. Australia at
    Sydney 20 June, 1970
    George Fairbairn (Wigan) v. France at Auckland
    (World Cup) 5 June, 1977
    John Woods (Leigh) v. France at Hull
    6 December, 1981
    David Stephenson (Wigan) v. Papua New Guinea
    at Wigan 24 October, 1987
    Paul Loughlin (St. Helens) v. Papua New Guinea
    at Port Moresby 22 May, 1988

Full back Eric Fraser, kicker of eight goals against Australia in 1958.

Full back George Fairbairn, a seven-goal haul against France in Auckland in 1977.

Utility back John Holmes, scorer of a record 26 points for Great Britain in the 1972 World Cup.

MOST POINTS IN A MATCH

26 (10g, 2t) by John Holmes (Leeds) v. New Zealand
at Pau, France (World Cup)
4 November, 1972

21 (9g, 1t) by Lewis Jones (Leeds) v. France at
Leeds 26 January, 1957
Neil Fox (Wakefield T.) v. France at
Wigan 3 April, 1963
Neil Fox (Wakefield T.) v. France at
Leigh 18 March, 1964

20 (10g) by Lewis Jones (Leeds) v. Australia at
Brisbane 3 July, 1954

(10g) Bernard Ganley (Oldham) v. France at
Wigan 23 November, 1957

(7g, 2t) Roger Millward (Hull K.R.) v.
Australia at Sydney 20 June, 1970

(8g, 1t) Joe Lydon (Wigan) v. France at Leeds
24 February, 1987

(5t) Martin Offiah (Widnes) v. France at
Leeds 16 February, 1991

(8g, 1t) Paul Eastwood (Hull) v. France at
Leeds 16 February, 1991

*Ellery Hanley, Britain's Man of the Series in the British
Coal Test series with the 1990 Kangaroos.*

GREAT BRITAIN

GREAT BRITAIN

1990-91 TEST REVIEW

Six out of 10. . .Great Britain's success rating from meetings with all four world Rugby League powers during a hectic 10-month Test timetable.

Malcolm Reilly's charges opened their 1990-91 round-the-world campaign with a drawn two-match Test series in Papua New Guinea, before celebrating a 2-1 triumph in New Zealand. The emotional 19-12 success at Wembley in October was the only victory in the autumn three-Test meeting with the touring Australians, the fast-improving Lions going on to register two record-breaking wins over the French in the new year.

The half dozen successes included two Tests carrying World Cup rating — in Papua and France — a 50 per cent haul to take Britain to second place in the table behind the unbeaten Australians.

The Test encounters with Papua New Guinea and New Zealand are chronicled in the chapter 1990 LIONS, while the triple meeting with Australia on British soil is detailed in the 1990 KANGAROOS section.

Rampant Great Britain passed the century of points in a double humiliation of the luckless French, rewriting the record books in both Perpignan and Leeds. The Anglo-French encounter in January established Britain's highest score and widest margin victory on French soil with a near perfect 45-10 performance, beating the 30-8 victory in Avignon two years earlier.

Stand off Garry Schofield battled against the strength-sapping effects of a virus to play a key part in the Perpignan rout, outstanding packman Denis Betts earning the British Coal Man of the Match award. Schofield scored two tries, had a hand in another and hit a drop goal against France, also having two other touchdowns disallowed before the virus took

its toll to force his withdrawal two minutes from the end.

Britain's forwards blasted through the French rearguard to establish the platform for half backs Shaun Edwards and Schofield to form the link with the backs. Britain's first touchdown set the pattern for some superb teamwork as Schofield finished off an intricate four-man move in front of the posts.

A precision pass from Schofield then put Betts through and he launched Martin Offiah on a 40-yard sprint for the first of his two tries. Betts, a main contributor in the build-up to the opening touchdown, was awarded a penalty try after kicking ahead in the 19th minute. The young Wigan back row forward continued to punish the French with his running and made the break that led to Offiah opening the tryscoring in the second half.

Edwards, revelling in the late opportunity to claim the scrum half role after the retirement from international football of Andy Gregory and the 11th-hour withdrawal of David Hulme, crossed for Britain's fourth try after good work by Hull hooker Lee Jackson to open up a 25-0 lead inside 22 minutes.

Then France produced a score as spectacular as any of Britain's with full back Christophe Auroy rounding off a 75-yard five-man raid. But Schofield popped up again to romp 30 yards for his second touchdown and, with Hull winger Paul Eastwood adding the goals to all five first-half tries, the French had already conceded more points than in any other home game against Britain.

Just before the break, a lazy pass from Schofield was snapped up by French centre David Fraisse, a target for Castleford, who raced 80 yards for France's last try, prop Marc Tisseyre's goal providing a half-time scoreline of 31-10.

Britain moved less effectively after the interval, although their defence tightened up to prevent any further French scores. Skipper Ellery Hanley set the example to head the tackle count with 26, followed by Andy Platt on 23, Hanley celebrating a record 18th match as British captain by achieving a record-equalling 12th win as skipper.

Offiah was unlucky to have two other touchdowns disallowed by impressive Australian referee Greg McCallum, making his third official trip to Europe. Platt highlighted a solid performance upfront by bumping off one defender and charging 20 yards for the seventh try, before Edwards rounded off the tryscoring with an interception.

Reilly awarded debuts to Widnes back row man Les Holliday and Wigan prop Ian Lucas, while substitutes St. John Ellis (Castleford) and Sheffield Eagles half back Mark Aston were brought on to make their first appearances.

The return fixture at Headingley, Leeds, three weeks later saw Britain resume where they had left off, running in 11 tries in a 60-4 rout despite heavy snow restricting their preparation programme to three sessions, only one of them on grass.

Reilly continued to celebrate his new full-time coaching contract by masterminding Great Britain to their highest-ever score against any country. France were not that bad a side, deserving to be at least level at the interval, but the home side produced exceptional teamwork and individual brilliance.

Offiah confirmed his status as one of the all-time great wingers with a British Test record five-try haul, all coming in a magical last half hour. Finally given the abundance of opportunities his rare talents deserve, the Widnes flier turned almost every one into a try, while creating another. It was a poetic performance of controlled pace and elusive running that included a tantalising liaison with the touchline.

After fewer than four seasons in Rugby League, Offiah leapt into fourth place in Britain's all-time tryscoring list with 19, while Schofield grabbed a hat-trick to take his total to 25, with only record cap Mick Sullivan ahead with 41 Test touchdowns.

Schofield also provided the final pass for two of Offiah's tries and his greater involvement in a commanding stand off display edged him ahead of the winger for the British Coal Man of the Match award.

All of Britain's 11 tries went to their backs, with three of them perfectly executed moves from the scrums that were straight out of the coaching manual. Yet it was the hardworking forwards, led by the inexhaustible Platt, who laid the foundations of success in a first half which gave the Lions a flattering 16-0 lead, boosted by a Schofield interception and Eastwood's four goals.

While the game was still a contest, Hull prop Andy Dannatt justified his late Test recall, after two appearances in 1985, with a succession of ground-devouring charges that helped sap French resistance. He also topped the tackle count with 23, ahead of Platt and Hanley.

Eastwood, who kept the goalkicking role despite the recall of St. Helens marksman Paul Loughlin, hit the target on eight successive occasions followed by five misses in a row. As the Airlie Bird also scored a try, the succession of misses left him — along with five-try Offiah — only one point short of the record 21 against France.

The record-breaking in the two-match series was rounded off by Hanley becoming Britain's most successful skipper by leading them to a 13th victory since being a stand-in captain in 1985. His 34th Test appearance put him into second place in the all-time Great Britain list.

FIRST BRITISH COAL TEST

27 January   **Perpignan**

GREAT BRITAIN 45		FRANCE 10
Steve Hampson (Wigan)	1.	Christophe Auroy (XIII Catalan)
Paul Eastwood (Hull)	2.	Eric Remirez (Carcassonne)
Daryl Powell (Sheffield E.)	3.	David Fraisse (Carcassonne)
Carl Gibson (Leeds)	4.	Guy Delaunay (XIII Catalan)
Martin Offiah (Widnes)	5.	Cyrille Pons (St. Gaudens)
Garry Schofield (Leeds)	6.	Gilles Dumas (St. Gaudens), Capt.
Shaun Edwards (Wigan)	7.	Patrick Entat (Hull)
Ian Lucas (Wigan)	8.	Marc Tisseyre (Pamiers)
Lee Jackson (Hull)	9.	Thierry Valero (Lezignan)
Andy Platt (Wigan)	10.	Thierry Buttignol (Avignon)
Denis Betts (Wigan)	11.	Jean-Pierre Magnac (XIII Catalan)
Les Holliday (Widnes)	12.	Daniel Verdes (Villeneuve)
Ellery Hanley (Wigan), Capt.	13.	Jacques Moliner (XIII Catalan)
Mark Aston (Sheffield E.)	14.	Denis Bienes (St. Gaudens)
Karl Fairbank (Bradford N.)	15.	Michel Roses (Le Baracares)
St. John Ellis (Castleford)	16.	Pierre Chamorin (St. Esteve)
Richard Eyres (Widnes)	17.	Abderazack Baba (XIII Catalan)

T: Schofield (2), Offiah (2), Edwards (2), Betts, Platt
G: Eastwood (6), Schofield (dg)
Substitutions:
Fairbank for Holliday (50 min.)
Ellis for Hampson (69 min.)
Eyres for Jackson (70 min.)
Aston for Schofield (79 min.)
Manager: Maurice Lindsay
Coach: Malcolm Reilly

T: Auroy, Fraisse
G: Tisseyre
Substitutions:
Charmorin for Verdes (13 min.)
Bienes for Dumas (35 min.)
Baba for Valero (51 min.)
Half-time 31-10
Referee: Greg McCallum
(Australia)
Attendance: 3,965

Scorechart

Minute	Score	GB	France
3:	Schofield (T)		
	Eastwood (G)	6	0
9:	Offiah (T)		
	Eastwood (G)	12	0
15:	Schofield (DG)	13	0
19:	Betts (T)		
	Eastwood (G)	19	0
22:	Edwards (T)		
	Eastwood (G)	25	0
27:	Auroy (T)	25	4
33:	Schofield (T)		
	Eastwood (G)	31	4
37:	Fraisse (T)		
	Tisseyre (G)	31	10
43:	Offiah (T)	35	10
61:	Platt (T)		
	Eastwood (G)	41	10
86:	Edwards (T)	45	10
	Scrums	8	11
	Penalties	3	3

SECOND BRITISH COAL TEST

16 February   **Leeds**

GREAT BRITAIN 60		FRANCE 4
Steve Hampson (Wigan)	1.	Christophe Auroy (XIII Catalan)
Paul Eastwood (Hull)	2.	Alain Bouzer (Toulouse)
Daryl Powell (Sheffield E.)	3.	David Fraisse (Carcassonne)
Paul Loughlin (St. Helens)	4.	Pierre Chamorin (St. Esteve)
Martin Offiah (Widnes)	5.	Cyrille Pons (St. Gaudens)
Garry Schofield (Leeds)	6.	Jacques Moliner (XIII Catalan)
Shaun Edwards (Wigan)	7.	Patrick Entat (Hull)
Andy Dannatt (Hull)	8.	Pierre Montgaillard (XIII Catalan)
Lee Jackson (Hull)	9.	Thierry Valero (Lezignan)
Andy Platt (Wigan)	10.	Thierry Buttignol (Avignon), Capt.
Richard Eyres (Widnes)	11.	Didier Cabestany (St. Esteve)
Karl Fairbank (Bradford N.)	12.	Daniel Verdes (Villeneuve)
Ellery Hanley (Wigan), Capt.	13.	Jean-Bernard Saumitou (Villeneuve)
St. John Ellis (Castleford)	14.	Jean-Pierre Magnac (XIII Catalan)
Roy Powell (Leeds)	15.	Marc Tisseyre (Pamiers)
Kevin Ellis (Warrington)	16.	Adolphe Alesina (Pamiers)
Keith England (Castleford)	17.	Eric Remirez (Carcassonne)

T: Offiah (5), Schofield (3), Eastwood, Hampson, Edwards

G: Eastwood (8)

Substitutions:

R. Powell for Eyres (56 min.)

S. Ellis for Hampson (64 min.)

K. Ellis for Loughlin (64 min.)

England for Fairbank (64 min.)

Manager: Maurice Lindsay

Coach: Malcolm Reilly

T: Pons

Substitutions:

Magnac for Cabestany (49 min.)

Remirez for Bouzer (54 min.)

Tisseyre for Montgaillard (64 min.)

Alesina for Auroy (71 min.)

Half-time: 16-0

Referee: Greg McCallum (Australia)

Attendance: 5,284

Scorechart

Minute	Score	GB	France				
15:	Eastwood (P)	2	0	52:	Edwards (T)		
21:	Schofield (T)				Eastwood (G)	34	0
	Eastwood (G)	8	0	54:	Offiah (T)		
26:	Eastwood (P)	10	0	56:	Eastwood (G)	40	0
37:	Eastwood (T)				Hampson (T)	44	0
	Eastwood (G)	16	0	62:	Offiah (T)	48	0
44:	Schofield (T)			67:	Offiah (T)	52	0
	Eastwood (G)	22	0	70:	Schofield (T)	56	0
49:	Offiah (T)			72:	Pons (T)	56	4
	Eastwood (G)	28	0	79:	Offiah (T)	60	4

	Scrums	7	3
	Penalties	9	8

Australian winger Michael Hancock fails to prevent Hull winger Paul Eastwood touching down in the first British Coal Test at Wembley.

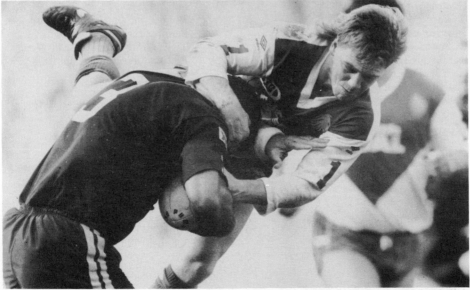

Great Britain full back Steve Hampson wraps up Kangaroo skipper Mal Meninga during the epic 1990 British Coal Test series.

TESTS

● Although early Tests were played under the titles of Northern Union or England, it is acceptable to regard them as Great Britain.
W-Won, D-Drawn, L-Lost refer to Great Britain.

GREAT BRITAIN v. AUSTRALIA

Date		Score	Venue	Attendance
12 Dec. 1908	D	22-22	QPR, London	2,000
23 Jan. 1909	W	15-5	Newcastle	22,000
15 Feb. 1909	W	6-5	Birmingham	9,000
18 Jun. 1910	W	27-20	Sydney	42,000
2 Jul. 1910	W	22-17	Brisbane	18,000
8 Nov. 1911	L	10-19	Newcastle	6,500
16 Dec. 1911	D	11-11	Edinburgh	6,000
1 Jan. 1912	L	8-33	Birmingham	4,000
27 Jun. 1914	W	23-5	Sydney	40,000
29 Jun. 1914	L	7-12	Sydney	55,000
4 Jul. 1914	W	14-6	Sydney	34,420
26 Jun. 1920	L	4-8	Brisbane	28,000
3 Jul. 1920	L	8-21	Sydney	40,000
10 Jul. 1920	W	23-13	Sydney	32,000
1 Oct. 1921	W	6-5	Leeds	32,000
5 Nov. 1921	L	2-16	Hull	21,504
14 Jan. 1922	W	6-0	Salford	21,000
23 Jun. 1924	W	22-3	Sydney	50,000
28 Jun. 1924	W	5-3	Sydney	33,842
12 Jul. 1924	L	11-21	Brisbane	36,000
23 Jun. 1928	W	15-12	Brisbane	39,200
14 Jul. 1928	W	8-0	Sydney	44,548
21 Jul. 1928	L	14-21	Sydney	37,000
5 Oct. 1929	L	8-31	Hull K.R.	20,000
9 Nov. 1929	W	9-3	Leeds	31,402
4 Jan. 1930	D	0-0	Swinton	34,709
15 Jan. 1930	W	3-0	Rochdale	16,743
6 Jun. 1932	W	8-6	Sydney	70,204
18 Jun. 1932	L	6-15	Brisbane	26,500
16 Jul. 1932	W	18-13	Sydney	50,053
7 Oct. 1933	W	4-0	Belle Vue, Manchester	34,000
11 Nov. 1933	W	7-5	Leeds	29,618
16 Dec. 1933	W	19-16	Swinton	10,990
29 Jun. 1936	L	8-24	Sydney	63,920
4 Jul. 1936	W	12-7	Brisbane	29,486
18 Jul. 1936	W	12-7	Sydney	53,546
16 Oct. 1937	W	5-4	Leeds	31,949
13 Nov. 1937	W	13-3	Swinton	31,724
18 Dec. 1937	L	3-13	Huddersfield	9,093
17 Jun. 1946	D	8-8	Sydney	64,527
6 Jul. 1946	W	14-5	Brisbane	40,500
20 Jul. 1946	W	20-7	Sydney	35,294
9 Oct. 1948	W	23-21	Leeds	36,529
6 Nov. 1948	W	16-7	Swinton	36,354
29 Jan. 1949	W	23-9	Bradford	42,000
12 Jun. 1950	W	6-4	Sydney	47,215
1 Jul. 1950	L	3-15	Brisbane	35,000
22 Jul. 1950	L	2-5	Sydney	47,178
4 Oct. 1952	W	19-6	Leeds	34,505
8 Nov. 1952	W	21-5	Swinton	32,421
13 Dec. 1952	L	7-27	Bradford	30,509
12 Jun. 1954	L	12-37	Sydney	65,884
3 Jul. 1954	W	38-21	Brisbane	46,355
17 Jul. 1954	L	16-20	Sydney	67,577
17 Nov. 1956	W	21-10	Wigan	22,473
1 Dec. 1956	L	9-22	Bradford	23,634
15 Dec. 1956	W	19-0	Swinton	17,542
14 Jun. 1958	L	8-25	Sydney	68,777
5 Jul. 1958	W	25-18	Brisbane	32,965
19 Jul. 1958	W	40-17	Sydney	68,720
17 Oct. 1959	L	14-22	Swinton	35,224
21 Nov. 1959	W	11-10	Leeds	30,184
12 Dec. 1959	W	18-12	Wigan	26,089
9 Jun. 1962	W	31-12	Sydney	70,174
30 Jun. 1962	W	17-10	Brisbane	34,766
14 Jul. 1962	L	17-18	Sydney	42,104
16 Oct. 1963	L	2-28	Wembley	13,946
9 Nov. 1963	L	12-50	Swinton	30,833
30 Nov. 1963	W	16-5	Leeds	20,497
25 Jun. 1966	W	17-13	Sydney	57,962
16 Jul. 1966	L	4-6	Brisbane	45,057
23 Jul. 1966	L	14-19	Sydney	63,503
21 Oct. 1967	W	16-11	Leeds	22,293
3 Nov. 1967	L	11-17	White City, London	17,445
9 Dec. 1967	L	3-11	Swinton	13,615
6 Jun. 1970	L	15-37	Brisbane	42,807
20 Jun. 1970	W	28-7	Sydney	60,962
4 Jul. 1970	W	21-17	Sydney	61,258
3 Nov. 1973	W	21-12	Wembley	9,874
24 Nov. 1973	L	6-14	Leeds	16,674
1 Dec. 1973	L	5-15	Warrington	10,019
15 Jun. 1974	L	6-12	Brisbane	30,280
6 Jul. 1974	W	16-11	Sydney	48,006
20 Jul. 1974	L	18-22	Sydney	55,505
21 Oct. 1978	L	9-15	Wigan	17,644
5 Nov. 1978	W	18-14	Bradford	26,447
18 Nov. 1978	L	6-23	Leeds	29,627
16 Jun. 1979	L	0-35	Brisbane	23,051

30 Jun. 1979	L	16-24	Sydney	26,837
14 Jul. 1979	L	2-28	Sydney	16,844
30 Oct. 1982	L	4-40	Hull C. FC	26,771
20 Nov. 1982	L	6-27	Wigan	23,216
28 Nov. 1982	L	8-32	Leeds	17,318
9 Jun. 1984	L	8-25	Sydney	30,190
26 Jun. 1984	L	6-18	Brisbane	26,534
7 Jul. 1984	L	7-20	Sydney	18,756
25 Oct. 1986	L	16-38	Man U. FC	50,583
8 Nov. 1986	L	4-34	Elland Rd, Leeds	30,808

* 22 Nov. 1986	L	15-24	Wigan	20,169
11 Jun. 1988	L	6-17	Sydney	24,202
28 Jun. 1988	L	14-34	Brisbane	27,103
* 9 Jul. 1988	W	26-12	Sydney	15,994
27 Oct. 1990	W	19-12	Wembley	54,569
10 Nov. 1990	L	10-14	Man U. FC	46,615
* 24 Nov. 1990	L	0-14	Elland Rd, Leeds	32,500

* Also World Cup match.

	Played	Won	Drawn	Lost	Tries	Goals	Dr	Pts for
Great Britain	105	51	4	50	255	260	6	1313
Australia	105	50	4	51	301	325	6	1605

GREAT BRITAIN-AUSTRALIA TEST MATCH RECORDS

Britain

Highest score: 40-17 Third Test at Sydney 19 July 1958 (Also widest margin win)

Most tries in a match: 4 by J. Leytham (Wigan) Second Test at Brisbane 2 July 1910

Most goals in a match: 10 by B. L. Jones (Leeds) Second Test at Brisbane 3 July 1954

Most points in a match: 20 by B. L. Jones (as above)
20 (7g,2t) by R. Millward (Hull K.R.) Second Test at Sydney 20 June 1970.

Biggest attendance: 54,569 First Test at Wembley, London, 27 Oct 1990

Australia

Highest score: 50-12 Second Test at Swinton, 9 Nov 1963 (Also widest margin win)

Most tries in a match: 3 by J. Devereux, First Test at QPR, London, 12 Dec 1908
3 by R. Gasnier, First Test at Swinton, 17 Oct 1959
3 by R. Gasnier, First Test at Wembley, 16 Oct 1963
3 by K. Irvine, Second Test at Swinton, 9 Nov 1963
3 by K. Irvine, Third Test at Sydney, 23 July 1966
3 by G. Miles, First Test at Old Trafford, Manchester, 25 Oct 1986
3 by M. O'Connor, First Test at Old Trafford, Manchester, 25 Oct 1986

Most goals in a match: 10 by M. Cronin, First Test at Brisbane, 16 June 1979

Most points in a match: 22 (5g,3t) by M. O'Connor First Test at Old Trafford, Manchester, 25 Oct 1986

Biggest attendance: 70,204 First Test at Sydney, 6 June 1932

● In a World Cup match at Perpignan, France, on 29 October 1972, R. Fulton scored 3 tries.

GREAT BRITAIN v. NEW ZEALAND

Date	Result		Venue	Crowd
25 Jan. 1908	W	14-6	Leeds	8,182
8 Feb. 1908	L	6-18	Chelsea	14,000
15 Feb. 1908	L	5-8	Cheltenham	4,000
30 Jul. 1910	W	52-20	Auckland	16,000
1 Aug. 1914	W	16-13	Auckland	15,000
31 Jul. 1920	W	31-7	Auckland	34,000
7 Aug. 1920	W	19-3	Christchurch	10,000
14 Aug. 1920	W	11-10	Wellington	4,000
2 Aug. 1924	L	8-16	Auckland	22,000
6 Aug. 1924	L	11-13	Wellington	6,000
9 Aug. 1924	W	31-18	Dunedin	14,000
2 Oct. 1926	W	28-20	Wigan	14,500
13 Nov. 1926	W	21-11	Hull	7,000
15 Jan. 1927	W	32-17	Leeds	6,000
4 Aug. 1928	L	13-17	Auckland	28,000
18 Aug. 1928	W	13-5	Dunedin	12,000
25 Aug. 1928	W	6-5	Christchurch	21,000
30 Jul. 1932	W	24-9	Auckland	25,000
13 Aug. 1932	W	25-14	Christchurch	5,000
20 Aug. 1932	W	20-18	Auckland	6,500
8 Aug. 1936	W	10-8	Auckland	25,000
15 Aug. 1936	W	23-11	Auckland	17,000
10 Aug. 1946	L	8-13	Auckland	10,000
4 Oct. 1947	W	11-10	Leeds	28,445
8 Nov. 1947	L	7-10	Swinton	29,031
20 Dec. 1947	W	25-9	Bradford	42,680
29 Jul. 1950	L	10-16	Christchurch	10,000
12 Aug. 1950	L	13-20	Auckland	20,000
6 Oct. 1951	W	21-15	Bradford	37,475
10 Nov. 1951	W	20-19	Swinton	29,938
15 Dec. 1951	W	16-12	Leeds	18,649
24 Jul. 1954	W	27-7	Auckland	22,097
31 Jul. 1954	L	14-20	Greymouth	4,240
14 Aug. 1954	W	12-6	Auckland	6,186
8 Oct. 1955	W	25-6	Swinton	21,937
12 Nov. 1955	W	27-12	Bradford	24,443
17 Dec. 1955	L	13-28	Leeds	10,438
26 Jul. 1958	L	10-15	Auckland	25,000
9 Aug. 1958	W	32-15	Auckland	25,000
30 Sept. 1961	L	11-29	Leeds	16,540
21 Oct. 1961	W	23-10	Bradford	19,980
4 Nov. 1961	W	35-19	Swinton	22,536
28 Jul. 1962	L	0-19	Auckland	14,976
11 Aug. 1962	L	8-27	Auckland	16,411
25 Sept. 1965	W	7-2	Swinton	8,541
23 Oct. 1965	W	15-9	Bradford	15,740
6 Nov. 1965	D	9-9	Wigan	7,919
6 Aug. 1966	W	25-8	Auckland	14,494
20 Aug. 1966	W	22-14	Auckland	10,657
11 Jul. 1970	W	19-15	Auckland	15,948
19 Jul. 1970	W	23-9	Christchurch	8,600
25 Jul. 1970	W	33-16	Auckland	13,137
25 Sept. 1971	L	13-18	Salford	3,764
16 Oct. 1971	L	14-17	Castleford	4,108
6 Nov. 1971	W	12-3	Leeds	5,479
27 Jul. 1974	L	8-13	Auckland	10,466
4 Aug. 1974	W	17-8	Christchurch	6,316
10 Aug. 1974	W	20-0	Auckland	11,574
21 Jul. 1979	W	16-8	Auckland	9,000
5 Aug. 1979	W	22-7	Christchurch	8,500
11 Aug. 1979	L	11-18	Auckland	7,000
18 Oct. 1980	D	14-14	Wigan	7,031
2 Nov. 1980	L	8-12	Bradford	10,946
15 Nov. 1980	W	10-2	Leeds	8,210
14 Jul. 1984	L	0-12	Auckland	10,238
22 Jul. 1984	L	12-28	Christchurch	3,824
28 Jul. 1984	L	16-32	Auckland	7,967
19 Oct. 1985	L	22-24	Leeds	12,591
2 Nov. 1985	W	25-8	Wigan	15,506
*9 Nov. 1985	D	6-6	Elland Rd, Leeds	22,209
*17 Jul. 1988	L	10-12	Christchurch	8,525
21 Oct. 1989	L	16-24	Man U. FC	18,273
28 Oct. 1989	W	26-6	Elland Rd, Leeds	13,073
*11 Nov. 1989	W	10-6	Wigan	20,346
24 Jun. 1990	W	11-10	Palmerston N.	8,073
8 Jul. 1990	W	16-14	Auckland	7,843
*15 Jul. 1990	L	18-21	Christchurch	3,133

*Also World Cup match.

	Played	Won	Drawn	Lost	Tries	Goals	Dr	Pts for
Great Britain	77	47	3	27	273	220	4	1293
New Zealand	77	27	3	47	177	222	1	1009

GREAT BRITAIN-NEW ZEALAND TEST MATCH RECORDS

Britain

Highest score: 52-20 First Test at Auckland, 30 July 1910 (Also widest margin win)

Most tries in a match: 4 by W. Boston (Wigan) First Test at Auckland, 24 July 1954
4 by G. Schofield (Hull) Second Test at Wigan, 2 Nov 1985

Most goals in a match: 7 by N. Fox (Wakefield T.) Third Test at Swinton, 4 Nov 1961
7 by E. Fraser (Warrington) Second Test at Auckland, 9 Aug 1958
Most points in a match: 16 (4t) by G. Schofield (Hull) Second Test at Wigan, 2 Nov 1985
Biggest attendance: 42,680 Third Test at Bradford, 20 Dec 1947

● In a World Cup match at Pau, France, on 4 November 1972, Britain won 53-19 with J. Holmes (Leeds) scoring 26 points from 10 goals and two tries.
In a World Cup match at Sydney on 8 June 1968, Bev Risman scored 7 goals.

New Zealand
Highest score: 32-16 Third Test at Auckland, 28 July 1984
Widest margin win: 19-0 First Test at Auckland, 28 July 1962
27-8 Second Test at Auckland, 11 Aug 1962
No player has scored three tries or more in a Test.
Most goals and points: 7g-14pts by D. White, Second Test at Greymouth, 31 July 1954
J. Fagan, First Test at Headingley, 30 Sep 1961
E. Wiggs, Second Test at Auckland, 20 Aug 1966
Biggest attendance: 34,000 First Test at Auckland, 31 July 1920
● In a World Cup match at Sydney, Australia, on 25 June 1957, W. Sorensen also scored 7 goals, 14 points.

GREAT BRITAIN v. FRANCE
● **Results since France were given Test match status.**

26 Jan. 1957	W	45-12	Leeds	20,221	7 Feb. 1971	L	8-16	Toulouse	14,960
3 Mar. 1957	D	19-19	Toulouse	16,000	17 Mar. 1971	W	24-2	St. Helens	7,783
10 Apr. 1957	W	29-14	St. Helens	23,250	6 Feb. 1972	W	10-9	Toulouse	11,508
3 Nov. 1957	W	25-14	Toulouse	15,000	12 Mar. 1972	W	45-10	Bradford	7,313
23 Nov. 1957	W	44-15	Wigan	19,152	20 Jan. 1974	W	24-5	Grenoble	5,500
2 Mar. 1958	W	23-9	Grenoble	20,000	17 Feb. 1974	W	29-0	Wigan	10,105
14 Mar. 1959	W	50-15	Leeds	22,000	6 Dec. 1981	W	37-0	Hull	13,173
5 Apr. 1959	L	15-24	Grenoble	8,500	20 Dec. 1981	L	2-19	Marseilles	6,500
6 Mar. 1960	L	18-20	Toulouse	15,308	20 Feb. 1983	W	20-5	Carcassonne	3,826
26 Mar. 1960	D	17-17	St. Helens	14,000	6 Mar. 1983	W	17-5	Hull	6,055
11 Dec. 1960	W	21-10	Bordeaux	8,000	29 Jan. 1984	W	12-0	Avignon	4,000
28 Jan. 1961	W	27-8	St. Helens	18,000	17 Feb. 1984	W	10-0	Leeds	7,646
17 Feb. 1962	L	15-20	Wigan	17,277	1 Mar. 1985	W	50-4	Leeds	6,491
11 Mar. 1962	L	13-23	Perpignan	14,000	17 Mar. 1985	L	16-24	Perpignan	5,000
2 Dec. 1962	L	12-17	Perpignan	5,000	*16 Feb. 1986	D	10-10	Avignon	4,000
3 Apr. 1963	W	42-4	Wigan	19,487	1 Mar. 1986	W	24-10	Wigan	8,112
8 Mar. 1964	W	11-5	Perpignan	4,326	*24 Jan. 1987	W	52-4	Leeds	6,567
18 Mar. 1964	W	39-0	Leigh	4,750	8 Feb. 1987	W	20-10	Carcassonne	2,000
6 Dec. 1964	L	8-18	Perpignan	15,000	24 Jan. 1988	W	28-14	Avignon	6,500
23 Jan. 1965	W	17-7	Swinton	9,959	6 Feb. 1988	W	30-12	Leeds	7,007
16 Jan. 1966	L	13-18	Perpignan	6,000	21 Jan. 1989	W	26-10	Wigan	8,266
5 Mar. 1966	L	4-8	Wigan	14,004	5 Feb. 1989	W	30-8	Avignon	6,500
22 Jan. 1967	W	16-13	Carcassonne	10,650	18 Mar. 1990	W	8-4	Perpignan	6,000
4 Mar. 1967	L	13-23	Wigan	7,448	7 Apr. 1990	L	18-25	Leeds	6,554
11 Feb. 1968	W	22-13	Paris	8,000	*27 Jan. 1991	W	45-10	Perpignan	3,965
2 Mar. 1968	W	19-8	Bradford	14,196	16 Feb. 1991	W	60-4	Leeds	5,284
30 Nov. 1968	W	34-10	St. Helens	6,080					
2 Feb. 1969	L	9-13	Toulouse	10,000	*Also World Cup match.				

	Played	Won	Drawn	Lost	Tries	Goals	Dr	Pts for
Great Britain	54	37	3	14	246	231	1	1275
France	54	14	3	37	101	133	4	597

GREAT BRITAIN-FRANCE TEST MATCH RECORDS

Britain
Highest score: 60-4 at Leeds, 16 February 1991. (Also widest margin win)
Most tries in a match: 5 by M. Offiah (Widnes) at Leeds, 16 February 1991
Most goals in a match: 10 by B. Ganley (Oldham) at Wigan, 23 November 1957
Most points in a match: 21 (9g,1t) by B.L. Jones (Leeds) at Leeds, 26 January 1957
21 (9g,1t) by N. Fox (Wakefield T.) at Wigan, 3 April 1963
21 (9g,1t) by N. Fox (Wakefield T.) at Leigh, 18 March 1964
Biggest attendance: 23,250 at St. Helens, 10 April 1957

France
Highest score: 25-18 at Leeds, 7 April 1990
Widest margin win: 19-2 at Marseilles, 20 December 1981
Most tries in a match: 3 by D. Couston at Perpignan, 17 March 1985
Most goals in a match: 7 by P. Lacaze at Wigan, 4 March 1967
Most points in a match: 14 by P. Lacaze (as above).
14 (4g,2t) by G. Benausse at Wigan, 17 February 1962
Biggest attendance: 20,000 at Grenoble, 2 March 1958
●In a World Cup match at Toulouse on 7 November 1954, there were 37,471

Additional Great Britain v. France

Pre-Test status
22 May 1952	L	12-22	Paris	16,466
24 May 1953	L	17-28	Lyons	
27 Apr. 1954	W	17-8	Bradford	14,153
11 Dec. 1955	L	5-17	Paris	18,000
11 Apr. 1956	W	18-10	Bradford	10,453

Other match
31 July 1982	L	7-8	Venice	1,500

GREAT BRITAIN v PAPUA NEW GUINEA
5 Aug. 1984	W	38-20	Mt. Hagen	7,510
*24 Oct. 1987	W	42-0	Wigan	9,121
*22 May 1988	W	42-22	Port Moresby	12,107
27 May 1990	L	18-20	Goroka	11,598
*2 Jun. 1990	W	40-8	Port Moresby	5,969

*Also World Cup

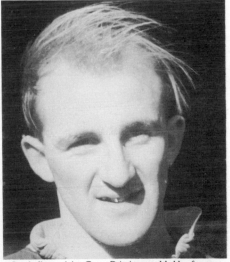

Lewis Jones, joint Great Britain record-holder for most points against France.

GREAT BRITAIN REPRESENTATION CLUB-BY-CLUB

Wigan beat their own record by fielding eight players in the Great Britain side which met Papua New Guinea at Wigan on 24 October 1987. The octet was backs Steve Hampson, David Stephenson, Joe Lydon, Shaun Edwards and Andy Gregory, plus forwards Brian Case, Andy Goodway and Ellery Hanley. The previous best of seven were backs Martin Ryan, Gordon Ratcliffe, Ernie Ashcroft, Jack Hilton and Tommy Bradshaw, plus forwards Ken Gee and Joe Egan in the 6-4 victory over Australia at Sydney on 12 June, 1950. Wigan also hold the record for the total of players selected with a remarkable 78.

Mick Sullivan gained Test honours with four clubs — Huddersfield (16), Wigan (19), St. Helens (10) and York (1). Billy Boston gained the most Test honours with a single club, making all 31 of his appearances for Britain while with Wigan.

Only six of last season's clubs have not had a player selected for Great Britain in Test or World Cup matches — Chorley, Bramley, Doncaster, Carlisle, Nottingham City and Trafford Borough. Of the extinct clubs only Broughton Rangers (later Belle Vue Rangers), Merthyr Tydfil, St. Helens Recs and the old Runcorn had players selected for Britain.

The following is a club-by-club register of Great Britain players. The figure in brackets after a player's name is the number of Great Britain appearances he made while serving the club under whose entry he is listed, and the number after the + sign indicates playing substitute. This is followed by the time span between his first and last British cap while at that club.

BARROW (19 players)
W. Burgess (16) 1924-29
W. Burgess (13) 1962-68
D. Cairns (2) 1984
C. Camilleri (2) 1980
C. Carr (7) 1924-26
F. Castle (4) 1952-54
R. Francis (1) 1947
H. Gifford (2) 1908
D. Goodwin (5) 1957-58
J. Grundy (12) 1955-57
P. Hogan (4 + 1) 1977-78
W. Horne (8) 1946-52
P. Jackson (27) 1954-58
J. Jones (1) 1946
B. Knowelden (1) 1946
E. Szymala (1 + 1) 1981
E. Toohey (3) 1952
L. A. Troup (2) 1936
J. Woods (1) 1933

BATLEY (4 players)
N. Field (1) 1963
F. Gallagher (8) 1924-26
C. Gibson (+1) 1985
J. Oliver (4) 1928

BRADFORD NORTHERN (31 players)
D. Barends (2) 1979
E. Batten (4) 1946-47
I. Brooke (5) 1966
L. Casey (5) 1979
G. Cordle (1) 1990
W. T. H. Davies (3) 1946-47
K. Fairbank (3 + 3) 1987-91
A. Fisher (8) 1970-78
P. Ford (7) 1987-88
T. Foster (3) 1946-48
J. Grayshon (11) 1979-82
E. Hanley (10 + 1) 1984-85
D. Hobbs (1 + 1) 1989
R. Jasiewicz (1) 1984
J. Kitching (1) 1946
A. Mann (2) 1908
K. Mumby (11) 1982-84
B. Noble (11) 1982-84
T. Price (1) 1970

J. Rae (1) 1965
W. Ramsey (+1) 1974
A. Rathbone (4 + 1) 1982-85
A. Redfearn (1) 1979
D. Redfearn (6 + 1) 1972-74
K. Skerrett (8) 1989-90
T. Smales (3) 1965
H. Smith (2) 1926
J. Thompson (1) 1978
K. Traill (8) 1950-54
E. Ward (20) 1946-52
F. Whitcombe (2) 1946

BROUGHTON/BELLE VUE RANGERS (8 players)
W. Bentham (2) 1924
L. Clampitt (3) 1907-14
E. Gwyther (6) 1947-51
A. Hogg (1) 1907
S. McCormick (2) 1948
D. Phillips (1) 1950
J. Price (2) 1921
J. Ruddick (3) 1907-10

CASTLEFORD (26 players)
A. Atkinson (11) 1929-36
K. Beardmore (13 + 1) 1984-90
W. Bryant (4 + 1) 1964-67
A. Croston (1) 1937
B. Cunniffe (1) 1937
W. J. Davies (1) 1933
D. Edwards (3 + 2) 1968-71
S. Ellis (+ 2) 1991
K. England (6 + 5) 1987-91
A. Hardisty (12) 1964-70
D. Hartley (9) 1968-70
K. Hepworth (11) 1967-70
S. Irwin (+ 4) 1990
J. Joyner (14 + 2) 1978-84
B. Lockwood (7) 1972-74
A. Marchant (3) 1986
R. Millward (1) 1966
S. Norton (2 + 1) 1974
D. Plange (1) 1988
M. Reilly (9) 1970
P. Small (1) 1962
G. Steadman (1) 1990
G. Stephens (5) 1979
D. Walton (1) 1965
J. Ward (3) 1963-64
K. Ward (14) 1984-89

DEWSBURY (6 players)
A. Bates (2 + 2) 1974
F. Gallagher (4) 1920-21
J. Ledgard (2) 1947
R. Pollard (1) 1950
M. Stephenson (5 + 1) 1971-72
H. Street (4) 1950

**FEATHERSTONE ROVERS
(15 players)**
T. Askin (6) 1928
C. Bibb (1) 1990
K. Bridges (3) 1974
T. Clawson (2) 1962
M. Dixon (2) 1962-64
S. Evans (5 + 3) 1979-80
Deryck Fox (9 + 2) 1985-90
Don Fox (1) 1963
D. Hobbs (7 + 1) 1984
G. Jordan (2) 1964-67
A. Morgan (4) 1968
S. Nash (16) 1971-74
P. Newlove (2 + 1) 1989
P. Smith (1 + 5) 1977-84
J. Thompson (19 + 1) 1970-77

FULHAM (1 player)
J. Dalgreen (1) 1982

HALIFAX (29 players)
A. Ackerley (2) 1952-58
A. Bassett (2) 1946
J. Beames (2) 1921
N. Bentham (2) 1929
H. Beverley (2) 1937
O. Burgham (1) 1911
A. Daniels (3) 1952-55
W. T. Davies (1) 1911
C. Dixon (1) 1968
P. Dixon (3 + 3) 1987-88
P. Eccles (1) 1907
T. Fogerty (+ 1) 1966
A. Halmshaw (1) 1971
N. James (1) 1986
R. Lloyd (1) 1920
A. Milnes (2) 1920
S. Prosser (1) 1914
D. Rees (1) 1926
C. Renilson (7 + 1) 1965-68
J. Riley (1) 1910
K. Roberts (10) 1963-66
A. Robinson (3) 1907-08
D. Schofield (1) 1955
J. Shaw (5) 1960-62
J. C. Stacey (1) 1920
J. Thorley (4) 1954
J. Wilkinson (6) 1954-55
F. Williams (2) 1914
D. Willicombe (1) 1974

HUDDERSFIELD (24 players)
J. Bowden (3) 1954
K. Bowman (3) 1962-63
B. Briggs (1) 1954
S. Brogden (9) 1929-33
J. Chilcott (3) 1914
D. Clark (11) 1911-20
D. Close (1) 1967
R. Cracknell (2) 1951
J. Davies (2) 1911
F. Dyson (1) 1959
B. Gronow (7) 1911-20
F. Longstaff (2) 1914
K. Loxton (1) 1971
S. Moorhouse (2) 1914
R. Nicholson (3) 1946-48
J. Rogers (7) 1914-21
K. Senior (2) 1965-67
T. Smales (5) 1962-64
M. Sullivan (16) 1954-57
G. Thomas (8) 1920-21
D. Valentine (15) 1948-54
R. Valentine (1) 1967
H. Wagstaff (12) 1911-21
H. Young (1) 1929

HULL (33 players)
W. Batten (1) 1921
H. Bowman (8) 1924-29

F. Boylen (1) 1908
R. Coverdale (4) 1954
M. Crane (1) 1982
L. Crooks (11 + 2) 1982-87
A. Dannatt (3) 1985-91
G. Divorty (2) 1985
J. Drake (1) 1960
W. Drake (1) 1962
P. Eastwood (7) 1990-91
S. Evans (2) 1982
V. Farrar (1) 1978
R. Gemmell (2) 1968-69
T. E. Gwynne (3) 1928-29
T. Harris (25) 1954-60
K. Harrison (3) 1990
M. Harrison (7) 1967-73
W. Holder (1) 1907
L. Jackson (8) 1990-91
A. Keegan (9) 1966-69
E. Morgan (2) 1921
S. Norton (9) 1978-82
W. Proctor (+ 1) 1984
P. Rose (1) 1982
G. Schofield (15) 1984-87
T. Skerrett (6) 1980-82
W. Stone (8) 1920-21
C. Sullivan (17) 1967-73
H. Taylor (3) 1907
R. Taylor (2) 1921-26
D. Topliss (1) 1982
J. Whiteley (15) 1957-62

**HULL KINGSTON ROVERS
(26 players)**
D. Bishop (+ 1) 1990
C. Burton (8 + 1) 1982-87
A. Burwell (7 + 1) 1967-69
L. Casey (7 + 2) 1977-83
G. Clark (3) 1984-85
A. Dockar (1) 1947
G. Fairbairn (3) 1981-82
J. Feetham (1) 1929
P. Flanagan (14) 1962-70
F. Foster (1) 1967
D. Hall (2) 1984
P. Harkin (+ 1) 1985
S. Hartley (3) 1980-81
P. Hogan (2 + 2) 1979
R. Holdstock (2) 1980
W. Holliday (8 + 1) 1964-67
D. Laws (1) 1986
B. Lockwood (1 + 1) 1978-79
P. Lowe (12) 1970-78
R. Millward (27 + 1) 1967-78
H. Poole (1) 1964
P. Rose (1 + 3) 1974-78
M. Smith (10 + 1) 1979-84
B. Tyson (3) 1963-67
D. Watkinson (12 + 1) **1979-86**
C. Young (5) 1967-68

HUNSLET (23 players)
W. Batten (9) 1907-11
H. Beverley (4) 1936-37
A. Burnell (3) 1951-54
H. Crowther (1) 1929
J. Evans (4) 1951-52
K. Eyre (1) 1965
B. Gabbitas (1) 1959
G. Gunney (11) 1954-65
D. Hartley (2) 1964
J. Higson (2) 1908
D. Jenkins (1) 1929
A. Jenkinson (2) 1911
W. Jukes (6) 1908-10
B. Prior (1) 1966
W. Ramsey (7) 1965-66
B. Shaw (5) 1956-60
G. Shelton (7) 1964-66
F. Smith (9) 1910-14
S. Smith (4) 1954
C. Thompson (2) 1951
L. White (7) 1932-33
R. Williams (3) 1954
H. Wilson (3) 1907

KEIGHLEY (1 player)
T. Hollindrake (1) 1955

LEEDS (68 players)
L. Adams (1) 1932
J. Atkinson (26) 1968-80
J. Bacon (11) 1920-26
R. Batten (3) 1969-73
J. Birch (1) 1907
S. Brogden (7) 1936-37
J. Brough (5) 1928-36
G. Brown (6) 1954-55
M. Clark (5) 1968
T. Clawson (3) 1972
D. Creasser (2 + 2) 1985-88
L. Crooks (1) 1989
W. A. Davies (2) 1914
K. Dick (2) 1980
R. Dickinson (2) 1985
P. Dixon (7 + 1) 1990
L. Dyl (11) 1974-82
A. Fisher (3) 1970-71
P. Ford (5) 1989
R. Gemmell (1) 1964
C. Gibson (10) 1990-91
J. Grayshon (2) 1985
R. Haigh (3 + 1) 1970-71
D. Hallas (2) 1961
F. Harrison (3) 1911
D. Heron (1 + 1) 1982
J. Holmes (14 + 6) 1971-82
S. Hynes (12 + 1) 1970-73
J. W. Jarman (2) 1914
D. Jeanes (3) 1972

D. Jenkins (1) 1947
B. L. Jones (15) 1954-57
K. Jubb (2) 1937
J. Lowe (1) 1932
P. Medley (3 + 1) 1987-88
I. Owens (4) 1946
S. Pitchford (4) 1977
H. Poole (2) 1966
R. Powell (13 + 6) 1985-91
D. Prosser (1) 1937
Keith Rayne (4) 1984
Kevin Rayne (1) 1986
B. Risman (5) 1968
D. Robinson (5) 1956-60
D. Rose (4) 1954
G. Schofield (16) 1988-91
B. Seabourne (1) 1970
B. Shaw (1) 1961
M. Shoebottom (10 + 2) 1968-71
B. Simms (1) 1962
A. Smith (10) 1970-73
S. Smith (10) 1929-33
D. Stephenson (4 + 1) 1988
J. Stevenson (15) 1955-58
S. Stockwell (3) 1920-21
A. Terry (1) 1962
A. Thomas (4) 1926-29
P. Thomas (1) 1907
J. Thompson (12) 1924-32
A. Turnbull (1) 1951
H. Waddell (1) 1989
D. Ward (12) 1977-82
W. Ward (1) 1910
F. Webster (3) 1910
R. Williams (9) 1948-51
H. Woods (1) 1937
G. Wriglesworth (5) 1965-66
F. Young (1) 1908

LEIGH (19 players)
K. Ashcroft (5) 1968-70
J. Cartwright (7) 1920-21
D. Chisnall (2) 1970
J. Darwell (5) 1924
S. Donlan (+ 2) 1984
D. Drummond (22) 1980-86
P. Foster (3) 1955
C. Johnson (1) 1985
F. Kitchen (2) 1954
J. Ledgard (9) 1948-54
G. Lewis (1) 1965
M. Martyn (2) 1958-59
W. Mooney (2) 1924
S. Owen (1) 1958
C. Pawsey (7) 1952-54
W. Robinson (2) 1963
Joe Walsh (1) 1971
W. Winstanley (2) 1910
J. Woods (7 + 3) 1979-83

MERTHYR TYDFIL (1 player)
D. Jones (2) 1907

OLDHAM (40 players)
A. Avery (4) 1910-11
C. Bott (1) 1966
A. Brough (2) 1924
T. Clawson (9) 1973-74
A. Davies (20) 1955-60
E. Davies (3) 1920
T. Flanagan (4) 1983-84
D. Foy (3) 1984-85
B. Ganley (3) 1957-58
A. Goodway (11) 1983-85
W. Hall (4) 1914
H. Hilton (7) 1920-21
D. Hobbs (2) 1987
D. Holland (4) 1914
R. Irving (8 + 3) 1967-72
K. Jackson (2) 1957
E. Knapman (1) 1924
S. Little (10) 1956-58
T. Llewellyn (2) 1907
J. Lomas (2) 1911
W. Longworth (3) 1908
L. McIntyre (1) 1963
T. O'Grady (5) 1954
J. Oster (1) 1929
D. Parker (2) 1964
D. Phillips (3) 1946
F. Pitchford (2) 1958-62
T. Rees (1) 1929
S. Rix (9) 1924-26
R. Sloman (5) 1928
A. Smith (6) 1907-08
I. Southward (7) 1959-62
L. Thomas (1) 1947
D. Turner (11) 1956-58
G. Tyson (4) 1907-08
H. Waddell (4) 1988
T. White (1) 1907
C. Winslade (1) 1959
A. Wood (4) 1911-14
M. Worrall (3) 1984

ROCHDALE HORNETS (8 players)
J. Baxter (1) 1907
J. Bennett (6) 1924
J. Bowers (1) 1920
T. Fogerty (1) 1974
E. Jones (4) 1920
M. Price (2) 1967
J. Robinson (2) 1914
T. Woods (2) 1911

RUNCORN (2 players)
J. Jolley (3) 1907
R. Padbury (1) 1908

**RUNCORN HIGHFIELD/
HUYTON/LIVERPOOL/WIGAN
HIGHFIELD (4 players)**
R. Ashby (1) 1964
W. Belshaw (6) 1936-37
N. Bentham (6) 1928
H. Woods (5) 1936

ST. HELENS (47 players)
C. Arkwright (+2) 1985
L. Aston (3) 1947
W. Benyon (5+1) 1971-72
T. Bishop (15) 1966-69
F. Carlton (1) 1958
E. Chisnall (4) 1974
E. Cunningham (1) 1978
R. Dagnall (4) 1961-65
D. Eckersley (2+2) 1973-74
A. Ellaby (13) 1928-33
L. Fairclough (6) 1926-29
J. Fieldhouse (1) 1986
A. Fildes (4) 1932
A. Frodsham (3) 1928-29
P. Gorley (2+1) 1980-81
D. Greenall (6) 1951-54
P. Groves (1) 1987
R. Haggerty (2) 1987
M. Hicks (1) 1965
N. Holding (4) 1984
R. Huddart (12) 1959-63
L. Jones (1) 1971
A. Karalius (4+1) 1971-72
V. Karalius (10) 1958-61
K. Kelly (2) 1972
B. Ledger (2) 1985-86
P. Loughlin (12+1) 1988-91
J. Mantle (13) 1966-73
S. McCormick (1) 1948
T. McKinney (1) 1957
R. Mathias (1) 1979
G. Moses (9) 1955-57
A. Murphy (26) 1958-66
F. Myler (9) 1970
G. Nicholls (22) 1973-79
H. Pinner (5+1) 1980-86
A. Platt (4+3) 1985-88
A. Prescott (28) 1951-58
A. Rhodes (4) 1957-61
J. Stott (1) 1947
M. Sullivan (10) 1961-62
J. Tembey (2) 1963-64
A. Terry (10) 1958-61
John Walsh (4+1) 1972
K. Ward (+2) 1990
J. Warlow (3+1) 1964-68
C. Watson (29+1) 1963-71

ST. HELENS RECS (5 players)
F. Bowen (3) 1928
A. Fildes (11) 1926-29
J. Greenall (1) 1921
J. Owen (1) 1921
J. Wallace (1) 1926

SALFORD (28 players)
W. Burgess (1) 1969
P. Charlton (17+1) 1970-74
M. Coulman (2+1) 1971
G. Curran (6) 1946-48
E. Curzon (1) 1910
T. Danby (3) 1950
C. Dixon (11+2) 1969-74
A. Edwards (7) 1936-37
J. Feetham (7) 1932-33
K. Fielding (3) 1974-77
K. Gill (5+2) 1974-77
J. Gore (1) 1926
C. Hesketh (21+2) 1970-74
B. Hudson (8) 1932-37
E. Jenkins (9) 1933-37
J. Lomas (5) 1908-10
T. McKinney (7) 1951-54
A. Middleton (1) 1929
S. Nash (8) 1977-82
M. Richards (2) 1974
A. Risman (17) 1932-46
J. Spencer (1) 1907
J. Ward (1) 1970
S. Warwick (2) 1907
D. Watkins (2+4) 1971-74
W. Watkins (7) 1933-37
P. Williams (1+1) 1989
W. Williams (2) 1929-32

**SHEFFIELD EAGLES
(2 players)**
M. Aston (+1) 1991
D. Powell (9+2) 1990-91

SWINTON (15 players)
T. Armitt (8) 1933-37
A. Buckley (7) 1963-66
F. Butters (2) 1929
W. Davies (1) 1968
B. Evans (10) 1926-33
F. Evans (4) 1924
J. Evans (3) 1926
K. Gowers (14) 1962-66
H. Halsall (1) 1929
M. Hodgson (16) 1929-37
R. Morgan (2) 1963
W. Rees (11) 1926-29
D. Robinson (12) 1965-67
J. Stopford (12) 1961-66
J. Wright (1) 1932

**WAKEFIELD TRINITY
(22 players)**
I. Brooke (8) 1967-68
N. Fox (29) 1959-69
R. Haigh (2) 1968-70
W. Horton (14) 1928-33
D. Jeanes (5) 1971-72
B. Jones (3) 1964-66
H. Kershaw (2) 1910
F. Mortimer (2) 1956
H. Murphy (1) 1950
H. Newbould (1) 1910
J. Parkin (17) 1920-29
C. Pollard (1) 1924
E. Pollard (2) 1932
H. Poynton (3) 1962
D. Robinson (5) 1954-55
G. Round (8) 1959-62
T. Skerrett (4) 1979
S. Smith (1) 1929
D. Topliss (3) 1973-79
D. Turner (13) 1959-62
D. Vines (3) 1959
J. Wilkinson (7) 1959-62

WARRINGTON (44 players)
J. Arkwright (6) 1936-37
K. Ashcroft (+1) 1974
W. Aspinall (1) 1966
W. Belshaw (2) 1937
N. Bentham (2) 1929
J. Bevan (8) 1974-78
T. Blinkhorn (1) 1929
E. Brooks (3) 1908
J. Challinor (3) 1958-60
N. Courtney (+1) 1982
W. Cunliffe (11) 1920-26
G. Dickenson (1) 1908
W. Dingsdale (3) 1929-33
D. Drummond (2) 1987-88
R. Duane (3) 1983-84
R. Eccles (1) 1982
K. Ellis (+1) 1991
J. Featherstone (6) 1948-52
M. Forster (2) 1987
E. Fraser (16) 1958-61
L. Gilfedder (5) 1962-63
R. Greenough (1) 1960
A. Gregory (1) 1986
M. Gregory (19+1) 1987-90
G. Helme (12) 1948-54
K. Holden (1) 1963
A. Johnson (6) 1946-47
K. Kelly (2) 1980-82
T. McKinney (3) 1955
J. Miller (6) 1933-36
A. Murphy (1) 1971
A. Naughton (2) 1954
T. O'Grady (1) 1961
H. Palin (2) 1947
K. Parr (1) 1968

A. Pimblett (3) 1948
R. Price (9) 1954-57
R. Ryan (5) 1950-52
R. Ryder (1) 1952
F. Shugars (1) 1910
G. Skelhorne (7) 1920-21
G. Thomas (1) 1907
D. Whitehead (3) 1971
J. Woods (+1) 1987

WHITEHAVEN (5 players)
V. Gribbin (1) 1985
W. Holliday (1) 1964
R. Huddart (4) 1958
P. Kitchin (1) 1965
A. Walker (1) 1980

WIDNES (42 players)
M. Adams (11+2) 1979-84
J. Basnett (2) 1984-86
K. Bentley (1) 1980
M. Burke (14+1) 1980-86
F. Collier (1) 1964
A. Currier (1) 1989
J. Davies (5+1) 1990
R. Dutton (6) 1970
K. Elwell (3) 1977-80
R. Eyres (1+2) 1989-91
J. Fieldhouse (6) 1985-86
R. French (4) 1968
L. Gorley (4+1) 1980-82
A. Gregory (8+1) 1981-84
I. Hare (1) 1967
F. Higgins (6) 1950-51
H. Higgins (2) 1937
L. Holliday (1) 1991
E. Hughes (8) 1978-82
D. Hulme (7+1) 1988-89
P. Hulme (3+2) 1988-89
A. Johnson (4) 1914-20
V. Karalius (2) 1963
G. Kemel (2) 1965
D. Laughton (4) 1973-79
J. Lydon (9+1) 1983-85
T. McCue (6) 1936-46
J. Measures (2) 1963
J. Mills (6) 1974-79
A. Myler (14) 1983-86
F. Myler (14+1) 1960-67
G. Nicholls (7) 1971-72
M. Offiah (20) 1988-91
D. O'Neill (2+1) 1971-72
M. O'Neill (3) 1982-83
H. Pinner (1) 1986
G. Shaw (1) 1980
N. Silcock (12) 1932-37
A. Tait (8) 1989-90
J. Warlow (3) 1971
D. Wright (+1) 1988
S. Wright (7) 1977-78

WIGAN (78 players)
R. Ashby (1) 1965
E. Ashcroft (11) 1947-54
E. Ashton (26) 1957-63
W. Ashurst (3) 1971-72
F. Barton (1) 1951
J. Barton (2) 1960-61
J. Bennett (1) 1926
D. Betts (10+1) 1990-91
D. Bevan (1) 1952
W. Blan (3) 1951
D. Bolton (23) 1957-63
W. Boston (31) 1954-63
T. Bradshaw (6) 1947-50
F. Carlton (1) 1962
B. Case (6+1) 1984-88
N. Cherrington (1) 1960
C. Clarke (7) 1965-73
P. Clarke (+1) 1990
A. Coldrick (4) 1914
F. Collier (1) 1963
J. Cunliffe (4) 1950-54
M. Dermott (2) 1990
S. Edwards (16+3) 1985-91
J. Egan (14) 1946-50
R. Evans (4) 1961-62
G. Fairbairn (14) 1977-80
T. Fogerty (1) 1967
P. Ford (1) 1985
W. Francis (4) 1967-77
D. Gardiner (1) 1965
K. Gee (17) 1946-51
H. Gill (14+1) 1981-88
A. Goodway (12) 1985-90
R. Goulding (5) 1990
J. Gray (5+3) 1974
A. Gregory (15) 1987-90
S. Hampson (9+1) 1987-91
E. Hanley (23) 1985-91
C. Hill (1) 1966
D. Hill (1) 1971
J. Hilton (4) 1950
T. Howley (6) 1924
W. Hudson (1) 1948
D. Hurcombe (8) 1920-24
B. Jenkins (12) 1907-14
K. Jones (2) 1970
R. Kinnear (1) 1929
N. Kiss (1) 1985
D. Laughton (11) 1970-71
J. Lawrenson (3) 1948
J. Leytham (5) 1907-10
I. Lucas (1) 1991
J. Lydon (13+1) 1986-90
B. McTigue (25) 1958-63
J. Miller (1) 1911
J. Morley (2) 1936-37
A. Platt (8) 1989-91
I. Potter (7+1) 1985-86
J. Price (1) 1924
R. Ramsdale (8) 1910-14

G. Ratcliffe (3) 1947-50
J. Ring (2) 1924-26
D. Robinson (1) 1970
M. Ryan (4) 1947-50
W. Sayer (7) 1961-63
J. Sharrock (4) 1910-11
N. Silcock (3) 1954
R. Silcock (1) 1908
D. Stephenson (5) 1982-87
J. Sullivan (25) 1924-33
M. Sullivan (19) 1957-60
G. Thomas (1) 1914
J. Thomas (8) 1907-11
S. Wane (2) 1985-86
E. Ward (3) 1946-47
L. White (2) 1947
D. Willicombe (2) 1974
W. Winstanley (3) 1911

**WORKINGTON TOWN
(9 players)**
E. Bowman (4) 1977
P. Charlton (1) 1965
B. Edgar (11) 1958-66
N. Herbert (6) 1961-62
W. Martin (1) 1962
V. McKeating (2) 1951
A. Pepperell (2) 1950-51
I. Southward (4) 1958
G. Wilson (3) 1951

YORK (7 players)
E. Dawson (1) 1956
H. Field (3) 1936
G. Smith (3) 1963-64
J. Stevenson (4) 1959-60
M. Sullivan (1) 1963
B. Watts (5) 1954-55
L. White (4) 1946

Scrum half Andy Gregory, Great Britain Test player while with Warrington, Widnes and Wigan.

314

GREAT BRITAIN TEAMS
...A 20-year review

The following is a compendium of Great Britain Test and World Cup teams since the start of the 1971-72 season.

Initials are included where more than one celebrated player shared a surname in the same era. Only playing substitutes are included on the teamsheet.

(WC): World Cup t: try g: goal dg: drop goal * captain

Salford centre Chris Hesketh, who appeared in all three 1971 Tests against New Zealand.

1971 New Zealand

Salford: 25 Sep

Lost 13-18

Whitehead (Warrington) 2g
Jones, L (St. Helens)
Benyon (St. Helens) 1t
Hesketh (Salford) 1t
Sullivan, C (Hull)
*Millward (Hull KR)
Nash (Featherstone)
Warlow (Widnes)
Karalius, A (St. Helens)
Jeanes (Wakefield)
Ashurst (Wigan) 1t
Coulman (Salford)
Mantle (St. Helens)
Sub: Edwards, D (Castleford)

1971 New Zealand

Castleford: 16 Oct

Lost 14-17

Edwards, D (Castleford)
Sullivan, C (Hull) 1t
Watkins, D (Salford) 1g
Hesketh (Salford)
Walsh, Joe (Leigh) 1t
*Millward (Hull KR) 1t
Murphy, A (Warrington)
Harrison, M (Hull)
Karalius, A (St. Helens)
Coulman (Salford) 1t
Dixon, C (Salford)
Mantle (St. Helens)
Haigh (Leeds)
Sub: Benyon (St. Helens)
Stephenson, M (Dewsbury)

1971 New Zealand

Leeds: 6 Nov

Won 12-3

Edwards, D (Castleford)
Sullivan, C (Hull)
Hesketh (Salford)
Holmes (Leeds) 2g,2dg
Atkinson, J (Leeds) 2t
*Millward (Hull KR)
Loxton (Huddersfield)
Harrison, M (Hull)
Karalius, A (St. Helens)
Jeanes (Wakefield)
Irving (Oldham)
Nicholls (Widnes)
Halmshaw (Halifax)
Sub: O'Neill, D (Widnes)

1972 France

Toulouse: 6 Feb

Won 10-9

Charlton (Salford)
*Sullivan, C (Hull) 1t
Holmes (Leeds) 2g
Benyon (St. Helens) 1t
Atkinson, J (Leeds)
Kelly (St. Helens)
Nash (Featherstone)
Harrison, M (Hull)
Karalius, A (St. Helens)
Jeanes (Wakefield)
Ashurst (Wigan)
Lowe, P (Hull KR)
Nicholls (Widnes)

1972 France

Bradford: 12 March

Won 45-10

Charlton (Salford) 1t
*Sullivan, C (Hull) 1t
Holmes (Leeds) 1t,6g
Benyon (St. Helens) 1t
Atkinson, J (Leeds) 1t
Kelly (St. Helens)
Nash (Featherstone)
Harrison, M (Hull)
Stephenson, M (Dewsbury) 1t
Jeanes (Wakefield) 1t
Ashurst (Wigan) 2t
Lowe, P (Hull KR) 1t
Nicholls (Widnes)
Sub: Walsh, John (St. Helens) 1t
Irving (Oldham)

1972 Australia (WC)

Perpignan: 29 Oct

Won 27-21

Charlton (Salford)
*Sullivan, C (Hull) 1t
Hesketh (Salford)
Walsh, John (St. Helens)
Atkinson, J (Leeds) 1t
O'Neill, D (Widnes) 1t
Nash (Featherstone)
Clawson (Leeds) 6g
Stephenson, M (Dewsbury) 1t
Jeanes (Leeds)
Lockwood (Castleford)
Lowe, P (Hull KR) 1t
Nicholls (Widnes)
Sub: Holmes (Leeds)

1972 France (WC)
Grenoble: 1 Nov
Won 13-4
Charlton (Salford)
*Sullivan, C (Hull) 1t
Hesketh (Salford)
Walsh, John (St. Helens)
Atkinson, J (Leeds)
O'Neill, D (Widnes)
Nash (Featherstone)
Clawson (Leeds) 2g
Stephenson, M (Dewsbury)
Lockwood, B (Castleford)
Dixon, C (Salford)
Lowe, P (Hull KR) 2t
Nicholls (Widnes)

1972 New Zealand (WC)
Pau: 4 Nov
Won 53-19
Charlton (Salford) 1t
*Sullivan, C (Hull) 1t
Hesketh (Salford) 1t
Walsh, John (St. Helens)
Atkinson, J (Leeds) 2t
Holmes (Leeds) 10g,2t
Nash (Featherstone) 1t
Jeanes (Leeds) 1t
Stephenson, M (Dewsbury) 1t
Lockwood (Castleford)
Irving (Oldham)
Lowe, P (Hull KR)
Nicholls (Widnes) 1t
Sub: Redfearn, D (Bradford)
      Karalius, A (St. Helens)

1972 Australia (WC)
Lyons: 11 Nov
Drew 10-10
Charlton (Salford)
*Sullivan, C (Hull) 1t
Hesketh (Salford)
Walsh, John (St. Helens)
Atkinson, J (Leeds)
Holmes (Leeds)
Nash (Featherstone)
Clawson (Leeds) 2g
Stephenson, M (Dewsbury) 1t
Jeanes (Leeds)
Lockwood, B (Castleford)
Lowe, P (Hull KR)
Nicholls (Widnes)
Sub: Irving (Oldham)

1973 Australia
Wembley: 3 Nov
Won 21-12
Charlton (Salford)
*Sullivan (Hull)
Hynes (Leeds)
Hesketh (Salford)
Atkinson, J (Leeds)
Topliss (Wakefield)
Nash (Featherstone) 1dg
Clawson (Oldham) 4g
Clarke (Wigan) 1t
Lockwood (Castleford) 1t
Nicholls (St. Helens)
Lowe, P (Hull KR) 2t
Batten (Leeds)

1973 Australia
Leeds: 24 Nov
Lost 6-14
Charlton (Salford)
*Sullivan (Hull)
Hynes (Leeds)
Hesketh (Salford)
Atkinson, J (Leeds)
Topliss (Wakefield)
Nash (Featherstone)
Clawson (Oldham) 3g
Clarke (Wigan)
Lockwood (Castleford)
Mantle (St. Helens)
Lowe, P (Hull KR)
Batten, R (Leeds)
Sub: Eckersley (St. Helens)
      Dixon, C (Salford)

1973 Australia
Warrington: 1 Dec
Lost 5-15
Charlton (Salford)
Smith, A (Leeds)
Hynes (Leeds)
Hesketh (Salford)
*Sullivan, C (Hull)
Eckersley (St. Helens)
Millward (Hull KR) 1t,1g
Clawson (Oldham)
Clarke (Wigan)
Harrison, M (Hull)
Nicholls (St. Helens)
Lowe, P (Hull KR)
Laughton (Widnes)
Sub: Watkins, D (Salford)
      Dixon, C (Salford)

1974 France
Grenoble: 20 Jan
Won 24-5
Charlton (Salford)
Fielding (Salford) 3t
Willicombe (Halifax) 1t
Hesketh (Salford)
Redfearn, D (Bradford)
Gill, K (Salford) 1t
Bates, A (Dewsbury)
Clawson (Oldham) 3g
Bridges (Featherstone)
Lockwood (Castleford)
Dixon, C (Salford)
Nicholls (St. Helens)
*Laughton (Widnes) 1t
Sub: Watkins, D (Salford)
      Gray (Wigan)

1974 France
Wigan: 17 Feb
Won 29-0
Charlton (Salford) 2t
Fielding (Salford)
Willicombe (Wigan) 1t
Hesketh (Salford)
Redfearn, D (Bradford) 2t
Gill, K (Salford)
Bates, A (Dewsbury)
Clawson (Oldham) 2g
Bridges (Featherstone)
Fogerty (Rochdale)
Dixon, C (Salford)
Nicholls (St. Helens)
*Laughton (Widnes) 1t
Sub: Watkins, D (Salford) 1g
      Gray (Wigan) 1t,1g

1974 Australia
Brisbane: 15 June
Lost 6-12
Charlton (Salford)
Redfearn, D (Bradford)
Watkins, D (Salford) 1g
*Hesketh (Salford)
Bevan, J (Warrington)
Millward (Hull KR)
Nash (Featherstone)
Clawson (Oldham) 2g
Bridges (Featherstone)
Mills (Widnes)
Dixon, C (Salford)
Thompson, J (Featherstone)
Nicholls (St. Helens)
Sub: Eckersley (St. Helens)
      Gray (Wigan)

1974 Australia
Sydney: 6 July
Won 16-11
Charlton (Salford)
Dyl (Leeds)
Eckersley (St. Helens)
*Hesketh (Salford)
Millward (Hull KR)
Gill, K (Salford) 1t
Nash (Featherstone)
Mills (Widnes)
Gray (Wigan) 3g,1dg
Thompson, J (Featherstone)
Dixon, C (Salford) 1t
Chisnall, E (St. Helens) 1t
Nicholls (St. Helens)
Sub: Norton (Castleford)

1974 Australia
Sydney: 20 July
Lost 18-22
Charlton (Salford)
Richards (Salford) 1t
Dyl (Leeds) 1t
*Hesketh (Salford)
Bevan, J (Warrington)
Gill, K (Salford)
Nash (Featherstone)
Clawson (Oldham)
Gray (Wigan) 6g
Thompson, J (Featherstone)
Dixon, C (Salford)
Chisnall, E (St. Helens)
Nicholls (St. Helens)
Sub: Millward (Hull KR)
Rose, P (Hull KR)

1974 New Zealand
Auckland: 27 July
Lost 8-13
Charlton (Salford)
Redfearn, D (Bradford)
Dyl (Leeds)
*Hesketh (Salford)
Bevan, J (Warrington) 1t
Gill, K (Salford)
Nash (Featherstone) 1t
Clawson (Oldham) 1g
Gray (Wigan)
Thompson, J (Featherstone)
Dixon, C (Salford)
Norton (Castleford)
Nicholls (St. Helens)
Sub: Ashcroft (Warrington)

1974 New Zealand
Christchurch: 4 Aug
Won 17-8
Charlton (Salford)
Redfearn, D (Bradford) 1t
Dyl (Leeds) 1t
Dixon, C (Salford)
Richards (Salford)
*Hesketh (Salford) 1t
Nash (Featherstone)
Mills (Widnes)
Gray (Wigan) 4g
Thompson, J (Featherstone)
Chisnall, E (St. Helens)
Norton (Castleford)
Nicholls (St. Helens)
Sub: Bates, A (Dewsbury)

1974 New Zealand
Auckland: 10 Aug
Won 20-0
Charlton (Salford)
Redfearn, D (Bradford)
Willicombe (Wigan)
Dyl (Leeds) 1t
Bevan, J (Warrington) 2t
*Hesketh (Salford) 1t
Nash (Featherstone)
Clawson (Oldham)
Gray (Wigan) 4g
Thompson, J (Featherstone)
Chisnall, E (St. Helens)
Dixon, C (Salford)
Nicholls (St. Helens)
Sub: Bates, A (Dewsbury)
Ramsey (Bradford)

1977 France (WC)
Auckland: 5 June
Won 23-4
Fairbairn (Wigan) 7g
Fielding (Salford)
Holmes (Leeds)
Dyl (Leeds) 1t
Wright, S (Widnes) 1t
*Millward (Hull KR) 1t
Nash (Salford)
Thompson, J (Featherstone)
Ward, D (Leeds)
Pitchford, S (Leeds)
Bowman, E (Workington)
Nicholls (St. Helens)
Hogan (Barrow)
Sub: Gill, K (Salford)
Casey (Hull KR)

1977 New Zealand (WC)
Christchurch: 12 June
Won 30-12
Fairbairn (Wigan) 6g
Wright, S (Widnes) 2t
Holmes (Leeds)
Dyl (Leeds)
Francis, W (Wigan)
*Millward (Hull KR) 1t
Nash (Salford)
Thompson, J (Featherstone)
Ward, D (Leeds)
Pitchford, S (Leeds)
Bowman, E (Workington) 1t
Nicholls (St. Helens) 1t
Hogan (Barrow) 1t
Sub: Casey (Hull KR)

1977 Australia (WC)
Brisbane: 18 June
Lost 5-19
Fairbairn (Wigan) 1g
Wright, S (Widnes)
Francis, W (Wigan)
Dyl (Leeds)
Fielding (Salford)
*Millward (Hull KR) 1t
Nash (Salford)
Thompson, J (Featherstone)
Ward, D (Leeds)
Pitchford, S (Leeds)
Bowman, E (Workington)
Nicholls (St. Helens)
Hogan (Barrow)
Sub: Holmes (Leeds)
Smith, P (Featherstone)

1977 Australia (WC)
Sydney: 25 June
Lost 12-13
Fairbairn (Wigan) 3g
Wright, S (Widnes)
Holmes (Leeds)
Dyl (Leeds)
Francis, W (Wigan)
*Millward (Hull KR)
Nash (Salford)
Thompson, J (Featherstone)
Elwell (Widnes)
Pitchford, S (Leeds) 1t
Bowman, E (Workington)
Casey (Hull KR)
Hogan (Barrow)
Sub: Gill, K (Salford) 1t
Smith, P (Featherstone)

1978 Australia
Wigan: 21 Oct
Lost 9-15
Fairbairn (Wigan) 3g
Wright, S (Widnes)
Hughes (Widnes)
Cunningham (St. Helens)
Bevan, J (Warrington) 1t
*Millward (Hull KR)
Nash (Salford)
Thompson, J (Bradford)
Ward, D (Leeds)
Rose, P (Hull KR)
Nicholls (St. Helens)
Casey (Hull KR)
Norton (Hull)
Sub: Holmes (Leeds)
    Hogan (Barrow)

1979 Australia
Brisbane: 16 June
Lost 0-35
Woods, J (Leigh)
Barends (Bradford)
Joyner (Castleford)
Hughes (Widnes)
Mathias (St. Helens)
Holmes (Leeds)
Stephens (Castleford)
Mills (Widnes)
Ward, D (Leeds)
Skerrett (Wakefield)
Nicholls (St. Helens)
*Laughton (Widnes)
Norton (Hull)
Sub: Evans, S (Featherstone)
    Hogan (Hull KR)

1979 New Zealand
Auckland: 21 July
Won 16-8
Fairbairn (Wigan) 1t,2g
Evans, S (Featherstone) 1t
Joyner (Castleford)
Smith, M (Hull KR) 1t
Hughes (Widnes) 1t
Holmes (Leeds)
Stephens (Castleford)
Casey (Bradford)
Ward, D (Leeds)
*Nicholls (St. Helens)
Hogan (Hull KR)
Grayshon (Bradford)
Adams, M (Widnes)
Sub: Lockwood (Hull KR)

1978 Australia
Bradford: 5 Nov
Won 18-14
Fairbairn (Wigan) 6g
Wright, S (Widnes) 2t
Joyner (Castleford)
Dyl (Leeds)
Atkinson, J (Leeds)
*Millward (Hull KR)
Nash (Salford)
Mills (Widnes)
Fisher (Bradford)
Lockwood (Hull KR)
Nicholls (St. Helens)
Lowe, P (Hull KR)
Norton (Hull)
Sub: Holmes (Leeds)
    Rose, P (Hull KR)

1979 Australia
Sydney: 30 June
Lost 16-24
Fairbairn (Wigan)
Barends (Bradford)
Joyner (Castleford) 1t
Woods, J (Leigh) 5g
Hughes (Widnes) 1t
Holmes (Leeds)
Stephens (Castleford)
*Nicholls (St. Helens)
Ward, D (Leeds)
Skerrett (Wakefield)
Casey (Bradford)
Grayshon (Bradford)
Adams, M (Widnes)
Sub: Evans, S (Featherstone)
    Watkinson (Hull KR)

1979 New Zealand
Christchurch: 5 Aug
Won 22-7
Fairbairn (Wigan) 5g
Evans, S (Featherstone) 1t
Joyner (Castleford)
Smith, M (Hull KR)
Hughes (Widnes) 1t
Holmes (Leeds)
Stephens (Castleford)
*Nicholls (St. Helens)
Ward, D (Leeds)
Skerrett (Wakefield)
Casey (Bradford) 1t
Grayshon (Bradford) 1t
Adams, M (Widnes)

1978 Australia
Leeds: 18 Nov
Lost 6-23
Fairbairn (Wigan)
Wright, S (Widnes)
Joyner (Castleford)
Bevan, J (Warrington) 1t
Atkinson, J (Leeds)
*Millward (Hull KR) 1t
Nash (Salford)
Mills (Widnes)
Fisher (Bradford)
Farrar (Hull)
Nicholls (St. Helens)
Lowe, P (Hull KR)
Norton (Hull)
Sub: Holmes (Leeds)
    Rose, P (Hull KR)

1979 Australia
Sydney: 14 July
Lost 2-28
Fairbairn (Wigan) 1g
Evans, S (Featherstone)
Joyner (Castleford)
Woods, J (Leigh)
Hughes (Widnes)
Topliss (Wakefield)
Redfearn, A (Bradford)
*Nicholls (St. Helens)
Ward, D (Leeds)
Casey (Bradford)
Hogan (Hull KR)
Grayshon (Bradford)
Norton (Hull)
Sub: Holmes (Leeds)
    Adams, M (Widnes)

1979 New Zealand
Auckland: 11 Aug
Lost 11-18
Fairbairn (Wigan) 1g
Evans, S (Featherstone)
Joyner (Castleford)
Smith, M (Hull KR) 1t
Hughes (Widnes) 1t
Holmes (Leeds)
Stephens (Castleford) 1t
Skerrett (Wakefield)
Ward, D (Leeds)
*Nicholls (St. Helens)
Casey (Bradford)
Grayshon (Bradford)
Adams, M (Widnes)
Sub: Woods, J (Leigh)
    Hogan (Hull KR)

1980 New Zealand
Wigan: 18 Oct
Drew 14-14
*Fairbairn (Wigan) 4g
Camilleri (Barrow) 1t
Joyner (Castleford)
Smith, M (Hull KR) 1t
Bentley (Widnes)
Hartley, S (Hull KR)
Dick (Leeds)
Holdstock (Hull KR)
Watkinson (Hull KR)
Skerrett (Hull)
Gorley, L (Widnes)
Grayshon (Bradford)
Casey (Hull KR)
Sub: Pinner (St. Helens)

1980 New Zealand
Bradford: 2 Nov
Lost 8-12
*Fairbairn (Wigan) 4g
Drummond (Leigh)
Joyner (Castleford)
Smith, M (Hull KR)
Camilleri (Barrow)
Kelly (Warrington)
Dick (Leeds)
Holdstock (Hull KR)
Elwell (Widnes)
Shaw, G (Widnes)
Casey (Hull KR)
Grayshon (Bradford)
Pinner (St. Helens)
Sub: Evans, S (Featherstone)
 Gorley, L (Widnes)

1980 New Zealand
Leeds: 15 Nov
Won 10-2
Burke (Widnes) 2g
Drummond (Leigh) 2t
Joyner (Castleford)
Evans, S (Featherstone)
Atkinson, J (Leeds)
Woods, J (Leigh)
Walker (Whitehaven)
Skerrett (Hull)
Elwell (Widnes)
*Casey (Hull KR)
Gorley, P (St. Helens)
Adams, M (Widnes)
Norton (Hull)

1981 France
Hull: 6 Dec
Won 37-0
Fairbairn (Hull KR) 1g
Drummond (Leigh) 2t
Smith, M (Hull KR)
Woods, J (Leigh) 1t,7g
Gill (Wigan) 3t
Hartley (Hull KR) 1t
Gregory, A (Widnes)
Grayshon (Bradford)
*Ward, D (Leeds)
Skerrett (Hull)
Gorley, L (Widnes)
Gorley, P (St. Helens)
Norton (Hull)
Sub: Burke (Widnes)
 Szymala (Barrow)

1981 France
Marseilles: 20 Dec
Lost 2-19
Burke (Widnes)
Drummond (Leigh)
Smith, M (Hull KR)
Woods, J (Leigh) 1g
Gill (Wigan)
Hartley (Hull KR)
Gregory, A (Widnes)
*Grayshon (Bradford)
Watkinson (Hull KR)
Skerrett (Hull)
Gorley, L (Widnes)
Szymala (Barrow)
Norton (Hull)
Sub: Gorley, P (St. Helens)

1982 Australia
Hull City FC: 30 Oct
Lost 4-40
Fairbairn (Hull KR)
Drummond (Leigh)
Hughes (Widnes)
Dyl (Leeds)
Evans, S (Hull)
Woods, J (Leigh)
*Nash (Salford)
Grayshon (Bradford)
Ward, D (Leeds)
Skerrett (Hull)
Gorley, L (Widnes)
Crooks, L (Hull) 2g
Norton (Hull)
Sub: D. Heron (Leeds)

1982 Australia
Wigan: 20 Nov
Lost 6-27
Mumby (Bradford) 3g
Drummond (Leigh)
Smith, M (Hull KR)
Stephenson, D (Wigan)
Gill (Wigan)
Holmes (Leeds)
Kelly, K (Warrington)
*Grayshon (Bradford)
Dalgreen (Fulham)
Skerrett (Hull)
Eccles (Warrington)
Burton (Hull KR)
Heron, D (Leeds)
Sub: Woods, J (Leigh)
 Rathbone (Bradford)

1982 Australia
Leeds: 28 Nov
Lost 8-32
Fairbairn (Hull KR)
Drummond (Leigh)
Stephenson, D (Wigan)
Smith, M (Hull KR)
Evans (Hull) 1t
*Topliss (Hull)
Gregory, A (Widnes)
O'Neill, M (Widnes)
Noble (Bradford)
Rose (Hull)
Smith, P (Featherstone)
Crooks, L (Hull) 2g,1dg
Crane (Hull)
Sub: Courtney (Warrington)

1983 France
Carcassonne: 20 Feb
Won 20-5
Burke (Widnes) 1g
Drummond (Leigh)
Joyner (Castleford) 1t
Duane, R (Warrington)
Lydon (Widnes) 1t,3g
Myler, A (Widnes)
Gregory, A (Widnes)
O'Neill, M (Widnes)
Noble (Bradford) 1t
Goodway (Oldham) 1t
*Casey (Hull KR)
Rathbone (Bradford)
Flanagan (Oldham)
Sub: Woods, J (Leigh)
 Smith, P (Featherstone)

1983 France
Hull: 6 March
Won 17-5
Mumby (Bradford) 4g
Drummond (Leigh)
Joyner (Castleford)
Duane, R (Warrington) 1t
Lydon (Widnes)
Myler, A (Widnes)
Gregory, A (Widnes) 1t
O'Neill, M (Widnes)
Noble (Bradford)
Goodway (Oldham)
*Casey (Hull KR)
Rathbone (Bradford)
Flanagan (Oldham)
Sub: Smith, P (Featherstone) 1t

1984 France
Avignon: 29 Jan
Won 12-0
*Mumby (Bradford)
Drummond (Leigh)
Duane, R (Warrington)
Foy, D (Oldham) 1t
Clark (Hull KR)
Lydon (Widnes)
Cairns (Barrow)
Rayne, Keith (Leeds)
Watkinson (Hull KR)
Goodway (Oldham) 1t
Worrall, M (Oldham)
Hobbs, D (Featherstone)
Hall (Hull KR)
Sub: Hanley (Bradford)
     Crooks, L (Hull) 2g

1984 France
Leeds: 17 Feb
Won 10-0
Mumby (Bradford)
Clark (Hull KR)
Joyner (Castleford)
Schofield (Hull)
Basnett (Widnes)
Hanley (Bradford)
Cairns (Barrow)
Rayne, Keith (Leeds)
*Noble (Bradford)
Ward, K (Castleford)
Jasiewicz (Bradford)
Hobbs, D (Featherstone) 5g
Hall (Hull KR)
Sub: Smith, M (Hull KR)
     Smith, P (Featherstone)

1984 Australia
Sydney: 9 June
Lost 8-25
Burke (Widnes) 2g
Drummond (Leigh)
Schofield (Hull) 1t
Mumby (Bradford)
Hanley (Bradford)
Foy, D (Oldham)
Holding (St. Helens)
Crooks, L (Hull)
*Noble (Bradford)
Goodway (Oldham)
Burton (Hull KR)
Worrall, M (Oldham)
Sub: Lydon (Widnes)
     Hobbs, D (Featherstone)

1984 Australia
Brisbane: 26 June
Lost 6-18
Burke (Widnes) 1g
Drummond (Leigh)
Schofield (Hull) 1t
Mumby (Bradford)
Hanley (Bradford)
Myler, A (Widnes)
Holding (St. Helens)
Rayne, Keith (Leeds)
*Noble (Bradford)
Crooks, L (Hull)
Burton (Hull KR)
Goodway (Oldham)
Worrall (Oldham)
Sub: Gregory, A (Widnes)
     Adams (Widnes)

1984 Australia
Sydney: 7 July
Lost 7-20
Burke (Widnes) 1g
Drummond (Leigh)
Schofield (Hull)
Mumby (Bradford)
Hanley (Bradford) 1t
Myler, A (Widnes)
Holding (St. Helens) 1dg
Hobbs, D (Featherstone)
*Noble (Bradford)
Case (Wigan)
Burton (Hull KR)
Goodway (Oldham)
Adams (Widnes)

1984 New Zealand
Auckland: 14 July
Lost 0-12
Burke (Widnes)
Drummond (Leigh)
Schofield (Hull)
Mumby (Bradford)
Hanley (Bradford)
Smith, M (Hull KR)
Holding (St. Helens)
Hobbs, D (Featherstone)
*Noble (Bradford)
Case (Wigan)
Burton (Hull KR)
Goodway (Oldham)
Adams (Widnes)

1984 New Zealand
Christchurch: 22 July
Lost 12-28
Burke (Widnes) 2g
Drummond (Leigh)
Hanley (Bradford) 1t
Mumby (Bradford)
Lydon (Widnes)
Myler, A (Widnes) 1t
Gregory, A (Widnes)
Hobbs, D (Featherstone)
*Noble (Bradford)
Case (Wigan)
Burton (Hull KR)
Goodway (Oldham)
Adams (Widnes)
Sub: Joyner (Castleford)
     Beardmore, K (Castleford)

1984 New Zealand
Auckland: 28 July
Lost 16-32
Burke (Widnes) 4g
Drummond (Leigh)
Hanley (Bradford) 1t
Mumby (Bradford) 1t
Lydon (Widnes)
Myler, A (Widnes)
Gregory, A (Widnes)
Hobbs, D (Featherstone)
*Noble (Bradford)
Case (Wigan)
Adams (Widnes)
Goodway (Oldham)
Flanagan (Oldham)
Sub: Donlan (Leigh)
     Joyner (Castleford)

1984 Papua New Guinea

Mount Hagen: 5 Aug

Won 38-20

Burke (Widnes) 1t,5g
Drummond (Leigh) 2t
Hanley (Bradford) 1t
Mumby (Bradford) 1t
Lydon (Widnes)
Myler, A (Widnes)
Gregory, A (Widnes)
Rayne, Keith (Leeds) 1t
*Noble (Bradford)
Goodway (Oldham)
Flanagan (Oldham)
Hobbs, D (Featherstone) 1t
Adams (Widnes)
Sub: Donlan (Leigh)
     Proctor (Hull)

1985 New Zealand

Leeds: 19 Oct

Lost 22-24

Burke (Widnes) 3g
Drummond (Leigh)
Schofield (Hull)
Hanley (Wigan) 1t
Lydon (Widnes) 1t,2g
Myler, A (Widnes)
Fox (Featherstone)
Crooks, L (Hull)
Watkinson (Hull KR)
Fieldhouse (Widnes)
Goodway (Wigan) 1t
Potter (Wigan)
*Pinner (St. Helens)
Sub: Arkwright (St. Helens)

1986 France (Also WC)

Avignon: 16 Feb

Drew 10-10

Burke (Widnes)
Drummond (Leigh)
Schofield (Hull)
Hanley (Wigan) 1t
Gill (Wigan)
Myler, A (Widnes)
Fox (Featherstone)
Crooks, L (Hull) 3g
Watkinson (Hull KR)
Wane (Wigan)
Potter (Wigan)
Fieldhouse (Widnes)
*Pinner (St. Helens)
Sub: Platt (St. Helens)

1985 France

Leeds: 1 March

Won 50-4

Edwards (Wigan)
Ledger (St. Helens)
Creasser (Leeds) 8g
Gribbin (Whitehaven) 1t
Gill (Wigan) 1t
Hanley (Bradford) 2t
Fox (Featherstone) 2t,1g
Dickinson (Leeds)
Watkinson (Hull KR) 1t
Dannatt (Hull)
*Goodway (Oldham)
Rathbone (Bradford)
Divorty (Hull) 1t
Sub: Gibson (Batley)
     Platt (St. Helens)

1985 New Zealand

Wigan: 2 Nov

Won 25-8

Burke (Widnes)
Drummond (Leigh)
Schofield (Hull) 4t
Hanley (Wigan)
Lydon (Widnes) 4g
Myler, A (Widnes)
Fox (Featherstone)
Grayshon (Leeds)
Watkinson (Hull KR)
Fieldhouse (Widnes)
Goodway (Wigan)
Potter (Wigan)
*Pinner (St. Helens) 1dg
Sub: Edwards (Wigan)
     Burton (Hull KR)

1986 France

Wigan: 1 March

Won 24-10

Lydon (Wigan)
Drummond (Leigh) 1t
Schofield (Hull) 1t,2g
Marchant (Castleford) 1t
Laws (Hull KR)
Myler, A (Widnes)
Fox (Featherstone)
Crooks, L (Hull) 2g
*Watkinson (Hull KR)
Fieldhouse (Widnes)
Rayne, Kevin (Leeds)
James (Halifax) 1t
Potter (Wigan)
Sub: Platt (St. Helens)

1985 France

Perpignan: 17 March

Lost 16-24

Johnson, C (Leigh)
Clark (Hull KR)
Creasser (Leeds) 1g
Foy, D (Oldham) 1t
Ford, P (Wigan) 2t
*Hanley (Bradford)
Fox (Featherstone)
Dickinson (Leeds)
Kiss (Wigan)
Wane (Wigan)
Dannatt (Hull)
Rathbone (Bradford)
Divorty (Hull) 1g
Sub: Harkin (Hull KR)
     Powell, R (Leeds)

1985 New Zealand (Also WC)

Elland Rd, Leeds: 9 Nov

Drew 6-6

Burke (Widnes)
Drummond (Leigh)
Schofield (Hull)
Edwards (Wigan)
Lydon (Widnes)
Hanley (Wigan)
Fox (Featherstone)
Grayshon (Leeds)
Watkinson (Hull KR)
Fieldhouse (Widnes)
Goodway (Wigan)
Potter (Wigan)
*Pinner (St. Helens)
Sub: Arkwright (St. Helens)
     Crooks, L (Hull) 3g

1986 Australia

Man. U. FC: 25 Oct

Lost 16-38

Lydon (Wigan) 1t
Marchant (Castleford)
Schofield (Hull) 2t
Hanley (Wigan)
Gill (Wigan) 1g
Myler, A (Widnes)
Fox (Featherstone)
Ward (Castleford)
*Watkinson (Hull KR)
Fieldhouse (Widnes)
Crooks, L (Hull) 1g
Potter (Wigan)
Goodway (Wigan)

1986 Australia
Elland Rd, Leeds: 8 Nov
Lost 4-34
Lydon (Wigan)
Ledger (St. Helens)
Schofield (Hull)
Marchant (Castleford)
Gill (Wigan)
Myler, A (Widnes)
Fox (Featherstone)
Ward (Castleford)
*Watkinson (Hull KR)
Fieldhouse (St. Helens)
Crooks, L (Hull)
Potter (Wigan)
Goodway (Wigan)
Sub: Edwards (Wigan)
    Platt (St. Helens)

1986 Australia (Also WC)
Wigan: 22 Nov
Lost 15-24
Lydon (Wigan) 2g
Gill (Wigan) 1g
Schofield (Hull) 2t,1dg
Stephenson (Wigan)
Basnett (Widnes)
Myler, A (Widnes)
Gregory, A (Warrington)
Ward (Castleford)
*Watkinson (Hull KR)
Crooks, L (Hull)
Burton (Hull KR)
Goodway (Wigan)
Pinner (Widnes)
Sub: Potter (Wigan)

1987 France (Also WC)
Leeds: 24 Jan
Won 52-4
Lydon (Wigan) 1t,8g
Forster (Warrington) 1t
Schofield (Hull)
Stephenson (Wigan)
Gill (Wigan)
*Hanley (Wigan) 2t
Edwards (Wigan) 2t
Hobbs (Oldham)
Beardmore, K (Castleford)
Crooks, L (Hull)
Goodway (Wigan) 1t
Haggerty (St. Helens)
Gregory, M (Warrington) 2t
Sub: Creasser (Leeds)
    England (Castleford)

1987 France
Carcassonne: 8 Feb
Won 20-10
Lydon (Wigan) 4g
Forster (Warrington)
Schofield (Hull)
*Hanley (Wigan) 1t
Gill (Wigan) 1t
Edwards (Wigan)
Gregory, A (Wigan)
Hobbs (Oldham)
Beardmore, K (Castleford) 1t
England (Castleford)
Burton (Hull KR)
Haggerty (St. Helens)
Gregory, M (Warrington)
Sub: Dixon (Halifax)

1987 Papua New Guinea (Also WC)
Wigan: 24 Oct
Won 42-0
Hampson (Wigan)
Drummond (Warrington)
Stephenson (Wigan) 7g
Lydon (Wigan) 1t
Ford (Bradford) 1t
Edwards (Wigan) 2t
Gregory, A (Wigan) 1t
Ward (Castleford)
Groves (St. Helens)
Case (Wigan)
Medley (Leeds) 1t
Goodway (Wigan)
*Hanley (Wigan) 1t
Sub: Woods (Warrington)
    Fairbank (Bradford)

1988 France
Avignon: 24 Jan
Won 28-14
Hampson (Wigan)
Drummond (Warrington) 1t
Schofield (Leeds) 2t
Loughlin (St. Helens) 3g
Offiah (Widnes) 1t
*Hanley (Wigan) 1t
Edwards (Wigan)
Ward (Castleford)
Beardmore, K (Castleford)
Waddell (Oldham)
Powell, R (Leeds)
Medley (Leeds)
Platt (St. Helens)
Sub: Creasser (Leeds) 1g
    Dixon (Halifax)

1988 France
Leeds: 6 Feb
Won 30-12
Hampson (Wigan)
Plange (Castleford) 1t
Schofield (Leeds) 1t,5g
*Hanley (Wigan) 2t
Ford (Bradford)
Edwards (Wigan)
Gregory, A (Wigan) 1t
Ward (Castleford)
Beardmore, K (Castleford)
Waddell (Oldham)
Powell, R (Leeds)
Dixon (Halifax)
Platt (St. Helens)
Sub: Stephenson (Leeds)
    Medley (Leeds)

1988 Papua New Guinea (Also WC)
Port Moresby: 22 May
Won 42-22
Loughlin (St. Helens) 7g
Ford (Bradford)
Schofield (Leeds) 2t
Stephenson (Leeds) 1t
Gill (Wigan) 2t
Edwards (Wigan)
Gregory, A (Wigan)
Ward (Castleford)
Beardmore, K (Castleford)
Case (Wigan)
Medley (Leeds) 1t
Gregory, M (Warrington) 1t
*Hanley (Wigan)
Sub: Hulme, D (Widnes)
    Dixon (Halifax)

1988 Australia
Sydney: 11 June
Lost 6-17
Loughlin (St. Helens) 1g
Ford (Bradford)
Schofield (Leeds)
Stephenson (Leeds)
Offiah (Widnes)
Hulme, D (Widnes)
Gregory, A (Wigan)
Ward (Castleford)
Beardmore, K (Castleford)
Dixon (Halifax)
Gregory, M (Warrington)
Platt (St. Helens)
*Hanley (Wigan) 1t
Sub: Gill (Wigan)
    Powell, R (Leeds)

1988 Australia
Brisbane: 28 June
Lost 14-34
Loughlin (St. Helens) 3g
Gill (Wigan)
Ford (Bradford) 1t
*Hanley (Wigan)
Offiah (Widnes) 1t
Hulme, D (Widnes)
Gregory, A (Wigan)
Ward (Castleford)
Beardmore, K (Castleford)
Powell, R (Leeds)
Dixon (Halifax)
Platt (St. Helens)
Gregory, M (Warrington)
Sub: Wright (Widnes)
     Hulme, P (Widnes)

1988 Australia (Also WC)
Sydney: 9 July
Won 26-12
Ford (Bradford) 1t
Gill (Wigan) 2t
Stephenson (Leeds)
Loughlin (St. Helens) 3g
Offiah (Widnes) 1t
Hulme, D (Widnes)
Gregory, A (Wigan)
Ward (Castleford)
Hulme, P (Widnes)
Waddell (Oldham)
Gregory, M (Warrington) 1t
Powell, R (Leeds)
*Hanley (Wigan)
Sub: Case (Wigan)

1988 New Zealand (Also WC)
Christchurch: 17 July
Lost 10-12
Ford (Bradford)
Gill (Wigan)
Stephenson (Leeds)
Loughlin (St. Helens) 1t,1g
Offiah (Widnes)
Hulme, D (Widnes) 1t
Gregory, A (Wigan)
Ward (Castleford)
Beardmore, K (Castleford)
Waddell (Oldham)
Gregory, M (Warrington)
Powell, R (Leeds)
*Hanley (Wigan)
Sub: Hulme, P (Widnes)

1989 France
Wigan: 21 Jan
Won 26-10
Tait (Widnes)
Ford (Leeds) 1t
Loughlin (St. Helens) 3g
Lydon (Wigan) 1t
Offiah (Widnes) 1t
Edwards (Wigan) 1t
Gregory, A (Wigan)
Ward (Castleford)
Beardmore, K (Castleford)
Waddell (Leeds)
Gregory, M (Warrington)
Powell, R (Leeds)
*Hanley (Wigan) 1t
Sub: Williams (Salford)
     Eyres (Widnes)

1989 France
Avignon: 5 Feb
Won 30-8
Tait (Widnes) 1t
Ford (Leeds) 2t
Williams (Salford) 1t
Lydon (Wigan) 3g
Offiah (Widnes)
Edwards (Wigan) 1t
Gregory, A (Wigan)
Ward (Castleford)
Beardmore, K (Castleford)
Crooks, L (Leeds)
Gregory, M (Warrington)
Powell, R (Leeds)
*Hanley (Wigan) 1t
Sub: Hampson (Wigan)
     England (Castleford)

1989 New Zealand
Man. U. FC: 21 Oct
Lost 16-24
Tait (Widnes) 1t
Ford (Leeds) 1t
Currier (Widnes)
Loughlin (St. Helens) 2g
Offiah (Widnes) 1t
Hulme, D (Widnes)
Gregory, A (Wigan)
Skerrett (Bradford)
Beardmore, K (Castleford)
Hobbs (Bradford)
Goodway (Wigan)
Platt (Wigan)
*Gregory, M (Warrington)
Sub: Edwards (Wigan)
     Newlove, P (Featherstone)

1989 New Zealand
Elland Rd, Leeds: 28 Oct
Won 26-6
Hampson (Wigan)
Ford (Leeds)
Newlove, P (Featherstone)
Loughlin (St. Helens) 5g
Offiah (Widnes) 1t
Edwards (Wigan) 1t
Hulme, D (Widnes)
Skerrett (Bradford)
Hulme, P (Widnes)
Platt (Wigan)
Goodway (Wigan) 2t
Powell, R (Leeds)
*Gregory, M (Warrington)
Sub: Hobbs (Bradford)
     Fox (Featherstone)

1989 New Zealand (Also WC)
Wigan: 11 Nov
Won 10-6
Tait (Widnes) 1t
Ford (Leeds)
Newlove, P (Featherstone)
Loughlin (St. Helens) 1g
Offiah (Widnes) 1t
Edwards (Wigan)
Hulme, D (Widnes)
Skerrett (Bradford)
Hulme, P (Widnes)
Platt (Wigan)
Goodway (Wigan)
Powell, R (Leeds)
*Gregory, M (Warrington)
Sub: Lydon (Wigan)
     England (Castleford)

1990 France
Perpignan: 18 Mar
Won 8-4
Tait (Widnes)
Lydon (Wigan)
Schofield (Leeds) 2g
Loughlin (St. Helens)
Offiah (Widnes) 1t
Edwards (Wigan)
Gregory, A (Wigan)
Skerrett (Bradford)
Beardmore, K (Castleford)
Platt (Wigan)
Gregory, M (Warrington)
Goodway (Wigan)
*Hanley (Wigan)
Sub: Powell, D (Sheffield)
     Betts (Wigan)

1990 France
Leeds: 7 Apr
Lost 18-25
Tait (Widnes) 1t
Cordle (Bradford) 1t
Schofield (Leeds)
Gibson (Leeds)
Offiah (Widnes) 1t
Steadman (Castleford) 3g
*Edwards (Wigan)
Skerrett (Bradford)
Beardmore, K (Castleford)
England (Castleford)
Betts (Wigan)
Fairbank, K (Bradford)
Gregory, M (Warrington)
Sub: Irwin (Castleford)
    Bishop (Hull KR)

1990 Papua New Guinea
Goroka: 27 May
Lost 18-20
Tait (Widnes)
Eastwood (Hull) 1t
Powell, D (Sheffield)
Davies (Widnes) 1t,3g
Gibson (Leeds)
Schofield (Leeds)
Goulding (Wigan) 1t
Powell, R (Leeds)
Jackson (Hull)
Dixon (Leeds)
Betts (Wigan)
Fairbank, K (Bradford)
*Gregory, M (Warrington)
Sub: Irwin (Castleford)
    England (Castleford)

1990 Papua New Guinea (Also WC)
Port Moresby: 2 June
Won 40-8
Tait (Widnes)
Eastwood (Hull) 1t
Davies (Widnes) 6g
Powell, D (Sheffield) 1t
Gibson (Leeds) 2t
Schofield (Leeds) 1t
Goulding (Wigan) 1t
Powell, R (Leeds)
Jackson (Hull)
England (Castleford)
Betts (Wigan)
Dixon (Leeds) 1t
*Gregory, M (Warrington)
Sub: Fox (Featherstone)
    Clarke (Wigan)

1990 New Zealand
Palmerston North: 24 June
Won 11-10
Bibb (Featherstone)
Davies (Widnes) 1t,1g
Lydon (Wigan)
Gibson (Leeds) 1t
Offiah (Widnes)
Schofield (Leeds) 1dg
Goulding (Wigan)
Skerrett (Bradford)
Dermott (Wigan)
England (Castleford)
Betts (Wigan)
Dixon (Leeds)
*Gregory, M (Warrington)
Sub: Powell, D (Sheffield)
    Powell, R (Leeds)

1990 New Zealand
Auckland: 8 July
Won 16-14
Lydon (Wigan)
Davies (Widnes) 2g
Powell, D (Sheffield)
Gibson (Leeds)
Offiah (Widnes) 1t
Schofield (Leeds) 1t
Goulding (Wigan)
Skerrett (Bradford)
Jackson (Hull)
England (Castleford)
Betts (Wigan) 1t
Dixon (Leeds)
*Gregory, M (Warrington)
Sub: Irwin (Castleford)
    Powell, R (Leeds)

1990 New Zealand (Also WC)
Christchurch: 15 July
Lost 18-21
Lydon (Wigan)
Davies (Widnes) 3g
Gibson (Leeds)
Powell, D (Sheffield)
Offiah (Widnes) 1t
Schofield (Leeds) 1t
Goulding (Wigan)
Skerrett (Bradford)
Dermott (Wigan)
England (Castleford)
Betts (Wigan)
Powell, R (Leeds) 1t
*Gregory, M (Warrington)
Sub: Irwin (Castleford)
    Dixon (Leeds)

1990 Australia
Wembley: 27 Oct
Won 19-12
Hampson (Wigan)
Eastwood (Hull) 2t,3g
Powell, D (Sheffield)
Gibson (Leeds)
Offiah (Widnes) 1t
Schofield (Leeds) 1dg
Gregory, A (Wigan)
Harrison (Hull)
Jackson (Hull)
Dixon (Leeds)
Betts (Wigan)
Powell, R (Leeds)
*Hanley (Wigan)
Sub: Fairbank (Bradford)
    Ward (St. Helens)

1990 Australia
Man. U. FC: 10 Nov
Lost 10-14
Hampson (Wigan)
Eastwood (Hull) 1g
Powell, D (Sheffield)
Gibson (Leeds)
Offiah (Widnes)
Schofield (Leeds)
Gregory, A (Wigan)
Harrison (Hull)
Jackson (Hull)
Platt (Wigan)
Betts (Wigan)
Dixon (Leeds) 1t
*Hanley (Wigan)
Sub: Loughlin (St. Helens) 1t
    Ward (St. Helens)

*Eleven-cap Sheffield Eagles centre
Daryl Powell.*

1990 Australia (Also WC)
Elland Rd, Leeds: 24 Nov
Lost 0-14
Hampson (Wigan)
Eastwood (Hull)
Powell, D (Sheffield)
Gibson (Leeds)
Offiah (Widnes)
Schofield (Leeds)
Gregory, A (Wigan)
Harrison (Hull)
Jackson (Hull)
Platt (Wigan)
Betts (Wigan)
Dixon (Leeds)
*Hanley (Wigan)
Sub: Davies (Widnes)
　　　Gregory, M (Warrington)
　　　Powell, R (Leeds)

1991 France (Also WC)
Perpignan: 27 Jan
Won 45-10
Hampson (Wigan)
Eastwood (Hull) 6g
Powell, D (Sheffield)
Gibson (Leeds)
Offiah (Widnes) 2t
Schofield (Leeds) 2t,1dg
Edwards (Wigan) 2t
Lucas (Wigan)
Jackson (Hull)
Platt (Wigan) 1t
Betts (Wigan) 1t
Holliday (Widnes)
*Hanley (Wigan)
Sub: Aston (Sheffield)
　　　Ellis, S (Castleford)
　　　Eyres (Widnes)
　　　Fairbank (Bradford)

1991 France
Leeds: 16 Feb
Won 60-4
Hampson (Wigan) 1t
Eastwood (Hull) 1t,8g
Powell, D (Sheffield)
Loughlin (St. Helens)
Offiah (Widnes) 5t
Schofield (Leeds) 3t
Edwards (Wigan) 1t
Dannatt (Hull)
Jackson (Hull)
Platt (Wigan)
Eyres (Widnes)
Fairbank (Bradford)
*Hanley (Wigan)
Sub: Ellis, K (Warrington)
　　　Ellis, S (Castleford)
　　　England (Castleford)
　　　Powell, R (Leeds)

Crunch tackle . . . by Great Britain scrum half Bobby Goulding on his opposite number, Gary Freeman, in the second Test in Auckland in July 1990.

GREAT BRITAIN RECORDS

Most appearances

46	Mick Sullivan*
33 + 1	Ellery Hanley
31	Billy Boston
31	Garry Schofield
29 + 1	Cliff Watson
29	George Nicholls
29	Neil Fox
28 + 1	Roger Millward
28	Alan Prescott
27	Phil Jackson
27	Alex Murphy
26	Eric Ashton
26	John Atkinson
25	Brian McTigue
25	Jim Sullivan
25	Tommy Harris

*Mick Sullivan's record number of appearances include a record run of 36 successive matches. In addition he played in two matches against France before they were given Test status.

Most tries

41, Mick Sullivan, also scoring two against France before they were given Test status.

Most goals and points

93 goals, (14 tries), 228 points, Neil Fox.

Longest Test careers

14 years   — Gus Risman
  1932 to 1946 (17 appearances)
13 years 9 months — Billy Batten
  1908 to 1921 (10 appearances)
13 years 6 months — Alex Murphy
  1958 to 1971 (27 appearances)
12 years 9 months — Roger Millward
  1966 to 1978 (28 + 1 appearances)
12 years 6 months — John Atkinson
  1968 to 1980 (26 appearances)
12 years 6 months — Terry Clawson
  1962 to 1974 (14 appearances)

Youngest Test player

Paul Newlove was 18 years 72 days old when he made his Great Britain Test debut as a 76th minute substitute in the first Test against New Zealand at Old Trafford, Manchester on 21 October 1989, making his full debut a week later. Born on 10 August 1971, he beat the previous record held by Shaun Edwards (born 17 October 1966) who was 18 years 135 days old when capped against France at Leeds on 1 March 1985.

Roger Millward (born 16 September 1947) was 18 years 37 days old when he was a non-playing substitute for the second Test against New Zealand at Bradford on 23 October 1965.

Oldest Test player

Jeff Grayshon (born 4 March 1949), was 36 years 8 months when he played in his last Test for Britain, against New Zealand at Elland Road, Leeds, on 9 November 1985.

Record team changes

The record number of team changes made by the Great Britain selectors is 10. This has happened on three occasions, all against Australia.

In 1929, Britain crashed 31-8 to Australia in the first Test at Hull KR and retained only three players for the second Test at Leeds where they won 9-3.

After their biggest ever defeat of 50-12 in the 1963 second Test at Swinton, Britain dropped nine players and were forced to make another change when Vince Karalius was injured and replaced by Don Fox. Britain stopped Australia making a clean sweep of the series by winning 16-5 at Leeds in the last Test.

Following the 40-4 first Test defeat at Hull City's soccer ground in 1982, the selectors again made 10 changes, not including substitutes, Britain going down 27-6 in the second Test at Wigan.

Britain have never fielded the same team for three or more successive Tests.

GREAT BRITAIN REGISTER

The following is a record of the 592 players who have appeared for Great Britain in 266 Test and World Cup matches.

It does not include matches against France before 1957, the year they were given official Test match status.

Figures in brackets are the total of appearances, with the plus sign indicating substitute appearances, e.g. (7 + 3).

For matches against touring teams, the year given is for the first half of the season.

World Cup matches are in bold letters except when also classified as Test matches. Substitute appearances are in lower case letters.

A - Australia, F - France, NZ - New Zealand, P - Papua New Guinea.

ACKERLEY, A (2) Halifax: 1952 A; 1958 NZ
ADAMS, L (1) Leeds: 1932 A
ADAMS, M (11+2) Widnes: 1979 Aa, NZ3; 1980 NZ; 1984 A2a, NZ3, P
ARKWRIGHT, C (+2) St. Helens: 1985 nz2
ARKWRIGHT, J (6) Warrington: 1936 A2, NZ; 1937 A3
ARMITT, T (8) Swinton: 1933 A; 1936 A2, NZ2; 1937 A3
ASHBY, R (2) Liverpool: 1964 F; Wigan: 1965 F
ASHCROFT, E (11) Wigan: 1947 NZ2; 1950 A3, NZ; 1954 A3, NZ2
ASHCROFT, K (5+1) Leigh: **1968 A**; 1968 F; 1969 F; **1970 F,NZ**; Warrington: 1974 nz
ASHTON, E (26) Wigan: **1957 A,NZ**; 1958 A2,NZ2; 1959 F, A3; 1960 F2; **1960 NZ,A**; 1961 NZ3; 1962 F3,A3; 1963 F,A2
ASHURST, W (3) Wigan: 1971 NZ; 1972 F2
ASKIN, T (6) Featherstone R: 1928 A3,NZ3
ASPINALL, W (1) Warrington: 1966 NZ
ASTON, L (3) St. Helens: 1947 NZ3
ASTON, M (+1) Sheffield E: 1991 f
ATKINSON, A (11) Castleford: 1929 A3; 1932 A3,NZ3; 1933 A; 1936 A
ATKINSON, J (26) Leeds: **1968 F,NZ**; 1970 A3,NZ3; **1970 A2,F,NZ**; 1971 F2,NZ; 1972 F2; **1972 A2,F,NZ**; 1973 A2; 1978 A2; 1980 NZ
AVERY, A (4) Oldham: 1910 A,NZ; 1911 A2

BACON, J (11) Leeds: 1920 A3,NZ3; 1921 A3; 1924 A; 1926 NZ
BARENDS, D (2) Bradford N: 1979 A2
BARTON, F (1) Wigan: 1951 NZ
BARTON, J (2) Wigan: 1960 F; 1961 NZ
BASNETT, J (2) Widnes: 1984 F; 1986 A
BASSETT, A (2) Halifax: 1946 A2
BATES, A (2+2) Dewsbury: 1974 F2,nz2
BATTEN, E (4) Bradford N: 1946 A2,NZ; 1947 NZ
BATTEN, R (3) Leeds: 1969 F; 1973 A2

BATTEN, W (10) Hunslet: 1907 NZ; 1908 A3; 1910 A2,NZ; 1911 A2; Hull: 1921 A
BAXTER, J (1) Rochdale H: 1907 NZ
BEAMES, J (2) Halifax: 1921 A2
BEARDMORE, K (13+1) Castleford: 1984 nz; 1987 F2; 1988 F2, P, A2, NZ; 1989 F2, NZ; 1990 F2
BELSHAW, W (8) Liverpool S: 1936 A3,NZ2; 1937 A; Warrington: A2
BENNETT, J (7) Rochdale H: 1924 A3,NZ3; Wigan: 1926 NZ
BENTHAM, N (10) Wigan H: 1928 A3,NZ3; Halifax: 1929 A2; Warrington: 1929(cont) A2
BENTHAM, W (2) Broughton R: 1924 NZ2
BENTLEY, K (1) Widnes: 1980 NZ
BENYON, W (5+1) St. Helens: 1971 F2,NZ,nz; 1972 F2
BETTS, D (10+1) Wigan: 1990 fF, P2, NZ3, A3; 1991 F
BEVAN, D (1) Wigan: 1952 A
BEVAN, J (6) Warrington: 1974 A2,NZ2; 1978 A2
BEVERLEY, H (6) Hunslet: 1936 A3; 1937 A; Halifax: A2
BIBB, C (1) Featherstone R: 1990 NZ
BIRCH, J (1) Leeds: 1907 NZ
BISHOP, D (+1) Hull KR: 1990 f
BISHOP, T (15) St. Helens: 1966 A3,NZ2; 1967 A3; 1968 F3; **1968 A,F,NZ**; 1969 F
BLAN, W (3) Wigan: 1951 NZ3
BLINKHORN, T (1) Warrington: 1929 A
BOLTON, D (23) Wigan: 1957 F3; 1958 F,A2; 1959 F,A3; 1960 F2; 1961 NZ3; 1962 F2,A,NZ2; 1963 F,A2
BOSTON, W (31) Wigan: 1954 A2,NZ3; 1955 NZ; 1956 A3; 1957 F5; **1957 F,A**; 1958 F; 1959 A; 1960 F; **1960 A**; 1961 F,NZ3; 1962 F2,A3,NZ; 1963 F
BOTT, C (1) Oldham: 1966 F
BOWDEN, J (3) Huddersfield: 1954 A2,NZ
BOWEN, F (3) St. Helens Rec: 1928 NZ3

BOWERS, J (1) Rochdale H: 1920 NZ
BOWMAN, E (4) Workington T: **1977 F, NZ, A2**
BOWMAN, H (8) Hull: 1924 NZ2; 1926 NZ2; 1928 A2,NZ; 1929 A
BOWMAN, K (3) Huddersfield: 1962 F; 1963 F,A
BOYLEN, F (1) Hull: 1908 A
BRADSHAW, T (6) Wigan: 1947 NZ2; 1950 A3,NZ
BRIDGES, K (3) Featherstone R: 1974 F2,A
BRIGGS, B (1) Huddersfield: 1954 NZ
BROGDEN, S (16) Huddersfield: 1929 A; 1932 A3, NZ3; 1933 A2; Leeds: 1936 A3,NZ2; 1937 A2
BROOKE, I (13) Bradford N: 1966 A3,NZ2; Wakefield: 1967 A3; 1968 F2; **1968 A,F,NZ**
BROOKS, E (3) Warrington: 1908 A3
BROUGH, A (2) Oldham: 1924 A,NZ
BROUGH, J (5) Leeds: 1928 A2,NZ2; 1936 A
BROWN, G (6) Leeds: **1954 F2,NZ,A**; 1955 NZ2
BRYANT, W (4+1) Castleford: 1964 F2; 1966 Aa; 1967 F
BUCKLEY, A (7) Swinton: 1963 A; 1964 F; 1965 NZ; 1966 F,A2,NZ
BURGESS, W (16) Barrow: 1924 A3,NZ3; 1926 NZ3; 1928 A3,NZ2; 1929 A2
BURGESS, W (14) Barrow: 1962 F; 1963 A; 1965 NZ2; 1966 F,A3,NZ2; 1967 F,A; 1968 F; Salford: 1969 F
BURGHAM, O (1) Halifax: 1911 A
BURKE, M (14+1) Widnes: 1980 NZ; 1981 fF; 1983 F; 1984 A3, NZ3, P; 1985 NZ3; 1986 F
BURNELL, A (3) Hunslet: 1951 NZ2; 1954 NZ
BURTON, C (8+1) Hull KR: 1982 A; 1984 A3, NZ2; 1985 nz; 1986 A; 1987 F
BURWELL, A (7+1) Hull KR: 1967 a; 1968 F3; **1968 A,F,NZ**; 1969 F
BUTTERS, F (2) Swinton: 1929 A2

CAIRNS, D (2) Barrow: 1984 F2
CAMILLERI, C (2) Barrow: 1980 NZ2
CARLTÓN, F (2) St. Helens: 1958 NZ; Wigan: 1962 NZ
CARR, C (7) Barrow: 1924 A2,NZ2; 1926 NZ3
CARTWRIGHT, J (7) Leigh: 1920 A,NZ3; 1921 A3
CASE, B (6+1) Wigan: 1984 A, NZ3; 1987 P; 1988 P, a
CASEY, L (12+2) Hull KR: **1977 f,nz,A**; 1978 A; Bradford N: 1979 A2,NZ3; Hull KR: 1980 NZ3; 1983 F2
CASTLE, F (4) Barrow: 1952 A3; 1954 A
CHALLINOR, J (3) Warrington: 1958 A,NZ; **1960 F**
CHARLTON, P (18+1) Workington T: 1965 NZ; Salford: **1970 nz**; 1972 F2; **1972 A2,F,NZ**; 1973 A3; 1974 F2,A3,NZ3
CHERRINGTON, N (1) Wigan: 1960 F
CHILCOTT, J (3) Huddersfield: 1914 A3
CHISNALL, D (2) Leigh: 1970 A; **1970 NZ**
CHISNALL, E (4) St. Helens: 1974 A2,NZ2
CLAMPITT, L (3) Broughton R: 1907 NZ; 1911 A; 1914 NZ

CLARK, D (11) Huddersfield: 1911 A2; 1914 A3; 1920 A3,NZ3
CLARK, G (3) Hull KR: 1984 F2; 1985 F
CLARK, M (5) Leeds: 1968 F2; **1968 A,F,NZ**
CLARKE, C (7) Wigan: 1965 NZ; 1966 F,NZ; 1967 F; 1973 A3
CLARKE, P (+1) Wigan: 1990 p
CLAWSON, T (14) Featherstone R: 1962 F2; Leeds: **1972 A2,F**; Oldham: 1973 A3; 1974 F2,A2,NZ2
CLOSE, D (1) Huddersfield: 1967 F
COLDRICK, A (4) Wigan: 1914 A3,NZ
COLLIER, F (2) Wigan: 1963 A; Widnes: 1964 F
CORDLE, G (1) Bradford N: 1990 F
COULMAN, M (2+1) Salford: 1971 f,NZ2
COURTNEY, N (+1) Warrington: 1982 a
COVERDALE, R (4) Hull: **1954 F2,NZ,A**
CRACKNELL, R (2) Huddersfield: 1951 NZ2
CRANE, M (1) Hull: 1982 A
CREASSER, D (2+2) Leeds: 1985 F2; 1987 f; 1988 f
CROOKS, L (12+2) Hull: 1982 A2; 1984 f, A2; 1985 NZ, nz; 1986 F2, A3; 1987 F; Leeds: 1989 F
CROSTON, A (1) Castleford: 1937 A
CROWTHER, H (1) Hunslet: 1929 A
CUNLIFFE, J (4) Wigan: 1950 A,NZ; 1951 NZ; 1954 A
CUNLIFFE, W (11) Warrington: 1920 A,NZ2; 1921 A3; 1924 A3,NZ; 1926 NZ
CUNNIFFE, B (1) Castleford: 1937 A
CUNNINGHAM, E (1) St. Helens: 1978 A
CURRAN, G (6) Salford: 1946 A,NZ; 1947 NZ; 1948 A3
CURRIER, A (1) Widnes: 1989 NZ
CURZON, E (1) Salford: 1910 A

DAGNALL, R (4) St.Helens: 1961 NZ2; 1964 F; 1965 F
DALGREEN, J (1) Fulham: 1982 A
DANBY, T (3) Salford: 1950 A2,NZ
DANIELS, A (3) Halifax: 1952 A2; 1955 NZ
DANNATT, A (3) Hull: 1985 F2; 1991 F
DARWELL, J (5) Leigh: 1924 A3,NZ2
DAVIES, A (20) Oldham: 1955 NZ; 1956 A3; **1957 F,A**; 1957 F2; 1958 F,A2,NZ2; 1959 F2,A; **1960 NZ,F,A**; 1960 F
DAVIES, E (3) Oldham: 1920 NZ3
DAVIES, J (5+1) Widnes: 1990 P2, NZ3, a
DAVIES, J (2) Huddersfield: 1911 A2
DAVIES, W (1) Swinton: 1968 F
DAVIES, W.A (2) Leeds: 1914 A,NZ
DAVIES, W.J (1) Castleford: 1933 A
DAVIES, W.T (1) Halifax: 1911 A
DAVIES, W.T.H (3) Bradford N: 1946 NZ; 1947 NZ2
DAWSON, E (1) York: 1956 A
DERMOTT, M (2) Wigan: 1990 NZ2
DICK, K (2) Leeds: 1980 NZ2
DICKENSON, G (1) Warrington: 1908 A
DICKINSON, R (2) Leeds: 1985 F2

DINGSDALE, W (3) Warrington: 1929 A2; 1933 A
DIVORTY, G (2) Hull: 1985 F2
DIXON, C (12 + 2) Halifax: 1968 F; Salford: 1969 F;
 1971 NZ; **1972 F**; 1973 a2; 1974 F2,A3,NZ3
DIXON, M (2) Featherstone R: 1962 F; 1964 F
DIXON, P (10 + 4) Halifax: 1987 f; 1988 f, F, p, A2;
 Leeds: 1990 P2, NZ2nz, A3
DOCKAR, A (1) Hull KR: 1947 NZ
DONLAN, S (+ 2) Leigh: 1984 nz, p
DRAKE, J (1) Hull: 1960 F
DRAKE, W (1) Hull: 1962 F
DRUMMOND, D (24) Leigh: 1980 NZ2; 1981 F2;
 1982 A3; 1983 F2; 1984 F, A3, NZ3, P; 1985
 NZ3; 1986 F2; Warrington: 1987 P;1988 F
DUANE, R (3) Warrington: 1983 F2; 1984 F
DUTTON, R (6) Widnes: 1970 NZ2; **1970 A2,F,NZ**
DYL, L (11) Leeds: 1974 A2,NZ3; **1977 F,NZ,A2**;
 1978 A; 1982 A
DYSON, F (1) Huddersfield: 1959 A

EASTWOOD, P (7) Hull: 1990 P2, A3; 1991 F2
ECCLES, P (1) Halifax: 1907 NZ
ECCLES, R (1) Warrington: 1982 A
ECKERSLEY, D (2 + 2) St.Helens: 1973 Aa; 1974 Aa
EDGAR, B (11) Workington T: 1958 A,NZ; 1961
 NZ; 1962 A3,NZ; 1965 NZ; 1966 A3
EDWARDS, A (7) Salford: 1936 A3,NZ2; 1937 A2
EDWARDS, D (3 + 2) Castleford: 1968 f; 1970 A;
 1971 NZ2nz
EDWARDS, S (16 + 3) Wigan: 1985 F,nzNZ; 1986 a;
 1987 F2, F; 1988 F2, P; 1989 F2, nzNZ2; 1990
 F2; 1991 F2
EGAN, J (14) Wigan: 1946 A3; 1947 NZ3; 1948 A3;
 1950 A3,NZ2
ELLABY, A (13) St.Helens: 1928 A3,NZ2; 1929 A2;
 1932 A3,NZ2; 1933 A
ELLIS, K (+ 1) Warrington: 1991 f
ELLIS, S (+ 2) Castleford: 1991 f2
ELWELL, K (3) Widnes: **1977 A**; 1980 NZ2
ENGLAND, K (6 + 5) Castleford: 1987 fF; 1989 f,
 nz; 1990 F, pP, NZ3; 1991 f
EVANS, B (10) Swinton: 1926 NZ; 1928 NZ; 1929
 A; 1932 A2,NZ3; 1933 A2
EVANS, F (4) Swinton: 1924 A2,NZ2
EVANS, J (4) Hunslet: 1951 NZ; 1952 A3
EVANS, J (3) Swinton: 1926 NZ3
EVANS, R (4) Wigan: 1961 NZ2; 1962 F,NZ
EVANS, S (7 + 3) Featherstone R: 1979 Aa2,NZ3;
 1980 NZnz; Hull: 1982 A2
EYRE, K (1) Hunslet: 1965 NZ
EYRES, R (1 + 2) Widnes: 1989 f; 1991 fF

FAIRBAIRN, G (17) Wigan: **1977 F,NZ,A2**; 1978 A3;
 1979 A2,NZ3; 1980 NZ2; Hull KR: 1981 F;
 1982 A2
FAIRBANK, K (3 + 3) Bradford N: 1987 p; 1990 F, P,
 a; 1991 fF

FAIRCLOUGH, L (6) St.Helens: 1926 NZ; 1928
 A2,NZ2; 1929 A
FARRAR, V (1) Hull: 1978 A
FEATHERSTONE, J (6) Warrington: 1948 A; 1950
 NZ2; 1952 A3
FEETHAM, J (8) Hull KR: 1929 A; Salford: 1932
 A2,NZ2; 1933 A3
FIELD, H (3) York: 1936 A,NZ2
FIELD, N (1) Batley: 1963 A
FIELDHOUSE, J (7) Widnes: 1985 NZ3; 1986 F2, A;
 St.Helens: 1986 A
FIELDING, K (3) Salford: 1974 F2; **1977 F**
FILDES, A (15) St.Helens Recs: 1926 NZ2; 1928
 A3,NZ2; 1929 A3; St.Helens: 1932 A,NZ3
FISHER, A (11) Bradford N: 1970 A2,NZ3; **1970 A**;
 Leeds: A; 1971 F2; Bradford N: 1978 A2
FLANAGAN, P (14) Hull KR: 1962 F; 1963 F; 1966
 A3,NZ; 1967 A3; 1968 F2; **1968 F,NZ**; 1970 A
FLANAGAN, T (4) Oldham: 1983 F2; 1984 NZ, P
FOGERTY, T (2 + 1) Halifax: 1966 nz; Wigan: 1967 F;
 Rochdale H: 1974 F
FORD, P (13) Wigan: 1985 F; Bradford N: 1987 P;
 1988 F, P, A3, NZ; Leeds: 1989 F2, NZ3
FORSTER, M (2) Warrington: 1987 F2
FOSTER, F (1) Hull KR: 1967 A
FOSTER, P (3) Leigh: 1955 NZ3
FOSTER, T (3) Bradford N: 1946 NZ; 1948 A2
FOX, Deryck (9 + 2) Featherstone R: 1985 F2, NZ3;
 1986 F2, A2; 1989 nz; 1990 p
FOX, Don (1) Featherstone R: 1963 A
FOX, N (29) Wakefield T: 1959 F,A2; 1960 F3; 1961
 NZ2; 1962 F3,A3,NZ2; 1963 A2,F; 1964 F; 1965
 F; 1966 F; 1967 F2,A; 1968 F3; 1969 F
FOY, D (3) Oldham: 1984 F, A; 1985 F
FRANCIS, R (1) Barrow: 1947 NZ
FRANCIS, W (4) Wigan: 1967 A; **1977 NZ,A2**
FRASER, E (16) Warrington: 1958 A3,NZ2; 1959 F2,A;
 1960 F3; **1960 F,NZ**; 1961 F,NZ2
FRENCH, R (4) Widnes: 1968 F2; **1968 A,NZ**
FRODSHAM, A (3) St.Helens: 1928 NZ2; 1929 A

GABBITAS, B (1) Hunslet: 1959 F
GALLAGHER, F (12) Dewsbury: 1920 A3; 1921 A;
 Batley: 1924 A3,NZ3; 1926 NZ2
GANLEY, B (3) Oldham: 1957 F2; 1958 F
GARDINER, D (1) Wigan: 1965 NZ
GEE, K (17) Wigan: 1946 A3,NZ; 1947 NZ3; 1948
 A3; 1950 A3,NZ2; 1951 NZ2
GEMMELL, R (3) Leeds: 1964 F; Hull: 1968 F;
 1969 F
GIBSON, C (10 + 1) Batley: 1985 f; Leeds: 1990 F,
 P2, NZ3, A3; 1991 F
GIFFORD, H (2) Barrow: 1908 A2
GILFEDDER, L (5) Warrington: 1962 A,NZ2,F;
 1963 F
GILL, H (14 + 1) Wigan: 1981 F2; 1982 A; 1985 F;
 1986 F, A3; 1987 F2; 1988 P, A2a, NZ

GILL, K (5+2) Salford: 1974 F2,A2,NZ; **1977 f,a**
GOODWAY, A (23) Oldham: 1983 F2; 1984 F, A3,
   NZ3, P; 1985 F; Wigan: 1985 NZ3; 1986 A3;
   1987 F, P; 1989 NZ3; 1990 F
GOODWIN, D (5) Barrow: 1957 F2; 1958 F,NZ2
GORE, J (1) Salford: 1926 NZ
GORLEY, L (4+1) Widnes: 1980 NZnz; 1981 F2;
   1982 A
GORLEY, P (2+1) St.Helens: 1980 NZ; 1981 Ff
GOULDING, R (5) Wigan: 1990 P2, NZ3
GOWERS, K (14) Swinton: 1962 F; 1963 F,A3; 1964
   F2; 1965 NZ2; 1966 F2,A,NZ2
GRAY, J (5+3) Wigan: 1974 f2,A2a,NZ3
GRAYSHON, J (13) Bradford N: 1979 A2,NZ3; 1980
   NZ2; 1981 F2; 1982 A2; Leeds: 1985 NZ2
GREENALL, D (6) St.Helens: 1951 NZ3; 1952 A2;
   1954 NZ
GREENALL, J (1) St.Helens Rec: 1921 A
GREENOUGH, R (1) Warrington: **1960 NZ**
GREGORY, A (24+1) Widnes: 1981 F2; 1982 A;
   1983 F2; 1984 a, NZ2, P; Warrington: 1986 A;
   Wigan: 1987 F, P; 1988 F, P, A3, NZ; 1989 F2,
   NZ; 1990 F, A3
GREGORY, M (19+1) Warrington: 1987 F2; 1988 P,
   A3, NZ; 1989 F2, NZ3; 1990 F2, P2, NZ3, a
GRIBBIN, V (1) Whitehaven: 1985 F
GRONOW, B (7) Huddersfield: 1911 A2, 1920
   A2, NZ3
GROVES, P (1) St. Helens: 1987 P
GRUNDY, J (12) Barrow: 1955 NZ3; 1956 A3; 1957
   F3; **1957 F,A,NZ**
GUNNEY, G (11) Hunslet: 1954 NZ3; 1956 A; 1957
   F3; **1957 F,NZ**; 1964 F; 1965 F
GWYNNE, T. E (3) Hull: 1928 A,NZ; 1929 A
GWYTHER, E (6) Belle Vue R: 1947 NZ2; 1950 A3;
   1951 NZ

HAGGERTY, R (2) St. Helens: 1987 F2
HAIGH, R (5+1) Wakefield T: **1968 A,F**; Leeds:
   1970 NZ,a; 1971 F,NZ
HALL, D (2) Hull KR: 1984 F2
HALL, W (4) Oldham: 1914 A3,NZ
HALLAS, D (2) Leeds: 1961 F,NZ
HALMSHAW, A (1) Halifax: 1971 NZ
HALSALL, H (1) Swinton: 1929 A
HAMPSON, S (9+1) Wigan: 1987 P; 1988 F2; 1989
   f, NZ; 1990 A3; 1991 F2
HANLEY, E (33+1) Bradford N: 1984 fF, A3, NZ3,
   P; 1985 F2; Wigan: 1985 NZ3; 1986 F, A; 1987
   F2, P; 1988 F2, P, A3, NZ; 1989 F2; 1990 F,
   A3; 1991 F2
HARDISTY, A (12) Castleford: 1964 F3; 1965 F,NZ;
   1966 A3,NZ; 1967 F2; 1970 A
HARE, I (1) Widnes: 1967 F
HARKIN, P (+1) Hull KR: 1985 f
HARRIS, T (25) Hull: 1954 NZ2; 1956 A3; 1957 F5;
   1957 F,A; 1958 A3,NZ,F; 1959 F2,A3; 1960 F2;
   1960 NZ

HARRISON, F (3) Leeds: 1911 A3
HARRISON, K (3) Hull: 1990 A3
HARRISON, M (7) Hull: 1967 F2; 1971 NZ2; 1972 F2;
   1973 A
HARTLEY, D (11) Hunslet: 1964 F2; Castleford: 1968
   F; 1969 F; 1970 A2,NZ2; **1970 A2,F**
HARTLEY, S (3) Hull KR: 1980 NZ; 1981 F2
HELME, G (12) Warrington: 1948 A3; 1954 A3,NZ2;
   1954 F2,A,NZ
HEPWORTH, K (11) Castleford: 1967 F2; 1970
   A3,NZ2; **1970 A2,F,NZ**
HERBERT, N (6) Workington T: 1961 NZ; 1962
   F,A3,NZ
HERON, D (1+1) Leeds: 1982 aA
HESKETH, C (21+2) Salford: 1970 NZ; **1970 NZ,a**;
   1971 Ff,NZ3; **1972 A2,F,NZ**; 1973 A3; 1974
   F2,A3,NZ3
HICKS, M (1) St.Helens: 1965 NZ
HIGGINS, F (6) Widnes: 1950 A3,NZ2; 1951 NZ
HIGGINS, H (2) Widnes: 1937 A2
HIGSON, J (2) Hunslet: 1908 A2
HILL, C (1) Wigan: 1966 F
HILL, D (1) Wigan: 1971 F
HILTON, H (7) Oldham: 1920 A3,NZ3; 1921 A
HILTON, J (4) Wigan: 1950 A2,NZ2
HOBBS, D (10+2) Featherstone R: 1984 F2, Aa, NZ3,
   P; Oldham: 1987 F2; Bradford N: 1989 NZnz
HODGSON, M (16) Swinton: 1929 A2; 1932 A3,NZ3;
   1933 A3; 1936 A3,NZ; 1937 A
HOGAN, P (6+3) Barrow: **1977 F,NZ,A2**; 1978 a; Hull
   KR: 1979 Aa,NZ,nz
HOGG, A (1) Broughton R: 1907 NZ
HOLDEN, K (1) Warrington: 1963 A
HOLDER, W (1) Hull: 1907 NZ
HOLDING, N (4) St. Helens: 1984 A3, NZ
HOLDSTOCK, R (2) Hull KR: 1980 NZ2
HOLLAND, D (4) Oldham: 1914 A3,NZ
HOLLIDAY, L (1) Widnes: 1991 F
HOLLIDAY, W (9+1) Whitehaven: 1964 F; Hull KR:
   1965 F,NZ3; 1966 Ff; 1967 A3
HOLLINDRAKE, T (1) Keighley: 1955 NZ
HOLMES, J (14+6) Leeds: 1971 NZ; 1972 F2; **1972
   Aa,NZ; 1977 F,NZ,Aa**; 1978 a3; 1979 A2a,NZ3;
   1982 A
HORNE, W (8) Barrow: 1946 A3; 1947 NZ; 1948 A;
   1952 A3
HORTON, W (14) Wakefield T: 1928 A3,NZ3; 1929 A;
   1932 A3,NZ; 1933 A3
HOWLEY, T (6) Wigan: 1924 A3,NZ3
HUDDART, R (16) Whitehaven: 1958 A2,NZ2;
   St.Helens: 1959 A; 1961 NZ3; 1962 F2,A3,NZ2;
   1963 A
HUDSON, B (8) Salford: 1932 NZ; 1933 A2; 1936
   A,NZ2; 1937 A2
HUDSON, W (1) Wigan: 1948 A
HUGHES, E (8) Widnes: 1978 A; 1979 A3,NZ3; 1982 A
HULME, D (7+1) Widnes: 1988 p, A3, NZ; 1989 NZ3

HULME, P (3+2) Widnes: 1988 Aa, nz; 1989 NZ2
HURCOMBE, D (8) Wigan: 1920 A2,NZ; 1921 A; 1924 A2,NZ2
HYNES, S (12+1) Leeds: 1970 A2,NZ2nz; **1970 A2,F,NZ**; 1971 F; 1973 A3

IRVING, R (8+3) Oldham: 1967 F2,A3; 1970 a,NZ; 1971 NZ; 1972 f; **1972 NZ,a**
IRWIN, S (+4) Castleford: 1990 f, p, nz2

JACKSON, K (2) Oldham: 1957 F2
JACKSON, L (8) Hull: 1990 P2, NZ, A3; 1991 F2
JACKSON, P (27) Barrow: 1954 A3,NZ3; **1954 F2,A,NZ**; 1955 NZ3; 1956 A3; **1957 F,NZ**; 1957 F5; 1958 F,A2,NZ
JAMES, N (1) Halifax: 1986 F
JARMAN, J W (2) Leeds: 1914 A2
JASIEWICZ, R (1) Bradford N: 1984 F
JEANES, D (8) Wakefield T: 1971 F,NZ2; 1972 F2; Leeds: **1972 A2,NZ**
JENKINS, B (12) Wigan: 1907 NZ3; 1908 A3; 1910 A,NZ; 1911 A2, 1914 A,NZ
JENKINS, D (1) Hunslet: 1929 A
JENKINS, D (1) Leeds: 1947 NZ
JENKINS, E (9) Salford: 1933 A; 1936 A3,NZ2; 1937 A3
JENKINSON, A (2) Hunslet: 1911 A2
JOHNSON, A (4) Widnes: 1914 A,NZ; 1920 A2
JOHNSON, A (6) Warrington: 1946 A2,NZ; 1947 NZ3
JOHNSON, C (1) Leigh: 1985 F
JOLLEY, J (3) Runcorn: 1907 NZ3
JONES, B (3) Wakefield T: 1964 F; 1965 F; 1966 F
JONES, B.L (15) Leeds: 1954 A3,NZ3; 1955 NZ3; 1957 F3; **1957 F,A,NZ**
JONES, D (2) Merthyr: 1907 NZ2
JONES, E (4) Rochdale H: 1920 A,NZ3
JONES, J (1) Barrow: 1946 NZ
JONES, K (2) Wigan: **1970 F,NZ**
JONES, L (1) St.Helens: 1971 NZ
JORDAN, G (2) Featherstone R: 1964 F; 1967 A
JOYNER, J (14+2) Castleford: 1978 A2; 1979 A3,NZ3; 1980 NZ3; 1983 F2; 1984 F, nz2
JUBB, K (2) Leeds: 1937 A2
JUKES, W (6) Hunslet: 1908 A3; 1910 A2,NZ

KARALIUS, A (4+1) St.Helens: 1971 NZ3; 1972 F; **1972 nz**
KARALIUS, V (12) St.Helens: 1958 A2,NZ2; 1959 F; **1960 NZ,F,A**; 1960 F; 1961 F; Widnes: 1963 A2
KEEGAN, A (9) Hull: 1966 A2; 1967 F2,A3; 1968 F; 1969 F
KELLY, K (4) St.Helens: 1972 F2; Warrington: 1980 NZ; 1982 A
KEMEL, G (2) Widnes: 1965 NZ2
KERSHAW, H (2) Wakefield T: 1910 A,NZ

KINNEAR, R (1) Wigan: 1929 A
KISS, N (1) Wigan: 1985 F
KITCHEN, F (2) Leigh: **1954 A,NZ**
KITCHIN, P (1) Whitehaven: 1965 NZ
KITCHING, J (1) Bradford N: 1946 A
KNAPMAN, E (1) Oldham: 1924 NZ
KNOWELDEN, B (1) Barrow: 1946 NZ

LAUGHTON, D (15) Wigan: 1970 A3,NZ2; **1970 A2,F,NZ**; 1971 F2; Widnes: 1973 A; 1974 F2; 1979 A
LAWRENSON, J (3) Wigan: 1948 A3
LAWS, D (1) Hull KR: 1986 F
LEDGARD, J (11) Dewsbury: 1947 NZ2; Leigh: 1948 A; 1950 A2,NZ; 1951 NZ; **1954 F2,A,NZ**
LEDGER, B (2) St. Helens: 1985 F; 1986 A
LEWIS, G (1) Leigh: 1965 NZ
LEYTHAM, J (5) Wigan: 1907 NZ2; 1910 A2,NZ
LITTLE, S (10) Oldham: 1956 A; 1957 F5; **1957 F,A,NZ**; 1958 F
LLEWELLYN, T (2) Oldham: 1907 NZ2
LLOYD, R (1) Halifax: 1920 A
LOCKWOOD, B (8+1) Castleford: **1972 A2,F,NZ**; 1973 A2; 1974 F; Hull KR: 1978 A; 1979 nz
LOMAS, J (7) Salford: 1908 A2; 1910 A2,NZ; Oldham: 1911 A2
LONGSTAFF, F (2) Huddersfield: 1914 A,NZ
LONGWORTH, W (3) Oldham: 1908 A3
LOUGHLIN, P (12+1) St. Helens: 1988 F, P, A3, NZ, 1989 F, NZ3; 1990 F, a; 1991 F
LOWE, J (1) Leeds: 1932 NZ
LOWE, P (12) Hull KR: 1970 NZ; 1972 F2; **1972 A2,F,NZ**; 1973 A3, 1978 A2
LOXTON, K (1) Huddersfield: 1971 NZ
LUCAS, I (1) Wigan: 1991 F
LYDON, J (22+2) Widnes: 1983 F2; 1984 F, a, NZ2, P; 1985 NZ3; Wigan: 1986 F, A3; 1987 F2, P; 1989 F2, nz; 1990 F, NZ3

McCORMICK, S (3) Belle Vue R: 1948 A2; St.Helens: A
McCUE, T (6) Widnes: 1936 A; 1937 A; 1946 A3,NZ
McINTYRE, L (1) Oldham: 1963 A
McKEATING, V (2) Workington T: 1951 NZ2
McKINNEY, T (11) Salford: 1951 NZ; 1952 A2; 1954 A3,NZ; Warrington: 1955 NZ3; St.Helens: **1957 NZ**
McTIGUE, B (25) Wigan: 1958 A2,NZ2; 1959 F2,A3; 1960 F2; **1960 NZ,F,A**; 1961 F,NZ3; 1962 F,A3,NZ2; 1963 F
MANN, A (2) Bradford N: 1908 A2
MANTLE, J (13) St.Helens: 1966 F2,A3; 1967 A2; 1969 F; 1971 F2,NZ2; 1973 A
MARCHANT, A (3) Castleford: 1986 F, A2
MARTIN, W (1) Workington T: 1962 F
MARTYN, M (2) Leigh: 1958 A; 1959 A

MATHIAS, R (1) St.Helens: 1979 A
MEASURES, J (2) Widnes: 1963 A2
MEDLEY, P (3+1) Leeds: 1987 P; 1988 Ff, P
MIDDLETON, A (1) Salford: 1929 A
MILLER, J (1) Wigan: 1911 A
MILLER, J (6) Warrington: 1933 A3; 1936 A,NZ2
MILLS, J (6) Widnes: 1974 A2,NZ; 1978 A2; 1979 A
MILLWARD, R (28+1) Castleford: 1966 F; Hull
    KR: 1967 A3; 1968 F2; **1968 A,F,NZ**; 1970
    A2,NZ3; 1971 F,NZ3; 1973 A; 1974 A2a; **1977
    F,NZ,A2**; 1978 A3
MILNES, A (2) Halifax: 1920 A2
MOONEY, W (2) Leigh: 1924 NZ2
MOORHOUSE, S (2) Huddersfield: 1914 A,NZ
MORGAN, A (4) Featherstone R: 1968 F2;
    1968 F,NZ
MORGAN, E (2) Hull: 1921 A2
MORGAN, R (2) Swinton: 1963 F,A
MORLEY, J (2) Wigan: 1936 A; 1937 A
MORTIMER, F (2) Wakefield T: 1956 A2
MOSES, G (9) St.Helens: 1955 NZ2; 1956 A; 1957
    F3; **1957 F,A,NZ**
MUMBY, K (11) Bradford N: 1982 A; 1983 F; 1984
    F2, A3, NZ3, P
MURPHY, A (27) St.Helens: 1958 A3,NZ; 1959
    F2,A; **1960 NZ,F,A**; 1960 F; 1961 F,NZ3; 1962
    F,A3; 1963 A2; 1964 F; 1965 F,NZ; 1966 F2;
    Warrington: 1971 NZ
MURPHY, H (1) Wakefield T: 1950 A
MYLER, A (14) Widnes: 1983 F2; 1984 A2, NZ2, P;
    1985 NZ2; 1986 F2, A3
MYLER, F (23+1) Widnes: **1960 NZ,F,A**; 1960 F;
    1961 F; 1962 F; 1963 A; 1964 F; 1965 F,NZ;
    1966 A,NZnz; 1967 F2; St.Helens: 1970
    A3,NZ3; **1970 A2,F**

NASH, S (24) Featherstone R: 1971 F,NZ; 1972 F2;
    1972 A2,F,NZ; 1973 A2; 1974 A3,NZ3; Salford:
    1977 F,NZ,A2; 1978 A3; 1982 A
NAUGHTON, A (2) Warrington: **1954 F2**
NEWBOULD, H (1) Wakefield T: 1910 A
NEWLOVE, P (2+1) Featherstone R: 1989 nzNZ2
NICHOLLS, G (29) Widnes: 1971 NZ; 1972 F2;
    1972 A2,F,NZ; St.Helens: 1973 A2; 1974
    F2,A3,NZ3; **1977 F,NZ,A**; 1978 A3; 1979
    A3,NZ3
NICHOLSON, R (3) Huddersfield: 1946 NZ;
    1948 A2
NOBLE, B (11) Bradford N: 1982 A; 1983 F2; 1984
    F, A3, NZ3, P
NORTON, S (11+1) Castleford: 1974 a,NZ2; Hull:
    1978 A3; 1979 A2; 1980 NZ; 1981 F2; 1982 A

OFFIAH, M (20) Widnes: 1988 F, A3, NZ; 1989 F2,
    NZ3; 1990 F2, NZ3, A3; 1991 F2
O'GRADY, T (6) Oldham: 1954 A2,NZ3;
    Warrington: 1961 NZ

OLIVER, J (4) Batley: 1928 A3,NZ
O'NEILL, D (2+1) Widnes: 1971 nz; **1972 A,F**
O'NEILL, M (3) Widnes: 1982 A; 1983 F2
OSTER, J (1) Oldham: 1929 A
OWEN, J (1) St.Helens Recs: 1921 A
OWEN, S (1) Leigh: 1958 F
OWENS, I (4) Leeds: 1946 A3,NZ

PADBURY, R (1) Runcorn: 1908 A
PALIN, H (2) Warrington: 1947 NZ2
PARKER, D (2) Oldham: 1964 F2
PARKIN, J (17) Wakefield T: 1920 A2,NZ3; 1921
    A2;1924 A3,NZ; 1926 NZ2; 1928 A,NZ; 1929 A2
PARR, K (1) Warrington: 1968 F
PAWSEY, C (7) Leigh: 1952 A3; 1954 A2,NZ2
PEPPERELL, A (2) Workington T: 1950 NZ; 1951
    NZ
PHILLIPS, D (4) Oldham: 1946 A3, Belle Vue R:
    1950 A
PIMBLETT, A (3) Warrington: 1948 A3
PINNER, R (6+1) St.Helens: 1980 nzNZ; 1985
    NZ3; 1986 F; Widnes: 1986 A
PITCHFORD, F (2) Oldham: 1958 NZ; 1962 F
PITCHFORD, S (4) Leeds: **1977 F,NZ,A2**
PLANGE, D (1) Castleford: 1988 F
PLATT, A (12+3) St. Helens: 1985 f; 1986 f, a;
    1988 F2, A2; Wigan: 1989 NZ3; 1990 F, A2;
    1991 F2
POLLARD, C (1) Wakefield T: 1924 NZ
POLLARD, E (2) Wakefield T: 1932 A2
POLLARD, R (1) Dewsbury: 1950 NZ
POOLE, H (3) Hull KR: 1964 F; Leeds: 1966 NZ2
POTTER, I (7+1) Wigan: 1985 NZ3; 1986 F2, A2a
POWELL, D (9+2) Sheffield E: 1990 f, P2, nzNZ2,
    A3; 1991 F2
POWELL, R (13+6) Leeds: 1985 f; 1988 F2, A2a,
    NZ; 1989 F2, NZ2; 1990 P2, nz2NZ, Aa; 1991 f
POYNTON, H (3) Wakefield T: 1962 A2,NZ
PRESCOTT, A (28) St.Helens: 1951 NZ2; 1952 A3;
    1954 A3,NZ3; 1955 NZ3; 1956 A3; 1957 F5;
    1957 F,A,NZ; 1958 F,A2
PRICE, J (6) Broughton R: 1921 A2; Wigan: 1924
    A2,NZ2
PRICE, M (2) Rochdale H: 1967 A2
PRICE, R (9) Warrington: 1954 A,NZ2; 1955 NZ;
    1956 A3; 1957 F2
PRICE, T (1) Bradford N: 1970 A
PRIOR, B (1) Hunslet: 1966 F
PROCTOR, W (+1) Hull: 1984 p
PROSSER, D (1) Leeds: 1937 A
PROSSER, S (1) Halifax: 1914 A

RAE, J (1) Bradford N: 1965 NZ
RAMSDALE, R (8) Wigan: 1910 A2; 1911 A2; 1914
    A3,NZ
RAMSEY, W (7+1) Hunslet: 1965 NZ2; 1966
    F,A2,NZ2; Bradford N; 1974 nz

RATCLIFFE, G (3) Wigan: 1947 NZ; 1950 A2
RATHBONE, A (4+1) Bradford N: 1982 a; 1983 F2;
  1985 F2
RAYNE, Keith (4) Leeds: 1984 F2, A, P
RAYNE, Kevin (1) Leeds: 1986 F
REDFEARN, A (1) Bradford N: 1979 A
REDFEARN, D (6+1) Bradford N: **1972 nz**; 1974
  F2,A,NZ3
REES, D (1) Halifax: 1926 NZ
REES, T (1) Oldham: 1929 A
REES, W (11) Swinton: 1926 NZ2; 1928 A3,NZ3;
  1929 A3
REILLY, M (9) Castleford: 1970 A3,NZ3; **1970 A2,F**
RENILSON, C (7+1) Halifax: 1965 NZ; 1967 a;
  1968 F3; **1968 A,F,NZ**
RHODES, A (4) St.Helens: **1957 NZ**; **1960 F,A**;
  1961 NZ
RICHARDS, M (2) Salford: 1974 A,NZ
RILEY, J (1) Halifax: 1910 A
RING, J (2) Wigan: 1924 A; 1926 NZ
RISMAN, A (17) Salford: 1932 A,NZ3; 1933 A3;
  1936 A2,NZ2; 1937 A3; 1946 A3
RISMAN, B (5) Leeds: 1968 F2; **1968 A,F,NZ**
RIX, S (9) Oldham: 1924 A3,NZ3; 1926 NZ3
ROBERTS, K (10) Halifax: 1963 A; 1964 F2; 1965
  F,NZ3; 1966 F,NZ2
ROBINSON, A (3) Halifax: 1907 NZ, 1908 A2
ROBINSON, Dave (13) Swinton: 1965 NZ; 1966
  F2,A3,NZ2; 1967 F2,A2; Wigan: 1970 A
ROBINSON, Don (10) Wakefield T: 1954 F2,NZ,A;
  1955 NZ; Leeds: 1956 A2; 1959 A2; 1960 F
ROBINSON, J (2) Rochdale H: 1914 A2
ROBINSON, W (2) Leigh: 1963 F,A
ROGERS, J (7) Huddersfield: 1914 A; 1920 A3;
  1921 A3
ROSE, D (4) Leeds: **1954 F2,A,NZ**
ROSE, P (2+3) Hull KR: 1974 a; 1978 Aa2; Hull:
  1982 A
ROUND, G (8) Wakefield T: 1959 A; 1962
  F2,A3,NZ2
RUDDICK, J (3) Broughton R: 1907 NZ2; 1910 A
RYAN, M (4) Wigan: 1947 NZ; 1948 A2; 1950 A
RYAN, R (5) Warrington: 1950 A,NZ2; 1951 NZ;
  1952 A
RYDER, R (1) Warrington: 1952 A

SAYER, W (7) Wigan: 1961 NZ; 1962 F,A3,NZ;
  1963 A
SCHOFIELD, D (1) Halifax: 1955 NZ
SCHOFIELD, G (31) Hull: 1984 F, A3, NZ; 1985
  NZ3; 1986 F2, A3; 1987 F2; Leeds: 1988
  F2,P,A; 1990 F2, P2, NZ3, A3; 1991 F2
SEABOURNE, B (1) Leeds: 1970 NZ
SENIOR, K (2) Huddersfield: 1965 NZ; 1967 F
SHARROCK, J (4) Wigan: 1910 A2,NZ; 1911 A
SHAW, B (6) Hunslet: 1956 A2; **1960 F,A**; 1960 F;
  Leeds: 1961 F

SHAW, G (1) Widnes: 1980 NZ
SHAW, J (5) Halifax: **1960 F,A**; 1960 F; 1961 F;
  1962 NZ
SHELTON, G (7) Hunslet: 1964 F2; 1965 NZ3;
  1966 F2
SHOEBOTTOM, M (10+2) Leeds: **1968 A,nz**; 1969
  F; 1970 A2a,NZ; **1970 A2,F,NZ**; 1971 F
SHUGARS, F (1) Warrington: 1910 NZ
SILCOCK, N (12) Widnes: 1932 A2,NZ2; 1933 A3;
  1936 A3; 1937 A2
SILCOCK, N (3) Wigan: 1954 A3
SILCOCK, R (1) Wigan: 1908 A
SIMMS, B (1) Leeds: 1962 F
SKELHORNE, G (7) Warrington: 1920 A,NZ3;
  1921 A3
SKERRETT, K (8) Bradford N: 1989 NZ3; 1990 F2,
  NZ3
SKERRETT, T (10) Wakefield T: 1979 A2,NZ2;
  Hull: 1980 NZ2; 1981 F2; 1982 A2
SLOMAN, R (5) Oldham: 1928 A3,NZ2
SMALES, T (8) Huddersfield: 1962 F; 1963 F,A;
  1964 F2; Bradford N: 1965 NZ3
SMALL, P (1) Castleford: 1962 NZ
SMITH, A (6) Oldham: 1907 NZ3; 1908 A3
SMITH, A (10) Leeds: 1970 A2,NZ3; **1970 A2**; 1971
  F2; 1973 A
SMITH, F (9) Hunslet: 1910 A,NZ; 1911 A3; 1914
  A3,NZ
SMITH, G (3) York: 1963 A; 1964 F2
SMITH, H (2) Bradford N: 1926 NZ2
SMITH, M (10+1) Hull KR: 1979 NZ3; 1980 NZ2;
  1981 F2; 1982 A2; 1984 f,NZ
SMITH, P (1+5) Featherstone R: **1977 a2**; 1982 A;
  1983 f2; 1984 f
SMITH, S (11) Wakefield T: 1929 A; Leeds: A2;
  1932 A3,NZ3; 1933 A2
SMITH, S (4) Hunslet: **1954 A,NZ,F2**
SOUTHWARD, I (11) Workington T: 1958 A3,NZ;
  Oldham: 1959 F2,A2; 1960 F2; 1962 NZ
SPENCER, J (1) Salford: 1907 NZ
STACEY, J.C (1) Halifax: 1920 NZ
STEADMAN, G (1) Castleford: 1990 F
STEPHENS, G (5) Castleford: 1979 A2,NZ3
STEPHENSON, D (9+1) Wigan: 1982 A2; 1986 A;
  1987 F, P; Leeds: 1988 f, P, A2, NZ
STEPHENSON, M (5+1) Dewsbury: 1971 nz; 1972
  F; **1972 A2,F,NZ**
STEVENSON, J (19) Leeds: 1955 NZ3; 1956 A3;
  1957 F5; **1957 F,A,NZ**; 1958 F; York: 1959 A2;
  1960 F2
STOCKWELL, S (3) Leeds: 1920 A; 1921 A2
STONE, W (8) Hull: 1920 A3,NZ3; 1921 A2
STOPFORD, J (12) Swinton: 1961 F; 1963 F,A2;
  1964 F2; 1965 F,NZ2; 1966 F2,A
STOTT, J (1) St.Helens: 1947 NZ
STREET, H (4) Dewsbury: 1950 A3,NZ

SULLIVAN, C (17) Hull: 1967 F; **1968 A,F,NZ**;
1970 A; 1971 NZ3; 1972 F2; **1972 A2,F,NZ**;
1973 A3
SULLIVAN, J (25) Wigan: 1924 A3,NZ; 1926 NZ3;
1928 A3,NZ3; 1929 A3; 1932 A3,NZ3; 1933 A3
SULLIVAN, M (46) Huddersfield: **1954 F2,NZ,A**;
1955 NZ3; 1956 A3; 1957 F3; **1957 F,A,NZ**;
Wigan: 1957 F2; 1958 F,A3,NZ2; 1959 F2,A3;
1960 F3; **1960 F,NZ,A**; St.Helens: 1961 F,NZ2;
1962 F3,A3,NZ; York: 1963 A
SZYMALA, E (1+1) Barrow: 1981 fF

TAIT, A (8) Widnes: 1989 F2, NZ2; 1990 F2, P2
TAYLOR, H (3) Hull: 1907 NZ3
TAYLOR, R (2) Hull: 1921 A; 1926 NZ
TEMBEY, J (2) St.Helens: 1963 A; 1964 F
TERRY, A (11) St.Helens: 1958 A2; 1959 F2,A3;
1960 F; 1961 F,NZ; Leeds: 1962 F
THOMAS, A (4) Leeds: 1926 NZ2; 1929 A2
THOMAS, G (1) Warrington: 1907 NZ
THOMAS, G (9) Wigan: 1914 A; Huddersfield: 1920
A3,NZ2; 1921 A3
THOMAS, J (8) Wigan: 1907 NZ; 1908 A3; 1910
A2,NZ; 1911 A
THOMAS, L (1) Oldham: 1947 NZ
THOMAS, P (1) Leeds: 1907 NZ
THOMPSON, C (2) Hunslet: 1951 NZ2
THOMPSON, J (12) Leeds: 1924 A,NZ2; 1928
A,NZ; 1929 A; 1932 A3,NZ3
THOMPSON, J (20+1) Featherstone R: 1970
A2,NZ2; **1970 A2,F,NZ**; 1971 Ff; 1974 A3,NZ3;
1977 F,NZ,A2; Bradford N: 1978 A
THORLEY, J (4) Halifax: **1954 F2,NZ,A**
TOOHEY, E (3) Barrow: 1952 A3
TOPLISS, D (4) Wakefield T: 1973 A2; 1979 A;
Hull: 1982 A
TRAILL, K (8) Bradford N: 1950 NZ2; 1951 NZ;
1952 A3; 1954 A,NZ
TROUP, L A (2) Barrow: 1936 NZ2
TURNBULL, A (1) Leeds: 1951 NZ
TURNER, D (24) Oldham: 1956 A2; 1957 F5; **1957
F,A,NZ**; 1958 F; Wakefield: 1959 A; 1960 F3;
1960 NZ,A; 1961 F,NZ; 1962 A2,NZ2,F
TYSON, B (3) Hull KR: 1963 A; 1965 F; 1967 F
TYSON, G (4) Oldham: 1907 NZ; 1908 A3

VALENTINE, D (15) Huddersfield: 1948 A3; 1951
NZ; 1952 A2; 1954 A3,NZ2; **1954 F2,NZ,A**
VALENTINE, R (1) Huddersfield: 1967 A
VINES, D (3) Wakefield T: 1959 F2,A

WADDELL, H (5) Oldham: 1988 F2, A, NZ; Leeds:
1989 F
WAGSTAFF, H (12) Huddersfield: 1911 A2; 1914
A3,NZ; 1920 A2,NZ2; 1921 A2
WALKER, A (1) Whitehaven: 1980 NZ

WALLACE, J (1) St.Helens Recs: 1926 NZ
WALSH, Joe (1) Leigh: 1971 NZ
WALSH, John (4+1) St.Helens: 1972 f; **1972
A2,F,NZ**
WALTON, D (1) Castleford: 1965 F
WANE, S (2) Wigan: 1985 F; 1986 F
WARD, D (12) Leeds: **1977 F,NZ,A**; 1978 A; 1979
A3,NZ3;1981 F; 1982 A
WARD, Edward (3) Wigan: 1946 A2; 1947 NZ
WARD, Ernest (20) Bradford N: 1946 A3,NZ; 1947
NZ2; 1948 A3; 1950 A3,NZ2; 1951 NZ3;
1952 A3
WARD, J (4) Castleford: 1963 A; 1964 F2; Salford:
1970 NZ
WARD, K (14+2) Castleford: 1984 F; 1986 A3; 1987
P; 1988 F2, P, A3, NZ; 1989 F2; St. Helens:
1990 a2
WARD, W (1) Leeds: 1910 A
WARLOW, J (6+1) St.Helens: 1964 F; **1968 f,NZ**;
1968 F; Widnes: 1971 F2,NZ
WARWICK, S (2) Salford: 1907 NZ2
WATKINS, D (2+4) Salford: 1971 f,NZ; 1973 a;
1974 f2,A
WATKINS, W (7) Salford: 1933 A; 1936 A2,NZ2;
1937 A2
WATKINSON, D (12+1) Hull KR: 1979 a; 1980
NZ; 1981 F; 1984 F; 1985 F, NZ3; 1986 F2, A3
WATSON, C (29+1) St.Helens: 1963 A2; 1966
F2,A3,NZ2; 1967 F,A3; 1968 F2; **1968 A,F,nz**;
1969 F; 1970 A3,NZ3; **1970 A2,F,NZ**; 1971 F
WATTS, B (5) York: **1954 F2,NZ,A**; 1955 NZ
WEBSTER, F (3) Leeds: 1910 A2,NZ
WHITCOMBE, F (2) Bradford N: 1946 A2
WHITE, L (7) Hunslet: 1932 A3,NZ2; 1933 A2
WHITE, L (6) York: 1946 A3,NZ; Wigan: 1947 NZ2
WHITE, T (1) Oldham: 1907 NZ
WHITEHEAD, D (3) Warrington: 1971 F2,NZ
WHITELEY, J (15) Hull: **1957 A**; 1958 A3,NZ; 1959
F2,A2; 1960 F; **1960 NZ,F**; 1961 NZ2; 1962 F
WILKINSON, J (13) Halifax: 1954 A,NZ2; 1955
NZ3; Wakefield T: 1959 A; 1960 F2; **1960
NZ,F,A**; 1962 NZ
WILLIAMS, F (2) Halifax: 1914 A2
WILLIAMS, P (1+1) Salford: 1989 fF
WILLIAMS, R (12) Leeds: 1948 A2; 1950 A2,NZ2;
1951 NZ3; Hunslet: 1954 A2,NZ
WILLIAMS, W (2) Salford: 1929 A; 1932 A
WILLICOMBE, D (3) Halifax: 1974 F; Wigan: F,NZ
WILSON, G (3) Workington T: 1951 NZ3
WILSON, H (3) Hunslet: 1907 NZ3
WINSLADE, C (1) Oldham: 1959 F
WINSTANLEY, W (5) Leigh: 1910 A,NZ; Wigan:
1911 A3
WOOD, A (4) Oldham: 1911 A2; 1914 A,NZ
WOODS, H (6) Liverpool S: 1936 A3,NZ2; Leeds:
1937 A
WOODS, J (1) Barrow: 1933 A

WOODS, J (7 + 4) Leigh: 1979 A3,nz; 1980 NZ; 1981
 F2; 1982 Aa; 1983 f; Warrington: 1987 p
WOODS, T (2) Rochdale H: 1911 A2
WORRALL, M (3) Oldham: 1984 F, A2
WRIGHT, D (+1) Widnes: 1988 a
WRIGHT, J (1) Swinton: 1932 NZ
WRIGHT, S (7) Widnes: **1977 F,NZ,A2**; 1978 A3
WRIGLESWORTH, G (5) Leeds: 1965 NZ; 1966
 A2,NZ2

YOUNG, C (5) Hull KR: 1967 A3; 1968 F2
YOUNG, F (1) Leeds: 1908 A
YOUNG, H (1) Huddersfield: 1929 A

Mick Worrall, three caps in 1984.

GREAT BRITAIN TOUR SUMMARIES

1910	P	W	D	L	T	For G	Pts	T	Against G	Pts
In Australia	14	9	1	4	76	56	340	51	47	247
In New Zealand	4	4	0	0	43	29	187	11	7	47
TOTAL	18	13	1	4	119	85	527	62	54	294

1914	P	W	D	L	T	G	Pts	T	G	Pts
In Australia	12	9	0	3	77	55	341	24	31	134
In New Zealand	6	6	0	0	46	28	194	12	13	62
TOTAL	18	15	0	3	123	83	535	36	44	196

1920	P	W	D	L	T	G	Pts	T	G	Pts
In Australia	15	12	0	3	83	64	377	48	42	228
In New Zealand	10	9	0	1	89	47	361	24	16	104
TOTAL	25	21	0	4	172	111	738	72	58	332

1924	P	W	D	L	T	G	Pts	T	G	Pts
In Australia	18	14	0	4	104	77	466	56	45	258
In New Zealand	9	7	0	2	64	40	272	25	21	117
TOTAL	27	21	0	6	168	117	738	81	66	375

1928	P	W	D	L	T	G	Pts	T	G	Pts
In Australia	16	11	1	4	67	60	321	43	45	219
In New Zealand	8	7	0	1	55	36	237	16	12	72
TOTAL	24	18	1	5	122	96	558	59	57	291

1932	P	W	D	L	T	G	Pts	T	G	Pts
In Australia	18	15	1	2	105	84	483	32	38	172
In New Zealand	8	8	0	0	65	52	299	17	18	87
TOTAL	26	23	1	2	170	136	782	49	56	259

1936

	P	W	D	L	T	G	Pts	T	G	Pts
In Australia	17	14	0	3	79	82	401	38	45	204
In New Zealand	8	8	0	0	52	27	210	8	16	56
TOTAL	25	22	0	3	131	109	611	46	61	260

1946

	P	W	D	L	T	G	Pts	T	G	Pts
In Australia	20	16	1	3	146	100	638	36	45	198
In New Zealand	7	5	0	2	35	20	145	12	21	78
TOTAL	27	21	1	5	181	120	783	48	66	276

1950

	P	W	D	L	T	G	Pts	T	G	Pts
In Australia	19	15	0	4	133	102	603	22	56	178
In New Zealand	6	4	0	2	37	25	161	16	20	88
TOTAL	25	19	0	6	170	127	764	38	76	266

1954

	P	W	D	L	For T	G	Pts	Against T	G	Pts
In Australia	*22	13	1	7	133	114	627	78	96	426
In New Zealand	10	8	0	2	60	56	292	14	32	106
TOTAL	*32	21	1	9	193	170	919	92	128	532

*One match abandoned. Scores included in points total.

1958

	P	W	D	L	T	G	Pts	T	G	Pts
In Australia	21	19	1	1	184	129	810	64	93	378
In New Zealand	9	8	0	1	88	61	386	18	27	108
TOTAL	30	27	1	2	272	190	1,196	82	120	486

1962

	P	W	D	L	T	G	Pts	T	G	Pts
In Australia	21	18	0	3	151	113	679	61	60	303
In New Zealand	9	6	0	3	73	50	319	35	28	161
TOTAL	30	24	0	6	224	163	998	96	88	464

1966

	P	W	D	L	T	G	Pts	T	G	Pts
In Australia	22	13	0	9	112	85	506	47	83	307
In New Zealand	8	8	0	0	57	47	265	10	24	78
TOTAL	30	21	0	9	169	132	771	57	107	385

1970

	P	W	D	L	T	G	Pts	T	G	Pts
In Australia	17	15	1	1	104	92	496	27	66	213
In New Zealand	7	7	0	0	61	37	257	9	24	75
TOTAL	24	22	1	1	165	129	753	36	90	288

1974

	P	W	D	L	T	G	DG	Pts	T	G	DG	Pts
In Australia	20	15	0	5	104	93	2	500	38	59	3	235
In New Zealand	8	6	0	2	37	32	0	175	8	27	0	78
TOTAL	28	21	0	7	141	125	2	675	46	86	3	313

1979

	P	W	D	L	T	G	DG	Pts	T	G	Pts
In Australia	18	13	1	4	66	73	3	347	39	68	253
In New Zealand	9	8	0	1	48	34	0	212	15	12	69
TOTAL	27	21	1	5	114	107	3	559	54	80	332

1984	P	W	D	L	T	G	DG	Pts	T	G	DG	Pts
In Australia	15	11	0	4	70	59	1	399	40	46	2	254
In New Zealand	8	4	0	4	32	25	1	179	21	21	0	126
In Papua New Guinea	1	1	0	0	7	5	0	38	4	2	0	20
TOTAL	24	16	0	8	109	89	2	616	65	69	2	400

1988	P	W	D	L	T	G	DG	Pts	T	G	DG	Pts
In Papua New Guinea	2	2	0	0	13	13	0	78	7	6	0	40
In Australia	13	8	0	5	59	47	0	330	42	36	1	241
In New Zealand	3	1	0	2	8	8	0	48	10	10	0	60
TOTAL	18	11	0	7	80	68	0	456	59	52	1	341

1990	P	W	D	L	T	G	DG	Pts	T	G	DG	Pts
In Papua New Guinea	5	4	0	1	31	24	0	172	7	15	2	60
In New Zealand	10	6	0	4	30	28	3	179	24	32	1	161
TOTAL	15	10	0	5	61	52	3	351	31	47	3	221

GREAT BRITAIN TOUR SQUADS TO AUSTRALIA AND NEW ZEALAND
Captains in bold

1910 Tour

J. Lomas (Salford)
A. Avery (Oldham)
J. Bartholomew (Huddersfield)
W. Batten (Hunslet)
F. Boylen (Hull)
E. Curzon (Salford)
J. Davies (Huddersfield)
F. Farrar (Hunslet)
T. Helm (Oldham)
B. Jenkins (Wigan)
T. Jenkins (Ebbw Vale)
W. Jukes (Hunslet)
H. Kershaw (Wakefield T.)
J. Leytham (Wigan)
T. Newbould (Wakefield T.)
R. Ramsdale (Wigan)
J. Riley (Halifax)
G. Ruddick (Broughton R.)
J. Sharrock (Wigan)
F. Shugars (Warrington)
F. Smith (Hunslet)
J. Thomas (Wigan)
W. Ward (Leeds)
F. Webster (Leeds)
W. Winstanley (Leigh)
F. Young (Leeds)

Managers: J. Clifford
(Huddersfield) and J.
Houghton (St. Helens)

1914 Tour

H. Wagstaff (Huddersfield)
J. Chilcott (Huddersfield)
J. Clampitt (Broughton R.)
D. Clark (Huddersfield)
A. Coldrick (Wigan)
W. Davies (Leeds)
A. Francis (Hull)
J. Guerin (Hunslet)
W. Hall (Oldham)
D. Holland (Oldham)
J. Jarman (Leeds)
B. Jenkins (Wigan)
A. Johnson (Widnes)
F. Longstaff (Huddersfield)
S. Moorhouse (Huddersfield)
J. O'Garra (Widnes)
W. Prosser (Halifax)
R. Ramsdale (Wigan)
J. Robinson (Rochdale H.)
J. Rogers (Huddersfield)
W. Roman (Rochdale H.)
J. Smales (Hunslet)
F. Smith (Hunslet)
G. Thomas (Wigan)
F. Williams (Halifax)
A. Wood (Oldham)

Managers: J. Clifford
(Huddersfield) and J.
Houghton (St. Helens)

1920 Tour

H. Wagstaff (Huddersfield)
J. Bacon (Leeds)
J. Bowers (Rochdale H.)
J. Cartwright (Leigh)
D. Clark (Huddersfield)
W. Cunliffe (Warrington)
E. Davies (Oldham)
J. Doyle (Barrow)
F. Gallagher (Dewsbury)
B. Gronow (Huddersfield)
H. Hilton (Oldham)
D. Hurcombe (Wigan)
A. Johnson (Widnes)
E. Jones (Rochdale H.)
R. Lloyd (Halifax)
A. Milnes (Halifax)
J. Parkin (Wakefield T.)
G. Rees (Leeds)
W. Reid (Widnes)
J. Rogers (Huddersfield)
G. Skelhorne (Warrington)
J. Stacey (Halifax)
S. Stockwell (Leeds)
W. Stone (Hull)
G. Thomas (Huddersfield)
A. Wood (Oldham)

Managers: S. Foster (Halifax)
and J. Wilson (Hull K.R.)

337

1924 Tour

J. Parkin (Wakefield T.)
J. Bacon (Leeds)
J. Bennett (Rochdale H.)
W. Bentham (Broughton R.)
H. Bowman (Hull)
A. Brough (Oldham)
W. Burgess (Barrow)
C. Carr (Barrow)
W. Cunliffe (Warrington)
J. Darwell (Leigh)
F. Evans (Swinton)
F. Gallagher (Batley)
B. Gronow (Huddersfield)
T. Howley (Wigan)
D. Hurcombe (Wigan)
E. Knapman (Oldham)
W. Mooney (Leigh)
C. Pollard (Wakefield T.)
J. Price (Wigan)
D. Rees (Halifax)
J. Ring (Wigan)
S. Rix (Oldham)
R. Sloman (Oldham)
J. Sullivan (Wigan)
J. Thompson (Leeds)
S. Whitty (Hull)

Managers: J.H. Dannatt (Hull) and E. Osborne (Warrington)

1928 Tour

J. Parkin (Wakefield T.)
T. Askin (Featherstone R.)
N. Bentham (Wigan Highfield)
F. Bowen (St. Helens Recs)
H. Bowman (Hull)
J. Brough (Leeds)
W. Burgess (Barrow)
O. Dolan (St. Helens Recs)
A. Ellaby (St. Helens)
B. Evans (Swinton)
J. Evans (Swinton)
L. Fairclough (St. Helens)
A. Fildes (St. Helens Recs)
A. Frodsham (St. Helens)
W. Gowers (Rochdale H.)
T. Gwynne (Hull)
B. Halfpenny (St. Helens)
W. Horton (Wakefield T.)
J. Oliver (Batley)
W. Rees (Swinton)
M. Rosser (Leeds)
R. Sloman (Oldham)
J. Sullivan (Wigan)
J. Thompson (Leeds)
W. Williams (Salford)
H. Young (Bradford N.)

Managers: G. Hutchins (Oldham) and E. Osborne (Warrington)

1932 Tour

J. Sullivan (Wigan)
A. Atkinson (Castleford)
L. Adams (Leeds)
S. Brogden (Huddersfield)
F. Butters (Swinton)
I. Davies (Halifax)
W. Dingsdale (Warrington)
A. Ellaby (St. Helens)
B. Evans (Swinton)
J. Feetham (Salford)
N. Fender (York)
A. Fildes (St. Helens)
M. Hodgson (Swinton)
W. Horton (Wakefield T.)
B. Hudson (Salford)
J. Lowe (Leeds)
E. Pollard (Wakefield T.)
A. Risman (Salford)
G. Robinson (Wakefield T.)
N. Silcock (Widnes)
S. Smith (Leeds)
J. Thompson (Leeds)
L. White (Hunslet)
W. Williams (Salford)
J. Woods (Barrow)
J. Wright (Swinton)

Managers: R. Anderton (Warrington) and G. Hutchins (Oldham)

1936 Tour

J. Brough (Leeds)
J. Arkwright (Warrington)
T. Armitt (Swinton)
A. Atkinson (Castleford)
W. Belshaw (Liverpool S.)
H. Beverley (Hunslet)
S. Brogden (Leeds)
E. Davies (Wigan)
A. Edwards (Salford)
H. Ellerington (Hull)
G. Exley (Wakefield T.)
H. Field (York)
F. Harris (Leeds)
M. Hodgson (Swinton)

B. Hudson (Salford)
E. Jenkins (Salford)
H. Jones (Keighley)
T. McCue (Widnes)
J. Miller (Warrington)
J. Morley (Wigan)
A. Risman (Salford)
N. Silcock (Widnes)
S. Smith (Leeds)
L. Troup (Barrow)
W. Watkins (Salford)
H. Woods (Liverpool S.)

Managers: R. Anderton (Warrington) and W. Popplewell (Bramley)

1946 Tour

A. Risman (Salford)
A. Bassett (Halifax)
E. Batten (Bradford N.)
G. Curran (Salford)
W. Davies (Bradford N.)
J. Egan (Wigan)
T. Foster (Bradford N.)
K. Gee (Wigan)
W. Horne (Barrow)
F. Hughes (Workington T.)
D. Jenkins (Leeds)
A. Johnson (Warrington)

J. Jones (Barrow)
J. Kitching (Bradford N.)
B. Knowelden (Barrow)
J. Lewthwaite (Barrow)
T. McCue (Widnes)
H. Murphy (Wakefield T.)
R. Nicholson (Huddersfield)
I. Owens (Leeds)
D. Phillips (Oldham)
M. Ryan (Wigan)
Edward Ward (Wigan)
Ernest Ward (Bradford N.)
F. Whitcombe (Bradford N.)
L. White (York)

Managers: W. Popplewell
(Bramley) and W. Gabbatt
(Barrow)

1950 Tour

E. Ward (Bradford N.)
E. Ashcroft (Wigan)
T. Bradshaw (Wigan)
J. Cunliffe (Wigan)
T. Danby (Salford)
A. Daniels (Halifax)
J. Egan (Wigan)
J. Featherstone (Warrington)
K. Gee (Wigan)
E. Gwyther (Belle Vue R.)
F. Higgins (Widnes)
J. Hilton (Wigan)
W. Horne (Barrow)
J. Ledgard (Leigh)
H. Murphy (Wakefield T.)
D. Naughton (Widnes)
F. Osmond (Swinton)
A. Pepperell (Workington T.)
D. Phillips (Belle Vue R.)
R. Pollard (Dewsbury)
G. Ratcliffe (Wigan)
M. Ryan (Wigan)
R. Ryan (Warrington)
H. Street (Dewsbury)
K. Traill (Bradford N.)
R. Williams (Leeds)

Managers: G. Oldroyd
(Dewsbury) and T. Spedding
(Belle Vue R.)

1954 Tour

R. Williams (Hunslet)
E. Ashcroft (Wigan)
W. Boston (Wigan)
J. Bowden (Huddersfield)
B. Briggs (Huddersfield)
A. Burnell (Hunslet)
E. Cahill (Rochdale H.)
F. Castle (Barrow)
J. Cunliffe (Wigan)
D. Greenall (St. Helens)
G. Gunney (Hunslet)
T. Harris (Hull)
G. Helme (Warrington)
J. Henderson (Workington T.)
P. Jackson (Barrow)
B. L. Jones (Leeds)
T. McKinney (Salford)
T. O'Grady (Oldham)
C. Pawsey (Leigh)
A. Prescott (St. Helens)
R. Price (Warrington)
N. Silcock (Wigan)
K. Traill (Bradford N.)
A. Turnbull (Leeds)
D. Valentine (Huddersfield)
J. Wilkinson (Halifax)

Managers: T. Hesketh
(Wigan) and H. Rawson
(Hunslet)

1958 Tour

A. Prescott (St. Helens)
A. Ackerley (Halifax)
H. Archer (Workington T.)
E. Ashton (Wigan)
D. Bolton (Wigan)
F. Carlton (St. Helens)
J. Challinor (Warrington)
A. Davies (Oldham)
B. Edgar (Workington T.)
E. Fraser (Warrington)
D. Goodwin (Barrow)
T. Harris (Hull)
R. Huddart (Whitehaven)
K. Jackson (Oldham)
P. Jackson (Barrow)
V. Karalius (St. Helens)

M. Martyn (Leigh)
B. McTigue (Wigan)
G. Moses (St. Helens)
A. Murphy (St. Helens)
F. Pitchford (Oldham)
I. Southward (Workington T.)
M. Sullivan (Wigan)
A. Terry (St. Helens)
J. Whiteley (Hull)
W. Wookey (Workington T.)

Managers: B. Manson
(Swinton) and T. Mitchell
(Workington T.)
Coach: J. Brough
(Workington T.)

1962 Tour

E. Ashton (Wigan)
D. Bolton (Wigan)
W. Boston (Wigan)
F. Carlton (Wigan)
G. Cooper (Featherstone R.)
B. Edgar (Workington T.)
R. Evans (Wigan)
N. Fox (Wakefield T.)
D. Fox (Featherstone R.)
E. Fraser (Warrington)
L. Gilfedder (Warrington)
N. Herbert (Workington T.)
R. Huddart (St. Helens)
B. McTigue (Wigan)
A. Murphy (St. Helens)
K. Noble (Huddersfield)
H. Poynton (Wakefield T.)
G. Round (Wakefield T.)
W. Sayer (Wigan)
J. Shaw (Halifax)
P. Small (Castleford)
I. Southward (Workington T.)
M. Sullivan (St. Helens)
J. Taylor (Hull K.R.)
D. Turner (Wakefield T.)
J. Wilkinson (Wakefield T.)

Managers: S. Hadfield
(Wakefield T.) and A. Walker
(Rochdale H.)
Coach: C. Hutton (Hull K.R.)

1966 Tour

H. Poole (Leeds)
W. Aspinall (Warrington)
T. Bishop (St. Helens)
I. Brooke (Bradford N.)
W. Bryant (Castleford)
A. Buckley (Swinton)
W. Burgess (Barrow)
C. Clarke (Wigan)
G. Crewdson (Keighley)
C. Dooler (Featherstone R.)
B. Edgar (Workington T.)
P. Flanagan (Hull K.R.)
T. Fogerty (Halifax)
K. Gowers (Swinton)
A. Hardisty (Castleford)
B. Jones (Wakefield T.)
A. Keegan (Hull)
J. Mantle (St. Helens)
F. Myler (Widnes)
W. Ramsey (Hunslet)
K. Roberts (Halifax)
D. Robinson (Swinton)
G. Shelton (Hunslet)
J. Stopford (Swinton)
C. Watson (St. Helens)
G. Wriglesworth (Leeds)

Managers: W. Spaven (Hull K.R.) and J. Errock (Oldham)

1970 Tour

F. Myler (St. Helens)
J. Atkinson (Leeds)
D. Chisnall (Leigh)
R. Dutton (Widnes)
D. Edwards (Castleford)
A. Fisher (Bradford N.)
P. Flanagan (Hull K.R.)
A. Hardisty (Castleford)
D. Hartley (Castleford)
K. Hepworth (Castleford)
C. Hesketh (Salford)
S. Hynes (Leeds)
R. Irving (Oldham)
D. Laughton (Wigan)
P. Lowe (Hull K.R.)
R. Millward (Hull K.R.)
T. Price (Bradford N.)

M. Reilly (Castleford)
D. Robinson (Wigan)
B. Seabourne (Leeds)
M. Shoebottom (Leeds)
A. Smith (Leeds)
C. Sullivan (Hull)
J. Thompson (Featherstone R.)
J. Ward (Salford)
C. Watson (St. Helens)

Manager: J. Harding (Leigh)
Coach: J. Whiteley (Hull)

1974 Tour

C. Hesketh (Salford)
K. Ashcroft (Warrington)
J. Atkinson (Leeds)
A. Bates (Dewsbury)
J. Bates (Dewsbury)
J. Bevan (Warrington)
J. Bridges (Featherstone R.)
J. Butler (Rochdale H.)
P. Charlton (Salford)
E. Chisnall (St. Helens)
T. Clawson (Oldham)
C. Dixon (Salford)
L. Dyl (Leeds)
D. Eckersley (St. Helens)
K. Gill (Salford)
J. Gray (Wigan)
J. Mills (Widnes)
R. Millward (Hull K.R.)
S. Nash (Featherstone R.)
G. Nicholls (St. Helens)
S. Norton (Castleford)
D. Redfearn (Bradford N.)
P. Rose (Hull K.R.)
J. Thompson (Featherstone R.)
D. Watkins (Salford)
D. Willicombe (Wigan)

Replacements during tour
W. Ramsey (Bradford N.) for J. Bates; M. Richards (Salford) for Atkinson

Manager: R. Parker (Blackpool B.)
Coach: J. Challinor (St. Helens)

1979 Tour

D. Laughton (Widnes)
M. Adams (Widnes)
D. Barends (Bradford N.)
L. Casey (Bradford N.)
S. Evans (Featherstone R.)
P. Glynn (St. Helens)
J. Grayshon (Bradford N.)
P. Hogan (Hull K.R.)
J. Holmes (Leeds)
E. Hughes (Widnes)
M. James (St. Helens)
J. Joyner (Castleford)
G. Liptrot (St. Helens)
B. Lockwood (Hull K.R.)
T. Martyn (Warrington)
R. Mathias (St. Helens)
J. Mills (Widnes)
R. Millward (Hull K.R.)
K. Mumby (Bradford N.)
S. Nash (Salford)
G. Nicholls (St. Helens)
S. Norton (Hull)
A. Redfearn (Bradford N.)
T. Skerrett (Wakefield T.)
M. Smith (Hull K.R.)
G. Stephens (Castleford)
C. Stone (Hull)
D. Ward (Leeds)
D. Watkinson (Hull K.R.)
J. Woods (Leigh)

Replacements during tour
J. Burke (Wakefield T.) for Mills; G. Fairbairn (Wigan) for Martyn; D. Topliss (Wakefield T.) for Millward

Managers: H. Womersley (Bradford N.) and R. Gemmell (Hull)
Coach E. Ashton (St. Helens)

1984 Tour*

B. Noble (Bradford N.)
M. Adams (Widnes)
R. Ashton (Oldham)
K. Beardmore (Castleford)
M. Burke (Widnes)
C. Burton (Hull K.R.)
B. Case (Wigan)
G. Clark (Hull K.R.)
L. Crooks (Hull)
S. Donlan (Leigh)
D. Drummond (Leigh)
R. Duane (Warrington)
T. Flanagan (Oldham)
D. Foy (Oldham)
A. Goodway (Oldham)
A. Gregory (Widnes)
E. Hanley (Bradford N.)
D. Hobbs (Featherstone R.)
N. Holding (St. Helens)
J. Joyner (Castleford)
J. Lydon (Widnes)
K. Mumby (Bradford N.)
A. Myler (Widnes)
M. O'Neill (Widnes)
H. Pinner (St. Helens)
W. Proctor (Hull)
Keith Rayne (Leeds)
G. Schofield (Hull)
M. Smith (Hull K.R.)
M. Worrall (Oldham)

Replacement during tour
J. Basnett (Widnes) for Duane

Managers: R. Gemmell (Hull)
and R. Davis (RLHQ)
Coach: Frank Myler (Oldham)

*One match in Papua New
Guinea

1988 Tour*

E. Hanley (Wigan)
K. Beardmore (Castleford)
B. Case (Wigan)
L. Crooks (Leeds)
P. Dixon (Halifax)
S. Edwards (Wigan)
K. Fairbank (Bradford N.)
M. Ford (Oldham)
P. Ford (Bradford N.)
C. Gibson (Leeds)
H. Gill (Wigan)
A. Gregory (Wigan)
M. Gregory (Warrington)
P. Groves (St. Helens)
R. Haggerty (St. Helens)
D. Hulme (Widnes)
P. Loughlin (St. Helens)
P. Medley (Leeds)
M. Offiah (Widnes)
A. Platt (St. Helens)
R. Powell (Leeds)
G. Schofield (Leeds)
D. Stephenson (Leeds)
H. Waddell (Oldham)
K. Ward (Castleford)
I. Wilkinson (Halifax)

Replacements during tour
D. Wright (Widnes) for
Edwards; A. Currier (Widnes)
and P. Hulme (Widnes) for
Schofield and Medley; R.
Eyres (Widnes) and J. Joyner
(Castleford) for Crooks, Dixon
and Platt

Managers: L. Bettinson
(Salford) and D. Howes
(RLHQ)
Coach: M. Reilly

*Including Papua New Guinea

1990 Tour*

M. Gregory (Warrington)
D. Betts (Wigan)
C. Bibb (Featherstone R.)
D. Bishop (Hull K.R.)
P. Clarke (Wigan)
J. Davies (Widnes)
M. Dermott (Wigan)
P. Dixon (Leeds)
P. Eastwood (Hull)
K. England (Castleford)
K. Fairbank (Bradford N.)
D. Fox (Featherstone R.)
C. Gibson (Leeds)
R. Goulding (Wigan)
S. Irwin (Castleford)
L. Jackson (Hull)
I. Lucas (Wigan)
J. Lydon (Wigan)
M. Offiah (Widnes)
D. Powell (Sheffield E.)
R. Powell (Leeds)
G. Price (Wakefield T.)
G. Schofield (Leeds)
R. Simpson (Bradford N.)
K. Skerrett (Bradford N.)
I. Smales (Featherstone R.)
G. Steadman (Castleford)
A. Sullivan (Hull K.R.)
A. Tait (Widnes)

Replacements during tour
J. Devereux (Widnes) for
Sullivan; D. Lyon
(Warrington) for Tait.

Manager: M. Lindsay (Wigan)
Coach: M. Reilly

*Papua New Guinea and
New Zealand only

ALL TIME TOUR RECORDS

IN AUSTRALIA
Highest score: 101-0 v. South Australia in 1914

Biggest defeat: 42-6 v. New South Wales in 1920 (Also *widest margin*)

Fewest defeats: 1 (and 1 draw) from 21 matches in 1958 and from 17 matches in 1970

Most defeats: 9 from 22 matches in 1966

Biggest attendances: 70,419 v. New South Wales (Sydney) in 1950

IN NEW ZEALAND
Highest score: 81-14 v. Bay of Plenty in 1962

Widest margin win: 72-3 v. Buller in 1928
72-3 v. North Island in 1958

Biggest defeat: 46-13 v. Auckland in 1962 (Also *widest margin*)

Fewest defeats: The tourists have won all their matches in the following years: 1910 (4 matches), 1914 (6), 1932 (8), 1936 (8), 1966 (8), 1970 (7).

Most defeats: 4 from 8 matches in 1984
4 from 10 matches in 1990

Biggest attendance: 35,000 v. Auckland in 1920

PLAYERS' FULL TOUR RECORDS
Most full appearances: 24 by Dick Huddart in 1958

Most tries: 38 by Mick Sullivan in 1958

Most goals and points: 127g, 278 pts by Lewis Jones in 1954

Most full tours: 3 Jonathan Parkin (1920, 1924, 1928)
Jim Sullivan (1924, 1928, 1932)
Joe Thompson (1924, 1928, 1932)
Augustus Risman (1932, 1936, 1946)
Brian Edgar (1958, 1962, 1966)
Roger Millward (1970, 1974, 1979)
● John Joyner (1979, 1984, 1988 as replacement)
● Garry Schofield (Full tours in 1984 and 1988, PNG and New Zealand only in 1990)

Biggest club representation: 8 by Wigan in 1950 — Ernie Ashcroft, Tommy Bradshaw, Jack Cunliffe, Joe Egan, Ken Gee, Jack Hilton, Gordon Ratcliffe, Martin Ryan

Brothers touring together: Bryn and Jack Evans (1928), Don and Neil Fox (1962), Alan and John Bates (1974), David and Paul Hulme (1988, Paul as replacement)

GREAT BRITAIN IN THE WORLD CUP

A — Australia, Fr — France, GB — Great Britain, NZ — New Zealand, PNG — Papua New Guinea

1954 in France   *Winners:* Great Britain

30 Oct.	Fr	22	NZ	13	Paris	13,240
31 Oct.	GB	28	A	13	Lyons	10,250
7 Nov.	GB	13	Fr	13	Toulouse	37,471
7 Nov.	A	34	NZ	15	Marseilles	20,000
11 Nov.	GB	26	NZ	6	Bordeaux	14,000
11 Nov.	A	5	Fr	15	Nantes	13,000

Play off

| 13 Nov. | GB | 16 | Fr | 12 | Paris | 30,368 |

Final Table

	P.	W.	D.	L.	F.	A.	Pts.
Great Britain	3	2	1	0	67	32	5
France	3	2	1	0	50	31	5
Australia	3	1	0	2	52	58	2
New Zealand	3	0	0	3	34	82	0

1957 in Australia   *Winners:* Australia

15 June	GB	23	Fr	5	Sydney	50,007
15 June	A	25	NZ	5	Brisbane	29,636
17 June	GB	6	A	31	Sydney	57,955
17 June	NZ	10	Fr	14	Brisbane	28,000
22 June	A	26	Fr	9	Sydney	35,158
25 June	GB	21	NZ	29	Sydney	14,263

Final Table

	P.	W.	D.	L.	F.	A.	Pts.
Australia	3	3	0	0	82	20	6
Great Britain	3	1	0	2	50	65	2
New Zealand	3	1	0	2	44	60	2
France	3	1	0	2	28	59	2

1960 in England   *Winners:* Great Britain

24 Sept.	GB	23	NZ	8	Bradford	20,577
24 Sept.	A	13	Fr	12	Wigan	20,278
1 Oct.	A	21	NZ	15	Leeds	10,773
1 Oct.	GB	33	Fr	7	Swinton	22,923
8 Oct.	A	3	GB	10	Bradford	32,773
8 Oct.	NZ	9	Fr	0	Wigan	2,876

Final Table

	P.	W.	D.	L.	F.	A.	Pts.
Great Britain	3	3	0	0	66	18	6
Australia	3	2	0	1	37	37	4
New Zealand	3	1	0	2	32	44	2
France	3	0	0	3	19	55	0

1968 in Australia   *Winners:* Australia
and New Zealand

25 May	A	25	GB	10	Sydney	62,256
25 May	Fr	15	NZ	10	Auckland	18,000
1 June	A	31	NZ	12	Brisbane	23,608
2 June	Fr	7	GB	2	Auckland	15,760
8 June	A	37	Fr	4	Brisbane	32,600
8 June	GB	38	NZ	14	Sydney	14,105

Final Table

	P.	W.	D.	L.	F.	A.	Pts.
Australia	3	3	0	0	93	26	6
France	3	2	0	1	26	49	4
Great Britain	3	1	0	2	50	46	2
New Zealand	3	0	0	3	36	84	0

Play off final

10 June	A	20	Fr	2	Sydney	54,290

Bev Risman, captain of the Great Britain 1968 World Cup squad in Australia and New Zealand.

1970 in England   *Winners:* Australia

21 Oct.	A	47	NZ	11	Wigan	9,586
24 Oct.	GB	11	A	4	Leeds	15,084
25 Oct.	NZ	16	Fr	15	Hull	3,824
28 Oct.	GB	6	Fr	0	Castleford	8,958
31 Oct.	GB	27	NZ	17	Swinton	5,609
1 Nov.	Fr	17	A	15	Bradford	6,215

Final Table

	P.	W.	D.	L.	F.	A.	Pts.
Great Britain	3	3	0	0	44	21	6
Australia	3	1	0	2	66	39	2
France	3	1	0	2	32	37	2
New Zealand	3	1	0	2	44	89	2

Play off final

7 Nov.	A	12	GB	7	Leeds	18,776

1972 in France   *Winners:* Great Britain

28 Oct.	Fr	20	NZ	9	Marseilles	20,748
29 Oct.	GB	27	A	21	Perpignan	6,324
1 Nov.	A	9	NZ	5	Paris	8,000
1 Nov.	GB	13	Fr	4	Grenoble	5,321
4 Nov.	GB	53	NZ	19	Pau	7,500
5 Nov.	A	31	Fr	9	Toulouse	10,332

Final Table

	P.	W.	D.	L.	F.	A.	Pts.
Great Britain	3	3	0	0	93	44	6
Australia	3	2	0	1	61	41	4
France	3	1	0	2	33	53	2
New Zealand	3	0	0	3	33	82	0

Play off final

11 Nov.	GB	10	A	10	Lyons	4,231

No further score after extra-time so Great Britain took the championship because they had scored the greatest number of points in the qualifying League table.

1977 in Australia   *Winners:* Australia
and New Zealand

29 May	A	27	NZ	12	Auckland	18,000
5 June	GB	23	Fr	4	Auckland	10,000
11 June	A	21	Fr	9	Sydney	13,231
12 June	GB	30	NZ	12	C'church	7,000
18 June	A	19	GB	5	Brisbane	27,000
19 June	NZ	28	Fr	20	Auckland	8,000

Final Table	P.	W.	D.	L.	F.	A.	Pts.
Australia	3	3	0	0	67	26	6
Great Britain	3	2	0	1	58	35	4
New Zealand	3	1	0	2	52	77	2
France	3	0	0	3	33	72	0

Play off final

25 June	A	13 GB	12 Sydney		24,457

1985-88 Series   *Winners:* Australia

1985

7 July	NZ	18 A	0 Auckland	19,000
9 Nov.	GB	6 NZ	6 Leeds	22,209
7 Dec.	Fr	0 NZ	22 Perpignan	5,000

1986

16 Feb.	Fr	10 GB	10 Avignon	4,000
29 July	A	32 NZ	12 Brisbane	22,811
17 Aug.	PNG	24 NZ	22 Port Moresby	15,000
4 Oct.	PNG	12 A	62 Port Moresby	17,000
22 Nov.	GB	15 A	24 Wigan	20,169
13 Dec.	Fr	0 A	52 Carcassonne	3,000

1987

24 Jan.	GB	52 Fr	4 Leeds	6,567
24 Oct.	GB	42 PNG	0 Wigan	9,121
15 Nov.	Fr	21 PNG	4 Carcassonne	5,000

1988

22 May	PNG	22 GB	42 Port Moresby	12,077
9 July	A	12 GB	26 Sydney	15,994
10 July	NZ	66 PNG	14 Auckland	8,392
17 July	NZ	12 GB	10 Christchurch	8,525
20 July	A	70 PNG	8 Wagga Wagga	11,685

Final Table	P.	W.	D.	L.	F.	A.	Pts.
Australia	7	5	0	2	252	91	12*
New Zealand	7	4	1	2	158	86	11*
Great Britain	8	4	2	2	203	90	10
P. N. Guinea	7	1	0	6	84	325	4*
France	5	1	1	3	35	140	3

*Awarded two points in lieu of France's non-fulfilment of fixtures Down Under.

Play off final

1988

9 Oct.	A	25 NZ	12 Auckland	47,363

GREAT BRITAIN WORLD CUP SQUADS

Captains in bold

1954 IN FRANCE

D. Valentine (Huddersfield)
W. Banks (Huddersfield)
H. Bradshaw (Huddersfield)
G. Brown (Leeds)
R. Coverdale (Hull)
G. Helme (Warrington)
P. Jackson (Barrow)
F. Kitchen (Leigh)
J. Ledgard (Leigh)

A. Naughton (Warrington)
D. Robinson (Wakefield T)
D. Rose (Leeds)
R. Rylance (Huddersfield)
S. Smith (Hunslet)
M. Sullivan (Huddersfield)
J. Thorley (Halifax)
B. Watts (York)
J. Whiteley (Hull)

Manager: G. Shaw (Castleford)

1957 IN AUSTRALIA

A. Prescott (St. Helens)
E. Ashton (Wigan)
W. Boston (Wigan)
A. Davies (Oldham)
J. Grundy (Barrow)
G. Gunney (Hunslet)
T. Harris (Hull)
P. Jackson (Barrow)
L. Jones (Leeds)

S. Little (Oldham)
T. McKinney (St. Helens)
G. Moses (St. Helens)
R. Price (Warrington)
A. Rhodes (St. Helens)
J. Stevenson (Leeds)
M. Sullivan (Huddersfield)
D. Turner (Oldham)
J. Whiteley (Hull)

Managers: W. Fallowfield (RL Secretary) and H. Rawson (Hunslet)

1960 IN ENGLAND

E. Ashton (Wigan)
W. Boston (Wigan)
J. Challinor (Warrington)
A. Davies (Oldham)
E. Fraser (Warrington)
R. Greenough (Warrington)
T. Harris (Hull)
V. Karalius (St. Helens)
B. McTigue (Wigan)

A. Murphy (St. Helens)
F. Myler (Widnes)
A. Rhodes (St. Helens)
B. Shaw (Hunslet)
J. Shaw (Halifax)
M. Sullivan (Wigan)
D. Turner (Wakefield T)
J. Whiteley (Hull)
J. Wilkinson (Wakefield T)

Manager: W. Fallowfield (RL Secretary)

1968 IN AUSTRALIA AND NEW ZEALAND

B. Risman (Leeds)
K. Ashcroft (Leigh)
J. Atkinson (Leeds)
T. Bishop (St. Helens)
I. Brooke (Wakefield T)
A. Burwell (Hull KR)
M. Clark (Leeds)

D. Edwards (Castleford)
P. Flanagan (Hull KR)
R. French (Widnes)
R. Haigh (Wakefield T)
R. Millward (Hull KR)
A. Morgan (Featherstone R)
C. Renilson (Halifax)

M. Shoebottom (Leeds)
C. Sullivan (Hull)
J. Warlow (St. Helens)
C. Watson (St. Helens)
C. Young (Hull KR)

Manager: W. Fallowfield (RL Secretary)   Coach: C. Hutton (Hull KR)

1970 IN ENGLAND

F. Myler (St. Helens)
K. Ashcroft (Leigh)
J. Atkinson (Leeds)
P. Charlton (Salford)
D. Chisnall (Leigh)
R. Dutton (Widnes)
A. Fisher (Bradford N & Leeds)

R. Haigh (Leeds)
D. Hartley (Castleford)
K. Hepworth (Castleford)
C. Hesketh (Salford)
S. Hynes (Leeds)
K. Jones (Wigan)
D. Laughton (Wigan)

M. Reilly (Castleford)
M. Shoebottom (Leeds)
A. Smith (Leeds)
J. Thompson (Featherstone R)
C. Watson (St. Helens)

Manager: J. Harding (Leigh)   Coach: J. Whiteley (Hull KR)

1972 IN FRANCE

C. Sullivan (Hull)
J. Atkinson (Leeds)
P. Charlton (Salford)
T. Clawson (Leeds)
C. Dixon (Salford)
C. Hesketh (Salford)
J. Holmes (Leeds)

R. Irving (Oldham)
D. Jeanes (Leeds)
A. Karalius (St. Helens)
B. Lockwood (Castleford)
P. Lowe (Hull KR)
S. Nash (Featherstone R)
G. Nicholls (Widnes)

D. O'Neill (Widnes)
D. Redfearn (Bradford N)
M. Stephenson (Dewsbury)
D. Topliss (Wakefield T)
John Walsh (St. Helens)

Manager: W. Spaven (Hull KR)   Coach: J. Challinor (St. Helens)

1977 IN AUSTRALIA AND NEW ZEALAND

R. Millward (Hull KR)
E. Bowman (Workington T)
L. Casey (Hull KR)
L. Dyl (Leeds)
K. Elwell (Widnes)
G. Fairbairn (Wigan)
K. Fielding (Salford)

W. Francis (Wigan)
K. Gill (Salford)
A. Hodkinson (Rochdale H)
P. Hogan (Barrow)
J. Holmes (Leeds)
S. Lloyd (Castleford)
S. Nash (Salford)

G. Nicholls (St. Helens)
S. Pitchford (Leeds)
P. Smith (Featherstone R)
J. Thompson (Featherstone R)
D. Ward (Leeds)
S. Wright (Widnes)

Manager: R. Parker (Blackpool B)   Coach: D. Watkins (Salford)

Great Britain Under-21 skipper Phil Clarke, British Coal
Man of the Match in Limoux.

UNDER-21s

UNDER-21s

Three weeks after inflicting a 48-2 humiliation on their French counterparts on foreign soil, Great Britain Under-21s crashed 16-6 at Wigan.

The dramatic turn-around was made all the more amazing by the depth of dominance in Limoux, the eight-try romp being an Under-21 record score in France. Coach Phil Larder, enjoying sole responsibility for the first time, made four changes for the return encounter, two of them players who were original choices for Limoux but forced to withdraw through injury. The French Espoirs, weakened by service call-ups for the Gulf War, wiped away the memory of the home rout to notch three tries to one in the Central Park meeting, switched from Huddersfield's Fartown because of heavy snow.

The 48-2 triumph at Limoux topped the 40-7 win in France in March 1987, but fell just short of the best-ever 54-6 success at St. Helens a fortnight later. Plaudits were in abundance after the international demolition job, with squad members being earmarked for the 1992 tour Down Under in the short term and the 1995 World Cup in Britain in the longer view.

Captain Phil Clarke was rated as British Coal Man of the Match, ahead of clubmate Bobby Goulding. The junior front row was outstanding, with two-try hooker Graham Southernwood being flanked by barn-storming prop forwards Gary Chambers and Craig Richards.

The powerful performance of the Under-21s was marred only by a bad-tempered brawl seven minutes from time after

26 January		Limoux

GREAT BRITAIN 48

Darren Moxon (Bradford N.)	1.
David Myers (Wigan)	2.
Chris Rudd (Warrington)	3.
Paul Newlove (Featherstone R.)	4.
Vince Fawcett (Leeds)	5.
Tommy Martyn (Oldham)	6.
Bobby Goulding (Wigan)	7.
Gary Chambers (Warrington)	8.
Graham Southernwood (Castleford)	9.
Craig Richards (Bradford N.)	10.
Steve McNamara (Hull)	11.
Gary Price (Wakefield T.)	12.
Phil Clarke (Wigan), Capt.	13.
Phil Darbyshire (Warrington)	14.
Michael Forshaw (Wigan)	15.
Tim Lumb (Hunslet)	16.
Michael Jackson (Hunslet)	17.

T: Southernwood (2), Goulding, Martyn, Fawcett, Clarke, Forshaw, Lumb
G: Rudd (8)
Substitutions:
Darbyshire for Newlove (Half-time)
Lumb for Martyn (47 min.)
Forshaw for Fawcett (48 min.)
Jackson for McNamara (60 min.)
Coach: Phil Larder

FRANCE 2

Eric Van Brussel (Carcassonne)
Emmanuel Correia (Pamiers)
Philippe Ricard (Albi)
Jean-Marc Garcia (St. Esteve)
Stephane Millet (St. Gaudens)
David Despin (Villeneuve), Capt.
Jean-Marc Koob (St. Esteve)
Stephane Martin (Lezignan)
Jean-Claude Gayral (Villefranche)
Yannick Sautrice (Pia)
Christophe Grandjean (Lezignan)
Luc Durand (Lyon)
Patrick Mons (Carcassonne)
Frederic Teixido (Limoux)
Lilian Hebert (St. Gaudens)
Jean-Charles Giorgi (Avignon)
Olivier Gagnon (Realmont)
G: Millet
Substitutions:
Hebert for Martin (Half-time)
Giorgi for Correia (Half-time)
Teixido for Sautrice (50 min.)
Gagnon for Mons (68 min.)
Half-time: 30-2
Referee: Brian Galtress (Bradford)
Attendance: 1,200

which Bradford referee Brian Galtress dismissed British full back Darren Moxon, for kicking, and French forward Christophe Grandjean, for punching. Both received a verdict of sending off sufficient.

On the centrally-heated Wigan pitch, the French bounced back to record a well-deserved three tries to one victory. While Britain fielded the same pack which had been so dominant, the French retained only one of the six and proved to be a much stronger unit.

Britain started as they had left off in Limoux, opening the scoring with a try from winger David Myers, created by Central Park teammate Goulding, who again spoilt himself by being sent to the sin bin in the 27th minute.

French referee Marcel Chanfreau did not endear himself to the British players or spectators, but his controversial decisions could not detract from the growing superiority of the visitors, who always looked the more assured.

British Coal Man of the Match, French stand off Pascal Fages, supported well for their first try, kicking through for Eric Van Brussel to touch down in the 23rd minute. Chris Rudd, who kicked an Under-21 record eight goals in Limoux, hit a penalty goal in the 35th minute, but within a minute debutant Tony Smith's pass was intercepted by Van Brussel, who sprinted 40 yards to the line to open up a 14-6 interval lead, substitute Stephane Millet completing the scoring with a penalty goal two minutes from time.

15 February		Wigan
GREAT BRITAIN 6		**FRANCE 16**
Gary Connolly (St. Helens)	1.	Daniel Carvet (Villeneuve)
David Myers (Wigan)	2.	Emmanuel Correia (Pamiers)
Chris Rudd (Warrington)	3.	David Despin (Villeneuve), Capt.
Paul Darbyshire (Warrington)	4.	Philippe Ricard (Albi)
Alan Hunte (St. Helens)	5.	Eric Van Brussel (Carcassonne)
Tony Smith (Castleford)	6.	Pascal Fages (Pia)
Bobby Goulding (Wigan)	7.	Raphael Delgado (Limoux)
Gary Chambers (Warrington)	8.	Christophe Grandjean (Lezignan)
Graham Southernwood (Castleford)	9.	Patrick Torreilles (Pia)
Craig Richards (Bradford N.)	10.	Lilian Hebert (St. Gaudens)
Steve McNamara (Hull)	11.	Patrick Costes (St. Esteve)
Gary Price (Wakefield T.)	12.	Frederic Teixido (Limoux)
Phil Clarke (Wigan), Capt.	13.	David Amat (Lezignan)
Tommy Martyn (Oldham)	14.	Yannick Sautrice (Pia)
Michael Forshaw (Wigan)	15.	Jean-Claude Gayral (Villefranche)
Stuart Spruce (Widnes)	16.	Stephane Millet (St. Gaudens)
Andy Burgess (Salford)	17.	Olivier Gagnon (Realmont)

T: Myers

G: Rudd

Substitutions:

Spruce for Connolly (16 min.)

Burgess for Chambers (47 min.)

Forshaw for Richards (47 min.)

Martyn for Smith (59 min.)

Coach: Phil Larder

Half-time: 6-14

T: Van Brussel (2), Fages

G: Torreilles, Millet

Substitutions:

Gagnon for Ricard (38 min.)

Sautrice for Hebert (63 min.)

Gayral for Delgado (64 min.)

Millet for Teixido (75 min.)

Referee: Marcel Chanfreau (France)

Attendance: 3,065

GREAT BRITAIN UNDER-21s RESULTS

25 Nov.	1984	W 24-8	v.	F	Castleford
16 Dec.	1984	W 8-2	v.	F	Albi
9 Oct.	1985	L 12-16	v.	NZ	Bradford
19 Jan.	1986	L 6-19	v.	F	St. Esteve
2 Feb.	1986	W 6-2	v.	F	Whitehaven
8 Mar.	1987	W 40-7	v.	F	St. Jean de Luz
21 Mar.	1987	W 54-6	v.	F	St. Helens
6 Mar.	1988	L 13-14	v.	F	Ausillon
19 Mar.	1988	L 4-8	v.	F	St. Helens
20 Jan.	1989	W 30-0	v.	F	Leeds
4 Feb.	1989	L 8-16	v.	F	Carpentras
20 Jan.	1990	W 22-0	v.	F	Villeneuve
16 Feb.	1990	W 20-6	v.	F	Doncaster
26 Jan.	1991	W 48-2	v.	F	Limoux
15 Feb.	1991	L 6-16	v.	F	Wigan

Key: F - France,
NZ - New Zealand

GREAT BRITAIN UNDER-21s REGISTER

The following is a register of appearances for Great Britain Under-21s since this classification of match was introduced in 1984.

Figures in brackets are the total appearances, with the plus sign indicating substitute appearances, e.g. (3+1).

Away matches are in bold letters. Substitute appearances are in lower case letters.

ALLEN, S. (1) St. Helens: 1984 F
ANDERSON, G. (4) Castleford: 1989 F, **F**; 1990 **F**, F

BECKWITH, M. (1+1) Whitehaven: 1986 f, **F**
BETTS, D. (4) Wigan: 1989 F, **F**; 1990 **F**, F
BIBB, C. (5) Featherstone R.: 1987 **F**, F; 1988 **F**; 1989 F, **F**
BISHOP, P. (1+1) Warrington: 1987 **F**, f
BOOTHROYD G. (1) Castleford: 1989 F
BURGESS, A. (+1) Salford: 1991 f

CARBERT, B. (3) Warrington: 1985 NZ; 1986 **F**, F
CASSIDY, F. (1+1) Swinton: 1988 **f**, F
CHAMBERS, G. (2) Warrington: 1991 **F**, F

CLARK, G. (2) Hull K.R.: 1984 F, **F**
CLARKE, P. (3) Wigan: 1990 **F**: 1991 **F**, F
CONNOLLY, G. (2) St. Helens: 1990 F, 1991 F
CONWAY, M. (1) Leeds: 1984 F
CREASSER, D. (5) Leeds: 1984 F, **F**; 1985 NZ; 1986 **F**, F
CRITCHLEY, J. (+1) Widnes: 1990 f
CROOKS, L. (2) Hull: 1984 F, **F**
CURRIER, A. (2) Widnes: 1984 F, **F**

DALTON, J. (3) Whitehaven: 1985 NZ; 1986 **F**, F
DANNATT, A. (6) Hull: 1984 F, **F**; 1985 NZ; 1986 F; 1987 **F**, F
DARBYSHIRE, P. (1+1) Warrington: 1991 f, **F**
DELANEY, P. (+2) Leeds: 1990 f, f
DERMOTT, M. (5) Wigan: 1987 **F**, F; 1988 **F**, **F**; 1989 F
DISLEY, G. (+1) Salford: 1987 f
DIVORTY, G. (6) Hull: 1984 F; 1985 NZ; 1986 F, **F**; 1987 **F**, F

EASTWOOD, P. (2) Hull: 1987 **F**, F
EDWARDS, S. (4) Wigan: 1984 F; 1985 NZ; 1987 **F**, F

FARRELL, A. (1+1) Huddersfield: 1989 f, **F**
FAWCETT, V. (3) Leeds: 1990 **F**, F; 1991 **F**
FLETCHER, M. (2) Hull K.R.: 1988 **F**, F
FORD, M. (3+1) Wigan: 1985 NZ; 1986 **F**; Leigh: 1987 f, **F**
FORSHAW, M. (+2) Wigan: 1991 f, f
FORSTER, M. (3) Warrington: 1985 NZ; 1986 **F**, F
FOX, D. (1) Featherstone R.: 1984 **F**

GILDART, I. (6) Wigan: 1988 **F**, F; 1989 F, **F**; 1990 **F**, F
GOULDING, B. (4) Wigan: 1990 **F**, F; 1991 **F**, F
GREGORY, M. (1) Warrington: 1984 **F**
GRIBBIN, V. (1+1) Whitehaven: 1984 f, **F**
GROVES, P. (3) Salford: 1984 F, **F**; 1985 NZ

HARCOMBE, K. (1) Rochdale H.: 1986 F
HARMON, N. (1+3) Warrington: 1988 f, **F**; 1989 f, f
HILL, B. (+1) Leeds: 1986 f
HILL, K. (3) Castleford: 1988 **F**, F; 1989 **F**
HUGHES, G. (1) Leigh: 1986 F
HULME, D. (2+1) Widnes: 1985 nz; 1986 **F**, F
HUNTE, A. (2) St. Helens: 1990 **F**, 1991 F

IRWIN, S. (4) Castleford: 1988 **F**; 1989 F, **F**; 1990 **F**

JACKSON, M. (+1) Hunslet: 1991 f
JOHNSON, E. (2) Leeds: 1988 **F**, F

LAY, S. (+1) Hunslet: 1989 f
LORD, G. (1) Castleford: 1988 **F**
LOUGHLIN, P. (2) St. Helens: 1987 **F**, F

LUCAS, I. (4) Wigan: 1988 **F**, **F**; 1989 F, **F**
LUMB, T. (+1) Hunslet: 1991 f
LYMAN, P. (3) Featherstone R.: 1985 NZ; 1986 **F**, F
LYON, D. (2) Widnes: 1985 NZ; 1986 **F**

McCORMACK, K. (2) St. Helens: 1987 **F**, F
McNAMARA, S. (2) Hull: 1991 **F**, F
MARTYN, T. (1+1) Oldham: 1991 **F**, f
MEDLEY, P. (2) Leeds: 1987 **F**, F
MOLLOY, S. (2) Warrington: 1990 **F**, F
MOUNTAIN, D. (+1) Castleford: 1987 f
MOXON, D. (1) Bradford N.: 1991 **F**
MYCOE, D. (1) Sheffield E.: 1990 **F**
MYERS, D. (2) Wigan: 1991 **F**, F

NEWLOVE, P. (5) Featherstone R: 1989 F, **F**;
    1990 **F**, F; 1991 **F**
NICKLE, S. (1) Sheffield E.: 1990 **F**

PARKER, W. (2) Hull K.R.: 1988 **F**, F
POWELL, R. (5) Leeds: 1984 F, **F**; 1985 NZ;
    1986 **F**, F
PRATT, R. (2) Leeds: 1988 **F**, F
PRICE, G. (5+1) Wakefield T.: 1988 f; 1989 F, **F**;
    1990 F; 1991 **F**, F
PRICE, R. (2) Hull: 1989 F, **F**
PROCTOR, W. (+1) Hull: 1981 f
PUCKERING, N. (4) Hull: 1986 **F**, F; 1987 **F**, F

RICHARDS, C. (2) Bradford N.: 1991 **F**, F
RIPPON, A. (1) Swinton: 1984 **F**
ROBINSON, S. (1) Halifax: 1988 F
ROEBUCK, N. (+1) Castleford: 1990 f
ROUND, P. (1+1) St. Helens: 1984 F, f
RUDD, C. (2) Warrington: 1991 **F**, F
RUSSELL, R. (1+1) Wigan: 1987 F; 1988 f

SAMPSON, D. (1) Castleford: 1988 **F**
SANDERSON, G. (4) Warrington: 1987 F, **F**;
    1988 **F**, F
SCHOFIELD, G. (2) Hull: 1984 **F**, F
SMITH, T. (1) Castleford: 1991 F
SOUTHERNWOOD, G. (4) Castleford: 1990 **F**, F:
    1991 **F**, F
SOUTHERNWOOD, R. (2) Castleford: 1989 F, **F**
SPRUCE, S. (+1) Widnes: 1991 f
STREET, T. (2) Leigh: 1989 F, **F**
SULLIVAN, A. (1) Hull K.R.: 1990 F
SUMNER, P. (1) Warrington: 1990 F

TURNER, R. (1) Warrington: 1990 F

WANE, S. (3) Wigan: 1984 **F**; 1985 NZ; 1986 **F**
WESTHEAD, J. (1+2) Leigh: 1985 nz; 1986 f, F
WRIGHT, D. (2) Widnes: 1987 **F**; 1988 **F**

GREAT BRITAIN UNDER-24s RESULTS

3 Apr. 1965	W 17-9	v.	F	Toulouse
20 Oct. 1965	W 12-5	v.	F	Oldham
26 Nov. 1966	L 4-7	v.	F	Bayonne
17 Apr. 1969	W 42-2	v.	F	Castleford
14 Nov. 1976	W 19-2	v.	F	Hull K.R.
5 Dec. 1976	W 11-9	v.	F	Albi
12 Nov. 1977	W 27-9	v.	F	Hull
18 Dec. 1977	W 8-4	v.	F	Tonneins
4 Oct. 1978	L 8-30	v.	A	Hull K.R.
14 Jan. 1979	W 15-3	v.	F	Limoux
24 Nov. 1979	W 14-2	v.	F	Leigh
13 Jan. 1980	W 11-7	v.	F	Carcassonne
5 Nov. 1980	L 14-18	v.	NZ	Fulham
10 Jan. 1981	W 9-2	v.	F	Villeneuve
16 Jan. 1982	W 19-16	v.	F	Leeds
21 Feb. 1982	W 24-12	v.	F	Tonneins
16 Jan. 1983	W 19-5	v.	F	Carpentras
11 Nov. 1983	W 28-23	v.	F	Villeneuve
4 Dec. 1983	W 48-1	v.	F	Oldham

GREAT BRITAIN UNDER-24s REGISTER
Since reintroduction in 1976

The following is a register of appearances for Great Britain Under-24s since this classification of match was reintroduced in 1976, until it was replaced by the new Under-21 level in 1984.

Figures in brackets are the total appearances, with the plus sign indicating substitute appearances, e.g. (7+3).

Away matches are in bold letters. Substitute appearances are in lower case letters.

ARKWRIGHT, C. (1) St. Helens: 1982 F
ASHTON, R. (3) Oldham: 1983 **F**, F, F

BANKS, B. (1) York: 1979 **F**
BELL, K. (2) Featherstone R.: 1977 F, **F**
BENTLEY, K. (+1) Widnes: 1980 nz
BURKE, M. (5) Widnes: 1979 F; 1980 **F**, NZ;
    1982 F; 1983 **F**
BURTON, B. (2) Castleford: 1976 F, **F**

CAIRNS, D. (2) Barrow: 1979 F; 1982 **F**
CASE, B. (3 + 1) Warrington: 1979 **F**; 1980 NZ: 1981 **F**; 1982 f
CLARK, G. (3) Hull K.R.: 1983 **F, F**, F
CRAMPTON, J. (4) Hull: 1976 F, **F**; 1977 F, **F**
CROOKS, L. (1) Hull: 1983 F

DICKINSON, R. (5) Leeds: 1976 F, **F**; 1977 F, **F**; 1978 A
DRUMMOND, D. (5) Leigh: 1979 F; 1980 **F**; 1981 **F**; 1982 F, **F**
DUANE, R. (2) Warrington: 1983 **F, F**
DUNN, B. (2) Wigan: 1983 **F**, F

ECCLES, R. (2) Warrington: 1978 A; 1979 F
ENGLAND, K. (+ 1) Castleford: 1983 f
EVANS, S. (3) Featherstone R.: 1980 NZ; 1981 **F**; Hull: 1982 **F**

FENNELL, D. (1) Featherstone R.: 1978 A
FENTON, S. (6) Castleford: 1977 F, **F**; 1979 F; 1980 **F**, NZ; 1981 **F**
FIELDHOUSE, J. (1 + 1) Warrington: 1983 **F**, f
FLANAGAN, T. (5) Oldham: 1980 NZ; 1981 **F**; 1983 **F, F**, F
FORD, Phil (1) Warrington: 1982 **F**
FOX, V. (1) Whitehaven: 1980 NZ
FOY, D. (2) Oldham: 1983 **F**, F

GIBBINS, M. (2) Featherstone R.: 1977 F, **F**
GILBERT, J. (2 + 1) Featherstone R.: 1977 **F**; 1977 f; 1981 **F**
GILL, H. (1) Wigan: 1982 F
GOODWAY, A. (2) Oldham: 1983 **F**, F
GREGORY, A. (1) Widnes: 1982 F

HALL, D. (+ 1) Hull K.R.: 1976 f
HANLEY, E. (2) Bradford N.: 1982 F; 1983 F
HARKIN, P. (1) Hull K.R.: 1981 **F**
HARTLEY, I. (1) Workington T.: 1979 **F**
HOBBS, D. (2) Featherstone R.: 1982 F, **F**
HOGAN, P. (2) Barrow: 1978 A; Hull K.R.: 1979 **F**
HOLDING, N. (4) St. Helens: 1979 **F**; 1980 **F**, NZ; 1983 **F**
HOLDSTOCK, R. (3) Hull K.R.: 1978 A; 1979 F; 1980 **F**
HORNBY, J. (2) Wigan: 1978 A; 1979 **F**
HYDE, G. (1 + 1) Castleford: 1980 NZ; 1982 f

JAMES, K. (1) Bramley: 1980 **F**
JOHNSON, B. (2) Castleford: 1982 F, **F**
JOYNER, J. (4 + 1) Castleford: 1976 f; 1977 F, **F**; 1978 A; 1979 **F**

LEDGER, B. (2) St. Helens: 1983 **F**, F
LIPTROT, G. (4) St. Helens: 1977 F, **F**; 1978 A; 1979 **F**
LYDON, J. (3) Widnes: 1983 **F, F**, F

MASKILL, C. (1) Wakefield T.: 1983 **F**
MOLL, D. (1) Keighley: 1983 **F**
MUMBY, K. (6) Bradford N.: 1976 F, **F**; 1977 F, **F**; 1978 A; 1981 **F**
MUSCROFT, P. (3) New Hunslet: 1976 F, **F**; 1978 A
MYLER, A. (3) Widnes: 1982 **F**; 1983 **F**, F
MYLER, J. (1 + 1) Widnes: 1982 f; **F**

NOBLE, B. (4) Bradford N.: 1982 F, **F**; 1983 **F**, F
NULTY, J. (2) Wigan: 1976 F, **F**

O'NEILL, M. (3 + 2) Widnes: 1980 nz; 1982 F, f; 1983 **F, F**
O'NEILL, P. (3) Salford: 1980 **F**, NZ; 1981 **F**
O'NEILL, S. (2) Wigan: 1979 **F**; 1981 **F**

PINNER, H. (4 + 4) St. Helens: 1976 F, **F**; 1977 f, f; 1978 a; 1979 f, **F**, 1980 **F**
POTTER, I. (4) Warrington: 1979 **F**; 1981 **F**; Leigh: 1982 F, **F**
PROCTOR, W. (1) Hull: 1983 **F**

RATHBONE, A. (+ 1) Leigh: 1979 f
RAYNE, Keith (2) Wakefield T.: 1979 F; 1980 **F**
RICHARDSON, T. (1) Castleford: 1979 **F**
ROE, P. (4) Bradford N.: 1976 F, **F**; 1977 F, **F**
RUDD, I. (1 + 1) Workington T.: 1979 f; 1980 **F**

SCHOFIELD, G. (+ 2) Hull: 1983 f, f
SHEPHERD, M. (2) Huddersfield: 1977 F, **F**
SKERRETT, T. (1) Wakefield T.: 1977 **F**
SMITH, D. (2) Leeds: 1976 F, **F**
SMITH, Malcolm (1) Wigan: 1979 **F**
SMITH, Mike (7) Hull K.R.: 1976 F, **F**; 1977 **F**; 1978 A; 1979 **F**, **F**; 1980 **F**
SMITH, P. (1) Featherstone R.: 1978 A
SMITH, R. (+ 1) Salford: 1983 f
STEPHENSON, D. (5) Salford: 1979 F; 1980 **F**, NZ; 1982 F; Wigan: 1982 **F**
SWANN, M. (1) Leigh: 1979 F
SYZMALA, E. (2) Barrow: 1976 F, **F**

THACKRAY, R. (1) Warrington: 1980 NZ
TIMSON, A. (2) Castleford: 1982 F, **F**
TURNBULL, S. (2) Salford: 1976 F, **F**

VAN BELLEN, G. (2) Bradford N.: 1980 NZ; 1982 **F**

WARD, D. (+ 2) Leeds: 1976 f, f
WARD, K. (3) Castleford: 1980 **F**, NZ; 1981 **F**
WHITFIELD, C. (1) Salford: 1981 **F**
WILKINSON, A. (1) Leigh: 1977 **F**
WOOD, J. (2) Widnes: 1977 F, **F**
WOODS, J. (5) Leigh: 1977 F, **F**; 1978 A; 1979 **F**, F
WORRALL, M. (3) Oldham: 1983 **F, F**, F

Wales prop Jim Mills dumps England's Roger Millward in the 1978 European Championship.

WALES

WALES

WALES RESULTS

The following is a list of all matches involving Wales which are recognised officially as full internationals.

Date	Opponent		Score	Venue	Attendance
1 Jan. 1908	New Zealand	W	9-8	Aberdare	15,000
20 Apr. 1908	England	W	35-18	Tonypandy	12,000
28 Dec. 1908	England	L	7-31	Broughton	4,000
4 Dec. 1909	England	L	13-19	Wakefield	4,000
9 Apr. 1910	England	W	39-18	Ebbw Vale	4,000
10 Dec. 1910	England	L	13-39	Coventry	4,500
1 Apr. 1911	England	L	8-27	Ebbw Vale	4,000
7 Oct. 1911	Australia	L	20-28	Ebbw Vale	7,000
20 Jan. 1912	England	L	5-31	Oldham	8,000
15 Feb. 1913	England	L	16-40	Plymouth	7,500
14 Feb. 1914	England	L	12-16	St. Helens	10,000
19 Jan. 1921	England	L	9-35	Leeds	13,000
10 Dec. 1921	Australia	L	16-21	Pontypridd	13,000
11 Dec. 1922	England	L	7-12	Herne Hill	3,000
7 Feb. 1923	England	W	13-2	Wigan	12,000
1 Oct. 1923	England	L	11-18	Huddersfield	11,066
7 Feb. 1925	England	L	22-27	Workington	14,000
30 Sept. 1925	England	L	14-18	Wigan	12,000
12 Apr. 1926	England	L	22-30	Pontypridd	23,000
4 Dec. 1926	New Zealand	W	34-8	Pontypridd	18,000
6 Apr. 1927	England	L	8-11	Broughton	6,000
11 Jan. 1928	England	L	12-20	Wigan	12,000
14 Nov. 1928	England	L	15-39	Cardiff	15,000
18 Jan. 1930	Australia	L	10-26	Wembley	16,000
18 Mar. 1931	England	L	18-23	Huddersfield	6,000
27 Jan. 1932	England	L	2-19	Salford	8,000
30 Nov. 1932	England	L	13-14	Leeds	4,000
30 Dec. 1933	Australia	L	19-51	Wembley	10,000
*1 Jan. 1935	France	L	11-18	Bordeaux	15,000
*10 Apr. 1935	England	L	11-24	Liverpool	7,100
*23 Nov. 1935	France	W	41-7	Llanelli	25,000
*1 Feb. 1936	England	W	17-14	Hull K.R.	17,000
*7 Nov. 1936	England	W	3-2	Pontypridd	12,000
*6 Dec. 1936	France	W	9-3	Paris	17,000
*29 Jan. 1938	England	W	7-6	Bradford	8,637
*2 Apr. 1938	France	W	18-2	Llanelli	20,000
*5 Nov. 1938	England	W	17-9	Llanelli	15,000
*16 Apr. 1939	France	L	10-16	Bordeaux	25,000
23 Dec. 1939	England	W	16-3	Bradford	15,257
9 Nov. 1940	England	L	5-8	Oldham	5,000
18 Oct. 1941	England	D	9-9	Bradford	4,339
27 Feb. 1943	England	L	9-15	Wigan	17,000
26 Feb. 1944	England	D	9-9	Wigan	16,028
10 Mar. 1945	England	L	8-18	Wigan	23,500
*24 Nov. 1945	England	W	11-3	Swansea	30,000
*24 Mar. 1946	France	L	7-19	Bordeaux	
*12 Oct. 1946	England	W	13-10	Swinton	20,213
*16 Nov. 1946	England	L	5-19	Swansea	25,000
*18 Jan. 1947	France	L	5-14	Marseilles	24,500
*12 Apr. 1947	France	W	17-15	Swansea	20,000
*20 Sept. 1947	England	W	10-8	Wigan	27,000
18 Oct. 1947	New Zealand	L	20-28	Swansea	18,283

*23 Nov. 1947	France	L	21-29	Bordeaux	26,000
*6 Dec. 1947	England	L	7-18	Swansea	10,000
*20 Mar. 1948	France	L	12-20	Swansea	6,500
*22 Sept. 1948	England	L	5-11	Wigan	12,638
*23 Oct. 1948	France	L	9-12	Swansea	12,032
20 Nov. 1948	Australia	L	5-12	Swansea	9,224
*5 Feb. 1949	England	W	14-10	Swansea	9,553
*10 Apr. 1949	France	L	0-11	Marseilles	30,000
*22 Oct. 1949	Other Nationalities	L	5-6	Abertillery	2,000
*12 Nov. 1949	France	W	16-8	Swansea	4,749
*1 Mar. 1950	England	L	6-11	Wigan	27,500
*14 Oct. 1950	England	L	4-22	Abertillery	8,000
*31 Mar. 1951	Other Nationalities	L	21-27	Swansea	5,000
*15 Apr. 1951	France	L	13-28	Marseilles	18,000
*19 Sept. 1951	England	L	11-35	St. Helens	20,918
*1 Dec. 1951	Other Nationalities	L	11-22	Abertillery	3,386
7 Dec. 1951	New Zealand	L	3-15	Bradford	8,568
*6 Apr. 1952	France	L	12-20	Bordeaux	15,678
*17 Sept. 1952	England	L	8-19	Wigan	13,503
*25 Oct. 1952	France	W	22-16	Leeds	10,380
*15 Apr. 1953	Other Nationalities	W	18-16	Warrington	8,449
*16 Sept. 1953	England	L	5-24	St. Helens	19,357
*7 Oct. 1953	Other Nationalities	L	5-30	Bradford	14,646
*13 Dec. 1953	France	L	22-23	Marseilles	25,000

St. Helens prop Mel James, holder of 11 Welsh caps between 1975 and 1981.

Seventeen-cap John Bevan, a 1973 recruit by Warrington from Cardiff RU.

7 Nov. 1968	England	W	24-17	Salford	6,002
9 Mar. 1969	France	L	13-17	Paris	6,189
*18 Oct. 1969	England	L	23-40	Leeds	8,355
*23 Oct. 1969	France	L	2-8	Salford	5,610
*25 Jan. 1970	France	W	15-11	Perpignan	11,000
*24 Feb. 1970	England	L	7-26	Leeds	9,393
16 Feb. 1975	France	W	21-8	Swansea	15,000
25 Feb. 1975	England	L	8-12	Salford	8,494
†2 Mar. 1975	France	L	7-14	Toulouse	7,563
†10 Jun. 1975	England	W	12-7	Brisbane	6,000
†14 Jan. 1975	Australia	L	13-30	Sydney	25,386
†28 Jun. 1975	New Zealand	L	8-13	Auckland	9,368
†20 Sept. 1975	England	L	16-22	Warrington	5,034
†19 Oct. 1975	Australia	L	6-18	Swansea	11,112
†2 Nov. 1975	New Zealand	W	25-24	Swansea	2,645
†6 Nov. 1975	France	W	23-2	Salford	2,247
*29 Jan. 1977	England	W	6-2	Leeds	6,472
*20 Feb. 1977	France	L	2-13	Toulouse	5,827
*15 Jan. 1978	France	W	29-7	Widnes	9,502
*28 May. 1978	England	L	13-60	St. Helens	9,759
*15 Oct. 1978	Australia	L	3-8	Swansea	4,250
*4 Feb. 1979	France	L	8-15	Narbonne	13,728
*16 Mar. 1979	England	L	7-15	Widnes	5,099
*26 Jan. 1980	France	L	7-21	Widnes	2,804
*29 Feb. 1980	England	L	9-26	Hull K.R.	7,557
*31 Jan. 1981	France	L	5-23	Narbonne	4,120
*18 Mar. 1981	England	L	4-17	Hull K.R.	4,786
8 Nov. 1981	England	L	15-20	Cardiff	8,102
24 Oct. 1982	Australia	L	7-37	Cardiff	5,617
14 Oct. 1984	England	L	9-28	Ebbw Vale	2,111

* European Championship
† World Cup

TOTALS

	P	W	D	L	F	A
England	58	15	2	41	677	1,106
France	28	10	0	18	377	400
Australia	9	0	0	9	99	231
New Zealand	6	3	0	3	99	96
Other Nationalities	5	1	0	4	60	101
GRAND TOTALS	106	29	2	75	1,312	1,934

● Wales won the European Championship in 1935-36, 1936-37 1937-38.

OTHER INTERNATIONAL MATCHES

Wales have been involved in five other matches which are not regarded as full internationals as follows:

17 Apr. 1937	Northern RL XIII	W	15-12	Newcastle	3,000
19 May. 1951	Empire XIII	L	16-29	Llanelli	6,500
19 May. 1955	France B	L	11-24	Nantes	
1 Mar. 1959	France	L	8-25	Toulouse	25,000
17 Feb. 1963	France	L	3-23	Toulouse	6,150

● A Welsh League XIII beat Australia 14-13 at Merthyr Tydfil on 16 January, 1909 and an Other Nationalities side made up entirely of Welshmen lost 33-16 to England at Workington on 5 February, 1921.

1975 AUSTRALIA AND NEW ZEALAND TOUR (Other than World Cup matches)

5 Jun. 1975	Ipswich (Aust)	W	35-13	Ipswich	4,000
18 Jun. 1975	Wellington (NZ)	W	52-8	Wellington	2,000
22 Jun. 1975	West Coast (NZ)	W	35-5	Greymouth	2,000
24 Jun. 1975	Canterbury (NZ)	W	25-18	Christchurch	2,500
1 Jul. 1975	Auckland (NZ)	L	5-31	Auckland	12,000
3 Jul. 1975	Maoris (NZ)	W	18-12	Rotorua	2,500

1975 World Championship squad in Australia and New Zealand
(World Cup and other matches)

Manager: R. Simpson (Castleford)
Coach: L. Pearce (Halifax)
Captain: D. Watkins (Salford)

	App	T	G	Pts
P. Banner (Salford)	6	1	0	3
B. Butler (Swinton)	4+2	0	0	0
K. Coslett (St. Helens)	7	1	10	23
E. Cunningham (St. Helens)	5	2	0	6
C. Dixon (Salford)	8	3	0	9
R. Evans (Swinton)	4+1	0	0	0
A. Fisher (Leeds)	5	2	0	6
W. Francis (Wigan)	7	2	0	6
J. Mantle (St. Helens)	5+3	1	0	3
R. Mathias (St. Helens)	9	10	0	30
J. Mills (Widnes)	6+1	2	0	6
M. Nicholas (Warrington)	2	2	0	6
P. Rowe (Blackpool B.)	2+3	2	0	6
C. Sullivan (Hull K.R.)	7+1	6	0	18
D. Treasure (Oldham)	8+1	2	1	8
G. Turner (Hull K.R.)	6	1	0	3
R. Wanbon (Warrington)	6+1	1	0	3
D. Watkins (Salford)	8+1	1	26	55
D. Willicombe (Wigan)	7+2	1	0	3
F. Wilson (St. Helens)	5+3	3	0	9
TOTALS		43	37	203

Roy Mathias, top tryscorer on the 1975 Wales visit Down Under.

David Watkins, skipper of the 1975 World Championship squad.

WALES TEAMS

● From 1975, when it revived after a gap of five years and continued until 1982 and on to 1984, before folding again.

1975 France

Swansea: 16 Feb

Won 21-8

Francis (Wigan)
Mathias (St. Helens) 1t
Willicombe (Wigan)
Wilson, F (St. Helens)
Bevan (Warrington) 2t
*Watkins (Salford) 1dg
Banner (Salford)
Mills (Widnes) 1t
Fisher (Leeds)
Mantle (St. Helens)
Nicholas (Warrington)
Dixon (Salford)
Coslett (St. Helens) 4g
Sub: Gallacher (Keighley)

1975 England

Salford: 25 Feb

Lost 8-12

Francis (Wigan)
Mathias (St. Helens)
Willicombe (Wigan)
Wilson, F (St. Helens)
Bevan (Warrington)
*Watkins (Salford) 1t, 1g, 1dg
Banner (Salford)
Mills (Widnes)
Evans (Swinton)
Mantle (St. Helens)
Dixon (Salford)
Gallacher (Keighley)
Coslett (St. Helens) 1g
Sub: Turner (Hull K.R.)
     Nicholas (Warrington)

1975 France (WC)

Toulouse: 2 March

Lost 7-14

Francis (Wigan)
Mathias (St. Helens)
Willicombe (Wigan)
Wilson, F (St. Helens) 1t
Richards (Salford)
*Watkins (Salford)
Banner (Salford)
Murphy (Bradford N.)
Evans (Swinton)
Butler (Swinton)
Dixon (Salford)
Mantle (St. Helens)
Coslett (St. Helens) 2g
Sub: Wallace (York)

1975 England (WC)

Brisbane: 10 June

Won 12-7

Francis (Wigan)
Sullivan (Hull K.R.) 1t
*Watkins (Salford) 3g
Willicombe (Wigan)
Mathias (St. Helens)
Treasure (Oldham) 1t
Banner (Salford)
Mills (Widnes)
Fisher (Leeds)
Wanbon (Warrington)
Dixon (Salford)
Cunningham, E. (St. Helens)
Coslett (St. Helens)
Sub: Wilson, F (St. Helens)
     Mantle (St. Helens)

1975 Australia (WC)

Sydney: 14 June

Lost 13-30

Francis (Wigan)
Sullivan (Hull K.R.)
*Watkins (Salford) 5g
Willicombe (Wigan)
Mathias (St. Helens)
Turner (Hull K.R.)
Treasure (Oldham)
Mills (Widnes)
Fisher (Leeds) 1t
Wanbon (Warrington)
Mantle (St. Helens)
Cunningham, E. (St. Helens)
Coslett (St. Helens)
Sub: Wilson (St. Helens)
     Rowe (Blackpool B.)

1975 New Zealand (WC)

Auckland: 28 June

Lost 8-13

Francis (Wigan) 1t
Sullivan (Hull K.R.)
*Watkins (Salford) 1g
Willicombe (Wigan)
Mathias (St. Helens)
Treasure (Oldham)
Banner (Salford)
Mills (Widnes) 1t
Fisher (Leeds)
Wanbon (Warrington)
Mantle (St. Helens)
Dixon (Salford)
Coslett (St. Helens)
Sub: Butler (Swinton)

1975 England (WC)

Warrington: 20 Sept

Lost 16-22

Francis (Wigan)
Sullivan (Hull K.R.)
*Watkins (Salford) 5g
Wilson, F (St. Helens)
Bevan (Warrington)
Treasure (Oldham)
Banner (Salford) 1t
Mantle (St. Helens)
Fisher (Castleford)
James (St. Helens)
Cunningham, E (St. Helens)
Gregory (Wigan)
Coslett (St. Helens) 1t
Sub: Turner (Hull K.R.)
     Rowe (Blackpool B.)

1975 Australia (WC)

Swansea: 19 Oct

Lost 6-18

*Watkins (Salford) 3g
Mathias (St. Helens)
Francis (Wigan)
Wilson, F (St. Helens)
Bevan (Warrington)
Turner (Hull K.R.)
Banner (Featherstone R.)
Mills (Widnes)
Fisher (Castleford)
Mantle (St. Helens)
Cunningham, E (St. Helens)
Dixon (Salford)
Coslett (St. Helens)
Sub: Rowe (Blackpool B.)

1975 New Zealand (WC)

Swansea: 2 Nov

Won 25-24

*Watkins (Salford) 5g
Mathias (St. Helens)
Wilson, F (St. Helens)
Willicombe (Wigan) 1t
Bevan (Warrington) 1t
Francis (Wigan) 2t
Banner (Featherstone R.)
Mills (Widnes)
Fisher (Castleford)
Murphy (Bradford N.)
Mantle (St. Helens) 1t
Gallacher (Keighley)
Gregory (Wigan)
Sub: Jones (Leigh)

1975 France (WC)
Salford: 6 Nov

Won 23-2

*Watkins (Salford) 4g
Mathias (St. Helens)
Wilson, F (St. Helens)
Willicombe (Wigan) 1t
Bevan (Warrington) 1t
Francis (Wigan) 1t
Banner (Featherstone R.) 1t
Mantle (St. Helens)
Evans (Swinton)
Murphy (Bradford N.)
Gregory (Wigan) 1t
Gallacher (Keighley)
Jones (Leigh)
Sub: Turner (Hull K.R.)
      Butler (Warrington)

1978 France
Widnes: 15 Jan

Won 29-7

Risman (Workington T.)
Mathias (St. Helens) 1t
Willicombe (Wigan)
Cunningham, E (St. Helens) 1t
Sullivan (Hull K.R.) 1t
*Francis (St. Helens) 1t
Woods (Widnes) 7g
Mills (Widnes) 1t
Evans (Salford)
James (St. Helens)
Nicholas (Warrington)
Shaw (Widnes)
Dixon (Salford)
Sub: Pritchard (Barrow)
      Jones (Leigh)

1979 France
Narbonne: 4 Feb

Lost 8-15

Box (Featherstone R.)
Sullivan (Hull K.R.)
*Watkins (Salford) 2g,1dg
Bevan (Warrington)
Juliff (Wakefield T.)
Francis (St. Helens)
Woods (Rochdale H.)
Murphy (St. Jacques)
Cunningham, T (Warrington)
James (St. Helens)
Skerrett (Wakefield T.)
Rowe (Huddersfield) 1t
Mathias (St. Helens)
Sub: Johns (Salford)
      Risman (Workington T.)

1977 England
Leeds: 29 Jan

Won 6-2

*Watkins (Salford)
Mathias (St. Helens)
Bevan (Warrington)
Cunningham, E (St. Helens) 1t
Richards (Salford)
Francis (Wigan)
Woods (Widnes) 1g
Mills (Workington T.)
Fisher (Castleford)
Mantle (Salford)
Nicholas (Warrington)
Dixon (Salford)
Rowe (Huddersfield) dg
Sub: Wilkins (Workington T.)

1978 England
St. Helens: 28 May

Lost 13-60

Watkins (Salford) 1g
Mathias (St. Helens)
Turner (Hull)
Willicombe (Wigan) 1t
Sullivan (Hull K.R.) 1t
*Francis (St. Helens)
Woods (Widnes) 1g
Mills (Widnes)
Evans (Salford)
James (St. Helens) 1t
Davies, F (New Hunslet)
Mantle (Leigh)
Cunningham, E (St. Helens)
Sub: Pritchard (Barrow)
      Jones (Leigh)

1979 England
Widnes: 16 Mar

Lost 7-15

Box (Featherstone R.) 1t,2g
Sullivan (Hull K.R.)
Risman (Workington T.)
Bevan (Warrington)
Juliff (Wakefield T.)
*Francis (St. Helens)
Woods (Rochdale H.)
Mills (Widnes)
Cunningham, T (Warrington)
James (St. Helens)
Skerrett (Wakefield T.)
Rowe (Huddersfield)
Mathias (St. Helens)
Sub: Prendiville (Hull)
      Nicholas (Warrington)

1977 France
Toulouse: 20 Feb

Lost 2-13

Wilkins (Workington T.)
Mathias (St. Helens)
Bevan (Warrington)
Treasure (Oldham)
Sullivan (Hull K.R.)
*Francis (Wigan)
Woods (Widnes) 1g
Mills (Widnes)
Fisher (Castleford)
Butler (Warrington)
Nicholas (Warrington)
Dixon (Salford)
Rowe (Huddersfield)
Sub: Curling (Warrington)
      Murphy (Bradford N.)

1978 Australia
Swansea: 15 Oct

Lost 3-8

*Watkins (Salford) 1g, 1dg
Sullivan (Hull K.R.)
Willicombe (Wigan)
Cunningham, E. (St. Helens)
Bevan (Warrington)
Francis (St. Helens)
Woods (Widnes)
Mills (Widnes)
Fisher (Bradford N.)
James (St. Helens)
Shaw (Widnes)
Skerrett (Wakefield T.)
Mathias (St. Helens)

1980 France
Widnes: 26 Jan

Lost 7-21

Box (Featherstone R.)
Juliff (Wakefield T.)
Diamond (Wakefield T.) 2g
Bevan (Warrington) 1t
Camilleri (Barrow)
*Francis (Oldham)
Flowers (Wigan)
James (St. Helens)
Parry (Blackpool B.)
Shaw (Widnes)
McJennett (Barrow)
Skerrett (Wakefield T.)
Mathias (St. Helens)
Sub: Griffiths (St. Helens)
      Seldon (St. Helens)

1980 England
Hull K.R.: 29 Feb
Lost 9-26
Box (Featherstone R.)
Prendiville (Hull)
Walters (Hull)
*Francis (Oldham)
Juliff (Wakefield T.) 1t
Woods (Hull) 3g
Flowers (Wigan)
James (St. Helens)
Parry (Blackpool B.)
Shaw (Widnes)
Seldon (St. Helens)
Bevan (Warrington)
Mathias (St. Helens)
Sub: Diamond (Wakefield T.)

1981 France
Narbonne: 31 Jan
Lost 5-23
Box (Wakefield T.)
Cambriani (Fulham)
Diamond (Wakefield T.)
*Bevan (Warrington)
Prendiville (Hull)
Wilson, D (Swinton) 1g
Woods (Hull)
James (St. Helens)
Parry (Blackpool B.) 1t
Owen, G (Oldham)
Skerrett (Hull)
Juliff (Wakefield T.)
Mathias (St. Helens)
Sub: Griffiths (St. Helens)
Owen, R (St. Helens)

1981 England
Hull K.R.: 18 Mar
Lost 4-17
Rule (Salford) 2g
Cambriani (Fulham)
Walters (Hull)
*Bevan (Warrington)
Juliff (Wakefield T.)
Wilson, D (Swinton)
Woods (Hull)
James (St. Helens)
Parry (Blackpool B.)
Owen, G (Oldham)
Skerrett (Hull)
Dixon (Hull K.R.)
Mathias (St. Helens)
Sub: Herdman (Fulham)

1981 England
Cardiff: 8 Nov
Lost 15-20
Pritchard (Cardiff C.)
Cambriani (Fulham)
Bayliss (St. Helens)
Fenwick (Cardiff C.) 4g
*Bevan (Warrington)
Wilson, D (Swinton) 1dg
Flowers (Wigan) 1t
James (St. Helens)
Parry (Blackpool B.)
David (Cardiff C.)
Shaw (Widnes)
Herdman (Fulham)
Ringer (Cardiff C.)
Sub: Prendiville (Hull) 1t
Owen, R (St. Helens)

1982 Australia
Cardiff: 24 Oct
Lost 7-37
Hopkins (Workington T.) 1g
Camilleri (Widnes)
Fenwick (Cardiff C.) 1g
*Bevan (Warrington)
Prendiville (Hull)
Hallett (Cardiff C.)
Williams (Cardiff C.) 1t
Shaw (Wigan)
Parry (Blackpool B.)
David (Cardiff C.)
Herdman (Fulham)
Juliff (Wigan)
Ringer (Cardiff C.)
Sub: McJennett (Barrow)

1984 England
Ebbw Vale: 14 Oct
Lost 9-28
Hallett (Bridgend) 2g
Camilleri (Bridgend)
Prendiville (Hull)
Davies, M (Bridgend)
Ford (Warrington)
Wilson, D (Swinton) 1t,1dg
Flowers, (Bridgend)
*Skerrett (Hull)
Preece (Bradford N.)
Shaw (Wigan)
McJennett (Barrow)
O'Brien (Bridgend)
Juliff (Wigan)
Sub: Johns (Blackpool B.)
Walters (Bridgend)

Kel Coslett, eight caps in 1975.

*Clive Sullivan, a 14-cap
Welsh career.*

*David Willicombe, a 13-cap tally
for Wales.*

WALES REGISTER
● Since 1975

Figures in brackets are the total appearances for Wales since 1975, with the plus sign indicating substitute appearances, e.g. (7 + 3).

A few players also played in the 1969-70 European Championship and this is shown as an additional total outside bracket, e.g. (11)2.

World championship matches are in bold letters. Substitute appearances are in lower case letters. A = Australia, E = England, F = France, NZ = New Zealand.

BANNER, P (9) Salford: 1975 F, E, **F, E, NZ.**
 Featherstone R: 1975 (cont.) **E, A, NZ, F**
BAYLISS, S (1) St. Helens: 1981 E
BEVAN, J (17) Warrington: 1975 F, E, **E, A, NZ, F**;
 1977 E, F; 1978 A; 1979 F, E; 1980 F, E;
 1981 F, E, E; 1982 A
BOX, H. (5) Featherstone R: 1979 F, E; 1980 F, E.
 Wakefield T: 1981 F
BUTLER, B (2 + 2) Swinton: 1975 **F, nz.** Warrington:
 1975 (cont.) f; 1977 F

CAMBRIANI, A (3) Fulham: 1981 F, E, E
CAMILLERI, C (3) Barrow: 1980 F. Widnes:
 1982 A. Bridgend: 1984 E
COSLETT, K (8)2 St. Helens: 1975 F, E, **F, E, A,
 NZ, E, A**
CUNNINGHAM, E (8) St. Helens: 1975 **E, A, E, A**;
 1977 E, 1978 F, E, A
CUNNINGHAM, T (2) Warrington: 1979 F, E
CURLING, D (+1) Warrington: 1977 f

DAVID, T (2) Cardiff C: 1981 E; 1982 A
DAVIES, F (1) New Hunslet: 1978 E
DAVIES, M (1) Bridgend: 1984 E
DIAMOND, S (2+1) Wakefield T: 1980 F, e; 1981 F
DIXON, C (10)3 Salford: 1975 F, E, **F, E, NZ, A**;
 1977 E, F; 1978 F. Hull K.R.: 1981 E

EVANS, R (5) Swinton: 1975 E, **F, F**; 1978 F;
 Salford: 1978 E

FENWICK, S (2) Cardiff C: 1981 E; 1982 A
FISHER, T (10)4 Leeds: 1975 F, **E, A, NZ.**
 Castleford: 1975 (cont.) **E, A, NZ**; 1977 E, F.
 Bradford N: 1978 A
FLOWERS, N (4) Wigan: 1980 F, E; 1981 E.
 Bridgend: 1984 E
FORD, Phil (1) Warrington: 1984 E
FRANCIS, W (19) Wigan: 1975 F, E, **F, E, A, NZ,
 E, A, NZ, F**; 1977 E, F. St. Helens: 1978 F, E,
 A; 1979 F, E. Oldham: 1980 F, E

GALLACHER, S (3+1) Keighley: 1975 f, E, **NZ, F**
GREGORY, B (3) Wigan: 1975 **E, NZ, F**
GRIFFITHS, C (+2) St. Helens: 1980 f; 1981 f

HALLETT, L (2) Cardiff C: 1982 A. Bridgend:
 1984 E
HERDMAN, M (2+1) Fulham: 1981 e, E; 1982 A
HOPKINS, L (1) Workington T: 1982 A

JAMES, M (11) St. Helens: 1975 **E**; 1978 F, E, A;
 1979 F, E; 1980 F, E; 1981 F, E, E
JOHNS, G (+2) Salford: 1979 f. Blackpool B: 1984 e
JONES, C (1+3) Leigh: 1975 **nz, F**; 1978 f, c
JULIFF, B (8) Wakefield T: 1979 F, E; 1980 F, E;
 1981 F, E: Wigan: 1982 A; 1984 E

McJENNETT, M (2+1) Barrow: 1980 F; 1982 a:
 1984 E
MANTLE, J (11+1)3 St. Helens: 1975 F, E, F, e,
 A, NZ, E, A, NZ, F; 1977 E; 1978 E
MATHIAS, R (20) St. Helens: 1975 F, E, **F, E, A,
 NZ, A, NZ, F**, 1977 E, F, 1978 F, E, A,
 1979 F, E; 1980 F, E; 1981 F, E
MILLS, J (13)4 Widnes: 1975 F, E, **E, A, NZ, A,
 NZ**; 1977 E, F; 1978 F, E, A; 1979 E
MURPHY, M (4+1) Bradford N: 1975 **F, NZ, F**;
 1977 f. St. Jacques, France: 1979 F

NICHOLAS, M (4+2) Warrington: 1975 F, e;
 1977 E, F; 1978 F; 1979 e

O'BRIEN, C (1) Bridgend: 1984 E
OWEN, G (2) Oldham: 1981 E, F
OWEN, R (+2) St. Helens: 1981 f, e

PARRY, D (6) Blackpool B: 1980 F, E; 1981 F, E, E;
 1982 A
PREECE, C (1) Bradford N: 1984 E
PRENDIVILLE, P (4+2) Hull: 1979 e; 1980 E;
 1981 F, e; 1982 A; 1984 E
PRITCHARD, G (1+2) Barrow: 1978 f, e;
 Cardiff C: 1981 E

RICHARDS, M (2)1 Salford: 1975 **F**; 1977 E
RINGER, P (2) Cardiff C: 1981 E; 1982 A
RISMAN, J (2+1) Workington T: 1978 F; 1979 f, E
ROWE, P (4+3)2 Blackpool B: 1975 **a, e, a.**
 Huddersfield: 1977 E, F; 1979 F, E
RULE, S (1) Salford: 1981 E

SELDON, C (1+1) St. Helens: 1980 f, E
SHAW, G (7) Widnes: 1978 F, A; 1980 F, E; 1981 E.
  Wigan: 1982 A; 1984 E
SKERRETT, T (7) Wakefield T: 1978 A; 1979 F, E;
  1980 F. Hull: 1981 F, E; 1984 E
SULLIVAN, C (10)4 Hull K.R.: 1975 **E, A, NZ, E**;
  1977 F; 1978 F, E, A; 1979 F, E

TREASURE, D (5) Oldham: 1975 **E, A, NZ, E**;
  1977 F
TURNER, G (3+3) Hull K.R.: 1975 e, **A**, e, **A**, f.
  Hull: 1978 E

WALLACE, R (+1) York: 1975 f
WALTERS, G (2+1) Hull: 1980 E. 1981 E.
  Bridgend 1984 e
WANBON, R (3)3+1 Warrington: 1975 **E, A, NZ**
WATKINS, D (14) Salford: 1975 F, E, **F, E, A, NZ,
  E, A, NZ, F**; 1977 E; 1978 E, A; 1979 F
WILKINS, R (1+1) Workington T: 1977 e, F
WILLIAMS, B (1) Cardiff C: 1982 A
WILLICOMBE, D (11)+2 Wigan: 1975 F, E, **F, E,
  A, NZ, NZ, F**; 1978 F, E, A
WILSON, D (4) Swinton: 1981 F, E, E; 1984 E
WILSON, F (7+2)4 St. Helens: 1975 F, E, **F, e, a,
  E, A, NZ, F**
WOODS, P (10) Widnes: 1977 E, F; 1978 F, E, A.
  Rochdale H: 1979 F, E. Hull: 1980 E; 1981 F, E

RECORDS

Highest score: 41-7 v. France at Llanelli 23 November, 1935 (Also widest margin win)
Highest score against: 60-13 v. England at St. Helens 28 May, 1978. (Also widest margin defeat)
Biggest home attendance: 30,000 v. England at Swansea 24 November, 1945
Most tries in a match: 4 by Will Davies (Halifax) v. Australia at Ebbw Vale 7 October, 1911
Most goals and points in a match: 14 (7g) by Johnny Thomas (Wigan) v. England at Tonypandy 20 April, 1908; Paul Woods (Widnes) v. France at Widnes 15 January 1978
Most appearances: 26 by Jim Sullivan (Wigan) 1921-39
Most tries in career: 9 by Arthur Daniels (Halifax) 1949-53; Alan Edwards (Salford, Bradford N) 1935-48
Most goals in career: 60 by Jim Sullivan (Wigan) 1921-39
Most points in career: 129 (60g,3t) by Jim Sullivan (Wigan) 1921-39

Glyn Shaw, a 1977 Widnes recruit from Neath RU, was capped seven times for Wales in a six-year international career.

Warrington packman Mike Nicholas, capped six times for Wales between 1975 and 1979.

New Zealand Test forward Brendon Tuuta, a September 1990 recruit for Featherstone Rovers.

TRANSFERS

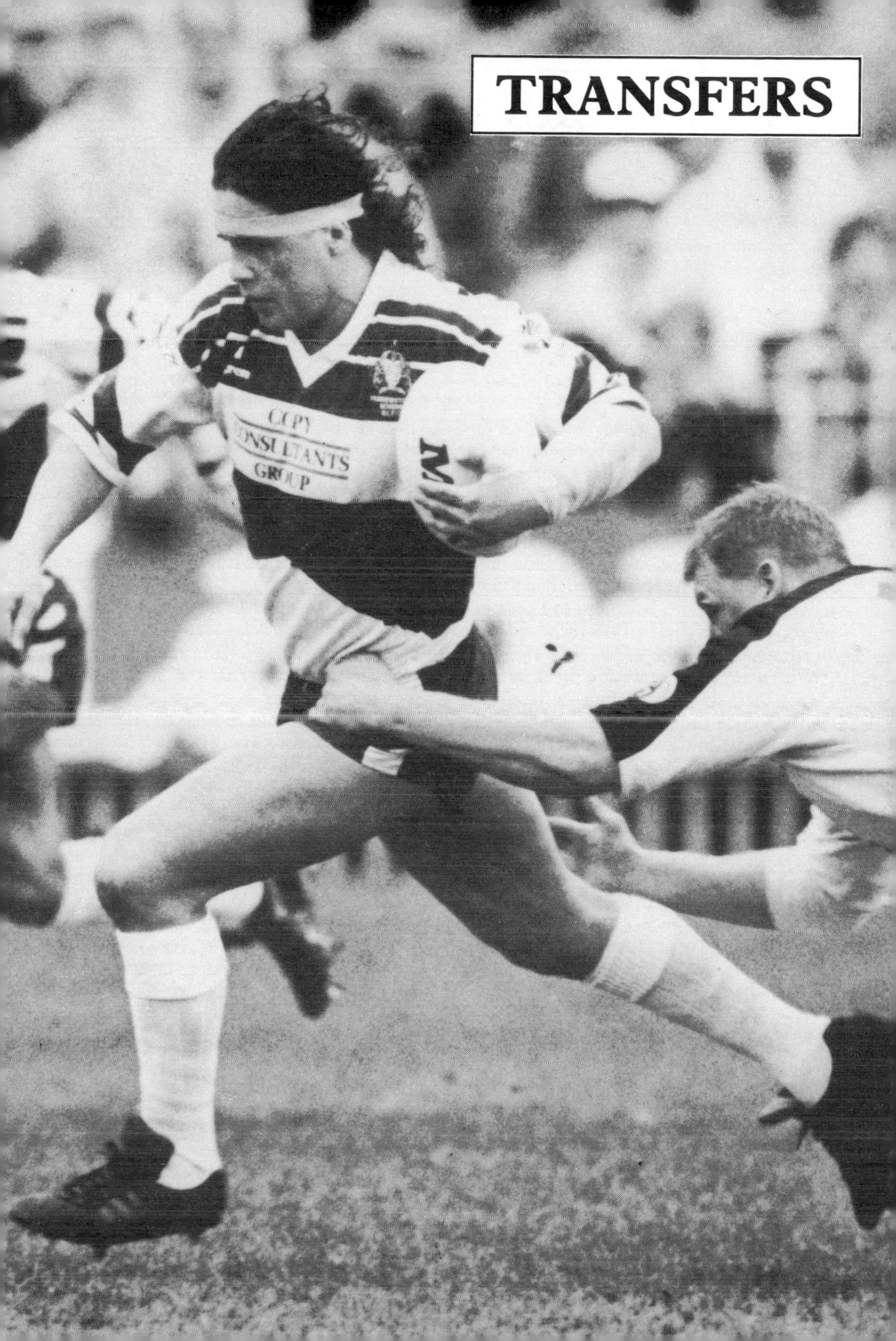

TRANSFERS

TRANSFER REVIEW
1 June 1990 to 31 May 1991

The biggest transfer fee during the period was the estimated £110,000 Leeds paid Warrington for 21-year-old prop Steve Molloy in September.

Featherstone Rovers doubled their club record fee when they signed Oldham's 24-year-old prop Leo Casey for £100,000 in July.

Another major transfer was Anthony Sullivan's move from Hull Kingston Rovers to St. Helens in May. There was some doubt about the reported fee, estimated to be around £100,000 for the 21-year-old, but it was almost certainly a record transfer fee for a winger. The previous record amount is also in some doubt. It involved Phil Ford's move from Bradford Northern to Leeds in a player-plus-cash deal in 1988 reckoned to be worth about £95,000.

With many clubs reporting financial difficulties there was a reduction in big-money transfer deals compared with the previous 12 months when there were five £100,000 or more moves.

Kelvin Skerrett would have been involved in a six-figure move except the Bradford Northern Test prop became a free agent at the end of the 1989-90 season and moved to Wigan without a transfer fee being paid.

Skerrett, however, signed a personal contract reported to be £225,000 for three years. The deal was clinched during Great Britain's tour of New Zealand and he was registered as a Wigan player on his return.

The total of transfers dropped from 187 to 125, but there was a big increase in the number of players joining clubs on loan — 94 against 26 the previous year, including the return of players to their original club.

There were four Tribunal hearings to decide disputed transfer fees: Paul Harkin from Bradford Northern to Leeds at £65,000, Ian Gormley from Salford to Rochdale Hornets at £60,000, Ikram Butt from Leeds to Featherstone Rovers for £30,000, and Chris Arkwright from St. Helens to Runcorn Highfield for a maximum of £6,000.

RUGBY UNION SIGNINGS

The total of 35 players being signed from Rugby Union was the highest for more than 10 years and double the previous year's figure. In 1983-84 only four Rugby Union players switched to professional Rugby League.

Four internationals were among the latest batch to leave the 15-a-side game with Welsh club Neath losing three stars — Rowland Phillips, Allan Bateman and Mark Jones.

Eddie Rombo became the first Kenyan international to switch codes when he signed for Leeds after impressing in the Wigan Sevens in August. The winger, who signed a three-year deal estimated at £100,000, made only nine first-team appearances during the season.

Warrington made a double swoop on Neath in September to sign Phillips and Bateman, having signed Wales B scrum half Kevin Ellis from Bridgend just before the end of the previous year's review.

Phillips, who played 10 times for Wales, signed a five-year contract reported to be worth about £100,000, but the forward made only four full first-team appearances during the season plus eight as substitute.

Bateman gained three Welsh caps before the centre signed a similar contract but made a bigger impression as he appeared 29 times including one as substitute.

Jones, who played 14 times for Wales, was the unluckiest of the Rugby Union signings as injury prevented the forward from appearing in Hull's first team during the season after clinching a five-year contract worth about £120,000 in October. At 6ft 5in and 18 stone he became one of the biggest players to play professional rugby.

Jones's signing came during the week that the Welsh Rugby Union called a special meeting to find ways of combatting the increasing number of players switching to Rugby League. A total of 14 internationals had left Wales in the last five years plus a few other top-ranking players, including Pontypool's B international full back, Matthew Silva, who joined Halifax during the season.

The relaxing of Union's amateur rules during the year, with the top players now able to earn many thousands of pounds off the field with rugby-related activities, led to speculation that fewer would be lured to League.

Other notable converts during the period were New Zealanders centre Darrall Shelford and scrum half Brett Iti to Bradford Northern, plus the latter's cousin, forward Clarry Iti, to Featherstone Rovers.

Jon Wray, the Morley and England B winger, signed for Castleford in October.

One of the most successful of the lesser known recruits was former Beverley RU captain Ian Marlow, who became a regular in Hull's pack and helped them to their surprise Stones Bitter Premiership final defeat of Widnes.

AMATEUR SIGNINGS

A total of 224 amateur Rugby League players turned professional compared with 249 in the previous period.

OVERSEAS SIGNINGS

The number of overseas players making first team appearances during the season reached record proportions for a second successive year, up from 158 to 168. And for the first time since 1982-83, New Zealanders outnumbered Australians 95 to 64.

The rise overall has continued despite the general overseas quota being reduced to three per club two years ago.

A record 95 New Zealanders made firstteam appearances last season, including a record 29 Test players. The previous records had been set a year earlier, with a total of 62 players including 19 Test men.

Of the 64 Australians to play first-team rugby last season only four had gained Test honours. The peak season for Australian recruits was 1986-87 with a total of 95.

Patrick Entat became the first Frenchman to play a full season in English Rugby League as the Test scrum half made 29 appearances for Hull.

Algerian-born Dazi Abdurahman joined Fulham from French club Chatillon and made six first-team appearances during the season.

Frenchmen became exempt from the overseas quota of three following a ruling in June 1990 by the Advisory Conciliation and Arbitration Service, who said there could be no restriction of movement on players from European common market countries. The decision followed Hull K.R.'s appeal that Test forward Daniel Divet should not count on their overseas quota after they signed him in May 1990. Ironically, after the ACAS ruling cleared Divet to play for Rovers, the Carcassonne forward said he no longer wished to move.

The following is a list of overseas players who made at least one first-team appearance during the 1990-91 season. The New Zealand register includes a few Pacific island-born players.

OVERSEAS REGISTER 1990-91

*Test players as at 1 June 1991

AUSTRALIA (64)

Tony Anderson	(Oldham)
Greg Austin	(Halifax, Hull K.R.)
Michael Booth	(Batley)
Darren Brown	(Trafford B.)
Russell Browning	(Fulham)
Tim Butler	(Dewsbury)
Peter Camroux	(Whitehaven)
Anthony Catton	(Carlisle)
Simon Chappell	(Runcorn H., Doncaster)
Jason Charlton	(Workington T.)
Lachlan Churchill	(Fulham)
Brett Clark	(Oldham)
*Noel Cleal	(Hull)
John Clifford	(Hunslet)
John Cogger	(Oldham)
Glen Coughlan	(Dewsbury)
David Cruickshank	(Fulham, Leigh)
Don Duffy	(Warrington)
Tim Dwyer	(Fulham)
Murray Fiechter	(Keighley)
Gary French	(Castleford)
Ian French	(Doncaster)
David Gallagher	(Rochdale H.)
Steve Gibson	(Salford)
Wally Gibson	(Huddersfield)
Craig Grauf	(Fulham)
Bob Grogan	(Bradford N., Rochdale H.)
Jeff Hardy	(Castleford)
Cavill Heugh	(Leeds)
Craig Hibberd	(Runcorn H.)
Bob Jackson	(Warrington)
David Jones	(Hunslet)
Ken Kerr	(Workington T.)
Steve Larder	(Castleford)
Mark Lee	(Fulham)
Peter Little	(Chorley)
Darren McCarthy	(Trafford B.)
Gary McFarlane	(Whitehaven)
Damien McGarry	(Hull)
Barry McGrath	(Nottingham C.)
Phil McKenzie	(Widnes)
Greg Mackey	(Hull)
Greg Manthey	(Fulham)
Stephen Mavin	(Trafford B.)
Ian Mellors	(Fulham)
Tony Mitchell	(Dewsbury, Halifax, Nottingham C.)
Shaun Mohr	(Fulham)
*Chris Mortimer	(Wakefield T.)
*Bryan Niebling	(Hull K.R.)
Chris O'Sullivan	(Warrington)
Greg Pearce	(Fulham)
Chris Perry	(Wakefield T.)
Darryl Pitt	(Fulham)
Paul Rees	(Batley)
Ian Russell	(Sheffield E.)
Aaron Sawyer	(Huddersfield)
Garry Schubert	(Carlisle)
Greg Shuttleworth	(Dewsbury, Huddersfield)
*Peter Tunks	(Salford, Sheffield E.)
Phil Veivers	(St. Helens)
Brad Webb	(Hull)
Paul White	(Hunslet)
Mark Wilkes	(Workington T.)
Bernard Wilkinson	(Fulham)

NEW ZEALAND (95)

Basil Ake	(Ryedale-York)
*Dean Bell	(Wigan)
Paul Bennett	(Nottingham C.)
Phil Bennett	(Nottingham C.)
Paul Bigg	(Trafford B.)
Frano Botica	(Wigan)
*Peter Brown	(Halifax, Leigh)
Robert Cheval	(Rochdale H.)
Trevor Clark	(Featherstone R.)
John Cleaver	(Nottingham C.)
John Collis	(Keighley)
*Shane Cooper	(St. Helens)
Shane Cummins	(Keighley, Nottingham C.)
Kevin Denton	(Carlisle)
Jason Donnelly	(Keighley)
Michael Dorreen	(Carlisle)
Reg Dunn	(Barrow)
Logan Edwards	(Swinton)
*Mark Elia	(Halifax)
*Esene Faimalo	(Widnes)
Mark Faumuina	(Ryedale-York)
Carl Findlay	(Carlisle)

*Clayton Friend	(Carlisle)	Peter Ropati	(Leigh)
Stuart Galbraith	(Rochdale H., Trafford B.)	*Tea Ropati	(St. Helens)
		Greig Rowe	(Carlisle)
*James Goulding	(Hull K.R.)	Craig Schumkel	(Nottingham C.)
Joe Grima	(Widnes)	*Adrian Shelford	(Wakefield T.)
Shaun Haereroa	(Keighley)	Darrall Shelford	(Bradford N.)
Carl Hall	(Doncaster)	Joe Smith	(Chorley)
Shane Hansen	(Salford)	*Kurt Sorensen	(Widnes)
Arnold Hema	(Nottingham C.)	Russell Stewart	(Huddersfield)
Bradley Hepi	(Carlisle)	Peter Subritzky	(Swinton)
Bradley Higgs	(Runcorn H.)	Tom Sutton	(Nottingham C.)
Greg Hiley	(Bradford N., Keighley)	*Kevin Tamati	(Salford)
		Nahu Timoko	(Carlisle)
*Shane Horo	(Whitehaven)	Mike Toomata	(Runcorn H., Trafford B., Whitehaven)
*Kevin Iro	(Wigan)		
*Tony Iro	(Leigh)	David Townsend	(Barrow)
Brett Iti	(Bradford N.)	*Paddy Tuimavave	(Workington T.)
Clarry Iti	(Featherstone R.)	Shane Tupaea	(Swinton)
Moses Keresome	(Barrow, Nottingham C.)	*Brendon Tuuta	(Featherstone R.)
		Andrew Vincent	(Bramley, Dewsbury)
Kerry Kite	(Nottingham C.)	Justin Wallace	(Bramley)
*Mike Kuiti	(Leeds)	*David Watson	(Hull K.R.)
*Francis Leota	(Salford, Sheffield E.)	*Graeme West	(Wigan)
*James Leuluai	(Doncaster, Ryedale York)	Sonny Whakarau	(Batley)
		Nigel White	(Carlisle)
Penieli Lia	(Widnes)	Aaron Whittaker	(Chorley)
Jason Lowrie	(Trafford B., Runcorn H.)	Dean Williams	(Workington T.)
		Sean Wilson	(Nottingham C.)
Charlie McAlister	(Oldham)	Walter Wilson	(Chorley)
Ken McIntosh	(Carlisle)	Robert Wilton	(Runcorn H.)
Loi Machee	(Nottingham C.)		
Des Maea	(Sheffield E.)	**FRANCE (2)**	
*Duane Mann	(Warrington)	Dazi Abdurahman	(Fulham)
*George Mann	(St. Helens)	*Patrick Entat	(Hull)
Vila Matautia	(Chorley, Doncaster)		
*Gary Mercer	(Warrington)	**KENYA (1)**	
Herbert Moore	(Hunslet)	Eddie Rombo	(Leeds)
Paul Nahu	(Bramley)		
*Tawera Nikau	(Ryedale-York)	**MOROCCO (1)**	
*Mark Nixon	(Rochdale H.)	Hussein M'Barki	(Fulham)
*Dane O'Hara	(Doncaster)		
Hitro Okesene	(Carlisle)	**SOUTH AFRICA (2)**	
Aaron Palelei	(Keighley)	Nick Du Toit	(Chorley, Wakefield T.)
*Sam Panapa	(Sheffield E.)	Adam Sada	(Fulham)
Mark Perry	(Carlisle)		
Neville Ramsey	(Doncaster, Halifax, Trafford B.)	**TONGA (3)**	
		Lawrence Johannson	(Fulham)
Peter Reinsfield	(Fulham)	Emosi Koloto	(Widnes)
Ian Rex	(Nottingham C.)	Armand Tuavao	(Runcorn H.)
*Joe Ropati	(Swinton)		

RECORD TRANSFERS

The first £1,000 transfer came in 1921 when Harold Buck joined Leeds from Hunslet, although there were reports at the time that another player was involved in the deal to make up the four-figure transfer. Other claims for the first £1,000 transfer are attached to Stan Brogden's move from Bradford Northern to Huddersfield in 1929. The following list shows how transfer fees have grown this century in straight cash deals only:

Season	Player	Position	From	To	Fee
1901-02	Jim Lomas	Centre	Bramley	Salford	£100
1910-11	Jim Lomas	Centre	Salford	Oldham	£300
1912-13	Billy Batten	Centre	Hunslet	Hull	£600
1921-22	Harold Buck	Wing	Hunslet	Leeds	£1,000
1929-30	Stanley Smith	Wing	Wakefield T.	Leeds	£1,075
1933-34	Stanley Brogden	Wing/centre	Huddersfield	Leeds	£1,200
1937-38	Billy Belshaw	Full back	Liverpool S.	Warrington	£1,450
1946-47	Bill Davies	Full back/centre	Huddersfield	Dewsbury	£1,650
1947-48	Bill Hudson	Forward	Batley	Wigan	£2,000
1947-48	Jim Ledgard	Full back	Dewsbury	Leigh	£2,650
1948-49	Ike Owens	Forward	Leeds	Castleford	£2,750
1948-49	Ike Owens	Forward	Castleford	Huddersfield	£2,750
1948-49	Stan McCormick	Wing	Belle Vue R.	St. Helens	£4,000
1949-50	Albert Naughton	Centre	Widnes	Warrington	£4,600
1950-51	Bruce Ryan	Wing	Hull	Leeds	£4,750
1950-51	Joe Egan	Hooker	Wigan	Leigh	£5,000
1950-51	Harry Street	Forward	Dewsbury	Wigan	£5,000
1957-58	Mick Sullivan	Wing	Huddersfield	Wigan	£9,500
1958-59	Ike Southward	Wing	Workington T.	Oldham	£10,650
1960-61	Mick Sullivan	Wing	Wigan	St. Helens	£11,000
1960-61	Ike Southward	Wing	Oldham	Workington T.	£11,002 10s
1968-69	Colin Dixon	Forward	Halifax	Salford	£12,000
1969-70	Paul Charlton	Full back	Workington T.	Salford	£12,500
1972-73	Eric Prescott	Forward	St. Helens	Salford	£13,500
1975-76	Steve Nash	Scrum half	Featherstone R.	Salford	£15,000
1977-78	Bill Ashurst	Forward	Wigan	Wakefield T.	£18,000
1978-79	Clive Pickerill	Scrum half	Castleford	Hull	£20,000
1978-79	Phil Hogan	Forward	Barrow	Hull K.R.	£35,000
1979-80	Len Casey	Forward	Bradford N.	Hull K.R.	£38,000
1980-81	Trevor Skerrett	Forward	Wakefield T.	Hull	£40,000
1980-81	George Fairbairn	Full back	Wigan	Hull K.R.	£72,500
1985-86	Ellery Hanley	Centre/stand off	Bradford N.	Wigan	£85,000
1985-86	Joe Lydon	Centre	Widnes	Wigan	£100,000
1986-87	Andy Gregory	Scrum half	Warrington	Wigan	£130,000
1987-88	Lee Crooks	Forward	Hull	Leeds	£150,000
1987-88	Garry Schofield	Centre	Hull	Leeds	£155,000
1989-90	Graham Steadman	Stand off	Featherstone R.	Castleford	£170,000

MOST MOVES

Geoff Clarkson extended his record number of transfers to 12 when he left Leigh for Featherstone Rovers on 27 October 1983. He played for 10 different English clubs and had a brief spell in Australia.

Clarkson, born on 12 August 1943 was 40 years old when he finished playing regular first team rugby in 1983-84. He turned professional with Wakefield Trinity in 1966 after gaining Yorkshire County forward honours with Wakefield Rugby Union Club.

Clarkson's club career in England is as follows:

1966 — Wakefield T.
1968 — Bradford N.
1970 — Leigh
1971 — Warrington
1972 — Leeds
1975 — York
1976 — Bramley
1978 — Wakefield T. and Hull K.R.
1980 — Bradford N. and Oldham
1981 — Leigh
1983 — Featherstone R.

1990-91 SIGNINGS

The following is a register of signings by clubs from 1 June 1990 to 31 May 1991. The right-hand column lists the club from which the player was recruited (ARL Amateur Rugby League, RU — Rugby Union).

In some instances a player who wishes to retain his amateur status is not registered although he may be named in the club's list of appearances.

Although this is a register of signings, it is possible to trace a club's transfers by scrutinising the right hand column.

Indicates where clubs have agreed to a player being signed 'on loan', a temporary transfer, the Rugby Football League prohibiting a subsequent transfer within 28 days. Where a player on loan has not been retained his return to his original club is also marked.

BARROW

Signed	Player	Club From
23.8.90	Fletcher, Andrew	Wakefield T.
23.8.90	Spears, Kevin	Lock Lane ARL
30.8.90	Cairns, David	Salford
6.9.90	*Rea, Kevin	Warrington
6.9.90	Rhodes, Stuart	Askam ARL
6.9.90	Roper, Kevin	Barrow Island ARL
6.9.90	Cartmel, Ian	Askam ARL
6.9.90	Archer, Darren	Marsh Hornets ARL
6.9.90	Jackson, Wayne	Dalton ARL
6.9.90	Simpson, Nigel	Dalton ARL
6.9.90	Payne, Darren	Holker Pioneers ARL
6.9.90	Jackson, Stephen	Dalton ARL
11.9.90	Peel, Phil	Panthers ARL
15.9.90	*Douglas, Ian	Wakefield T.
17.9.90	Norton, Stephen	Wakefield T.
21.9.90	Dunn, Reg	Southern United, NZ
21.9.90	Townsend, David	Richmond, NZ
21.9.90	Blackwood, Mark	Kells ARL
21.9.90	Campbell, Gary	Holker Pioneers ARL
25.9.90	Keresoma, Moses	Otahuhu RU, NZ
13.10.90	Wood, Mark	RU
11.1.91	Howse, Stephen	Whitehaven
10.2.91	Wild, John	
27.2.91	Westwood, Gary	Barrow Island ARL
25.3.91	*Kay, Tony	St. Helens

BATLEY

Signed	Player	Club From
6.7.90	Redick, Paul	Shaws ARL
2.8.90	Bavister, Maurice	Shaws ARL
2.8.90	Madden, Michael	Firths ARL
15.8.90	Sheridan, Mark	Batley Boys ARL
15.8.90	Craven, Nigel	Batley Boys ARL
20.8.90	Booth, Michael	Emerald, Aus
20.8.90	Crossley, John	Ryedale York
24.8.90	Thornton, Gary	Wakefield T.
13.9.90	Child, Darren	Morley RU
16.10.90	Rees, Paul	South Newcastle, Aus
19.10.90	Whakarau, Sonny	Upper Hutt, NZ
12.11.90	Speight, Darren	Batley Victoria ARL
23.11.90	*Pratt, Richard	Hull K.R.
29.12.90	Ledgers, Simon	Batley Victoria ARL
29.12.90	Maguire, Mick	Shaws ARL

BRADFORD NORTHERN

Signed	Player	Club From
3.7.90	Powell, Daio	Middleton, ARL
18.7.90	Iti, Brett	Suburbs RU, NZ
20.7.90	Shelford, Darrall	Ngongotaha RU, NZ
16.8.90	Lee, Darren	Middleton ARL
12.10.90	Hiley, Gregory	Mount Albert, NZ
8.1.91	Gumbs, Hugh	West Bowling ARL
8.2.91	Godfrey, Heath	Keighley
13.3.91	Grogan, Bob	Rochdale H.

BRAMLEY

Signed	Player	Club From
2.7.90	Evans, David	Staffordshire Poly ARL
24.8.90	*Fletcher, Thomas	Doncaster
28.8.90	Haigh, Colin	Redhill ARL
14.9.90	Jones, Keith	Doncaster
14.9.90	Bettney, Neville	Normanton ARL
20.9.90	Wallace, Justin	Linwood, NZ
12.10.90	Timson, Andy	Doncaster
12.10.90	Nahu, Paul	Ngongotaha, NZ
1.11.90	*Hall, Gary	Featherstone R.
2.11.90	Blankley, Dean	Castleford
9.11.90	Vincent, Andrew	NZ
10.11.90	Clawson, Neil	Oldham
8.12.90	*Hall, Gary	Featherstone R.
14.12.90	Clark, Andrew	Bramley RU
18.1.91	Dickinson, Roy	Halifax
20.1.91	*Charles, Marquis	Hull
24.1.91	*Harker, Keith	Ryedale-York
25.1.91	*Fagan, Gary	Ryedale-York
25.1.91	*Walsh, Chris	Halifax
25.1.91	*Kemp, Martin	Halifax
25.1.91	Smith, Neil	Leeds
25.1.91	Rayner, Gary	Dudley Hill ARL
25.1.91	Devine, Paul	Ryedale-York
5.3.91	*Gill, Henderson	Bradford N.

CARLISLE

Signed	Player	Club From
6.8.90	Chapman, John	Glasson ARL
6.8.90	Lay, Robert	Widnes Tigers ARL
6.8.90	Lunt, Peter	Aspatria ARL
6.8.90	Seagar, Stewart	Kells ARL
13.8.90	Rowe, John	Sunderland ARL
23.8.90	Friend, Clayton	North Sydney, Aus
30.8.90	Davies, Lee	Broughton Red Rose ARL
30.8.90	Cowgill, David	Aspatria RU
7.9.90	Okesene, Hitro	Manukau, NZ
7.9.90	Timoko, Nahu	Manukau, NZ
7.9.90	Denton, Kevin	Ryde Eastwood, NZ
7.9.90	Rowe, Greig	Penzance RU
28.9.90	McIntosh, Ken	Northcote, NZ
9.10.90	Dorreen, Michael	Addington, Canterbury, NZ
12.10.90	Buglass, Barry	Cockermouth ARL
19.11.90	Catton, Anthony	Valleys, Aus
27.11.90	Charlton, Gary	Whitehaven
18.1.91	Jefferson, Michael	Askam ARL
18.1.91	Burns, Anthony	Glasson ARL
15.3.91	*Hewer, Gary	Whitehaven
22.5.91	Ackerman, Robert	Leeds

CASTLEFORD

Signed	Player	Club From
7.8.90	Atkins, Garry	Ryedale-York
12.10.90	Fletcher, Paul	Hull
24.10.90	Wray, Jonathan	Morley RU
12.11.90	Hay, Andrew	Redhill ARL
20.4.91	Middleton, Simon	Knottingley RU

CHORLEY

Signed	Player	Club From
30.7.90	Smith, Joe	NZ
1.8.90	McGuigan, Paul	RU
13.8.90	Eccles, Bob	Trafford B.
15.8.90	Wakefield, Stuart	Swinton
15.8.90	Hankey, Stephen	Rose Bridge ARL
15.8.90	Newton, Anthony	St. Cuthberts ARL
20.8.90	Sharkey, Michael	St. Patricks ARL
24.8.90	Meadows, Kevin	Trafford B.
2.9.90	*Sedgwick, Peter	Huddersfield
3.9.90	Roberts, Paul	Trafford B.
14.9.90	Du Toit, Nick	Barrow
14.9.90	Ramsdale, Dennis	Wigan
28.9.90	Whittaker, Aaron	Halswell, Christchurch, NZ
28.9.90	Wilson, Walter	Halswell, Christchurch, NZ
9.10.90	Shaw, Mark	Trafford B.
8.11.90	Matautia, Vila	Otahuhu, NZ
31.12.90	Little, Peter	Past Brothers, Aus
1.3.91	Bolton, Mark	St. Patricks ARL

DEWSBURY

Signed	Player	Club From
1.7.90	Dickinson, Andy	Huddersfield
2.7.90	Durnin, Paul	Runcorn H.
15.8.90	Ingham, Gareth	Bramley
15.8.90	Kelley, Richard	Shaw Cross ARL
23.8.90	Van Bellen, Gary	Sheffield E.
24.8.90	Barnes, John	Eastmoor ARL
24.8.90	Garnett, Paul	Oldham St. Annes ARL
24.8.90	Slater, Mark	BRK Gildersome ARL
20.9.90	Saville, Mark	Siddal RU
26.9.90	Vincent, Andrew	NZ
31.10.90	Mitchell, Tony	Chinchilla, Aus
8.11.90	*Marsden, Bob	Rochdale H.
22.11.90	Shuttleworth, Greg	Huddersfield
23.11.90	Stephenson, William	Deighton ARL
3.12.90	Vasey, Chris	Leeds
14.1.91	*Drummond, Barry	Featherstone R.
18.1.91	Hughes, Paul	Featherstone R.
21.5.91	Delaney, Paul	Leeds
21.5.91	Worthy, Paul	Leeds

DONCASTER

Signed	Player	Club From
22.8.90	Price, Darren	Castleford
22.8.90	Sunderland, Tony	Doncaster
22.8.90	Holmes, Gary	Oulton ARL
22.8.90	Heptinstall, Jason	Hunslet
24.8.90	O'Hara, Dane	Hull
24.8.90	Ellis, Mark	Walnut Warriors ARL
24.8.90	Watkin, Darren	Middleton ARL
28.8.90	Fenton, Wayne	Batley
4.9.90	*Cass, Mark	Hull
7.9.90	Sheldon, Ian	Wakefield T.
7.9.90	Race, Wayne	Bramley

7.9.90	Hall, Carl	Linwood, NZ
7.9.90	French, Ian	North Sydney, Aus
12.10.90	Chappell, Simon	Briarcroft RU
1.11.90	*Patrick, Shaun	Hull
13.11.90	Matautia, Vila	Samoa
2.12.90	Holmes, David	Halifax
10.12.90	Barnes, Stephen	Lock Lane ARL
3.1.91	Pell, Richard	Cutsyke ARL
12.1.91	*Murphy, Kieron	Fulham
18.1.91	Brookfield, Paul	Hull Dockers ARL
18.1.91	Leuluai, James	Ryedale-York
27.1.91	*Holmes, David	Halifax
14.2.91	Miller, Tony	Oldham
12.3.91	*Close, David	Sheffield E.
2.4.91	Marsh, Richard	Stanley Rangers ARL
10.4.91	Labourn, Terry	Shaws ARL

FEATHERSTONE ROVERS

Signed	Player	Club From
3.7.90	Beaumont, Jonathon	Travellers Saints ARL
3.7.90	Booth, Craig	Travellers Saints ARL
3.7.90	Dickenson, Robert	Travellers Saints ARL
3.7.90	Jepson, John	Travellers Saints ARL
3.7.90	Longstaff, Spencer	Travellers Saints ARL
3.7.90	Minter, Steven	
3.7.90	Smith, Michael	Travellers Saints ARL
3.7.90	Wood, Jason	Travellers Saints ARL
26.7.90	Casey, Leo	Oldham
9.8.90	Butt, Ikram	Leeds
14.9.90	Tuuta, Brendon	Western Suburbs, Aus
20.9.90	Simpson, Frank	Huddersfield
5.10.90	Morrisey, Gary	Southern Suburbs, Aus
9.11.90	Simpson, Owen	Keighley
16.11.90	*Carlyle, Brendon	Ryedale-York
14.12.90	Goulbourne, Alexander	Northern Dairies ARL
18.1.91	Smelt, Roger	Travellers Saints ARL

FULHAM

Signed	Player	Club From
20.8.90	Reinsfield, Peter	Hukanui, NZ
20.8.90	McInerney, Paul	Balmain, Aus
20.8.90	Helg, Albert	St. Mary's College, NZ
20.8.90	Peart, Barrington	Fulham Travellers ARL
20.8.90	Winstanley, Chris	
20.8.90	Scott, Conrad	St. Mary's ARL
28.8.90	Cruickshank, David	South Sydney, Aus
28.8.90	Rotheram, David	West London Institute ARL
29.8.90	Burt, Keith	RU
30.8.90	Callow, Steve	West London Institute ARL
14.9.90	Roberts, Steve	
28.9.90	Abdurahman, Dazi	Chatillon XIII, France
28.9.90	Stevens, Andrew	Hornsey Lambs ARL
16.10.90	Manthey, Gregory	Northern Suburbs, Aus
18.10.90	Dwyer, Tim	Eastern Suburbs, Aus
30.10.90	Churchill, Lachlan	Sawtell, Aus
6.11.90	Corcoran, Colin	
13.11.90	Koellner, Michael	South Sydney, Aus
5.12.90	Wilkins, Brett	RU

5.12.90	Scarlett, Richard	Peckham ARL
5.1.91	Sada, Adam	Ashville College
5.1.91	Holderness, Kevin	Essex Scimitars RU
21.1.91	Wilkinson, Bernard	Essex Scimitars RU
29.2.91	Nolen, Craig	Brothers, Aus

HALIFAX

Signed	Player	Club From
24.8.90	Platt, Alan	Leigh
24.8.90	Southernwood, Roy	Castleford
24.8.90	Keebles, Michael	Dudley Hill ARL
24.8.90	Heslop, Simon	Dudley Hill ARL
30.8.90	Roberts, Lea	Ovenden ARL
6.9.90	Richardson, Gary	Calder Valley ARL
13.9.90	Wilson, Warren	Leeds
14.9.90	*Jowett, Chris	Huddersfield
14.9.90	Wilkinson, Bernard	Cowra, Aus
19.9.90	Austin, Greg	Hull K.R.
2.10.90	Elia, Mark	Canterbury Bankstown, Aus
7.10.90	Ramsey, Neville	NZ
12.10.90	Bancroft, Phil	Glenora, NZ
2.11.90	Barker, Andrew	Queensbury ARL
23.11.90	Irvine, Jimmy	Hull K.R.
23.11.90	*Grimoldby, Nick	Sheffield E.
27.11.90	Robinson, Christopher	Dudley Hill ARL
3.12.90	*Puckering, Neil	Doncaster
18.1.91	Brooke-Cowden, Mark	Salford
21.1.91	Brown, Peter	Leigh
21.1.91	Dunn, John	Park Amateurs ARL
18.2.91	Sharp, Henry	Dudley Hill ARL
7.3.91	Dixon, Paul	Old Crossleyans RU
13.3.91	Silva, Matthew	Pontypool RU
19.3.91	*Francis, Norman	Oldham
15.4.91	Robert, David	Ovenden ARL
15.4.91	Pickles, Damieon	Siddall ARL
16.4.91	Maugrandra, Richard	Siddall ARL
6.5.91	Watson, David	Hull K.R.

HUDDERSFIELD

Signed	Player	Club From
1.7.90	Wells, Trevor	St. Josephs ARL
4.7.90	McTigue, Mick	Salford
24.8.90	Meillam, Paul	York All Blacks ARL
24.8.90	Hawkyard, Colin	Oldham
24.8.90	Parr, Chris	St. Patricks ARL
24.8.90	Barker Scholes, Damon	Paddock ARL
24.8.90	Maskery, Graham	Leigh Miners ARL
24.8.90	Royston, Paul	West Bowling ARL
28.8.90	*O'Donnell, Damien	Castleford
11.9.90	Staniforth, Tony	Featherstone R.
17.9.90	*Seabourne, Peter	Bradford N.
21.9.90	Mountain, Gary	Lock Lane ARL
22.9.90	Bean, Chris	Greetland Allrounder ARL
22.9.90	Gregg, Carl	Siddall ARL
28.9.90	Stewart, Russell	New Zealand
8.10.90	Sawyer, Aaron	Mount Pritchard, Aus
11.10.90	*Mallinder, Paul	Wakefield T.

Hull scrum half Patrick Entat, the first Frenchman to play a full season in English club football.

HUNSLET

Signed	Player	Club From
18.7.90	Coyle, Michael	Middleton, ARL
14.8.90	*Lidbury, Steven	Sheffield E.
25.9.90	White, Paul	Brothers Rockhampton, Aus
27.9.90	Precious, Andrew	York All Blacks ARL
9.10.90	Jones, David	Atherton Roosters, Aus
9.10.90	Clifford, John	Tully, Aus
19.10.90	Bucktrout, Terry	Panthers ARL
9.11.90	Moore, Herbert	Mangere East, NZ
15.11.90	*Cartwright, Phil	Sheffield E.
23.11.90	Bell, Keith	Featherstone R.
25.11.90	*Waites, Brian	Batley
6.1.91	Daniel, Alan	Queens ARL
23.1.91	*Halafihi, Nick	Sheffield E.
23.1.91	Bettney, Neville	Normanton ARL
22.2.91	*Carlyle, Brendan	Ryedale-York
5.3.91	*White, Paul	Ryedale-York
28.3.91	Wilson, Sean	Parkside ARL

KEIGHLEY

Signed	Player	Club From
2.8.90	Farrell, Carlton	Deighton Woolpack ARL
2.8.90	James, Anthony	Deighton Woolpack ARL
10.8.90	*Mitchell, Patrick	Leeds
13.8.90	Burke, Mick	Oldham
13.8.90	Wooler, Mark	—
13.8.90	Cox, Dave	Worth Village ARL
13.8.90	Beardsmore, Nigel	Panthers ARL
28.8.90	Nelson, David	Huddersfield
28.8.90	Kelly, Haydn	Bramley
15.9.90	Gascoigne, Andrew	Bramley
25.9.90	Collis, John	Manuran, NZ
26.9.90	Donnelly, Jason	NZ
28.9.90	Malcolm, Trevor	West Bowling ARL
8.10.90	Haereroa, Shaun	North Beach, NZ
12.10.90	Burks, Jake	Siddal ARL
22.10.90	Cummins, Shane	Nottingham C.
22.10.90	Wardle, Chris	Park Amateurs ARL
30.10.90	Priestley, Raymond	Dudley Hill ARL
6.11.90	Hiley, Gregory	Mount Albert, NZ
12.11.90	Fiechter, Murray	Fortitude Valleys, Aus
18.11.90	Dixon, Paul	Halifax RU
30.11.90	Palelei, Aaron	Otahuhu, NZ
7.2.91	*Needham, David	Halifax
19.3.91	Stephenson, Andrew	Clayton ARL
19.3.91	Stephenson, Philip	Clayton ARL
24.3.91	Eyres, Andy	Widnes
24.3.91	*Chick, Stuart	Warrington
24.3.91	McLean, Brian	—
25.3.91	*Mirfin, Phillip	Castleford
25.3.91	*Race, Wayne	Doncaster
6.4.91	Plath, Andre	St. Marys London ARL
5.3.91	Wasyliw, John	Halifax RU

HULL

Signed	Player	Club From
12.7.90	Entat, Patrick	Avignon, Fr
25.7.90	Marlow, Ian	Beverley RU
14.8.90	Dearlove, Andrew	British Gas ARL
20.8.90	Webb, Brad	Kempsey, Aus
12.10.90	Jones, Mark	Neath RU
4.1.91	McGarry, Damien	Balmain, Aus
14.1.91	Heptinstall, Jason	Doncaster
25.2.91	Durham, Steve	Bramley
2.4.91	Nolan, Gary	NDLB ARL

HULL KINGSTON ROVERS

Signed	Player	Club From
14.7.90	Hoe, Sean	ARL
14.7.90	Cook, Graham	Greatfield Juniors ARL
14.7.90	Crane, Michael	Greatfield Juniors ARL
20.8.90	Sodje, Bright	Blackheath, RU
24.8.90	Chatfield, Gary	Eureka ARL
28.8.90	Watson, Dave	Ryedale-York
14.9.90	Goulding, James	Newcastle Knights, Aus
28.9.90	Jackson, Wayne	West Hull ARL
7.10.90	Hadi, Stephen	ARL
31.1.91	*Moore, Darren	Halifax

Kenyan Eddie Rombo, a July 1990 capture by Leeds.

LEIGH

Signed	Player	Club From
3.7.90	Brennan, Brian	Leigh East ARL
16.7.90	Bleakeley, Michael	Leigh Miners ARL
16.7.90	Entwistle, Paul	Silver Well ARL
15.8.90	Cannon, Peter	Crosfields ARL
24.8.90	Woods, John	Rochdale H.
14.9.90	Iro, Tony	Manly, Aus
20.9.90	*Bridge, Russell	Fulham
20.12.90	Sullivan, Andrew	Rochdale H.
14.1.91	Irwin, Anthony	Terrigal Wamberal, Aus
4.2.91	Waterworth, Keith	Swinton
12.2.91	*Gittins, Thomas	Chorley
12.2.91	*Ellis, Jeff	Chorley
16.2.91	*Cruickshank, David	Fulham

NOTTINGHAM CITY

Signed	Player	Club From
17.8.90	*Cooper, Colin	Leeds
20.8.90	Chappell, Anthony	Doncaster
20.8.90	Wilson, Sean	NZ
20.8.90	Riley, Malcolm	Mansfield
20.8.90	Crellin, Martin	Mansfield
20.8.90	Edridge, Lee	Clowne ARL
20.8.90	Jackson, Dean	Clowne ARL
20.8.90	Wood, Richard	Clowne ARL
20.8.90	Jackson, Darryl	Clowne ARL
20.8.90	Robson, Duncan	Castleford RU
7.9.90	Toder, Jai	Shirebrook
10.9.90	Rex, Ian	NZ
10.9.90	Schumkel, Craig	NZ
10.9.90	Cleaver, John	NZ
10.9.90	Keresoma, Moses	NZ
17.9.90	Fraser, Mark	South London ARL
17.9.90	Quinn, John	South London ARL
17.9.90	Townsend, Jeff	South London ARL
19.9.90	*Portz, Karl	Carlisle
21.9.90	Machee, Loi	Richmond
21.9.90	Busby, David	Featherstone R.
26.9.90	Sutton, Thomas	Mount Albert, NZ
26.9.90	Kite, Keri	Mount Albert, NZ
28.9.90	*Gregoire, Don	Dewsbury
28.9.90	*Moore, John	Dewsbury
19.10.90	Holland, Michael	RU
1.11.90	McGrath, Barry	Quinndi, Aus
24.11.90	*Coop, Chris	Keighley
23.12.90	Gillespie, Michael	St. Josephs ARL
5.1.91	Bennett, Paul	RU
5.1.91	Bennett, Philip	RU
16.1.91	Francis, Donovan	Derby RU
19.1.91	*Burgess, Mark	Dewsbury
21.1.91	Stoppard, Shane	Shirebrook
20.2.91	Pattison, Ian	Clowne ARL
20.2.91	Butler, Lee	Clowne ARL
3.3.91	Burgess, Mark	Dewsbury
10.3.91	Taylor, Adrian	Clowne ARL
15.3.91	*Cooper, Paul	Dewsbury
21.3.91	*Meehan, Gary	Huddersfield
6.4.91	Hare, Tyrone	Notts Crusaders ARL

LEEDS

Signed	Player	Club From
2.7.90	Harkin, Paul	Bradford N.
3.7.90	Anderson, John	Lock Lane ARL
3.7.90	Cole, Paul	Stanley ARL
3.7.90	Deakin, Leigh	Heworth ARL
3.7.90	Judge, Chris	Heworth ARL
23.7.90	Maloney, Francis	St. John Fisher ARL
24.7.90	Rombo, Eddie	Mean Machine RU, Kenya
19.9.90	Wane, Shaun	Wigan
21.9.90	Stephens, Gareth	Lock Lane ARL
23.9.90	Molloy, Stephen	Warrington
5.2.91	Cocker, Paul	Travellers Rest ARL
14.2.91	Hughes, Darren	Redhill ARL

OLDHAM

Signed	Player	Club From
1.7.90	Pyke, Derek	Widnes
16.8.90	Duane, Ronnie	Warrington
31.8.90	Francis, Norman	Leeds
16.10.90	Eckersley, Chris	Saddleworth Rangers ARL
26.10.90	Barrow, Paul	Thatto Heath ARL
19.3.91	Longstaff, Simon	Halifax
9.4.91	Warburton, Stephen	Woolston ARL

ROCHDALE HORNETS

Signed	Player	Club From
23.7.90	O'Neill, Mike	Widnes
17.8.90	Gormley, Ian	Salford
17.8.90	Whitfield, Colin	Halifax
17.8.90	Gartland, Stephen	Oldham St. Annes ARL
20.8.90	Belle, Adrian	Oldham St. Annes ARL
20.8.90	Kay, Martin	Oldham St. Annes ARL
20.8.90	Calland, Matthew	Oldham St. Annes ARL
14.9.90	Holding, Neil	St. Helens
14.9.90	Grogan, Robert	Gold Coast, Aus
17.9.90	Gallagher, Dave	Western Suburbs, Aus
17.9.90	Nixon, Mark	Hornby, NZ
17.9.90	Williams, Michael	Golbourne, ARL
16.10.90	*Lever, David	St. Helens
16.10.90	Halsall, Ian	St. Patricks ARL
22.10.90	Ramsey, Neville	Richmond, NZ
9.11.90	Galbraith, Stuart	Trafford B.
9.11.90	Abram, Darren	Trafford B.
20.12.90	*Dunn, Brian	Leigh
11.1.91	*Dean, Mick	Leigh
14.3.91	Cheval, Robert	Ealing ARL

RUNCORN HIGHFIELD

Signed	Player	Club From
7.10.90	Hibberd, Craig	Lakes United, Aus
18.10.90	Arkwright, Chris	St. Helens
18.10.90	*Lowrie, Jason	Northcote Tigers, NZ
18.10.90	*Toomata, Mike	Northcote Tigers, NZ
1.11.90	Goulding, Dean	St. Judes ARL
1.1.91	Cooney, Paul	Clock Face ARL
11.1.91	Toomata, Mike	Trafford B.
17.1.91	*Turner, Stuart	Widnes
18.1.91	*Forber, Gary	Swinton
25.1.91	Johnson, William	Dewsbury
29.1.91	Barrow, Norman	Thatto Heath ARL
30.1.91	Wakefield, Stuart	Swinton
31.1.91	Tinsley, Edward	Thatto Heath ARL
3.2.91	Chappell, Simon	Halifax
3.2.91	Littler, Paul	Thatto Heath ARL
2.3.91	*Brown, Andrew	Swinton
18.3.91	*Turner, Stuart	Widnes
2.4.91	*Brown, Andrew	Swinton

RYEDALE-YORK

Signed	Player	Club From
23.7.90	Devine, Paul	Stanningley ARL
23.7.90	Fellows, Darren	Middleton ARL
23.7.90	Harker, Keith	Stanningley ARL
23.7.90	Howarth, Richard	Lock Lane ARL
23.7.90	Martin, Kevin	Normanton ARL
23.7.90	McCarthy, Martin	Fryston ARL
23.7.90	Pinkney, Nicolas	Greatfield ARL
23.7.90	Pryce, Stephen	West Bowling ARL
9.8.90	*Timson, Andrew	Doncaster
24.8.90	Leuluai, James	Wakefield T.
20.9.90	*Vasey, Chris	Leeds
28.9.90	Nikau, Tawera	Otahuhu, NZ
18.10.90	Faumuina, Mark	Otahuhu, NZ
1.11.90	Pallister, Alan	York All Blacks ARL
1.11.90	Dickinson, Robert	York Civil Service ARL
11.1.91	*Lidbury, Steven	Sheffield E.
18.1.91	*Cornforth, Philip	Bradford N.
21.1.91	Fowler, Richard	Heworth ARL
18.2.91	*Cornforth, Philip	Bradford N.
22.2.91	*Wilkinson, Shaun	Hunslet
22.2.91	*Warrener, Stan	Hunslet
22.3.91	*James, Neil	Leeds
25.3.91	*Ackerman, Rob	Leeds

ST. HELENS

Signed	Player	Club From
6.7.90	Ward, Kevin	Castleford
25.8.90	Ropati, Tea	NZRL
30.8.90	Casey, Sean	—
14.9.90	*Forber, Gary	Swinton
18.1.91	Dudley, Steven	Thatto Heath ARL
29.4.91	Sullivan, Anthony	Hull K.R.
29.4.91	Davies, Glynn	Leigh Easts ARL

SALFORD

Signed	Player	Club From
30.8.90	Tamati, Kevin	Warrington
11.9.90	Tunks, Peter	Penrith, Aus
13.9.90	Gilfillan, John	Wigan
20.9.90	Hansen, Shane	Northcote NZ
19.10.90	Swift, Philip	Saddleworth Rangers ARL
25.10.90	Quigley, Jonathan	Leigh Miners ARL
23.11.90	Leota, Francis	Sheffield E.
30.11.90	Horrigan, Liam	Woolston ARL
21.1.91	O'Connor Terence	Widnes Tigers ARL
29.1.91	Gelling, Brian	Swinton
31.1.91	Stephenson, David	Leigh
12.3.91	Dean, Michael	Leigh
10.4.91	Finney, Ian	Widnes Tigers ARL
10.4.91	Ainsworth, Stephen	Widnes St. Maries ARL
25.4.91	Young, David	Leeds
2.1.91	Barratt, David	Rochdale H.
10.4.91	Finney, Ian	Widnes Tigers ARL
10.4.91	Ainsworth, Stephen	Widnes St. Maries ARL
25.4.91	Young, David	Leeds
21.5.91	Randall, Craig	Leigh Miners ARL

SCARBOROUGH PIRATES

Signed	Player	Club From
10.4.91	Hill, Kenneth	Castleford

SHEFFIELD EAGLES

Signed	Player	Club From
23.7.90	Moore, Thomas	Hunslet Parkside ARL
23.7.90	Dyer, Peter	Hoyland ARL
23.7.90	Wilson, Clive	—
2.8.90	Wilby, Tim	Hull
20.8.90	Panapa, Sam	Teatatu, NZ
7.9.90	Russell, Ian	Illawarra, Aus
29.10.90	*Pearce, Gary	Hull
22.11.90	Tunks, Peter	Salford
11.12.90	Mumby, Keith	Bradford N.
3.1.91	*Warrener, Stanley	Hunslet
11.1.91	Lewis, Peter	Bramley
21.1.91	Maea, Desmond	Otahuhu, NZ
21.2.91	*Bateman, Andy	St. Helens
6.3.91	*Price, Richard	Hull
19.5.91	Davidson, Jason	Junior Eagles ARL

SWINTON

Signed	Player	Club From
30.8.90	Clark, Jason	St. Annes ARL
6.9.90	Pimlott, John	St. Annes ARL
26.9.90	Ratu, Emon	Smallbridge
19.10.90	Griffiths, Darren	Rose Bridge ARL
19.10.90	Boucher, Philip	St. Annes ARL
19.10.90	Smith, Ian	St. Annes ARL
22.10.90	Kennett, Paul	Tondu RU
14.1.91	Best, Brian	St. Annes ARL
28.1.91	*McNicol, Tony	Carlisle
31.1.91	*Murdoch, Gary	Carlisle
5.2.91	Herbert, Steve	Trafford B.
20.2.91	*Frodsham, Tommy	St. Helens
20.2.91	Daintith, Ian	Farnworth ARL
7.3.91	Wilkinson, Chris	Dewsbury
1.4.91	Leyland, Martin	Thatto Heath ARL
9.5.91	Prince, Glen	Langworthy ARL

TRAFFORD BOROUGH

Signed	Player	Club From
16.8.90	Greaves, Alan	Crosfields ARL
16.8.90	Slater, Neil	Thatto Heath ARL
6.9.90	Osman, Cassim	Leigh Miners ARL
21.9.90	Nuttall, Nicholas	Folly Lane ARL
27.9.90	Maloney, David	Leigh Miners ARL
28.9.90	Reid, Terence	Crosfields ARL
12.10.90	Galbraith, Stuart	Northcote Tigers, NZ
12.10.90	Sumner, Richard	Leigh Miners, ARL
26.10.90	Bigg, Paul	Innsfail Brothers, NZ
1.11.90	Lowrie, Jason	Northcote Tigers, NZ
9.11.90	*Bamber, Simon	Rochdale H.
22.12.90	Bent, Peers	Leigh Miners ARL
1.3.91	*Webb, Vinny	Rochdale H.
9.4.91	Farrall, Lee	Crosfields ARL

South African Nick Du Toit, a September 1990 recruit for Wakefield Trinity.

WAKEFIELD TRINITY

Signed	Player	Club From
23.8.90	Webster, Mark	St. Helens
30.8.90	*Carter, Darren	Doncaster
14.9.90	Shelford, Adrian	Manly, Aus
14.9.90	Jones, David	St. Patricks ARL
28.9.90	Byrne, Ged	Wigan
28.9.90	Mortimer, Chris	Penrith, Aus
28.9.90	Du Toit, Nick	Chorley
28.9.90	Wilson, Stephen	Dewsbury Celtic ARL
31.12.90	Wright, Nigel	Stanley Rangers ARL
31.12.90	Colbeck, Mark	Eastmoor ARL
31.12.90	Goddard, Richard	Stanley Rangers ARL
16.1.91	Spencer, Gary	Leeds

WARRINGTON

Signed	Player	Club From
9.8.90	Bennett, Andrew	Woolston Rovers ARL
11.9.90	Dusher, Mark	Hull Boys ARL
26.9.90	O'Sullivan, Chris	Canberra Raiders, Aus
28.9.90	Duffy, Don	Carlisle
28.9.90	Phillips, Rowland	Neath RU
28.9.90	Bateman, Allan	Neath RU
12.10.90	Westhead, John	Leigh
5.12.90	Tees, Gary	Barrow
21.1.91	Boyle, Chris	Katoomba, Aus
7.4.91	Hodkinson, Colin	Leigh Miners ARL

WHITEHAVEN

Signed	Player	Club From
24.8.90	Rae, Neil	Whitehaven RU
24.8.90	Routledge, John	Egremont RU
6.9.90	Turley, Norman	Trafford B.
7.9.90	Pugsley, Stuart	Leigh East ARL
20.9.90	Camroux, Peter	Balmain, Aus
20.9.90	McFarlane, Gary	Balmain, Aus
11.10.90	Toomata, Mike	Trafford B.
26.10.90	Cosgrove, Neale	Kells ARL
2.11.90	Burns, David	Kells ARL
9.11.90	*Brown, David	Trafford B.
9.11.90	*Richardson, David	Barrow
11.1.91	Maguire, Stephen	Barrow
11.1.91	Beckwith, Mark	Barrow
21.1.91	Batley, Stephen	Workington T.
8.3.91	*Pollard, Damien	Carlisle
8.3.91	*Rea, Stephen	Carlisle
8.3.91	*Kendall, David	Carlisle

WIDNES

Signed	Player	Club From
23.7.90	Ogburn, Carl	Simms Cross ARL
23.7.90	Hunter, Brian	Farnworth ARL
23.7.90	McCurrie, Steve	Hensingham ARL
23.7.90	Tyrer, Christian	Leigh Rangers ARL
7.8.90	Wynne, Stephen	Golborne Parkside ARL
13.8.90	Whitfield, Darren	Wigan St. Judes ARL
21.8.90	Evans, Nicholas	Woolston ARL
17.10.90	Faimalo, Esene	Upper Hutt, NZ
29.11.90	Davidson, Paul	Hensingham, ARL
21.1.91	Lia, Penieli	Upper Hutt, NZ

WIGAN

Signed	Player	Club From
24.6.90	Skerrett, Kelvin	Bradford N.
1.8.90	*Bridge, Russell	Fulham
15.9.90	Moran, Shaune	Golborne Parkside ARL
26.9.90	Chambers, Steven	Golborne Parkside ARL
21.1.91	Hainsworth, Gregory	—

WORKINGTON TOWN

Signed	Player	Club From
14.7.90	Ashton, Ray	Leeds
24.7.90	Oglanby, Martin	Glasson Rangers ARL
22.8.90	Chick, Stuart	Leeds
22.8.90	Scott, Ian	Carlisle
22.8.90	Atherton, Mark	Netherhall RU
22.8.90	Hyncica, John	Egremont ARL
22.8.90	Stansfield, Ivan	Seddon Atkinson ARL
24.8.90	McLean, Ian	St. Annes ARL
29.8.90	Graham, John	Carlisle
20.9.90	Wilkes, Mark	Carlisle
29.9.90	*Roskell, Mark	Warrington
3.10.90	Armstrong, Colin	Hull K.R.
19.10.90	Williams, Dean	Northcote Tigers NZ
22.11.90	Kerr, Ken	Canterbury, Aus
22.11.90	Tuimavave, Paddy	Northcote Tigers, NZ
14.12.90	Simpson, Colin	Nottingham C.

Stones Bitter Man of Steel 1991, Garry Schofield.

AWARDS

THE 1991 MAN OF STEEL AWARDS

Launched in the 1976-77 season, the Rugby Football League's official awards are presented to the Man of Steel, the personality judged to have made the most impact on the season; the First and Second Division Players of the Year, decided by a ballot of the players; the Young Player of the Year, under-21 at the start of the season; the Coach of the Year and Referee of the Year, all chosen by a panel of judges.

The official award scheme was sponsored by Trumanns Steel from inception in 1977 to 1983, brewers Greenall Whitley taking over in 1984 until 1989. Stones Bitter introduced a three-year £50,000 sponsorship in 1990.

Stones Bitter Man of Steel

A cheque for £4,000 and a £300 silver champagne goblet were presented to Leeds skipper **Garry Schofield**. Appointed vice-captain of Great Britain, he was the only player to feature in all 10 Tests during the year. Rated Man of the Match in all three Tests in New Zealand, he was automatic Man of the Series, also gaining the Man of the Match rating against France at Leeds. Schofield scored eight tries and three drop goals in the 10 Tests. He graduated to second place in the all-time Great Britain tryscoring chart and third place in the tally of Test caps, despite still being only 25. Passed the 200-try landmark during the year and figured in the top ten try chart. Voted the Leeds Player of the Year by a record margin and was the recipient of the Ernest Ward Trophy as Great Britain Player of the Year.

Stones Bitter First Division Player of the Year

Widnes utility back **Jonathan Davies** topped the poll of fellow Stones Bitter Championship players. The first-ever Welsh winner of a Man of Steel award, he broke the Widnes points in a season record with 342 and equalled the points in a match record with 34. Davies, who was capped six times during the year, was top goal and points scorer on the 1990 Lions tour.

Stones Bitter Second Division Player of the Year

His fellow players' choice in the twin ballot was Ryedale-York back row forward **Tawera Nikau**. The Kiwi Test man played in all 25 games during his stay, scoring three tries, his impressive form earning a lucrative new contract with First Division Castleford.

Stones Bitter Young Player of the Year

Wigan second row man **Denis Betts** took the award at the third attempt, having been runner-up in the previous two years. He missed only one of Great Britain's 10 Tests during the year, including the 1990 tour Down Under. Earned Man of the Match rating in France and was awarded the Lance Todd Trophy at Wembley. Betts was the only player to appear in all of Wigan's 39 matches.

Stones Bitter Referee of the Year

Kippax whistler **John Holdsworth** received his fourth title in 11 years. Top of the assessment chart, he was chosen by the French to take charge of their two Tests with Australia in the autumn of 1990 and selected by the Australians to control their three Tests with New Zealand in the summer of 1991. Also appointed for the 1991 Stones Bitter Premiership final.

Stones Bitter Coach of the Year

Australian **John Monie** earned top rating for the second successive season, Wigan becoming the first club to repeat a Cup-League double. The Stones Bitter Championship was clinched in their last match, their fourth game in seven days. Best attacking and defensive records in the First Division.

● Each of the above five category winners received £1,000 and a £250 silver wine goblet.

THE MAN OF STEEL AWARDS ROLL OF HONOUR

	Man of Steel	1st Division Player	2nd Division Player	Young Player	Coach	Referee
1977	David Ward (Leeds)	Malcolm Reilly (Castleford)	Ged Marsh (Blackpool B.)	David Ward (Leeds)	Eric Ashton (St. Helens)	Billy Thompson (Huddersfield)
1978	George Nicholls (St. Helens)	George Nicholls (St. Helens)	John Woods (Leigh)	John Woods (Leigh)	Frank Myler (Widnes)	Billy Thompson (Huddersfield)
1979	Doug Laughton (Widnes)	Mick Adams (Widnes)	Steve Norton (Hull)	Steve Evans (Featherstone R.)	Doug Laughton (Widnes)	Mick Naughton (Widnes)
1980	George Fairbairn (Wigan)	Mick Adams (Widnes)	Steve Quinn (Featherstone E.)	Roy Holdstock (Hull K.R.)	Peter Fox (Bradford N.)	Fred Lindop (Wakefield)
1981	Ken Kelly (Warrington)	Ken Kelly (Warrington)	John Crossley (York)	Des Drummond (Leigh)	Billy Benyon (Warrington)	John Holdsworth (Kippax)
1982	Mick Morgan (Carlisle)	Steve Norton (Hull)	Mick Morgan (Carlisle)	Des Drummond (Leigh)	Arthur Bunting (Hull)	Fred Lindop (Wakefield)
1983	Allan Agar (Featherstone R.)	Keith Mumby (Bradford N.)	Steve Nash (Salford)	Brian Noble (Bradford N.)	Arthur Bunting (Hull)	Robin Whitfield (Widnes)
1984	Joe Lydon (Widnes)	Joe Lydon (Widnes)	David Cairns (Barrow)	Joe Lydon (Widnes)	Tommy Dawes (Barrow)	Billy Thompson (Huddersfield)
1985	Ellery Hanley (Bradford N.)	Ellery Hanley (Bradford N.)	Graham Steadman (York)	Lee Crooks (Hull)	Roger Millward (Hull K.R.)	Ron Campbell (Widnes)
1986	Gavin Miller (Hull K.R.)	Gavin Miller (Hull K.R.)	Derek Pyke (Leigh)	Shaun Edwards (Wigan)	Chris Anderson (Halifax)	Fred Lindop (Wakefield)
1987	Ellery Hanley (Wigan)	Andy Gregory (Wigan)	John Cogger (Runcorn H.)	Shaun Edwards (Wigan)	Graham Lowe (Wigan)	John Holdsworth (Kippax)
1988	Martin Offiah (Widnes)	Steve Hampson (Wigan)	Peter Smith (Featherstone R.)	Shaun Edwards (Wigan)	Doug Laughton (Widnes)	Fred Lindop (Wakefield)
1989	Ellery Hanley (Wigan)	David Hulme (Widnes)	Darryl Powell (Sheffield E.)	Paul Newlove (Featherstone R.)	Graham Lowe (Wigan)	John Holdsworth (Kippax)

(continued)

| 1990 | Shaun Edwards (Wigan) | Andy Goodway (Wigan) | John Woods (Rochdale H.) | Bobby Goulding (Wigan) | John Monie (Wigan) | Robin Whitfield (Widnes) |
| 1991 | Garry Schofield (Leeds) | Jonathan Davies (Widnes) | Tawera Nikau (Ryedale-York) | Denis Betts (Wigan) | John Monie (Wigan) | John Holdsworth (Kippax) |

NOMINEES:

1977 *1st Division Player:* Bruce Burton (Castleford), Vince Farrar (Featherstone R.). *2nd Division Player:* Jeff Grayshon (Dewsbury), Keith Hepworth (Hull). *Young Player:* Jimmy Crampton (Hull), Harry Pinner (St. Helens). *Coach:* Keith Cotton (Featherstone R.), Mal Reilly (Castleford). *Referee:* Joe Jackson (Pudsey), Mick Naughton (Widnes).

1978 *1st Division Player:* Roger Millward (Hull K.R.), Harry Pinner (St. Helens). *2nd Division Player:* Phil Hogan (Barrow), Mick Morgan (York). *Young Player:* Neil Hague (Leeds), Keith Mumby (Bradford N.). *Coach:* Eric Ashton MBE (St. Helens), John Mantle (Leigh). *Referee:* Ron Campbell (Widnes), Fred Lindop (Wakefield).

1979 *1st Division Player:* Brian Lockwood (Hull K.R.), Tommy Martyn (Warrington). *2nd Division Player:* Barry Banks (York), John Wolford (Dewsbury). *Young Player:* Mick Burke (Widnes), John Woods (Leigh). *Coach:* Billy Benyon (Warrington), Arthur Bunting (Hull). *Referee:* Fred Lindop (Wakefield), Billy Thompson (Huddersfield).

1980 *1st Division Player:* Len Casey (Hull K.R.), George Fairbairn (Wigan). *2nd Division Player:* Mick Blacker (Halifax), John Wolford (Dewsbury). *Young Player:* Steve Hubbard (Hull K.R.), Harry Pinner (St. Helens). *Coach:* Maurice Bamford (Halifax), Arthur Bunting (Hull). *Referee:* Ron Campbell (Widnes), Billy Thompson (Huddersfield).

1981 *1st Division Player:* Mick Adams (Widnes), Tommy Martyn (Warrington). *2nd Division Player:* Arnie Walker (Whitehaven), Danny Wilson (Swinton). *Young Player:* Paul Harkin (Hull K.R.), Keith Mumby (Bradford N.). *Coach:* Reg Bowden (Fulham), Peter Fox (Bradford N.) *Referee:* Ron Campbell (Widnes), Fred Lindop (Wakefield).

1982 *1st Division Player:* Jeff Grayshon (Bradford N.), Andy Gregory (Widnes). *2nd Division Player:* Denis Boyd (Carlisle), Alan Fairhurst (Swinton). *Young Player:* Lee Crooks (Hull), Andy Gregory (Widnes). *Coach:* Doug Laughton (Widnes), Alex Murphy/Colin Clarke (Leigh). *Referee:* Gerry Kershaw (York), Billy Thompson (Huddersfield).

1983 *1st Division Player:* Bob Eccles (Warrington), David Topliss (Hull). *2nd Division Player:* Tommy David (Cardiff C.), Mike Lampkowski (Wakefield T.). *Young Player:* Ronnie Duane (Warrington), Andy Goodway (Oldham). *Coach:* Alex Murphy (Wigan), Frank Myler (Oldham). *Referee:* John Holdsworth (Leeds), Fred Lindop (Wakefield).

1984 *1st Division Player:* Garry Schofield (Hull), John Woods (Leigh). *2nd Division Player:* Lynn Hopkins (Workington T.), John Wolford (Hunslet). *Young Player:* Gary Divorty (Hull), Garry Schofield (Hull). *Coach:* Arthur Bunting (Hull), Roger Millward (Hull K.R.). *Referee:* Derek Fox (Wakefield), Fred Lindop (Wakefield).

1985 *1st Division Player:* Harry Pinner (St. Helens), Gary Prohm (Hull K.R.). *2nd Division Player:* Terry Langton (Mansfield M.), Peter Wood (Runcorn H.). *Young Player:* Deryck Fox (Featherstone R.), Andy Platt (St. Helens). *Coach:* Arthur Bunting (Hull), Colin Clarke/Alan McInnes (Wigan). *Referee:* Fred Lindop (Wakefield), Stan Wall (Leigh).

1986 *1st Division Player:* Steve Ella (Wigan), John Fieldhouse (Widnes). *2nd Division Player:* John Henderson (Leigh), Graham King (Hunslet). *Young Player:* Paul Lyman (Featherstone R.), Roy Powell (Leeds). *Coach:* Roger Millward (Hull K.R.), John Sheridan (Doncaster). *Referee:* John Holdsworth (Kippax), Robin Whitfield (Widnes).

1987 *1st Division Player:* Lee Crooks (Hull), Ellery Hanley (Wigan). *2nd Division Player:* Andy Bateman (Hunslet), Les Holliday (Swinton). *Young Player:* Paul Loughlin (St. Helens), Kevin McCormack (St. Helens). *Coach:* Chris Anderson (Halifax), Alex Murphy (St. Helens). *Referee:* Kevin Allatt (Southport), Fred Lindop (Wakefield).

1988 *1st Division Player:* Martin Offiah (Widnes), Kurt Sorensen (Widnes). *2nd Division Player:* Deryck Fox (Featherstone R.), Hugh Waddell (Oldham). *Young Player:* Paul Medley (Leeds), Steve Robinson (Halifax). *Coach:* Alex Murphy (St. Helens), Barry Seabourne (Bradford N.). *Referee:* John Holdsworth (Kippax), Ray Tennant (Castleford).

1989 *1st Division Player:* Andy Gregory (Wigan), Kelvin Skerrett (Bradford N.). *2nd Division Player:* Cavill Heugh (Barrow), Chris Johnson (Leigh). *Young Player:* Grant Anderson (Castleford), Denis Betts (Wigan). *Coach:* Peter Fox (Featherstone R.), Brian Smith (Hull). *Referee:* Ray Tennant (Castleford), Robin Whitfield (Widnes).

1990 *1st Division Player:* Deryck Fox (Featherstone R.), Andy Platt (Wigan). *2nd Division Player:* David Bishop (Hull K.R.), John Cogger (Oldham). *Young Player:* Denis Betts (Wigan), Anthony Sullivan (Hull K.R.). *Coach:* Tony Barrow (Oldham), Brian Johnson (Warrington). *Referee:* John Holdsworth (Kippax), Colin Morris (Huddersfield).

1991 *1st Division Player:* Andy Gregory (Wigan), George Mann (St. Helens). *2nd Division Player:* Steven Kerry (Salford), Peter Ropati (Leigh). *Young Player:* Phil Clarke (Wigan), Craig Richards (Bradford N.). *Coach:* Ray Ashton (Workington T.), Doug Laughton (Widnes). *Referee:* Brian Galtress (Bradford), Jim Smith (Halifax).

STONES BITTER TEAM OF THE MONTH AWARDS 1990-91

Introduced in the 1979-80 season, the scheme acknowledges the adjudged Team of the Month in both Division One and Two.

A panel of judges representing Stones Bitter and the Rugby League selected the two monthly winners, the First Division winners receiving £500, the Second Division £350, plus a framed citation.

The awards were sponsored for the first four seasons by Shopacheck before Lada Cars took over in the 1983-84 season and introduced the first-ever Team of the Year title. Stones Bitter took over the sponsorship in 1987-88, the 1991 Team of the Year, **Wigan,** receiving £1,500.

	First Division	Second Division
Aug./Sept.	Widnes	Salford
Oct.	Hull	Fulham
Nov.	Wakefield T.	Swinton
Dec.	Warrington	Keighley
Jan.	Castleford	Workington T.
Feb.	Widnes	Batley
Mar.	Wigan	Doncaster
Apr./May	Wigan	Salford

Team of the Year
1983-84: Widnes
1984-85: Hull K.R.
1985-86: Halifax
1986-87: Wigan
1987-88: Widnes
1988-89: Wigan
1989-90: Wigan
1990-91: Wigan

WALLACE ARNOLD – SUNDAY MIRROR ENTERTAINER AWARDS 1990-91

Introduced in 1986-87, the scheme was sponsored by Wallace Arnold and promoted by the *Sunday Mirror*.

Each month a player was chosen as Entertainer of the Month to receive a Wallace Arnold holiday voucher for £400. The Entertainer of the Year was awarded a £1,500 holiday voucher, the 1991 winner being Great Britain vice-captain and Leeds skipper **Garry Schofield**.

Entertainer of the Month

Sept.	Emosi Koloto (Widnes)
Oct.	Garry Schofield (Leeds)
Nov.	Dave Watson (Hull K.R.)
Dec.	Deryck Fox (Featherstone R.)
Jan.	Kevin Ellis (Warrington)
Feb.	Martin Offiah (Widnes)
Mar.	Frano Botica (Wigan)
Apr./May	Denis Betts (Wigan)

Entertainer of the Year

1987:	Ellery Hanley (Wigan)
1988:	Martin Offiah (Widnes)
1989:	Martin Offiah (Widnes)
1990:	Deryck Fox (Featherstone R.)
1991:	Garry Schofield (Leeds)

TRAVELEADS TOP FAN 1991

Sheffield Eagles fan John Lack (43) won the 1991 Traveleads awards as official Supporter of the Year, with a prize of a £4,500 holiday for two coinciding with the second and third Tests in Australia in 1992 against the touring Great Britain side.

STONES BITTER TOP SCORERS AWARDS 1990-91

Launched in the 1976-77 season, the scheme was designed to reward the top try and goal scorers in the League. Sponsored by Stones Bitter, the 1991 awards were worth £25 a try and £5 a goal.

For the fourth successive season, the top try merchant was Widnes winger **Martin Offiah** who touched down 49 times to earn a prize cheque for £1,225.

The top marksman was Salford scrum half **Steve Kerry** who hit the target 177 times to qualify for a prize pay out of £885.

New Zealander Dave Watson, Entertainer of the Month in November 1990.

WAR OF THE ROSES

LANCASHIRE v. YORKSHIRE RESULTS

All county championship matches except where stated.

Date	Result		Score	Venue	Attendance
7 Dec. 1895	Yorkshire	won	8 - 0	Oldham	9,059
29 Feb. 1896	Lancashire	won	8 - 3	Huddersfield	5,300
21 Nov. 1896	Lancashire	won	7 - 3	Oldham	15,000
20 Nov. 1897	Yorkshire	won	7 - 6	Bradford P.A.	11,000
5 Nov. 1898	Yorkshire	won	20 - 9	Salford	8,000
4 Nov. 1899	Lancashire	won	16 - 13	Halifax	9,000
3 Nov. 1900	Lancashire	won	24 - 5	Rochdale	18,000
15 Feb. 1902	Yorkshire	won	13 - 8	Hull	15,000
15 Nov. 1902	Lancashire	won	13 - 0	Salford	14,000
14 Nov. 1903	Lancashire	won	8 - 0	Leeds	11,000
12 Nov. 1904	Yorkshire	won	14 - 5	Oldham	8,500
4 Nov. 1905	Lancashire	won	8 - 0	Hull	8,000
3 Nov. 1906	Lancashire	won	19 - 0	Salford	5,000
2 Nov. 1907	Yorkshire	won	15 - 11	Halifax	7,000
31 Oct. 1908	Lancashire	won	13 - 0	Salford	5,000
4 Nov. 1909	Yorkshire	won	27 - 14	Hull	6,000
7 Nov. 1910	Lancashire	won	17 - 3	Wigan	2,000
25 Jan. 1912	Lancashire	won	13 - 12	Halifax	3,199
16 Dec. 1912	Yorkshire	won	20 - 8	Oldham	4,000
10 Dec. 1913	Yorkshire	won	19 - 11	Huddersfield	3,500
24 Sept. 1919	Lancashire	won	15 - 5	Broughton	5,000
21 Oct. 1920	Yorkshire	won	18 - 3	Hull	7,000
4 Oct. 1921	Yorkshire	won	5 - 2	Rochdale	4,000
7 Dec. 1922	Match drawn	—	11 - 11	Hull K.R.	8,000
8 Dec. 1923	Lancashire	won	6 - 5	Oldham	8,000
29 Nov. 1924	Lancashire	won	28 - 9	Halifax	6,000
12 Dec. 1925	Lancashire	won	26 - 10	St. Helens	13,000
30 Oct. 1926	Lancashire	won	18 - 13	Wakefield	9,000
29 Oct. 1927	Lancashire	won	35 - 19	Warrington	12,000
3 Nov. 1928	Lancashire	won	33 - 10	Halifax	6,520
22 Mar. 1930	Lancashire	won	18 - 3	Rochdale	4,000
18 Oct. 1930	Yorkshire	won	25 - 15	Wakefield	9,000
17 Oct. 1931	Lancashire	won	11 - 8	Warrington	10,049
*29 Oct. 1932	Yorkshire	won	30 - 3	Wakefield	4,000
25 Sept. 1933	Yorkshire	won	15 - 12	Oldham	2,000
*9 Jan. 1935	Match drawn	—	5 - 5	Leeds	1,500
12 Oct. 1935	Lancashire	won	16 - 5	Widnes	6,700
21 Oct. 1936	Lancashire	won	28 - 6	Castleford	7,648
12 Feb. 1938	Lancashire	won	10 - 9	Rochdale	3,653
*26 Oct. 1938	Match drawn	—	10 - 10	Leeds	3,000
10 Nov. 1945	Lancashire	won	17 - 16	Swinton	11,059
9 Nov. 1946	Yorkshire	won	13 - 10	Hunslet	5,000
12 Nov. 1947	Lancashire	won	22 - 10	Wigan	6,270
3 May 1949	Lancashire	won	12 - 3	Halifax	7,000
5 Oct. 1949	Lancashire	won	22 - 13	Warrington	15,000

(Continued)

Date	Result		Score	Venue	Attendance
18 Oct. 1950	Yorkshire	won	23 - 15	Huddersfield	6,547
10 Oct. 1951	Yorkshire	won	15 - 5	Leigh	11,573
28 Apr. 1953	Yorkshire	won	16 - 8	Hull	8,400
14 Oct. 1953	Lancashire	won	18 - 10	Leigh	12,870
6 Oct. 1954	Yorkshire	won	20 - 10	Bradford	8,500
26 Sept. 1955	Lancashire	won	26 - 10	Oldham	8,000
26 Sept. 1956	Lancashire	won	35 - 21	Hull	8,500
23 Sept. 1957	Yorkshire	won	25 - 11	Widnes	6,200
24 Sept. 1958	Yorkshire	won	35 - 19	Hull K.R.	5,000
29 Oct. 1958	Yorkshire	won	16 - 15	Leigh	8,500
11 Nov. 1959	Yorkshire	won	38 - 28	Leigh	6,417
31 Aug. 1960	Lancashire	won	21 - 20	Wakefield	15,045
9 Oct. 1961	Lancashire	won	14 - 12	Leigh	4,970
26 Sept. 1962	Yorkshire	won	22 - 8	Wakefield	7,956
11 Sept. 1963	Lancashire	won	45 - 20	St. Helens	11,200
23 Sept. 1964	Yorkshire	won	33 - 10	Hull	7,100
10 Nov. 1965	Yorkshire	won	16 - 13	Swinton	5,847
21 Sept. 1966	Lancashire	won	22 - 17	Leeds	10,528
24 Jan. 1968	Lancashire	won	23 - 17	Widnes	8,322
25 Sept. 1968	Yorkshire	won	10 - 5	Hull K.R.	6,656
3 Sept. 1969	Lancashire	won	14 - 12	Salford	4,652
13 Jan. 1971	Yorkshire	won	32 - 12	Castleford	2,000
24 Feb. 1971	Yorkshire	won	34 - 8	Castleford	4,400
29 Sept. 1971	Yorkshire	won	42 - 22	Leigh	4,987
11 Oct. 1972	Yorkshire	won	32 - 18	Castleford	2,474
19 Sept. 1973	Lancashire	won	17 - 15	Widnes	3,357
25 Sept. 1974	Yorkshire	won	20 - 14	Keighley	1,219
16 Oct. 1974	Lancashire	won	29 - 11	Widnes	3,114
20 Dec. 1975	Yorkshire	won	17 - 7	Wigan	700
1 Mar. 1977	Yorkshire	won	18 - 13	Castleford	2,730
††19 Oct. 1977	Lancashire	won	33 - 8	Widnes	5,056
27 Sept. 1978	Lancashire	won	23 - 7	Widnes	4,283
12 Sept. 1979	Yorkshire	won	19 - 16	Castleford	2,738
24 Sept. 1980	Lancashire	won	17 - 9	Widnes	1,593
9 Sept. 1981	Yorkshire	won	21 - 15	Castleford	1,222
26 May 1982	Yorkshire	won	22 - 21	Leigh	1,738
WR11 Sept. 1985	Yorkshire	won	26 - 10	Wigan	6,743
WR17 Sept. 1986	Yorkshire	won	26 - 14	Leeds	5,983
WR16 Sept. 1987	Yorkshire	won	16 - 10	Wigan	9,748
WR21 Sept. 1988	Yorkshire	won	24 - 14	Leeds	8,244
WR20 Sept. 1989	Yorkshire	won	56 - 12	Wigan	10,182

* Match abandoned but result stands   †† Queen's Jubilee match   WR War of the Roses
● There were also a few Lancashire-Yorkshire matches played during the war years but not of a competitive nature.

SUMMARY

Yorkshire won 42   Lancashire won 41   Drawn 3

LANCASHIRE REGISTER

The following is a register of current players who have appeared for Lancashire, including fixtures other than the War of the Roses. Each played at least one first team game last season.

ARKWRIGHT, C. (4) St. Helens

BENTLEY, K. (4) Widnes
BYRNE, G. (1) Wigan

CASE, B. (3) Warrington 2, Wigan
COTTRELL, A. (+1) Leigh
CULLEN, P. (2) Warrington
CURRIER, A. (1) Widnes

DERMOTT, M. (1) Wigan
DOWD, B. (+1) Widnes
DRUMMOND, D. (4) Leigh 3, Warrington
DUANE, R. (1) Warrington

ECCLES, R. (3) Warrington
EDWARDS, S. (2+1) Wigan
EYRES, R. (1+1) Widnes

FIELDHOUSE, J. (2+2) Warrington +2, Widnes 2
FORBER, P. (1) St. Helens
FORSTER, M. (2) Warrington

GILDART, I. (+1) Wigan
GREGORY, A. (9) Widnes 3, Warrington 2, Wigan 4
GREGORY, M. (4) Warrington
GROVES, P. (1) St. Helens

HAGGERTY, R. (+1) St. Helens
HAMPSON, S. (3) Wigan
HENDERSON, J. (1+1) Leigh
HOLDING, N. (2) St. Helens
HULME, D. (1+1) Widnes
HULME, P. (2) Widnes
HUMPHRIES, A. (1) Warrington

LEDGER, B. (1) St. Helens
LOUGHLIN, P. (2) St. Helens
LYDON, J. (4) Widnes, Wigan 3

McCORMACK, K. (1) St. Helens
McCULLOCH, N. (+1) Leigh
McGINTY, W. (1+1) Warrington
MEADOWS, K. (1) St. Helens
MYLER, A. (2) Widnes

OFFIAH, M. (1) Widnes
O'LOUGHLIN, Keiron (4+1) Wigan 2+1, Widnes, Salford
O'NEILL, M. (9) Widnes
O'NEILL, S. (3) Wigan

PENDLEBURY, J. (1) Salford
PLATT, A. (2) St. Helens, Wigan
POTTER, I. (5) Warrington 2, Leigh 2, Wigan
PRESTON, M. (2) Wigan
PYKE, D. (3) Leigh 2, Widnes

ROBERTS, M. (2) Warrington
ROUND, P. (2) Oldham

STEPHENSON, D. (6) Salford 2, Wigan 4

WANE, S. (1+1) Wigan
WHITFIELD, C. (4+1) Salford 3, Wigan +1, Halifax
WILLIAMS, P. (+1) Salford
WOODS, J. (6) Leigh 3, Warrington
WRIGHT, D. (1) Widnes

LANCASHIRE TEAMS . . . A REVIEW

Lancashire team line-ups since the introduction of the Rodstock War of the Roses in September 1985, including opposition other than Yorkshire.

1985 Yorkshire

Wigan: 11 Sept.

Lost 10-26

Burke (Widnes) 1g
Ledger (St. Helens)
Stephenson (Wigan)
Keiron O'Loughlin (Salford)
Lydon (Widnes)
A. Myler (Widnes)
A. Gregory (Warrington) 1t
M. O'Neill (Widnes)
Webb (Warrington)
Forber (St. Helens)
Eccles (Warrington) 1t
Fieldhouse (Widnes)
Pendlebury (Salford)
Subs: Edwards (Wigan)
      Wane (Wigan)

1986 Yorkshire

Leeds: 17 Sept.

Lost 14-26

Lydon (Wigan)
Forster (Warrington)
R. Duane (Warrington)
Stephenson (Wigan) 1t, 3g
Basnett (Widnes) 1t
Edwards (Wigan)
A. Gregory (Warrington)
Pyke (Leigh)
Liptrot (St. Helens)
Fieldhouse (Widnes)
Arkwright (St. Helens)
Platt (St. Helens)
M. Gregory (Warrington)
Subs: Henderson (Leigh)
      Haggerty (St. Helens)

1987 Yorkshire

Wigan: 16 Sept.

Lost 10-16

Hampson (Wigan) 1t
McCormack (St. Helens)
Cullen (Warrington)
Whitfield (Halifax) 1g
D. Wright (Widnes)
Woods (Warrington)
A. Gregory (Wigan)
Case (Wigan)
Dermott (Wigan)
Humphries (Warrington)
Round (Oldham) 1t
Potter (Wigan)
M. Gregory (Warrington)
Subs: McCulloch (Leigh)
      McGinty (Warrington)

1987 Papua New Guinea
St. Helens: 14 Oct.

Drew 22-22

Hampson (Wigan)
Drummond (Warrington)
Lydon (Wigan) 1t, 1g
Henderson (Leigh) 1t
Offiah (Widnes)
Edwards (Wigan) 2t
A. Gregory (Wigan)
Pyke (Leigh)
Groves (St. Helens)
Round (Oldham)
M. Gregory (Warrington)
Roberts (Warrington) 1t
Arkwright (St. Helens)
Subs: D. Hulme (Widnes)
      Cottrell (Leigh)

1988 Yorkshire
Leeds: 21 Sept

Lost 14-24

Lydon (Wigan)
Thackray (Widnes) 1t
Currier (Widnes) 1t
Loughlin (St. Helens) 1g
Preston (Wigan)
D. Hulme (Widnes)
A. Gregory (Wigan)
Pyke (Widnes)
Kiss (Wigan)
Wane (Wigan)
M. O'Neill (Widnes)
P. Hulme (Widnes)
Roberts (Warrington)
Subs: Dowd (Widnes) 1t
      R. Eyres (Widnes)

1989 Yorkshire
Wigan: 20 Sept

Lost 12-56

Hampson (Wigan)
Forster (Warrington)
Loughlin (St. Helens) 2g
Cullen (Warrington)
Preston (Wigan) 1t
Byrne (Wigan)
A. Gregory (Wigan)
M. O'Neill (Widnes)
P. Hulme (Widnes)
Platt (Wigan)
McGinty (Warrington)
Eyres (Widnes)
M. Gregory (Warrington) 1t
Subs: Williams (Salford)
      Gildart (Wigan)

YORKSHIRE REGISTER
The following is a register of current players who have appeared for Yorkshire, including fixtures other than the War of the Roses. Each played at least one first team game last season.

BEARDMORE, K. (3) Castleford
BELL, K. (4) Featherstone R.
BIBB, C. (1) Featherstone R.
BURTON, C. (3) Hull K.R.

CREASSER, D. (1+1) Leeds
CROOKS, L. (2) Hull, Leeds

DANNATT, A (+1) Hull
DICK, K. (3) Leeds
DICKINSON, R. (3+1) Leeds
DIXON, P. (3+1) Halifax 2+1, Leeds

EASTWOOD, P. (1) Hull

FAIRBANK, K. (1) Bradford N.
FLETCHER, A. (4) Wakefield T.
FOX, D. (7) Featherstone R.

GIBSON, C. (7) Batley 2, Leeds 5
GILL, H. (3) Wigan
GOODWAY, A. (4) Wigan
GRAYSHON, J. (14) Dewsbury 9, Bradford N. 5

HANLEY, E. (4) Wigan
HERON, D. (2+4) Leeds
HILL, B. (1) Leeds
HOBBS, D. (6+1) Featherstone R. +1, Oldham 2, Bradford N. 4
HYDE, G. (1) Castleford

IDLE, G. (1+1) Bramley +1, Bradford N.

JOYNER, J. (12) Castleford

KAY, A. (1) Hunslet
KELLY, A. (1) Hull K.R.

LYMAN, P. (1+2) Featherstone R.

McCALLION, S. (1) Halifax
MARCHANT, A. (4) Castleford
MASON, A. (4+2) Bramley (2+1), Wakefield T. 2+1
MEDLEY, P. (+2) Leeds, Bradford N.
MUMBY, K. (9) Bradford N.

NASH, S. (10) Featherstone R. 5, Salford 5
NEWLOVE, P. (1) Featherstone R.
NOBLE, B. (2) Bradford N.

POWELL, D. (1) Sheffield E.
POWELL, R. (3) Leeds
PRICE, G. (1) York
PRYCE, G. (1) York

RAYNE, Keith (+1) Leeds
RAYNE, Kevin (2) Wakefield T.

SCHOFIELD, G. (3) Hull, Leeds 2
SKERRETT, K. (2) Bradford N.
SMITH, G. (+1) York
SMITH, M. (1) Hull K.R.
STEADMAN, G. (1+2) York, Featherstone R. 1+1
STEPHENS, G. (6) Castleford

VAN BELLEN, G. (2) Bradford N.

WARD, K. (2) Castleford
WATKINSON, D. (2) Hull K.R.
WILKINSON, I. (2) Leeds, Halifax

YORKSHIRE TEAMS . . . A REVIEW

Yorkshire team line-ups since the introduction of the Rodstock War of the Roses in September 1985, including opposition other than Lancashire.

1985 Lancashire
Wigan: 11 Sept.
Won 26-10
Kay (Hunslet)
Gibson (Batley)
Hyde (Castleford) 1t
Mason (Bramley) 2t
Laws (Hull KR)
Joyner (Castleford)
Fox (Featherstone) 3g
Hill (Leeds)
Watkinson (Hull KR)
M. Morgan (Oldham)
Hobbs (Oldham) 1t
Burton (Hull KR)
D. Heron (Leeds) 1t
Subs: Lyman (Featherstone)
      Dannatt (Hull)

1985 New Zealand
Bradford: 23 Oct.
Won 18-8
Mumby (Bradford)
Gibson (Batley) 1t
Creasser (Leeds)
Schofield (Hull) 1dg
Mason (Bramley)
Hanley (Wigan) 1t, 1dg
Fox (Featherstone) 2g
Grayshon (Bradford)
Noble (Bradford)
T. Skerrett (Hull)
L. Crooks (Hull)
Goodway (Wigan) 1t
D. Heron (Leeds)
Subs: Steadman (York)
      Lyman (Featherstone)

1986 Lancashire
Leeds: 17 Sept.
Won 26-14
Wilkinson (Leeds)
Gibson (Leeds)
Marchant (Castleford) 1t
Hanley (Wigan) 1t
Gill (Wigan) 1t
Joyner (Castleford)
Fox (Featherstone)
Kelly (Hull KR)
Noble (Bradford)
Hobbs (Oldham) 5g
P. Smith (Featherstone)
Price (York)
Lyman (Featherstone) 1t
Subs: Mason (Bramley)
      Medley (Leeds)

1987 Lancashire
Wigan: 16 Sept.
Won 16-10
Wilkinson (Halifax)
Gibson (Leeds)
Marchant (Castleford) 1t
Mason (Wakefield)
Gill (Wigan) 1t
Hanley (Wigan) 1t
Fox (Featherstone) 1g
Ward (Castleford)
K. Beardmore (Castleford)
Hobbs (Bradford) 1g
L. Crooks (Leeds)
Burton (Hull K.R.)
Goodway (Wigan)
Sub: Dixon (Halifax)

1987 Papua New Guinea
Leeds: 27 Oct.
Won 28-4
Mumby (Bradford)
Eastwood (Hull)
Marchant (Castleford) 1t
Gibson (Leeds) 3t
Mason (Wakefield)
Joyner (Castleford)
Fox (Featherstone)
Hobbs (Bradford) 2g
McCallion (Halifax)
Powell (Leeds)
Burton (Hull K.R.)
K. Fairbank (Bradford) 1t
Dixon (Halifax)
Subs: Creasser (Leeds) 1t
      D. Heron (Leeds)

1988 Lancashire
Leeds: 21 Sept.
Won 24-14
Roockley (Castleford)
Gill (Wigan) 1t
Schofield (Leeds) 1t
Marchant (Castleford) 1t
Gibson (Leeds)
Hanley (Wigan) 1t
Fox (Featherstone)
Hobbs (Bradford) 4g
K. Beardmore (Castleford)
K. Skerrett (Bradford)
Dixon (Halifax)
Powell (Leeds)
Goodway (Wigan)
Subs: Steadman (Featherstone)
      D. Heron (Leeds)

1989 Lancashire
Wigan: 20 Sept
Won 56-12
Bibb (Featherstone)
Gibson (Leeds)
Schofield (Leeds) 1t
D. Powell (Sheffield)
Newlove (Featherstone) 2t
Steadman (Castleford) 2t, 4g
Fox (Featherstone) 1t
K. Skerrett (Bradford)
K. Beardmore (Castleford)
Dixon (Leeds)
Hobbs (Bradford) 1t, 4g
R. Powell (Leeds)
Goodway (Wigan) 2t
Subs: Mason (Wakefield)
      Medley (Bradford) 1t

1985 Yorkshire loose forward Dave Heron.

1985 White Rose hooker David Watkinson.

COUNTY CHAMPIONSHIP TITLES
(including joint titles)

Lancashire	34
Yorkshire	24
Cumbria	16
Cheshire	1

Year	Winner	Year	Winner
1895-96	Lancashire	1937-38	Lancashire
1896-97	Lancashire	1938-39	Lancashire
1897-98	Yorkshire	1945-46	Lancashire
1898-99	Yorkshire	1946-47	Yorkshire
1899-1900	Lancashire	1947-48	Lancashire
1900-01	Lancashire	1948-49	Cumberland
1901-02	Cheshire	1949-50	Undecided
1902-03	Lancashire	1950-51	Undecided
1903-04	Lancashire	1951-52	Yorkshire
1904-05	Yorkshire	1952-53	Lancashire
1905-06	Lancashire Cumberland	1953-54	Yorkshire
1906-07	Lancashire	1954-55	Yorkshire
1907-08	Cumberland	1955-56	Lancashire
1908-09	Lancashire	1956-57	Lancashire
1909-10	Cumberland Yorkshire	1957-58	Yorkshire
1910-11	Lancashire	1958-59	Yorkshire
1911-12	Cumberland	1959-60	Cumberland
1912-13	Yorkshire	1960-61	Lancashire
1913-14	Undecided	1961-62	Cumberland
1919-20	Undecided	1962-63	Yorkshire
1920-21	Yorkshire	1963-64	Cumberland
1921-22	Yorkshire	1964-65	Yorkshire
1922-23	Lancashire Yorkshire	1965-66	Cumberland
1923-24	Lancashire	1966-67	Cumberland
1924-25	Lancashire	1967-68	Lancashire
1925-26	Lancashire	1968-69	Yorkshire
1926-27	Lancashire	1969-70	Lancashire
1927-28	Cumberland	1970-71	Yorkshire
1928-29	Lancashire	1971-72	Yorkshire
1929-30	Lancashire	1972-73	Yorkshire
1930-31	Yorkshire	1973-74	Lancashire
1931-32	Lancashire	1974-75	Lancashire
1932-33	Cumberland	1975-76	Yorkshire
1933-34	Cumberland	1976-77	Yorkshire
1934-35	Cumberland	1977-78	Not Held
1935-36	Lancashire	1978-79	Lancashire
1936-37	Lancashire	1979-80	Lancashire
		1980-81	Cumbria
		1981-82	Cumbria
		1982-83	Yorkshire

REFEREES

REFEREES' HONOURS 1990-91

Silk Cut Challenge Cup final:
Jim Smith

Regal Trophy final:
Jim Smith

Stones Bitter Premiership final:
John Holdsworth

Second Division Premiership final:
Brian Galtress

Grunhalle Lager Lancashire Cup final:
Alan Burke

John Smiths Yorkshire Cup final:
Jim Smith

France v Australia (2):
John Holdsworth

Under-21 France v Great Britain:
Brian Galtress

CIS Insurance Charity Shield:
Colin Morris

SENIOR REFEREES 1991-92

KEVIN ALLATT (Southport)
Date of birth: 29.12.42
Grade Two: 1970-71
Grade One: 1972-73
Premiership Trophy 1986-87
Lancashire Cup 1983-84, 1988-89
Yorkshire Cup 1987-88 (+replay)
Lancashire v Yorkshire 1975-76

DAVID ASQUITH (York)
Date of birth: 20.6.53
Grade One: 1989-90

GEOFF BERRY (Batley)
Date of birth: 26.4.54
Grade Two: 1981-82
Grade One: 1983-84

ALAN BURKE (Oldham)
Date of birth: 21.1.57
Grade One: 1987-88
Lancashire Cup 1990-91

DAVID CAMPBELL (St. Helens)
Date of birth: 9.10.54
Grade One: 1989-90

DAVE CARTER (Widnes)
Date of birth: 29.11.55
Grade One: 1984-85
France v Great Britain Under-21s 1988-89

JOHN CONNOLLY (Wigan)
Date of birth: 30.9.59
Grade One: 1990-91

ROBERT CONNOLLY (Wigan)
Date of birth: 30.9.59
Grade One: 1990-91

PAUL CRASHLEY (Wakefield)
Date of birth: 1.8.50
Grade One: 1989-90

STEVE CROSS (Hull)
Date of birth: 23.3.50
Grade One: 1986-87

STUART CUMMINGS (Widnes)
Date of birth: 17.11.60
Grade One: 1991-92

BRIAN GALTRESS (Bradford)
Date of birth: 8.10.51
Grade One: 1988-89
Second Division Premiership 1990-91
France v Great Britain Under-21s 1990-91

STEPHEN HAIGH (Ossett)
Date of birth: 5.4.45
Grade Two: 1980-81
Grade One: 1983-84

JOHN HOLDSWORTH (Kippax)
Date of birth: 25.1.47
Grade Two: 1979-80
Grade One: 1980-81
Challenge Cup 1986-87,1989-90
John Player Trophy 1985-86, 1986-87, 1988-89
Premiership Trophy 1980-81, 1987-88, 1988-89,
   1990-91
Lancashire Cup 1982-83, 1985-86
World Club Challenge 1987-88
France v Australia (2) 1990-91
Wales v England 1980-81
Great Britain v Rest of World 1988-89
RL Chairman's XIII v Papua New Guinea 1987-88
Cumbria v Yorkshire 1981-82
France v Great Britain Under-24s 1982-83
War of the Roses 1987-88
Charity Shield 1987-88, 1989-90

JOHN KENDREW (Castleford)
Date of birth: 22.4.50
Grade Two: 1982-83
Grade One: 1983-84
Lancashire v Papua New Guinea 1987-88

GERRY KERSHAW (Easingwold)
Date of birth: 24.10.43
Grade Two: 1969-70
Grade One: 1970-71
Challenge Cup 1980-81
Lancashire Cup 1980-81
Floodlit Trophy 1973-74
Regal Trophy 1973-74, 1989-90
Wales v England 1981-82
Wales v Australia 1982-83
France v Great Britain Under-24s 1981-82
Lancashire v Yorkshire 1971-72
Lancashire v Cumbria 1972-73
Cumbria v Other Nationalities 1974-75
Cumbria v Lancashire 1978-79, 1980-81
War of the Roses 1989-90

COLIN MORRIS (Huddersfield)
Date of birth: 14.3.57
Grade One: 1989-90
Premiership Trophy 1989-90
France v Great Britain Under-21s 1989-90
Charity Shield 1990-91

IAN OLLERTON (Wigan)
Date of birth: 31.3.53
Grade One: 1990-91

JIM SMITH (Halifax)
Date of birth: 2.3.44
Grade Two: 1977-78
Grade One: 1983-84
Challenge Cup 1990-91
Regal Trophy 1990-91
Yorkshire Cup 1990-91
Lancashire Cup 1986-87

RUSSELL SMITH (Castleford)
Date of birth: 24.1.64
Grade One: 1991-92

COLIN STEELE (Dalton-in-Furness)
Date of birth: 11.9.60
Grade One: 1987-88
Cumbria v France 1988-89

RAY TENNANT (Castleford)
Date of birth: 7.4.49
Grade One: 1985-86
Challenge Cup 1988-89
New Zealand v Australia (3) 1989
European Club Championship 1988-89
Lancashire Cup 1989-90
Charity Shield 1988-89
Cumbria v Papua New Guinea 1987-88

CHARLIE TIDBALL (Wakefield)
Date of birth: 25.12.48
Grade One: 1987-88

PAUL VOLANTE (Birstall)
Date of birth: 30.6.52
Grade One: 1983-84

JOHN WHITELAM (Hull)
Date of birth: 11.5.53
Grade One: 1988-89

ROBIN WHITFIELD (Widnes)
Date of birth: 26.11.43
Grade Two: 1979-80
Grade One: 1980-81
Challenge Cup 1982-83, 1985-86
Yorkshire Cup 1981-82, 1988-89
Second Division Premiership 1987-88, 1988-89, 1989-90
France v Australia (2) 1982-83
France v New Zealand (2) 1989-90
New Zealand v Australia 1983
Australia v New Zealand (3) 1986
Yorkshire v Lancashire 1981-82
War of the Roses 1988-89

Bradford referee Brian Galtress, a double honour in 1990-91.

THE ALLIANCE

SLALOM LAGER ALLIANCE
FINAL TABLES 1990-91

FIRST DIVISION

	P.	W.	D.	L.	FOR	AGAINST	Pts.
Hull	26	24	0	2	729	336	48
Hull K.R.	26	18	0	8	616	424	36
Castleford	26	16	0	10	690	527	32
Oldham	26	14	0	12	488	514	28
Wigan	26	13	1	12	596	553	27
Leeds	26	13	0	13	680	569	26
Halifax	26	12	2	12	546	604	26
St. Helens	26	12	1	13	660	601	25
Warrington	26	12	0	14	621	600	24
Featherstone R.	26	10	2	14	559	591	22
Widnes	26	11	0	15	628	691	22
Wakefield T.	26	10	0	16	466	590	20
Salford	26	8	0	18	488	663	16
Leigh	26	6	0	20	374	878	12

● Bottom two clubs relegated

SECOND DIVISION

	P.	W.	D.	L.	FOR	AGAINST	Pts.
Bradford N.	24	20	0	4	900	354	40
Workington T.	24	18	1	5	517	411	37
Rochdale H.	24	17	1	6	521	355	35
Carlisle	24	15	3	6	632	311	33
Hunslet	24	16	1	7	572	445	33
Dewsbury	24	14	2	8	490	389	30
Sheffield E.	24	14	0	10	636	489	28
Batley	24	13	1	10	481	399	27
Swinton C.	24	12	2	10	534	463	26
Doncaster	24	11	1	12	405	377	23
Ryedale-York	24	9	0	15	460	453	18
Huddersfield	24	9	0	15	507	555	18
Barrow	24	9	0	15	361	562	18
Fulham	24	9	0	15	352	568	18
Keighley	24	7	1	16	448	636	15
Bramley	24	7	0	17	332	734	14
Trafford B.	24	6	0	18	395	596	12
Whitehaven	24	3	1	20	257	703	7

● Top two clubs promoted

SLALOM LAGER ALLIANCE CHALLENGE CUP 1991

First Round

Batley	14	Trafford B.	8
Bradford N.	38	Wigan	15
Castleford	32	Carlisle	12
Hull K.R.	30	Bramley	4
Hunslet	10	Hull	60
Keighley	16	Doncaster	22
*Leeds		Barrow	
Oldham	16	Huddersfield	8
Rochdale H.	72	Whitehaven	6
Ryedale-York	2	Featherstone R.	8
St. Helens	23	Halifax	10
Sheffield E.	22	Dewsbury	20
Wakefield T.	50	Fulham	6
Warrington	26	Leigh	16
Widnes	22	Salford	24
Workington T.	2	Swinton C.	14

*Tie awarded to Leeds

Second Round

Batley	18	Salford	23
Castleford	28	Swinton C.	4
Doncaster	26	Sheffield E.	1
Featherstone R.	18	Warrington	8
Hull	36	Rochdale H.	8
Leeds	30	Wakefield T.	14
Oldham	34	Hull K.R.	8
St. Helens	21	Bradford N.	36

Third Round

Bradford N.	39	Salford	10
Doncaster	12	Featherstone R.	24
Hull	34	Leeds	6
Oldham	12	Castleford	18

Semi-Finals

Castleford	28	Featherstone R.	8
Hull	8	Bradford N.	10

Final

Bradford N.	25	Castleford	4

SLALOM LAGER ALLIANCE PLAYER OF THE YEAR

1986: Steve Gill (Castleford)
1987: Shaun Fairhurst (Leigh)
1988: Mike O'Hara (Blackpool S.)
1989: Alan Moses (Barrow)
1990: Tim Lumb (Hunslet)
1991: Shaun Brown (Salford)

LANCASHIRE COUNTY CHALLENGE SHIELD 1990-91

First Round

Barrow	16	Widnes	24
Farnworth	8	Trafford B.	24
Leigh	24	Rochdale H.	23
Oldham	28	Workington T.	10
St. Helens	56	Fulham	24
Salford	24	Whitehaven	16
Swinton	18	Carlisle	4
Warrington	24	Wigan	28

Second Round

Oldham	14	Wigan	16
St. Helens	46	Swinton	14
Trafford B.	8	Salford	24
Widnes	38	Leigh	12

Semi-Finals

Widnes	30	St. Helens	18
Wigan	30	Salford	18

Final

Wigan	22	Widnes	10

YORKSHIRE SENIOR COMPETITION CHALLENGE CUP 1990-91

Preliminary Round

Featherstone R.	40	Castleford	22

First Round

Bradford N.	20	Sheffield E.	0
Bramley	13	Halifax	54
Dewsbury	20	Huddersfield	18
Doncaster	14	Batley	15
Hull K.R.	16	Hull	20
Hunslet	29	Keighley	22
Ryedale-York	14	Leeds	20
Wakefield T.	32	Featherstone R.	35

Second Round

Bradford N.	24	Leeds	14
Dewsbury	12	Batley	16
Hull	30	Halifax	8
Hunslet	44	Featherstone R.	12

Semi-Finals

Bradford N.	48	Batley	4
Hunslet	16	Hull	46

Final

Bradford N.	6	Hull	4

POT POURRI

DIARY OF LANDMARKS

1895   August 29... the beginning. The Northern Rugby Football Union formed at The George Hotel, Huddersfield, following the breakaway from the English RU by 21 clubs who wanted to pay players for taking time off work to play.

September 7... season opens with 22 clubs.

Joseph Platt appointed Rugby League Secretary.

1897   April 24... Batley won the first Northern Union — later Rugby League — Challenge Cup final.

Line-out abolished and replaced by punt from touch.

All goals to be worth two points.

1898   Professionalism allowed but players must be in full-time employment.

1899   Scrum if player cannot release the ball after a tackle.

1901   Punt from touch replaced by 10-yard scrum when ball is carried into touch.

1902   Two divisions introduced.

Punt from touch abolished completely. Touch-finding rule introduced with the ball having to bounce before entering touch.

1905   Two divisions scrapped.

Lancashire and Yorkshire County Cup competitions inaugurated.

1906   Thirteen-a-side introduced, from traditional 15.

Play-the-ball introduced.

1907   First tour — New Zealand to England. The tour party were RU 'rebels'.

First Top Four play-off for championship.

1908   Australia and New Zealand launch Rugby League.

First Australian tour of England.

1910   First British tour of Australia and New Zealand.

1915   Competitive rugby suspended for duration of First World War.

1919   Competitive rugby resumed in January.

1920   John Wilson appointed Rugby League Secretary.

1922   Title of Northern Rugby Football Union changed to Rugby Football League.

Goal from a mark abolished.

1927   First radio broadcast of Challenge Cup Final — Oldham v. Swinton at Wigan.

1929   Wembley staged its first RL Challenge Cup final — Wigan v. Dewsbury.

1932   London exhibition match under floodlights at White City — Leeds v. Wigan.

1933   France staged its first Rugby League match — an exhibition between England and Australia in Paris.

London Highfield, formerly Wigan Highfield, became capital's first Rugby League team, also first to play regularly under floodlights.

1934   A French squad made a short tour of England before Rugby League was officially launched in France.

1935   European Championship introduced, contested by England, France and Wales.

1939   Second World War. Emergency war-time competitions introduced.

1945   War-time emergencies over.

Bill Fallowfield appointed Rugby League Secretary.

1946   First all-ticket match — Hull v. Hull K.R.

1948   King George VI became first reigning monarch to attend Rugby League match — Wigan v. Bradford Northern Cup final at Wembley.

First televised match — at Wembley — but shown only in London area.

Wembley's first all-ticket final.

International Board formed.

1949   Welsh League formed.

1950   Italian squad made brief tour of England.

1951   First televised match in the North — Britain v. New Zealand at Swinton.

First floodlights installation by Northern club, Bradford Northern.

1952   First nationally televised Challenge Cup final — Workington Town v. Featherstone Rovers.

1954   First World Cup, staged in France.

393

1955	London staged series of televised floodlit matches for the Independent Television Association Trophy. Welsh League disbanded.
1956	Sunday rugby for amateurs permitted by the Rugby Football League.
1962	Two divisions reintroduced, with Eastern and Western Divisions also formed.
1964	Substitutes allowed for injuries, but only up to half-time. Two division and regional leagues scrapped. One league system with Top-16 play-off for championship.
1965	BBC-2 Floodlit Trophy competition began with regular Tuesday night series. Substitutes allowed for any reason up to and including half-time. English Schools Rugby League formed.
1966	Four-tackle rule introduced for Floodlit Trophy competition in October, then for all games from December.
1967	First Sunday fixtures played, two matches on December 17th.
1969	Substitutes allowed at any time. University Rugby League Association formed.
1971	John Player Trophy competition launched.
1972	Six-tackle rule introduced. Timekeepers with hooter system to signal end of match introduced. Colts League formed.
1973	Two divisions re-introduced. March 4... British Amateur Rugby League Association formed.
1974	Drop goal value halved to one point. Had been reduced earlier in international matches. David Oxley appointed Rugby League Secretary. David Howes appointed first full-time Public Relations Officer to the Rugby Football League. National Coaching Scheme launched.

1975	Premiership Trophy competition launched.
1976	Differential penalty introduced for technical scrum offences.
1977	County Championship not held for first time since 1895, excluding war years. Anglo-Australian transfer ban agreed.
1978	Papua New Guinea admitted as full members of International Board.
1981	Rugby League Professional Players' Association formed.
1982	County Championship scrapped.
1983	January 1... Sin bin introduced. Try value increased to four points. Handover after sixth tackle introduced, among several other new or amended laws following meeting of International Board. Anglo-Australian transfer ban lifted.
1984	Alliance League introduced in reserve grade reorganisation.
1985	First Charity Shield match played in Isle of Man. War of the Roses launched on Lancashire v. Yorkshire county of origin basis. Relegation-promotion reduced to three down, three up.
1986	Relegation-promotion altered for one year only to four down, two up to provide a 14-strong First Division for the 1987-88 season.
1987	Division Two Premiership Trophy competition launched. New players' contracts system introduced.
1988	Colts scrapped for new youth scheme. Six-man League Board of Directors appointed, plus first-ever Controller of Referees, ex-match official Fred Lindop.
1989	First-ever Sales Marketing Executive, Mike Turner, appointed by the League.
1990	Russia introduced Rugby League and sent 90-man squad of players and officials on three-match tour to Britain.
1991	Russian eight-club league launched. Three divisions introduced for 1991-92 season.

DISCIPLINARY RECORDS

This sub-section is a compilation of sendings off and disciplinary verdicts for first team players.

The following information is based on the workings of the League's Disciplinary Committee which meets weekly during a season.

Not guilty finding for Leeds scrum half Paul Harkin.

DISMISSALS .... A five-year review

The following is a review of the number of first team dismissals in each season since 1986-87.

The 1990-91 tally of 115 dismissals, 19 of whom were found not guilty, was 57 down on the previous season.

— indicates where a club was not in existence.

	1990-91	1989-90	1988-89	1987-88	1986-87
Barrow	5	5	4	4	4
Batley	4	1	2	1	7
Bradford N.	3	5	2	2	2
Bramley	5	4	2	4	3
Carlisle	4	0	4	9	3
Castleford	4	6	4	3	1
Chorley	7	3	—	—	—
Dewsbury	5	3	3	5	3
Doncaster	4	2	1	3	2
Featherstone R.	1	4	1	2	0
Fulham	1	4	0	0	6
Halifax	3	8	1	1	2
Huddersfield	1	7	3	0	4
Hull	1	3	1	2	5
Hull K.R.	3	3	3	1	4
Hunslet	6	6	5	2	1
Keighley	5	10	3	5	7
Leeds	5	3	0	2	1
Leigh	1	7	3	6	2
Nottingham C.	2	5	7	2	6
Oldham	3	6	3	4	3
Rochdale H.	5	3	3	5	1
Runcorn H.	3	3	6	3	3
Ryedale-York	3	7	3	4	3
St. Helens	1	6	3	1	3
Salford	5	4	2	2	5
Sheffield E.	2	3	4	0	3
Swinton	1	4	2	3	3
Trafford B.	2	9	2	2	4
Wakefield T.	2	6	1	5	5
Warrington	2	4	2	3	6
Whitehaven	3	6	3	3	2
Widnes	2	6	2	2	4
Wigan	7	8	3	5	3
Workington T.	4	8	3	5	5
Totals	**115**	**172**	**91**	**101**	**116**

DISCIPLINARY ANALYSIS 1990-91

The following is a club-by-club disciplinary record for last season, showing the players sent off in first team matches and the findings of the League's Disciplinary Committee.

The committee's verdict is featured in the brackets after the player's name, each number indicating the match ban imposed. SOS stands for sending off sufficient and NG for not guilty. A suspension reduced or increased on appeal is shown as follows, 6 to 4.

During 1988-89 the totting-up system for sin-bin suspensions was abandoned. Previously two points were issued for a 10-minute temporary dismissal, a one-match ban being imposed when the total reached six. Instead, the sin bins were recorded and taken into account when considering a full dismissal.

The 1984-85 season was the first time video action other than official BBC or ITV tapes could be offered in evidence. Seven cases were considered by the committee after viewing a video, the player not having been dismissed.

Bradford Northern packman Karl Fairbank, who missed the 1991 Regal Trophy final through suspension.

Club	Total sent off	Dismissed Player	Number of Sin Bins
Barrow	5	S. Clayton (4 to 2, 4), P. Crarey (4), S. Rhodes (4), R. Dunn (2)	20
Batley	4	N. Hartley (2), J. Stainburn (2), P. Rees (NG), S. Parrish (1)	12
Bradford N.	3	K. Fairbank (1, 3), B. Noble (SOS)	11
Bramley	5	P. Lister (4, 2), N. Clawson (2), J. Wallace (1), S. Durham (1)	20
Carlisle	4	T. Catton (4), C. Friend (NG), G. Charlton (NG), B. Williams (NG)	15
Castleford	4	J. Hardy (1), D. Sampson (SOS), D. Plange (SOS), P. Fletcher (4)	8
Chorley	7	J. Mayo (4), T. Hodson (2), M. Edwards (NG, SOS), C. Briscoe (2), J. Duffy (5), B. Eccles (2)	11

Dewsbury	5	D. Watkinson (2), C. Whitehead (2), P. Hughes (3), G. Coughlan (2), D. Hall (4)	8
Doncaster	4	A. Pennant (SOS, 4), C. Hall (SOS), R. Pell (4)	12
Featherstone R.	1	B. Tuuta (2)	6
Fulham	1	P. Reinsfeld (1)	14
Halifax	3	J. Lyons (2), D. Fairbank (4), J. Irvine (4)	8
Huddersfield	1	G. Senior (4)	6
Hull	1	K. Harrison (4)	9
Hull K.R.	3	D. Bishop (NG), B. Niebling (4), D. Lightfoot (4)	2
Hunslet	6	R. Sampson (2, NG), T. Lumb (2, NG), S. Wilkinson (4), S. Warrener (SOS)	8
Keighley	5	G. Coulter (NG), M. Fairbank (6), A. Fairbank (2), R. Priestley (2), C. Farrell (2)	10
Leeds	5	P. Harkin (NG), P. Dixon (4, 1), C. Maskill (3), S. Irving (2)	16
Leigh	1	P. Brown (2)	7
Nottingham C.	2	N. Rudd (6), K. Portz (2)	9
Oldham	3	D. Platt (2), P. Round (SOS), J. Cogger (2)	8
Rochdale H.	5	K. Marriott (SOS), S. Turner (4), M. Hall (4), M. O'Neill (SOS), M. Nixon (4)	12
Runcorn H.	3	N. Barrow (4), S. Turner (2), D. Hine (4)	17
Ryedale-York	3	A. Timson (4), B. Ake (2, 3)	11
St. Helens	1	P. Forber (NG)	7
Salford	5	C. Whiteley (6), T. Evans (4, SOS), F. Cassidy (SOS), J. Gilfillan (2 to 1)	5
Sheffield E.	2	D. Nelson (SOS), A. Farrell (2)	7
Swinton	1	J. Ropati (4)	7
Trafford B.	2	K. Jones (2), D. McCarthy (NG)	5
Wakefield T.	2	J. Thompson (SOS), N. Du Toit (SOS)	4
Warrington	2	D. Drummond (NG), M. Forster (4)	11
Whitehaven	3	S. Howse (NG), G. Mounsey (NG), G. McFarlane (SOS)	9
Widnes	2	E. Koloto (4), J. Grima (NG)	11
Wigan	7	S. Edwards (1), K. Skerrett (4, 2), E. Hanley (2 to 1), J. Lydon (NG), A. Gregory (NG), M. Dermott (2)	10
Workington T.	4	A. McMullen (SOS), P. Penrice (SOS), C. Falcon (4), R. Ashton (NG)	13

SPONSORSHIP

This updated sub-section is a record of the sponsorship programme under the control of the Rugby Football League.

1990-91 COMPETITIONS:

Silk Cut Challenge Cup	£300,000
Regal Trophy	£275,000
Stones Bitter Championship and Premiership	£250,000
British Coal Tests	£190,000
CIS Insurance Charity Shield	£ 17,000

	£1,032,000
Awards:	£ 50,000
Miscellaneous:	£ 75,000
GRAND TOTAL	£ 157,000

COMPETITION SPONSORSHIP

The following is a review of sponsorship of the game's major competitions.

SILK CUT CHALLENGE CUP

	Prel.	1st	2nd	3rd	S.F.	R.U.	Winners	Development Fund	Total
	£	£	£	£	£	£	£	£	£
1979	—	750	1,160	2,000	3,555	6,555	12,555	4,500	60,000
1980	—	750	1,160	2,000	3,555	6,555	12,555	19,500	75,000
1981	—	750	1,160	2,000	3,555	6,555	12,555	29,500	85,000
1982	1,000	1,000	1,400	2,400	4,325	8,000	14,555	30,000	100,000
1983	1,000	1,000	1,400	2,400	4,325	8,000	14,555	40,000	110,000
1984	1,000	1,000	1,400	2,400	4,325	8,000	14,555	48,000	120,000
1985	1,100	1,100	1,500	2,500	4,500	9,000	16,000	47,600	130,000
1986	1,100	1,100	1,500	2,500	4,500	9,000	16,000	57,600	140,000
1987	1,200	1,200	1,650	2,750	4,500	9,000	16,000	58,200	150,000
1988	1,200	1,200	1,800	3,000	5,000	10,000	18,000	62,000	160,000
1989	1,300	1,300	2,000	3,250	5,500	11,000	20,000	62,600	170,000
1990	2,000	2,000	3,250	5,000	8,500	16,000	30,000	111,000	275,000
1991	2,250	2,250	3,500	5,500	9,000	17,000	32,000	120,000	300,000

● Sponsored by State Express 1979-84

REGAL TROPHY

	Prel.	1st	2nd	3rd	S.F.	R.U.	Winners	Development Fund	Total
	£	£	£	£	£	£	£	£	£
1971-72	—	—	—	—	1,000	2,500	5,000	—	9,500
1972-73	—	150	300	450	1,000	2,500	5,000	—	16,100
1973-74	—	150	300	450	1,000	2,500	5,000	—	16,100
1974-75	—	150	300	450	1,000	2,500	5,000	—	16,100
1975-76	—	300	450	600	1,500	3,000	6,000	—	22,800
1976-77	—	400	550	700	1,500	3,000	6,000	—	25,600
1977-78	—	450	600	750	1,750	3,500	8,000	—	30,000
1978-79	—	550	700	900	1,750	3,500	8,000	—	33,000
1979-80	—	600	800	1,000	2,000	4,000	8,500	—	36,500
1980-81	—	600	800	1,000	2,000	4,000	8,500	3,500	40,000
1981-82	700	700	900	1,175	2,500	4,500	9,000	7,000	50,000
1982-83	700	700	900	1,175	2,500	5,000	10,000	10,500	55,000
1983-84	700	700	900	1,175	2,500	5,000	10,000	15,500	60,000
1984-85	750	750	1,000	1,500	2,500	5,000	10,000	20,000	75,000
1985-86	750	750	1,000	1,500	2,750	5,500	11,000	26,000	80,000
1986-87	800	800	1,100	1,700	3,000	6,000	12,000	26,200	85,000
1987-88	1,100	1,100	1,600	2,825	4,750	9,000	16,000	65,000	150,000
1988-89	1,250	1,250	1,850	3,175	5,250	10,000	18,000	74,000	170,000
1989-90	1,740	1,745	2,750	4,800	8,250	15,500	28,000	100,000	250,000
1990-91	2,000	2,000	3,250	5,000	8,500	16,000	30,000	110,000	275,000

● Under the John Player banner from 1971-1989

STONES BITTER

	Championship winners	R.U.	2nd Division winners	R.U.	Premiership winners	R.U.	2nd Division Premiership winners	R.U.	Development Fund	Total
	£	£	£	£	£	£	£	£	£	£
1980-81	6,000	—	3,000	—	4,000	—	—	—	42,000	55,000
1981-82	10,000	—	6,000	—	6,000	—	—	—	48,000	70,000
1982-83	12,000	—	7,000	—	7,000	—	—	—	54,000	80,000
1983-84	12,000	—	7,000	—	7,000	—	—	—	59,000	85,000
1984-85	13,000	—	9,000	—	8,000	—	—	—	60,000	90,000
1985-86	13,000	—	9,000	—	8,000	—	—	—	65,000	95,000
1986-87	20,000	8,000	10,000	4,000	9,000	3,500	4,000	1,500	60,000	120,000
1987-88	20,000	8,000	10,000	4,000	9,000	3,500	4,000	1,500	70,000	123,000
1988-89	25,000	10,000	12,000	5,000	10,000	4,000	5,000	2,000	77,000	150,000
1989-90	40,000	15,000	18,000	7,500	15,000	6,000	8,000	3,000	112,500	225,000
1990-91	44,000	16,500	20,000	8,250	17,000	6,750	9,000	3,500	125,000	250,000

● Sponsored by Slalom Lager from 1980-86

GRUNHALLE LAGER LANCASHIRE CUP

	Winners £	Total £
1976	1,000	4,000
1977	1,500	5,000
1978	1,800	5,500
1979	1,900	6,000
1980	2,530	10,000
1981	2,700	11,000
1982	3,000	11,500
1983	3,200	12,500
1984	3,400	13,250
1985	3,400	13,250
1986	4,300	17,000
1987	4,600	18,600
1988	5,000	19,000
1989	5,000	21,000
1990	6,000	25,000

● Sponsored by Burtonwood Brewery 1976-85

YORKSHIRE CUP

	Sponsor	Winners £	Total £
1972	Esso	800	4,000
1973	Esso	1,500	6,000
1974	Esso	1,400	6,000
1975	Esso	1,200	6,000
1976	Esso	1,200	6,000
1977	Esso	1,600	8,000
1978	Esso	2,000	9,000
1979	Esso	2,000	9,500
1980	Websters Brewery	2,750	13,000
1981	Websters Brewery	3,000	14,000
1982	Websters Brewery	2,500	15,000
1983	Philips Video	2,500	15,000
1984	Philips Video	2,500	15,000
1985	John Smiths	2,500	5,000
1986	John Smiths	2,500	12,500
1987	John Smiths	3,000	12,500
1988	John Smiths	3,500	27,500
1989	John Smiths	5,000	35,000
1990	John Smiths	5,000	35,000

QUEEN'S HONOURS

Eight Rugby League players have been awarded the MBE by Her Majesty the Queen for their services to the game.

Player	Awarded MBE	GB Caps	Career	Clubs
Eric Ashton	June 1966	26	1955-69	Wigan
Geoff Gunney	June 1970	11	1951-73	Hunslet
Clive Sullivan	January 1974	17	1961-85	Hull, Hull K.R., Oldham, Doncaster
Chris Hesketh	January 1976	21 + 2	1963-79	Wigan, Salford
Roger Millward	January 1983	28 + 1	1963-80	Castleford, Hull K.R.
Neil Fox	June 1983	29	1956-79	Wakefield T., Bradford N., Hull K.R., York, Bramley, Huddersfield
David Watkins	January 1986	2 + 4	1967-82	Salford, Swinton, Cardiff C.
Ellery Hanley	January 1990	33 + 1	1978-	Bradford N., Wigan

ATTENDANCES

CLUB ATTENDANCE REVIEW

The following is a review of clubs' home attendances for league matches from 1982-83.

The main figure is the individual club's average gate for league games during that season. The figure in brackets indicates an upward or downward trend compared with the previous season.

Also indicated is the division the club competed in that season, i.e.

1 — First Division, 2 — Second Division.

Club	82-83	83-84	84-85	85-86	86-87	87-88	88-89	89-90	90-91
Barrow	1 3852 (−310)	2 3218 (−450)	1 2728 (−490)	2 1926 (−802)	1 2664 (+738)	2 1624 (−1040)	2 1594 (−30)	1 1997 (+403)	2 962 (−1035)
Batley	2 916 (−136)	2 864 (−52)	2 1015 (+151)	2 930 (−85)	2 744 (−186)	2 859 (+115)	2 924 (+65)	2 1506 (+582)	2 1188 (−318)
Bradford N.	1 4920 (−896)	1 5316 (+386)	1 4251 (−1065)	1 3975 (−276)	1 4312 (+377)	1 4723 (+411)	1 4969 (+246)	1 5584 (+615)	1 5274 (−310)
Bramley	2 809 (−119)	2 759 (−50)	2 858 (+99)	2 831 (−27)	2 737 (−94)	2 858 (+121)	2 1004 (+146)	2 982 (−22)	2 805 (−177)
Bridgend	2 854 (−1154)	2 581 (−273)	2 510 (−70)	—	—	—	—	—	—
Carlisle	1 1924 (−1172)	2 752 (+244)	2 986 (−368)	2 618 (+171)	2 789 (+171)	2 763 (−26)	2 678 (−85)	2 574 (−104)	2 781 (+207)
Castleford	1 3548 (−243)	1 4288 (+740)	1 3217 (−1071)	1 3701 (+430)	1 4758 (+1057)	1 4520 (−738)	1 6580 (+2060)	1 6428 (152)	1 6019 (−409)
Chorley	—	—	—	—	—	—	—	2 806 —	2 690 (−116)
Dewsbury	2 779 (−269)	2 706 (−73)	2 995 (+189)	1 1819 (+824)	2 669 (−1150)	2 658 (−41)	2 772 (+114)	2 1227 (+455)	2 955 (−272)
Doncaster	2 441 (−115)	2 255 (−186)	2 266 (+11)	2 689 (+423)	2 1543 (+854)	2 1450 (−93)	2 1906 (+456)	2 1965 (+59)	2 1458 (−507)
Featherstone R.	1 2647 (−159)	1 3032 (+385)	1 2541 (−491)	1 2320 (−221)	1 2606 (+286)	2 1879 (−727)	1 4379 (+2500)	1 4269 (−110)	1 4722 (+453)
Fulham	2 2688 (−1633)	1 2238 (−450)	2 949 (−1289)	2 817 (−132)	2 684 (−133)	2 615 (−69)	2 588 (−27)	2 841 (+253)	2 557 (−284)
Halifax	1 2270 (−548)	2 1254 (−1016)	1 3497 (+2243)	1 4944 (+1447)	1 4891 (−53)	1 6521 (+1630)	1 8022 (+1501)	2 5921 (−2101)	2 4458 (−1463)
Huddersfield	2 776 (−409)	2 699 (−77)	2 905 (+206)	2 678 (−227)	2 524 (−154)	2 601 (+77)	2 1114 (+513)	2 1634 (+520)	2 1306 (−328)
Hull	1 11525 (−1665)	1 10679 (−846)	1 8525 (−2154)	1 6245 (−1280)	1 5538 (−707)	1 5111 (−427)	1 6804 (+1693)	1 6218 (−586)	1 6699 (+481)
Hull K. R.	1 7379 (−1344)	1 6966 (−413)	1 6715 (−215)	1 4855 (−1860)	1 4651 (−204)	1 4186 (−465)	1 5298 (+1111)	2 4851 (−447)	1 4952 (+101)
Hunslet	2 1195 (+451)	2 1338 (+143)	1 2246 (+908)	2 722 (−1524)	1 1050 (+338)	1 2678 (+1050)	2 947 (−1731)	2 1046 (+99)	2 767 (−279)

Club	82-83	83-84	84-85	85-86	86-87	87-88	88-89	89-90	90-91
Keighley	2 1085 (−491)	2 734 (−351)	2 822 (+88)	2 685 (−137)	2 445 (−240)	2 958 (+503)	2 961 (+3)	2 936 (−25)	2 985 (+49)
Leeds	1 5893 (+294)	1 6542 (+649)	1 7330 (+788)	1 6928 (−402)	1 6393 (−535)	1 9911 (+3518)	1 12060 (+2149)	1 12251 (+191)	1 11102 (−1149)
Leigh	1 4617 (−1322)	1 4434 (−183)	1 3822 (−612)	2 2710 (−1112)	1 4232 (+1522)	1 4516 (+284)	2 2346 (−2170)	1 4568 (+2222)	2 1719 (−2849)
Nottingham C.	—	—	2 1020 —	2 487 (−553)	2 368 (−119)	2 368 —	2 560 (+192)	2 577 (+17)	2 255 (−322)
Oldham	1 3721 (+1326)	1 4138 (+417)	1 4562 (+424)	1 4333 (−229)	1 3915 (−418)	2 3790 (−125)	1 5759 (+1696)	2 4401 (−1358)	1 5094 (+693)
Rochdale H.	2 619 (−269)	2 538 (−81)	2 542 (+4)	2 1267 (+725)	2 877 (−390)	2 1106 (+229)	2 1027 (−79)	2 2510 (+1483)	1 2542 (+32)
Runcorn H.	2 224 (−161)	2 172 (−52)	2 509 (+337)	2 363 (−146)	2 331 (−35)	2 515 (+184)	2 298 (−217)	2 453 (+155)	2 632 (+179)
Ryedale-York	2 1685 (−1992)	2 1215 (−470)	2 1528 (+313)	1 2828 (+1300)	2 1520 (−1380)	2 1406 (−114)	2 2021 (+615)	2 2495 (+474)	2 1857 (−638)
St. Helens	1 4543 (−319)	1 4656 (+113)	1 7336 (+2680)	1 6022 (−1314)	1 7341 (+1391)	1 8417 (+1076)	1 9514 (+1097)	1 8555 (−959)	1 7391 (−1164)
Salford	2 1928 (−476)	1 2399 (+471)	2 1795 (−604)	1 2520 (+725)	1 2826 (+306)	1 3747 (+921)	1 5470 (+1723)	1 3720 (−1750)	2 2314 (−1406)
Sheffield E.	—	—	2 885 —	2 698 (−187)	2 708 (+10)	2 847 (+139)	2 838 (−9)	1 4038 (+3200)	1 4031 (−7)
Southend Invicta	—	2 731 —	2 216 (−515)	—	—	—	—	—	—
Swinton	2 1314 (−253)	2 1077 (−237)	2 1590 (+513)	1 2706 (+1116)	2 1622 (−1084)	1 2987 (+1365)	2 1435 (−1543)	2 1678 (+243)	2 1737 (+59)
Trafford B.	2 679 (−89)	2 625 (−54)	2 555 (−70)	2 534 (−21)	2 475 (−59)	2 922 (+447)	2 512 (−410)	2 780 (+294)	2 638 (−142)
Wakefield T.	2 2344 (−1372)	1 3483 (+1139)	2 1568 (−1915)	2 1714 (+146)	1 2637 (+923)	2 2416 (−221)	1 5151 (+2735)	1 5428 (+277)	1 4848 (−580)
Warrington	1 3824 (−14)	1 4059 (+235)	1 3801 (−258)	1 3618 (−183)	1 4172 (+554)	1 4974 (+820)	1 4893 (−81)	1 5412 (+519)	1 5915 (+503)
Whitehaven	2 1742 (−968)	1 1639 (−103)	2 1540 (−99)	2 1878 (+333)	2 1800 (−78)	2 1772 (−28)	2 1310 (−462)	2 961 (−349)	2 1035 (+74)
Widnes	1 4703 (−782)	1 4687 (−16)	1 4266 (−421)	1 4019 (−247)	1 3840 (−179)	1 6262 (+2422)	1 8648 (+2386)	1 7858 (−790)	1 6793 (−1065)
Wigan	1 7426 (+1929)	1 7479 (+53)	1 10056 (+2577)	1 12515 (+2459)	1 12732 (+217)	1 13021 (+289)	1 14543 (+1519)	1 13973 (−570)	1 14493 (+520)
Workington T.	1 1470 (−499)	2 934 (−536)	1 920 (−14)	2 702 (−218)	2 653 (−49)	2 737 (+84)	2 774 (+37)	2 691 (−83)	2 1426 (+735)

COMPETITION ATTENDANCE REVIEW

		82-83	83-84	84-85	85-86	86-87	87-88	88-89	89-90	90-91
FIRST	Total	1,113,915	1,140,548	1,137,195	1,100,329	1,162,666	1,060,296	1,327,192	1,173,815	1,168,407
DIVISION	Av.	4,641	4,752	4,738	4,585	4,844	5,826	7,292	6,450	6,420
SECOND	Total	321,226	279,673	266,730	310,311	217,552	381,825	298,776	515,687	371,398
DIVISION	Av.	1,181	914	953	1,014	863	1,364	1,067	1,754	1,263
LEAGUE TOTALS	Total	1,435,141	1,420,221	1,403,925	1,410,640	1,380,218	1,442,121	1,625,968	1,689,502	1,539,805
(1st & 2nd)	Av.	2,803	2,601	2,700	2,584	2,805	3,121	3,519	3,549	3,235
R.L. CUP	Av.	8,355	8,399	8,497	8,280	6,965	8,764	8,666	7,339	6,748
REGAL	Av.	4,219	3,893	4,881	4,232	4,122	3,570	4,987	4,876	3,515
PREMIER	Av.	10,099	8,136	10,115	9,273	15,154	13,462	15,856	16,796	12,483
10,000 + (No. of)		37	26	27	36	43	46	59	54	43

20,000-plus crowds . . . . A 10-year review
All matches except the Rugby League Challenge Cup final at Wembley

26,771	Britain v. Australia	First Test	Hull C. FC	30 Oct. 1982
23,216	Britain v. Australia	Second Test	Wigan	20 Nov. 1982
26,031	Hull v. Castleford	RL Cup semi-final	Elland Rd, Leeds	2 Apr. 1983
20,569	Hull v. Hull K.R.	Division One	Hull	8 Apr. 1983
20,077	St. Helens v. Wigan	RL Cup round 3	St. Helens	11 Mar. 1984
25,237	Hull v. Hull K.R.	Yorks Cup final	Hull C. FC	27 Oct. 1984
26,074	St. Helens v. Wigan	Lancs Cup final	Wigan	28 Oct. 1984
25,326	Hull v. Hull K.R.	John Player final	Hull C. FC	26 Jan. 1985
20,982	Hull v. Castleford	RL Cup semi-final	Leeds	6 Apr. 1985
20,968	Hull v. Castleford	RL Cup semi-final replay	Leeds	10 Apr. 1985
22,209	Britain v. New Zealand	Third Test	Elland Rd, Leeds	9 Nov. 1985
21,813	Wigan v. St. Helens	Division One	Wigan	26 Dec. 1985
23,866	Hull K.R. v. Leeds	RL Cup semi-final	Elland Rd, Leeds	29 Mar. 1986
32,485	Hull K.R. v. Leeds	RL Cup semi-final replay	Elland Rd, Leeds	3 Apr. 1986
28,252	Wigan v. St. Helens	Lancs Cup semi-final	Wigan	1 Oct. 1986
30,622	Wigan v. Australia	Tour	Wigan	12 Oct. 1986
20,180	Oldham v. Wigan	Lancs Cup final	St. Helens	19 Oct. 1986
50,583	Britain v. Australia	First Test	Manchester U. FC	25 Oct. 1986
30,808	Britain v. Australia	Second Test	Elland Rd, Leeds	8 Nov. 1986
20,169	Britain v. Australia	Third Test	Wigan	22 Nov. 1986
21,214	St. Helens v. Wigan	Division One	St. Helens	26 Dec. 1986
21,144	Warrington v. Wigan	John Player final	Bolton W. FC	10 Jan. 1987
20,355	Wigan v. St. Helens	Division One	Wigan	17 Apr. 1987
22,457	Wigan v. Halifax	Premiership semi-final	Wigan	10 May 1987
38,756	Warrington v. Wigan	Premiership final	Manchester U. FC	17 May 1987

(continued)

36,895	Wigan v. Manly	World Club Challenge	Wigan	7 Oct. 1987
20,234	Wigan v. Warrington	Lancs Cup final	St. Helens	11 Oct. 1987
23,809	Wigan v. St. Helens	Division One	Wigan	27 Dec. 1987
25,110	Wigan v. Leeds	RL Cup round 2	Wigan	14 Feb. 1988
20,783	Salford v. Wigan	RL Cup semi-final	Bolton W. FC	12 Mar. 1988
20,534	Halifax v. Hull	RL Cup semi-final	Leeds	26 Mar. 1988
25,117	Hull v. Halifax	RL Cup semi-final replay	Elland Rd, Leeds	30 Mar. 1988
21,812	St. Helens v. Wigan	Division One	St. Helens	1 Apr. 1988
35,252	St. Helens v. Widnes	Premiership final	Manchester U. FC	15 May 1988
22,968	Castleford v. Leeds	Yorks Cup final	Elland Rd, Leeds	16 Oct. 1988
20,709	Widnes v. Wigan	John Player final	Bolton W. FC	7 Jan. 1989
26,080	Leeds v. Widnes	RL Cup round 2	Leeds	26 Feb. 1989
26,529	Warrington v. Wigan	RL Cup semi-final	Manchester C. FC	25 Mar. 1989
21,076	Wigan v. St. Helens	Division One	Wigan	12 Apr. 1989
40,194	Hull v. Widnes	Premiership final	Manchester U. FC	14 May 1989
30,786	Widnes v. Canberra	World Club Challenge	Manchester U. FC	4 Oct. 1989
20,346	Britain v. New Zealand	Third Test	Wigan	11 Nov. 1989
27,075	Wigan v. St. Helens	Division One	Wigan	26 Dec 1989
23,570	Leeds v. Wigan	Division One	Leeds	4 Mar 1990
26,489	St. Helens v. Wigan	R.L. Cup semi-final	Manchester U. FC	10 Mar 1990
24,462	Wigan v. Leeds	Division One	Wigan	10 Apr. 1990
40,796	Bradford N. v. Widnes	Premiership final	Manchester U. FC	13 May 1990
24,814	Wigan v. Australia	Tour	Wigan	14 Oct. 1990
54,569	Britain v. Australia	First Test	Wembley	27 Oct. 1990
46,615	Britain v. Australia	Second Test	Manchester U. FC	10 Nov. 1990
32,500	Britain v. Australia	Third Test	Elland Rd, Leeds	24 Nov. 1990
29,763	Wigan v. Widnes	Division One	Wigan	9 Apr. 1991
42,043	Hull v. Widnes	Premiership final	Manchester U. FC	12 May 1991

1990-91 ATTENDANCE ANALYSIS

FIRST DIVISION

Total............................ 1,168,407
Average 6,420

Wigan increased their home gate by 520 a match to top the gates chart for the seventh successive season with an average home attendance of 14,493. Leeds again commanded second spot with an average of 11,102. Half of the 14 clubs recorded an increase in gates, notably promoted Oldham despite an immediate return to the Second Division. Gates fell by a minimal 0.46 per cent compared with the 1989-90 figures of 1,173,815 and 6,450.

SECOND DIVISION

Total.......................... 371,398
Average.......................... 1,263

Following the previous season's 64 per cent increase in gates due to the presence of well supported Hull K.R. and Oldham, there was a 28 per cent decrease during 1990-91 compared with the corresponding figures of 515,687 and 1,754. Halifax topped the gates chart for the second successive season with an average home attendance of 4,458, Salford being the only other club to break the 2,000-mark with a gate of 2,314. Eleven of the 21 Second Division sides recorded average gates of below 1,000, while only six clubs increased their support.

LEAGUE CHAMPIONSHIP

Aggregate 1,539,805
Average 3,235

The average attendance for the 35 clubs in both divisions, staging a total of 476 matches, was down 8.9 per cent compared with the previous figure of 1,689,502 and 3,549.

SILK CUT CHALLENGE CUP

The 1991 Challenge Cup trail attracted a total of 249,670 to the 37 ties, providing the season's top gate of 75,532 for the Wembley final. The average of 6,748 was a 12.7 decrease on the 1990 figure of 7,339.

REGAL TROPHY

A total of 137,066 were attracted to the 39 ties, including two replays. The average gate of 3,515 was 28 per cent down on the 1990 figure of 4,876.

STONES BITTER PREMIERSHIP

The end of season top-eight competition was attended by a total of 87,378 spectators, the average gate for the seven ties being 12,483. This was a 25.6 per cent decrease on the 1990 figures of 117,578 and 16,796. The 1991 tournament featured a record attendance for the Premiership final of 42,043 at Manchester United's Old Trafford ground.

SECOND DIVISION PREMIERSHIP

There was a 4.4 per cent decrease in the seven ties, including a replay, before the Old Trafford double header final. The total turnout of 24,676 provided an average gate of 3,525, compared with the 1990 figure of 3,938.

GREENALLS LANCASHIRE CUP

Gates for the 16-tie Red Rose competition increased by 3.6 per cent with a total turnout of 82,116 providing an average attendance of 5,132. The comparative 1989-90 returns were 79,237 and 4,952.

JOHN SMITHS YORKSHIRE CUP

The 17 ties attracted a total of 86,431 supporters for an average gate of 5,084, a 19.2 per cent decrease on the previous season's average of 5,633.

FIVE-FIGURE CROWDS

There was a total of 43 five-figure crowds, the Silk Cut Challenge Cup final at Wembley again topping the chart with 75,532. Wembley was also the venue for the first British Coal Test between Great Britain and Australia, which produced a British record Test crowd of 54,569. The fifth Stones Bitter Premiership double-header at Manchester United's Old Trafford again beat the competition record with a crowd of 42,043. Wigan broke the 20,000-barrier twice with a tour fixture against the Kangaroos and a virtual title decider with Widnes in the Stones Bitter Championship. In all matches, Wigan attracted a total of 13 five-figure home crowds, ahead of Leeds with 11, the next best being Widnes with four. The 10,000-plus gates were divided into the following categories:

League 24
Australian Tour 8
Challenge Cup 4
Lancashire Cup 2
Yorkshire Cup 2
Regal Trophy 1
Premiership Trophy 1
Charity Shield 1

STONES BITTER CHAMPIONSHIP

	1990-91 Average	Annual Difference
Wigan	14493	(+520)
Leeds	11102	(−1149)
St. Helens	7391	(−1164)
Widnes	6793	(−1065)
Hull	6699	(+481)
Castleford	6019	(−409)
Warrington	5915	(+503)
Bradford Northern	5274	(−310)
*Oldham	5094	(+693)
*Hull K.R.	4952	(+101)
Wakefield Trinity	4848	(−580)
Featherstone Rovers	4722	(+453)
Sheffield Eagles	4031	(−7)
Rochdale Hornets	2542	(+32)

*Promoted 1989-90

SECOND DIVISION

	1990-91 Average	Annual Difference
Halifax	4458	(−1463)
*Salford	2314	(−1406)
Ryedale-York	1857	(−638)
Swinton	1737	(+59)
*Leigh	1719	(−2849)
Doncaster	1458	(−507)
Workington Town	1426	(+735)
Huddersfield	1306	(−328)
Batley	1188	(−318)
Whitehaven	1035	(+74)
Keighley	985	(+49)
*Barrow	962	(−1035)
Dewsbury	955	(−272)
Bramley	805	(−177)
Carlisle	781	(+207)
Hunslet	767	(−279)
Chorley	690	(−116)
Trafford Borough	638	(−142)
Runcorn Highfield	632	(+179)
Fulham	557	(−284)
Nottingham City	255	(−322)

*Relegated 1989-90

FIXTURES

PRINCIPAL DATES 1991-92

1991

25 August	CIS Insurance Charity Shield (Gateshead)
1 September	Stones Bitter League campaign opens
15 September	County Cups (Round 1)
18 September	Rodstock War of the Roses (Headingley, Leeds)
25 September	County Cups (Round 2)
2 October	Foster's World Club Challenge
9 October	County Cups (Semi-Finals)
19 October ⎱	Lancashire Cup Final
20 October ⎰	Yorkshire Cup Final
27 October	British Coal International: Wales v. Papua New Guinea (Swansea City FC)
30 October	British Coal International: Great Britain Under-21s v. Papua New Guinea (Headingley, Leeds)
3 November	Humberside v. Papua New Guinea (Boulevard, Hull)
5 November	Cumbria v. Papua New Guinea (Derwent Park, Workington)
9 November	British Coal Test: Great Britain v. Papua New Guinea (Central Park, Wigan)
16/17 November	Regal Trophy (Round 1)
23/24 November	Regal Trophy (Round 2)
30 Nov/1 Dec	Regal Trophy (Round 3)
7 December	Regal Trophy (Semi-Final 1)
21 December	Regal Trophy (Semi-Final 2)

1992

11 January	Regal Trophy Final
25/26 January	Silk Cut Challenge Cup (Round 1)
8/9 February	Silk Cut Challenge Cup (Round 2)
16 February	British Coal Test: France v. Great Britain
22/23 February	Silk Cut Challenge Cup (Round 3)
7 March	British Coal Test: Great Britain v. France
14 March	Silk Cut Challenge Cup (Semi-Final 1)
28 March	Silk Cut Challenge Cup (Semi-Final 2)
21 April	Stones Bitter Divisional Premiership (Round 1)
26 April	Stones Bitter Premiership (Round 1) Stones Bitter Divisional Premiership (Round 2)
2 May	Silk Cut Challenge Cup Final (Wembley)
10 May	Stones Bitter Premiership (Semi-Finals) Stones Bitter Divisional Premiership (Semi-Finals)
17 May	Stones Bitter Premiership Final Stones Bitter Divisional Premiership Final (Old Trafford, Manchester)

STONES BITTER CHAMPIONSHIP

SUNDAY, 1st SEPTEMBER, 1991

Bradford N.	v.	Hull K.R.	3.00
Castleford	v.	Wigan	3.30
Halifax	v.	Featherstone R.	3.00
Hull	v.	St. Helens	3.15
Swinton	v.	Wakefield T.	3.00
Warrington	v.	Salford	3.00
Widnes	v.	Leeds	3.00

SUNDAY, 8th SEPTEMBER, 1991

Featherstone R.	v.	Swinton	3.30
Hull K.R.	v.	Halifax	3.15
Leeds	v.	Hull	3.00
St. Helens	v.	Warrington	3.00
Salford	v.	Castleford	3.00
Wakefield T.	v.	Bradford N.	3.30
Wigan	v.	Widnes	3.00

SUNDAY, 15th SEPTEMBER, 1991
COUNTY CUPS — ROUND 1

SUNDAY, 22nd SEPTEMBER, 1991

Bradford N.	v.	Salford	3.00
Castleford	v.	Leeds	3.30
Halifax	v.	Wakefield T.	3.00
Hull	v.	Wigan	3.15
Swinton	v.	St. Helens	3.00
Warrington	v.	Featherstone R.	3.00
Widnes	v.	Hull K.R.	3.00

WEDNESDAY, 25th SEPTEMBER, 1991
COUNTY CUPS — ROUND 2

SUNDAY, 29th SEPTEMBER, 1991

Featherstone R.	v.	Bradford N.	3.30
Hull K.R.	v.	Warrington	3.15
Leeds	v.	Swinton	3.00
St. Helens	v.	Castleford	3.00
Salford	v.	Widnes	3.00
Wakefield T.	v.	Hull	3.30

SUNDAY, 6th OCTOBER, 1991

Bradford N.	v.	Leeds	3.00
Castleford	v.	Widnes	3.30
Halifax	v.	St. Helens	3.00
Hull	v.	Salford	3.15
Swinton	v.	Hull K.R.	3.00
Warrington	v.	Wakefield T.	3.00
Wigan	v.	Featherstone R.	3.00

WEDNESDAY, 9th OCTOBER, 1991
COUNTY CUPS — SEMI FINALS

SUNDAY, 13th OCTOBER, 1991

Featherstone R.	v.	Hull	3.30
Hull K.R.	v.	Castleford	3.15
Leeds	v.	Warrington	3.00
St. Helens	v.	Bradford N.	3.00
Salford	v.	Halifax	3.00
Wakefield T.	v.	Wigan	3.30
Widnes	v.	Swinton	3.00

SATURDAY/SUNDAY, 19/20th OCTOBER, 1991
LANCASHIRE/YORKSHIRE COUNTY CUP FINALS

SUNDAY, 20th OCTOBER, 1991

Halifax	v.	Hull K.R.	3.00
Hull	v.	Bradford N.	3.15
St. Helens	v.	Salford	3.00
Swinton	v.	Wigan	3.00
Wakefield T.	v.	Leeds	3.30
Warrington	v.	Castleford	3.00
Widnes	v.	Featherstone R.	3.00

SUNDAY, 27th OCTOBER, 1991

Castleford	v.	Featherstone R.	3.30
Hull K.R.	v.	Wakefield T.	3.15
Leeds	v.	St. Helens	3.00
Salford	v.	Hull	3.00
Wigan	v.	Halifax	3.00

WALES v. PNG — SWANSEA

SUNDAY, 3rd NOVEMBER, 1991

Bradford N.	v.	Castleford	3.00
Featherstone R.	v.	Salford	3.30
Halifax	v.	Widnes	3.00
Swinton	v.	Warrington	3.00
Wakefield T.	v.	St. Helens	3.30
Wigan	v.	Leeds	3.00

COMBINED HUMBERSIDE v. PNG
BOULEVARD, HULL

TUESDAY, 5th NOVEMBER, 1991
CUMBRIA v. PNG

SATURDAY, 9th NOVEMBER, 1991
BRITISH COAL TEST:
GREAT BRITAIN v. PNG
CENTRAL PARK, WIGAN

SUNDAY, 10th NOVEMBER, 1991

Castleford	v.	Halifax	3.30
Hull	v.	Swinton	3.15
Leeds	v.	Featherstone R.	3.00
St. Helens	v.	Hull K.R.	3.00
Salford	v.	Wigan	3.00
Warrington	v.	Bradford N.	3.00
Widnes	v.	Wakefield T.	3.00

SUNDAY, 17th NOVEMBER, 1991
REGAL TROPHY — ROUND 1

SUNDAY, 24th NOVEMBER, 1991
REGAL TROPHY — ROUND 2

SATURDAY/SUNDAY,
30th NOVEMBER/1st DECEMBER, 1991
REGAL TROPHY — ROUND 3

SUNDAY, 1st DECEMBER, 1991

Bradford N.	v.	Widnes	3.00
Featherstone R.	v.	St. Helens	3.30
Halifax	v.	Hull	3.00
Hull K.R.	v.	Salford	3.15
Swinton	v.	Leeds	3.00
Wakefield T.	v.	Warrington	3.30
Wigan	v.	Castleford	3.00

SATURDAY, 7th DECEMBER, 1991
REGAL TROPHY — SEMI-FINAL (1)

SUNDAY, 8th DECEMBER, 1991

Castleford	v.	Hull K.R.	3.30
Hull	v.	Featherstone R.	3.15
Leeds	v.	Bradford N.	3.00
St. Helens	v.	Swinton	3.00
Salford	v.	Wakefield T.	3.00
Warrington	v.	Halifax	3.00
Widnes	v.	Wigan	3.00

SUNDAY, 15th DECEMBER, 1991

Bradford N.	v.	Warrington	3.00
Featherstone R.	v.	Leeds	3.30
Halifax	v.	Salford	3.00
Hull K.R.	v.	St. Helens	3.15
Swinton	v.	Castleford	3.00
Wakefield T.	v.	Widnes	3.30
Wigan	v.	Hull	3.00

SATURDAY, 21st DECEMBER, 1991
REGAL TROPHY — SEMI-FINAL (2)

THURSDAY, 26th DECEMBER, 1991

Bradford N.	v.	Halifax	3.30
Castleford	v.	Hull	11.30
Featherstone R.	v.	Wakefield T.	11.30
Salford	v.	Swinton	3.00
Widnes	v.	Warrington	3.00
Wigan	v.	St. Helens	3.00

SUNDAY, 29th DECEMBER, 1991

Leeds	v.	Hull K.R.	3.00

WEDNESDAY, 1st JANUARY, 1992

Halifax	v.	Bradford N.	3.00
Hull	v.	Hull K.R.	3.15
Leeds	v.	Salford	3.00
St. Helens	v.	Widnes	3.00
Wakefield T.	v.	Castleford	3.30
Warrington	v.	Wigan	3.00

SUNDAY, 5th JANUARY, 1992

Bradford N.	v.	Hull	3.00
Featherstone R.	v.	Halifax	3.30
Hull K.R.	v.	Swinton	3.15
Salford	v.	St. Helens	3.00
Warrington	v.	Leeds	3.00
Widnes	v.	Castleford	3.00
Wigan	v.	Wakefield T.	3.00

SATURDAY, 11th JANUARY, 1992
REGAL TROPHY FINAL

SUNDAY, 12th JANUARY, 1992

Bradford N.	v.	Wigan	3.00
Castleford	v.	Salford	3.30
Hull	v.	Warrington	3.15
Leeds	v.	Widnes	3.00
St. Helens	v.	Featherstone R.	3.00
Swinton	v.	Halifax	3.00
Wakefield T.	v.	Hull K.R.	3.30

SUNDAY, 19th JANUARY, 1992

Castleford	v.	Bradford N.	3.30
Halifax	v.	Wigan	3.00
Hull K.R.	v.	Featherstone R.	3.15
St. Helens	v.	Wakefield T.	3.00
Salford	v.	Leeds	3.00
Warrington	v.	Swinton	3.00
Widnes	v.	Hull	3.00

SUNDAY, 26th JANUARY, 1992
SILK CUT CHALLENGE CUP — ROUND 1

SUNDAY, 2nd FEBRUARY, 1992

Bradford N.	v.	St. Helens	3.00
Featherstone R.	v.	Warrington	3.30
Hull	v.	Halifax	3.15
Leeds	v.	Castleford	3.00
Swinton	v.	Widnes	3.00
Wakefield T.	v.	Salford	3.30
Wigan	v.	Hull K.R.	3.00

SUNDAY, 9th FEBRUARY, 1992
SILK CUT CHALLENGE CUP — ROUND 2

SUNDAY, 16th FEBRUARY, 1992

Halifax	v.	Swinton	3.00
Hull K.R.	v.	Leeds	3.15
Salford	v.	Featherstone R.	3.00
Warrington	v.	Hull	3.00

SUNDAY, 23rd FEBRUARY, 1992
SILK CUT CHALLENGE CUP — ROUND 3

FRIDAY, 28th FEBRUARY, 1992

Salford	v.	Bradford N.	3.00

SUNDAY, 1st MARCH, 1992

Castleford	v.	Warrington	3.30
Featherstone R.	v.	Hull K.R.	3.30
Hull	v.	Wakefield T.	3.15
St. Helens	v.	Leeds	3.00
Widnes	v.	Halifax	3.00
Wigan	v.	Swinton	3.00

SUNDAY, 8th MARCH, 1992

Bradford N.	v.	Featherstone R.	3.00
Castleford	v.	St. Helens	3.30
Wakefield T.	v.	Halifax	3.30
Warrington	v.	Hull K.R.	3.00

SATURDAY, 14th MARCH, 1992
SILK CUT CHALLENGE CUP — SEMI-FINAL (1)

SUNDAY, 15th MARCH, 1992

Featherstone R.	v.	Castleford	3.30
Halifax	v.	Warrington	3.00
Hull K.R.	v.	Widnes	3.15
Leeds	v.	Wigan	3.00
Swinton	v.	Bradford N.	3.00

SUNDAY, 22nd MARCH, 1992

Hull	v.	Leeds	3.15
St. Helens	v.	Halifax	3.00
Swinton	v.	Featherstone R.	3.00
Widnes	v.	Bradford N.	3.00
Wigan	v.	Salford	3.00

SATURDAY, 28th MARCH, 1992
SILK CUT CHALLENGE CUP — SEMI-FINAL (2)

SUNDAY, 29th MARCH, 1992

Castleford	v.	Swinton	3.30
Featherstone R.	v.	Widnes	3.30
Hull K.R.	v.	Wigan	3.15
Leeds	v.	Wakefield T.	3.00
St. Helens	v.	Hull	3.00
Salford	v.	Warrington	3.00

SUNDAY, 5th APRIL, 1992

Bradford N.	v.	Wakefield T.	3.00
Featherstone R.	v.	Wigan	3.30
Swinton	v.	Hull	3.00
Warrington	v.	St. Helens	3.00
Widnes	v.	Salford	3.00

SUNDAY, 12th APRIL, 1992

Halifax	v.	Castleford	3.00
Hull	v.	Widnes	3.15
Salford	v.	Hull K.R.	3.00
Wakefield T.	v.	Swinton	3.30
Wigan	v.	Bradford N.	3.00

FRIDAY, 17th APRIL, 1992

Bradford N.	v.	Swinton	3.00
Castleford	v.	Wakefield T.	7.30
Hull K.R.	v.	Hull	3.15
Leeds	v.	Halifax	7.30
St. Helens	v.	Wigan	3.00
Warrington	v.	Widnes	3.00

MONDAY, 20th APRIL, 1992

Halifax	v.	Leeds	3.00
Hull	v.	Castleford	3.15
Hull K.R.	v.	Bradford N.	3.15
Swinton	v.	Salford	3.00
Wakefield T.	v.	Featherstone R.	3.30
Widnes	v.	St. Helens	3.00
Wigan	v.	Warrington	3.00

SECOND DIVISION

SUNDAY, 1st SEPTEMBER, 1991

Leigh	v.	Ryedale-York	3.30
Rochdale H.	v.	Carlisle	3.00
Sheffield E.	v.	Oldham	3.15
Workington T.	v.	Fulham	3.00

SUNDAY, 8th SEPTEMBER, 1991

Carlisle	v.	Sheffield E.	2.30
Oldham	v.	Leigh	3.00
Rochdale H.	v.	Fulham	3.00
Ryedale-York	v.	Workington T.	3.15

SUNDAY, 15th SEPTEMBER, 1991
COUNTY CUPS — ROUND 1

SUNDAY, 22nd SEPTEMBER, 1991

Fulham	v.	Sheffield E.	3.00
Leigh	v.	Carlisle	3.30
Rochdale H.	v.	Ryedale-York	3.00
Workington T.	v.	Oldham	3.00

WEDNESDAY, 25th SEPTEMBER, 1991
COUNTY CUPS — ROUND 2

SUNDAY, 29th SEPTEMBER, 1991

Carlisle	v.	Workington T.	2.30
Fulham	v.	Leigh	3.00
Oldham	v.	Rochdale H.	3.00
Ryedale-York	v.	Sheffield E.	3.15

SUNDAY, 6th OCTOBER, 1991

Fulham	v.	Oldham	3.00
Rochdale H.	v.	Leigh	3.00
Ryedale-York	v.	Carlisle	3.15
Sheffield E.	v.	Workington T.	3.15

WEDNESDAY, 9th OCTOBER, 1991
COUNTY CUPS — SEMI-FINALS

SUNDAY, 13th OCTOBER, 1991

Carlisle	v.	Fulham	2.30
Leigh	v.	Sheffield E.	3.30
Oldham	v.	Ryedale-York	3.00
Workington T.	v.	Rochdale H.	3.00

SATURDAY/SUNDAY 19/20th OCTOBER, 1991
LANCASHIRE/YORKSHIRE COUNTY CUP FINALS

SUNDAY, 20th OCTOBER, 1991

Carlisle	v.	Oldham	2.00
Fulham	v.	Ryedale-York	3.00
Leigh	v.	Workington T.	3.30
Sheffield E.	v.	Rochdale H.	3.15

SUNDAY, 27th OCTOBER, 1991

Oldham	v.	Sheffield E.	3.00
Ryedale-York	v.	Leigh	3.15
Workington T.	v.	Fulham	3.00

SUNDAY, 3rd NOVEMBER, 1991

Fulham	v.	Rochdale H.	3.00
Leigh	v.	Oldham	3.30
Sheffield E.	v.	Carlisle	3.15
Workington T.	v.	Ryedale-York	3.00

TUESDAY, 5th NOVEMBER, 1991
CUMBRIA   v.   PNG

SATURDAY, 9th NOVEMBER, 1991
BRITISH COAL TEST:
GREAT BRITAIN   v.   PNG
CENTRAL PARK, WIGAN

SUNDAY, 10th NOVEMBER, 1991

Carlisle	v.	Leigh	2.00
Fulham	v.	Sheffield E.	3.00
Oldham	v.	Workington T.	3.00
Ryedale-York	v.	Rochdale H.	3.15

SUNDAY, 17th NOVEMBER, 1991
REGAL TROPHY — ROUND 1

SUNDAY, 24th NOVEMBER, 1991
REGAL TROPHY — ROUND 2

**SATURDAY/SUNDAY,
30th NOVEMBER/1st DECEMBER, 1991**
REGAL TROPHY — ROUND 3

SUNDAY, 1st DECEMBER, 1991

Fulham	v.	Leigh	3.00
Rochdale H.	v.	Oldham	3.00
Workington T.	v.	Carlisle	3.00

SATURDAY, 7th DECEMBER, 1991
REGAL TROPHY — SEMI-FINAL (1)

SUNDAY, 8th DECEMBER, 1991

Carlisle	v.	Ryedale-York	2.00
Leigh	v.	Rochdale H.	3.30
Oldham	v.	Fulham	3.00
Workington T.	v.	Sheffield E.	3.00

SUNDAY, 15th DECEMBER, 1991

Fulham	v.	Carlisle	3.00
Rochdale H.	v.	Workington T.	3.00
Ryedale-York	v.	Oldham	3.15
Sheffield E.	v.	Leigh	3.15

SATURDAY, 21st DECEMBER, 1991
REGAL TROPHY — SEMI-FINAL (2)

THURSDAY, 26th DECEMBER, 1991

Carlisle	v.	Workington T.	2.00
Leigh	v.	Fulham	3.30
Oldham	v.	Rochdale H.	3.00
Ryedale-York	v.	Sheffield E.	3.15

SUNDAY, 29th DECEMBER, 1991

Sheffield E.	v.	Ryedale-York	3.15

WEDNESDAY, 1st JANUARY, 1992

Leigh	v.	Oldham	3.30

SUNDAY, 5th JANUARY, 1992

Fulham	v.	Ryedale-York	3.00
Oldham	v.	Carlisle	3.00
Rochdale H.	v.	Sheffield E.	3.00
Workington T.	v.	Leigh	3.00

SATURDAY, 11th JANUARY, 1992
REGAL TROPHY FINAL

SUNDAY, 12th JANUARY, 1992

Carlisle	v.	Rochdale H.	2.00
Fulham	v.	Workington T.	3.00
Leigh	v.	Ryedale-York	3.30
Oldham	v.	Sheffield E.	3.00

SUNDAY, 19th JANUARY, 1992

Carlisle	v.	Sheffield E.	2.00
Fulham	v.	Rochdale H.	3.00
Ryedale-York	v.	Workington T.	3.15

SUNDAY, 26th JANUARY, 1992
SILK CUT CHALLENGE CUP — ROUND 1

SUNDAY, 2nd FEBRUARY, 1992

Leigh	v.	Carlisle	3.30
Rochdale H.	v.	Ryedale-York	3.00
Sheffield E.	v.	Fulham	3.15
Workington T.	v.	Oldham	3.00

SUNDAY, 9th FEBRUARY, 1992
SILK CUT CHALLENGE CUP — ROUND 2

SUNDAY, 16th FEBRUARY, 1992

Fulham	v.	Oldham	3.00
Rochdale H.	v.	Leigh	3.00
Ryedale-York	v.	Carlisle	3.15
Sheffield E.	v.	Workington T.	3.15

SUNDAY, 23rd FEBRUARY, 1992

Carlisle	v.	Fulham	2.00
Leigh	v.	Sheffield E.	3.30
Oldham	v.	Ryedale-York	3.00
Workington T.	v.	Rochdale H.	3.00

SILK CUT CHALLENGE CUP — ROUND 3

SUNDAY, 1st MARCH, 1992

Fulham	v.	Workington T.	3.00
Rochdale H.	v.	Carlisle	3.00
Ryedale-York	v.	Leigh	3.15
Sheffield E.	v.	Oldham	3.15

SUNDAY, 8th MARCH, 1992

Leigh	v.	Workington T.	3.30
Oldham	v.	Carlisle	3.00
Ryedale-York	v.	Fulham	3.15
Sheffield E.	v.	Rochdale H.	3.15

SATURDAY, 14th MARCH, 1992
SILK CUT CHALLENGE CUP — SEMI-FINAL (1)

SUNDAY, 15th MARCH, 1992

Carlisle	v.	Leigh	2.00
Oldham	v.	Fulham	3.00
Ryedale-York	v.	Rochdale H.	3.15
Workington T.	v.	Sheffield E.	3.00

SUNDAY, 22nd MARCH, 1992

Fulham	v.	Carlisle	3.00
Rochdale H.	v.	Workington T.	3.00
Sheffield E.	v.	Leigh	3.15

SATURDAY, 28th MARCH, 1992
SILK CUT CHALLENGE CUP — SEMI-FINAL (2)

SUNDAY, 29th MARCH, 1992

Carlisle	v.	Oldham	2.00
Leigh	v.	Fulham	3.30
Rochdale H.	v.	Sheffield E.	3.00
Workington T.	v.	Ryedale-York	3.00

SUNDAY, 5th APRIL, 1992

Leigh	v.	Rochdale H.	3.30
Oldham	v.	Workington T.	3.00
Ryedale-York	v.	Fulham	3.15
Sheffield E.	v.	Carlisle	3.15

SUNDAY, 12th APRIL, 1992

Carlisle	v.	Rochdale H.	2.30
Ryedale-York	v.	Oldham	3.15
Sheffield E.	v.	Fulham	3.15
Workington T.	v.	Leigh	3.00

FRIDAY, 17th APRIL, 1992

| Carlisle | v. | Ryedale-York | 2.30 |
| Rochdale H. | v. | Oldham | 3.00 |

SUNDAY, 19th APRIL, 1992

| Sheffield E. | v. | Ryedale-York | 3.15 |

MONDAY, 20th APRIL, 1992

Oldham	v.	Leigh	3.00
Rochdale H.	v.	Fulham	3.00
Workington T.	v.	Carlisle	3.00

THIRD DIVISION

SUNDAY, 1st SEPTEMBER, 1991

Batley	v.	Whitehaven	3.15
Bramley	v.	Keighley C.	3.30
Chorley	v.	Dewsbury	3.00
Doncaster	v.	Nottingham C.	3.00
Highfield	v.	Trafford B.	3.00
Hunslet	v.	Barrow	3.30
Scarborough P.	v.	Huddersfield	3.00

SUNDAY, 8th SEPTEMBER, 1991

Barrow	v.	Doncaster	2.30
Dewsbury	v.	Hunslet	3.15
Huddersfield	v.	Batley	3.30
Keighley C.	v.	Chorley	3.15
Nottingham C.	v.	Scarborough P.	3.00
Trafford B.	v.	Bramley	3.30
Whitehaven	v.	Highfield	3.30

SUNDAY, 15th SEPTEMBER, 1991
COUNTY CUPS — ROUND 1

SUNDAY, 22nd SEPTEMBER, 1991

Batley	v.	Nottingham C.	3.15
Bramley	v.	Huddersfield	3.30
Chorley	v.	Barrow	3.00
Doncaster	v.	Dewsbury	3.00
Highfield	v.	Keighley C.	3.00
Hunslet	v.	Trafford B.	3.30
Scarborough P.	v.	Whitehaven	3.00

WEDNESDAY, 25th SEPTEMBER, 1991
COUNTY CUPS — ROUND 2

SUNDAY, 29th SEPTEMBER, 1991

Barrow	v.	Highfield	2.30
Dewsbury	v.	Bramley	3.15
Huddersfield	v.	Doncaster	3.30
Keighley C.	v.	Batley	3.15
Nottingham C.	v.	Hunslet	3.00
Trafford B.	v.	Scarborough P.	3.30
Whitehaven	v.	Chorley	3.30

SUNDAY, 6th OCTOBER, 1991

Batley	v.	Barrow	3.15
Bramley	v.	Nottingham C.	3.30
Doncaster	v.	Trafford B.	3.00
Highfield	v.	Dewsbury	3.00
Hunslet	v.	Keighley C.	3.30
Scarborough P.	v.	Chorley	3.00
Whitehaven	v.	Huddersfield	3.30

SUNDAY, 13th OCTOBER, 1991

Barrow	v.	Bramley	2.30
Chorley	v.	Batley	3.00
Dewsbury	v.	Scarborough P.	3.15
Huddersfield	v.	Highfield	3.30
Keighley C.	v.	Doncaster	3.15
Nottingham C.	v.	Whitehaven	3.00
Trafford B.	v.	Hunslet	3.30

SATURDAY/SUNDAY, 19/20th OCTOBER, 1991
LANCASHIRE/YORKSHIRE COUNTY CUP FINALS

SUNDAY, 20th OCTOBER, 1991

Batley	v.	Huddersfield	3.15
Bramley	v.	Chorley	3.30
Hunslet	v.	Highfield	3.30
Keighley C.	v.	Barrow	3.15
Scarborough P.	v.	Nottingham C.	3.00
Trafford B.	v.	Dewsbury	3.30
Whitehaven	v.	Doncaster	3.30

SUNDAY, 27th OCTOBER, 1991

Barrow	v.	Scarborough P.	2.30
Chorley	v.	Hunslet	3.00
Dewsbury	v.	Whitehaven	2.30
Doncaster	v.	Bramley	3.00
Highfield	v.	Batley	2.15
Huddersfield	v.	Trafford B.	3.30
Nottingham C.	v.	Keighley C.	3.00

SUNDAY, 3rd NOVEMBER, 1991

Batley	v.	Chorley	2.30
Bramley	v.	Dewsbury	3.30
Doncaster	v.	Huddersfield	3.00
Highfield	v.	Nottingham C.	2.15
Hunslet	v.	Whitehaven	3.30
Scarborough P.	v.	Keighley C.	3.00
Trafford B.	v.	Barrow	3.30

TUESDAY, 5th NOVEMBER, 1991

CUMBRIA   v.   PNG

SATURDAY, 9th NOVEMBER, 1991

BRITISH COAL TEST:
GREAT BRITAIN v. PNG
CENTRAL PARK, WIGAN

SUNDAY, 10th NOVEMBER, 1991

Barrow	v.	Hunslet	2.30
Chorley	v.	Scarborough P.	3.00
Dewsbury	v.	Doncaster	2.30
Huddersfield	v.	Bramley	3.30
Keighley C.	v.	Highfield	3.15
Nottingham C.	v.	Batley	3.00
Whitehaven	v.	Trafford B.	3.30

SUNDAY, 17th NOVEMBER, 1991

REGAL TROPHY — ROUND 1

SUNDAY, 24th NOVEMBER, 1991

REGAL TROPHY — ROUND 2

SATURDAY/SUNDAY,
30th NOVEMBER/1st DECEMBER, 1991

REGAL TROPHY — ROUND 3

SUNDAY, 1st DECEMBER, 1991

Batley	v.	Keighley C.	2.30
Bramley	v.	Whitehaven	3.30
Doncaster	v.	Chorley	3.00
Highfield	v.	Barrow	2.15
Hunslet	v.	Nottingham C.	3.30
Scarborough P.	v.	Dewsbury	3.00
Trafford B.	v.	Huddersfield	3.30

SATURDAY, 7th DECEMBER, 1991

REGAL TROPHY — SEMI-FINAL (1)

SUNDAY, 8th DECEMBER, 1991

Barrow	v.	Trafford B.	2.30
Batley	v.	Doncaster	2.30
Chorley	v.	Bramley	3.00
Huddersfield	v.	Dewsbury	3.30
Hunslet	v.	Scarborough P.	3.30
Nottingham C.	v.	Highfield	3.00
Whitehaven	v.	Keighley C.	3.30

SUNDAY, 15th DECEMBER, 1991

Bramley	v.	Barrow	3.30
Dewsbury	v.	Chorley	2.30
Doncaster	v.	Whitehaven	3.00
Highfield	v.	Huddersfield	2.15
Keighley C.	v.	Hunslet	3.15
Scarborough P.	v.	Batley	3.00
Trafford B.	v.	Nottingham C.	3.30

SATURDAY, 21st DECEMBER, 1991

REGAL TROPHY — SEMI-FINAL (2)

SUNDAY, 22nd DECEMBER, 1991

Keighley C.	v.	Huddersfield	3.15
Scarborough P.	v.	Doncaster	3.00

THURSDAY, 26th DECEMBER, 1991

Barrow	v.	Whitehaven	2.30
Batley	v.	Dewsbury	12.00
Chorley	v.	Trafford B.	3.00
Hunslet	v.	Bramley	3.00

SUNDAY, 29th DECEMBER, 1991

Nottingham C.	v.	Doncaster	3.00
Huddersfield	v.	Scarborough P.	3.30

WEDNESDAY, 1st JANUARY, 1992

Bramley	v.	Hunslet	3.30
Dewsbury	v.	Batley	2.30
Trafford B.	v.	Chorley	3.30

SUNDAY, 5th JANUARY, 1992

Bramley	v.	Trafford B.	3.30
Chorley	v.	Huddersfield	3.00
Dewsbury	v.	Barrow	2.30
Doncaster	v.	Keighley C.	3.00
Highfield	v.	Scarborough P.	2.15
Whitehaven	v.	Nottingham C.	3.30

SATURDAY, 11th JANUARY, 1992

REGAL TROPHY FINAL

SUNDAY, 12th JANUARY, 1992

Barrow	v.	Chorley	2.30
Batley	v.	Highfield	2.30
Huddersfield	v.	Whitehaven	3.30
Keighley C.	v.	Bramley	3.15
Nottingham C.	v.	Dewsbury	3.00
Scarborough P.	v.	Hunslet	3.00
Trafford B.	v.	Doncaster	3.30

SUNDAY, 19th JANUARY, 1992

Barrow	v.	Nottingham C.	2.30
Bramley	v.	Scarborough P.	3.30
Chorley	v.	Keighley C.	3.00
Dewsbury	v.	Trafford B.	2.30
Doncaster	v.	Highfield	3.00
Hunslet	v.	Huddersfield	3.30
Whitehaven	v.	Batley	3.30

SUNDAY, 26th JANUARY 1992
SILK CUT CHALLENGE CUP — ROUND 1

SUNDAY, 2nd FEBRUARY, 1992

Dewsbury	v.	Keighley C.	2.30
Doncaster	v.	Batley	3.00
Highfield	v.	Whitehaven	2.15
Huddersfield	v.	Chorley	3.30
Nottingham C.	v.	Bramley	3.00
Scarborough P.	v.	Barrow	3.00

SUNDAY, 9th FEBRUARY, 1992
SILK CUT CHALLENGE CUP — ROUND 2

SUNDAY, 16th FEBRUARY, 1992

Barrow	v.	Huddersfield	2.30
Batley	v.	Bramley	2.30
Chorley	v.	Nottingham C.	3.00
Hunslet	v.	Doncaster	3.30
Keighley C.	v.	Scarborough P.	3.15
Trafford B.	v.	Highfield	3.30
Whitehaven	v.	Dewsbury	3.30

SUNDAY, 23rd FEBRUARY, 1992

Highfield	v.	Chorley	2.15
Keighley C.	v.	Nottingham C.	3.15
Whitehaven	v.	Hunslet	3.30

SILK CUT CHALLENGE CUP — ROUND 3

SUNDAY 1st MARCH, 1992

Bramley	v.	Doncaster	3.30
Chorley	v.	Whitehaven	3.00
Dewsbury	v.	Highfield	2.30
Huddersfield	v.	Keighley C.	3.30
Hunslet	v.	Batley	3.30
Nottingham C.	v.	Barrow	3.00
Scarborough P.	v.	Trafford B.	3.00

SUNDAY, 8th MARCH, 1992

Barrow	v.	Dewsbury	2.30
Batley	v.	Scarborough P.	2.30
Highfield	v.	Bramley	2.15
Huddersfield	v.	Nottingham C.	3.30
Trafford B.	v.	Whitehaven	3.30

SATURDAY, 14th MARCH, 1992
SILK CUT CHALLENGE CUP — SEMI-FINAL (1)

SUNDAY, 15th MARCH, 1992

Doncaster	v.	Barrow	3.00
Highfield	v.	Hunslet	2.15
Keighley C.	v.	Trafford B.	3.15
Nottingham C.	v.	Chorley	3.00
Scarborough P.	v.	Bramley	3.00

SUNDAY, 22nd MARCH, 1992

Barrow	v.	Batley	2.30
Bramley	v.	Highfield	3.30
Chorley	v.	Doncaster	3.00
Dewsbury	v.	Nottingham C.	2.30
Trafford B.	v.	Keighley C.	3.30
Whitehaven	v.	Scarborough P.	3.30

SATURDAY, 28th MARCH, 1992
SILK CUT CHALLENGE CUP — SEMI-FINAL (2)

SUNDAY, 29th MARCH, 1992

Batley	v.	Hunslet	3.15
Chorley	v.	Highfield	3.00
Doncaster	v.	Scarborough P.	3.00
Keighley C.	v.	Dewsbury	3.15
Nottingham C.	v.	Huddersfield	3.00
Whitehaven	v.	Bramley	3.30

SUNDAY, 5th APRIL, 1992

Bramley	v.	Batley	3.30
Highfield	v.	Doncaster	3.00
Huddersfield	v.	Barrow	3.30
Hunslet	v.	Chorley	3.30
Keighley C.	v.	Whitehaven	3.15

SUNDAY, 12th APRIL, 1992

Barrow	v.	Keighley C.	2.30
Dewsbury	v.	Huddersfield	3.15
Doncaster	v.	Hunslet	3.00
Nottingham C.	v.	Trafford B.	3.00
Scarborough P.	v.	Highfield	3.00

FRIDAY, 17th APRIL, 1992

Huddersfield	v.	Hunslet	3.30
Trafford B.	v.	Batley	7.30
Whitehaven	v.	Barrow	3.30

MONDAY, 20th APRIL, 1992*

Batley	v.	Trafford B.	3.15
Hunslet	v.	Dewsbury	3.30

*Subject to Monday 20th April being declared a League Match Day by the Rugby League Council, bearing in mind the stage of the divisional trophy play-offs.

ROTHMANS FOOTBALL YEARBOOK 1991-92   JACK ROLLIN £14.95
ROTHMANS RUGBY UNION YEARBOOK 1991-92   STEPHEN JONES £13.95
ROTHMANS SNOOKER YEARBOOK 1991-92   JANICE HALE £13.95

Queen Anne Press offers an exciting range of quality titles by both established and new authors. All of the books in this series are available from:
Queen Anne Press Paperbacks
Cash Sales Department,
P.O. Box 11,
Falmouth,
Cornwall,
TR10 9EN.

Alternatively you may fax your order to the above address. Fax No. 0326 76423.

Payments can be made as follows: Cheque, postal order (payable to Macdonald & Co (Publishers) Ltd) or by credit cards, Visa/Access. Do not send cash or currency. UK customers: please send a cheque or postal order (no currency) and allow 80p for postage and packing for the first book plus 20p for each additional book up to a maximum charge of £2.00.

B.F.P.O. customers please allow 80p for the first book plus 20p for each additional book.

Overseas customers including Ireland, please allow £1.50 for postage and packing for the first book, £1.00 for the second book, and 30p for each additional book.

NAME (Block Letters) ....

ADDRESS ....

....

....

      I enclose my remittance for _____

      I wish to pay by Access/Visa Card

      Number ....

      Card Expiry Date ....